SOME SORT OF GENIUS

A LIFE OF WYNDHAM LEWIS

PAUL O'KEEFFE

COUNTERPOINT
BERKELEY

Library of Congress Cataloging-in-Publication Data is available
ISBN 978-1-61902-530-1

Cover image © National Portrait Gallery

COUNTERPOINT
2560 Ninth Street, Suite 318
Berkeley, CA 94710
www.counterpointpress.com

Printed in the United States of America
Distributed by Publishers Group West

10 9 8 7 6 5 4 3 2 1

CONTENTS

ONE

F^A 1008

The typography of this page, along with every other external surface of the world, impresses itself upon the brain through a threefold relay of neurones: rods and cones, ganglion cells and optic nerve fibres.

Light, projecting images of objects in the temporal or outer fields of vision, strikes the retinal surfaces closest to the nose. Fibres conduct these images along the right and left optic nerves, into the cranial cavity and through the dura mater, until they cross at the optic chiasma. Fibres from the left nasal retina then pass along the right optic tract, those from the right passing along the left, to the primary visual centres at the base of the brain, and from there to the occipital lobes at the rear. Images of objects positioned between the temporal, in what are known as the nasal, fields are registered by the outer retinae and communicated more directly: bypassing the junction at the centre of the optic chiasma, fibres from the right eye run along the right optic nerve and tract, those from the left eye along the left optic nerve and tract. The central field, represented by the macular region at the centre of the retina, splits down the middle in each eye, half belonging to the temporal and half to the nasal field. The bundle of fibres from the macular region of each retina run along the optic nerves to the optic chiasma. There the bundles divide. Half the fibres from each eye pass along the right tract, half along the left.

Extensive damage to one of the optic nerves will destroy the sight in the eye to which it belongs. Similar damage to one of the optic tracts will cause a loss of the nasal field in one eye and of the temporal field in the other. Damage to the optic chiasma will eliminate the temporal vision of both eyes.

Below the chiasma, embedded in bone, lies the pituitary gland. About a centimetre across, it occupies a small depression in the base of the skull, protected by bony ridges front and back. The appearance of this depression suggests its name: the sella turcica or Turkish saddle. In its healthy state the pituitary gland is not connected with the mechanism of sight.

The Pathology Museum on the ground floor and mezzanine of Westminster Medical School in Horseferry Road was dismantled in 1986, when government rationalisation of the Health Service merged it with

Charing Cross Hospital.* As they awaited transfer to other premises, the cluttered ranks of old, disease-tattered human organs formed grotesque collages in corridors, offices and storerooms. Amongst this grisly, formalin-preserved lumber, the dexter half of a man's brain lay sealed in its perspex container, the label barely legible: F^A 1008. It was occasionally retrieved from the chaotic limbo of exhibits for the edification of medical students learning about cerebral tumours.

The longitudinal cross-section of F^A 1008 shows a pituitary gland swollen to a solid ovoid mass, six centimetres in height and four centimetres from front to back and from side to side; it is the size of a moderately developed hen's egg. The bottom of this morbid excrescence was some two centimetres lower than the original site of the gland, because, in its inexorable growth, it had burst apart the ridges of the sella turcica and forced the bone itself downwards. Its bulbous upper extremity, meanwhile, pushed on into the floor of the midbrain, compressing the third ventricle and flattening the optic chiasma to the thinness of paper. The tumour was pink in section and stippled with blood vessels. Because of its age and slow growth, parts of the outer surface had calcified like eggshell.

Sight began to fail in 1937 as the tumescent gland encroached on the chiasma causing a gradual loss of vision, starting with the temporal field, in the left eye. By 1946 the temporal field of the right eye had also become affected as the tumour expanded further to atrophy the optic fibres at this sensory junction box. By 1950, vision in the left eye had been practically obliterated and only a small window in the lower central field stayed open. The pupil was almost fixed in direct light. With the destruction of the chiasma nearly complete, only the central field of the right eye remained and even this limited vista had the grainy texture of a mist, creeping across the mouth of a tunnel, as the right optic tract was also invaded. The blue-grey mist was not of uniform density and a movement of the head could bring small details into focus: a friend's waistcoat, a nose, a bald scalp. But such splinters of perception gradually dulled as the thickening mist became less and less distinguishable from the outer darkness. However, darkness never entirely overwhelmed the narrow island of sight and in this sensory twilight visitors could still be discerned as shadows and a sunlit window as a blurred rectangular patch of slightly lighter grey.

Blindness, although the most devastating, was not the only effect of the tumour. The pituitary gland controls the hormonal balance of the body. An adult male victim of pituitary disorder might suffer in one of two ways:

* The Horseferry Road building was demolished in the late 1990s and today the Pathology Museum is housed in Hammersmith.

overactivity or hyperpituitarism produces 'Acromegaly': an ape-like coarsening of the features, abundance of hair and enlargement of bones in hands and feet; underactivity or hypopituitarism, 'Feminism': poor beard, thinning or absence of pubic, armpit and chest hair, smooth skin and loss of sexual function. The man whose last organic remnant is preserved as F^A 1008 was afflicted by the latter condition. Four years before he died a female acquaintance noted his 'queer white skin, unlined face and hands . . . Like an old frog.'

The tumour blinded and emasculated, but did not kill him. Autopsy revealed an enlarged heart, while microscopic examination of a section of kidney showed grossly distended arteries. Hypertension, or chronic high blood-pressure, had caused renal failure and the level of urea in the blood accordingly rose to ten times the norm. The result was uraemic coma. Bronchopneumonia finally engorged the lungs with pus. Doctors call this 'the old man's friend'.

Death in the subdistrict of Westminster South was registered on the eighth of March 1957 by the deceased's widow: died seventh of March, Westminster Hospital, Percy Wyndham Lewis, Male, 72 years, of Studio A, 29 Notting Hill Gate, Kensington, Artist and Author.

TWO

Tracks

The deceased was not 72. He was 74.

Over half a century earlier, in February 1900, the estranged wife of Charles Edward Lewis made a solemn declaration at the Mansion House in the City of London, in accordance with the Statutory Declarations Act. Her only son had been born on the 18th day of November 1882, at Amherst, Nova Scotia, in the Dominion of Canada. The declaration was being made, she claimed, because there had been no Registry of Births in Amherst at that time and, as a result, the boy did not have a birth certificate. In his 18th year, the last of the 19th century, and for the price of a shilling stamp, it was belatedly certified by Anne Stuart Lewis and the Lord Mayor of London that Percy Wyndham Lewis had been born.

With no other documentation to back his mother's statement, an individual's birthdate becomes a matter of hearsay. For a man who was to spend the major part of his life creating an aura of mystery and drama around his vigorously self-promoted personality, the lack of a birth certificate would be a symbolic but potent advantage. It would afford him the opportunity, denied to those who had embarked upon more conventionally documented lives, of retrospective choice in the time, place and circumstances of his birth. It would shroud the fantastic event in mystery. Evasion would become a lifelong habit: evasion of creditors, of infatuated women, of importunate offspring.

The lack of a birth certificate meant that he could invent himself.

In 1949 he would give future biographers an account of the nativity, understated but nonetheless marked out for portentous embroidery. 'It was on the North American continent,' he claimed, 'and the cradle was a ship moored to the side of a wharf.'

An earlier account was more definitive as to the natal vessel. But it was discrepant as to date and place, from his mother's testimony, by three years and 150 miles:

November 18, 1885, on . . . yacht of American registry (Portland, Maine),

4

belonging to the Portland Yacht Club off Campobello, Nova Scotia, Canada.

This much is true: Wyndham Lewis's father owned a 28-ton sloop, *Wanda*, of Canadian registry (St John, New Brunswick). Campobello is an island just west of the Maine border and part of the province of New Brunswick. It lies at the mouth of an immense inlet 170 miles long and 50 miles wide. Noted for strong currents and the highest tides in the world, the difference between high and low water in its upper reaches is as great as 50 feet.

It may have been that the child was told a swashbuckling version of his birth at the yarn-spinning father's knee. It may have been that the two facts, the father's ownership of a boat and the son's birth in Nova Scotia, became conflated into a single colourful family legend. Either way the story, unquestioned, became chronicled: that Wyndham Lewis was born on a yacht in the Bay of Fundy.

Leaving aside the improbability of a man embarking upon a boating trip with a nine-months-pregnant wife, in winter and in such potentially perilous waters, one constituent of the myth is exploded by Lloyd's of London, whose yacht register lists the *Wanda* as having been built by J. T. Logan at Rothesay, New Brunswick, in 1883, the year after Charles Lewis's son first saw the light of day.

It would have been satisfying to discover that truly inclement weather, a storm or hurricane perhaps, prevailed in the Bay of Fundy on 18 November 1882. Satisfying, not in order to add drama and excitement to the otherwise uneventful early pages of a biography, but in the interests merely of mundane truth: to preclude decisively the shipboard birth that Lewis later claimed for himself. Unfortunately no such tempestuous conditions were forecast for the Maritime Provinces the day before in Saint John's *Daily Sun*: 'moderate to fresh northwest to north winds; fair weather; stationary or slightly lower temperature.' Between the 17th and the 20th the temperature continued to fall, rivers iced over and a storm appeared to threaten.

But no storm came and no conclusive proof can be found that Lewis was not born on a yacht, apart from the fact that the only such vessel his father was ever documented as owning was built a year too late to serve as 'cradle' to his son.

However, there was something extraordinary about the weather that weekend, something far more awe-inspiring than storm or hurricane. Had family legend passed on to Lewis the actual atmospheric conditions prevailing across the Maritime Provinces and the western United States on the 17th and 18th, and indeed the 19th and 20th of November 1882, he would have had no need to enlist an as yet unbuilt sloop to add the lustre of distinction to his nativity.

Telegraph operators at the Western Union Building in Saint John reported crimson sparks showering from their apparatus whenever it was touched, and at one point the entire signal board of the central telephone office 'was ablaze with electric fire'. It was referred to as an 'electric storm', but the *Daily Evening News* of 18 November clarified the term:

> It is scarcely proper to call the electric disturbance a storm. The air simply becomes heavily charged with electricity, which takes to the wires, and creates on them wavy currents, which generally antagonize the current of the battery operating the wire, making a general confusion, and the transmission of messages difficult, and at times ... almost or quite impossible.

An experiment was made with the quadruplex wire running from Bangor, Maine, to North Sydney, Cape Breton Island. Each end of the wire was earthed and, without the aid of generator or battery, conversation was carried on and messages transmitted across the seven hundred miles between the two points. It was hailed as 'one of the most remarkable feats accomplished in telegraphy'.

As if this were not enough excitement to commemorate the birth of a child to Charles and Anne Lewis, the electrical disturbance also gave rise to the most spectacular phenomenon of the northern skies: the Aurora Borealis. From Halifax, Nova Scotia, to as far west as Chicago the reports came in: 'fully two thirds of the sky is ablaze tonight with auroral light of many colours.'

*

At the opposite end of Fundy to the island of Campobello, just inland of a stretch of water called the Cumberland Basin, lies the town of Amherst. There, according to his mother's sworn statement, and in all probability on dry land, Percy Wyndham Lewis was born. It was to be home for the first six months of the child's life.

Amherst, in Cumberland County, Nova Scotia, was an expanding town drawing revenue from the lumber business and from the fertile farmland of the Tantramar Marshes that surrounded it. The 1881 census numbered the population at 1,800. A year later, when Oscar Wilde arrived by train from Saint John on the last leg of his epic North American tour, it had almost doubled. Nevertheless, Wilde had been amazed at the smallness of the population when a correspondent for the *Morning Herald* interviewed 'beauty's latest evangel' in his room at Lamy's Hotel. 'Do you tell me that it has only three thousand inhabitants? Why, I never spoke in a town so small as that', he told the reporter. 'I consider it a beautiful little place.' And the population were amazed at 'wild Oscar', as they called him, dressed in knee breeches and black silk hose, addressing them on the Decorative Arts in the Amherst Academy of Music, six weeks before Wyndham Lewis was born.

*

Seven years before, Charles Lewis had taken 16-year-old Anne Prickett from her mother's boarding house in Upper Norwood, South London. They were married on 23 February 1876, at St Stephen's Church, Camberwell. He was 33, a mutton-chop-sideburned Civil War veteran, with an army career behind him distinguished by gallantry and considerable recklessness. He possessed a highly treasured document, signed 14 October 1868 by President Abraham Lincoln, granting him the nominal rank of Captain by Brevet, in recognition of his 'gallant and meritorious services during the war'.

According to War Department records he had entered the Military Academy of West Point as cadet on 1 July 1861, tendered his resignation three and a half months later on account of weak eyesight, and a year later enlisted in the 130th New York Volunteer Infantry in August 1862. This regiment became the 19th New York Cavalry and was subsequently known as the 1st New York Dragoons. Charles was made Sergeant three days after enlisting, then in October he was promoted to 2nd Lieutenant.

At Manassas Junction, on 17 October 1863, he led 15 men to capture an unoccupied enemy earthwork and, having taken it, proceeded, against orders, to attack another. While galloping towards this second, unauthorised, objective he was shot through the left groin. The exit wound had not healed by the following January and it was not until April that he was pronounced fit enough for active duty. Then, only a month later, on 7 May, in an action at Todd's Tavern, two days into the gruelling Battle of Wilderness, he was taken prisoner. The next six months were spent in a variety of Confederate prisons. He was confined at Libby Prison in Virginia, Macon in Georgia, at Roper Hospital in Charleston, South Carolina, and finally at a poorly guarded camp at Columbia. From here, on 4 November, he escaped with two other Union officers. It took them a month to walk the two hundred miles through Confederate territory from Columbia to their own lines at Knoxville, Tennessee. Some time during the four-month period of convalescence from this ordeal, Charles was evidently able to demonstrate that his virile processes were unaffected by the earlier wound to the groin. It was a demonstration, however, necessitating treatment for primary syphilis in April 1865.

He had by this time been promoted to 1st Lieutenant and was a hero in his home town, where he wrote a first account of his daring exploits for the local paper, the *Nunda News*. 'ESCAPE FROM REBEL PRISON' was subtitled: 'A long and Perilous journey through the Mountains, Narrow Escape, Interesting Incidents'. It told of being chased by Rebel guards and bloodhounds, the privations of cold and hunger, and crossing the Great Smoky Mountains in thick snow and constantly under threat from attacks by marauding bands of hostile Indians known to be prowling the area.

Married, Charles worked for his brother William's firm in Montreal: W. F. Lewis & Company, wine merchants.* As the wife of a travelling liquor salesman, Anne was to become used to temporary accommodation and long periods left alone while Charles plied his wares across western Canada.

*

Most miserable day feeling not well at all. Hear of diphtheria in the hotel.

The first brief entry in Anne Lewis's 1883 diary records a bleak New Year's Monday at Lamy's Hotel, Amherst, where Oscar Wilde had been interviewed, reclining on a black bearskin rug and sipping tea, only three months before.

Anne's fears for the health of her month-old baby were understandable. Five years earlier, in a Quebec hotel, she had borne a child that breathed for an hour and died. She had just turned 18 and apart from Mrs Geddes, the midwife, she was alone. The news was cabled to her husband in Montreal. Perhaps because of the disparity in age between Charles and his 'darling little wife' his reaction seemed strangely detached: a father consoling his daughter over the loss of a cherished puppy:

> I sympathise deeply with you about the little one as I know you had set considerable store by it and even I had got to liking the idea of your having the little companion of your own.

Delayed by business, he had promised to get up to see her inside a week. She had received letters from her mother in August and September 1877,

---

* Charles was the fourth of eight siblings. William was the eldest, followed by Flora Matilda (b.1837), known as 'Tilly'. George Howard Lewis (b.1840) was three years older than Charles, then came Albert (b.1846), Henry (b.1848), Julius (b.1850) and Mary (b.1853).

anticipating: 'longing to see your baby how proud we shall be'; urging caution in gynaecological matters: 'ask the nurse, with my love, to take care how she binds you up of all things'; fussing:

> I hope you will like what I have sent you . . . everything the baby will need for the next two months, at any rate. I will then all being well get the short clothes ready. Mrs Bray sent in a very pretty satin hood, but as you will see I could not get it in, it will do when you come home.

And she had the letter in October consoling her, telling her there was another little angel in heaven waiting for them:

> it is hard to say Oh Father not my will but thine be done, but we know not what is good for us; but the disappointment is none the less, and I am truly grieved, that it did not please our Heavenly Father to spare your baby.

She had sent her daughter the box of baby clothes from England in early September, tempting mortality. They had arrived in time for the child's birth and death. 'You must put the little things safely away', she told Anne, 'don't look at them dear.'

In Lamy's Hotel, five years on, memories of that first fruitless labour must have made her small son's grip on life seem frighteningly tenuous, especially with suspicion of diphtheria in the hotel. The choking scourge of infants thrived in the colder months of the year. It started with a redness and soreness of the throat. This inflammation generated a tough livid membrane, sometimes spreading over the whole inner surface of the larynx and trachea. The accumulation and folding of the membrane could eventually close off the respiratory tract, causing death by asphyxiation. It would be seven years before an antitoxin was developed to cure the disease and another 23 years before there was a hope of preventing it by immunisation.

Rumour of the disease that New Year's Day prompted hasty packing and a move to healthier accommodation, 'much warmer and more comfortable', four days later.

Today an establishment called the Elm Tree Tavern stands on the corner of Victoria Street and Station Road, the railway line running alongside. From the sidewalk nothing can be seen through the smoked glass of the windows and crush-barred double doors, but to the left of the bar at the far end of the long single-storey building, a black and white photograph hangs on the garishly papered wall between two flashing fruit machines. Blurred by the non-reflective glass, the photograph shows the Terrace Hotel that once occupied this site.

It was to the Terrace Hotel that Charles Lewis and his wife moved with their six-week-old son, fleeing the diphtheria scare at Lamy's. For the next five months, Anne would grow accustomed to the blasts of steam whistles as the clanging locomotives crossed Victoria Street within 50 feet of her and her baby, east to Halifax or west to Saint John, New Brunswick.

During those five months, according to her diary, Anne saw little of her husband. She recorded Charles's departure for Montreal on 6 January and his unexpected return on 11 February, his departure for St John and Eastport, his return ten days later. He was then away for the latter half of March, the whole of April and most of May. Occasionally he sent her a cheque for $50, enabling her to pay for their board, the washing, milk, and for a series of nursemaids: Miss O'Neill, Mary Niles, Annie and Clara Emree.

The baby was christened, Percy Wyndham, on 26 January, in an Anglican ceremony conducted at Christ Church, Amherst, by the Reverend George Townshend. Anne's schedule of his comings and goings suggests that Charles was not present. The child's forenames, however, were probably his father's choice and they may have commemorated an exotic hero from his military career.

Sir Percy Wyndham was an English soldier of fortune.* He had served in the French Navy, British artillery, Austrian cavalry and, during the Risorgimento, under General Garibaldi at the battles of Palermo and Capua. In the latter theatre of war he reached the rank of Lieutenant-Colonel and was knighted in the field by King Victor Emmanuel. In 1861 he came to America and joined the Union Army as Colonel of the First New Jersey Cavalry, a rank he held until the end of 1863. He cut a dashing figure with moustaches a foot wide.

Military records show the paths of Sir Percy Wyndham and the 21-year-old 2nd Lieutenant Lewis coinciding from 13 September to 17 October 1883, when the 19th New York and the 1st New Jersey Cavalry were in action together. The coincidence ceased, at least as far as the 2nd Lieutenant was concerned, the day a Confederate rifle bullet passed through his groin.

If Percy Wyndham Lewis ever knew the reason for the particular conjunction of his forenames he never recorded the fact. Had he known of the dashing namesake he might have been less adamant in suppressing 'Percy' in adult life. It would come to be regarded as a personal affront to

* 'Sir Percy Wyndham: Soldier of Fortune', Leslie Edwards and Paul Edwards, *Lewisletter 5*, Newsletter of the Wyndham Lewis Society, Autumn 1995.

call him anything but 'Wyndham Lewis', 'Lewis' or, in the case of certain favoured intimates, 'Wyndham'.

*

Although she had numerous acquaintances in Amherst the winter of 1883 seems, for the most part, to have been a tedious time for Anne. Unchronicled blank days in the little diary were interspersed with health anxieties: 'saw the Doctor about Baby as was very uneasy'; with mundane post-natal procedures: 'had my breast strapped'; with foul weather and abortive engagements: 'very stormy day. Was to have dined at the Douglas's'. A full day was defined in terms of social contacts. One Thursday was particularly busy: 'out to dinner at Mrs Douglas's, called on Mrs Main, Mrs Dickey, Miss Townshend, Mrs Townshend, Mrs Boggs.' There was an invitation to the Masonic Ball on the first Saturday in February. It was a big affair and on Friday the Terrace Hotel was full. But she made no mention of having attended. There would have been constraints upon an unaccompanied married woman.

April was a particularly lonely and trying month. In the first week the baby was sufficiently ill, or she sufficiently nervous, to necessitate a Sunday visit to the doctor. The undisclosed sickness had abated by Wednesday but at the weekend she was exhausted. 'Have felt vexed and worried all the week . . . feeling quite miserable – very unwell in the evening'. Towards the end of the month her diary entries were a monotonous litany of isolation: Wednesday, 'quite alone'; Thursday, 'alone'; Tuesday, 'had no one with me'; Wednesday, 'quite alone'; Sunday, 'at home all day. Nothing new.'

Then, when Charles returned from Montreal on 25 May, they started packing. A week later, Friday 1 June, they went to Moncton. 'Left Amherst', she wrote, 'and so glad to go.'

On 7 June they moved on from Moncton to the seaside town of Shediac, 14 miles away, on the Cumberland Strait between New Brunswick and Prince Edward Island, where Anne was to stay for the next three months. The place was noted for its oysters, fine sandy beaches and the warmest sea bathing north of the US Carolinas. Although Charles spent just as much time away from her as before, it was summer and the weather pleasant. She was able to take the baby's occasional sickness in her stride, although getting advice from a Dr Harrison just in case. When her friend Mrs Ryan came over from Moncton they had a drive out to Hopewell Cape, no doubt to see what the Baedeker described as 'remarkable rocks of red sandstone, sculpted into fantastic shapes by the powerful tides'. The baby's first tooth appeared above the gum and nine days later the second, and Anne duly recorded both events. In July she was able to go bathing and, one Friday evening, danced and had 'quite a pleasant time'. August passed with less to report and in early September she received a telegram from Charles in Montreal 'advising remove to Jacquet River'. She packed and, three days later, boarded the train at Moncton, with 'Percy good as possible during the journey', arriving in Jacquet River at eight in the evening.

The reason for the move to this angling resort in the far north of New Brunswick is not known and, although Anne pronounced herself 'quite well pleased with the surroundings', they were there for less than a month. The interlude was notable for three momentous diary entries. The 17th of September was Anne's 24th birthday, an occasion that brought Charles from Montreal to stay with her for a week. The following day Percy was ten months old and, a week later, his eighth tooth appeared.

On 2 October they left Jacquet River, arriving in Montreal on the 3rd, and five words in Anne's diary recorded an end to hotel living:

Took possession of our house.

Provisions bought and carefully noted in the first week marked a significant stake in domestic stability for the family:

7lbs of white sugar
7lbs of brown sugar
7lbs of soda
7lbs of soap
a pound and a half of coffee
2lbs of butter
2lbs of rice
2lbs of bacon
3 dozen eggs
oatmeal
2 finnan haddies
2 pots of preserves
a peck and a half of potatoes
one peck of apples.

A servant, Mary O'Neill, was hired for $11 a month

Anne's Post Office passbook, renewed in January of the following year, gave the address as number 14, Fort Street. In the southern part of the city, rue du Fort, as it is now, runs between Dorchester West and Sherbrooke West, the latter said to have been the handsomest residential street in Montreal. It was close to the village of Lachine, the yachting resort, and

Charles and his wife drove there with his brother William and sister-in-law Maggie on their first Sunday in the city.

A familiar pattern re-established itself as Charles left for the Eastern Townships on 9 October and was gone a week. He was back for two days and then away again. Anne stayed behind, making careful note of her activities: taking the baby out, tending to him when he was sick from eating too much, engaging a plumber to fit pipes to something downstairs, visiting Maggie, shopping.

The baby's first birthday, 18 November, was the last significant date in Anne's 1883 diary. Thereafter, no trace exists of the family's movements in the city of Montreal and province of Quebec.

By the time they left, Percy was in his fifth year.

*

Anne's third Post Office Pass Book, issued September 1887, was sent to her on Campobello Island, New Brunswick, and a Liverpool and London Globe Insurance policy in the name of Charles Edward Lewis suggested he owned or rented property in Welshpool, the largest hamlet on this ten-mile-long resort for summer visitors. They wintered at Saint John, New Brunswick.

By the spring of 1888, the family had moved across the Canadian border, to Portland, Maine. Here Charles became the proud owner of the 48-foot sloop, *Wanda*.

Family tradition had it that they lived near to a reservation of Micmac Indians, and Lewis recalled: 'my mother painting pictures of the farmhouse where we lived, my father writing books inside it'.

My infant mind was filled with the hubbub of battles. A part of the garden was converted into the field of the 'Wilderness' . . . I could not help imbibing from my very American father . . . a lot about the Civil War.

While not always reliable, his memory, as to both age and place, seemed, in this case, consistent: 'at 6 years old I frisked and frolicked with other little American boys on the New English coast.' Older children of a neighbouring family, 'the Collis boys', taught young Percy his first swear words, much to his mother's horror, and once he was butted by a goat he had approached thinking it a sheep.

They cannot have spent as long as a year in Portland. 'At around the age of six', Lewis declared, again with some accuracy, 'I arrived in England, a small American.' This was towards the end of 1888.

George Howard Lewis, President of Bell, Lewis & Yates Coal Mining Company of Buffalo, NY, and a man of considerable wealth, agreed to provide his younger brother with a six-monthly stipend of $500. The first payment was sent on 7 January 1889 together with a letter wishing his brother's income were 'a little larger' and hoping it would increase in time. When George died in October 1897, Charles had received a total of $9,000.

*

For the next three years, Charles, his wife and child left little trace. For a time they lived together in Eastbourne, and later on the Isle of Wight. Then husband and wife separated. Anne took her son to live with his maternal grandmother in Norwood, while Charles remained in Ryde.

Mrs Prickett's boarding house, 'Ravenstone' in Farquhar Road, was a large establishment employing a live-in domestic staff of 11 and able to cater for around 20 paying guests. The 68-year-old widow's sister-in-law, Frances Prickett, also lived with her, together with an elderly retainer, Mrs Tompkins.

Percy played in the rolling grassy parkland surrounding the Crystal Palace under his mother's careful supervision, exchanging this, at intervals, for the heartier holiday pastimes of sea and shoreline with his father.

THREE

'Am greatly disappointed in the boy and have unpleasant misgivings regarding his future'

'So it is' said I.

'All hands shorten sail' shouted Mortar.

There was a great hubub [*sic*] in which I had a good share.

'Now boys lower the dinghy and Charlie do you think you could get in and steer, and have Brown, Donagan and Hayward in with you to row' said Mortar.

'Obey orders, sir' said I.

The real force of the storm had abated, and [in] thick mist [only a] gusty wind made the sloop go. Now getting into the dinghy and rowing or sailing about was a very simple thing. We rowed away from the sloop into the darkness, and soon saw something black looming ahead.

So began 'Good Times', Percy Wyndham Lewis's earliest surviving literary composition. Pencilled across 30 pages of lined paper in a tiny green and black covered exercise book, it was illustrated with childish drawings of figures in profile: schoolcapped boys carrying muskets, hatchets and cutlasses confront feathered savages armed with shields, spiked clubs and spears. Creatures of the son's imagination, they were doubtless born out of the father's stories of his epic redskin-threatened journey from Confederate prison to Union lines of 1864. The setting was a tropical island, familiar to readers of Defoe or Stevenson, although Campobello and the Isle of Wight would have figured in the child's mind as well. And the action began aboard a sloop, the only type of vessel heard of at his father's knee. Significantly, the young author of 'Good Times' divided his father's two forenames between his narrator, 'Charlie', and the castaway explorer who organises the boys' resistance against the cannibals: 'Sir Edward More'.

*

In 1892 Charles was renting a place called Laurel Cottage at 7 West Street,

15

in Ryde. Here he kept 'a stack of dogs', and elsewhere in the neighbourhood a shadowy female companion with whom he later confessed to have 'lived as man and wife' since the previous year. Anne may have been aware of this but still entertained hopes that some time her husband 'would be willing to bury any old differences' and that they 'might have started afresh'. He held out no such hope and, for the time being, seemed content for their marriage to hang in limbo awaiting some event to trigger its collapse.

Meanwhile, he suspected 'the old people', his mother-in-law, Frances Prickett and Mrs Tompkins, were turning his son against him. This at least was his explanation for the boy's behaviour in April 1892, when the ten-year-old came to Laurel Cottage for a holiday.

'He sneers at me', Charles complained, 'and abuses Polly.' Whether the object of the child's abuse on this occasion was his father's mistress or one of his dogs is not clear, but Percy was evidently enjoying himself. He pulled down half the branches of a laurel tree in the garden and Charles feared his landlord would come down on him for the damage. On another day the boy disappeared until 8 o'clock in the evening. Eventually his father had had enough and wrote to Anne demanding she take him back to Norwood where, he was inclined to think, the child was apt to behave himself better.

Nevertheless, before the boy's pattern of mischief established itself, Charles had been well pleased with him. 'He looks first-rate', Anne was told, 'brown as a berry.' And one Tuesday, father and son stood companionably on the beach at Ryde, watching the big guns firing from the naval base at Portsmouth on the other side of the Solent. This spectacle provided the boy with a climax to his first attempt at literary narrative:

> a thunderous roar, and a great shot come crashing through the building, and swept the natives away with it. Then roar after roar and shot after shot came crashing over the Island . . . We went on the beach and saw a cloud of smoke on the sea and the British ensign. We cheered, and we cheered and cheered.

But the 'good times' were all too fleeting that spring holiday and, leaving the mutilated laurel behind him, Percy was returned to his mother with an ominous judgement on his head:

> Am greatly disappointed with the boy and have unpleasant misgivings regarding his future.

*

Charles gave up Laurel Cottage with the idea of moving to the East Sussex coast. However, finding everything too expensive, in December 1892 he rented another property in Ryde. Number 5, Partlands Avenue, known as Winchester Villa, was 'very comfortable and a great improvement on Laurel Cottage'. He was 'about out of funds' and asked Anne to lend him £3 to tide him over until his $500 remittance from George arrived in January. On second thoughts, he told her, she 'might send £5 to save sending more a few days later.' She sent him the £5, which went on squaring tradesmen's bills, 'coal and things', then came a request for £3 more by return of post. Husband's letters to wife demanding money were a strange prefiguration of son's letters to mother a decade later.

Charles had also been promised a lump sum of $5,000 by George, which he hoped would not affect his six-monthly remittance, and some of which he thought of sinking into a dairy and poultry farm.

He spent Christmas at Winchester Villa, on account, he said, of a sick dog, but he planned to visit Norwood during the first week of January in order to take Percy skating before the ice melted. This was in spite of the strain and embarrassment he now felt whenever he saw his wife.

His family in America had no inkling of their marital difficulties. When brother George and his wife Kate stopped off in London that March on their way back to Buffalo after wintering in the South of France, Charles, Anne and Percy presented an apparently united front to greet them. Only one thing puzzled George. Charles talked of putting aside $2,000 of his expected $5,000 in trust for Percy, as if making provision for an uncertain future. But when George mentioned the matter to Anne, the day before they left London, he was surprised to discover she knew nothing about it.

Charles accompanied George and Kate back to America for a brief visit. Meanwhile, Anne took Percy for a holiday at Winchester Villa in his absence. It is probable that the time they spent in one another's company in London before Charles embarked was the last she ever saw of her husband.

Landing at New Jersey on 1 April, George and Kate continued by train to Buffalo while Charles stayed for most of the month with his younger sister Mary's family at Edgewater, Bergen County, on a high bank over the Hudson River nearly opposite Central Park. He behaved scandalously. 'Charley went off with [Mary's] house maid a pretty English girl', George reported later. 'Mary of course was grieved and astonished.'

The brief dalliance cannot have been of much importance to Charles, because he left it behind when he sailed for Southampton at the beginning of May. But, casual though the affair had been, it served him as a pretext to broaden the rift with Anne and make a bid for freedom. He began, a week after his return to Ryde, with a confession apparently pre-empted by word from his scandalised sister in New Jersey. 'I must admit (as you seem already to have found out) that I have misconducted myself with another woman – you know who.' The first letter he wrote to her on Monday 15 May bluntly hammered home the irretrievable ruin of their marriage. 'You and I can never by any possible chance come together again', he told her. He would have liked to visit Percy in Norwood on his way home from New Jersey: 'but it has come to such a pass that to see him I must subject myself to the embarrassment of seeing you too and our relations have been so strained [in] late years as to have culminated in a situation painful alike to you and to me.'

Her husband's affair with a housemaid did not come as a complete surprise to Anne. She was already aware of the longer-established liaison at Ryde, and Charles reminded her of that as he pressed his case further. 'It is useless to deny it longer especially as the old relation is still maintained and will continue to the end. She and I have lived as man and wife for going on two years.' He concluded his letter: 'you will no doubt be happier so far as I am concerned to put me where I deserve to be out of your mind and life.' And he signed it: 'Yours unfaithfully.'

As if the business could not be settled in one letter, he wrote her a second on the same day. Having outlined the problem in the morning, as it were, he proposed a solution in the afternoon:

As man and wife intercourse has long ceased between us. To go on so with a tie that galls each one to the bone is intolerable – Scrap it! You have a good substantial ground for divorce: *cruelty, neglect, desertion – adultery.* Let us be free once more.

Curiously, in this second letter he seemed to forget the woman referred to earlier in the day, with whom he had 'lived as man and wife for going on two years'. Instead he appeared to be demanding his freedom so as to be able to marry someone else entirely. And if Annie refused to divorce him he would proceed with his plans regardless. 'If . . . it be your intention to *keep me in chains* I will go back to America where I am unknown and probably marry if I can a good and conscientious woman as I require that companionship.' With this consummate piece of emotional blackmail he placed his fate entirely in her hands. 'There is but one way to save me from the pains and penalties of adultery, perchance bigamy. You know what that is.'

With steely control and a fluency testifying to months if not years of mental rehearsal, she replied by return of post. She told him of the pain his letters had caused her, admitted that some of the fault lay with her but at the same time professed to have loved him 'fondly and devotedly' and would have continued loving him had she been treated with consideration. She then made it clear that she intended to devote herself singlemindedly to her son:

> I will never get a divorce. I think so much of Percy and am so desirous of his wellbeing both now and in the future (in fact he is the only interest in life that I have) that I could not mar his youth so greatly as to have it ever said that his parents were divorced.

She sent a copy of this, with copies of her husband's letters, to his brother George, who for as long as he could kept news of Charles's behaviour from his immediate family. He wrote to Anne that Charles 'seems to have become lost to all sense of duty or loyalty . . . He has forfeited my love and respect and I have no desire for intercourse with him.' Sister 'Tilly' Chisholm in Oakville was of the same mind when she eventually found out: 'About Charles, the less said the better perhaps. I cannot bear to think of his despicable conduct and hope I may never see him again.'

Charles soon left Ryde, moved north and took a small cottage in Bunbury Heath, Cheshire. George continued to send the remittance of $500 each January and July, 'simply because he is my brother', he explained. This allowed Charles to live in the idleness to which he was accustomed. He told George that he had a horse which he rode a great deal and that he was fairly comfortable. 'But [he] bemoans his lonely fate', George reported to Anne, 'and being cut off from everyone. Mentioned his boy in particular and seemed to malign the fate he had brought upon himself.' Stung by varying degrees of remorse, guilt, loneliness and self-pity, Charles tried to explain, if not excuse, his behaviour. 'I can't quite understand what could have come over me . . . to bring matters to such a pass, but I had been boozing a good deal and got in a wrong way.'

Meanwhile George promised to provide for his sister-in-law. 'As for yourself', he assured her, 'don't be uneasy. I will send you £100 a year for the present and will always be your good friend.' He gave her advice about the sale of her mother's boarding house business and a profitable investment of the proceeds. Acting as her agent he invested the bulk of the £1,200 she sent him in property and land at interest of 6 per cent, and the residue with Bell, Lewis & Yates Mining at 5 per cent. George also gave advice when Anne later set herself up in the laundry business.

For part of 1894 she stayed at Winchester Villa, her husband's former address in Ryde. This was the home address recorded by the County School in Bedford, where the 11-year-old Percy was now a boarder. Only one letter to his mother survives from this educational establishment, largely concerned with the 'good time' he was having. He was in the third form and hoped soon to be in the fourth. He had got an exeat to go into the town the day before 'and fooled about the whole afternoon'. He had been forbidden a boat trip on the river because he could not swim but did not seem too unhappy about it. He wrote of his friends, the catalogue of names and assessments showing him to be a normal, happy, gregarious child: 'Marshall is a nice chap, but a deuce of a prig. Waldram is all right . . . Jones is not a bad fellow, but a deuce of a fool. Thorpe sextus is an ass too. Mansell Jones is a fine fellow. So's Boby [sic] Clarke, a chap of about sixteen, I work with. I say, there are a lot of big fellows in our form.'

In August his Uncle Albert, a Toronto lawyer, wrote to the boy, forwarding money from his father. Charles had evidently persuaded his brother to act as intermediary and a large part of Albert's letter was concerned with impressing upon his nephew the desirability of his parents divorcing:

> I do not intend to interfere between you and your mother or between her and your father – but should think if she looks at it from the pecuniary standpoint only, it would be worth more to her to make some arrangement with your father and sever the tie than to hold onto it and get little return while he lives and in the event of his death get nothing. I do not suppose there is any prospect of their coming together again – probably neither desires it or intends it . . . There is probably no love or affection lost on either side and all in all it seems to me to be reduced to a matter of dollars and cents.

Albert must have believed that at almost 12 years of age the child was old enough to form a judgement upon such matters. Despite its opening remarks the letter clearly encouraged the boy to side with his father. It must have been difficult for Percy to ignore the implications for his own future of the words that followed:

> If . . . you run counter to [Charles's] view, you will probably not get much assistance from him. In this case he may be and probably is a better judge than your mother – the mother does not always see things in these cases with the cool judgement of the father.

The letter concluded with an incidental and rather predictable piece of career advice: 'Unless you have pre-eminent ability in art, I should think business the safer course to follow.'

Anne never divorced her husband and by October 1894 had settled with her mother in Ealing, North London. Part of the proceeds from the sale of 'Ravenstone' had enabled Mrs Prickett to buy a detached house: no. 8 Mount Avenue. Unlike most of the neighbouring properties, it did not have a name but Anne called it 'Amherst' in commemoration of her only son's place of birth. Despite Percy's ambition to graduate from the third form to the fourth at Bedford County School, his mother had him move closer to her new home. He was to board at Castle Hill School, about half a mile away from 'Amherst'. His Aunt Tillie in Oakville marvelled that he did not seem homesick and thought the experience of boarding was the best thing for him. 'It will teach him self reliance and application', she declared, 'and a bit of human nature as well.' He arrived during the final term of 1894, and following the Christmas holiday he was much engrossed with the development of a new skill, wood carving, with the active encouragement of the School Principal. 'Mr Morgan has given me permission to practice [*sic*] in the playground shed', he reported to his mother.

*

Details of Charles's life following the final break with Anne are few, but from hints dropped in his letters, a broad outline emerges. 'I have without realising it soon enough,' he wrote, 'got myself entangled in a way that makes my extrication seem next to impossible.' The woman with whom he was now living* had become pregnant, and some time towards the end of 1894 or at the beginning of 1895 she bore him a daughter: Ethel Evelyn.

By the time Ethel was three years old, 'a most beautiful, intelligent and lovable little thing', the woman who passed as Charles's wife was 'in many respects an invalid and her mental faculties greatly impaired'. One unguarded statement suggests that an actual wedding ceremony had taken place. 'She thinks she is married to me', he confided to Anne, 'and in that respect I have deceived and wronged her grievously.' This would not be the last time Charles Lewis was to commit bigamy.

Some time during the next four years, the unidentified woman who had borne his daughter probably died. When he left England in 1901 to settle permanently in America, Charles styled himself 'widower'. He was 58 and accompanied by his seven-year-old daughter, and another young woman, of 23, called Lillian Natalie Phipps.

*

Wyndham Lewis's final report from Castle Hill School, for the term ending 17 December 1896, ranged from 'Fair' in Scripture and Algebra, to 'Very Fair' in Arithmetic, English History, Geography, Mapping and Latin, to

---

* This may have been the same woman he was involved with in Ryde. On the other hand it may have been someone else entirely.

'Good' in English Grammar, Parsing, Analysis and Euclid, to 'Very Good' in Spelling, Punctuation and Writing. For French he received 27 marks out of 100 but he was pronounced 'stronger than the mark would imply'. Art was not among the 12 listed disciplines. His conduct was described as 'very good on the whole'.

It is not certain where the money came from to continue his education, from his mother or from the erratic contributions made by his wayward father, but in January 1897, having just turned 14, Lewis entered Mr George Stallard's House at Rugby School. At first he appeared to take a full part in the hearty activities of the place. During his first term he played the school's particular species of football for his house four times. By March, 'footer' was finished, he reported, and 'brookjumping' had commenced. And he was eager for his mother to come to the Sports. 'I have got in a fairly high running set', he told her. Fridtjof Nansen, the Norwegian explorer, visited on 3 March to give a lecture about his expedition to the North Pole and Lewis was clearly proud that the proceedings had been reported in the press. 'I was there', he told his mother.

But his passage through the school was not academically remarkable. Records show he was placed in the second lowest form, where he remained for the next four terms. He moved up a form in the fifth term, up one more in the term following, and then left.

He appeared in two House photographs. The first, in the summer of '97, shows a group of 50-odd boys and young men, standing, sitting and crosslegged in front of a Tudor arched door. The bearded Stallard sits in the middle. Lewis is towards the back and on the outer edge of the closely packed mass of faces. His dark-haired, handsome and unsmiling features are partly obscured by the head of a boy wearing a particularly ill-fitting jacket in front of him. A year later he had moved from the Lower Middle to the Upper Middle School, exchanged the broad Eton shirt collar for a stiff, jaw-chafing stand collar, but was otherwise little changed. The face was, perhaps, slightly less full. He still did not smile.

In retrospect, Lewis was to take pride in his undistinguished academic showing at Rugby, in the punishment he claims was meted out to him and in the stoicism with which he bore it:

> Scarcely did I learn how to spell, certainly. Masters, noticing this, and pretending it was my fault, took advantage of the fact to beat me unmercifully. They gave me a note to hand to my Housemaster. When he read it he beat me too. But I understood it was their fun, and being quite healthy didn't mind.

This account is untrustworthy in one respect, however. Lewis's spelling, punctuation and writing had been deemed 'Very Good' in his previous school, earning him 90 marks out of a possible 100, and the letters he wrote home to his mother from Rugby confirm that assessment. Good spelling is not an accomplishment that can be lost so easily in changing schools. If he was beaten it would have been as a result of other misdemeanours, and his summary of the time at Rugby, 'two years of kicking balls and being beaten for neglect of work', was probably nearer the mark.

Even so, it may be that he received fewer beatings than he claimed and that the image of himself as reprobate and rebel, even at that early age, was one that he carefully fostered in later life. He certainly expressed a schoolboy's admiration for the notable miscreants among his contemporaries. He wrote in great excitement to his mother about a boy who was 'bunked' – expelled – for stealing from a shop in the town. He also described to her the ritualised fate of another boy who had suffered "a 'sixth licking" '. This was a beating from every 'sixth' or prefect in the House. He explained that it was only the second time this awesome punishment had been given since the House was founded. But in conversation nearly 50 years later, Lewis altered the story in two fundamental respects. Firstly, he conferred the historic notoriety upon himself, and secondly, changed the nature of the ordeal to improve his story. Marshall McLuhan recalled hearing the enhanced version:

He . . . was very proud of being the only Rugby man until his time who had ever been given the 'sixth licking' – six full-scale lashings by a prefect in one day. When he had achieved his fifth licking, and having no wish to forgo the distinction of the sixth, he at once proceeded to the prefect's door, with tennis racket and ball, and began to bounce the ball vigorously against the prefect's door.

*

On 1 October 1897, at his home in Buffalo, George Lewis experienced a sharp pain in his chest on sitting down to dinner. His doctor was called but by the time he arrived the pain had abated. Late the same night the pain returned and the doctor was called again. While awaiting his arrival, George sat down in an armchair, and in the early hours of 2 October he died. He was 57 years old and he left to his heirs a large and complicated estate, of whose full value nobody seemed quite sure. George had made his will five years before, whilst preparing to visit Europe and before Charles abandoned his wife and son. As a result, no mention was made of Anne. 'I feel sure he intended providing for you and doing less for Charley', Tilly told her. 'As it is, Charley will come in to quite a large sum . . . I hope [he] will do the fair thing to you and Percy but he is such a queer character it is hard to tell.'

Charles's share of his brother's estate was to be 14 per cent, a sum Albert Lewis estimated variously at $67,000, then at a more realistic $56,000. When he wrote to Anne in the immediate aftermath of George's death, and cheered by the higher of Albert's estimates, Charles was generous with his promises. 'Whatever it be, you shall have half, you and Percy, and all to go to Percy on my death excepting a certain sum sufficient for my child [Ethel] here to live respectably and get a fair education.'

But even Albert's lower estimate of what constituted a 14 per cent share turned out to be over-optimistic. And Charles was dismayed to discover that the executors of his brother's estate insisted upon counting the six-monthly remittances paid him over the years as advances on his inheritance. It was calculated that since January 1889 he had received a total of $9,000. By the end of 1899, two years after George's death, the sum of only $21,000 was being mentioned by Albert as his brother's probable share.

*

Lewis's school holidays were spent with his mother at resorts on the south and east coasts. One year they stayed at Weymouth in Dorset, the next was spent strolling the flat grey wastes of shingle at Southwold in Suffolk, where Anne had rented a cottage. Nearly half a century later Lewis remembered Walberswick, the adjacent town, and recommended a pleasant walk along a dyke there to T. S. Eliot. Mother and son also visited Paris for 'some weeks every year', but he left only one brief account of the first impressions made on him by that city:

> It was then I first frequented the galleries, the Louvre and Luxembourg. On several occasions we stayed I recall at a pension in the rue d'Alger, which was full of books – the library of George Augustus Sala, whose widow I think ran it.

The rue d'Alger is a sidestreet running between the rue de Rivoli and the rue St Honoré. If Sala's widow ran a pension there it must have been some time after 1896, the year of the writer's death, that Lewis and his mother stayed. Lewis confessed himself indifferent to the books, 'but the unnumerable [sic] oil-paintings in the museums, in one big lazy blur of cupids, shipwrecks, madonnas and fat women, exercised a pleasurable mesmerism.'

Back at Rugby he painted in oils in his half of the tiny study he shared with another boy:

Instead of poring over my school books, there I would sit and copy an oil painting of a dog. I remember a very big boy opening the door of the study, putting his big red astonished face inside, gazing at me for a while (digesting what he saw – the palette on my thumb, the brush loaded with pigment in the act of dabbing) and then, laconic and contemptuous, remarking 'You frightful Artist!' closed the study door – and I could hear his big slouching lazy steps going away down the passage to find some more normal company.

When the House Master discovered what was going on under his roof, Lewis was sent for and his sketches and paintings examined. Stallard, probably relieved to find the boy skilled at something, however lacking in academic rigour, arranged for him to have personal tuition from the drawing master. Thomas Mitchener Lindsay, an 'old Scot, a beautiful silver moustache shading his red lips, gargled away . . . in a Glasgow accent, but gave [his pupil] much practice in the portrayal of plaster casts, and provided [him] with reports of unrestrained enthusiasm.'

Although he had moved up two forms to the Upper Middle School, halfway through the Michaelmas Term of 1897 his position in the new form of 28 boys was 28th. His mid-term report reflected this. 'Is not doing much work' was underlined. He was 'very unpunctual'. His English was 'not nearly his best', also underlined. His Latin and French were 'very weak' and the words 'makes little effort' were underlined, as were 'poor' in Mathematics, 'lazy' and 'not good' in Physics and 'very slow' in Chemistry.

Only in Drawing was there a glimmer of promise. The initials V.F. – 'Very Fair' on a four-point scale of Good, Fair, Moderate and Bad – placed him just below 'Good'. But even this fell somewhat short of the 'reports of unrestrained enthusiasm' Mr Lindsay was said to have given him.

His Tutor underlined that he was 'very variable in Preparation' and went on: 'Sometimes works well, but often falls far short of being really industrious.' His House Master said he was 'thoroughly idle' and underlined the words twice. 'As bad a report as can well be imagined,' pronounced his Head Master, not so much given to underlining as his colleagues, but no less emphatic in his phraseology: 'He must work or go.'

Stallard had already written to Mrs Lewis, expressing the opinion that her son might be better placed at an educational institution where he could concentrate exclusively on the only activity he appeared to have a vocation for. At the age of 16 Lewis was enrolled at the Slade School of Drawing, Painting and Sculpture.

FOUR

'They must have a very high opinion of him to consider him dangerous'

The Slade School runs along the northern side of University College at the Euston Road end of Gower Street. The neo-classical Portland stone façade comprises two storeys. Projecting from the centre is a domed semi-rotunda, its upper storey ribbed with Corinthian pillars. Double doors give access to a small half-circle of entrance hall, and only a few paces across its stone flags, a flight of stone stairs ascends to a landing, then branches to right and left and out of sight. In the early days the ladies would climb these stairs to the right, attending Life Classes in a room on the first floor. Gentlemen drew from the model in another part of the building. In the centre of the wall, between the two branches of the staircase, a large roundel commemorates the benefactor whose legacy had helped found the School. Alongside the words ARTIUM LIBERALIUM PATRONUS and the date MDCCCLXXI, a seated angel points to the name FELIX SLADE.

The wealthy lawyer and connoisseur had died in 1868, leaving his collection of books, prints and glass to the nation, together with £35,000 to provide chairs of Fine Art at Oxford, Cambridge and London. Digby Wyatt was appointed Professor in Cambridge and John Ruskin in Oxford. University College, London, voted a further £5,000 to provide a purpose-built Art School. It opened in October 1871 under the Professorship of Edward John Poynter. During the five years he held the post, Poynter established a system of art education based upon the French tradition in which students spent as short a time as possible drawing from plaster casts in the Antique Room, progressing rapidly to working from the living model. Alphonse Legros, who succeeded Poynter in 1892, his teaching conducted exclusively in French, consolidated the Slade's emphasis on the importance of serious, accurate draughtsmanship.

By 1899 the formidable Frederick Brown, Legros's successor, was in charge. Randolph Schwabe* remembered him as 'about fifty years of age,

---

* Student at the Slade 1900–6. Slade Professor from 1930 until his death in 1948.

a rather grim figure in a black frock coat . . . grey hair, moustache and chin-tuft, protruding jaw, grave eyes behind spectacles'. He had established a reputation as a teacher at the Westminster Art School before becoming Slade Professor in 1892, bringing many of his Westminster students with him. 'His masseter muscles were prominent,' Schwabe recalled, 'as if his teeth were permanently clenched, and this gave him the look of one who would stand no nonsense. Nor did he.' Perhaps because Art was a field of human endeavour more prone than most to moral laxity, Brown ensured that an almost monastic discipline was maintained. Smoking was not permitted in the corridors. Fraternisation between lady and gentleman students was discouraged. One young man, observed saying good morning to a young woman in the corridor, was taken aside and informed that the Slade was an Art School and not a matrimonial agency. Fraternising or even speaking with models was expressly forbidden.

Brown's assistant was a Fellow of the Royal College of Surgeons. He was well over six feet tall, long and angular of limb, with large ears, hooded eyes and a hooked nose near vertical in profile. Henry Tonks taught drawing, the backbone of the Slade tradition, and his instruction always referred back to skeleton and musculature, with constant insistence upon anatomical accuracy in drawing. According to Schwabe: 'This was the important thing in our lives – drawing. "Action, Construction, Proportion", we were told.'

When Wyndham Lewis arrived from his final term at Rugby, a large canvas, five foot by seven foot, had recently been hung above and to the right of the Slade Roundel, over the stairs leading to the Ladies' Life Room. It showed a bearded man holding a tall cross with a snake coiled around the top of it. With his left arm raised he pointed towards the reptile, while around him men, women and naked children gesticulated wildly in fear or adoration. Beyond the complicated mass of figures, a wooded and rocky landscape stretched into the distance, clouds and lightning reflecting the portentous event. The 1898 Summer Prize painting, *Moses and the Brazen Serpent*, challenged all who entered the Slade to equal or surpass it.

The first person Lewis encountered in the poky entrance hall would have been Campion. The tattooed former soldier who served the Slade School as Beadle occupied a box to the left of the door, from where he could see everyone entering or leaving the building. He may have proudly pointed out to Lewis the gleaming, freshly varnished virtuosity hanging above their heads, and told him it was the work of Augustus John, the 'Slade School ingenious', who had departed in triumph the previous July with the £30 Summer Prize money in his pocket and the aura of legend about him. The Beadle might even have felt it incumbent upon him as a Slade servant to instil in new students the ambition to emulate so shining an example.

Campion would have directed the newcomer to a heavy cloth-bound ledger where he was to sign his name. Here, as everywhere else in the building apart from the Antique Room, where the ladies worked alongside the gentlemen, the sexes were strictly segregated. 'LADIES' signed the left-hand page, 'GENTLEMEN' the right, and below these blue printed headings an alphabet of blue capital letters descended four columns per page, leaving sufficient space below each to register all students of that initial. Each morning Campion would turn the leaf, inscribe day and date at the top of the left-hand page and ensure that each student signed on entry. Sometimes the first of a particular initial to arrive would incorporate the printed letter into his signature. Michael Carmichael Carr invariably did this: writing an 'M' on one side and 'arr' on the other, he allowed the capital 'C' to represent the initials of both his forename and his surname.

Below the large blue 'L' on the right-hand page the new student wrote 'P. Lewis'.

Percy Wyndham Lewis passed through the Slade's doors as a student for the first time on the morning of Monday 9 January 1899. Two and a half years later he would be thrust violently through the same doors in the opposite direction, leaving a whiff of tobacco smoke hanging in the air behind him.

After signing in on his first day he would have been directed up the stairs to the left and through the second door he came to on the upper corridor. Here in the Antique Room he began his formal artistic training. He was put to work sitting astride a low, narrow bench known as a 'donkey', his drawing board propped against the wooden 'T'-shaped structure at one end of it, a pencil in his right hand and a lump of fresh bread, supplied by Campion, for rubbing out, in his left. Everyone started in the Antique Class copying from casts of *Discobolus* and the decapitated, dismembered masterpieces of Ancient Greece. Even John, the 'greatest draughtsman since Michelangelo', according to Tonks, had to serve his time among the plaster casts.

Since the Slade Session ran from October to June, Lewis had already missed one term. His fees for the remainder of the Session were settled by two payments of seven guineas per term, together with £1.11.6 for a two-term course of Anatomy lectures. This invaluable adjunct to the teachings of Henry Tonks, conducted by the University College Professor of Anatomy, G. D. Thane, was intended to have special reference to the requirements of art students. The Course consisted of 20 lectures, delivered Mondays and Thursdays at 4 in the afternoon throughout the second and third terms, 'treating chiefly of the Bones, Joints, and Muscles; and . . . illustrated by demonstrations on the Living Model'.

Apart from sparse registration records, the signing-in books contain the only evidence by which Lewis's passage through the Slade may be traced. Admittedly, such evidence is not an entirely reliable guide to a student's routine. A signature on a particular day does not constitute proof positive that the student actually attended classes or did any work. It merely shows that he was present in the entrance hall that particular morning. It is said that, in the early 1920s, Ben Nicholson conscientiously signed the book each morning and then conscientiously played billiards for the rest of the day. Also, although it would have been one of Campion's duties to preside over the signing-in book and, knowing all the students by name, ensure that nobody signed in on behalf of someone else, there are occasional instances in which the divergent handwriting of a signature from day to day shows that a student was being covered for by his friends.

Lewis's first two months seemed to establish a pattern of diligence. Six days a week, with the exception of one day in January and four days in February, he signed in under Campion's watchful eye. A couple of obviously forged scrawls testify to moments when Campion's attention must have been distracted and a friend wrote in Lewis's name as well as his own. But for the most part the startling variations in the style of his signature are consistent only with the calligraphic flourishes of adolescent experimentation.

Lewis had just turned 16. Having abandoned his public school career early he was still very much a schoolboy when he arrived at the Slade, and considerably younger than his fellow students. Spencer Frederick Gore, the first man he spoke to that day, was four years his senior. William Crampton Gore (no relation) was older by five years, as was F.H.S. Shepherd. Harold Gilman, at 23, was even older and Arthur Croft Mitchell older still at 26. With one or more of these friends Lewis would hurry along Grafton Street at the start of the midday break. The luncheon room in Shoolbred's department store, 151–158 Tottenham Court Road, provided homely fare at a moderate price. 'Veal and ham pie and swiss roll and cream – a great deal of cream', he recalled, 'was how I was nourished as a student.'

With another friend, he lunched at Frascati's. Herman Hildesheim was also in his twenties. During the War he would change his forename to Hubert and his surname to Hilton in deference to anti-German feeling. Albert Rothenstein, another Slade contemporary, would become Rutherston for the same reason. But when Hildesheim began taking his lunch with Lewis, it was the possibility of another sort of racial prejudice that concerned him. Having lunched together two or three times Hildesheim confided, with some embarrassment, that he was Jewish and asked Lewis if he minded: 'my first experience', Lewis recalled, 'of that ghastly problem of an ostracised race.'

At another point in their acquaintance, Lewis confided something to Hildesheim. Badly scared by a Gower Street doctor's diagnosis, he sought his Jewish friend's advice. Hildesheim took the patient to see his brother Oscar, a recently qualified medical man, who was able to assure Lewis that the genital rash he complained of was not, as he feared, syphilis. Half a century later he still remembered the favour. 'Your brother . . . immediately blew away that bogey for me', he reminded his old Slade comrade.

Hildesheim painted his young friend's portrait in oils, the only surviving likeness of him as a Slade student. It is a mediocre piece of work, showing an adolescent blessed with near feminine good looks, darkly dressed and sitting against a brown background. The hands, accentuated against the blackness of the jacket, are particularly unconvincing. The head is cocked to the left, the eyes directed up to the right. By the time it was presented to the sitter his sight had deteriorated to such an extent that he was mercifully spared the necessity of passing polite comment on it.

After his death, Lewis's widow had to be restrained by friends from taking a pair of nail scissors to the canvas and separating the idealised head from the offending hands.

It is not known how long Lewis spent slaving over drawings of dusty plaster casts, only that such slaving was a prerequisite of further advance at the Slade. 'All Students', the prospectus decreed, '(except those specially exempted by the Professor) will . . . be required to draw from the Antique until judged sufficiently advanced to draw from the Life.' Some had to wait longer than others. William Rothenstein, when Legros was Professor, endured a full year's incarceration with the Antique, eventually leaving the Slade without ever graduating to the Life.

But most people under Brown's regime spent half a term before being granted permission to attend the Life Room during the last three quarters of an hour of the afternoon. This initial graduation from plaster to flesh was known as 'short poses'. It was the time when the model would relax from the statuesque posture the senior students had been copying all day, to take up a number of poses of three or four minutes' duration. For a further trial period the student would continue working from the Antique and attending 'short poses' at the end of each day until the Professor and his Assistant deemed him ready to join the Gentlemen's Life Class full time.

It was the largest room in the building. Along the corridor to the right of the entrance hall, past the tangled intricacies of Laocoön and his sons wrestling the serpent, a cast too heavy and unwieldy to have reached the Antique Room, and down a flight of stairs, Room 10 was actually in the basement of the Slade but it rose through two storeys.

The model posed all day on a high platform or 'throne', contours of the body unvaried by shadow in the even north light from five tall windows at first-floor height and a skylight. Students squatted astride their donkeys in a semicircle to struggle with the formal complexities of the man or woman before them. The throne had to be high enough for students at the back of the semicircle to get a clear view. In later years as many as three models would pose at a time. Smaller groups of students clustered around each model and the thrones were proportionally lower.

The height of the throne in Lewis's day can be gauged from the large black chalk drawing, another example of the great Augustus John's brilliant facility, which hung on the wall of the Life Room: 'a hairy male nude,' Lewis remembered, 'arms defiantly folded and bristling moustache, commemorated his powers with almost a Gascon assertiveness.' The feet of this figure were enormous, testifying to the steep angle from which the Slade star had squinted up to draw it. Glaring loftily from the summit of corded neck, folded arms, dramatically foreshortened torso and powerful thighs, the tour de force of observational draftsmanship had been left there to inspire or intimidate the aspirants toiling, scratching and rubbing out below. Shoulder-high along the north wall ran a narrow, lipped shelf where lesser students' work would be propped up for comparison and criticism by Tonks.

While there can be no reliable evidence of when Lewis joined these aspirants, it is possible to speculate on when his probationary period in the Antique Class came to an end and he was able to feel secure in the routine of Room 10.

After two months of apparently assiduous attendance, signing the book daily, Lewis's trail abruptly evaporates. After 27 February, with the single exception of a Tuesday in March, his name vanishes from the daily roll for the rest of that term. Likewise for the whole of the following term, from 17 April to 1 July, not one tangled scribble of lines, however illegible, can be found below the blue capital 'L' to show he even entered the building.

But it is difficult to believe that he could be absent this length of time and still gain the experience and do the work that would bring him the accolades in figure drawing of the following year. Also, this four-month lacuna was only the beginning of a trend that would last throughout his remaining time at the Slade. Out of a total of 461 days that its doors were open to him, he signed the book only 226 times.

When a student failed to sign the book it did not necessarily mean that he had been absent. Campion opened the Slade's doors and the signing-in book before the beginning of classes at 9.30 each morning. At 11 he put the book away until the following day. Anyone arriving later than 11 would therefore not register.

The most likely explanation for the lack of signatures in March, April, May and June was that Lewis consistently arrived late. An explanation for this suddenly relaxed pattern of behaviour was that, after two months laboriously proving his mettle with attacks upon *Discobolos*, by the end of February 1899 he had secured his place among the senior students in the Life Room.

Lewis must have lost or destroyed nearly every life drawing he executed in Room 10. One exception is the pencil drawing of a nude male, weight resting on the right leg, left leg slightly forward and hands loosely clasped behind the back, now in the Strang Collection of Prints and Drawings, University College, London. Lewis sat to the model's right, towards the extremity of the crescent of students and far enough from the throne to allow him to keep the figure in proportion. He worked hard and, judging from the pentimenti around the legs, used up a lot of bread in erasures. The drawing won Tonks's approval. It was retained by the Slade and the peppering of tiny holes in the corners of the paper testify to the number of times it must have been taken from a plan chest, pinned to a drawing board, propped on the shelf of the Life Room and shown to later students as an example of good figure drawing.

It was while Lewis was in Room 10 one day that the door opened and he caught a first glimpse of the 'Slade School ingenious' himself. 'A tall bearded figure, with an enormous black Paris hat, large gold ear-rings decorating his ears, with a carriage of the utmost arrogance, strode in and the whisper "John" went round the class. He sat down on a donkey . . . tore a page of banknote paper out of a sketch book, pinned it upon a drawing board, and with a ferocious glare at the model (a female) began to draw with an indelible pencil.' Lewis joined the crowd that gathered behind the legend and watched him work.

John's visit and impromptu demonstration, recalled 50 years later, created a stir among the students jostling to see. It became apparent that John's style had departed from the 'grand manner' championed by Tonks and epitomised by the heroic hairy figure that dominated the Gentlemen's Life Room. Instead: 'a squat little figure began to emerge upon the paper . . . A modern Saskia was taking shape upon the banknote paper: drawings that followed all came out of the workshop of Rembrandt Van Rhyn. Needless to say everyone was tickled to death.' When he had finished, John abruptly left the room. 'We watched in silence this mythical figure depart.'

Over the following weeks 'the squalor of the Dutch, rather than the noble rhetoric of the cinquecento' spread like a virus. 'Tonks's life was a hell on earth . . . However tall and graceful the model might be, displaying her

32

young English charms . . . Tonks was presented, as he went his rounds . . . with nothing but dumpy little images.'

After a half-century, Lewis may have exaggerated John's responsibility for this trend. Another Slade contemporary, Hubert L. Wellington, recalled that '1899 was the year of the Rembrandt exhibitions at the Royal Academy and the Print Room of the British Museum, both arousing keen interest and study in the School.'

Wherever this fashion for 'Dutch squalor' came from, Lewis participated for a time. 'I tried my hand at it, but found [the drawings] did not come out very well.' The densely crosshatched pen and ink composition *An Oriental Design*, with its pendulous-bellied odalisque dressed in harem pants and jewellery, is one such experiment. No others have survived. Eventually he reverted to a Master that would have been more to Tonks's liking. 'I went back to a version of my own of Signorelli.'

If Lewis was copying Luca Signorelli, the 15th-century draftsman second in his day only to Michelangelo, this would probably have been some time towards the end of 1899 after Lewis's first excursion to the Department of Prints and Drawings at the British Museum. His signature appeared for the first time in the Students' Room visitors' book on Saturday 7 October. Later he spoke of being 'directed' thither, by Tonks, to study the draftsmanship of Raphael and Michelangelo. However, Lewis found more in the British Museum than he had been sent to study. And while he followed Tonks's instructions and copied and learnt from the great Western masters of form and sinuous line, his attention was also drawn to artefacts the Assistant Professor would have certainly dismissed.

In the late 1940s an American critic, preparing an article on Lewis's early work, wrote to the artist wondering whether he was correct in recognising Polynesian influences. Lewis replied that indeed there had been such influences and that they originated in his visits to the Department of Prints and Drawings while he was at the Slade. 'I had always to pass between cases full of more savage symbols on my way to the shrines of the cinquecento', he told James Thrall Soby.

Prints and Drawings was at that time located in the eastern corner of the upper floor. Lewis would have got there by going up the main staircase and through the Prehistoric Saloon and the Roman British Room; the Students' Room of the Department of Prints and Drawings was straight ahead on the other side of the Asiatic Saloon. This route did not in fact take him 'between cases full of . . . savage symbols' on his way to copy Michelangelo, but only a slight detour left at the Asiatic Saloon brought him into the great East Gallery which housed the Ethnographic Collections: 'Oceanic, African and American sections,' according to Baedeker, 'each containing a great variety of objects illustrating the habits, dress, warfare, handicrafts, etc., of the less civilised inhabitants of the different quarters of the globe.'

With his first two terms at the Slade behind him, he was absorbing influences from two broad cultures: the one, trumpeted by Tonks as the apogee of civilisation; the other despised by him as primitive, but soon to inspire a generation of Expressionists, Post-Impressionists and Cubists.

In 1947, prompted by James Thrall Soby to recall those early visits to the British Museum, he leafed through an old sketchbook. It contained copies of a grotesque man with a swollen underlip by Leonardo and of athletes by Michelangelo. On other pages there were sketches of Pacific Island masks.*

*

At the Museum he would be taken up by another circle of acquaintances. As at the Slade these were men considerably older than himself. The poet and engraver Thomas Sturge Moore, for instance, was 12 years his senior. Laurence Binyon, poet and assistant keeper of Prints and Drawings, was 13 years older, while R. A. Streatfield, assistant keeper of Printed Books, music critic of the *Daily Graphic* and soon to become the literary executor of Samuel Butler, was older by some 16 years. And it was probably at the Museum that he met another older man: a self-styled architect, freemason and occult philosopher by the name of William Stirling.

*

The records of University College indicate three payments of seven guineas apiece for the 1899/1900 Session. Mrs Lewis was paying her son's fees term by term, despite the fact that she could have saved herself three guineas in October 1899 by paying the full Sessional fee of 18 guineas. This suggests that her resources were stretched to the limit and that her son's art education continued upon an extremely precarious economic footing. Lewis entered his name in the Slade's signing-in book on the morning of the first day of the 1899–1900 Session, 2 October. He did not sign again until a fortnight later, the 16th. Out of a total of 66 days that term he arrived early enough to sign the book on only 21 occasions. Such erratic timekeeping can hardly have gone unnoticed by the authorities, and the pattern of signatures in the following term suggests he might have received a warning from Professor Brown. Throughout January and February he seemed to make an

* The sketchbook's present whereabouts are unknown.

effort and his name was to be found in the book every day. Nevertheless on at least one occasion the name seems to have been written by someone else.

For a time he appeared to be a model Slade student, and was one of 36 to be awarded a Certificate in Figure Drawing. The time spent studying and copying at the British Museum and the previous year's Anatomy Course had evidently not been wasted. His homage to Signorelli may also have reflected well on him, together with his abandonment of the habit for Dutch pastiche.

The Certificate in Figure Drawing was nothing more than a validation by Tonks of a level of competence in the Life Room. A more exclusive and indeed lucrative prize was still to come.

*

From the beginning of 1900, students entering the Department of Prints and Drawings were required to supply a name and address on every visit. Previously only a signature had been called for. This welcome innovation allows Lewis's movements to be roughly traced for the next eight years. The Visitors Books yield the first evidence of what was to become a significant and characteristic trend in Lewis's future life: a bewildering frequency in changes of address.

For the first few months of 1900 his stated residence was 24 Fitzroy Street. Once, in May, he wrote 3 Brookfield, Highgate, his mother's address. Then, in November, he moved from 20 Bloomsbury Street to 38 Queens Square. By February 1901 he had moved to 34 Milman's Street, off Cheyne Walk. After spending April with his mother he was at 1 Margaretta Terrace, Oakley Street, until September when he could be found briefly at 7 Beaufort Street. He then moved to 4 Limerston Street until very nearly the end of the year. In January 1902 he was again at Margaretta Terrace, then again at 24 Fitzroy Square before returning, in February, to 4 Limerston Street. In April he was at 59 or 159 Church Street, Chelsea, before returning in May to Fitzroy Street, where he stayed, this time for the most part at no. 8, but latterly at no. 37, until the end of the year.

'He liked to shroud himself in mystery', William Rothenstein recalled. 'After hiding for weeks he would suddenly reappear, having been, he would declare, in Sweden, or in some remote country; and he would hint at a conquest. His 'conquests' seemed for the most part to be Swedes, Germans, Poles or Russians, shadowy figures whom one heard of, but never met.'

Rothenstein was never sure whether he had ever left London. Indeed, there is no reason to believe he had been further abroad than his mother's house in Highgate.

*

If Lewis's regular attendance in January and February 1900 was the result of a caution from the Professor, he might have been further encouraged to make an effort by the suggestion that greater diligence and compliance with the Slade's regimen could, along with his undoubted talent, get him elected to a Scholarship.

Felix Slade's will had provided for the award of six Scholarships valued at £35 per annum and tenable for a period not exceeding three years. Two of these Scholarships were awarded each year to students who had shown a proficiency in drawing, painting or sculpture. John had received one in 1896. It was during his industrious first two months of 1900 that Lewis entered the running.

Regulations stated that competitors had to provide certificates of birth proving them to be under 21 at the date of the election. It was to tender this proof that Mrs Lewis, in mid-February, made her solemn declaration at the Mansion House: 'My son Percy Wyndham Lewis was born on the 18th day of November 1882 at Amherst, Nova Scotia, and was therefore on the 18th day of November last seventeen years old and no more.'

Having stated his intention to compete for the Scholarship he apparently slipped back into old habits, failing to sign the book for the rest of the term. But he signed again on 18 April, the first day of the following term, and thereafter daily until 26 May.

At a meeting of the College Council at the beginning of June, Lewis was elected to a two-year Scholarship on the basis of his figure drawing. As a condition of the award, one of the submitted drawings was retained by the Slade: a nude boy in black chalk, knees bent, back horizontal and right arm stretched down as if in the act of picking something off the floor.

According to a 1927 draft of autobiographical detail written in the third person, becoming a Scholar made Lewis a cynosure of the life room. 'So great was his precocious dexterity that groups of students would gather round ... to watch him work.' Sitting astride the donkey with his contemporaries craning their necks to look over his shoulders at the emerging drawing, he must have felt as if cast in the glowing role of a previous Scholar: Augustus John.

More important so far as his mother was concerned, the Scholarship provided £35 per annum for the next two years. It meant that she was able to settle the whole of the 1900/1 Sessional fee in one payment of 18 guineas that October.

The £35 per annum did not come entirely free of obligation or responsibility. Lewis's duties, shared with the other Scholar of 1900,

William Rothenstein's younger brother Albert, were 'giving assistance to the Slade Professor in the maintenance of order in the Schools, in superintending, under his direction, the younger Students'.

He began the 1900–1901 Session conscientiously enough. A fortnight into the term, on 15 October, he signed in and made a note beside his name, commemorating the uniquely early hour of his arrival that morning: twenty minutes past nine. One of his duties as a Scholar was to start the Life Class off at 9.30 by setting the model's pose for the day. His routine of early rising was short-lived, however, and after the end of November, when it came to posing the model: 'I was seldom there to do that.' His work routine slackened off as well. 'I preferred smoking and reading the paper or talking in the drying room to painting the nude.'

If Lewis was aware of the final paragraph in regulations governing the tenure of his Scholarship, he evidently did not allow it to alter his behaviour:

> The Council will have the right to withdraw a Scholarship at any time from a Scholar whose attendance and diligence are not satisfactory to the Slade Professor, or whose general conduct may make it desirable to remove him or her from the Schools.

He lasted only one complete Session as a Scholar: from October 1900 to June 1901. Despite the fact that a further £35 awaited him for the second year of his Scholarship, he did not even enrol the following October for the 1901/2 Session. Later, in the third-person account, he would explain his abrupt departure in a manner reflecting best upon himself: 'like many other well-known artists of advanced views, dissatisfied with the traditional training supplied at an art-school, he completed his apprenticeship by himself.' But there is also a more honest account: 'the same thing occurred there as had already befallen me [at Rugby] – only this time it was more violent, since they were paying me, not I paying them. My scholarship was taken away from me and I was shown the door.'

The actual circumstances of the expulsion were witnessed by Randolph Schwabe. It happened towards the end of the summer term and 10 June was the last day Lewis's signature appeared in Campion's book. It seems he lit a cigarette in the entrance hall while Professor Brown was watching him. Smoking was prohibited in the corridors of the Slade, partly out of consideration for the lady students. The corridors, and especially the entrance hall, were parts of the building in which a mingling of the sexes was unavoidable at one time of the day or another. When he stood at the bottom of the stairs and calmly applied the match to his cigarette, Lewis knew he was being observed by Brown, either from the landing above or from the door to the Professor's study to the right of the staircase. The gesture was not only a flagrant breach of discipline, it was a display of studied arrogance and a defiant challenge to Brown to do something about it. And it was probably just the excuse he was waiting for. By his own admission Lewis had been a long way from fulfilling the responsibilities and duties of his Scholarship.

In later years Schwabe would tell the story to illustrate what a powerful man Fred Brown could become when roused. The renegade Scholar was seized, and hurled bodily through the double doors into the quadrangle beyond.

Campion was given instructions that Lewis be refused entry should he attempt to come back. When the reprobate returned some days later to obtain a model's address, Campion followed orders and turned him away at the threshold. It was said that Brown once summoned a student to his office, having seen him talking to Lewis on the top deck of a bus in the King's Road, and issued dire warnings of the bad influence. Lest it be thought that Lewis exaggerated this flattering notoriety, corroboration came from Spencer Gore writing to Hubert Wellington in 1902:

> So bitterly do the authorities of the Slade dislike Lewis that anyone going in for a prize or Scholarship is apparently first questioned and his former life examined to find out 'whether he is a friend of Lewis'. Seems to me that this is nearly as good for him as being great friends with them, as they must have a very high opinion of him to consider him dangerous.

FIVE

'The poet' and mentors

He had begun writing verse at the Slade. 'He hesitated between writing and painting', was how William Rothenstein remembered it. 'I recall no compositions by Lewis – the imaginative and romantic side of his nature he put into his poems and into his daily life.' One sonnet, 'To Doubt', if Lewis's recollection in 1942 was correct, his 'earliest literary product, written about 16th year', was especially commended:

> Death's incorruptible minister is Doubt,
> Whose very name of Hope is eloquent:
> And so the interest in this changeful plot
> Is kept at whiteheat till the curtain drop:
> Doubt is the sole tonic that sustains the mind,
> The key note of this universe entire, –
> Self-conscious certainty is Doubt, – and blind
> God-worship is Doubt's sanctified attire.
>
> God fashioned us in Doubt, – for Eden trees
> Were planted there in God's initial doubt:
> This brief respite Fate grants us doth but tease
> Us into hope, where Certainty could not.
>
> Doubt's Universal empire doth but show
> God fears a certain Anarchy of Woe.

'So young', marvelled William Rothenstein, looking up from the page and eyeing him closely, 'and yet as wise as I am.' Rothenstein had been introduced to Lewis's verse by William Stirling and had thought it 'strange and interesting'.

During the opening chapters of a novel, *The Apes of God*, that Lewis would publish 30 years later, a young poet is introduced, his fresh green talent discussed:

'. . . he has written one most lovely poem. I will show it to you.'

'Thank you. I should like to read it very much. Is it in free verse? I suppose so.'

'Not at all – it is in a quite traditional metre. Absolutely the youngest generation, sir, do not write in free verse – they have gone back to quite traditional forms . . . It is only, you will find, the thirties and forties that believe in violent experiment – the very youngest generation . . . are classical to a man!'

An admirer of the poetry and, probably, a covert admirer of the handsome young poet himself, William Stirling was a 40-year-old bachelor who worked as Demonstrator in the Department of Architecture at University College. Also a student of mystical philosophy, his only published work, *The Canon*, had appeared in 1897. It was subtitled 'An exposition of the Pagan Mystery Perpetuated in the Cabala as the Rule of the Arts'. He was acquainted with W. B. Yeats, who thought him 'sooner or later . . . certain to do good work'. But despite his leanings towards the esoteric, even Yeats was baffled by Stirling's obsessions:

He showed me a quantity of designs for some sort of a pagan temple which seemed very imaginative – I couldn't follow his numerical speculations & indeed had no great trust in them, but he lit on all sorts of interesting things by the way.

Rothenstein said of him that he had 'an exquisite and lovable nature'. He was 'self-sufficing and knew hardly anyone'. He was an avid collector of books which, Rothenstein suspected, he starved himself to buy. His cultivation of the young poet also incurred expense.

Lewis, 'so young then that everything is misty', nevertheless remembered being taken by Stirling to Buszard's, the palatial confectioners on the corner of Oxford Street and Ramillies Street, and treated to Meringue Chantilly: 'I was inordinately greedy and probably did not have to be pressed very much to eat three or four.' He admitted, in retrospect, that Stirling, who supported a sister and aged mother from a slender income, could ill afford such lavish entertainment and would have had to fast for several days thereafter.

The tall, beautiful, black-haired 19-year-old with a schoolboy's taste for Meringue Chantilly, passively enjoying the blandishments of an older man, would be recognisable in the tall, beautiful, black-haired, moronic hero of *The Apes of God*, gushed over by the sexually indeterminate Horace Zagreus:

'Mr Boleyn is only nineteen . . . He has a great future – of course as yet he is too young to have done much, but he has written one most lovely poem.'

And Stirling's Freemasonry and mystical interests would be recalled in the esoteric claptrap of Mr Zagreus's preparations for the role of First Conjuror to Lord Osmund's Lenten Party: 'Ace, tray, cinque, size. How many letters are there in my name? Are there enough to fill the points of space?'

William Stirling lived in a small dark flat at 8 York Buildings in the area known as the Adelphi, between the Strand and the Embankment. He displayed marked signs of paranoia, believing himself to be spied upon by a fellow tenant, the young actor Harley Granville Barker.

Just before Rothenstein left London for Berlin, in March 1902, Stirling gave him a copy of *The Canon*. When they said goodbye, Stirling touched him lightly on the cheek with his fingertips. Rothenstein claimed to have had a feeling they would never meet again.

In that same month Lewis lent Stirling a packet of his sonnets to read.

A couple of weeks later, on 7 April, the author of *The Canon*, 'being of sound mind', wrote a will leaving all his goods to his sister Anne and appointing Rothenstein as his literary executor. He sealed the envelope and left it on his sitting-room table. Then he entered his bedchamber, opened a razor and cut his throat. The first gash drenched his shirt with blood but left him alive. He removed his collar and tie, stripped off the bloodstained shirt and, unaccountably, put on a clean one. This action gave the *Daily Express* its headline: SUICIDE'S TOILET. Stirling then slashed his throat a second time and slowly bled to death.

Nobody had seen him since 2 April. The police were informed and his rooms entered on the 24th. By this time Stirling had been dead for seventeen days. The rats that swarmed the area so close to the river had gnawed his ankles, ears, fingers and, according to the *Daily Express*, 'other parts of the body'.

At the inquest a neighbour described him as being 'a hard student, something of a recluse, and eccentric'. The deceased's second cousin testified that, so far as he knew, Stirling had nothing preying upon his mind but that he was a disappointed man. 'He was a very clever architect, but had not been successful.'

Not mentioned at the inquest was the fact that, unsuccessful in his profession or not, he had just received promotion in the Department of Architecture and was, at the time of his death, Assistant to the Professor.

Despite the initial assertion of his will, the inquest jury returned a verdict that 'Deceased committed suicide while of unsound mind.'

Among Stirling's papers Will Rothenstein found a sheaf of sonnets.

In the Rare Books and Manuscript Collections of the Carl A. Kroch

Library at Cornell University, Ithaca, New York, is an envelope containing 44 sheets of manuscript and typescript. On the envelope is the following note:

> These poems were mainly written in about 18th year: all before 20th certainly. Of no value, but better be kept. It is certainly not my desire to have these not very interesting early efforts published. I should be very sorry to think that after my death they might be dragged out and published by some literary promoter, for mercenary reasons. – On the other hand, I do not destroy them because Sir William Rothenstein has a duplicate of them. A long time ago (when I was about 19 years old) I gave the set now in the possession of Rothenstein to a man called Stirling to read . . . A few weeks after I gave him the poems he committed suicide . . . Sir W.R. was his literary executor or something; anyhow the poems came into his possession. At first I believe he thought they were Stirling's. Then he discovered they were mine. Very improperly Sir William Rothenstein did not return them to me but stuck to them. There the matter still stands. If I succeed in getting them back I will destroy them. Anyhow, I hope they will never see the light.

> Wyndham Lewis. Toronto. 1942.

*

Thomas Sturge Moore, poet and engraver, was another older man who offered guidance:

> While still a teenager . . . instead of preparing for the University you switched to a course of . . . purely technical art-training . . . Consider what otherwise you would have been taking in . . . Your intellect is that of a schoolboy. But you have to make up for the world you lost in pure art-training. The intellect demands that.

With these words, a character in Lewis's last completed novel began the belated completion of its young protagonist's education. And it would not be taking too great a liberty, melding fact with fiction, to imagine Moore, at his home in Holland Park, addressing his young protégé in similar terms.

Many years later, beyond one world conflict and halfway through another, Lewis wrote from Canadian exile to Moore's old address, not knowing if the letter had a chance of finding his old friend, even if it successfully braved bombs and torpedoes in its Atlantic crossing. He remembered a Golden Age:

How calm those days were before the epoch of wars and social revolutions when you used to sit on one side of your worktable and I on the other, and we would talk – with trees and creepers of the placid Hampstead domesticity beyond the windows, and you used to grunt with a philosophic despondency I greatly enjoyed. It was the last days of the Victorian world of artificial peacefulness – of the R.S.P.C.A. and London bobbie, of 'slumming' and Buzzards [sic] cakes. As at that time I had never even heard of anything else, it seemed to my young mind in the order of nature. You – I suppose – knew it was all like the stunt of an illusionist. You taught me many things. But you never taught me that.

*

Lewis was first formally introduced to Augustus John, by William Rothenstein, in the summer of 1902, shortly after John's return from Liverpool. Lewis's studio was only a few doors away at 8 Fitzroy Street. As he and Rothenstein approached the top-floor flat at number 18 they heard a baby crying: 'this patriarch had already started upon his Biblical courses'. The meeting began a friendship that would last until Lewis's death.

It was mainly of Rothenstein and John, and probably also Walter Sickert whom he met around this time, that Lewis wrote:

> The only people of eminence I was in touch with as a beginner were painters . . . They overlooked in me the budding artist but accorded a generous recognition to something else . . . And to these elders I was known as a 'poet'. The Fine Arts they imagined were already in good hands, namely their own.

John would refer to him for years to come as 'the poet'.

For his part Lewis regarded the glamorous older man with unabashed hero worship. For the rest of his life he would sport variations of the broad-brimmed black hat he had first seen John wearing at the Slade. He picked up the abandoned drawings that John had torn from his sketch pad, ripped up and discarded. He took them away, carefully stuck the pieces together and found an album to keep them in.

John's charcoal drawing of 'the poet', aged 20, was a marked contrast to Hildesheim's oil of a few years before. It was not just a better portrait: it captured a cast of feature that either had not been there before or that Hildesheim had missed. The three-quarter profile showed Lewis's boyish good looks to have filled out slightly, giving the face a sensual quality reinforced by the cupid's bow of the lips. The eyes, half covered by the drop of the lids, had a calculating, slightly cruel look. The same portrait, scratched with a needle onto polished copper and bitten by nitric acid, accentuated these features and subtly transformed the face. Inked and pressed into paper the etched plate left a reversed, heavily shaded, rather sinister version of the charcoal original. It threw into prominence the dark bags under the brooding hooded eyes, the puffy cheeks and jowls and the voluptuous mouth. John had made him look like a debauched schoolboy.

SIX

Bohemian trappings

In January of 1903 he moved from Fitzroy Street to Great Ormond Street, where he lived – at two different addresses – for most of that year. On 24 August John's wife Ida wrote to his sister Gwen with the news that Lewis had gone to Spain with Spencer Gore. This was his first taste of foreign travel unaccompanied by his mother.

The advertisement described Eliza Briggs's 'first class English pension' as being 'airy' with electric light and a lift. Terms were moderate and available on application to: Miss Briggs, Calle Mayor, 92, Madrid.

'I think Madrid in the really winter time ... must be an extremely dangerous place, and one's life would be crowded with precautions and not worth living, – like walking on thin ice.' Hypochondria was a characteristic feature of Lewis's letters to his mother, and she encouraged such anxiety in her only child. He had contracted a cold almost as soon as he arrived and felt exhausted for the first ten days. He developed a painfully ulcerated throat, but a physician friend of Miss Briggs told him that everybody in Madrid, including the Queen and half the Court, had ulcerated throats.

Despite the poor health both were suffering, Lewis and Gore rented a studio and furnished it, the younger man keeping account of everything they spent for his mother:

15 pesetas for a good coke stove
8 pesetas for the pipes
5 pesetas for two chairs
3 or 4 pesetas for a sort of table
1½ pesetas for a deal box
30 pesetas for a carpet

They would be able to sell the furnishings back for half the price when they left. The exchange rate stood at 33 pesetas to the pound at this time; their rent for the pension was equivalent to about 38 shillings each and the studio 4 shillings. 'Models are cheap here: three pesetas for three hours. So if we spend three pesetas each a day we'll have no lack of work.'

[Miss] Briggs – say 38/-
studio –   say 4/-
models –   say 12/-
———
£2.14

'We go to bed at 10 and get up at 8 without the least variety, and spend no money outside, as there's nothing worth spending it on.'

Every week Mrs Lewis sent him a cheque for £6 which he collected from the offices of Thomas Cook in the Carrera San Jeronimo.

In mid-September, about a fortnight or so after their arrival, he was ill again. 'I think I have caught a fresh cold (a slight one). I still have the old one. Gore's not well either. I suppose I must stay here another month, and see the run of the studio out but dare not longer . . . We're not well chiefly because of the change – extreme change – of climate, I suppose, and change of food: we eat an awful lot here.'

They visited the Prado. Lewis told his mother that they had seen a room full of Goya drawings. This was the 'Salón de Goya', on the ground floor to the left of the vestibule, and contained, not only pen and ink and crayon drawings, but portraits and the series of scenes from Spanish life originally executed as tapestry designs. Lewis copied Goyas and, years later, also claimed to have 'studied the principles of the red Venetian grounds' in the Prado.

At least one, unfortunately anonymous, contact was made in Madrid's artistic community:

We . . . visited an artist, (ridiculous person,) and to do so hired a conveyance. I've never had a more exciting twenty minutes than that cab drive: we had our side-step smashed by a carriage, stopped the traffic several times, quarrelled with everybody, were turned out of main street for frightening a mule-team and using bad language, dived into dark narrow lane, and, finding large cart facing us, turned round, having first driven onto pavement, and nearly into a shop window: we reached the artist at last, and found him, as I said, a ridiculous person.

*

Before coming home he thought of extending his travels. 'I rather think that I should like to go to Italy . . . before returning to England; as I am going there soon, it would be cheaper to go while I'm abroad.' It was to be, however, another 20 years, and in the glamorous company of Nancy Cunard, before he made his only excursion to Italy.

46

Leaving the climatic perils of Madrid behind, they probably returned to London in mid to late October. On 30 December he was signing the British Museum visitors' book and giving 18 Fitzroy Street as his new address.

In January 1904 he moved to 8 Fitzroy Street and, towards the end of the month, north to 4 St Georges Square* near Regent's Park, where he would remain until June. In August he moved to 5 The Mall, Park Hill Road, Hampstead.

*

There is evidence that his mother's business was in difficulties at this time. A letter from T. B. Bowe & Co., Thames Soap Works in Brentford, to Anne's West Middlesex Laundry acknowledged the receipt of £26 with the balance of the bill to be paid in four days' time. Mrs Lewis had allowed her debt to remain unpaid for six months, despite an agreed credit limit of three months, taking advantage of the leniency the company had shown her in the past. She was warned that steps would be taken to see that overdue accounts were paid if she failed, in future, to keep within her terms of credit.

This crisis did not prevent her from taking a short holiday with her son, and towards the end of August she joined him in Holland. Lewis was in Haarlem for the best part of two months. Part of his time was spent in Room III of the Municipal Museum, where the west wall was occupied by ten Frans Hals paintings from which he was copying. There must also have been something to interest him at the Teyler Museum, because the guest book records two visits. On 1 September he was there with his mother. He went again, three weeks later, and this time he was joined by the young Dutch painter Lodewijk Schelfhout,† a new acquaintance. 'Louis' Schelfhout would be responsible for getting Lewis his first, rather unsalubrious, lodgings in Paris a month or so later.

Following his mother's departure he stayed on at a pension where, by October, he had compromised himself by dallying with the daughter of the house – an attractive but 'very stupid, uninteresting and not in the least exciting' girl called Lesbie. 'I have taken certain opportunities to bestow a kiss upon her blanched brow,' he wrote home, 'and may perhaps have stroked her bosom, but . . . I have done nothing more.' His mother might have been reminded of her husband's abuse of hospitality with the pretty English housemaid in New Jersey a decade earlier.

His attentions, far from outraging his hosts, gave Lesbie's parents reason for hope. The father began talking of marriage and asked questions about his

* Now Chalcot Square.
† (1881–1943)

family. The girl's mother dropped blatant hints as to the attractions of such a match: 'Of course the furniture will go to my dear little Lesbie.' Lewis was greatly amused by this: 'it's the sort of remark Mamas make in Dickens's books.' Loud arguments were overheard in the next room. 'I think that I am often the subject of these disputes.'

It was a good story, and the picaresque situation in which he found himself was obviously relished in the telling.

He instructed his mother to send him, poste restante, enough money to effect a hasty departure. Another letter, 'with nothing much in it', sent to his lodgings would allow him the subterfuge that pressing family business called him back to London.

He had finished copying Hals and there was nothing to keep him in Haarlem.

Then, before sending the letter, he seems to have had second thoughts about leaving just then. He could, after all, stay on for a fortnight with comparative safety. 'I don't see what possible thing these people could do to annoy me, beyond the beastly hinting the whole time that I might marry their daughter; and I may even exaggerate that.' He intended coming back to London, at the latest, in the last three days of October, so as to be in time for the New English Art Club's sending-in day on 5 November. As no work of Lewis's appeared in the NEAC show the following April, it is not clear whether he arrived back in time or not.

*

In November or December he went to Paris. His first address was a room at 41 rue Denfert-Rochereau, sublet to him by the family of Louis Schelfhout – a wretched, Zolaesque menage of uncertain number. He was their sole tenant and only source of income. They were out of work and ill-looking. Salvation, in the form of two Spanish lodgers, was expected imminently, but in the meantime they clung desperately to the young Englishman, spending the two napoleons (40F) he gave them each week on paying their own rent and furnishing the Spaniards' accommodation. The tottering economic edifice of this blighted household would occasionally be shored up by a visit to the Mont de Piété in the rue de Rennes. 'They pawned something this morning,' he told his mother, 'I suppose to get my dinner with.'

His embarrassment gave rise to absurd qualms: having earlier borrowed a couple of francs from one of the Schelfhouts, he was worried about paying the money back too promptly, in case 'they would suspect that I know of their pawnings'.

He was to become familiar with the workings of the Mont de Piété, which would in turn loom large in importance for the German protagonist of his first novel, *Tarr*. Like Otto Kreisler, he would leave his 'frac' as hostage in the heavily guarded establishment on the corner of the rue de Rennes and the boulevard Raspail.

Meanwhile, he was anxious to find somewhere else to live. 'I can't work [at the Schelfhouts'] for various and obvious reasons that I needn't detail', he told his mother. The acquisition of a studio was therefore a priority.

A valuable source of information on this subject was a man who had been with him at the Slade. D.I.V. Gatty from Rotherham was an enviable figure: on an allowance of only £3 a week he had a good studio and 'models more or less in abundance'. Studios in Paris were cheap, Lewis was told, 'you can get a studio here for £28 a year that would be £50 or £60 in London', and once installed there would be no shortage of models. On the corner of the rue de la Grande-Chaumière and the boulevard du Montparnasse, they stood on the pavement waiting for casual hire: 'le Marché aux Modèles'. National distinctions were a consideration for the discerning painter. 'Italian models here are very cheap, – you can often arrange with them for a napoleon a week, – the french models a franc an hour.'

The 22-year-old who saw Paris in the autumn of 1904 was gauche and easily unsettled by female company. Walter Sickert had given him a letter of introduction to the sculptress Kathleen Bruce, later to marry the Arctic explorer Robert Falcon Scott. She gave him tea in a room lit only by a fire, the gloom hiding his embarrassment. He felt that she had hardly enough clothes on for the time of year. She was four years his senior and had lived in Paris since 1901 – an ideal contact for a young man who needed an introduction to the city and, perhaps, a little mothering. He asked her about the Bohemian fundamentals: 'the likelihood of getting a studio and a mistress, and the price of cigarettes'. She was able to arrange the first requirement in the week before Christmas, leaving him to acquire the second for himself.

Lewis's first Paris studio was below Miss Bruce's, at 22 rue Delambre, just round the corner from the Café du Dôme. Its great advantage, as he explained to his mother, was that it was being let for only one or two months. A more conventional let in Paris was for the minimum of a year, involving a much greater payment of rent in advance. His proximity to the English sculptress, however, caused him some initial disquiet: 'I don't much relish that aspect of it.' Although exploiting the benefits of Miss Bruce's local knowledge to the full, he seemed to distance himself from her, to maintain his privacy and present the image of a man with no attachments or encumbrances. This would be a characteristic trait in all his future relationships with women.

The studio was light enough, furnished with bed, cups and saucers, and a good stove; 'the only thing that seems expensive here are coals'. The rent was 50 francs per month; '10 or 11 shillings a week'. This, he told his mother, was cheap. 'There is a *femme de ménage* that does your room any morning for *trente centimes*: that, four times a week, would be 1/-, which is cheap also.'

So far as the studio and its rent are concerned, it is instructive to consider the experience of another young painter, one year older than Lewis. Pablo Picasso settled in Paris in the spring of 1904. The studio he occupied for the next five years in the legendary 'Bateau Lavoir' in Montmartre cost him 15F a month. It had no furniture, no gas or electricity. There was one filthy toilet and one water tap serving 30 studios. This was a cheap studio. Lewis's, by comparison, was positively salubrious.

He took over the studio on 19 December but continued to sleep and take his meals at 41 rue Denfert-Rochereau, 'till the Schelfhouts get a bit settled', he explained. The Spaniards were expected to arrive on New Year's Day.

He had also become infested with a type of vermin: 'where I got them heaven knows, but I have a species of crabs in my head.' This necessitated a haircut, the purchase of a comb and also a bottle of poisonous lotion to be rubbed into the scalp night and morning. He included a sketch of the offender, enlarged by a third and enclosed in a small square in the text of a letter to his mother: a dot with legs. 'Are they lice, think you?'

Now that he had the use of a studio he was able to start work in earnest. The project was a grandiose one: 'a series of paintings and drawings of the creation of the world'. How far the series progressed is not known because nothing from this period has survived. He must have been astute enough to realise that painting and drawing on the theme of the creation of the world would, in all likelihood, not lead to immediate prosperity. He was accordingly also pursuing more commercial goals. 'I have been busy trying drawings (caricatures) for the Paris papers, which certainly seem very successful in themselves, but the french joke is the difficulty.' There is no evidence that he succeeded in placing any of this material.

He had secured the services of a model: six days a week for 24F. Once he had moved into the studio and shaken off the expense of bed and board chez Schelfhout he worked out he would be 15F or so to the good, and 'be able to afford a few other models for an hour or so occasionally'.

Meanwhile Miss Bruce was introducing him to the Montparnasse community. He went with her to Midnight Mass on Christmas Eve in the company of a French artist, a Member of Parliament and an Irish girl. Afterwards, they all went back to the French painter's studio and drank champagne.

On 3 January 1905 he abandoned his room in the rue Denfert-Rochereau and began sleeping in his studio, thereby making a considerable saving and leaving the Schelfhouts to their fate.

SEVEN

'No likelihood of complications'

Later that month came a windfall. Albert Lewis wrote to Anne enclosing a cheque from her husband for £51, the sterling equivalent of $250. It was made out to Percy Wyndham Lewis. Her husband had not written himself, she told her son, 'which shows he is deeply incensed. What I think has happened is that Albert has told him it is impossible for him not to send *something*, so this is probably his contribution for the year. – It will provide you with funds at your present expenditure for 4 months, and by that time (May) you ought to be able to produce something saleable, and my anxiety about you will be eased.' She instructed him to endorse the cheque on the back and return it to her immediately for banking. He was also to write to his Uncle Albert acknowledging the cheque and send her the letter for posting. This was to ensure it was franked from London. 'I don't think it would be wise to say you are in Paris as possibly they would think you were simply amusing yourself.'

*

By the beginning of February, his lease up in the rue Delambre, Lewis moved into a studio at 19 rue Mouton-Duvernet, just off avenue d' Orléans (now avenue du Général Leclerc). He had it for another short let of three months at something under 200F (£8) for that period: 'about 14/- to 16/- ... may be 17/- a week'. This was slightly more than he had been paying, and the new place was not ideal. A large but not very good studio, the light was 'extremely bad for painting' and the rue Mouton-Duvernet rather too remote for his liking from the boulevard du Montparnasse. Nevertheless he wrote enthusiastically about the cosmopolitan social whirl he was enjoying. 'I am going to a conference tonight to help get Gorki out of prison, whereat Anatole France is going to speak. I've seen a lot of very remarkable things ... I've been, for example, to Russian dances, – am going to one on Saturday, by the way, and I have also entered Maxim's without the expense of a sou.'
He was also eager for information about the Memorial Exhibition of the

late J. M. Whistler opening at the New Gallery in Regent Street on 22 February and about the exhibition of French Impressionists at the Grafton Gallery which was due to close a few days later. He hurried back to London to see them both and his return to Paris left him with a three-day headache, 'the after effects of . . . being shaken up crossing the Channel, without being sick'. He supplied his mother with a detailed bulletin. 'For the last few days I have been blessed with an extremely bad cold in the throat and head, and a feeling of general weakness, and have done no work which is worse; today my cold is very bad, and I shall buy some sort of medicine.' He was inclined to give full rein to his hypochondria when writing to his mother. To Augustus John, on the other hand, he was stoic in the main: 'I am suffering, as you will be concerned to hear, from an attack of influenza; but to give the devil his due, it is an excuse for a week's holiday.'

He had also forgotten how old he was. 'Am I 22 or 23 years old; please let me know by return of post.' He gave his mother no explanation as to why the information was needed.

In April he acquired what, next to a studio, was the most important Bohemian prerequisite: a mistress. He had mentioned a 'German lady' to his mother while he was suffering from his cold, but at the time he was showing interest in the beautiful young wife of Stephen Hawais, the future poet, Mina Loy. The German lady had felt slighted by his attentions in that quarter. 'I don't very much mind,' he told his mother, '*tant pis – pour elle.*' And he was also maintaining amatory options in another direction: a 'Norwegian lady' to whom he planned to make a proposal of marriage – or so he told his mother. But it was the young Fräulein who won through in the end and appeared to make most of the running in consummating the affair:

> The German lady came round to see me one day and to my unquenchable amazement asked me to kiss her, and threw herself into my arms, and kissed me with unabated vigour for three hours.

Her name was Ida Vendel, and she was in Paris with her elder sister Hedwig to study art. Her father, a merchant, had died in 1902. The family was Catholic and Ida was the third of six children. Born in Elberfeld in 1879, she was 26 years old, three years his senior, when she threw herself at Lewis. This was a possible reason for enquiring of his mother how old he was. He may have been calculating the precise age gap.

The pasteboard photograph she gave her lover shows a placid, rounded face and jaw-line, with high cheekbones shaded by a wide-brimmed straw hat decorated with fabric flowers. The strong nose and chin are ill-matched to a slightly receding lower lip. A necklace and medallion is tied, choker fashion, around a sturdy throat. Her gaze is disengaged, directed down to the right of the camera lens.

'I think there is no likelihood of complications', Lewis told his mother, 'if there were I could easily go away, – but in this case I think all is for the best.'

He was pleased with his acquisition. 'It saves me a lot of trouble and expense to have a beautiful and nicely bred mistress.' It must have given him considerable satisfaction that Ida had been drawn to him: evidence of sexual magetism which, he hoped, might soon rival that of his polygamous role model, Augustus John. After all, if he could attract one, he could attract others.

With money from London he was able to move from his less than satisfactory studio in the rue Mouton-Duvernet to one closer to the hub of Montparnasse. A studio at 90 rue d'Assas was being sublet for a couple of months by two ladies who intended travelling to Spain. It had very good light, was furnished, and there was even a small back garden. The ladies were offering it for less than the rent and only a little more than he was paying for accommodation off the avenue d'Orléans. Further advantages were a good big English bath and a separate WC and water tap. He would also be able to save money on models by getting friends to pose: 'girls who perhaps wouldn't like the appearance of my present studio and couldn't come so far either'.

He told his mother that the opportunity had to be taken or lost within the fortnight. The ladies' journey to Spain was entirely dependent upon their subletting the studio and, since their excursion tickets were due to expire in a week or so, they would not be disposing of the studio at all if their departure was much delayed.

He probably left debts behind him, either to the concierge at 19 rue Mouton-Duvernet or to tradesmen in the vicinity. Whatever it was, he never again felt comfortable in the area south of the place Denfert-Rochereau. The following year Augustus John moved with his brood to a house in the rue Dareau. 'You have a studio near my old dwelling', Lewis told him. 'I shall never be able to visit you there.'

*

By September he was in Holland with Ida Vendel at a small coastal resort, north of Rotterdam, called Noordwijk aan Zee. Baedeker described it as 'the most prettily situated watering place on the Dutch coast' and with 'numerous German visitors'. Lewis had originally planned the holiday with his mother, but she had to remain in London attempting to find a tenant for the flat she owned in South Hampstead, at 5 Pembroke Mansions, Canfield Gardens. Without the promise of that income, she did not dare to risk the expense of travel.

'A magnificent prospect of the surging sea, the bijou white bathing machines and all the attractions sought by the town-weary toiler': this was the view Lewis described from the dining room of the Villa Cato, where he and Ida had a large bedroom. He was also renting a moderately priced studio. In his letters home he affected the German *Kleiner*, little one, when referring to Ida. He also laboured with an obscure running joke which may have had its basis in the image of his partner as a convenient economic resource: 'my German garden', he called her, or 'my German allotment', or even 'the German back-yard is hard up, though always willing to lend.' He was soon in her debt to the tune of 55F and was anxious to start repayments. 'It wouldn't matter at all if our relations were certain, and I had faced the woeful possibility of a marriage, but I haven't, so I want to be clear *monetarily* with her by Christmas.' This down-to-earth cynicism was partly intended to convince his mother of the practical and economic benefits of the liaison to his artistic career. 'She poses for me regularly, and I reap a rich harvest; – I certainly couldn't have such a model in London for less than 15/- a week for the number of hours.' She posed for two hours every morning. 'I am in clover as far as models go.'

He had consolidated the start he made during his last months in Paris and was, by his own account, producing excellent work in Noordwijk. The hyperbolic tone he adopted to his mother contained a healthy element of self-mockery. 'I begin to see my way to some Parnassus: though my road, like all those apart and high-lying, is uncertain and rocky enough: let us pray together that there will be some commercial aspect at the turn of the hill.' But the September weather had broken up and days were grey and chilly. He was afflicted by diarrhoea and headaches. 'Why have I headaches?' he asked. 'I didn't have such things once, not so long ago.'

Then, at the beginning of October, Ida received word from Elberfeld that a friend was ill and she made rapid plans to leave. Lewis was, in retrospect, to have suspicions about this abrupt departure, but at the time his only concerns were climatic and practical. 'I don't want to stay here any longer than I can help alone, as the weather is miserable, and I can't work without my model.' He prepared to return to London. His mother sent him the requisite £2.10s. to get him home. She could spare no more.

The gravity of Anne's financial position at this time might be judged by the fact that she wrote to her husband's sister Tilly and asked for a loan to help her over 'a difficult time' with her ailing laundry business. She told her son it was to see what response she would get, rather than with any definite hope of help. Tilly replied that she was sorry for her sister-in-law's straits but that her own expenses were so great she could spare nothing. She said that Charles was 'the proper person' to help and sent Anne's letter to Albert, who in turn promised to try and find him, but claimed to be 'by no means sure of his present address'.

Charles had in fact been living in Portland, Maine, since 1901 with his daughter Ethel and the young woman he had brought with him from England, Lillian Phipps. 'We were foolish to let [him] leave . . . without a definite settlement', Anne complained, 'and I am afraid little chance now of ever getting it.' She was unaware that Charles had aquired yet another dependent, when Lillian bore him a son, Alexander. It was to be another seven years before the child was given a spurious legitimacy when Charles Lewis contracted what may have been his second bigamous marriage.

Although unable to offer Anne financial aid, Tilly had one suggestion to make: 'It appears to me the business you are in is not suited to you, and if you spend more money on it, might mean sending good money after bad. Would it not be better to get rid of it . . . and do something else, for instance you would make an excellent saleswoman in a store.'

For Lewis, a regime of fierce austerity appeared to loom. 'The one thing is, we *know* now' – and his mother's words may or may not have impressed themselves on his mind as he packed to leave Noordwijk aan Zee – 'we have only what we can get for ourselves and if you can help yourself a little, I daresay I can worry through unless anything very bad turned up, or my health was *much* worse than at present.'

He arrived in London on Thursday morning, 5 October. A visit to the British Museum two days later records he was staying with a Slade friend, Cuthbert Hamilton, at 16 Fitzroy Street. Less than a fortnight later he had found new quarters close by: 'a room, rather large with a north light, 1st floor unfortunately and so perhaps a little dark . . . for 7/- or 7/6.' Grafton Street, now Grafton Way, ran from Gower Street, across Tottenham Court Road and Whitfield Street, along the southern side of Fitzroy Square and ended at Cleveland Street. Number 59 was between Tottenham Court Road and Whitfield Street and was just around the corner from Shoolbred & Co., purveyors of the veal and ham pie and the swiss roll and cream that had nourished him as a student.

His new address was scrawled alongside a poem he was working on: 'To Lust':

> O thou whose home is Heaven's wilderness,
> Who call'st thyself of Heaven, yet art no more
> Eternal citizen than some rude kess
> And dweller in waste lands all states ignore.

Not one driven hence – once mentioned in God's grace
And of our age and blood, but thou and thine,
Bear all the rude integrity of race,
And passion of an elemental line.

Each human mind, beyond life's centring bound,
Communal aims in which all minds are massed,
Are unreclaimed Life's haunting depths around,
Of desert ages and the lonely past.

No mind's true heaven participation knows,
In this Love, too, with Lust more lonely grows.

Through this exquisitely structured but barely comprehensible stream of verbiage runs a tenuous theme: the dichotomy between Love and Lust. It may have been the feared consequences of the latter which accounted for his next bout of continental travel.

He had no sooner moved in to 59 Grafton Street than he was off again, travelling light, and still hard up after a frantic last-minute trawl to get his fare. He had managed to sell a drawing to Macklem, a Canadian friend from the Slade, for a pound. This was probably the first cash he had ever received for his skills. He had high hopes that Macklem would be a more substantial buyer in the future. 'The drawing he chose, though one of the good ones, was very quickly done, and of no importance to me, so it's a pound well in my pocket.' But he still needed more and certain avenues of acquisition were closed to him. 'I am on such excellent terms with John that I don't want to slacken them by a loan. So I suppose I'd better drop on Macklem for an extra 10/-, which will make thirty.' He also had a book of William Blake poetry to sell. He would be able to borrow another pound when he met up with Ida.

By 8 o'clock on the evening of Wednesday 25 October he was sitting on the Great Eastern boat train at Liverpool Street Station with a second-class return ticket to Hamburg via Harwich and the Hook of Holland. The ticket was valid for 45 days but he did not intend to be away for long. His luggage comprised one small bag.

His movements during the following week are obscure. Presumably he met Ida in Hamburg and he may have gone with her to Elberfeld. But by travelling on with her to Paris he wasted his return ticket from Hamburg to London. His mother complained that he did not even bother to try to sell it. 'You might have got nearly half price for it.' She was at some pains to keep track of her errant son's movements. By the time she wrote to him poste restante at Hamburg he had already left and never received her letter. When she wrote to him on 4 November she was clearly irritated. 'I think you quite foolish to tear about Europe in the uncertain state of finances.' By this time he was in Paris and had decided to marry Ida.

He had mentioned the prospect of marriage, albeit negatively, as a 'woeful possibility', while they were in Holland. His mother had also pronounced upon the subject. 'It is a pity that you are not earning enough to keep a wife . . . but it is of course impossible to burden yourself at present with all sorts of responsibilities.'

Nevertheless, she now made enquiries at St Pancras Town Hall, carefully weighing the cost of the union. 'If you get a licence costing £2.17s', she told him, 'you can get married the next day – after giving notice. If on the other hand, you publish the notice only, you have to wait *three weeks*, this however only costs 9/7d – a saving of £2.8s.' Lewis seemed insistent that the wedding take place in London. Hedwig Vendel would be accompanying her sister and Mrs Lewis was harassed at the prospect of entertaining and finding accommodation for the two young ladies. She suggested that her son come home immediately, persuade Ida and Hedwig to go to a boarding house for a few days before the wedding, and then he could move into the Pembroke Mansions flat with his bride on 20 November. As ever Mrs Lewis, despite harbouring reservations, remained indulgent. 'Well dear boy, I hope the step you are going to take is not out of the frying pan into the fire, but I daresay you will be quite as well off as you are alone.' She thought, however, that things would be altogether less complicated if the ceremony took place in Elberfeld. Hedwig felt the same. 'It is the man's job to go to the country of the woman for marriage', she told her prospective brother-in-law, 'one could get married as quietly in Germany as in England and in less time also.'

His determination to marry Ida was puzzling. Still completely dependent upon the small amounts of money he could scrounge from his mother, he was barely in a position to support himself. The added responsibility of a wife seemed unthinkable.

At Noordwijk in September there had been no hint that he was prepared to commit himself. On the contrary, he wanted to be free of all financial obligations towards Ida by Christmas. Their relations were uncertain and he was content that they remain so. But a month later he was rushing to meet her in Hamburg and, during the following week, announcing their engagement. The time-scale might suggest that in October Ida believed herself to be pregnant. If her lover received word from her to that effect, then his subsequent reckless journey across Europe can be interpreted as an action of panic, his proposal of marriage an obligation. And, in the summer of the following year, a line of rankling complaint from a letter supports the hypothesis: '. . . and the way you were frightened when there was the danger of a baby? That hurt me very much, Percy.'

She was not pregnant. He did not marry her. Something happened early in November 1905 that made Lewis abandon her in Paris and return to London alone. Precisely how it happened is uncertain, but it is clear that the discovery of something in his fiancée's past shook his confidence in her completely and made him retrospectively and, according to Ida's friend and confidante Hanni Simons, pathologically jealous.

The 35-year-old Fräulein Simons was confronted by Lewis one morning in her apartment at 11 rue Léopold-Robert. He was flourishing letters and photographs and demanding an explanation. His obvious agitation scared her considerably. 'How dreadfully suspicious you are', she told him, 'not only towards Ida but towards me – towards everybody. It's a sort of illness in you.'

Before she met him, Ida had been involved with a fellow German expatriate in Paris called Linnenkampf. The crisis can be partially reconstructed from an eight-page letter written in faulty but eloquent English that Hanni Simons sent to Lewis on 17 November. In it she endeavoured to repair the damage done to Ida's reputation and, so, to her engagement to the Englishman. It appeared that at least one of the letters Lewis waved in her face was from Linnenkampf, libelling his ex-mistress. 'How *can* he say he had doubts in Ida's purity', Hanni protested in turn.

Thirteen years later, in Lewis's first published novel, *Tarr*, the fictionalised chronicle of his relationship with Ida, Otto Kreisler turns to the eponymous English painter – estranged fiancé of Bertha Lunken – and says: 'You want to know what I think of the Lunken? – She's a sly prostitute, that's what she is!'

Hanni's commentary and the details of what Ida had confided to her friend of her past relations with Linnenkampf show the degree to which Lewis used the raw material of this affair in his novel. There, in outline, was Kreisler: buffoon, rapist, and festering scandal in the German bourgeois-bohemian community of Montparnasse:

> I will only say a few words of that brute of Linnenkampf. The more I think of his behaviour the more I detest and disdain him . . . it was *he* who had led a life full of base sensuality and frivolity! . . . Ida told me that she was tormented by a certain sensuality of his kisses [which] reminded her of his past life.

There, in Ida's allegedly altruistic relationship with Linnenkampf, was a model for the tortuous self-justifications of Bertha compromised by her connection with a social pariah:

she hoped he would learn to be pure at her side, that she would help him
to be good and strong and all that . . . And I am quite sure that this sort of
pity and wish to help and to save is the only reason . . . why girls so often
love a man who is not at all [worthy] of their love.

According to Hanni, Ida had not told Lewis about Linnenkampf because
she was afraid of his jealous outbursts. As a result she entangled herself in a
web of lies and deceptions which, when the facts became known to him,
made her earlier affair appear more serious than perhaps it was. Hanni at
first blamed her for the break-up, telling her that it would not have
happened had she been more open from the beginning. And Hanni received
an angry outburst from her friend in return. 'She wished me only that I
should come to suffer under suspicion as *she* had suffered and *then*
condemn her.' After Lewis's departure, Ida shut herself up in her apartment
at 225 rue de l'Université. She did not go out, she ate irregularly and saw no
one, apart from Hanni and occasionally her sister. The letter Lewis received
in London was scattered with glimpses of this emotional desolation. 'She is
terribly alone . . . She is living with you as intensely as if you were there . . .
her whole being lights up when she speaks of you, not of you as you were in
the last days and in the days of suspicion but of "Percy" in general.' And
Hanni described her as 'au bout de ses forces', a phrase used frequently by
the fictionalised Ida – Bertha Lunken.

According to Hedwig, Ida had decided to stay in Paris for the winter and
not attempt to contact Lewis. She hoped that, given time, his faith in her
might be restored and a reconciliation effected. 'I will never marry Percy if
he does not believe me,' she told her sister.

Towards the end of November Lewis sent her a telegram. 'I believe you.
Come.' She left for London the same night.

But the reconciliation was short-lived. No sooner had she written to
friends in Hamburg announcing her engagement, than the atmosphere of
tension and suspicion returned. In Paris Hedwig received letters from both
sides of the acrimonious divide. Ida wrote expressing concern for Lewis's
state of mind, while he seems to have written obsessively of his own
unhappiness, of the consequences to him alone of marrying Ida or rejecting
her. Hedwig's reply was a furious condemnation of his treatment of her
sister and his compulsive raking over of her earlier associations. Alongside
Herr Linnenkampf, another shadowy rival had meanwhile emerged from
Ida's past, a sculptor called Neumann, for whom she may or may not have
posed. 'Even if you were tormented by all the devils in hell', Hedwig told
Lewis:

you should keep everything to yourself and not mention a single doubt. It would not even be generous on the man's part to remind a woman of her past mistake, but to torment her with a thing which does not exist and which is pure imagination of his brain is infamous, above all when the man has promised by a telegram that the thing was finished.

Of his vacillation about marrying Ida, she was equally blunt:

you will break the life of a woman. After the relations you have had with Ida her life will be lost if you do not get married. The thing that counts is my mother's chagrin and the useless embarrassment that has been caused her.

But elsewhere in the letter she was of the opinion that marriage to Lewis would be a degradation. 'I hope that she will have too much pride to become the wife of a man who considers her a spoiled thing and who would only marry her so as not to be alone.' She concluded her tirade:

you have treated Ida like a ball in a game which one throws from right to left from left to right until one is tired of the game then one throws it in the corner for good.

Ida, meanwhile, was staying with Mrs Lewis. It was the first time the two women had met. 'Personally I like Ida', she said later, 'and . . . shall always think her a good and generous minded girl; it is her misfortune to be very tactless.' Perhaps Lewis's mother proved to be a mediating influence because, by the time Ida left England, the shaky engagement had once more been re-established. She arrived home in Elberfeld on 5 January and, among family and friends, any doubts she harboured about Lewis's intentions were evidently kept to herself. 'I play the role of happy fiancée', she told him:

Everyone is very interested in me, and in you, everyone always asks me: what is your Percy doing – does he write? Then people invite me out, and if I say no, they reply, oh naturally, you don't have time . . . you write all day long to your darling Percy! I return home and the first thing my mother says to me is: Percy has not yet written!

She had waited for ten days. When the six-page letter arrived she found it cold and impersonal. 'I read it, and I read it again, I turned all the pages and looked for a kiss! a tiny word of love! nothing, nothing, nothing!!' Three days later he sent her a photograph of himself, wearing a greatcoat and looking like a consumptive Russian anarchist.

Lewis was playing for time. As incapable of committing himself fully to Ida as he was of breaking with her, he allowed her to continue thinking herself engaged while he confided his irresolution to his mother and waited for something to happen. 'I don't think as things are I could marry that girl, and it's awful for one reason and another . . . to have to gain time as it were. But I suppose all will arrange itself.'

EIGHT

'To put an end gradually'

Pursuing his self-regulated course of artistic training, the 23-year-old Lewis went to Munich at the beginning of 1906. He caught the boat train from Liverpool Street station on Saturday evening, 27 January, and the steamer from Harwich got him to the Hook of Holland in the early hours of the next morning. He assumed there was a customs post at Rotterdam and made the half-hour train journey expecting to be reunited with his bag there. He arrived to discover that the bag had been held up by customs back at the Hook. Assurances from officials that it would catch him up within three hours proved optimistic. It was Sunday and, not relishing the prospect of a day waiting in Rotterdam, he decided to press on, breaking his journey south in Elberfeld.

The town boasted a unique form of public transport: built only six years before, the overhead suspension railway or *Schwebebahn* ran eight miles from Elberfeld to Barmen along the River Wupper.* A decade later Lewis briefly recalled the industrial splendours of his fiancée's *Heimat* in the Vorticist enthusiasm of the second and final outburst of *BLAST*, comparing them with New York, a city he had not yet visited: 'this modern jungle is not without its beauty (what do you think of 21st Street or the town of Elberfeld?)'

He regarded visiting Ida as weakness getting the better of him, but he did not expect to stay long. The baggage-handler at Rotterdam assured him his luggage would get to Elberfeld about two hours after he did. This assurance also proved optimistic, and he had to stay with Ida for three days before the slow goods train arrived with his bag and he could continue his journey to Munich.

'The only effect my visit to Ida had on me was to make me sadder.' He gave her some of the drawings he had done in Paris before their holiday in Noordwijk. They probably included two she had been particularly eager to possess: a figure composition of two men, one apparently dead, with a little child, and a small portrait head of a woman, perhaps of Ida herself, in red and black. 'Some of the best,' he told his mother, 'I think that was well.'

---

* Elberfeld and Barmen now form the city of Wuppertal.

'About Ida, I am in an impasse, a moral cul-de-sac. God knows what to do. I don't however look towards marriage as a solution, and I suppose that with infinite pain I shall drift away, and other interests eventually help me to forget the strongest and most unfortunate attachment I'm ever likely to have.' As if to spare himself the pain of a sharp break with her, he chose to follow a course of inaction which would ultimately be more damaging and demoralising for Ida: it amounted to a gruelling piecemeal severance of relations. 'I'm going . . . to put an end gradually to any *absolute* hopes of marriage she may have.'

He arrived in Munich on the first day of February. The Carnival was in full swing and offered some distraction from his emotional troubles. The pre-Lenten festivities, or *Fasching*, begin the day after Epiphany, on 7 January and continue for anything from four to nine weeks, reaching a climax on the Sunday before Lent with an immense street parade taking hours to pass through the centre of town. *Fasching* ends on Shrove Tuesday, which in 1906 fell on 27 February.

He had been in Munich for a full week when he made himself known, as the law demanded, to the German police. He informed them that his profession was *'Kunstmaler'*, his religion 'protestant' and his year of birth 1883. He was apparently still experiencing difficulty remembering how old he was.

When he registered with the police he was staying at the Pension Stephanie in Amalienstrasse. He had stayed at another establishment during the week between his arrival in Munich and his visit to police headquarters. The Pension Bellevue in Theresienstrasse boasted proximity to museums, theatres and concert halls and comfortably furnished rooms for 4 marks per night. Evidently finding this unsatisfactory for one reason or another, he moved to 85 Amalienstrasse, where he secured a room for $3\frac{1}{2}$ marks. The Pension Stephanie was run by a family called Muffat and occupied the 1st, 2nd and 3rd floor of the building. On the ground floor was the Restaurant Parcival.

'The pension is cheap and naturally disagreeable', he told his mother. The food served by Frau Muffat he found particularly distasteful. 'There is always veal for dinner . . . and that doesn't agree with me very well; and 3 times out of 4 the meat, if other than veal is dry and without nourishment and soaked in gravy, – also a beastly vegetable predominates, which haunts my slumbers.' A tenuous literary association partly compensated for the atrocious bill of fare and Lewis took it to be a good omen. 'I find to my inexpressible delight that IBSEN inhabited the room in front of mine in the pension for 6 weeks!'

Amalienstrasse runs through the heart of the student and artistic quarter of the city. Opposite Pension Stephanie the building of an extension to the University began in 1906, and two hundred yards or so to the left, at the top of the street, a huge Italianate pile loomed, stretching over 800 feet from east to west, the flight of steps to its main entrance flanked by a pair of equestrian bronze statues. 'Imposing' or 'ostentatious' according to the changing judgement of Baedeker, the Akademie der bildenden Künste still dominates the head of Amalienstrasse.

But it was down the street, away from the naked martial figures of Castor and Pollux, that Lewis went in the evening to pursue his artistic education. Two hundred yards in the opposite direction was Schellingstrasse. Here, on the ground floor of number 23, was what the Munich Adressbuch listed as Privatzeichenschule von Moritz Heymann, where students could draw from a nude model for 6 pfennigs a session.

In later life Lewis would recall attending 'Heymann's Academy'. He also referred to it as 'Papa Heymann's Munich Academy', despite the fact that Moritz Heymann was no older than 37 at the time. It probably amounted to nothing grander than an *ad hoc* night class in Heymann's studio. It was never registered with the police as a commercial business and therefore does not appear in Heymann's records at the Munich City Archive.

Whatever its worth as a centre of artistic excellence, 23 Schellingstrasse was useful in providing social contacts, and only three days after his arrival in Munich he had secured an invitation to a formal dance, or *Bal Paré*, on 14 February. He would be expected to attend either *en frac* or *en costume* and remembered the unworn black suit, opera hat and cloak reposing in a chest of drawers at his mother's house in Hanwell. If she sent them registered post immediately it would save him the considerable expense of hiring evening dress for his Carnival debut. 'I will never again have occasion to wear them,' he told her.

The *Bal Paré* was 'very amusing but rather expensive'. The ticket cost him 3 marks but he had also to buy a rosette before he was allowed inside. Then there were various, unspecified, 'articles of attire'. In all, the evening set him back about 10 marks, which he resolved to make up from his allowance by gradual economies 'and avoid *Bal Parés* in future'.

He was having German lessons with a young woman, another contact perhaps from Heymann's Privatzeichenschule, but the sessions seemed only to serve as an excuse to brood at length to his mother:

I don't enjoy them very much, and have in fact very little interest left in young ladies in general, and only a real desire to meet some day a woman that I can take seriously, and that will help me to forget Ida. I suffer very much about all this, and spend many hours of great despondency; I don't see any prospect of this feeling passing, and must resign myself to it, and go on with my life in spite of it, and not wait for it to depart in idleness and misery: p'raps work cures best. – On the other hand I see no prospect of my ever being able to live with Ida, that would be another form of suffering, with many disadvantages to boot.

But he continued to vacillate about informing the object of his deliberations: 'p'raps the time even yet has not come for me to be able definitely to say anything.'

Meanwhile Ida was oblivious. She sent him a food hamper and affectionate letters with the salutation '*Schatz*' – treasure. 'I slept well last night, thinking that you were next to me, caressing my head and the whole of your little woman. – Percy I love you – and your love is all that I want in my life.' She received a regular allowance from a relative or friend called Lilly. Upon hearing of Ida's engagement, this patroness promised to continue the payments for an additional three years. The news prompted Lewis to briefly reconsider his position: 'it's really rather a temptation to marry her, even for this mess of potage,' he told his mother. But he immediately thought better of it. 'I think with this money you give me . . . , and what I must earn in the near future, whatever it may be, I should be freer and happier for the moment, – and infinitely freer afterwards.'

He had told Ida that he might break his journey back to London at Cologne, a relatively short distance for her to travel from Elberfeld, and she was keen to meet him there. 'I want to see you, my sweet, I want to see that you live and that you love me . . . any day is good for me.' But he was still not sure when he would be setting out.

On registering with the police he had been asked how long he intended staying in Munich. The word '*unbestimmt*' was written on his form: uncertain. Much depended upon whether he could find himself a studio to work in, and for a time he believed he had succeeded. A fifth-floor atelier with good light and a big stove: 'it is 20 marks a month, – and there are some people underneath that will . . . furnish it for 5 marks a month, bed included. This seems too good to be true.' And so it proved. The day before he was to move in, the present tenant informed him that she had been let down over another studio and that she would not be moving after all. It was a bitter disappointment. 'After this blow, my energy really deserted me. I felt it was really too bad of Fortune to play with me in this fashion, and despaired of ever getting settled in this ill-omened city.'

Only the *Fasching* made an impression on him and he, by his own account, made a great impression on the *Fasching*. A crowd of young artists insisted on standing him drinks. They said he had the look of a portrait by the popular Munich painter Franz Lenbach: 'a doubtful compliment', he felt. His good looks also attracted female attention as the beery and socially promiscuous atmosphere created a holiday intimacy of strangers:

> Several women asked me to accompany them without my having so much as looked at them; a magnificent Parisienne cocotte called me and caressed me under the nose of her entreteneur for a considerable time. I made crowds of acquaintances and have any number of appointments.

A year later he would try to persuade Augustus John to return with him, promising a Crown Princess for his dance partner.

He was careful to reassure his mother that his allowance was not being squandered: he could enjoy himself, even in his customary state of penury:

> I spent nothing to speak of – an ordinary 'redoute' costs a mere entrance, and a glass of beer is all one need drink, once inside. – I bought a 'passe-partout', 5 marks, for the Luitpold Café, an enormous place where everyone goes before and after and during the Balls, and which is really the centre of the carnival; there are always thousands of people there, and one walks from one salle to another, and needn't drink at all, unless one wants to.

He spent the '*interrement*', the last night of the festivities, with a group of young German officers, who no doubt also bought him drinks, 'who spoke French very well, and were more agreeable than the average student.' And as the *Fasching* reached its heated climax late that Shrove Tuesday night an amorous adventure seemed in the offing:

> one very pretty little woman . . . rushed up to me and embraced me and I'm going to meet her next Tuesday . . . she was most particularly struck with me and I with her:– she told all my friends that I 'pleased her from every point of view', and that I had the coldest mouth she had ever met with and that she would take French lessons with me.

'So I have grown extremely vain,' he told his mother, 'though none the less unhappy.' The addendum was a reminder, to himself it seemed as much as to her, of his mental anguish, temporarily forgotten amongst the heady blandishments of the Luitpold Café. He believed the strain of the unresolved predicament left behind in Elberfeld might have affected his health, although he was forced to admit that a half-hour of nausea and heart palpitation experienced during the revelry had less to do with his emotional troubles than with an unsatisfactory dinner and four hours of energetic dancing.

And in the cold light of Ash Wednesday, the *Fasching* finished, he again took stock. 'Face to face with the old question, more than ever I can neither forget Ida, nor can I marry her.' The old doubts remained and festered. 'I am convinced that my suspicions are well-founded . . . I think p'raps if she told me I might suffer less.' And he had probably canvassed his new acquaintances on the subject of racial and sexual characteristics. Prejudice confirmed prejudice: 'the more I think of her conduct with me, and the more I hear of German women, the more sure I am.'

With the festivities over and his hopes of settling himself in a studio blighted, there was nothing to keep him in Munich. He told his mother he intended staying another two or three weeks; but only one week later he left. This was 6 March: the same day, incidentally, he had planned to meet the 'pretty little woman' who had been so impressed with the coldness of his mouth. He informed the police of his destination: Koblenz.

What attraction this garrison town at the confluence of Rhine and Mosel held for him is a mystery. The young officers who had befriended him may have spoken of it. It boasted one of the biggest and most powerful fortresses in the world: Ehrenbreitstein had been painted by Turner, and was built on a spectacularly precipitous crag 400 feet above the Rhine. There was also a colossus standing on the tongue of land where the Mosel flows into the Rhine: Kaiser Wilhelm I on horseback with a winged figure proffering him the laurel-wreathed imperial crown. The bronze statuary alone reared nearly 50 feet high, and this was more than doubled by a massive base reached by 107 stone steps. 'This is', according to Baedeker, 'one of the most impressive purely personal monuments in the world, and dominates the landscape in all directions.'

Such wonders may of course have held little fascination for him, and a more likely explanation for his visit was that Ida had persuaded him to meet her there. She had been prepared to rendezvous in Cologne, and Koblenz was only another 50 miles south. But such a meeting can only be a matter of speculation. All the bureaucratic paraphernalia of arrival and departure that might have recorded their names in Koblenz during March 1906 were destroyed, along with 85 per cent of the city and the colossal statue of Kaiser Wilhelm I, by Allied bombing in the last war.

*

He was soon back in Paris and there was friction in the correspondence with his mother. 'Received your letter this morning', he wrote, 'burnt it.' The spat apparently followed further demands for money. He was staying in a hotel at 26 rue Servandoni and had found an apartment that suited him, but he urgently needed the three months' rent (140F) before he could move in.

'You know that the quarter in France begins the 15 of April – that is to say, tomorrow – and if I take the apartment tomorrow or in two weeks time, I still pay as from tomorrow – and each day that I remain at the hotel, it means, so to speak, paying two rentals.'

He had great creative plans. 'I'm going to stay in Paris until I've written five sonnets as good as any five of Baudelaire's,' he told Augustus John, 'then I'm going into the country *d'entamer quelque vaste projet.*' He used the word '*entamer*' – to broach or to open – he explained, because he always felt that a project, once imagined by him, existed: 'as gold does in the earth and only needed the energy to demonstrate its existence.'

This 'vast project' may have been a work he told John about in another letter: 'I am writing a poem in the form of St Agnes Eve, as to length etc., recounting the loves of a god for a mortal woman. I am trying to recreate as impressively as possible, in precision of surroundings, unsparing psychology ... intensity of emotion, the strangeness of such a union, – treating it, in fact, in a "modern" spirit, although mystical and ideally as well.' From what followed it seemed as if he had in mind a piece of scholarly pornography: 'creating in the first place, an *actual* woman; and not contenting myself with introducing the god the *first* time into her chamber, make him persist in his visits: – what a field for romantic thought!' It is not known how far the project progressed. Nothing remotely comparable to Lewis's outline has survived.

He also claimed to have written 30 sonnets the previous week; 'or rather, a succession of poems, in three parts, in the sonnet form.' When he had completed the sequence with 20 or 30 more he proposed calling it 'Preludes of Life'.

'But my projects multiply: – I hope, without speaking of them now, at some future time to submit to you some of the least abortive of their results.' That such modesty might or might not have been entirely justified, John could judge for himself from the following piece from the same letter:

> And like a dolorous tomb haunted of laughter;
> And like a mad man's lips haunted of song,
> And tender melodies the heart did throng, –
> Like wild birds that this ruin'd soul's hereafter
> Did n'ere forsake, – dead love had fed so long: –
> And like a passion worn with bitter wrong,
> Remembering in sleep love's hours, and after
> Waking beneath love's thong.

He invariably wrote to John about his literary projects, never on the subject of painting or drawing. In truth he seemed far too daunted by 'the

Slade School ingenious' even to discuss art with him, let alone lay brush to canvas or charcoal to paper in his vicinity. He could feel equal or superior to John only in the realm of literature. Often he seemed to act as tutor to his friend, and his letters became reading lists. He recommended to John's notice Baudelaire's *Petits Poèmes en Prose*, 'and to your memory the entire works of Voltaire'. He urged upon him Stendhal's *La Vie d'Henri Brulard*. Hearing that John had finished the second volume of *Crime and Punishment* in French translation, he wanted his opinion of the ending. Lewis was invariably ahead of John in his reading and was now engrossed in Dostoevsky's *Krotkaia*, 'another terrible book'.* Here he found quoted a line of Goethe† which sent him off determined to read 'every word of *Faust* forthwith'.

As to his 'matrimonial projects': they had failed. 'I think in any case that I will not follow after this illusion.' And he told John that he was looking for a mistress: 'not with very much verve, it's true, but still I am looking for one.'

It was spring in Paris and his overheated imagination was mightily charged by the women he saw in the streets. Dissatisfied for the moment with Ida and her compatriots he found himself lustfully preoccupied with the Parisienne and her transcendence of a particularly unbecoming Teutonic fashion. 'French women are wearing reform dresses, stolen from the Germans just now; it's extraordinary how they transfigure this heretofore bottomless abortion; there can even be no mistaking the exact situation of the slit in their rump, although one knows that the actual bottom lies some four inches beneath the habitual padding.'

Apart from expounding such adolescent bawdry, he was incapable of confiding the true and troubled state of his private life to John, being far franker on this score with his mother. But he does appear to have discussed the problem of Ida with John, even if only in the abstract. Answering a query from Alick Schepeler, John told her: 'My poet has not got married yet, no – one obstacle, he lacks a lady – another – how is he to be sure of her when she's found? I can't advise him on so slim an hypothesis – can I – still he keeps consulting me.' John, after all, was a profound authority on the subject. Lewis had noticed a book on his shelf called *The Evolution of Sex* and, 'although hardly knowing what it might contain, supposed [his] mind must be full of accouplements, masculine pangs, choice of sex by smell etc., and . . . was overcome with awe at the knowledge [he] must possess . . . after months of handy practice, backed by this hand-book.'

* Usually published, in English translation, as 'Krotkaya' or 'A Gentle Creature' in collections of Dostoevsky short stories. However, Lewis was presumably reading the French translation by E. Halpérine, published as a separate volume in Paris, 1886, as *Krotkaïa*.
† A conflation of two speeches by Mephistopheles from *Faust Part One*, quoted by Dostoevsky: 'Je suis une fraction de cette fraction de l'être, qui veut faire le mal et qui fait le bien.' (I am a part of that part of being, who wishes to do evil and who does good.')

But however much he consulted John on the hypothetical subject of Ida Vendel, he kept her actual existence a secret. Ida herself appears to have been aware of this: 'you always try to hide me in front of your friends,' she accused him, 'why, are you ashamed of me?'

For a young man of Lewis's jealous temperament and personal insecurity, keeping her away from the libidinous John was perhaps understandable, but the closeting of his sexual partners, even with no potential predator in sight, was to become an obsessive characteristic of his future life.

In June, his three-month lease in Paris having expired, Lewis set out to explore the Normandy coast with John, who was looking for a quiet place by the sea where he could bring his wife, his mistress and their brood for the summer.

Ste-Honorine-des-Pertes appears only on the largest-scale maps. It lies between Port-en-Bessin to the east and St Laurent-sur-Mer to the west, and the nearest town, Bayeux, is about six miles away. When Lewis returned, in August to join the ménage at this remote spot, Ida was holidaying separately nearly 40 miles south of them, near Flers. He paid a visit at her request: 'this cost me a little.' His personal hygiene had presumably left much to be desired: 'dirtiness', she wrote, 'that terrible disease of yours!!' In her long, demanding letter she encapsulated the emotional imbalance of their relationship:

> The Egotism, that you have shown in millions of small and great things, – this egotism is horrible! and it makes me very cold, – it makes me so ill, – because you reveal to me that your love is not true or great enough, – in nature, everywhere you see that the creature who loves sacrifices itself for the loved one, – you would never do that even in the smallest things! – and that makes me so sad, Percy, I find it so shameful to ask.

A strange blend of vituperation and affection, the letter finished warmly:

> if my dirty little vagabond comes to visit me maybe one more time (perhaps Sunday) – I ask him to be like a prince in his appearance – worthy of being gazed on by the blue eyes of his queen who loves him so much.

The holiday with John's extensive family at Ste-Honorine seems to have begun well. The French tourists sang 'Won't you come 'ome Bill Bailey?' to them as they passed and Lewis cut a dash on the beach in his Rugby school blazer, a pair of white trousers, white hat and cholera belt. 'He came back full of the beauties of sea bathing', John wrote to Alick, 'that is to say he had been viewing the girls frolicking in the water from a prominent position . . .

He assures me there were at least 10 exquisite young creatures with fat legs.'
He had bought his finery, apart from the Rugby blazer, in Bayeux and
succeeded in saving one and a half francs by haggling. He was also
cultivating a beard, 'just to see'. Lewis's posturings provided a constant
source of amusement for John. 'To-day I laughed so much over the poet's
plans that I wept.'

But apart from such light relief it was an appalling holiday. They were
plagued with flies and became ill in the soporific summer heat. 'I can't do a
stroke, no, not a stroke of work', Lewis told his mother. 'I can hardly lift up
my arm for quite half of the day.' It was not only the enervating climate that
he found so maddening. 'I want also to do some painting very badly . . . but
near John I can never paint, since his artistic personality is much too strong,
and he much more developed naturally, and this frustrates any effort.'

John was creatively paralysed too, and his gloom was pervasive. He was
also losing patience with Lewis. This had been evident in June when the two
men reconnoitred the Normandy coast together in preparation for the
holiday. 'The poet irritates me – he is always asking for *petits suisses* which
are unheard of in this country and his prudence is boundless.' It was a
character trait Lewis assigned to his literary self-portrait a decade later:

> He had never eaten oysters before. Prudence had prevented him . . . 'You
> are a savage, Tarr! . . . You are afraid of typhoid, and your palate is as
> conservative as an ox's!'

'What a mistake it is to have a friend – or having one ever to see him. I don't
like the cut of the poet's clothes nor the shape of his hat . . . He is getting
more and more bourgeois looking I regret to say, and fonder of his meals
than ever. As regards eating he has the undeveloped tastes of a fastidious
schoolboy.' In turn, Lewis complained to his mother that he never had
enough to eat *chez* John. Partly to supplement his diet, he took to eating at a
pension in hopes of seeing a Scottish girl who was holidaying nearby. He
had admired her bathing; 'a raw creature' according to John, 'who guffaws
in her Glasgow manner before and after each remark.'

The oppressive atmosphere and his inability to work made Lewis
desperate to cut short his stay after only ten days. Another call upon the
limited maternal coffers – 'send me an extra 50 francs,' he wrote, 'the words
stick in my mouth, but they must be said' – made escape possible. 'I'd
apologise for all this sad expense if I felt better: I'm really too done up even
to express my regrets on that score.'

He would go to Honfleur or Dieppe and find himself a cheap room. John
received a letter from Honfleur. Lewis was staying at 59 rue Dupuits and
warning him against reading Strindberg's *Chimie* with its 'laboratorical

gibberish' and Huysmans's 'nauseating' *La Cathédrale*. He had just finished a life of Flaubert and reread *Madame Bovary* 'with boundless delight' and filled half a page of his letter with a lengthy quotation from it. 'My reading has been, and continues to be, one might almost say "wild" lately.' He was in the middle of Anatole France's *M. Bergeret de Paris* and had just read the 1903 Nobel Laureate Bjørnsterne Bjørnson's 'rather insignificant' *La Fille de la pêcheuse* and Hugo's *Derniers jours d'un condamné à mort*, notable only for one or two expressions of thieves' slang. Finally, Prévost's *Manon Lescaut* was 'another dolly' he had in his bag. He asked John if he knew of it and thought that 'life in those times must have been extremely ridiculous'.

*

Contrary to the wishes of his mother, who was anxious that he come back to London and abandon his doomed liaison, Lewis returned to Paris. 'I felt you and Ida were bound to part sooner or later', she told him afterwards, 'but you could not drag yourself away from her as you know; you ought then to have had sufficient resolution to stay away.'

*

He was in London in November applying for a Reader's card to the British Library. Harold Gilman wrote the reference, assuring the authorities that he had known the applicant for many years and that he was a bona fide student. Lewis stated that he was 'by profession a writer' and that the chief subject of his studies would be the literature of the Middle Ages. No explanation can be found for this arcane specification. Perhaps he had been advised that admittance was granted only to students who could prove their research areas were not to be catered for by other libraries. He gave his address as 14 Whiteheads Grove, Chelsea.

Later that month he returned to Paris and took a room in the Hôtel de la Haute Loire at the crossing of the boulevards Raspail and Montparnasse. Thinly disguised, this *carrefour* became the topographical focus for the action of *Tarr*:

> a convenient space, where the Boulevard du Paradis and Boulevard Pfeifer cross with their electric trams.=In the middle is a pavement island, like vestige of submerged masonry.=Italian models festoon it in symmetrical human groups.*

---

* The eccentric punctuation mark (=) in this passage is reproduced from the first American edition of the novel and was consistent with Lewis's written style at the time. The first English edition normalised it to a long dash or hyphen.

He had started negotiating for a studio about a hundred yards away in the rue de la Grande-Chaumière. His hotel room commanded a majestic view of the cypress trees and tombs in the Cimetière Montparnasse back along the boulevard Raspail. 'I wish I could have room and studio as well.'

Taking the studio would incur the usual expenses: a quarter's rent in advance, a stove, table, candles. To supplement the £2 a week and extras his mother sent him he was becoming financially embroiled with Ida again. His policy of gradually easing himself out of her life still left her available as a temporary source of cash. But she was about to travel to Elberfeld for Christmas and was attempting to call in earlier debts. 'She is abusing me for not having any money to give her, – the £2 is naturally lost and I had borrowed during that miserable visit to Paris a little more than that and . . . now I shall have to borrow something from her to buy my furniture with.' He did not find her abuse particularly daunting, and indeed now seemed to be on fairly amicable terms with her. She was a generous girl and had offered him some sticks of furniture from her own meagre store. 'A few little things I can get from Ida for the moment, although I want eventually to be independent of this *aimable* lady even down to a spoon.' The most pressing consideration was the rent for three months, payable on 1 January: 'perhaps Ida can give me the 150 francs,' he told his mother, 'though I should prefer that you could pay that as soon as possible.' He may have foreseen the vexation that would result for him in being indebted to Ida. His mother was the only person in his life whom he could be financially dependent upon and not end up resenting.

While he was at the Haute Loire and preparing to occupy his studio, he instructed his mother to send his money to a safe address in the rue d'Assas and when writing to him at the hotel cautioned her about mentioning her business activities. This was the Rugby School nurtured snobbery of a painfully self-conscious young man terrified of the stigma that might attach to him if his friends found out that his mother took in washing for a living: 'don't talk about Laundries, as the place is full of Americans, and anyone might open the letter.'

Despite his qualms about venturing near his old haunts off the avenue d'Orléans, he spent Christmas under the fecund roof of 77 rue Dareau, where John had installed his women and children. Perhaps because he was an only child Lewis appeared to enjoy the company of infants and tried to entertain the precocious brood with stories. It was a challenging audience. 'They called me a "smutty thing" and a "booby", because I insisted that a lion could climb up a beanstalk, – nay had done so, in my presence.' His host had been extending his paternity and both wife and mistress were pregnant. 'I think John will end by building a city, and being worshipped as the sole man therein – the deity of Masculinity.' Clearly fascinated by the idea of this seraglio, he was slightly disgusted by its sordid day-to-day realities: 'one of the first wife's children has contracted the indelicate habit of spitting at one of the second wife's children while having his bath.' He had developed an antipathy towards John's wife, Ida, and this, he thought, justified the unconventional domestic arrangements. 'Mrs John has changed very much and is no longer pretty, and I no longer have any pity for her: – I don't see how John could do otherwise than perquisition another woman: – but she seems changed . . . I don't like her a bit.'

His hostility to Ida John was not reciprocated. For her part, she had always found him a delightful companion. 'What a refreshment in the desert to see Lewis,' she had once written, 'I love him as a brother.'

Just over two months after Lewis spent Christmas in the rue Dareau and communicated his opinions of Mrs John, she would be dead, 'of peritonitis and a heap of other things' following the birth of her fifth baby.

*

Officially installed in 16 rue de la Grande-Chaumière from New Year's Day 1907, Lewis began work. As if to justify all the expenses she had incurred and to convince her that he might soon be in a position to support himself, he sent his mother a meticulous prospectus:

I have roughly the following plan of campaign: . . . I will do a dozen extremely careful heads in pen and ink, to which I may add an etching or two; with these I might at once get some portraits to do since they will be extremely good. – Then I'm going to do 2 or 3 series of illustrations, – say twenty or thirty drawings – 5 or 6 'finished' in your sense of the word, to always have ready to show; – additionally I will have a portfolio of various studies, nudes, heads etc. – to back up 'the sets' – this will take me all my time till May or April. I will then along with these do as much painting as ever I can, but set myself no task, as yet merely studying: I must so to speak go into training in that matter, and will as soon as possible take up a picture, but it would be useless to do that at once; – still, we'll see how that goes in a month or so. I'm convinced that success in art is only a matter of common sense with a matter of disposing of one's work, and a certain amount of discipline in the doing of it . . . roughly, what I'm doing, it may not sound very much, but is a most sound programme – the dozen heads in ink are a most important item, as I have done one or two that please extremely, in popular quarters . . . of course there's a great deal of grind and one has to be very hard on oneself, reject inefficient work, slovenly work etc. – never work in a tired fashion etc. – the beer and skittles are not so far away, I hope however.

75

Like the literary projects he mentioned to John the previous spring, none of the promised pen and ink drawings, etchings or paintings have survived, if, indeed, they were ever made. In fact, nothing of any significance is known to exist from Lewis's hand between his departure from the Slade in 1901 and the year 1909.

Whatever work was under way in his new studio, considerable creative attention was being paid to his personal appearance. 'I have bought a wonderful new hat, which makes me look ever so much more handsome. I'm going to buy a fur collar as soon as I can see one cheap . . . a long one that buttons onto the coat. I let my hair hang down underneath the hat: the effect is astonishing.' The beard he had experimented with in Normandy had been removed, leaving a drooping moustache. Profile and full-face sketches were included as marginalia in the letter to his mother. He ran into a contemporary from the Slade before Christmas and had been delighted to discover his Bohemian image had proved impenetrable. 'To show how changed I am, Everett . . . talked to me for 10 minutes and left me without recognising me! I met him again today; he had seen Gore the night before and Gore had told him that he had seen me – it is 4 years since I saw Everett.' Henry Everett was as impressed with the work Lewis was doing as he was with his appearance. 'I have at once an adherent and a model; – I showed some drawings to Everett . . . he said they were a million times better than he had ever imagined they could be, as good as John etc. etc. – and that, since he had seen my drawings, he would sit as often as I like. – I'm not sure I want him to sit as often as all that, still every little helps.'

There was another reunion. 'Ida is here, and warily I renew my relationship with her.' He assured his mother that marriage was still out of the question and indeed often reiterated this when the subject of Ida came up in his letters. He seemed to be using his mother as sounding board for a long, repetitive and self-reassuring monologue:

> I couldn't, quite simply call my soul my own if I were married to her; as since I don't by any means like her as well as I did, and wish to call my soul very much my own, – and even shouldn't mind calling other people's also, if they were so disposed, – I think marriage dwindles steadfastly; – my affair with her has 'lowered my temperature' in the matter of good spirits, gaiety, a good many degrees, generally speaking I feel a little bit heavier hearted all round, – but marrying her would be no solution to this, – quite the contrary.

He also hinted at fresh grounds for suspicion. 'I . . . have my own opinions about her fidelity at Elberfeld latterly, but refuse to worry myself about it.' His apparent indifference to her real or imagined infidelities signalled a change of attitude. From this time on her continued presence in Paris and his obligation to her were constant irritants:

> I don't see her very often, that is I see her every day or so, and get abused if I don't go to see her, but my visits are short and always disagreeable; I don't remember having spent an agreeable half hour with her for many a month. I don't know whether she imagines that that is the way to make oneself liked: I don't suppose she does, as the idea would be too original for her; I suppose she's so nervous that she doesn't know what to do with herself, and that 'scenes', quarrels are the only means of letting off steam. – nice for me, isn't it?

The suffocating tension of these volatile meetings became raw material for the psychologically charged interviews between Bertha and Tarr:

> An intense atmosphere of Teutonic suicide permeated everything. He could not move an eyelid or a muscle without wounding or slighting something. It was like being in a dark kitchen at night, where you know at every step you will put your foot on a beetle.

Unable to extricate himself from this attrition, he sounded off in the most vindictive terms to his mother:

> I've not seen Ida for a day or so, and wish from the bottom of my heart that she were in the bottom of the sea – it reached a climax the other day, when in one gigantic effort she seemed to have wished to fuse all her most disagreeable qualities into one; – I suppose every human creature has their possibilities of nastiness and malevolent propensities, but they are of little use to one once they have manifested them: – happily I have a tender feeling in another direction, which may ripen into covetousness; then farewell stinking german bitch.

These brutal letters may have provoked painful memories for Mrs Lewis of the callous treatment she had suffered when abandoned by her philandering husband 14 years before. In one of his tirades her son was tactless enough to indicate the parallel. 'I think I may go a step further than my august father, and say that there are "too many bitches in this *world*".'

Nothing is known about the object of the 'tender feeling' that he hoped would soon supplant Ida, but according to John he was often so besotted, and Alick Schepeler received regular bulletins.

'Lewis announced the other day that he was loved! At last! It seems he had observed a demoiselle in a restaurant who whenever he regarded her sucked her cheeks in slightly and looked embarrassed – the glorious fact was patent then – *l'amour*! he means to follow this up like a bloodhound.' It would be tempting to see in this 'demoiselle', glimpsed across a restaurant, a prototype of the fabulous Anastasya Vasek in *Tarr*. Anastasya, also first encountered in a restaurant by the smitten Kreisler, is the dazzling antithesis of the homely Bertha Lunken. However, if John is to be believed, one new romantic interest turned out to be a good deal less than dazzling:

> Last night I met Lewis in a café where there's good music and he announced he was waiting for the most beautiful woman in Paris – an Englishwoman – this of course made me excited – at last she arrives – a great gawk with an addled brain in which float vague amorphous fragments, like vegetables in a soup. She is very embarrassed and wishes to appear more so. She gazes at me tactlessly and makes me want to say something shocking – I do. – without any appreciable effect. She talks French in the mincing English fashion. She attacks Lewis's bowler and wants to know if I understand French politics. I ask Lewis if he remembers those long nights upon the Nile. He says 'Ah! in Flood-time'. He becomes very *intrigué* and tries to look occult, that is to say becomes transparent, almost naked. I induce her to drink something. She sips a little and pretending that the quite innocuous mixture has mounted to her head, pushes it away dramatically. She says drink makes her indiscreet if not frank. We implore some little confidence on the strength of a mouthful of marc-cassis. She declines with some nervousness; perhaps she has nothing to confess – handy. She finishes the marc-cassis. We leave and she loses her tram home; we conduct her inexorably to her door.

Lewis also took to haunting the Cabaret Bobino and yearned after the fleshly performers on the stage. This was a waste of time to the seasoned campaigner, John: '*Cependant, il ne trouve pas son affaire – le nigaud*.*'

But despite looking elsewhere, no definitive break with Ida had been made and the affair dragged on throughout the early months of 1907. When his mother contemplated a visit in April or May, Lewis tried to arrange things so that the two women would meet as little as possible. 'I've come to that stage at which I positively hate the sight of her, and I think we would amuse ourselves better without her.' By this time Mrs Lewis had begun to send Ida money. She was paying off her son's debts in instalments. Lewis appeared to distance himself from these transactions. 'Oh, so it's the £40 interest that bothers Ida: she says she's very hard up, and I can quite believe it: send it to her if you can.'

---

* Simpleton or booby.

NINE

'Doubts that he is a shit are still graver'

Financial obligations to his mistress may have contributed to the souring of their relations. This at least was his mother's opinion. 'I think had you or Ida had sufficient money to be very independent you would probably have continued on much better terms.' Throughout his life Lewis consistently bit the hands that fed him. Debts become humiliating only when they are brought to the debtor's attention. For Lewis, humiliation invariably turned, defensively, to antagonism.

And money had now become a cause of friction with Augustus John. 'As to Lewis,' he wrote to Alick, 'I'm done with that type. Recently I happened to mention I could do with a few pounds he owed me . . . I did not press him at all – but his manners are so bad and fatuous and really end by being offensive, one does expect a little frankness from those we treat on terms of equality. He said he would talk privily to me.'

However, it was Lewis who felt himself to be the injured party, his pretext being a supposed slight he suffered at John's hands, one night at the Café du Dôme. A lady said to John: 'Perhaps you'd like to talk alone with Mr. Lewis.' John replied: 'I'd rather go to bed.' Lewis 'was Ass enough to take offence at this,' John told Alick, 'for after a while he rose and offered a lymphatic hand all round and departed.' An exchange of letters followed. Lewis was verbose and pretentious. 'The next morning I received a scrawl from him . . . in which he "saw no reason why a *fâcheux* [regrettable] acquaintance should continue any longer", this enveloped of course in idiotic tergiversation.' John replied, couching his letter in a style mimicking Lewis's:

> Renouncing the illusions I had nourished with my heart's blood for years, and amongst them (*bien entendu*) that of my own sagacity, and permitting myself that linguistic licence if not that stylistic obscurity which serve you, at the same time for *'protection d'adornment'*, I briefly confess your note, once deciphered, proves you too 'poltroon', too *'mesquin'*, too *'bête'* to make the loss of the acquaintance referred to a matter for sorrow. – Alas! it is the acquaintance I have cause to regret! But let us congratulate each other – each in his own way has gained something.

The crisis allowed John to tackle Lewis over a character trait that had evidently been a source of irritation to him for some time:

> you have never it seems to me given the idea of friendship a chance – it would appear that you live in fear of intrusion and can but dally with your fellows momentarily as Robinson Crusoe with his savages.

John was perceptive. Lewis rigorously compartmentalised his affairs; the confidences other men entrusted to friends being shared only with his mother.

It was not only to friends that he could sometimes prove irritating. Some idea of the effect his company had on passing acquaintances can be found in a letter from Duncan Grant to Lytton Strachey in February. Grant and Lewis got to know each other quite well three or four years later, but in 1907 their only relationship was that of neighbours. Grant had a studio in the rue Delambre where Lewis had rented one a few years before, and on the opposite side of the *carrefour* to his present studio. 'I have begun to have depressing intervals,' Grant complained to Strachey:

> not because I have no one to talk to but because on the contrary there's someone turned up to whom I have to talk. He's a poet-painter called Lewis who always feeds at the same places as I do and my gorge simply rises when ever I see him. And just because he talks about interesting things I have to answer and so I suppose he thinks I like him. But really it's too awful – I simply descend into the depths of despair and gloom after seeing him – and I cannot decide whether my feelings are absurd or silly, but I certainly think all his hopelessly *mesquin** and putrid. You will think all this is mere hysterics perhaps it is, but it's very odd that any one should have the power of making one go into them. Today I took up a book and read directly he began to speak, but ugh! tomorrow he'll most likely ask me why I did it.

At the Dôme the precociously brilliant young man was observed in full conversational flow by Euphemia, the wife of Henry Lamb. Listening while he expounded, perhaps, on the books he was currently reading, and noting the effect of inadequate hygiene on his complexion, she remarked to her companion that he was so bloody clever it was coming out of his face in spots.

Lewis had spent six months at the studio in the rue de la Grande-Chaumière and, since the second quarter's rent was due to run out on 30 June, he made preparations to leave Paris. 'I got the 3 pounds, paid all up,

* Interestingly, both Grant and John applied the same word to Lewis: *mesquin* (mean, petty).

80

the concierge, bought a box for 4 francs as I have collected certain things here and it is easier for porterage, – paid 5½ francs for a suit that I had absolutely forgotten was in Mont Piété, – a relic of the Schelfhout days.' He intended spending a month in Dieppe with friends, returning to London for a short time and then taking an August holiday in Brittany. Mrs Lewis counselled against the latter excursion. 'I really think Brittany far too hot for pleasure in August. You know how you felt last year at St. Honorine; I should not think you want to repeat that experience.' She was planning to join him. 'Why not try the northern coast between Boulogne and Ostend; there's a place called Malo les Bains close to Dunkerque – which is very bracing and healthy and there is Berck near Boulogne; these are both small quiet places, and would suit me very well for a couple of weeks. Also a consideration, the fare would be much less for you as well as for me than going to Brittany.'

He kicked his heels in Paris for a fortnight while his (unidentified) friends delayed their departure. He had just written to his mother to tell her that the Dieppe trip was off and he was coming home, when they made a move. 'We arrived very late and the ladies of the party, once out of the train, were becoming tired and firmly refused to move a step except in the direction of a definite shelter; at last we came across a "*Maison de Famille*" in which, to my chagrin, I have installed myself.' He soon moved into cheaper quarters – '6 francs, all included, a day' – at the Hôtel du Rocher and instructed his mother to send him three pounds.

He had left behind him in Paris the emotional wreckage of his affair with Ida. It had evidently been clumsily concluded. Late in June Ida wrote to Mrs Lewis. 'She . . . said she was very unhappy so I gathered that you had had an *extra violent* disagreement . . . you have wasted each other's time, strained your affection to its utmost limits, and now have parted, I am sure, in a very unbefitting manner.' His mother felt things might have been more tactfully handled. 'Would not it, under all circumstances, have been much nicer and more politic to have said goodbye amiably and have left for your summer excursion leaving it vague and indefinite as to *when* and *where* you were to again meet.' It seemed as if the tortured affair might at last have been over. 'I've had a lesson in the matter of women such as I shan't forget in a hurry.' But his mother had as little faith in his ability to learn as in his strength of will. 'Although you feel weary of her now, very likely indeed by the autumn you will be wanting to follow her to Germany, if she goes there.' She knew her son well. The emotional immaturity he evinced throughout his unhappy dealings with Ida made him unable to let her go. A monotonous pattern of alienation and pursuit was the result. Later, in *Tarr*, he would be able to rationalise his behaviour:

The mandates of the governing elements in our nature, resolves, etc., were childish enough things. His resentment against Bertha, and resolve to quit, would always be there. There was room in life for the satisfaction of this impulse, and the equally strong one to see her again.

But Ida was soon to find her own way out of the stagnant absurdity of this affair. She found it in a banal manner – no 'Teutonic suicide', she – that would absolve Lewis of all responsibility towards her and gain for herself the security she had sought in vain for the previous two years.

*

Lewis's planned month in Dieppe, due to the late start, was now reduced to about ten days; 'the best thing I can do is to come back . . . to London, stay there a bit and talk things over a bit, (perhaps attack a publisher or two) and then join John in the country . . . or if not John some other friend.'

Ruffled feelings had now been smoothed and there was an opportunity of spending the summer at another little resort on the Normandy coast, Équihen, near Boulogne, where John was staying with Dorelia and the children. He had been a widower since March.

*

After Dieppe Lewis's movements are difficult to trace. Although he intended visiting London to see his mother and 'attack a publisher or two' there is no evidence that he did so. He probably did not go to Équihen. Instead, despite maternal pressure, he went to Brittany and by 27 July he was at Doëlan in Finistère with the painter Henry Lamb.* John wrote to Lamb recalling his fussy companion of the previous year. 'Lewis no doubt misses his petits Suisses.'

Passing through the town of Gestel, about seven miles east of Doëlan, Lewis and Lamb encountered a scene of picturesque poverty:

sitting on a bench near the church we found two remarkable figures, a young man raggedly clothed, with a strange reckless face, and an old man bent over and leaning on a heavy stick. The latter was largely built, his legs half naked, and a dark metallic, salmon colour; and his feet thrust into the straw of his enormous sabots, one ankle swollen and wounded . . . he

* Keith Clements, *Henry Lamb: the Artist and his Friends*, 1985, claims the two men were in Brittany together in 1909 or 1910. Lewis, however, was in London during the summer of 1909 and considering the views he was expressing to Augustus John concerning Lamb in 1910, neither date seems likely.

sat motionless beside his insouciant and listless companion. With a heavy grey mat of hair, he was dark-skin'd and . . . the flesh was pucker'd round his eyes into innumerable deep wrinkles, as though some torrid sun were constantly in his eyes . . . He look'd at us steadily when we spoke to him and answer'd our questions slowly. My companion ask'd him if he would be painted; he made no difficulty. When asked where was his home . . . he replied simply, with that deep and tragic voice . . . 'On the stones' ('sur les pierres',): it was there that he sat the greater part of the day, on the cobbles, to receive alms.

In 1935, invited to write an account of his earliest creative experiences for an anthology called *Beginnings*, Lewis recalled the portrayal of this beggar, deprived of sight to make him additionally wretched, as a demonstration of how to separate the visual from the literary:

I was painting a blind Armorican [Breton] beggar. The 'short story' was the crystallisation *of what I had to keep out of my consciousness while painting*. Otherwise the painting would have been a bad painting . . . A lot of discarded matter collected there, as I was painting or drawing, in the back of my mind – in the back of my consciousness. As I squeezed out *everything* that smacked of literature from my vision of the beggar, it collected at the back of my mind. It imposed itself upon me as a complementary creation.

While he carefully preserved the literary relic of his meeting with the beggar, the complementary creation in oils, gouache or charcoal was, along with the rest of his early output, subsequently discarded and, in all probability, deliberately destroyed.

That summer of 1907, with Henry Lamb, was his first experience of the primitive Breton environment. It would take another extended visit the following summer, the most part travelling alone, for the experience to crystallise into publishable stories.

*

Towards the end of 1907 his whereabouts are known, his activities obscure. The British Museum visitors' book puts him at 81 Alwiche Road on 18 October and at 5 Adelaide Road, a lodging house, on 13 December. In between, late in November, he went to North Wales for a fortnight. He sent his mother a picture postcard of four Welsh shrimp women, written in French against prying local eyes. He had adopted the same practice in Germany and would do so again in Spain. 'Don't send postcards written in French', his mother implored him. 'So tiresome when you write such *tiny* scratchings.' He became stranded without money and was finally rescued from the Pengwern Arms, Ffestiniog, by a timely and ill-afforded cheque. It covered a hotel bill of £1.12.6, 2/6 for tips, and 13/6 excursion train fare back to London.

There is no clue as to what he was doing in Wales. The winter weather would appear to preclude sketching, and even the glories of Ffestiniog, extolled by Lord Lyttelton and quoted in the guide books,* must have been bleak in early December. Three miles away the jagged lines and facets of the vast grey slate quarries of Blaenau may have fed an embryonic interest in the harshness of abstract form.

*

Back in London in January 1908, John had no idea where he was and this may not have been unconnected with the fact that 'that devil Lewis' was still in his debt. 'He's a cool card with other people's money', John complained to Lamb, 'I don't know how much of mine he's calmly appropriated, without so much as a "thank you". One gets from him merely elaborately explicit promises to pay.' When they did meet, at the theatre in February, relations were a little frosty and John kept him at arm's length. 'We accosted each other with casual punctiliousness. My doubts that he is a shit are still graver than formerly.'

John's resentment was, as ever, shortlived and by the summer he was addressing Lewis in terms of friendship again. He had even, by autumn, bestowed upon him the title of honorary Romany: Rai.

*

In March he was living at 4 High Street, Ealing, where Sturge Moore wrote, inviting him to a poetry reading at the small Queen's Hall in Langham Place. 'It might be worth your while to turn up there even if you don't intend to read, as it is quite informal . . . Of course if you like to show us your operatic style we should be delighted.'

By the end of April he was in Paris again, soon to depart for his customary summer holiday. This one would last seven months.

His mother was once more weathering an acute economic crisis with her

---

* 'With a few mundane attractions thrown in, "a loving wife, a bosom friend, and a good set of books," a former Lord Lyttelton once wrote that he could "pass an age here and think it a day." ' (M.J.B. Baddeley, B.A., and C. S. Ward, M.A., *North Wales Part I*, 8th edition – revised, Thomas Nelson & Sons, London, Edin., Dublin, & N.Y., 1909.)

failing laundry business. She was also worried about her son's health. In desperation she wrote two postcards to her husband: one to New London, Connecticut, the last address she had for him, and another, care of his brother Albert in Toronto. Their son, she told him, was suffering from neurasthenia and his doctor had ordered him to go away to the country for several months. She implored Charles to help him as her means were small. Her appeal remained unanswered for the best part of three months.

'Neurasthenia', the catch-all complaint of that period, might have been used to describe a number of physical and mental symptoms, including loss of energy, insomnia, aches and pains (especially in the chest and abdomen), depression, irritability, and reduced concentration. Whatever the precise nature of Lewis's malady before he left Paris, the journey to Northern Spain by way of Bayonne and San Sebastián is unlikely to have improved his condition. Also, he spilt and lost the medicine he had brought with him on the train. He waited in León for a replacement prescription to be sent from England.

At the end of May he travelled from León to Vigo on the northwest coast where he stayed, initially, at the Hotel Europa; then, according to an account published a couple of years later, in furnished, third-floor lodgings on the Calle Real.* He told his mother he did not like Vigo but she urged him to stay a while as the Atlantic air would do him good. A week later he was still feeling ill and depressed.

He caught the Royal Mail Steam Packet from Vigo on 18 June. The voyage to Cherbourg took two days and his 3rd class passage, including food, cost him £2.

From Cherbourg he travelled down into Brittany. His movements may be traced only from references in letters to him. None of his own letters has survived. On 10 July, a letter from John was addressed to him at the Hôtel Kerfany, Moëlan. By the 16th he had moved on, had been north to Quimperlé, staying at an inn run by one Morin. From there he went south again: either to the small bathing resort of Le Pouldu, or three miles east along the coast to Doëlan.

Lewis's observations of his second Breton holiday would appear in the *English Review* the following year, and in *The Tramp* and *The New Age* during the two years following that.

At Doëlan he lodged at an inn by the slipway on the east side of the harbour, known locally, for reasons no one could remember, as 'Peste' and presided over by a man of Spanish extraction called Peron. This was to be

* 'A Spanish Household', *The Tramp: An Open Air Magazine*, I (June–July 1910).

the model for one of his earliest exercises in the creation of character.* He described the formidable figure of Peron, thinly disguised as 'Bestre', a year later in an article published by the *English Review*:

> his Spanish origin is visible in his face. He is a large man, grown naively corpulent: one can see by his movements that the gradual and insidious growth of his stomach has not preoccupied him in the least . . . Sunburnt, with a large yellow-white moustache, his little eyes protrude with a cute strenuosity of expression. When he meets anyone for the first time his mouth remains open, with his cigarette-end adhering to the lower lip; he assumes an expression of expectancy and repressed amusement, like a man accustomed to nonplussing and surprising people.

Towards the end of July Lewis hired a bicycle. Practical advice mingled with dire warnings came from his mother. 'I daresay it would do you good, but if you hire the machine be sure to get it cleaned and the tyres looked to each day . . . Also be careful not to be run down by a motor on the road, nor to coast down long hills and get smashed . . . and you don't want to *scorch* on the bike as that is not good for your heart.' A nail in one of his canvas shoes grazed a toe and infection set in. 'It is most dangerous to get matter in your feet', she told him, 'as there is so much danger of blood poisoning and you might get that by wearing a coloured sock if the skin is broken and if the foot swells it is not to be neglected. I would see a doctor if I were you, and adopt the proper remedies.' As for his other ailments, she thought time would heal:

> I hope you will soon be feeling better. I think your stomach is as much in fault as anything and if you can really get your stomach right, the other horrible feelings will pass away. I have no doubt there are many people who suffer as you do, but I trust yours is only temporary after all.

And, perhaps to instil in him a measure of concern beyond himself, she added:

> I am feeling very ragged myself, but as you know I don't have many distractions and almost constant bother and anxiety of one sort and another, so that it is hardly surprising that sometimes I feel tired out.

He probably did not tell his mother about the gonorrhoea he had

---

* According to a letter from Lytton Strachey to Ottoline Morrel (22 October 1912), leafing through a back issue of the *English Review* Strachey discovered Lewis's story and immediately recognised the protagonist from the inn at Döelan where he had stayed in 1911. Topographical details are from Keith Clements' *Henry Lamb* . . . , p. 93.

contracted in Spain. He confided news of this Bohemian rite of passage completed to John, and the venereal veteran feigned outrage. 'My poor Lewis, I am distressed to hear of your persistent illness ... But fly and linger not, if that young woman can really represent the manners of the Spanish fair sex. Effrontery indeed! Is this Spanish frankness?'

He might have caught this, his first dose of 'clap', in San Sebastián, in León or even during the time he spent in Vigo, perhaps from the Galician servant in the house where he roomed on the Calle Real. He named her La Flora in the short prose sketch published a couple of years later in *The Tramp*: 'a tall, lithe and handsome fisher girl. Her eyebrows always raised in weary, affected fatalism, her mouth hanging in affected brutal listlessness, she was very fond of notice and had the best of hearts.'

Wherever it was contracted, this did not commemorate his only sexual experience that summer. Lingering infection notwithstanding, he appears to have had a further adventure after leaving Vigo. Once again, he confided it to John who, in turn, thought the liaison sufficiently pertinent for communication to Robert Andrew Scott Macfie, Honorary Secretary of the Gypsy Lore Society in Liverpool:

> I have recently taken it upon myself ... to confer the title Rai upon a friend of mine – one Percy Wyndham Lewis – whose qualifications – rather historical or anthropological than linguistic, viz. – he having coupled and lived in a state of copulation with a wandering Spanish romi in Brittany – seemed to me ... to merit the honourable and distinctive title of our confraternity.

If this were not enough, yet another candidate for the young man's attentions was to be found in a bookshop in Lorient. She, it seems, was of a higher social class than her predecessors: 'the daughter of [a] Spanish hidalgo'.

Evidently these affairs, sordid or romantic, consummated or frustrated, and united by a common nationality, preoccupied him as he continued his travels. Across an unused quarter of the folded sheet of another letter from John, 'the poet' wrote a single pencilled word of four block capitals, and underneath a large number of other tiny words in neat columns. It was a complete conjugation of the Spanish verb AMAR: to love.

*

Mrs Lewis's economic difficulties were temporarily eased in July when her appeal to Charles for a contribution towards their 'neurasthenic' offspring's convalescence was finally answered. It came in the form of a cheque made out to Percy Lewis for the sum of £40 18s., the stirling equivalent of $200, and was sent to her by Charles's brother Albert. 'Now I believe myself', she told her son, 'that your father has sent the money to your Uncle Alb – but does not wish him to say *he* has sent, as he doesn't want to establish a precedent.' She instructed him to endorse the cheque and return it to her by registered post. She would keep it as 'a reserve fund' from which he could buy himself an overcoat in the autumn. But she cautioned him: 'We do not know what we may want . . . and it is as well to be prepared and only get the strictly necessary things.'

Charles's timely, if anonymous, intervention enabled Mrs Lewis to embark on her previously arranged holiday in Brittany with comparative financial security. She was accompanied by her friends, Mr and Mrs Castell, and planned to spend some time with her son. By mid-August they were all together, staying at the Lion d'Or in Quimperlé.

A single dated diary entry of Monday 17 August records an excursion to Le Pouldu and their return by way of Clohars during the boozy aftermath of a *pardon*. Essentially local religious festivals, *pardons* took place throughout Brittany during the summer months. Apart from the processions and the canopied display of sacred effigies, there were wrestling matches, acrobats, dancing and copious drinking. Something of the primitive nature of such outbursts of faith and exuberance caught Lewis's imagination. 'These fetes are essentially *orgies*', he wrote excitedly that evening in the Lion d'Or, syntax almost out of control and his pen scratching out and altering the spidery hand to near illegibility:

> It is the renunciation and dissipation at stated times, of everything that a peasant has of disorder'd, exalted, that in us that will not be contain'd in ordinary life; all that there is left of rebellion against life, fate, routine in the peasant. All these people bring all their indignations, all their revolts, and bewilder'd dreams, and sacrifice them here, pay their supreme tribute to Fate, instead of keeping jealously their passions and reveries hidden in their hearts, they come here and fling all to the winds, leave themselves bare, make a bonfire of what the intelligence tells us is most precious.

It was eventually visual abstractions of these dancing peasants, and not studies of mendicant and *saltimbanque*, reminiscent, perhaps, of blue and pink Picassos, that would figure strongly in the subsequent paintings and drawings he allowed to survive.

*

On the 21st they moved to Plouhinec for four or five days and then to Le

Faouët, staying under the inn roof of a man by the name of Portier for a week or so. Then, leaving her travelling companions, the Castells, at St Malo, Mrs Lewis sailed home on 5 September. The parting letter to her son rustled with maternal care and caution: *'Don't get wet, don't drink water or unboiled milk.'*

Her son stayed on at Le Faouët, chez Portier, using this as his base for the next two months. He continued cycling in the area despite his mother's dire warnings not to *'scorch'* on the bike. Later in September he contemplated an excursion to the wilder shores of the Finistère peninsula pursued, again, by maternal concern: 'don't go to the Pointe du Raz or the Baie des Trépassés *alone* as the road is dangerous (I suppose the cliffs are unsafe) and there have been a good many accidents there the guide books say.' Indeed, Baedeker promised 'an almost constantly wild and tempestuous sea-view' but warned visitors:

> It is hazardous to proceed to the N[orth], towards the *Enfer de Plogoff* and the *Baie des Trépassés*, without minute instructions and precautions (guide advisable; 1 fr.).

*

Returning from her holiday, Mrs Lewis found her business in as parlous a state as when she had left. She was £15 overdrawn at the bank and most weeks there seemed to be a scramble to call in sufficient from her tardily paying customers to cover wages. She also had staffing problems. Her carman, it seems, had had three horses in as many months, each one having been returned to Pickford's in such poor condition that the hire company suspected him of selling the animals' feed on the side. 'Added to this the fellow seems to have got slacker and slacker', Anne complained, 'and dirtier and dirtier.' Eventually Pickford's refused to send any more horses until he was dismissed.

Also, Lillie, her live-in bookkeeper and packer, was leaving to get married. While this boded a much greater workload for herself until a replacement could be found, Mrs Lewis found some consolation in the thought that her late mother's sister-in-law, Fanny Prickett, still a permanent fixture in the house, would no longer have an object to hand for her constant nagging. The domestic tensions had been largely the fault of 'this cantankerous old woman', although Lillie's 'little airs too were tiresome' and cannot have helped matters.

She had envisaged her son returning to London towards the end of September but, on reflection, decided that she could not afford to send him sufficient funds until business improved. He was to stay where he was while the weather was fine, probably into November. In the meantime, she told him: 'get your writing done, and then you can see.' The last reference suggests he was already consciously working up his Breton experiences for publication on his return to London.

By October he had moved around so much that his belongings, hostages to outstanding rent, were lodged at a series of inns over about 90 square miles. His mother advised a complex scheme of manoeuvre in order to rationalise the situation:

> collect all your things at one place, instead of three. Better go to Pont Scorff and come back to Quimperlé by train via Lorient and leave the things there, Quimperlé, till you want to leave for Paris, and get your things at Portiers sent to Quimperlé by the Courrier, then it will only mean the [Hôtel] Kerfany things to be conveyed to Quimperlé in preparation for departure.

*

Towards the end of November Mrs Lewis hired an accountant and his assessment of her business was not encouraging. She had taken £200 less, up to the first of that month, than she had taken in 1907. Her profits for the year amounted to £250. And in December she had an accumulation of money to find. She had to pay her staff's wages, a coke bill for £10, the water bill, the gas bill, together with her own and her son's living expenses 'and a few other odd pounds'.

And she had to send £5 to Ida. There had been references to other payments in September and October. Then, in November, she mentioned that Ida had not sent her a receipt for the last month's money but that this was perhaps understandable:

> I suppose she is not feeling very well just now as she expects the baby in December.

Payments of £5 per month by a mother to her son's heavily pregnant former mistress might constitute strong evidence for an attribution of paternity. It has been assumed that Lewis made Ida pregnant and then callously abandoned her, leaving his mother to support the girl through her lonely gestation. Significance has been found in Part VII of *Tarr*, in which the protagonist marries his ex-mistress in order to legitimise another man's child. This has been interpreted as autobiographical revisionism: the author absolving himself of guilt and responsibility by rewriting an action as fiction.

However, a letter from the Hansa-Hotel at Wiesbaden, on 20 August

1908, goes a long way to confounding the tragic legend. 'My dear Missis Lewis,' it began, 'I think you will have your holy days now but I hope this letter will follow you.' It was signed 'Ida Elfreide Follot'. She was on holiday, cruising along the Rhine with her husband. She seemed very happy. She told Mrs Lewis that her sister Hedwig would be in London in September and would like to visit Percy if he were there. 'And I would be happy to hear that Percy too is well! and healthy – does he work?'

Nowhere in the scribbled broken English was there the slightest hint of harboured animosity from a wronged and abandoned mistress.*

Mrs Lewis's monthly £5 cheques most likely represented repayment of her son's debts, the discharge of a purely financial obligation. No more.

*

Mrs Lewis's final words to her son in the letter of 25 November suggesting he return to London by the first week in December might have stood as a useful injunction for the rest of his life:

Don't get into debt or *borrow any money*.

---

* Of course, Ida's letter only indicates that she was happily married at the time she was expecting her baby. It offers no conclusive proof that Lewis was not the father. After all, Follot might have married Ida to legitimise the child, in which case the fictional denouement of *Tarr* followed even closer upon fact than has been realised. But for a baby to be expected some time between the first and the thirty-first of December it would need to have been conceived between the first and thirty-first of March. Lewis can definitely be placed in London for much of that month. The British Museum alone offers him an alibi for the 14th, 18th, 19th and 20th.

TEN

First essays and the futility of pot-boiling

When Lewis arrived back in London in December 1908 he had just turned 26 years old. In the same month, the first issue of a new publication appeared which was to give his literary career a start. The *English Review* was a periodical, its editorial admitted, 'of what is commercially described as "of the 'heavy' order," . . . a periodical devoted to the arts, to letters and ideas'.

Also awaiting him was a letter from Sturge Moore which can only have encouraged his literary ambitions:

> I often think of your sonnets and I wish I could read them again and had a more detailed recollection of them. Of all the poetry which I have read by my contemporaries . . . it is those sonnets which gave me most the sense of a new possibility, a new creation, and consequently there is no writer whom I more desire to accompany and communicate with.

Since Moore numbered among his friends Laurence Binyon and W. B. Yeats, this was praise indeed.

Lewis was now working on short prose pieces based upon his travels in Northern France and Spain. He would visit Moore and his wife and read them aloud. 'The Brittany sketches often return to my mind and always strengthen my conviction of their value', Moore told him. 'Bring some more Ms please. It is a great pleasure to us both to listen.'

And it was as a writer, albeit one with close conections to the world of the visual arts, that Moore introduced him, in April, to W. B. Yeats. Yeats, however, recalled nothing of the conversation apart from a diatribe about Henry Lamb and Dorelia McNeill. 'The day before yesterday', he wrote:

> I met a young poet called Lewis who is an admirer of Augustus John . . . He says that John's mistress has taken another admirer, a very clever young painter who does not admire John's work, and this influences her, and so she does not give John the old 'submissive admiration', and this is bad for John, and she has done it all for vengeance because John will not marry her. Lewis is very angry and thinks John should leave her. What does he owe to her or her children?

The fact that John had established reciprocal relations with Lamb's wife, Euphemia, the woman who had made the jibe in the Café du Dôme about Lewis's cleverness erupting in spots, may have escaped his notice. Lewis's concern for John seemed a particular preoccupation. Several months later he was still telling Moore what a 'very bad way' his friend was in:

> not so much in what he is actually doing, which seems to be portraits of Mayors and Mayoresses but in his state of mind. That cursed family of children is his excuse, but that sickening bitch he has attached himself to is the reason, or at least his accomplice in the muzzling of his genius.

A door slammed shut in Lewis's face early the following year would show the feelings Dorelia harboured for him in return.

The May issue of the *English Review* devoted 11 of its 200–odd pages to the first literary endeavour to appear under the byline of P. Wyndham Lewis. Elsewhere between the dark blue paper wrappers was a tribute to Algernon Charles Swinburne, who had died the previous month, poetry by Sturge Moore and the prose of Conrad, Dostoevsky, Norman Douglas and W. H. Hudson.

If testimony of the *Review*'s editor, the notoriously unreliable Ford Madox Hueffer,* is to be believed, Lewis, looking like a Russian conspirator, in a black coat and cape and wearing a Latin-Quarter hat, confronted him on a dark stairway and pressed the manuscript of 'The "Pole" ' into his hands before departing without a word. Another version from the same source has a similarly dressed but more voluble Lewis cornering Hueffer in his bathroom, announcing himself as a man of genius and proceeding to read the essay aloud while the editor of the *English Review* sat in the tub, nonchalantly plying his sponge.

The following month's *English Review* carried another article, 'Some Innkeepers and Bestre', immortalising Peron of Doëlan. Seeing it in print, Lewis was disgusted by its 'unpardonably poor jokes . . . garrulity and carelessness'.

By July he had moved from Ealing to 14B Whitehead's Grove, Chelsea, and was writing to Sturge Moore with the news that he had just finished writing a story which featured a duel and a German protagonist. He had not had time to work on it properly but would send his mentor the manuscript to hear what he thought of it, 'prepared . . . for your curses and abuse at the unfinished state of the writing'. This is the earliest recorded reference to a major novel in the making. But the 'story' of Otto Kreisler's duel would have to undergo considerable expansion and a great many accretions over the next eight or nine years before it would emerge as such.

* Later Ford Madox Ford.

A month or so later he seemed disenchanted with the *English Review*'s editor: 'Hueffer is a shit of the most dreary and uninteresting type' he told Moore. For his last article, 'Les Saltimbanques', published in August, he had received 'a dirty little cheque' for £4.10s. He admitted that he should have sent it back in disgust, but he 'was damnably hard up'. Nevertheless it was in that unremunerative direction that his 'Otto Kreisler' appeared destined. 'Because of its awkward length and tone . . . no other magazine would have it.'

Meanwhile John had been in London and taken Lewis to dinner at the Carlton with a lawyer from New York, a collector of contemporary art and literary manuscripts, by the name of John Quinn. Lewis heard that he had supported Yeats but, having quarrelled with the poet, now felt 'a void of Genius in his life':

> So he is recklessly attaching John, with the strings of his purse: – he has bought a set of 140 etchings, a ten foot picture, a portrait of himself, thousands of drawings, and if John were twice as industrious as he is he could not satisfy the thirst for pictures that Quinn has repeatedly hinted the obscure Future will be salt with!

Eventually Lewis himself was to become a beneficiary of this man's enthusiastic if fickle patronage. But this was only after Quinn came under the influence of a fellow American, a champion of the 'modern', who convinced him, for a time, of Lewis's worth.

Despite his reservations about the *English Review* and 'that ignoble fellow-being and slippery customer', its editor, Lewis hoped to be appointed Foreign Correspondent soon. Certain of Hueffer's remarks had at least given the impression that this was what he had in mind. 'Troublesome as the monthly article would be,' Lewis reasoned, 'it would be nothing compared to the uncertainties of other work.' He also thought of writing a Paris column for the *Manchester Guardian* or *Liverpool Courier*. But nothing came of any of these projects.

Nevertheless, with the grand total of 30 pounds already received from his articles, and with a view perhaps to gathering material for his prospective journalistic enterprises, he was able to go to Paris. He planned to spend several months there. 'I feel it is high time I began some work of another kind', he told Moore. 'I shall spend the next six months, in any case, in working for myself.'

*

That autumn in Paris 'something happened', Lewis told John later the following year. What precisely occurred is unclear, but it appears that Lewis quarrelled with a number of people John held in high regard, resulting in yet another cooling of relations between the two men. The personalities, if not the circumstances, involved may be deduced from three long rambling reconciliatory letters. Euphemia Lamb was responsible for some of the unpleasantness. She accused Lewis of boasting in a letter that she had made love to him and, furthermore, that she had been laying loud claims to a bill for several meals he was supposed to owe her.

He had also 'quarrelled definitely' with Euphemia's husband. 'Harry Lamb', he told John, 'is one of the elements out of which your estrangement with me has grown.' The reasons for the quarrel are, once again, obscure but they may have had something to do with money Lewis owed to his former travelling companion and stories spread by him 'and received enthusiastically, of course, by the ladies', resulting in Lewis, to his 'great astonishment', being viewed as 'above all a "fellow", a scamp'.

There was another individual, referred to as the ' "High Priest of Elemental Passion", alias "The Crow" ', that John received the benefit of his views upon:

> He is a spotty-waistcoated, pot-bellied, cockney-voiced little shit, with a truculent journalistic attitude in life; just the sort of boy the girls like. He was coy and indulged in the luxury . . . of calling me names. I agree with the generality of mankind in considering that this luxury should be made as expensive as possible . . . I would take it out of his dirty carcass only a 'High Priest Assaulted' would be such a good advertisement for him.

*

Late in 1909 or early 1910, his money spent and 'at the end of [his] tether', he prepared to return to London, to plunge, as he put it, 'dans les affaires du nouveau'. He was in grotesque company: a living comedy of dependence. 'I am bringing some Spaniards over with me', he announced to Moore:

> one to buy six suits of clothes, – another to have his pimples cured, – a third is coming because he dare not let the man with the pimples out of his sight, as he is his only means of support, – having lived with him and on him for several years now, he is very jealous of his benefactor's pimples, and when the latter grows despondent, or broods on some vague plan of curing once and for all his disfigurement, he who is his shadow sees ruin staring him in the face.

He promised to bring this bizarre troupe to the Vienna Café and introduce them to Moore and his circle.

Following certain abusive remarks made about Harry Lamb to Dorelia, Lewis found himself snubbed on the doorstep of 153 Church Street. 'Dorelia is the object of my most sympathetic admiration', he protested to John, who was staying in the South of France:

> And I am quite content to maintain my admiration at a distance. Indeed, with no intention of approaching *her*, although filled with the most simple and respectful feelings for her . . . I went to your house to get your Arles address. I had an inner door slammed in my face, and your address brought to me by a serving woman grinning from ear to ear.

He hoped that what he had said to Dorelia of a 'careless and haphazard nature' concerning her friend had not been 'mistaken for strenuous plotting'.

*

He had initial difficulties placing his stories and sketches of Breton life outside of the *English Review*. He sent one piece, 'Père François', about a deranged vagrant, to *Blackwood's Magazine*, who returned it to him with thanks and the explanation that their readers were 'chiefly army men, and that it was too subtle for them'. Thereafter he secured the services of a literary agent, J. B. Pinker. He had, by this time, written a novel, perhaps the 'work of another kind' he mentioned in September. It was a light-hearted adventure concerning a criminal gang's plot to kidnap the elderly beneficiary of a will and substitute an actor to impersonate her while they laid hands on her fortune. He told Pinker he thought of calling it *The Three Mrs Dukes*, or *Khan & Company* or even *A Will Happily Revised*. By his own admission it was a 'miserable pot-boiler', written to make money and enable him to complete more serious work. 'Otto Kreisler', he had decided, was to be expanded into something more substantial and he was anxious, even with a novel at that conceptual stage, to differentiate its author from the writer of *Khan & Company*. He told Pinker that 'James Sed' was to be his pseudonym for the latter.

All these considerations proved academic, however, because Pinker, having given the manuscript due consideration, pronounced it 'not marketable'. Lewis retrieved it from the agent's office and resolved to do nothing more about it, regarding the experience as 'a lesson showing the futility of pot-boiling'. He also requested Pinker to return him the four articles he had been trying to place, believing he could do better. 'I can probably place all of them', he wrote, 'if I have them at once, and as they are unmarketable, in a different way, this chance may not recur.'

The story about the tramp found a place in the appropriately named publication *The Tramp: an Open Air Magazine*, edited by Douglas Goldring, as did the three other 'unmarketable' prose pieces and a poem over the following two years. One of these, 'A Breton Innkeeper', shared the pages of the August issue with a translation of Filippo Tommaso Marinetti's first Futurist Manifesto, a document that included the delirious sentiments:

> we wish to exalt the aggressive movement, the feverish insomnia, running, the perilous leap, the cuff and the blow. We will destroy museums, libraries, and fight against moralism, feminism and all utilitarian cowardice ... We intend to glorify the love of danger, the custom of energy, the strength of daring. The essential elements of our poetry will be courage, audacity and revolt.

Marinetti had lectured at the Lyceum Club earlier in 1910, 'adorned with diamond rings, gold chains and hundreds of flashing white teeth'. It is not known whether Lewis attended, but he was clearly aware of the tenor of these diatribes when he wrote to John in the spring, having heard his friend had made the acquaintance of a pioneer of experimental flight in the South of France:*

> I am to tell people then that you have become a Futuriste, and that we may expect to hear any day now that you have flown in at one of the galleries of the Louvre and put your foot through the Mona Lisa?

This was Lewis's first recorded reference to the Italian movement, but it was to be another year or so before he had direct dealings with Marinetti beyond their coincidental proximity in *The Tramp*.

As for the manuscript of *Khan & Company*, it eventually surfaced in a London junk shop in the late 1950s. It was published in 1977 as *Mrs Dukes' Millions*, a title Lewis himself had never even considered.

*

For much of 1910 he was living in Chelsea, at 51 Danvers Street, off Cheyne Walk. From here he wrote the three long letters to John explaining and excusing the social intrigues of the previous autumn and winter.

Reference was also made to another bout of venereal disease. Whether this was a recrudescence of the gonorrhoea contracted in Spain, or a new infection, is not known. Lewis, however, viewed the troublesome complaint

---

* Albert Bazin. See Michael Holroyd, *Augustus John*, London, 1996, pp. 317–18.

with equanimity and replied to John's queries with a certain swagger, referring to it in the terms he might have used towards a domestic pet. 'The clap, thank you, is growing up a fine healthy clap. The slight disturbance its entrance into my private life caused, has quieted down, and it has become in due course, and to all appearances definitely an inmate. It is not, however, at all troublesome. Its needs are few. I feed it from a bottle morning and night, voilà tout.'

Also, in the early months of 1910, he claimed to have finished what he described as 'an "analytic novel" about a German student'. He explained to John that this was the result of 'working over material and work a year old' and that the language was 'not "travaillé", any beauty it may possess depending on the justness of the psychology, – as is the case in the Russian novels.' He believed it to be 'a great thing to have ready to one's hand a good many forms, – novel, jaunty or vernacular essay, ... etc.'

ELEVEN

'Paint run mad'

During a lecture to the Heretics Club in Cambridge in 1924, Mrs Virginia Woolf made the famous assertion: 'On or about December 1910 human character changed.' She was not quite sure, precisely, when this change in character occurred:

> I am not saying that one went out, as one might into a garden, and there saw that a rose had flowered, or that a hen had laid an egg. The change was not sudden and definite like that. But a change there was nevertheless; and since we must be arbitrary, let us date it about the year 1910.

She observed a change in the behaviour of her cook. Before December 1910, the cook stayed downstairs in the kitchen. After December 1910 she was forever popping up into the drawing room to borrow the *Daily Herald* or ask advice about a hat.

1910 was a curious year. If there was a change in human character in general, and in the behaviour of Mrs Woolf's domestic staff in particular, there was a quite extraordinary lack of change in the political landscape of the House of Commons. 1910 began with a General Election in which the Liberals and Tories tied at 273 seats each and a Liberal government led by Mr Asquith continued in power with the support of 42 Labour MPs and 82 Irish Nationalists. And the year ended with another General Election. This time the Liberals and Tories tied again with 272 seats each and the Liberal government led by Mr Asquith continued in power with the support of 42 Labour MPs and 84 Irish Nationalists.

Sandwiched between these two nearly identical elections, 1910 was a year of momentous events.

It was the year that Dr Crippen poisoned his wife, became the first criminal to be apprehended with the help of radio waves, and was hanged.

It was the year that Suffragettes mobbed the Prime Minister and forced a member of his Cabinet to retire, hurt, to his bed.

It was the year that the Welsh miners came out on strike in support of the dockers and the cavalry was sent in to quell riots in Pontypridd and Tonypandy.

It was the year Haley's Comet came within 13 million miles of the Earth and was seen in the night sky for the first time since 1835.

It was the year that King Edward VII died and King George V succeeded him.

And it was the year that the term Post-Impressionism was invented in a short thoroughfare running between the top of Dover Street and Bond Street.

*

No. 7 Grafton Street was flanked by the premises of a Court Milliner and a dressmaker. On an upper floor was the office of the Kennel Club.

The exhibition which opened at the Grafton Galleries on Guy Fawkes Night, 1910, came about almost by chance. Roger Fry, painter, art critic and editor of the *Burlington Magazine*, heard that the gallery had a gap in its programme and he persuaded the director to let him organise an exhibition of contemporary French painting. A secretary, Desmond MacCarthy, was appointed for a fee of £100 to handle the business side. Fry himself worked for nothing, deeming it a privilege to introduce the work of French painters he so much admired to the English public. It was not expected that the exhibition would make any money from sales, but in the unlikely event that it did, MacCarthy was told he could expect a half share of the profits, the other half going to the Gallery.

The first public announcement appeared at the bottom of page 13 of *The Times* of 1 October:

> An exhibition of pictures by the Post-Impressionists of France will be held at the Grafton Galleries during November, December and January. Among the artists of this School who will be represented are Cézanne, Van Gogh, Gauguin and Matisse.

The term 'Post-Impressionism' had been a late invention. The artists included did not belong to a school of painting as such and Fry knew it. All they had in common was that they had developed forms of visual expression beyond Impressionism and beyond the scientific and slavishly realistic representation of the world. Fry claimed they were 'cutting away the merely representative element in art to establish more and more firmly the fundamental laws of expressive form in its barest, most abstract elements'. But some term was required to pull all the very different painters and styles together. Just before the announcement appeared in *The Times*, Fry became exasperated and, on the basis that they had come after the Impressionists, decided on the concept 'Post-Impressionism'. About 250 paintings, drawings and sculptures were assembled. The artists most represented were Gauguin by 36 canvases, Cézanne by 22, and Van Gogh by 19.

As if to soften the impact of modern painting for the timid English public, Fry included nine works by an already acknowledged master and called the exhibition 'Manet and the Post-Impressionists'. Manet's *A Bar at the Folies Bergère* was the most expensive work on show and was insured for £10,000, according to the *Daily Express*, a record for a modern painting.

It should not be forgotten that this revolutionary exhibition, described by Desmond MacCarthy in a memoir written in the Forties as 'The Art-Quake of 1910', was grouped around the work of four dead painters. Cézanne had been dead for four years, Gauguin for seven, Van Gogh for twenty and Manet himself for over a quarter-century. They were, nevertheless, relatively unknown in England.

Twenty-two other artists were represented, including Derain, Vlaminck, Matisse and Picasso. According to Laurence Binyon's account in the *Saturday Review*, the exhibition was set out to afford visitors a gradual immersion in the 'modern':

> By an admirably discreet arrangement, reminding one of a Turkish bath, the shock of the revelation is only administered by degrees. In the first room you need scarcely be uneasy; Manet reigns there, and Manet is already a classic; in the second room the temperature is more exciting, you are in the face of Gauguin and Van Gogh; and only when sufficiently acclimatised need you venture yet further into the wild realms of Matisse and his peers.

Fry would exhibit much 'wilder' examples of the work of Matisse and Picasso at the same gallery two years later. This time he erred on the side of caution. Of the two, it was Matisse who drew most of the critical fire. His startlingly coloured portrait, *Girl with Green Eyes*, excited a great deal of comment, mainly along the lines of unfavourable comparison with the products of an average nursery. One of the two Picasso paintings on the other hand, *Nude Girl with a Basket of Flowers*, was well received, called 'a fine thing, almost an exquisite thing' in *The Builder* and even compared, albeit to its disadvantage, to the work of Whistler in the *Fortnightly Review*.

'This show will be a great affair', Fry told a friend the month before it opened. 'I am preparing for a huge campaign of outraged British philistinism.' He was not disappointed.

The gentlemen of the press enjoyed themselves immensely. The *Daily Express* correspondent spoke for the majority of his colleagues:

> It is paint run mad. The aim of the Post-Impressionists is not to paint

objects as they strike the human eye but simply to convey emotion by means of paint. They are invariably successful but one may cavill at the fact that the emotion expressed is too often that of a sick headache.

The exhibition was an enormous success. 25,000 people paid a shilling each and passed through the turnstile during the following three months. As the hordes of English men and women came to grips with the newest trends in art to reach their shores, the general mood was hilarity. 'It is all titter and cackle', wrote the critic from *The New Age*:

> well dressed women go about saying: 'How awful! A perfect nightmare, my dear!' 'Did you ever? Too killing! How they can!' They are like dogs to music; it makes them howl, but they can't keep away. Men with tall hats are funny over the exhibits, saying: 'This is a horse; No this is a horse; This is a man.' All through the galleries I am pursued by the ceaseless hee-haw of a stage duke with a monocle.

Desmond MacCarthy, who as secretary observed the phenomenon daily, recalled a couple who seemed to have stepped out of a Bateman cartoon:

> A stout, elderly man of good appearance, led in by a young woman, went into such convulsions of laughter on catching sight of Cézanne's portrait of his wife that his companion had to take him out and walk him up and down in the fresh air.

And Wilfrid Scawen Blunt, writing in his diary ten days after the show opened, expressed the views of the public without a sense of humour:

> The exhibition is either an extremely bad joke or a swindle. I am inclined to think the latter, for there is no trace of humour in it. Still less is there a trace of sense or skill or taste, good or bad, or art or cleverness. Nothing but that gross puerility which scrawls indecencies on the walls of a privy. The drawing is on the level of that of an untaught child of seven or eight years old, the sense of colour that of a tea tray painter, the method that of a schoolboy who wipes his fingers on a slate after spitting on them. There is nothing at all more humorous than that, at all more clever ... Apart from the frames, the whole collection should not be worth £5, and then only for the pleasure of making a bonfire of them.

Sir William Richmond RA wrote a letter to the *Morning Post*. He hoped that in the remaining years of his long life he would never again feel, as he had whilst walking through the Grafton Galleries, ashamed of being a painter:

For a moment there came a feeling of terror lest the youth of England, young promising fellows, might be contaminated there. On reflection I was reassured that the youth of England, being healthy, mind and body, is far too virile to be moved save in resentment against the providers of this unmanly show.

Oliver Brown, later director of the Leicester Galleries and, incidentally, Wyndham Lewis's dealer, remembered being buttonholed by an elderly academician as he entered the exhibition. This individual, who may have been Sir William Richmond himself, cried out earnestly: 'Don't go in, young man, it will do you harm. The pictures are evil.'

*

During the year that Mrs Woolf judged human character to have changed, the name of P. Wyndham Lewis had become known, to the readership of a couple of periodicals at least, as belonging to a writer of short clever travel pieces and character sketches of the inmates of French and Spanish hotels. During the very month in which Mrs Woolf estimated the change as occurring, subscribers to *The Tramp* would have encountered a 13-verse poem called 'Grignolles (Brittany)'.* He had written it earlier in the year, sent it to John in the South of France as a peace offering, 'a very small, insignificant present', and hoped to make him the bigger present of a book of verse before long. He was 'going to do nothing but poetry', he declared, now that his 'analytic novel' was finished. Clearly, it was as a writer, not as a painter, that he saw himself. He was 28 years old and a decade separated him from the promising young winner of the 1900 Slade Scholarship. During that decade he had had eight articles published and exhibited only one drawing – *Study of a Girl's Head* – in the 32nd Exhibition of Modern Pictures held by the New English Art Club at the Dudley Gallery in April and May 1904. It was as a writer, not as a painter, that anyone else would have seen him towards the end of 1910.

As he was in London at the time 'Manet and the Post-Impressionists' was creating such a stir, it is likely that he visited the exhibition on at least one occasion. However there is no definitive evidence that he did so. It is probable that he would have seen nothing there that he had not already seen in Paris. He was certainly aware of Picasso and Matisse. He had mentioned them to Moore the previous year, although without making further comment beyond an enquiry as to whether his friend had seen any of their paintings.

* The name of this town 'grown bald with age' was 'fabulous' he told John. It may have been derived from the French word *grignotage*: erosion.

And he made only one documented reference to the major upheaval in the art world, writing to Moore, who was out of the country in February 1911. He made no mention of the contents of the exhibition, and confined his remarks only to the furore it had caused:

> I suppose the Post-Impressionists' Christmas in London, and the 'ahurissement' of the citizens, you will, in one way or another, have heard about?

More importantly, in the same letter, he announced that he had 'included once more various plastic arts' in his 'already extensive programme' and he looked forward to Moore's return when he would place before him 'the first fruits of [his] new enterprise'. A tone of modest apology for this distraction from literary endeavour was belied by his obvious confidence in the quality of the work:

> The first misgivings you will feel on hearing I have again become an idolator (as [Eric] Gill describes all artists) are, you will be glad to hear, without reason. I have already quite justified this step.

It is tempting to suggest that the resumption of artistic activity was stimulated, or even inspired, by a visit to 'Manet and the Post-Impressionists'.

TWELVE

'Dunk' and Hoel

In December 1910 or January 1911, at the home of the painter Robert Bevan, Lewis met Kate Lechmere, a woman with whom he was later to have a brief affair and a slightly longer business partnership. He invited her to dinner, but Lechmere later recalled that he seemed distracted and hardly spoke to her throughout the meal. Afterwards, at the Café Royal, he confided to her the cause of his preoccupation. He had just learned that his relations with a 'shopgirl' had entered a new and potentially complicated phase.

The daughter of a bookmaker, Olive Johnson was 19 or 20 years old when she became pregnant by Lewis. Whether she was, in the strictest sense, a 'shopgirl' at the time is not known. In 1914 she worked for a branch of Fuller's Ltd – the 'American Confectioners'; in 1917 she had an unspecified job in a London hotel, and when she married in 1922 she described herself as a 'waitress (restaurant)'.

Olive can be identified as the model for two drawings, both dated 1911. One shows her asleep, seen from below and to one side, a heavy straight line marking the edge of her jaw. The other drawing is an angular, frontal portrait in pencil and wash: eyes downcast in the broad, truncated wedge of face, a dark cedilla of hair hanging down against one side of the forehead. The title is *Mamie*,* a contraction of the French *ma mie*: 'my beloved'. But it was Olive's dark colouring which accounted for the other *nom d'amour* with which Lewis graced her. 'Dunk' was short for the German *die Dunkle*: 'dark-haired woman'. She was the first serious atttachment Lewis had formed since Ida Vendel.

*

In March a major piece of work appeared to be nearing completion. It was a novel called *The Bourgeois-Bohemians*, an expansion of the ' "analytic novel"

---

* This was the title given in a sale catalogue of 1927. The identification of Olive Johnson as the subject of this drawing was made possible by comparison with photographs taken of her in the 1940s. Despite the passage of well over 30 years, the likeness is unmistakable.

about a German student' of the previous year, which, in turn, was an expansion of the 'story' called 'Otto Kreisler' of 1909. 'It has been a long time on the way', he told Moore. 'It is better than it could have been at any other time. But you must wait a year or two for a really satisfactory novel from me.' The provisional title, 'Bourgeois-Bohemians', would be retained for Part III of the novel as eventually published, but 'a year or two' was an optimistic projection for this long-awaited delivery.

Meanwhile, products of his enterprise in 'various plastic arts', mentioned the previous month, were soon to be held up to critical scrutiny. In spring a new Society was formed out of disaffection with the New English Art Club. Under the Presidency of Spencer Gore, with James Manson Bolivar as Secretary and with a further 14 members, the Camden Town Group came into being. The membership comprised Augustus John, Walter Sickert, Lucien Pissarro, Robert Bevan, Harold Gilman, Charles Ginner, Henry Lamb, Malcolm Drummond, Walter Bayes, James Dickson Innes, Maxwell G. Lightfoot, William Ratcliffe, J. Doman Turner and Wyndham Lewis. There had been some disagreement about whether Lewis should be invited to join, but Gilman, probably supported by Gore, was insistent and he was duly elected.

On 14 June 1911 the first Camden Town Group exhibition opened in basement premises at 24 Bury Street, St James: The Carfax Gallery. Members were entitled to show four reasonably sized works, space at the Carfax being at a premium.

Lewis exhibited only two. They were ink drawings and, according to the catalogue, esoterically if unimaginatively titled: *The Architect (no. 1)* and *The Architect (no. 2)*.

He had, he said, assumed his contributions would go unnoticed, but was gratified when they were singled out for special vilification. In view of the treatment meted out by many critics to paintings by Cézanne, Gauguin, Van Gogh and Matisse only six months before at the Grafton Galleries, Lewis could be excused for regarding critical hostility as a hallmark of excellence and he gleefully quoted Moore the tenor of the reviews:

> The critics would begin: 'Despite the alarming announcement of the character of this "Group", we find that amongst this band of honest, hard-working young men (with one exception) that good old English conservatism has saved them from the excesses' etc. Then the next paragraph would begin: 'That one exception is Mr Wyndham Lewis, whose blackguardly, preposterous, putrid' etc. But invariably!

It was probably P. G. Konody's review in the *Observer* that he was paraphrasing:

I was neither shocked nor repelled by the work of this group of intensely serious artists who, with perhaps one exception, show neither eccentricity nor a desire to *épater le bourgeois*, but are clearly inspired by the longing for self expression in what each considers the most suitable language. The exception is Mr Wyndham Lewis, whose pen-drawings . . . are executed in an amateurish, laboured method of crosshatching, which is painfully at variance with the artist's grotesque affectation of archaism.

The *Sunday Times* reviewer found the exhibition on the whole conservative but expressed the same proviso as Konody:

A few visitors may be shocked at the elongated noses in the squarely drawn heads by Mr Wyndham Lewis . . . but with the exception of these two pen drawings I cannot recall any exhibit which could justifiably be described even as 'queer'.

And the *Morning Post* critic betrayed a distaste for advanced architecture as well as advanced art:

As an imaginary portrait of the man who designed most of the modern buildings in London, it may be welcomed as a caricature nearer the truth than perhaps the artist intended . . . Mr Lewis, who enjoys a high reputation among his friends as poet and draughtsman, introduces a note of insincerity that is well enough in criticism but regrettable in serious art, and entirely foreign to the present exhibition.

But if he expected praise and reassurance from Sturge Moore he was disappointed. Although dismissing the critics' reaction on the grounds that 'fools will behave like bulls if you wave the proper coloured rag', he dismissed his friend's work equally bluntly:

As to your drawings, you know what I think of them . . . I believe you have put your head into a pudding bag, aesthetically speaking, and hope you will take it out again before it is too late.

*

Having made his first, however negative, impression upon the London art world, Lewis stayed the summer of 1911 in Dieppe with Olive Johnson. He spent over three months adding more material to his novel, expanding it to between 400 and 500 manuscript pages. This was the same novel he had told Moore that he was 'finishing' in March, and John the previous year that he had 'finished'. When he wrote to Moore again from Dieppe in October, the first three chapters, as eventually published, had yet to be written and the action began with the English protagonist's parting interview with his German mistress. It ended with another interview, presumably the one in which Tarr proposes marriage to Bertha in order to legitimise another man's child. Between 'these two psychological pillars' the rest of the story – Kreisler's running amok in Parisian expatriate society, the rape, the duel, the suicide – hung 'like a grotesque tapestry'. He thought of calling it *Between Two Interviews* but, on reflection, felt that *Otto Kreisler's Death* would be preferable. Although the final seven-part structure of the novel had been established by this time, considerable further expansion was to take place before publication seven years later.

Olive, meanwhile, had spent the summer preparing for an altogether less protracted labour. The vacation may have been arranged to spare her the disapproval her condition would have aroused in London, where she was known to be unmarried. In Dieppe they passed as man and wife, at least as far as the locals were concerned. As for other English visitors, Olive would probably have been subject to the same sequestration Lewis always imposed upon the women in his life. It is unlikely, for example, that he would have taken her to any of Walter Sickert's little Saturday afternoon receptions. His eminent colleague from the Camden Town Group was on his honeymoon, having married Christine Drummond Angus at the end of July. His family were with him as well and Lewis had sport at their expense in his letter to Sturge Moore:

> . . . the brother without any teeth, the one-eyed brother, the one without any brains and also his poor paralytic old mother. How with so many infirmities they manage to get even so far as Dieppe is a mystery to me.

The long letter Lewis wrote to Sturge Moore in October made no mention of Olive. Nor did it refer, except in the most oblique terms, to the birth of his son: 'This Dieppe is . . . an odious place', he declared. 'I will tell you, when I see you, why I came here.'

Hoel Lewis was born at half-past four in the afternoon of 4 September at 11 rue d'Eu, in Le Pollet, the fisherman's quarter on the eastern side of Dieppe harbour. Lewis registered his son's birth at the Mairie two days later. Charles Ginner, who was staying four doors away, and Louis Jules Daniel, a local waiter, were the witnesses. Lewis informed the Registrar that he and Olive had been married in London on 2 June 1909. His stated occupation was '*étudiant*'. Olive, he declared, was '*sans profession*'. Their address in London was 'Regent's Park'. This last detail was not too far from the truth, as it could apply to either of Lewis's two known addresses of

1911. 32 Albert Street and 34 Arlington Road, although properly Mornington Crescent, are both close to the Park.

Hoel, the only forename given in the Dieppe registration, is of Breton origin. Eighteen years later a solicitor's clerk, on a visit to a North London prison, would learn that the boy's full name was 'Hoel Briniley'. From an early age, however, he went by the less exotic soubriquet of Peter.

*

'I shall now, henceforth, devote myself to painting', Lewis told Moore as he wrote 'the last few pages' of his novel. He had already, towards the end of August, managed to do a few weeks' painting in preparation for the second Camden Town Group Exhibition. Presumably, having then taken up his novel again in late September or early October and, 'the Lord be praised, finished it', he spent the rest of his time in Dieppe working on the three canvases, all of them now lost, that he intended showing at the Carfax Gallery in December.

Two of the titles suggest they evolved from the Le Pollet environment of sailors and bustling fish markets: *Au Marché* and *Port de Mer*. This last was bought at the exhibition by Augustus John for 20 guineas. Lewis recalled that it was 'a largish canvas . . . [of] two sprawling figures of Normandy fishermen, in mustard yellows and browns.' When John died in 1961 his estate contained no pictures by Lewis but Dorelia remembered *Port de Mer* as showing 'two men with a bright orange background, but it mysteriously vanished'.

The third painting, *Virgin and Child*, despite the title's religious connotations, was probably based on the mundane spectacle of Olive and the newly born Hoel. A year later he painted another variation on the same theme in which, despite a considerable degree of stylisation, the broad features of 'Dunk' are clearly recognisable.

*

He had told Moore that he would be back in London by about 10 November. However he spent his return fare on a trip to Paris and arrived back later than expected.

The second Camden Town Group exhibition opened on 1 December. Again Lewis's work attracted critical hostility. Even so, *The Times* appeared to err on the side of caution, conceding that he ought to be given benefit of doubt. 'Mr Wyndham Lewis exhibits three geometrical experiments which many people will take for bad practical jokes. They are not that, but this geometrical art needs great beauty of material, as in mosaic or stained glass, or else a very strong emotion to carry it off. Without either or both of these it is merely diagrammatic, as in Mr Lewis's pictures.'

The *Athenaeum* critic dismissed the three canvases in the final sentence of his review. 'Mr Wyndham Lewis's exhibits appear to us a somewhat formless compromise between two conventions hardly as yet ripe for criticism.'

Frank, if friendly, criticism came again privately from Sturge Moore:

> the Fishermen I like a little only not your use of paint which lacks any approach to exquisiteness always desirable in proportion as art is empty of import. But we shall not agree yet awhile on this subject.

However, the most heated assault came from within the ranks of the Camden Town Group itself. Lucien Pissarro wrote to Gore: 'I am quite upset by what I saw this afternoon at the . . . exhibition. The pictures of Lewis are quite impossible! Either ours is a serious movement or else a farce! I don't feel inclined to let my pictures remain if he persists in showing these particular canvases. I was not consulted when he was asked to join our society – we all took him from Gilman's recommendation without knowing his work. If the principle of the group were like the A.A.A.,* I would say nothing, but as we are quite a closed society I don't see why we should put up with such rubbish.'

The day after the private view most of the Group met at 19 Fitzroy Street to decide whether membership was to be extended beyond the original 16. Lewis was vocal in the majority who favoured increase. Pissarro, finding himself in a minority of four that included Sickert as chairman, and presumably with Lewis's three canvas atrocities still deeply branded on his memory, argued against. The debate was, however, put into perspective by Harold Gilman, who pointed out the futility of increasing membership while the basement premises at the Carfax Gallery could not provide sufficient space for even the present 16 to show more than four works each. The Camden Town Group remained 'a closed society'.

---

* The Allied Artists Association, set up by Frank Rutter in 1908. It did not have a jury, there was no limit on membership, and annual exhibitions were held in the vast circus of the Royal Albert Hall.

THIRTEEN

'I have a sort of idea he's a genius'

In March 1912 the Sackville Gallery hosted an 'Exhibition of Works by the Italian Futurist Painters'. There were 35 paintings crammed into the Sackville's three poky rooms. Umberto Boccioni, Carlo Carrà, Luigi Russolo, Gino Severini, as well as Giacomo Balla, who did not exhibit, had grouped themselves around the charismatic figure of F. T. Marinetti, and espoused the sentiments of his first Futurist Manifesto of 1909. They had published manifestos of their own describing the fluctuating reality they sought to express on canvas:

> all things move, all things run, all things are rapidly changing. A profile is never motionless before our eyes, but it constantly appears and disappears. On account of the persistency of an image upon the retina objects constantly multiply themselves . . . Thus a running horse has not four legs, but twenty, and their movements are triangular . . . Our bodies penetrate the sofas upon which we sit, and the sofas penetrate our bodies. The motor bus rushes into the houses which it passes, and in their turn the houses throw themselves upon the motor bus and are blended with it.

The Sketch ran a full-page spread reproducing assorted works by Boccioni and Russolo. Above the five jagged and discordant images was the headline: WHAT DO YOU THINK OF IT – SERIOUSLY? And with picture titles like *The street enters the house* and *What I was told by the Tramcar*, the exhibition gave the public more than enough scope for amusement.

*

Later that year, a two-minute walk away from the Sackville Galleries, the enterprise of another flamboyant foreigner provided more exclusive entertainment. On Wednesday 26 June 1912, in a cellar underneath the offices of a Scotch tweed manufacturer at 9 Heddon Street, a new nightclub was launched. A prospectus had been issued the month before, setting out its attractions:

The Club will open at 8.30 pm daily. From 9 o'clock to 11.30 a varied programme, with the tendency of a return of art to intuition and simplicity, will be given . . . The audience will sit around small tables. The cellars will be stocked by connoisseurs . . . From 11.30 Suppers – artistic suppers – . . . Spanish gypsies will play, Neapolitans sing, English poets say their verses, dancers dance.

The author of this eccentrically couched advertisement, and the presiding genius of the Cabaret Theatre Club, was the second wife of August Strindberg. She was born Frida Uhl, daughter of a councillor to the Viennese Court. Married to the Swedish playwright for a little over a year, she divorced him in 1896, but retained his name.

In his autobiography, Augustus John claimed that it was in 1910, and while she was in pursuit of Wyndham Lewis, that Madame Strindberg first introduced herself to him. They had a brief affair and thereafter the formidable Austrian stalked John assiduously. 'I admit that the sight of Mme Strindberg bearing down on me in an open taxi-cab, a glad smile of greeting on her face, shaded with a hat turned up behind and bearing a luxuriant outcrop of sweetpeas – this sight, I confess, unnerved me.'

A goodly crowd of members and their guests and a smattering of critics arrived on that Wednesday night. Heddon Street is an H-shaped cul-de-sac off the west side of Regent Street. The entrance to the club was, according to the man from *The Times*, 'a sort of man hole' from which descended a flight of steps to a large chamber with a stage raised a foot or so from the floor level, covered by deep blue curtains and occupying a third of the wall space on the right as one entered. The raftered ceiling was picked out in green and white. The furniture was simple: bentwood chairs and small round tables. This was the 'Cave of the Golden Calf'. Madame Strindberg, plastered in chalk-white make-up, greeted her guests wrapped in a thick fur coat which even the stifling heat at the latter part of the evening did not persuade her to remove.

The entertainment was organised and introduced by Mme Bokken Lasson, a cabaret artiste of some note in her native Norway, who sang to a mandolin accompaniment. There were no wings to the stage, so performers entered from the audience. Mlle Aggersholm, another Scandinavian, told fairy tales and would have been 'even more delightful', in the opinion of the *Sunday Times* critic, 'if she did not seem so intensely convinced of her powers to please.' Miss Margaret Morris danced barefoot to the melodies of Grieg. Mr Dalhousie Young played the piano and 'imagined that he was amusing'. A more successful comic turn was provided by Mr Stacey Aumonier, 'whose very countenance spelt laughter, and whose words, often inaudible, and wilfully independent of his subject, created continuous joy'.

His deadline pressing, the *Times* correspondent had to leave early, but noted that the programme contained 'enough . . . to carry it far beyond the hour when all good newspapers are sent to press . . . and . . . must have kept the cave-dwellers happy till dawn.' He missed what his more relaxed colleague on the *Sunday Times* described as 'the best number of all, the Spanish dances of Señor Mathias, dances fraught with the spirit of Spain and the passion of the Spanish blood.'

Both correspondents mentioned the décor. 'The walls were decorated with a kind of futurist paintings,' noted *The Times*, 'but they were infantile and not funny, imitation of what one sees across the water.' And the *Sunday Times* reported 'mural decorations representing we should not care to say what precise stage beyond Impressionism – they would easily, however, turn into appalling goblins after a little too much supper.'

Spencer Gore had been in overall charge of the cellar's decoration. He himself painted the huge mural of a deer-hunting scene blazing with primary colour running the length of one wall. He also designed a complementary tiger hunt to run the length of another wall, but may have passed this commission to Charles Ginner. Jacob Epstein turned a pair of iron pillars into totem poles with plaster cladding which he then painted. And it fell to Eric Gill to fashion the Cave's eponymous calf. Carved in Hopton Wood stone and gilded, it stood a little under one and a half feet high and less than two feet from nose to tail. Another version of this rather endearing little animal was fashioned in bas-relief to be hung outside the club's entrance.

Apart from the garish Post-Impressionist murals by Gore and Ginner, other decorations that might have caused distress to inebriate patrons in the early hours of the morning were executed by Lewis.

A drop-curtain at the back of the small stage showed chunky orange nudes and yellow horses on a shoreline. There were brown shapes in the upper part of the composition. What might be the hulls of boats reflected in water, and perhaps an outrigger canoe, suggests it was intended as a Polynesian scene drawn from memories of the Oceanographic collections at the British Museum, studied on his circuitous forays to the Department of Prints and Drawings whilst at the Slade.

It cannot be said with any degree of certainty what Lewis's other contributions were, apart from designs for posters and programme and menu covers. The club's prospectus contained a Study for a Wall Decoration, but whether this was executed in time for the opening in June 1912, or at all, is not known. A contract survives, probably from the following year, commissioning 'two paintings' from him, together with 'two screens and the arrangement and decoration of the walls' for £60.

Madame Strindberg must have had extraordinary powers of persuasion, because Gore, Ginner, Gill and Epstein carried out their work on only extravagant promises of payment. They were probably left unpaid when the enterprise collapsed two years later. Lewis, on the other hand, a more tenacious negotiator, seems to have insisted upon a less nebulous financial arrangement. According to his contract he was to receive a downpayment of £5 and the rest in three instalments: £20 by 10 o'clock on 27 September 1913, £20 on 1 October and a further £15 a fortnight later on 15 October.

*

In the arena of the Royal Albert Hall, when the 5th Allied Artists Salon opened in July 1912, one work in particular caught the eye of *The Nation*'s art critic, Roger Fry. The enormous canvas, numbered 1013 in the catalogue, could not fail to be noticed. *Kermesse** was nearly nine feet square and presented what a New York auction catalogue of the 1920s would describe as 'a cubistic rendering of three festive figures, the central in rich yellow, the others in varying shades of red and purple'. But, according to contemporary descriptions, there were in fact more than three figures. In the middle was a woman, seen from behind. The broad Breton skirt arched out to the left as her shoulders sloped right in the movements of the dance. The woman's partner was for the most part concealed, his face appearing in the V-shaped space made by her sloping left shoulder and her head. These figures appeared to be 'kissing one another on the mouth', Ramiro de Maeztu wrote in *The New Age*. Another critic noted the man's 'two wicked-looking eyes' in the dead centre of the composition. On the left of the canvas, according to Maeztu, one figure appeared to offer wine to another, seated, figure. While on the right a fifth figure, of indeterminate sex, poured a stream of wine in the general direction of its face. The curves of the Breton skirt and the cigar-shaped trunks and limbs of the other figures provided invertebrate comparisons to most of the critics: 'some terrible battle of extermination between murderous insects'; 'some gigantic fantastic insects descended upon earth from some other planet'; 'crabs in anguish', 'boiled lobster legs'.

Fry regarded Lewis as the only artist who had risen to the challenge of the Albert Hall:

His design . . . is the only thing that survives the ordeal of being placed in

---

* Another lost painting. The composition can be reconstructed from an etching, 'Viewing "Kermesse" ', by Horace Brodzky, sketched during its exhibition at the Penguin Club in New York in 1917, and from surviving studies.

such ample surroundings. All the rest of the pictures disappear – they might have something to say in other surroundings, but they do not attain to any sufficient constructive unity to impose a definite idea here. Mr Lewis, on the contrary, has built up a design which is tense and compact. His quantities and volumes have decisive relations to one another: long before one has begun to inquire what it represents, one has the impression of something plastic brought about by deliberately intentional colour oppositions. When we begin to look more closely, we find indeed that the rhythm of these elementary geometric forms is based upon the rhythm of the human figure. The rhythm is not merely agreeable and harmonious, but definitely evocative of a Dionysiac mood. For the moment, doubtless, many people will fail to allow themselves to be influenced by this design, simply because they are not accustomed to exert the passive attention of such a rhythmic disposition of abstract units of form as this art demands. They are familiar enough with such an attitude in music, but they are apt to turn crusty when it is demanded of them by a painter. Fortunately, in the Albert Hall there is a method by which any willing spectator may get a new aperçu of such methods of design. Let him look down into the arena from the gallery, and at this vast distance he will not be disturbed by the absence of a merely descriptive form, and may see how expressive of a particular mood this abstract harmony is; also, it may dawn upon him that it has singular force and beauty of colour.

Clive Bell in *The Athenaeum* also instructed the reader to take the lift to the gallery. From that height:

> having shed all irrelevant prejudices in favour of representation, he will be able to contemplate it as a piece of pure design . . . he cannot fail to be impressed by the solidity of the composition, to which the colour is not an added charm, but of which it is an integral part; he will feel that the picture holds together as a unity in the way that a sonata by Beethoven holds, in a way that nothing else does in this exhibition.

Bell even gave to his reservations the lustre of praise, as when he suggested that the viewer, having made an effort to get up to the gallery:

> will feel a certain dissatisfaction which may cause him to inquire whether Mr Lewis has altogether succeeded in expressing himself. We believe that he has not. There is a laboriousness about this work which seems to represent the artist's unsuccessful struggle to realise in paint his mental conception; and it is for this reason that we admire it rather as a promise of something great than as an achievement.

The *Times* correspondent, while finding the picture 'not intelligible', nevertheless mounted a grudging defence, buried in which was a confession that his own critical faculties might be at fault:

> we are persuaded that the artist means something by it, because the design, considered abstractly, has a lucidity and precision we have never found in pure nonsense pictures such as the works of most of the Futurists. We have to deal here with the same problem that presents itself in very obscure poetry. We cannot judge its merits until we understand it; and we are right perhaps to be impatient with an artist who produces something so difficult to understand. Still there is rhythm which leads us to believe that the sense is obscure not wanting.

Augustus John found his appreciation of the picture hampered by the irritating presence at his elbow of 'that wretched fellow Rutter'. He admitted to Lewis that he could not, as yet, fully grasp the principles of the work, nervertheless:

> I was greatly impressed . . . and the impression increases as I think of it. In spite of the perplexing and unaccustomed elements of the design I recognise the energy and grandeur of the conception and am positively moved by it as to the beating of drums and blowing of horns and thumping of feet. It is to me a revelation of dynamic art . . . For this vivifying and magnificent effort, accept my gratitude.

*

Lewis spent August and part of September in Dunkerque, completing a series of drawings intended to illustrate a folio edition of *Timon of Athens*, to be published by 'an almost derelict firm' in Surrey Street, off the Aldwych end of the Strand.

Marjorie Tripp, of Evelyn Benmar & Co., had advanced him £20 of her own money before he left, in the hopes of persuading her partner to back the project fully. Lewis had left her some of the initial drawings which she showed to Benmar, anxiously watching his face for a reaction. She observed his lip curl and his nostrils pinch.

'My good girl that's mania not art!' he said.

There was silence as he studied the designs. Then: 'a strange, rather puzzled, childish look . . . as the drug began to work, and at last . . . a flushed cheek and bright eye', and he gripped her shoulder.

'Marjie – I verily believe there *is* something in this!' he exclaimed. 'Look at those Amazons – look at – by God I think you've got hold of something – What sort of a chap is Lewis?'

'I have a sort of idea he's a genius,' she replied.

Lewis had told Miss Tripp he would be back in London on 15 September and his mother reminded him of this fact on the 20th. Having just scraped together the £4 to get him home she was anxious that he should see the publisher as early as possible on Monday the 23rd. The balance of his money was to come when he delivered the rest of the drawings, and Mrs Lewis needed it '*awfully*'. She chided her son on his lack of professionalism:

> Your great fault is want of punctuality and you will have to stop and correct this if you are going to make headway, as it is a shocking fault from the business point of view.

He was in London by 22 September, staying with Cuthbert Hamilton at 16 Fitzroy Street for three days before moving into a large dark, north-facing first-floor room at 35 Greek Street, Soho. It was next door to the 'Petit Savoyard' and opposite the 'Coach and Horses'. The rent was 7/6 a week but Lewis had hoped to beat the landlord down to 7/-.

In his review of the Allied Artists Salon, Roger Fry mentioned that *Kermesse* had been originally intended for the Cabaret Theatre Club. Whether this was so or not, the painting did indeed find a temporary home on the stairs leading down to the 'Cave of the Golden Calf'. Madame Strindberg, having seen it at the Albert Hall but unable, or unwilling, to pay the full purchase price of £30, rented the canvas for a period of three months, from October 1912 until January 1913. For this she paid Lewis £10 on the understanding that, should she wish to purchase it outright at any time during the three months, she would pay him the balance of £20. She also undertook to insure the picture against 'fire, water and accident' and that 'should any such damage occur whether slight or of a serious nature' the sum of £20 would still be forfeit.

*

Just under two years after the scandalous success of 'Manet and the Post-Impressionists' at the Grafton Galleries, the 'Second Post-Impressionist Exhibition' opened at the same location on 5 October 1912. This purported to be a more international survey of modern artistic trends than its precursor, being devoted to works from three different countries. Responsibility for the selection of the 257 or so paintings and sculptures was shared by three men: Roger Fry chose the French section; Boris Anrep the Russian, and Clive Bell the English.

Bell called at Greek Street to make his selection of Lewis's pictures. He chose two large canvases and a number of drawings, including six crowded gouaches intended as illustration for *Timon of Athens*. The *Athenaeum* critic thought these 'one of the most noteworthy features of the exhibition'. He went on:

> Mr Wyndham Lewis . . . is claimed as a disciple of Picasso, and his work being far more intelligible than many of the later ones of the Frenchman, he may be charged by some with being a mere popularizer. We should rather regard him as . . . a consolidating influence, laying stress in his pursuit of abstract significance of form on its geometric elements, but with a clear conviction, denied to Picasso, that it is almost impossible to have significant form quite divested of function.

The term 'significant form' suggests the review was written by Clive Bell himself who, as one of the organisers of the exhibition, preserved his anonymity by neither signing nor initialling his contribution.

P. G. Konody, covering the exhibition for the *Observer*, noticed a parson, standing in front of Lewis's large *Mother and Child*, raise his protesting hands as if at a blasphemy. This was possibly another version of the *Virgin and Child* he had exhibited the year before at the Carfax Gallery. As reproduced in *The Sketch*, the presentation of Olive's features had undergone a startling abstraction by 1912. The truncated wedge of *Mamie* had crystallised into a grim pentagonal mask on top of a long neck, thrust up like a basalt column from the body's mass of overlapping arcs and planes, amongst which the child appeared embedded. Legs apart and bent at the knees, froglike, he lay on a diagonal axis across the monumental mother's chest. Her protective right arm, crossing the smaller figure, ended in a hand that looked like a big bundle of cutlery.

The Second Post-Impressionist Exhibition was even more successful than the first, attracting an estimated 50,000 visitors through the Grafton's turnstile. It was initially to have run until the end of December but was extended through January 1913.

1912 ended as the previous year had ended, with a Camden Town Group exhibition, the third, at the Carfax Gallery. This time Lewis showed only one painting, albeit a large one. *Dance* was priced at £30, the same as *Kermesse* and therefore probably of comparable size. The *Times* critic set the seal on Lewis as a rising young man in the art world by craving 'intelligibility':

> Mr Wyndham Lewis is a cubist and his 'Dance' seems to belong to a different world from all the other pictures in the room. We feel that it might be quite intelligible to the man in the moon, that it is indeed intelligible to Mr Wyndham Lewis. For, though we see no dance in it, we

do see a kind of geometrical logic in the design, which gives us more pleasure than we get from a quite commonplace and intelligible picture. But whether this pleasure would increase or disappear if we lived with the picture and whether it would gradually become intelligible we cannot tell. We only know that we like this better than most cubist pictures; but one cannot like a picture very much if one does not know what it represents.

The *Athenaeum* critic offered cautious praise: 'with the majority of the exhibitors the readiness not only to accept homely subjects, but also to treat them in a homely fashion is doubtless allied to a deep distrust of, if not scorn for, invention and imagination. Mr Wyndham Lewis is at least an exception to this rule, and his important contribution "Dance" . . . is the more valuable as combating what might become a merely negative characteristic of the exhibition.' While it was 'not quite so good' as his group of *Timon of Athens* drawings at the Grafton, 'it is by far the best large painting that he has done.' If the *Times* critic liked it without understanding it, this correspondent devoted a half paragraph to a formal analysis:

> The design has the momentary, precarious balance of a kaleidoscopic pattern, and we feel that the raising or depression of the poised toe of one of the figures would induce an immediate shifting of all the other angles of the structure. Much no doubt has been sacrificed to the violence of the play of these angles – greater elasticity of movement, for example, might easily have been secured without departing from the chosen convention, had the artist consented to the notation of the slight tilt of a pelvis, the slight bending of a supporting limb, whereby the weight of a figure poised on one leg is distributed and the balance maintained. The imaginative interest of the dance is somewhat lessened by the formal starring of the figure from the centre, which makes it a rather obviously mechanical marionette.

*

Meanwhile 'the almost derelict firm' of Evelyn Benmar & Co. was undergoing a change of identity. Benmar himself appears to have departed and Marjorie Tripp, the remaining proprietor, persuaded Douglas Gold-ring, editor of *The Tramp*, to undertake 'the honorary task of pulling it together'. The firm was renamed 'Max Goschen' for reasons Goldring could not afterwards recollect. Tripp's original plan of publishing a folio edition of *Timon of Athens* with illustrations by Lewis also came in for modification. It was decided to issue the plates separately in portfolio form, under the imprint of 'The Cube Press' and in advance of the actual book.* Sample sets were run off by the printers in haste and sent to the Carfax and Grafton Galleries to attract orders from visitors to the third Camden Town Group and Second Post-Impressionist Exhibitions. A flyer was issued:

> In response to a repeated demand, a limited number of Sets of the Drawings have been put up separately in a portfolio for the benefit of Collectors, and those who desire the Pictures for framing. The Drawings have been reproduced with the utmost care and by the most costly means. Price 10/6 Net.

In December Lewis sent Miss Tripp two letters: the first protesting that his designs would lose their significance outside the context of Shakespeare's play and arguing that their advance publication would inevitably harm sales of the book when it finally appeared; the second complaining about the poor quality of the reproductions. Tripp replied in frosty tones, considerably at odds with the geniality of her former correspondence. She told him that the firm of Max Goschen, late Evelyn Benmar & Co., was under no contract with him regarding the publication of *Timon of Athens* 'with or without [his] plates at any particular time, or in any particular way'. As for his second letter, she assured him the portfolio at the Carfax had been hurriedly printed but that all due care would be taken with the rest:

> since having been already at enormous expense, trouble and annoyance and pains over the production of your drawings, it is, as it always has been, our intention to give them and our sales of them, the best possible chance.

The portfolio, as eventually published,† contained 16 plates, six of them in colour. Richard Aldington canvassed opinion for his column in *The Egoist*. 'One youthful person' of his acquaintance said they looked like 'a cacophony of sardine-tins', a 'distinguished novelist' thought that the cover resembled 'a child's Christmas mechanical motor-car'. Aldington himself hung them around his room:

---

* Douglas Goldring claimed that this was due to a blunder. 'Unfortunately [Marjorie Tripp] had the text printed off without the blocks being fitted in to the places designed for them, so these, much to Lewis's justifiable wrath, had to be issued in a separate portfolio. The whole venture was thus rather a fiasco.' (*South Lodge* pp. 63–4) However, the publication of a separate portfolio in advance of the book was deliberately planned. Max Goschen's eventual decision not to publish the book as well was probably due to doubts as to the commercial viability of the enterprise.

† The publication date is not known. Copies were in existence by 8 December 1912 and Tripp promised Lewis they would all be ready by the end of the week. However, because the only review of the portfolio appeared in *The Egoist* of 1 January 1914, it has been widely assumed that publication took place in late 1913.

though I do not know what they represent, and do not even know whether they mean to represent anything, I get a great deal of pleasure from them. The drawing of Act IV which looks rather like a lot of cinders thrown into a big black spider's web delights me; at night I sit opposite it, smoking my pipe, and all sorts of curious ideas come out of it and take shape and curl away, and I never get tired and the picture never gets dull.

Lewis's fears that the portfolio would harm sales of the book proved, if not groundless, then certainly irrelevant. No edition of *Timon of Athens*, folio or otherwise, with or without illustrations, was ever published by Max Goschen.

*

In something under two years Lewis had undergone a remarkable development, from a poet and writer of occasional prose pieces to an artist whose work wrenched critical attention away from acres of other men's canvas in the Albert Hall or wherever else it was shown. With no more than six paintings and about ten drawings exhibited to his credit he was sustaining comparison with one of the leading figures of the continental avant-garde. He had produced, in *Kermesse*, what was by all accounts as potent an icon of modern painting as Picasso's *Les Demoiselles d'Avignon*. He had also made influential friends in Roger Fry and Clive Bell. These were men who recognised his worth and, with the power of the literary and artistic freemasonry of Bloomsbury behind them, could ease his future career in those fields. But by the end of the following year he had made influential enemies of them both.

FOURTEEN

The laughing woman

Lewis called Kate Lechmere 'Jacques' because she was reading Jean-Jacques Rousseau when he first met her. His long black hair suggested to her a *nom d'amour* for him: 'Golliwog'. He took charge of her reading, urging on her the 'disreputable Slav literature' of Dostoevsky and Gorki. They were lovers briefly, probably in 1912, and, if the postscript on one letter is anything to go by, their relations were affectionate. 'As many kisses as the envelope will hold', he wrote. 'The rest I keep in my mouth for you.' In retrospect Kate Lechmere viewed their short affair and subsequent friendship as 'most amicable . . . most amusing and entertaining'. She must have laughed a great deal. It might indeed be said that her laugh became an inspiration to him.

The whereabouts of Olive Johnson, consigned to the background of his life for the time being, is uncertain. Hoel, known as Peter, was probably being looked after by Lewis's mother.

*

There was a dispute over money as the Second Post-Impressionist Exhibition came down at the end of January 1913. 'When the time came to pay artists their share of the purchase amounts of pictures sold, Roger [Fry] insisted upon deducting a higher commission without any explanation or apology to the painters. Most of them meekly accepted what they were given, but Wyndham Lewis, at best of times a bilious and cantankerous man, protested violently. Roger was adamant in ignoring him and his demands.' This at least was the partisan recollection of Leonard Woolf.

Lewis's work had excited considerable attention, and sales of his work may, as a result, have been brisk. No records survive as to how brisk, nor of the commission Fry claimed and Lewis disputed. But, perhaps as a result of this unpleasantness, Fry did not include Lewis's work in the slimmed-down version of the exhibition he sent to Liverpool in February. When Lewis discovered the slight he wrote to Fry for an explanation and received the reply: 'I forgot to ask if you had anything to send.' Lewis wrote back, apparently more in sorrow than in anger:

122

all other contributors . . . were asked . . . if their paintings or drawings . . . should be sent . . . The implication is obvious. I am animated by most cordial sentiments as regards yourself and your activities. But to continue in an atmosphere of special criticism and illwill . . . would have manifest disadvantages, as well as being distasteful, to me.

Such disadvantages, of course, were primarily financial. Failure to have his work shown in Liverpool meant one less chance of selling. 'An attitude of denigrement on your part, or abscence of cordiality', he told Fry, 'might hurt my stomach as well as my vanity.'

Some sort of reconciliation must have been arrived at, because in late March Lewis participated in one further exhibition organised by Fry. This was the Grafton Group show at the Alpine Club Gallery in Mill Street. The Group comprised Fry himself, Vanessa Bell, Duncan Grant, Frederick Etchells and Lewis. There were also paintings by Winifred Gill, Etchells's sister Jessie, Cuthbert Hamilton, Edward Wadsworth, Spencer Gore, Christopher Nevinson, and other non-members, including contributions by Wassily Kandinsky and Max Weber. All these artists exhibited 'by invitation'. Critics were somewhat nonplussed by Fry's policy of showing works anonymously. There were no names and no titles, the catalogue consisting only of a sequence of numbers: one to sixty. This was intended to give the viewer 'a fresh impression of [the work] without the slight and almost unconscious predilection which a name generally arouses'. The policy irritated C. Lewis Hind, writing for the *Daily Chronicle*: 'It is not difficult to discover the parents of most of the pictures, but why try?' Many of the works he found 'refreshed by talent' but 'none deluged by genius'. He recalled a picture of 'smiling, archaic women' and references from other sources identify this as Lewis's contribution to the show.

The *Pall Mall Gazette* correspondent mentioned a large cartoon of three women as being 'a synthesis of laughter'. The *Daily Telegraph* critic, having presumably been told which was Lewis's picture and, in the absence of a title in the catalogue, supplying one of his own, wrote: 'If his composition of life size figures, Three Women, is not a picture, hardly, indeed a work of art at all, it is a very powerful design of its kind.' Kate Lechmere remembered a painting which comprised three portraits of herself with large grinning faces and folded arms.

According to Lewis, a 'large paper-picture' was destroyed, 15 years later, in a flooded cellar of the Tate Gallery. The description, 'an over-lifesize gouache of three smiling women' predominantly 'reddish' in colour, coincides with what little is known of the work exhibited in the Grafton Group exhibition. Its progress from the Alpine Club Gallery to the bottom of several fathoms of muddy Thames water is a confused tale of not one, but two lost pictures, differentiated in the documentation of the time by nothing more than a single definite article.

A month after the large cartoon was shown in the Grafton Group exhibition, anonymous, untitled, and 'undistinguished even by a number', another large cartoon appeared at the Goupil Gallery. This time the catalogue gave it a number: 139, an attribution: P. Wyndham Lewis, and also a title: *The Laughing Woman*.

Prior to his embarkation for Flanders with the Royal Garrison Artillery in 1917, Lewis compiled an inventory of his work in which 'a large paper roll, cartoon, "The Laughing Woman" ' was listed. A photograph shows the angular figure of a grinning woman, recognisable, even in semi-abstraction, as Kate Lechmere. A curved shape to the left of the head might represent a rounded window or recess. This detail suggests the picture may have been based upon a section of the three-figure composition shown at the Alpine Club Gallery in which the *Athenaeum* critic had noticed 'arched alcoves' in the background. Also clearly visible in the photograph are horizontal and vertical lines showing the work to be made of several sheets of paper. Left behind in 1917 with Helen Saunders, this was clearly the 'large paper roll' mentioned in his inventory. There is another photograph which shows how large it was. Lewis, clad in waistcoat, scarf and overcoat, stands in front of the framed cartoon and, by happy chance, another picture, the precise size of which is known, was leaning against it when the photograph was taken. From the relatively modest dimensions of *Smiling Woman Ascending a Stair*, coincidentally another grinning image of Kate Lechmere, *The Laughing Woman* can be proportionately calculated to somewhere over six feet high and four feet wide.

This substantial cartoon, hung in the Goupil Gallery that April, was part of an exhibition mounted by the Contemporary Art Society. Presided over by Lord Howard de Walden, the CAS had been formed in 1910, its purpose 'the acquisition of Works of Modern Art for loan or gift to Public Galleries'. The 18-man committee included Charles Aitken, director of the Tate Gallery, Edward Marsh, Private Secretary to Winston Churchill, the First Sea Lord, Roger Fry and Clive Bell. Members of the Committee were appointed buyers in rotation for six-month periods. This meant that no single individual's taste would be discernible in the overall accumulation of works in the Society's possession. On show at the Goupil Gallery were recent acquisitions, including John's portrait of Dorelia, *The Smiling Woman*, which may incidentally have provided inspiration for the jagged likenesses of Kate Lechmere.

The Society's 'recent acquisitions' were augmented by loans of which Lewis's *The Laughing Woman* was one.

*

At the end of May Roger Fry wrote to his friend G. Lowes Dickinson that his new enterprise, 'Omega Workshops Ltd., Artist Decorators', intended to introduce Post-Impressionist design to the domestic furnishings of the cultured classes, was under way: 'I've *got* to make it pay or goodness knows what'll become of me, let alone the group of artists who are already dependent on it. God knows how they lived before they got their thirty shillings a week from my workshop.'

The painters of the Grafton Group formed Fry's core workforce: Duncan Grant, Frederick Etchells, Vanessa Bell and Lewis. It expanded to include Cuthbert Hamilton, Edward Wadsworth, Henri Gaudier-Brzeska, Winifred Gill, Nina Hamnett, and a designer of stained glass, John 'Jock' Turnbull.

But the purchasers of artefacts designed and made in the first-floor rooms of the large Adam house at 33 Fitzroy Square would be unaware of who had made what. Fry insisted on anonymity for all contributions, the only signature being the company stamp: the last letter of the Greek alphabet.

From memories of the Omega's early days recorded by Winifred Gill, Lewis emerges as a self-conscious, rather ridiculous figure, who was 'building up what would now be called a public "image" '.

Without realising it, he afforded Miss Gill a rare glimpse of this image cultivation. She was resting on a bedstead in the back showroom, concealed by a shadow to the left of the window and opposite the door. It was late afternoon and getting dark. 'Suddenly the door burst open and in rushed Wyndham Lewis carrying a large paper bag which he threw onto a small table.' The bag contained an outsize cloth cap made in a large black and white check material: the height of fashion. 'Lewis . . . tried it on in front of the looking glass on the mantel piece. He cocked it slightly to one side to his satisfaction, then, taking a few steps backward, raised his hand as though to shake hands with someone and approached the mirror with an ingratiating smile. He backed again and tried the effect of a sudden recognition with a look of surprised pleasure. Then, cocking the cap at a more dashing angle his face froze and he turned and glanced over his shoulder with a look of scorn and disgust.' Throughout this embarrassing would-be solitary performance, the reluctant spy feigned sleep, terrified at what he might do to her if he discovered he had been observed. Finally Lewis snatched the cap from his head, thrust it back into its paper bag and left. She heard his boots clattering down the stairs. The coast clear she went back to the studio and recounted the incident to her fellow worker, 'Jock' Turnbull. 'Ye were never nearer being murdered in yer life,' he told her, 'no man could have let yer live.'

On another occasion she remembered a black sombrero, the first royal blue shirt she had ever seen, and carefully clipped oblongs of whisker in front of each ear: 'sideboards'. Capitalising upon his dark good looks, the 'image' was now unmistakably Spanish and Miss Gill thought (mistakenly) that he had just returned from a visit to that country.

It was a day in late July and he was lounging at a table in the main workroom, his long legs stretched out in front of him. A friend appeared in the doorway and Lewis asked:

'Been to the show?'

'No, have you?'

'. . . . There this morning.'

'Oh, anything worth seeing?'

'. . . . Very fine head by Brancusi.'

The friend departed and Lewis raised his hand in farewell: 'Adios'. Miss Gill explained that the four dots represented 'a portentous intake of breath issuing in a rich, deliberate speech'. She recalled that a few minutes later, somebody else popped their head round the door:

'Been to the show?'

'No, have you?'

'. . . . There this morning.'

'Oh, anything worth seeing?'

'. . . . Very fine head by Brancusi.'

'Adios.'

In all he conducted the identical exchange no less than three times.

The show referred to was at the Albert Hall – the sixth London Salon of the Allied Artists' Association – and Constantin Brancusi was represented by three heads, two in brass and one in stone. Lewis himself contributed two drawings and a large oil singled out for special notice by Roger Fry in *The Nation*:

'Group' . . . is more completely realised than anything he has shown yet. His power of selecting those lines of movement and those sequences of mass which express his personal feeling, is increasing visibly. In this work the mood is Michaelangelesque in its sombre and tragic intensity. Mr Lewis is no primitive.

Despite such fulsome praise, Lewis still suspected Fry of undervaluing his work. He would not have forgotten being passed over when the Second Post-Impressionist Exhibition transferred to Liverpool.

Although Miss Gill could not recall seeing Lewis do anything at 33

Fitzroy Square apart from pose in front of a mirror and chat to passing acquaintances, he did in fact do some work to earn the 30 shillings a week Fry paid him. A screen showing circus performers cavorting on its four panels figured prominently in a photograph of the Omega Showroom in the *Daily News and Leader*. He also produced a set of nine fan-shaped figurative designs for lampshades. Perhaps in an effort to shock her, Lewis told Miss Gill that he intended four of the designs to be viewed as a sequence: 'stages in the bargaining between a roué and a procuress for the purchase of a young woman'.

*

At a committee meeting on 9 June, Clive Bell was appointed six-monthly buyer for the Contemporary Art Society with effect from 1 July. During his term of duty he bought seven pictures: a Duncan Grant, a Lucien Pissarro, a Harold Squire, a Cuthbert Hamilton, a Frederick Etchells, a still life by Jessie Etchells and *Laughing Woman* by Wyndham Lewis.

Lack of a definite article in the title noted in CAS minutes is the first clue that the picture Bell purchased was not the cartoon exhibited at the Goupil Gallery as *The Laughing Woman*. In Lewis's 1917 inventory, distinct from the 'large paper roll', left with Miss Saunders, was:

'Laughing Woman' painting in possession of the *Contemporary Art Society*.

In late June or early July it seemed as if Lewis was planning to paint a canvas for Bell's consideration. 'I'm afraid the Society would never let me buy outright a picture that I had not seen', Bell told him. 'I liked the cartoon so much that, unless you are going to do something very different, I can't doubt that I shall like the picture; but I'm afraid I must reserve a right of final judgement.' The cartoon Bell had liked so much was probably the large gouache from the Grafton Group Exhibition showing three laughing versions of Kate Lechmere. He told Lewis it reminded him of Giotto. Along with Cézanne, Giotto was probably much in Bell's thoughts in the latter half of 1913 as he prepared his little book, *Art*, for publication. Every picture he considered purchasing for the CAS would have been rigorously measured, as an example of 'significant form', against Cézanne or the 14th-century master of the Arena frescoes at Padua. The arches in the background of Lewis's picture, the 'archaic' figures and, if it bore any resemblance to *Smiling Woman Ascending a Stair*, the muted colour and stylised fall of drapery, may all have combined to bring Giotto to mind.

Lewis did not produce the promised canvas. He must have persuaded
Bell to buy the gouache cartoon for the Contemporary Art Society instead.
In August he received a cheque for £50, and plans were made to mount the
paper onto canvas. The job was to be carried out in Vanessa's studio and
Bell made fretful preparations. 'My wife tells me that stretching a big canvas
is a complicated affair and two men's job. Do be sure to send capable
workmen: it would be too maddening if anything were to miscarry.' There
was even a space on the end wall of the studio where it could be hung for the
time being. Fashionable taste had moved on and a large canvas, *The
Childhood of Pyramus*, by Augustus John, bought five years before, had
recently been sold. 'The chains and hooks remain', said Bell, adding that it
would be interesting to see the new picture on the wall. 'If you see your men
before they start you might tell them to bring screws, tools, etc. Perhaps it
would amuse you to come and see it when in place? or to supervise the work
of hanging.'

FIFTEEN

'*Ça, c'est trop fort!*'

There was an undercurrent of tension and intrigue in the Bells' home at 46 Gordon Square on the day in early August that *Laughing Woman* was stretched and hung. While Lewis was in the studio supervising the workmen, a whispered exchange occurred in a neighbouring room. Concerned that Lewis felt his work was unappreciated at the Omega, Roger Fry asked Clive Bell if he had any idea what grounds the painter had for this belief.

Bell was clearly embarrassed by the question. Lewis had previously complained about Fry, in confidence, and a likely cause of complaint was the major commission that had come the Omega's way during the previous month. If Lewis had at that time known the full background to this commission, he would not have confined himself to grumbling privately to Clive Bell. Following the discovery of certain facts, two months later, a great many more people were to hear his views on Roger Fry and the Omega Workshop.

But in early August there was only a suspicion that his work was not appreciated. Put on the spot by Fry while Lewis was out of the room seeing to the hanging of his picture, Bell was diplomatic. He told Fry that Lewis thought he did not care for his circus screen. Bell felt this was a sensible thing to say because he had frequently heard Fry praise the screen and was fairly sure that he liked it. It was intended as a tactful way of letting the Omega director know that Lewis may 'have been given a false impression of his views'.

If Fry was worried that one of his artists felt undervalued, he did not seem to make an immediate effort to redress the suspicion once *Laughing Woman* was up on the wall and everybody gathered round to look at it. When he wrote to Lewis, Bell attempted to make up for the somewhat lukewarm initial response. 'Fry and my wife – who may have seemed a little cold at first – liked it better and better till at last they became thoroughly enthusiastic.' Unfortunately this enthusiasm was only manifested after Lewis had departed. 'To be sure', Bell gushed on, 'I think my wife likes it almost, if not quite as much as I do from the first. Only she is not demonstrative.'

As he was leaving, Lewis took Bell to one side at the door and cautioned him, belatedly, to say nothing whatsoever about him to Fry. 'I don't reproach myself with any treachery', Bell wrote before getting into bed, 'because after you had asked me to say nothing, nothing was said by me.'

Laughing Woman probably remained on the end wall of the Gordon Square studio, secured by the hooks and chains that had once secured John's *Childhood of Pyramus*, until December, when Bell's period as buyer for the Contemporary Art Society came to an end and he handed it over to the committee with his six other purchases. Bought 'through Bloomsbury influence', this was the last time Bloomsbury influence would be exercised to Lewis's benefit.

In February of the following year *Laughing Woman* went to Liverpool, part of a CAS exhibition at the Sandon Studio Society in School Lane, where it was shown with other challenging pictures in a separate category of 'Decorative Cartoons'. The Roscoe Professor of Architecture at the University of Liverpool, Charles Reilly, conceded in the *Daily Post* that Lewis 'at any rate allows himself pleasant colour if he deals in forms of nightmare shape'. From Liverpool the exhibition went to Sheffield and then to Leicester.

Returning from the provinces it was stored with the rest of the CAS's holdings in a cellar room at the Tate Gallery.

*

The loud slamming of a front door followed by a French exclamation from the top of a flight of stairs brought to an end Lewis's connection with the Omega Workshop and with its director.

In July, P. G. Konody was asked by the *Daily Mail* to recommend a suitable 'Futurist' artist to decorate a room for the Ideal Home Exhibition at Olympia in October. Mme Strindberg, having had some experience in commissioning modern interior design, suggested he give the organisers Gore's name and address. She wrote to Gore separately, telling him: 'For God's sake don't recommend another man but make the money YOUR-SELF.' Nevertheless it was with a joint commission in mind that a *Daily Mail* agent wrote inviting Gore to the Ideal Home Exhibition offices in Fleet Street a couple of days later. At this preliminary meeting the agent told Gore that a room 'in an advanced style' was required and, consulting a slip of paper, said that two other artists had been recommended to share the work: Roger Fry and Wyndham Lewis. Gore was then asked to contact the other two and arrange a further meeting 'to fix it up'. The painter went directly to Fitzroy Square with an illustrated brochure of the previous year's exhibition. Neither Fry nor Lewis was in when he called, but he explained the offer to Duncan Grant and asked him to pass the message to Fry, suggesting he contact the agent. Gore left the brochure and departed.

At this point in mid-July only Gore, the anonymous *Daily Mail* agent, and now Grant knew about the proposed commission.

Thereafter the affair became a tangled comedy of misunderstandings and missed opportunities for explanation, erupting, in early October, into a row that split the London avant-garde down the middle. Central to the dispute was Lewis's charge that Fry had stolen the commission for the Omega Workshop and cut out two of the artists for whom it had originally been intended. Fry's guilt or innocence would seem to hinge upon whether or not he received the message Gore left at Fitzroy Square.

Fifty years later Duncan Grant could not remember Gore's visit on the day in question but thought it likely that he might have received the message but forgotten to pass it on to Fry. Be that as it may, somehow or other Fry, as director of the Omega Workshop, was given the *Daily Mail* commission without any conditions as to the artists he would employ.

Fry claimed, in a letter to Gore on 5 October, that the *Daily Mail* people had approached him directly and that they had made no mention of any other collaborators. But Fry altered his story less than a fortnight later in another letter to Gore dated 18 October:

> as you very unfortunately did not deliver the message yourself I think you must take my word for it that I never got it with sufficient clearness to make me consider it as compared with what I thought the quite authoritative full statement of the *Daily Mail*.

In other words the message had been passed on but had become garbled. The version that Fry received may then have been that the *Daily Mail* were anxious to commission someone to design and furnish a room and would he, as Omega director, care to come and discuss the matter further? Even if Lewis and Gore had been mentioned by the agent at the subsequent meeting, Fry would doubtless have quoted company policy: 'the Omega produces its work anonymously and would not expect to have the work distributed beforehand by outsiders amongst various artists.'

The first Lewis heard of the matter was when Fry told him Omega had secured the prestigious commission and would he care to carve a mantelpiece? Feeling his talents would not be shown to best advantage by a lowly piece of woodworking, Lewis claimed that he asked Fry about painting wall decorations instead. He was told that there would be no wall decorations. 'Nothing at all,' said Fry, 'just a few irregular spaces of colours. No decorations.' Fry later testified that Lewis had wanted to do the carving. 'It was his own suggestion and I considered it the most interesting and important job in the whole work ... I didn't tell him there would be no [wall] decoration.'

Then, in August, Lewis left for his customary summer holiday. Frederick Etchells accompanied him to Dieppe: 'Lewis had an address and recommendation from Sickert when we arrived, and it turned out to be a charming place in the working-class quarter which would only house one of us. We tossed a coin for it and Lewis won. But I managed to find two pretty rooms at an old douanier's with a great big Napoleonic bed. So I said to Lewis, "I'll come and look you up in the morning", and when I did I found him sitting on a table surrounded by between 80 and 100 dead bugs. He had been up all night killing them with a hammer. I laughed and laughed, so we had a tiff over that.'

Further testimony of his activities was provided by Lytton Strachey in a letter to Dorelia: 'Did you know that your friend Lewis has been spending his Summer in Dieppe, pursuing bonnes along the plage? – and alas! pursuing in vain.'

A photograph shows Lewis in the bosom of the Sickert family and friends. Long black hair parted down the middle, sporting a thin black moustache and with a light-coloured, flat-crowned felt hat resting on his knee, he sits on a bench next to Sickert's mother and second wife, Christine. Lewis is the only member of the group who looks at the camera as if consigning the moment and his presence there to posterity.

Olive Johnson joined him in Dieppe and a letter from his mother suggests the visit was not a happy one: 'I am sorry your holiday has not been successful. Personally I think it is rather a mistake to return to a place you have liked under different conditions.' This referred to the summer of two years before. The letter continued: 'I believe if you had taken the child to some English seaside place, you would have enjoyed it more.' Olive must have brought their son Peter with her. On 4 September mother and father might have commemorated the child's second birthday in his place of birth. And there may even have been a possibility of history repeating itself, because Olive was pregnant again. However, there is no record in Dieppe from that year of a child's birth to parents named Lewis or Johnson, so it must be assumed that their daughter, Betty, was born after Olive's return to London.

Another sentence in his mother's letter suggests that the carving of the mantelpiece for Omega had not been executed when Lewis left for his holiday, but that he intended carving it when he returned. 'Perhaps after you have done Fry's work', she told him, 'you can have another little holiday in Paris and enjoy it more.'

He did go to Paris, in late October, but by then the Omega's 'Post-Impressionist Room' had been completed and installed at Olympia without a mantelpiece, carved or otherwise, and Lewis would never work for Fry again.

Arriving back from Dieppe he discovered painted panels destined for the walls of the Ideal Home drawing room all around the Workshop in Fitzroy Square. This would have confirmed the suspicions he had harboured two months before that Fry did not appreciate his work. The grainy coloured photograph of the Omega installation that appeared in the *Illustrated London News* showed three semi-abstract compositions of dancers not entirely unlike the figures in Lewis's studies for *Kermesse*. Clearly this part of the commission would have suited his talents better than the carving of a mantelpiece.

It was a chance meeting with Gore on 4 or 5 of October that brought matters to a head. Lewis would have lost no time in confronting Fry with what Gore had to tell him: that the Ideal Home commission was originally offered to three individual artists, himself among them, rather than to Fry and a group of anonymous 'workmen' constituting the Omega Workshop.

He was backed up by Etchells, Cuthbert Hamilton and Edward Wadsworth when he went to see Fry.

Angry voices might have been heard coming from no. 33, disrupting the Sunday quiet of Fitzroy Square: Lewis accusing Fry of stealing the commission from himself and Gore; Fry protesting that their names had never been mentioned; Lewis reiterating the charges and accusing Fry of calling Gore a liar; perhaps the disparate voices of Etchells, Hamilton and Wadsworth raised in confused support. Finally there was the clatter of four pairs of boots on the stairs and the thunderous boom of the front door being slammed.

In the silence that followed, Fry was heard to say to no one in particular: 'Ça, c'est trop fort!'

*

The following weekend a three-page typed circular was sent out from Lewis's studio in Brecknock Road to Fry's friends and clients:

> Understanding that you are interested in the Omega Workshops, we beg to lay before you the following discreditable facts:
> (1) That the Direction of the Omega Workshops secured the decoration of the 'Post-Impressionist' room at the Ideal Home Exhibition by a shabby trick.

And there was a second charge.

A day or two before the revelations of his chance meeting with Gore, Lewis had received a letter from Frank Rutter, curator of the Leeds City Art Gallery and founder of the AAA, asking for two or three paintings for the 'Post-Impressionist and Futurist' show he was organising at the Doré Galleries later in the month. Rutter told him that this was the second time he had written with this request and had he not received the letter sent care of the Omega Workshop? Lewis had not. Rutter had also written to Fry asking for Etchells's address, and stating his intention of inviting the latter to contribute also. Rutter, it seems, had been 'given to understand that Mr Etchells had no pictures ready and would have none till 1914. This statement of Mr Fry's was not only unauthorised but untrue.' Hence, the further charge:

(2) . . . the suppression of information in order to prevent a member from exhibiting in a Show of pictures not organised by the Direction of the Omega.

By the time copies of the round robin, signed by Lewis, Wadsworth, Etchells and Hamilton, had been delivered to people having an interest in the Omega Workshop, Fry was out of the country. Just before leaving for Villeneuve-les-Avignon, in fact while he was packing to go, Fry claims he discovered the letter from Rutter to Lewis. Forwarding it on 10 October, he explained that he had opened and read it before realising that it had been addressed to someone else. 'I . . . can only suppose that you [Lewis] had left it about and that it had got put among my things.'

With Fry on holiday, his friends rallied round to deal with the attack as best they could.

'We have had a day of it!' Vanessa Bell wrote to him on 12 October. In the morning Molly MacCarthy had telephoned to say she had received the round robin. She thought Fry must have given Lewis and his friends cause for anger, while Desmond MacCarthy believed that he should defend himself. Fry had other enemies who would derive great satisfaction from the schism. Vanessa's brother Adrian Stephen and Duncan Grant came round to lend support. Grant and Vanessa went to see Etchells that afternoon to try to get him to see that whether he and Lewis were right or wrong about Fry, they had 'behaved monstrously' in writing the circular letter without first accusing him to his face. They talked for two hours and it was only with great difficulty that Etchells could be made to see their point. 'When he did see it he simply said that he didn't agree.' Regarding his specific accusation that Fry had told Rutter that he had nothing to send to the Doré Gallery,

Vanessa had a disloyal thought about her friend. 'I only hope [you] *didn't* say that Etchells had no paintings! Apparently he had several.'

She and Grant returned to Gordon Square. By this time Desmond MacCarthy had come round and he and Clive were drafting letters which Fry might possibly send to answer the accusations. 'I think it rather depends on whether Rutter and the *Daily Mail* produce clear evidence.' By late afternoon Leonard Woolf had joined the discussion. He was for Fry taking no notice of the charges. Clive Bell was inclined to agree. 'The whole thing's a matter of character and surely yours is good enough to stand a little scurrilous rhetoric. Everyone who knows what's what will draw his own conclusions from the style of the circular . . . What about saying nothing, or at any rate about waiting before you say anything?'

The following day Bell met Lewis by chance in Bond Street. Lewis came forward and said: 'I hope you're not very upset!' 'Oh no,' replied Bell, 'not in the least.' They walked on together, Lewis claiming that he had had to use politics to defend his interests because he 'had his way to make'. Bell told him that he thought the circular was 'a silly and suburban affair which would convince no one of anything but the folly of the writers'.

'Suburban' was perhaps the most pejorative adjective in Clive Bell's vocabulary. He used it again in a letter to Lewis the following day: 'you ought not to bombard the town with pages of suburban rhetoric. The vulgarity of the thing! And the provincialism! That's what I mind. You don't belong in the suburbs, so what the devil are you doing there?'

Faced with Bell's obvious disapproval as they walked down Bond Street and into Piccadilly, Lewis seemed to have second thoughts about his attack on Fry. He put the responsibility for the round robin on Etchells, Hamilton and Wadsworth, explaining that it was not the sort of thing he liked doing. He hoped that his former colleagues at the Omega were not hurt by the remarks about 'Prettiness',* that he for one had not wanted to put in that sort of thing. Lewis had not been in a conciliatory mood to start with and his 'admissions were only made as he saw that he might have made himself rather foolish over this letter and so tended to make light of it.'

This account of the conversation was communicated by Bell to his wife and by her to Fry. It was therefore not only far from being impartial but was also at third hand — a fact that Vanessa admitted to Fry: 'But of course you won't take my report of their conversation as pretending to be accurate.'

Vanessa told Fry that Bell got the impression that 'they are all longing for

* 'As to [Omega's] tendencies in Art, they alone would be sufficient to make it very difficult for any vigorous art-instinct to long remain under that roof. The Idol is still Prettiness, with its mid-Victorian languish of the neck, and its skin is "greenery-yallery", despite the Post-What-Not fashionableness of its draperies.'

you to reply. Lewis was very much disappointed that you had not rushed back from France at once! What they would really like would be an action for libel.' This does seem to be the case, because Lewis had already engaged the services of a solicitor in preparation for such an eventuality. On 18 October, when no response had come from Fry, Vandercom & Co. charged Lewis two guineas and regretted the affair had not gone further. 'I am very sorry to hear that the letter failed to arouse Roger Fry, and I hope that you have succeeded in impressing some of his supporters.'

G. Lowes Dickinson, for one, was far from impressed. 'I have received from you a libellous letter dealing with the affairs of the Omega Workshop', he wrote to Lewis. 'You must be as stupid as you are malicious to send such a letter to Mr Fry's friends, who all know him to be incapable of any such conduct as you describe. I trust you will not trouble me further with these sordid intrigues.'

The allegations contained in the round robin were certainly libellous, and Lewis was perhaps fortunate that Fry took no action. On the charge of stealing the Ideal Home commission, all that Lewis could direct at Fry was the word of Spencer Gore. Fry, however, could defend himself with documentary proof to the contrary. The day after Bell's conversation with Lewis, Vanessa went to the Ideal Home Exhibition offices at Olympia and the secretary, Mr F. G. Bussy, furnished her with a letter confirming Fry's story:

> The commission to furnish and decorate a room at Olympia was given by the *Daily Mail* to Roger Fry without any conditions as to the artists he would employ. In the conversation between our representative and Mr Roger Fry, there was no question of collaboration between Omega Workshops and any other artist or artists. The names of Mr Spencer Gore and Mr Wynham [sic] Lewis were not mentioned by our representative to Mr Roger Fry so far as he can remember, neither do we recollect having any interview with either of the latter gentlemen.

That Fry came by one Ideal Home commission honestly is proved. What will never be known for certain is whether he had been aware of another, earlier offer, from a different official, which he chose to ignore. Perhaps he had been guilty of misappropriation by default and for this reason, even with Mr Bussy's affidavit, he did not pursue a libel action.

A month after Lewis and his lieutenants slammed out of 33 Fitzroy Square, Fry was maintaining silence: 'I think people are in hopes of something dramatic on my part to get things on the move again. But I think I shall not oblige.'

*

It can readily be assumed that the Ideal Home affair was the main topic of conversation, gossip and speculation at the Private View of the Post-Impressionist and Futurist Exhibition from 10 until 6 o'clock on 16 October. Those present at the Doré Galleries who had received a copy of the round robin earlier in the week would know that Roger Fry was alleged to have lied to the exhibition organiser, Frank Rutter, when he told him that Frederick Etchells had no work to show. Recipients of the circular would also have known that a letter, in connection with this same exhibition, and addressed to Wyndham Lewis at the Omega Workshop, had mysteriously gone astray. And anybody present, taking a break from conversation about such matters to cast an eye over the Doré's walls, would probably have remarked upon the absence of any works by Vanessa Bell, Duncan Grant and Roger Fry.

And when another exhibition opened at the Alpine Club Galleries two months later in January 1914 the *Athenaeum* correspondent noted that the names, 'Mrs Clive Bell, Mr Roger Fry, and Mr Duncan Grant', on the outside of the catalogue now represented the sole members of the Grafton Group.

The schism was complete.

*

Towards the end of October Lewis went to Paris for a couple of days, 'to transact a little piece of business' he told Cuthbert Hamilton. It may have been on this occasion that he visited Gertrude Stein for the first time. She remembered he was tall and thin and looked like 'a young frenchman on the rise' and that 'his feet were very french, or at least his shoes':

he came and told all about his quarrel with Roger Fry. Roger Fry had come in not many days before and had already told all about it. They told exactly the same story only it was different, very different.*

If Lewis also mentioned to Miss Stein his irritation with Madame

---

* Stein also recalled: '[Lewis] used to come and sit and measure pictures. I can not say that he actually measured with a measuring-rod but he gave all the effect of being in the act of taking very careful measurement of the canvas, the lines within the canvas and everything that might be of use.' Ernest Hemingway gave a more spiteful version, quoting Stein telling him: 'I call him "the Measuring Worm" . . . He comes over from London and he sees a good picture and takes a pencil out of his pocket and you watch him measuring it on the pencil with his thumb. Sighting on it and measuring it and seeing exactly how it is done. Then he goes back to London and does it and it doesn't come right. He's missed what it's all about.' (*A Moveable Feast* p. 98)

Strindberg that month, she did not record the fact. But according to the letter he wrote Hamilton from Paris, this was another business relationship strained to breaking point. The two artists had collaborated to devise a shadow play for the Cabaret Theatre Club. *Ombres Chinoises* was performed on 26 October. During the preparations an argument blew up between Hamilton and Madame Strindberg over the black screens necessary for the performance. Apologising for withholding support from his colleague during this 'bustle', Lewis showed that where money, or the promise of money, was concerned, he could exercise considerable restraint. Despite the 'many ridiculous vexations' of 'that beastly Cabaret' he did not wish to alienate the proprietress:

> I must still try and get something out of it; I am so hard up, and it serves to fill up the necessary gaps financially . . . – I assure you I was far more exasperated, if anything, than you were, and only held back for that reason, that I knew I should say too much: or rather only did so on the strict promise to myself that if she repeated it I would clear out and leave her 'en panne'.

This suggests that he had received something for his labours and that necessary financial gaps had been filled by Madame Strindberg. However the balance of his £60, promised so precisely in three instalments, payable by 10 o'clock on 27 September and on 1 and 15 October, had still not materialised. By November his patience was at an end. 'The Strindberg has broken down my phlegm at last', he told Hueffer, 'and I am thinking of writs to regain what is due to me. I have often, for absurd sentimental reasons . . . consented to help her anew. But she is a hard and godless old ape.'

SIXTEEN

Blast

zang – tumb – tumb – zang – zang – tuuumb
tatatatatatatata   picpacpampacpacpicpampampac
uuuuuuuuuuuuuuuu   ZANG-TUMB-TUMB-TUMB-
TUUUUM

In an upstairs room of the Florence Restaurant, Rupert Street, on 18 November, at a dinner given in his honour, Signor Marinetti declaimed his poem about the siege of Adrianople, phonetically reproducing the sounds of machine-gun and rifle fire, artillery bombardment, and high explosive. Downstairs the band was playing one of the most popular tunes of 1913:

> You maaade me looove you
> I didn't wanna do it – I didn't wanna do it . . .

The melody made little impression on the Futurist leader's vocal onslaught. 'It was a matter of astonishment what Marinetti could do with his unaided voice', Lewis recalled:

> He certainly made an extraordinary amount of noise. A day of attack upon the Western Front, with all the 'heavies' hammering together, right back to the horizon was nothing to it. My equanimity when first subjected to the sounds of mass-bombardment in Flanders was possibly due to my marinettian preparation – it seemed 'all quiet' to me by comparison.

Christopher Nevinson organised the dinner, aided and abetted by Lewis. Fellow admirers of Marinetti at this stage, there may even have been some rivalry between the two Englishmen when it came to greeting their celebrated guest. David Bomberg remembered an argument in Madame Strindberg's Cave. 'Lewis was threatening to punch Nevinson for daring to claim that when Marinetti stepped off the Golden Arrow bringing him into the Victoria platform no. 19 it was Lewis and not Nevinson who kissed Marinetti's hand first.'

The Italian had a full programme of personal appearances. Two days before the Florence Restaurant dinner he had lectured on 'The Art of Noise' at the Cabaret Theatre Club and he would be speaking on 'Futurism and the Plastic Arts' at the Doré Galleries in New Bond Street two days later, surrounded by Rutter's 'Post-Impressionist and Futurist Exhibition'. There were rumours that a gang of troublemakers would try to disrupt this occasion and the Doré's director, a man called Fishburn, was nervous lest any harm come to the works of art in his care. He was especially protective of a large composition by Robert Delaunay incorporating the Eiffel Tower, a biplane, a ferris wheel and rugby players and entitled *The Cardiff Football Team*. Nevinson felt Fishburn's anxiety to be groundless. 'I don't think they will chuck anything even if the fools come', he told Lewis.

The identity of these anti-Futurists is not known. Nevinson could not have anticipated, however, that, seven months later, Lewis himself would lead another gang of troublemakers to the same gallery and disrupt a lecture he was giving alongside Marinetti.

*

'I am going to the Picture Ball, if you please, as a Futurist picture designed by Wyndham Lewis!' Edward Marsh wrote to Elliot Seabrooke on 30 November. The Private Secretary to Winston Churchill had just returned from visiting Stanley Spencer in Cookham when he encountered the sombreroed Lewis for the first time:

> He is very magnificent to look at, but I don't think he liked me, and I suspected him of pose, so we shan't be friends. Hoping to strike a chord, I told him I had spent the day with Stanley Spencer and he said, 'I don't know him, is he a painter?' which must have been put on.

Throughout November *The Times* had devoted many column-inches to preparations for 'The Picture Ball' to be held at the Albert Hall on 3 December. The purpose of this lavish event was to raise money for the London Invalid Kitchens, a scheme to relieve the sufferings of 'the sick poor of all denominations' in Southwark, Bermondsey, Hoxton, Stepney and Canning Town.

Carefully posed in a glittering series of living pictures and presenting what was intended to be a history of world art from ancient Egyptian to Modern, the cream of London Society would be participating in the extraordinary spectacle.

Lady Muriel Paget, Honorary Secretary of the charity, had contacted Nevinson through the Doré Galleries and he had written to Lewis:

> She wants some tableaux vivants of five well known 'cubist' or futurist

paintings! and wants to know if we will help her and she also murmured something about you and me 'dining with her and arranging things' but I don't think there is any money in it . . . [She] seems to think it is a fearful difficult job and imagines it will need the combined brains of Etchells, Hamilton, Wadsworth and myself under your command . . . Though I promised her nothing I thought it as well not to refuse and offend the good Lady as I was given to understand she was a buyer.

On the night, the floor of the Albert Hall was raised to the level of the lowest tier of boxes and the orchestra and organ concealed by a vast black velvet curtain. Five 'frames' had been cut in the curtain and in these, standing on a specially erected platform, the participants showed themselves.

'Exquisite beyond conception,' the *Daily Mirror* gushed the following morning, 'beautiful beyond believing, unforgettable and haunting was the brilliant picture provided by the historic Picture Ball . . . It was easily the most fashionable and the most brilliant function of the season.' As for the eagerly awaited 'Futurist' contribution, Nevinson's and Lewis's designs, realised by a pair of Chelsea artists, the Misses Forestier, did not disappoint. 'The costumes beggar description and include long necks and nightmare faces.' Edward Marsh's best friend would not have recognised him as he posed with right arm raised to shoulder height, his head completely enclosed in a high tapering tube surmounted by a curious box-like structure. A photograph of Marsh's 'quaint dress' was featured on the *Mirror*'s back page, alongside one of Sir Denis Anson, garbed in a shiny dark robe, his face covered by a circular mask, all eyes and nose, and carrying a small abstract picture. Two drawings by Lewis had been reproduced the day before the Ball. In one, called 'The Birth of Futurism', designs for Marsh's and Anson's costumes could be made out and the correspondent hoped that the performers would 'not be expected to remain at the impossible angles of the figures . . . as otherwise they [could not] expect to enjoy the evening'. The other drawing, referred to as 'The Culmination of Futurism', was a complicated improvisation of jagged and curvilinear forms. The caption read: 'How [this] will be shown is, for the moment, a secret which is locked in the costumier's breast.'

The *Manchester Guardian* reported that the Futurist tableau was 'menacing and geometrical and disturbing' and 'made some people laugh'. It was 'a good note to end on', the *Times* correspondent felt, 'a gentle let-down, so to speak, from the heights of classic art into the merriment of a Christmas carnival'. Nevinson told Lewis that 'the crowd . . . shouted for us half an hour . . . but fortunately Tree's Dramatic Academy stepped into the breach and gave an exhibition of dancing.' Dressed as fairies, the children pranced in, scattering sweets and crackers to the ladies.

It was estimated that the Hall contained 4,000 people when the dancing was at its height. The startling contrasts of high art, contemporary lunacy and ragtime were not lost on 'Rambler', the *Mirror*'s gossip columnist: 'I saw futurist figures, Egyptian maidens, Japanese flower girls and Italian ladies who might have stepped out of Botticelli, dancing to the strains of "The Robert E. Lee".'

Unable or unwilling to attend the festivities himself, Lewis had, in Nevinson, a friend prepared to look after his interests. During the evening he ran into Lady Drogheda and all but clinched a commission for Lewis that promised to be more challenging than the designing of tableaux vivants and considerably more lucrative. She told Nevinson that if Lewis sent her his estimates for decorating her dining room she would accept them.

*

'I hope you are considering the question of taking steps of forming an organisation of your own that will protect you from abuses that Roger Fry's regime seemed to accentuate rather than diminish.' The solicitor Lewis had hired in anticipation of legal action from the direction of Fitzroy Square had proffered this advice in October. At the beginning of the new year 1914 Kate Lechmere wrote from Nice with just such a proposition: an atelier of the French type, enrolling students who would paint there during the week, receiving instruction and criticism from more experienced artists at weekends. Lechmere had inherited money and was willing to get the enterprise started. Thereafter, it would be financed by student fees and by the sale of decorative objects made on the premises. It could offer serious competition to Fry's outfit.

Plans for a journal had been initiated even earlier than Lechmere's proposal. Nevinson had even suggested a name for it. 'Blast' as the title, and 'Vortex' as an image that would eventually be wedded to it, had been mentioned, independently, within a two-day period in the last fortnight of 1913. On 17 December Edward Wadsworth wrote to Lewis: 'I have not been able to think of another name for *Blast* and I am not convinced yet really that *Blast* is bad . . . In any case I don't think we ought to change the name unless for something *better*.'

Two days later Ezra Pound wrote to a fellow American poet, William Carlos Williams: 'You may get something slogging away by yourself that you would miss in The Vortex – and that we miss.'

By the New Year Nevinson's bombastic title had been definitely agreed upon and *The New Age* of 8 January 1914 contained the first published reference:

> a magazine, to be named 'Blast', will shortly appear under the editorship of Mr Wyndham Lewis to provide a platform for the discussion of Cubism and other aesthetic phenomena.

Pound's 'Vortex' was held in reserve for another six months.

Lewis and Pound had first encountered one another at the Vienna Café near the British Museum, probably in late 1908 and in the company of their respective mentors: Sturge Moore and Laurence Binyon. Pound recalled that Binyon effected the introduction: 'His bull-dog, me as it were against old Sturge M[oore]'s bull-dog.' It was a friendship begun in mutual suspicion – Lewis only spoke to the red-haired American at their third meeting – but by late 1913 they were partners in an enterprise intended to revolutionise English art. They presided over a tea party to formulate lists of people and institutions which editorial policy would support and those it would deplore. These lists were to be headed 'BLESS' and 'BLAST'. Douglas Goldring was present:

> It was a solemn occasion except, I suspected, for the two prophets – who, when unobserved by the disciples, occasionally exchanged knowing grins – and for myself, who had frequently to suppress irreverent giggles. There were, I suppose, more than twenty people present, and Jessie Dismorr, an advanced painter and poetess . . . was ordered by the Master [Lewis], after a counting of heads, to get tea for us.

Goldring remembered that Nevinson was present, and William Roberts, also probably Henri Gaudier-Brzeska, together with 'several young men who resolutely wore their black hats and endeavoured unsuccessfully to look "tough" '.

It was Goldring, with his experience as editor of *The Tramp*, who was chief adviser on the practicalities of publishing. He found Lewis a small printer in Harlesden 'humble enough blindly to carry out his instructions' for the typographically eccentric organ. For its unquestioning services, the firm of Leveridge and Company found itself among the ranks of the Blessed.

*

Also Blessed was Madame Strindberg. During the last days of the Cabaret Theatre Club, prior to the liquidation sale in February, she wrote to Lewis inviting him to what must have been something in the nature of a wake. It was to be 'a special night . . . reuniting all the "founders" of the Cabaret'. She asked him to bring along all the 'interesting people' he knew and to keep them together so that she could 'feed them safely and cheaply . . . without the others knowing it'. Otherwise she would have to invite the whole room, 'which won't do.' He was to bring the Countess Drogheda if he liked, 'and other Duchesses . . . anybody to see the thing in its greatest glory. *Also critics.*'

Ever optimistic, Madame Strindberg planned to relaunch the Cabaret in new and palatial premises within four weeks. She proposed renaming it the 'Blast Club'.

But she still owed him money, and legend has it that one night, in her absence, Lewis took control of the till at the door to the Cave. When enough money had been taken in entrance fees to cover what was owed him, he pocketed it and left. Another story has an altercation, ending with Lewis kicking the lady down a flight of stairs.*

The Blast Club never opened.

*

Meanwhile, Roger Fry was still suffering from the aftershocks of the Ideal Home row. 'The Lewis group have got hold of *The New Age* critic and he's written an amazing thing', he told Duncan Grant. An article on the Second Grafton Group show at the Alpine Club lacerated the Omega director and his coterie and the wording left no doubt as to which side of the schism the correspondent's sympathies lay:

> the departure of Mr Wyndham Lewis, Mr Etchells, Mr Nevinson and several others has left concentrated in a purer form all the worked-out and dead elements in the movement. It has become increasingly obvious that Mr Fry and his group are nothing but a kind of backwater.

And the critic was not content merely with pointing out the general failings of the group. He clearly had knives out for Fry personally:

---

* The source of these stories was Mrs Spencer Gore. Richard Cork substantiates the first with a reference in the minute book of the Club to Lewis being employed, at £8 a week, as 'an unofficial assistant' to Madame Strindberg. (See *Art Beyond the Gallery*, p 189.) This, Cork argues, would have given him access to the till for the unorthodox settlement of his account. However, the 'Mr Percy Wyndham' referred to in the minutes on 25 December 1913 cannot have been the man known to everyone present at the meeting – Gore, Ginner, Konody and Madame Strindberg herself – as 'Lewis' or 'Mr Lewis'. In the same Christmas Day entry 'Mr Wyndham' was said to be advising his employer on what other establishments charged as entrance fee to members' guests. This 'unofficial assistant', with expert knowledge of London nightclubs, that Lewis would not have possessed, was, in short, merely a coincidental near-namesake.

He . . . accomplishes the extraordinary feat of adapting the austere
Cezanne into something quite fitted for chocolate boxes.* It is too
tedious to go on mentioning mediocre stuff.

This critical belligerent, T. E. Hulme, shared a lecture platform with Lewis
at the Kensington Town Hall when they each addressed the Quest Society
on the subject of Modern Art. Hulme spoke of the distinction between Vital
Art and Geometric Art. He read with his face buried in his text and was
barely audible. Lewis, sitting in the body of the hall with Kate Lechmere,
kept whispering to her: 'You've got to hold your head up when you speak in
public.' He was next to mount the platform, spoke rapidly in a husky voice
and, seeming to address himself entirely to the paper he was reading from,
fared no better than his predecessor. According to Ezra Pound, writing in
The Egoist, both men's remarks were 'almost wholly unintelligible'. Lewis
'compared the soul to a bullet'. He went on to say 'that you could set a loaf
of bread in an engine shop and that this would *not* cause said loaf to produce
cubist pictures.' There was a third lecturer that the *Egoist* correspondent
modestly forbore to identify. Pound 'stole the show', according to Kate
Lechmere, 'made a very good speech and read some poetry'. Lewis
muttered to her afterwards that the audience had only been impressed on
account of his accent. 'It's rather a joke hearing poetry read by an
American', he told her.

*

Whatever the estimate Lewis submitted to Lady Drogheda for painting her
dining room, it was accepted without question. About the same time he told
Mrs Percy Harris that for a 'large decoration' he would ask £50, this being
the sum which the Contemporary Art Society had paid him for the large
gouache, *Laughing Woman*, which he thought 'not exorbitant'. And six
months later he agreed to paint six wall panels for a room in the American
novelist Mary Borden Turner's house for £250.

Lady Drogheda's dining room at 40 Wilton Crescent was undergoing a
funereal transformation to the Countess's eccentric specifications. Carpet
and ceiling were of so dark a green as to seem black, and the walls were
covered in panels of similarly near-black velvet. Each panel was bordered by
a three-inch-wide vertical strip of bevelled mirror set into the wall.

Lewis's more colourful contribution, barely mooted by Her Ladyship on
the night of the Picture Ball, was complete just under three months later.

* Fry was sometimes called, by his detractors, 'Chocolate Fry', because of his family connection with
the confectionery manufacturers.

On either side of the fireplace were thin vertical strips bearing a chevroned design in vermilion, and flanking the ebony-framed mirrored overmantel were tall abstractions on nine-inch-wide panels. High up, between the unrelieved sombre velvet of the walls and the old gold of the cornice, a nine-inch-wide frieze painted in 'vivid light reds, dark greens and other tints' ran almost the entire perimeter of the room. *Vanity Fair* described this, one of the most arresting features of the room, as a 'rioting mass of colours, each vying with the other in brilliance, quite irrespective of form, meaning, or design – colour for colour's sake, so to speak'. The frieze was interrupted at only one point. Filling the space between the top of the doorframe and the cornice was a rectangular abstract composition entitled *The Dancing Ladies*.

The Countess opened her home to invited guests on Thursday, 26 February, from 3 o'clock until 7, 'to see the Frieze Paintings and a small collection of drawings'. A press release listed 27 notables as having been present (29 counting the artist and Her Ladyship). They included the US Ambassadress, the Spanish Ambassador, Greek and Chilean Ministers and an assortment of Barons, Baronesses and other titled persons. Sir Claude Philips, art critic of the *Daily Telegraph*, was there together with other representatives of the press. The only artists mentioned apart from Lewis were Jacob Epstein and John, although Wadsworth also received an invitation and promised to come early with his wife.

Many years later John recalled the afternoon for comic effect in a *Sunday Times* article: 'Among the exhibits hung a picture described as a portrait. Although taken from the back, the artist had included an attractive pair of breasts, apparently attached to the subject's shoulder-blades! . . . I thought it was going too far myself but, wisely, I think, made no comment. After all, I might have been mistaken. What I took to be the lady's black hair might have been her face in shadow or something; you never can tell.' That was in 1958. The day after his actual visit he had told Dorelia it was 'a perfectly bloody show'.

The press release concluded: 'Mr Wyndham Lewis is shortly to do wall paintings in two other well known houses.' This claim may have been a fabrication. Further commissions were to come but only later in the year. Nevertheless it would have done no harm to impress on Lady Drogheda's wealthy guests that the artist was willing to take on further work of a similar nature.

*

A more modest commission came from Lady Cunard. Hosting a large dinner party for an 'American millionaire', she required Post-Impressionist knick-knacks as little presents for the 'rich and influential' guests. Lewis's appetite was whetted by the words 'American millionaire', 'rich' and 'influential'. Wadsworth was to make 25 handkerchiefs, Nevinson 25 candle shades, Lewis 25 fans and Hamilton 25 of something else. They were to be paid 10/- per item, £50 in all, and had three days to deliver the goods. Lady Cunard said that if they could not do the job she would have to go to Omega. The prospect of taking £50 worth of business from Roger Fry would have appealed to Lewis. 'I hope that you and your friends will be able to make an impression on Mr Roger Fry,' the solicitor from Vandercom & Co. had told him. 'I fancy that this can only be done through his pocket.'

In early March Fry wrote to Duncan Grant: 'The Lewis gang do nothing else even now but abuse me. Brzeska, who sees them, says he's never seen such a display of vindictive jealousy among artists.'

About this time 'the Lewis gang' occupied premises rented for them by Kate Lechmere on the first floor of a four-storey building at 38 Great Ormond Street: The Rebel Art Centre. Lechmere had a small flat on the top floor back which she decorated, according to *Vanity Fair*, with 'black doors in cream walls, and black curtains in addition to the usual orgies of colour'. Downstairs on the first floor, a dividing wall was demolished and rooms enlarged. 'The studio walls were painted pale lemon yellow and the doors Chinese red.' Several artists, among them Hamilton, Wadsworth and Lewis, were said to be decorating the studio with large mural paintings and friezes. 'It will be the only room in Europe', the Prospectus claimed, 'where artists belonging to the New Movement in art have had so free a hand, and done work on this scale.'

There was an office and, finally, 'an extra room for Lewis and his prospective pupils to paint in'. This was to be the Art School.

*

'The First Exhibition of Works by Members of the London Group' opened on 4 March 1914 at the Goupil Gallery. 'The London Group really consists of two groups', the *Times* correspondent explained. 'One of these may be said generally to derive from Mr Walter Sickert, the other from M. Picasso.' Gore, Gilman, Ginner and Bevan comprised the former subgroup, Lewis, Bomberg, Wadsworth, Hamilton, Etchells, Nevinson, Gaudier-Brzeska and Epstein, the latter.

'A champagne glass with something that looks uncommonly like a lady's leg' was how the *Telegraph* critic described one of three drawings by Lewis:

The Enemy of the Stars. The catalogue described it as a drawing for sculpture and it may indeed have been intended to compete with Epstein's small flenite figures that T. E. Hulme had rated so highly in December's issue of *The New Age*.

At the private view Lechmere and Hulme stood in front of the drawing. She had been asked by Lewis to steer the critic towards it. Hulme professed to like it but thought it top-heavy. The couple laughed together about something or other and Lewis, watching with Wadsworth from across the room, formed the bitter conviction that they were ridiculing his work.

In his *New Age* review Hulme, in fact, deemed *The Enemy of the Stars* to be a 'quite remarkable drawing'. But he also wrote, with reference to Lewis's larger compositions, *Eisteddfod* and *Christopher Columbus*, that they failed because of a lack of coherence and control:

> His sense of form seems to me to be sequent rather than integral, by which I mean that one form probably springs out of the preceding one as he works, instead of being conceived as a whole.

This was a passable definition of doodling.

Lewis had been the inadvertent instigator of Lechmere's liaison with Hulme. If Lechmere's recollections were accurate, it must have been a little before the Goupil opening that, with characteristic secrecy, Lewis arranged for the *New Age* critic to visit the premises in Great Ormond Street, having first ascertained that his co-director had a luncheon engagement. But her appointment fell through and he was obliged to introduce her to Hulme. They liked one another immediately, and Lewis became alarmed at a potentially dangerous shift in the system of alliances that, for him, controlled the delicate balance of power in art politics. His reasoning seemed to be that if Hulme extended his sphere of influence, through Lechmere, to Great Ormond Street, then it would not be long before he himself was ousted in favour of Hulme's man. 'Epstein is Hulme,' he told Lechmere over dinner, 'Hulme is Epstein.'

If a story told by William Roberts many years later is to be believed, there must have been considerable tension in the Goupil Gallery on the evening of the First London Group opening. While Lewis was glaring at his ex-mistress and business partner sharing a joke with the burly *New Age* critic, he himself was the object of vengeful intrigue from another painter.

When the Group's pictures were hung the day before, David Bomberg secured an excellent central position for his large kaleidoscopic abstract canvas, *In the Hold*. This was the biggest picture in the show and he considered himself fortunate that it would be seen to its greatest possible advantage. He had made arrangements, after the private view, to spend the rest of the evening with Lewis and Roberts on his home turf, the East End. They were to dine at Harry Steinwoolf's Jewish restaurant in the Whitechapel Road. 'There was to be Palestinian wine,' Roberts recalled:

> Wiener Schnitzel, Russian cigarettes and Russian Lemon tea, and to make our evening's entertainment complete, Bomberg had promised to bring a couple of black-haired, dark-eyed East End Rebeccas.

After dinner they had tickets for a Yiddish play at the Pavilion Theatre opposite the restaurant. But on the day of the opening, arriving early at the Goupil Gallery, Bomberg made a discovery which rather dampened his celebratory mood.

The coveted central position he had claimed for his picture the day before was now occupied by Lewis's *Christopher Columbus. In the Hold* had been rehung elsewhere.

Justifiably furious, the painter modified his arrangements. Instead of the promised 'dark-eyed East End Rebeccas' he arrived at Steinwoolf's in the company of his elder brother Mo. A professional pugilist, he exercised his ring craft under the sobriquet 'American Mowie'.

Nothing was said until after the soup. Then, very loudly, Bomberg demanded: 'Say, Wyndham, what do you mean by taking my picture down and sticking your own up in its place?' Lewis attempted to protest. Then, unable to justify his action and finding himself in a part of town unfamiliar to him, in hostile company and sitting opposite a man who fought with his fists for a living, he got up, threw his theatre ticket down on the table and fled.

*

It may have been as a result of insecurity arising from the Lechmere/Hulme alliance that Lewis insisted their business be placed upon a proper legal footing. He was given a certificate for 510 deferred shares in the company called, for official, administrative and legal purposes, the Cubist Art Centre Limited. It was agreed that his controlling interest should be maintained, in the event of further shares being allotted to Miss Lechmere, by the transfer of 50 per cent of such shares to him. However, in order to safeguard her unequal investment in the company, it was further agreed and understood that any dividends accruing from his shares, for a period of six months from 3 April, would belong to her.

Miss Lechmere paid the £50 in solicitor's fees. Mr Rayner the solicitor was formally blessed for his services to the movement several months later.

Miss Lechmere also supplied money for a new suit to be tailored for

Lewis – one befitting his role as Managing Director of the Rebel Art Centre. The jacket had a black and white check lining and a fold ran down the side of the trouser legs together with a stitched band. When he wore the suit for the first time she either did not notice or neglected to comment. She remembered him with his hands in the jacket pockets, violently flapping it open and shut to show off the lining and remarking how unobservant women are.

She remembered minor arguments: Lewis stamping up and down the room growling 'bloody bitch!' over and over again. And once, when she was unwell and in bed in her flat on the top floor, he stood over her and whacked the mattress with a walking stick, shouting: 'I will not be bullied!'

*

At the end of March the Rebel Arts Centre opened its doors to the press. There were photographs in the *Daily Mirror*: Wadsworth perched on top of a stepladder hanging one of his pictures above a mantelpiece, Hamilton looking on, Nevinson holding the ladder, and Lewis leaning on the mantelpiece hat in hand and looking nowhere in particular. Another showed Lewis, also standing on a ladder, holding brush and palette, working on a section of mural in the corner of a room. A third showed Lechmere in the act of drawing back an expanse of drapery designed by Hamilton.

A prospectus was printed offering membership of the Centre for a guinea. Privileges were 'Free Entrance for the space of one year . . . to all Lectures, Meetings and Picture Exhibitions' and half-price admission 'for any dances or social entertainments that may be arranged'. Members might also attend regular 'Saturday afternoon meetings of artists from 4 to 6 pm'.

It was impossible to supply a complete lecture programme because:

> much depends, in getting such men to lecture as we intend, on arrangements that have to fit in with their stay in London and other engagements, and can be made only a week or two ahead.

Signor Marinetti was expected to lecture, and did so on Wednesday 6 May at 8.45. Admission was by ticket and cost 5 shillings. Ezra Pound lectured on 30 May, his subject, ' "Imagisme," the most vital movement in English poetry to-day, and in which he is the principal mover'. It was hoped that the Futurist Painters would consent to address a meeting during the run of their forthcoming exhibition at the Doré Gallery and it was the management's intention 'also to ask some great innovator in music, Schoenburg [*sic*] or Scrabine [*sic*], when they are next in London, to lecture'. The experience of only one other lecturer is documented. Ford Madox Hueffer spoke 'absentmindedly in a tail coat', according to Douglas Goldring, who was unable to recall the topic. Kate Lechmere remembered the lecture's spectacular climax. Lewis's monumental nine-foot-high painting, *Plan of War*, fell forward off the wall behind Hueffer. The two-foot-wide heavy wooden frame detached itself from the canvas and clattered to the floor, leaving the huge abstraction balanced harmlessly on the speaker's head.

The Art School was to open on 26 April. There were to be three terms of three months each per year and fees were payable at five guineas a quarter. Hours would be from 10 o'clock until 5, five days a week. Mr Wyndham Lewis was to visit daily as professor. The educational regime over which he would preside was liberal to say the least. 'The principal object of this school', the Prospectus declared:

> will be to help any student to do what he most wants to do. If he prefers to play the fiddle to drawing he can do that, so long as he does not annoy his neighbour. The academic basis of drawing will not be neglected. But those who are evidently meant for a child's paradise will be left with their wit, skill and ingenuousness. Instruction will approach them on tip-toe.

Only two prospective students presented themselves: a young man who wanted to design gas brackets and a lady pornographer too embarrassed to show her erotic drawings to Kate Lechmere. 'Lewis had to go and look at them behind a door', Lechmere recalled.

Lewis's co-director complained later that he made no effort to recruit students and the Art School very quickly came to nothing.

*

Christopher Nevinson's father, the journalist Henry Nevinson, addressed a letter to the publisher John Lane. 'Let me introduce to you my son . . . and his friend Wyndham Lewis . . . revolutionary artists of Futurist fame, who want to consult you about bringing out an artistic magazine they have in mind.' By May Lane had agreed to handle *Blast* in England, the United States and Canada and to do his best to push sales in each country. It would retail at 2/6 but Lane was to receive 1,000 copies without charge on the understanding that he expend £50 on advertising. On all copies sold beyond 1,000, the editor would be paid at the rate of 1 shilling per copy.

*

On Saturday 16 May Lewis was at the Leeds Arts Club to open an exhibition of Futurist, Cubist and Post-Impressionist work that Frank

Rutter had organised. He gave a short speech in which he outlined three movements of modern painting. Cubism and Expressionism were the longest established, he said, Futurism the most recent. It is difficult to decide whether his explanation of Futurist aesthetics was as muddled and obscure as it appeared when the *Yorkshire Post* reported it:

> Supposing they wanted to give a feeling of two human beings attracted or repelled, or without any feeling to each other, the only way was to give something of their essence, two organisms that were more than the eyes, the ears, and the legs, which one knew as the characteristics of men. In a futurist picture they got all the instincts and life of the man.

Afterwards there were questions from the floor and one wag, a Mr C. B. Howdill, suggested that 'the man in the street' might be excused for thinking that the paintings on show at the Leeds Arts Club were the work of madmen. He did not, he hastened to add, hold this view himself as he would not condemn anything just because he did not understand it. Then, producing a bundle of sketches that he described as 'thought forms', he asked for the speaker's comments. Evidently disconcerted, Lewis replied that people who drew things that could not be seen were certainly mad and he held up one of the drawings for the audience to see. It appeared to consist of a formless blob of paint. Besides, he said that it was not the drawing of a thought but of a flower and he pointed out the stalk. Mr Howdill said that the speaker's criticism proved that he condemned without understanding. Later in the discussion when Lewis declined, through 'natural modesty and shyness', to give an explanation of his own drawing *Time*, Mr Howdill came back at him saying it was his duty to explain the picture and accusing the artist of wanting 'to keep his new-found heaven to himself'.

*

Another aesthetic discussion occurred in a London toilet while Signor Marinetti was sluicing himself down with cold water from the washbasin after delivering one of his strenuous public performances. Nearly everything the excitable Italian said seemed to end with an exclamation mark:

> 'You are a futurist, Lewis!'
> 'No', Lewis replied.
> 'Why don't you announce that you are a futurist!'
> 'Because I am not one.'
> 'Yes. But what's it matter!'
> 'It's most important.'

'Not at all! Futurism is good. It is all right.'

'Not bad. It has its points. But you Wops insist too much on the Machine. You're always on about these driving belts, you are always exploding about internal combustion. We've had machines here in England for a donkey's years. They're no novelty to *us*.'

'You have never understood your machines! You have never known the *ivresse* of travelling at a kilomctre a minute. Have you ever travelled at a kilometre a minute?'

'Never. I loathe anything that goes too quickly. If it goes too quickly, it is not there.'

'It is not there! It is *only* when it goes quickly that it *is* there!'

'That is nonsense. I cannot see a thing that is going too quickly.'

'See it – see it! Why should you want to *see*? But you *do* see it. You see it multiplied a thousand times. You see a thousand things instead of one thing.'

'That's just what I don't want to see. I prefer *one* thing.'

'There is no such thing as *one* thing.'

'There is if I wish to have it so. And I wish to have it so.'

'You are a monist!'

'All right. I am not a futurist anyway. *Je hais le mouvement qui déplace les lignes.*'

'And you "never weep" – I know, I know. *Ah zut alors!* What a thing to be an Englishman!'

'I hate movement that blurs the lines.' Lewis's riposte exposed the aesthetic and stylistic gulf between Futurism and his own sharply defined, crystalline abstractions. Allowing for a degree of caricature in the portrait of an emotional Italian whose questions emerge as exclamations, this debate, recalled by Lewis many years later, remains a fair summary of the differences between the two movements.

There was a growing realisation that if the English movement, based at 38 Great Ormond Street and led by Lewis, was to gain any credibility at all, it would not be under Marinetti's welcoming banner. The event which turned the intellectual differences into an actual rupture was the publication in the *Observer*, on Sunday 7 June, of 'Vital English Art, Futurist Manifesto', jointly signed by Marinetti and Nevinson. It called for the 'support, defence and glorification of the great Futurist painters or pioneers and advance-forces of vital English Art – ATKINSON, BOMBERG, EPSTEIN, ETCHELLS, HAMILTON, NEVINSON, WADSWORTH, WYNDHAM LEWIS.'

That it implied Lewis, Etchells, Wadsworth and the rest were Futurists was an affront. Nevinson's appending of the Rebel Art Centre address to his signature made it seem as if the others concurred. Repudiation, definition and the drawing up of battle lines at once became necessary.

Five days later, at 8.45 in the evening, Marinetti and Nevinson were to share a platform at the Doré Gallery. 'The Manifesto of Vital English Art' was to be read aloud and Nevinson would give a lecture. Lewis made his preparations:

> I assembled in Greek Street a determined band of miscellaneous anti-futurists. Mr Epstein was there; Gaudier-Brzeska, T. E. Hulme, Edward Wadsworth and a cousin of his called Wallace,* who was very muscular and forcible, according to my eminent colleague, and he rolled up very silent and grim. There were about ten of us. After a hearty meal we shuffled bellicosely round to the Doré Gallery.

That night, during Nevinson's lecture, the word 'Vorticist' was heard in public for the first time. It was a measure of how out of touch he was with the discussions at Great Ormond Street that, while he was aware of the name coined by Pound and finally adopted by Lewis, he had evidently never heard it spoken. As a result he hardened the 'c' and pronounced it 'Vortickist', giving rise to Gaudier's sibilant and repeated correction from the floor: 'Vorticiste! Vorti-CCC-iste!'

There were other interruptions. When Nevinson declared: 'Only bad work goes on forever. No one would take the 'Mona Lisa' as a gift. Nobody wants a singer to go on singing all day', someone shouted 'I don't agree!' And when, concluding a reading of the Vital English Art Manifesto, he shouted: '*Hurrah* for motors! *Hurrah* for speed! *Hurrah* for lightning!' someone set off a fire cracker in the centre doorway.

While Gaudier stayed resolutely on his feet in the middle of the audience, hissing 'Vorti-ccc-iste' at the speaker, Lewis and the rest of his party 'maintained a confused uproar'.

*

If Hulme was indeed one of that 'determined band of anti-futurists', standing comradely shoulder to shoulder with Lewis on the night of 12 June, then it must have been at a later date that Lewis attempted to strangle him.

The tension caused by Hulme's relationship with Lechmere finally broke one Tuesday evening, and the serio-comic climax has become the stuff of

---

* Wadsworth's cousin was in fact called Norman Wallis and his name was soon to appear among the blessed.

legend. It might be imagined as a series of jerky sepia scenes from the early days of the motion picture, played out to a frenetic tinkling piano accompaniment: Lewis and Lechmere arguing in a restaurant somewhere in the West End, Lewis perhaps reiterating his assertion that 'Epstein is Hulme and Hulme is Epstein'; at length Lewis standing up from the table and swearing his intention to murder Hulme, then rushing out into the night; Lechmere chasing him along Piccadilly, shouting silently, a caption reading: 'PLEASE DON'T KILL HIM! PLEASE DON'T!'; Lewis arriving wild-eyed at 67 Frith Street, running up the stairs, bursting into Hulme's first-floor salon and grasping the philosopher by the throat; finally Hulme manhandling his attacker out into the street, upending him and hanging him by the trouser turn-ups from the iron railings in Soho Square.

The legend has a tenuous claim to veracity in that it was Lewis himself who reported the humiliating incident. 'I never see the summer house [in the centre of the Square] without remembering how I saw it upside down.'

*

Towards the end of June the Harlesden printer had completed his labours and *Blast* was ready for publication. It was at this late stage that John Lane discovered an obscenity at the bottom of page 48. 'It was verbally understood between us', he reminded Lewis, 'that the Review would deal almost entirely with art and that there would be no sexual disagreeableness or anything which could possibly be construed into libel in it.' It was doubtless to avoid contravening the libel laws that no reference had been made to Roger Fry.* Both printer and publisher were legally responsible and, if the esoteric drift of Pound's short poem 'Fratres Minores' went unnoticed in Harlesden, it was certainly not lost on John Lane himself:

> With minds still hovering above their testicles
> Certain poets here and in France
> Still sigh over established and natural fact
> Long since fully discussed by Ovid.
> They howl. They complain in delicate and exhausted metres
> That the twitching of three abdominal nerves
> Is incapable of producing a lasting Nirvana.

Before any distribution could take place, Lane insisted that the first line, with its intimate anatomical reference, together with the final two-line

---

* C. B. Fry was blasted in his namesake's place; at an imaginative stretch the cricketer's initials might have been made to stand for 'Chocolate Box'.

description of sexual orgasm, be inked out by hand. This piece of drudgery fell to the women at the Rebel Arts Centre: Jessica Dismorr and Helen Saunders. At the end the offending lines could still just be read through the ink. Lewis believed this helped sales.

'At the moment of going to press I have received a copy of "Blast" – at last actually out.' Richard Aldington could almost be heard panting as he beat *The Egoist*'s deadline. The title page was dated 20 June, but the blacking out of Pound's indelicacies had delayed things and it was not until 1 July 1914 that *Blast* made its appearance, or at least had its appearance noted. 'It is a huge pink periodical of 160 pages', Aldington went on. 'The title "Blast" is printed diagonally across both covers. There is no time for detailed criticism, but from a hasty glance through the manifestos and some of the contributions, I can declare that this is the most amazing, energised, stimulating production I have ever seen.'

It was edited by Lewis, who also wrote a substantial part of its contents. 'Enemy of the Stars' was a strange hybrid of play and novella, replete with dark metaphor. There was an appreciation of Spencer Gore, who had died on 27 March, and 20 pages of 'Vortices and Notes', culminating in the lines:

Our Vortex is proud of its polished sides.
Our Vortex will not hear of anything but its disastrous polished dance.
Our Vortex desires the immobile rhythm of its swiftness.
Our Vortex rushes out like an angry dog at your Impressionistic fuss.
Our Vortex is white and abstract with its red-hot swiftness.

Although uncredited, Lewis was also responsible for the two manifestos. The first, typographically the most startling, Blasted England, France, Humour, Aestheticism, and the Victorian Age. It Blessed England, France, English Humour, and the Hairdresser as one who brought order to overgrown chaotic nature. The Blast and Bless lists, compiled by Lewis and Pound, and solemnly read out over tea some months before to the young, tough-looking men in their black hats, was a catalogue of despised establishment figures and personal *bêtes noires* on the one hand, and friends, rebels, suffragettes, music hall performers, and prizefighters, on the other. There were more candidates for Blessing than for Blasting, and some of those favoured are puzzling choices. It is not known for instance what 'The Pope', Pius X, had done to impress Lewis and Pound, while the identity of 'Jenny' and the reason for her benediction will perhaps never be known.

The other manifesto was a more serious statement. It consisted of seven series of numbered aphorisms, combining to assert that, not only should an art be organic with its time but also with its place, 'that what is actual and vital for the South, is ineffectual and unactual in the North.' The harsh and austere abstractions produced by Lewis and his colleagues were claimed to be consonant with the Northern climate and fundamentally at odds with the products of Marinetti and his followers who, 'in their . . . Futuristic gush over machines, aeroplanes, etc.', were 'the most romantic and sentimental "moderns" to be found'. Eleven names were appended: 'Signatures for Manifesto'. As editor of *Blast* and leader of the movement, 'Wyndham Lewis' – his middle name now part of his surname – ensured that he would climactically succeed 'E. Wadsworth', at the end of the alphabetical list, rather than be buried in the ranks between 'C. Hamilton' and 'E. Pound'.

Most commentators mentioned the cover, but there was some confusion as to exactly what colour it was. Ford Madox Hueffer writing in *Outlook* observed in passing that it was purple and *The Times* agreed. *The Athenaeum*, *New Weekly* and *New Statesman*, on the other hand, thought it was magenta, while *The Little Review* described it as 'something between magenta and lavender, about the colour of a sick headache'. *The Egoist* was content to call it pink, the *Observer* 'pucey pink', while the *Pall Mall Gazette* attempted even greater precision with 'chill flannelette pink', adding that the colour 'recalls the catalogue of some cheap Eastend draper, and its contents are of the shoddy sort that constitutes the Eastend draper's stock.' *Poetry* said it was cerise. John Cournos remembered it as 'scarlet'. Living in Ezra Pound's old room at no. 10 Church Walk, the young American poet did not mind the chimes from St Mary Abbots that had plagued his predecessor and led to 'Rev. Pennyfeather (Bells)' being immortalised in damnation. Instead, it was the Sunday hymn singing from the nonconformist household opposite that got on Cournos's nerves, and he showed his displeasure by placing a copy of *Blast* in the window with its black letters filling an entire pane: 'miraculously the noise stopped each time I tried this.'

Inside, a portentous motif appeared on a number of pages: a black cone on a vertical thread or axis. It was based on a coastguard signal consisting of shiny, tarred canvas stretched between a small wooden ring and a large one, three feet in diameter, and hoisted to warn of gales: the storm cone. Raised point downwards it was known as a 'south cone', anticipating a gale from the south. Point upwards, a 'north cone' – as in the pages of *Blast* – warned of a northerly gale: a blast from the north. It was the English avant-garde's answer to the Futurist invasion of London from the Latin south.

1 July was the hottest day of the year, with a temperature, recorded at the Kensington Observatory, of 90 degrees in the shade. In the Home Counties violent thunderstorms provided an apt accompaniment to *Blast*'s appearance. With war only a month away such coincidence was to seem, in retrospect, ominous. Twenty-eight years later, midway through another world war, on 26 April 1942, Ezra Pound sat behind a microphone in an

Italian radio studio and delivered his weekly short-wave lecture to the English-speaking world. It was an activity for which he would later be caged, threatened with the gallows and spend 12 years in an institution for the criminally insane. That evening in 1942 he recalled an anecdote told him by a niece of the actor-manager Sir Herbert Beerbohm Tree. It was a memory from a vanished 'languid era', a split-second vision of black, magenta and green seen through rain-blurred glass to which time and future events would lend significance:

> Waaal, the Trees and their circle were havin' tea on the lawn . . . with due paraphernalia, large silver tea urns etc. and up come a storm, thunder and lightenin', and the family naturally plunged indoors . . . *Blast* had been left solitary there on the lawn, and the niece and Sir Herbert gazed elegiacally from the drawing room window on the scene . . . A FLASH of lightening lit up the lawn. There in its solitude, huge on the flaring magenta cover, the black letters vivid, the word BLAST was written. Possibly someone ventured out to rescue the treasure, now valued of second hand book sellers, but more probably no one did.

There was to be another house party later in July, in the Scottish Borders. Just south of the Berwickshire county town of Duns, Charterhall was the country home of Major Algernon Richard Trotter of Mortonhall, Midlothian. It was usually leased out during the close season, to be reoccupied by the Major's family and friends in time for the start of grouse shooting on 12 August. That particular year the grouse were spared by the men of this distinguished military family. The Trotters did not occupy the house again until 1918, by which time two of the Major's three brothers had been killed in action.

Mary Borden Turner, whose Scottish husband had rented it for the summer, hated the place. 'It is like a Glasgow suburb', she wrote to Lewis. 'The big house is of an unclean grey colour. It is the middle class mansion: the awful and sinister mean between the castle and the hovel . . . It says "I am large and comfortable, built for breeding and my children are the backbone of the country." I hate it.' She also hated the great fat yew trees that hemmed the house in on all sides, 'smug, squat, all of a uniform green, that stand about motionless, too self-possessed to be affected by the wind'. Charterhall irritated her like clothes chafing raw skin. Douglas, her husband, told her that if she made up her mind to it she could be happy there. 'But why should I?' she demanded.

She had already found happiness in an affair with Lewis begun a month or so earlier. 'You make everyone else seem flat,' she had told him, 'just as your pictures make other pictures look dull . . . It doesn't matter does it, whether I understand your technique or not as long as I adore you, not too stupidly? . . . I am happy with that delicious "malaise" that comes when one is obsessed by another personality.' Her happiness was not entirely unalloyed. 'You hurt me. I can't go on like this. You must be considerate and human', she told him after he had invited her to a party at John Lane's where he got drunk and left without seeing her. 'I could love you madly and give you pleasure if you'd take just a little trouble to be courteous.' Nevertheless, she found him 'nicer than anyone else, even when unshaved'.

She seized every opportunity to escape from her Scottish border exile.

*

A *Blast* dinner was held at the Dieudonné Restaurant, Ryder Street, in the West End of London, on Wednesday 15 July. Guests were charged ten shillings and sixpence and invited for 8 o'clock.

Kate Lechmere sat between Arthur Symons and Gaudier-Brzeska. The sculptor arrived late, after everyone else was seated, depositing a small marble fawn on Pound's plate in lieu of payment for his meal.

A man was overheard to say that he had abandoned reading *Blast* and had given it to his children in the hope that they would make more sense of it. Lewis tapped the table and told the guest he had insulted Miss Lechmere, who had paid for the magazine and had 50 copies piled up underneath her chair.

Mary Borden Turner was present, grateful to be free from the stultifying atmosphere of Charterhall, where she had left her husband the day before. But the *Blast* dinner does not seem to have been a happy experience for her either. She and Lewis quarrelled. 'Something ugly, unpleasant has grown up suddenly out of our intercourse', she wrote to him the following night from the Savoy. 'Two odourless acids mixed, may make a bad smell. We get on each other's nerves. We are bored with each other. We offend each other.' What happened between them at the Dieudonné is unclear but, while it did not terminate their friendship, it seems to have marked the end of their brief affair:

> Let us abandon this attempted intimacy and take refuge in a more gentle formality or a more formal gentleness.

A little over a week after the *Blast* dinner the fragile business relationship between the two directors of the Rebel Art Centre also came to an end. The trouble started on the morning of 23 July, when Kate Lechmere called in at the studio to collect her copies of *Blast*. Jessica Dismorr gave them to her and she took them up to her flat. She was expecting Harold Monro to call the following day and she hoped to sell him 30 copies at cost price for the Poetry Bookshop. Later in the day, while she was out, Helen Saunders went up to the flat and retrieved them. She had been given strict instructions that no copies be allowed out of the studio and her doglike devotion to Lewis made his word law. Miss Saunders was perhaps overanxious to please.

Earlier that week she had written him a highly emotional, largely incoherent letter in which she pleaded for some clarification in their relationship. 'I keep trying to tell you that I want you to help me out of the clouds – if you don't want me please let me go and I will try and be something else. I can't live in this half-way country any more – it is too pleasant.' She seemed profoundly unsure of herself and her talents; she saw herself as an unetched metal plate inviting the bite of the acid: 'I think you ought to help me because I am such satisfactorily unpromising raw material like a sheet of zinc – just what a good vorticist ought to like.'

She had offered to take charge of the Rebel Art Centre for the latter half of the week while he was away. 'Will you write instructions if there is anything you want me to do.'

So when Lechmere confronted her on that Thursday demanding the return of her copies of *Blast*, the zealous custodian's sole concern was the protection of Lewis's interests. To Miss Lechmere's claim that she was entitled to 40 copies, Miss Saunders replied 'that Mr Lewis had told Miss Dismorr that Mr Lewis did not intend letting Miss Lechmere have these copies.' Miss Saunders was then told that if she did not hand over the *Blast*s forthwith Miss Lechmere would exercise her power as co-director and shut up the Rebel Art Centre until Mr Lewis's return.

Miss Saunders capitulated. That night Miss Lechmere wrote Lewis a full and very bad-tempered account of the affair.

Monro did not buy the disputed pile of *Blast*s after all. The only other outlet she could think of was John Lane. When Lewis returned and heard that she had sold copies of his journal back to its publisher he was furious. He presumably thought Lane would assume *Blast* was not selling well and therefore have doubts about its commercial viability.

A sheet of Rebel Art Centre notepaper was dispatched on the Saturday with the ominous message: 'I am coming tomorrow morning to make the arrangements that your behaviour necessitates. W. Lewis'.

The row that blew up the following day, 26 July, finally persuaded Miss Lechmere to withdraw from the enterprise. 'After your language and behaviour of this morning I think it is better that matters should be wound up as soon as possible.'

The following Thursday Wadsworth wrote to apologise for not meeting

Lewis the previous afternoon. 'I couldn't have got there until after 3.30 . . . by which time you would be already in the new premises.' This suggests that Lewis took Lechmere's deadline seriously. She went out on Wednesday afternoon and returned to find the place stripped of its furnishings. 'So ended the Rebel Art Centre.'

*

Evidently reconciled following the misunderstanding at the Dieudonné Restaurant, Lewis spent the last weekend before war was declared with Mrs Turner and her husband at Charterhall.

Ford Madox Hueffer was there with Violet Hunt, and Pound was to have come but did not. There were others in the party but neither Hueffer nor Lewis mentioned who. Not so jaded as his hostess, Hueffer thought Charterhall delightful: 'the turf of the Scottish lawns was like close, fine carpeting and the soft Scottish sunshine and the soft Scottish showers did the heart good.' Like many memories of the last days of peace this, recalled in 1931, evoked a paradise soon to be lost. They sat on the lawn in the sun and read aloud to each other. Hueffer read from *Blast* the first instalment of his novel, *The Saddest Story*. Mrs Turner read from James Joyce's first novel that was being serialised in *The Egoist*.

The London newspapers came to Duns by way of Edinburgh, bringing word of the deepening international crisis. A conversation occurred one morning over breakfast. Mrs Turner thought a war involving England was unlikely:

'There won't be any war, Ford', she said. 'Not here. England won't go into a war.'

'England will', Ford replied.

'England will! But Ford, England has a Liberal Government. A Liberal Government cannot declare war.'

At this point Lewis joined the discussion:

'Of course it can't. Liberal Governments can't go to war. That would not be liberal. That would be conservative.'

Ford was silent.

'Well, Ford', said his hostess. 'You don't agree!'

'I don't agree,' came the emphatic reply, 'because it has always been the Liberals who have gone to war. It is *because* it is a Liberal Government that it *will* declare war.'

A chauffeured Rolls-Royce was at their disposal, and on 3 August some of the party were driven off to play golf. They dropped Lewis near Duns and he walked in to town and bought a London paper: 'GERMANY

DECLARES WAR ON RUSSIA'. This event had actually occurred two days before, on Saturday the 1st, but reports in the dailies only appeared on the Bank Holiday Monday. In the regional papers, like the *Northern Echo*, news of the breakdown in diplomatic manoeuvres between the German ambassador and Russian foreign minister in St Petersburg had to compete with a report of the first day of the Morpeth Games, Saturday's other noteworthy event. 'MORPETH OLYMPIAD', a poster for one newspaper proclaimed in violet lettering, 'RECORD CROWD'.

By the time the party returned from the golf links to pick up their companion, Lewis had bought a selection of the London papers. As an ironic counterpoint to the grave news, he also secured the 'Morpeth Olympiad' poster, and this was stuck up in Charterhall. 'It appeared to the household an adequate expression of the great Nation to which they belonged.'

Lewis left Charterhall ahead of the main party, and travelled overnight back to London. He was in a train packed with naval reservists, under mobilisation orders and making for Chatham. There were sentries lining the bridges at Newcastle and stacks of rifles on the station platform. The country would very soon, as Hueffer had so confidently predicted, be at war.

SEVENTEEN

Clap

During the first months of the war Lewis had a studio in Fitzroy Street and was living in a two-room flat at no. 4 Percy Street let by a couple called Pierce. The ground floor was occupied by Phelon & Moore Ltd, Motorcycle Manufacturers. Three doors along the street to the left was the celebrated establishment run by Rudolf Stulik: the Restaurant de la Tour Eiffel.

Inviting Jessica Dismorr to tea in early January 1915, he suggested they meet somewhere close to his home, the ABC Tea Rooms, perhaps, in Oxford Street between Frascati's Restaurant and Rathbone Place. He referred to recent legislation brought in under the Defence of the Realm Act restricting the movement of aliens. 'I am supposed not to wander very far,' he told her, 'like German subjects.' Confinement to the close environs of Percy Street was due to his suffering considerable physical discomfort from recently contracted gonorrhoea.

Among the contents of a battered, black, metal deeds box in Dean Farrar Street, Westminster,* are three minimally punctuated letters written variously in pencil and purple wax crayon. They chart an ignoble phase in Lewis's relationship with Olive Johnson following the birth of their second child, Betty. Carefully preserved, they were sealed in an envelope inscribed by Lewis:

> Confession of infidelity . . . (It was 'the Spaniard' referred to who gave her the clap, and then she afterwards gave it to me. Hence the row).

Just after Easter, in April 1914, Olive was seen out with another man. 'I am not surprised at your seeing me,' she wrote to Lewis:

> it was impossible for me to go on any longer without somebody, but at the same time it is only natural that I think much more of you than any man

---

* The offices of Bircham & Co., Solicitors managing the Wyndham Lewis Memorial Trust. The cache of papers stored there was withheld by the Trustees from the main collection of Lewis's papers, sold to Cornell University in the 1960s and 1970s.

and that is why I should always be looking for you. I simply go with him because I am very lonely, and miserable there is no alternative I asked you and begged of you to come back to me, and you refused me time after time it is very hard when you cant have the one you love, but I want you, and I shall always want you. You practically told me to find a man and I suppose I shall go from bad to worse.

Worse indeed followed, and the man she had found for herself, an unnamed Spaniard, infected her with gonorrhoea. 'I have had an unfortunate life,' she told Lewis, 'and you are the only one who could do anything for me and you wont.'

Despite her despairing tone, she still hoped they might continue to meet occasionally. She worked in a branch of 'Fullers', the American Confectioners, during the daytime but thereafter she was free. 'Will you see me one evening . . . I could see you Sunday or Monday evening or any evening next week . . . I should like to go to a Cinema with you.' The letter was signed with 'love from your Dunkie'.

As with his first mistress, Ida Vendel, so it was with Olive. Lewis seemed incapable of effecting a clean break with her, and when he resumed sexual relations in the first months of war he contracted gonorrhoea.

Lewis was of course no stranger to the infection. His first 'dose' had been six years before with, coincidentally, another Spaniard responsible. He contracted it again in early 1910. Late in 1913 – around the same time, incidentally, that Olive was being delivered of their second child – he announced to Richard Aldington, over dinner, that he had clap. Aldington cast his mind back to an afternoon a week or so before when Lewis had borrowed his razor and shaving brush. After using them he declared 'he had been copulating for three days.' The recently married Aldington was appalled in retrospect at the potential danger to himself and his young wife of an infected shaving brush. Beyond the newlywed squeamishness of the Aldington household there was little stigma attached to the venereal condition among Lewis's circle of friends. Frederick Etchells, about this time, apologised for some minor offence, saying: 'Just now I'm sick to death of clap and poverty and inactivity – these can be the only reasons for any unfortunate impression I may have given you.' And he gave Lewis the reassurance of his continued friendship: 'Leaving cunts on one side, you're the only person in London I really care to see or talk to.'

Late in 1914, as the discharging and stinging symptoms of his latest dose manifested themselves, Lewis took Sickert's advice: 'treat it as a bad cold that lasts for a long time . . . The treatments that dispose of it quickly are all of them apt to lead to complications.'*

The septicaemia resulting from this neglect immobilised him at his flat and ruled out early enlistment in the armed forces. 'Any violent movement or exertion redoubled the septacaemia', he wrote later. 'I had to get well first, before my King and Country could benefit by my martial intervention. Probably the micro-organism saved my life.' A further benefit of the micro-organism was that it enforced the painful leisure to complete *Tarr*, the novel he had been working on for so long.

His fitful convalescence followed a cyclical pattern. Confined to bed for sometimes ten days at a time he had his meals sent up from the Tour Eiffel. He drank no wine with his meals as this aggravated the condition. After a time he felt better. 'There was not a sign of a discharge', he passed water without pain and thought it was all over. He left his bed and resumed normal activities: leapt onto buses, ate his meals at the Tour Eiffel with 'a bottle, perhaps, of one of Stulik's less celebrated marks'. But then, oxalic acid in the red wine inflamed the barely healed urethral lesion and the symptoms returned. Another bedridden period ensued, followed by a recession of symptoms, then 'some wine with . . . dinner, only a glass or two, and the bloody thing came on again.'

It was during the first months of war that he met Guy Baker. A former captain in the Indian Army, Baker was in his forties. He had a chronic skin condition which broke out in unsightly rashes and he was tortured by rheumatism. Later, when unaccountably accepted for active service in the army, he is said to have nearly broken his right arm energetically saluting a superior officer, and had to wear it in a sling for weeks after. He and Lewis got on famously. Baker had no artistic pretensions but sufficient money to build up a small collection of his friend's drawings and gouaches which he eventually bequeathed to the Victoria and Albert Museum. Substituting the name of one tradesman for another, Lewis wrote him into the second chapter of his novel as 'Butcher'. They had encountered one another during one of Lewis's intermittent bouts of mobility, at the Tour Eiffel. In subsequent periods of invalidity Baker paid regular visits to the flat with cigarettes and newspapers, and the two men would discuss the latest war news and compare symptoms, 'cursing together the micro-organism and all its works'.

Curses were doubtless heaped upon the unfortunate carrier of the 'micro-organism': Olive Johnson. The content of these conversations might be

---

* The quotation is taken from a manuscript at Cornell and first published as 'Wyndham Lewis's *Cantleman-Crowdmaster* sections seven and eight', edited by Robert Edward Murray, *Enemy News* 35, Winter 1992. Although the advice is attributed to a fictional character, 'that old devil Samber', Lewis told Geoffrey Grigson that it originally came from Sickert.

guessed at from misogynistic outbursts in the chapters of *Tarr* being written at this time:

> Think of all the . . . liaisons that you know in which some frowsy or foolish or doll-like or log-like bitch accompanies everywhere the form of an otherwise sensible man, a dumbfounding, disgusting and septic ghost!

Lewis was not content with Olive's verbal 'confession of infidelity'. He appeared to be demanding what amounted to a signed affidavit that she had transmitted the disease. A humiliation too far, she rebelled, lashing back at him with a sad little note in early January:

> I have admitted that I had it 3 weeks before you. There is no need for me to write it down, that sort of thing would never be mentioned in my life, and I am not in a law suit or anything like that I think you are disgusting asking me to write it down, what do you think I am. I am very angry at all this it makes me feel feed [*sic*] up with every thing. do not depress me too much or else I shall do away with my self.

This was the most explicit written statement of responsibility he was able to extract from her and the folded scrap of paper, scrawled across both sides, was carefully preserved with the others.

The demand for such sordid documentary evidence might be explained by a desire to punish Olive with a task akin to the schoolchild's enforced repetition of what it must not do. Or perhaps her remark about a lawsuit was nearer the truth than she suspected, and Lewis was storing ammunition to fight any subsequent action for breach of promise she might bring against him.

At the very least it may have absolved him of responsibility for Olive and assuaged any guilt he might feel when he at last succeeded in abandoning her. The scrap of paper referring to her transgression proved, despite his own infidelities, despite his negligence and carelessness of her feelings, despite any past or future cruelty he might inflict upon her, that for once, lying in bed at the top of 4 Percy Street, early in 1915, he was the injured party.

The longest in that pathetic clutch of letters labelled 'Confession of infidelity' was resigned to parting. She quite understood that he did not wish to see her again:

> you must know at the bottom of your heart that I rearly [*sic*] love you I have come to the time when I must say it, and rearly feel it. If I could only have said this 2 years ago, and you could have said the same to me I am

sure we should have been very very happy, but I am afraid it has all been a mistake or something wrong. Well it is no use talking. I can see what course you intend to take.

Only the injured party's strongest conviction of righteousness could have made his emotions proof against the tugging of Olive's farewell:

> I do hope you will find life easier in future without me to worry you . . . I felt very depressed yesterday and the Manager told me I must be in love. I only just saved myself from breaking down . . . I hope this letter will not tire you, but I hope you will read it through, because it is the last long letter I shall write to you, I have said all I have got to say with every good wish for your health and happiness. From your broken hearted Dunk.

But the postscript was a reminder that certain responsibilities still existed between them. Peter and his sister Betty were still in the care of Mrs Lewis but their mother had access to them when her employment at Fullers permitted. 'I shall have one day off next week', she wrote, 'if I let you know the day before will you arrange about kiddies?'

*

During one of the periods when infirmity was in recession he wrote to Pound: 'I am doing a power of painting. If I get my head blown off when I am pottering about Flanders, I shall have left something.' Despite the war, he felt he had reason for optimism:

> The excellent Mrs Turner is going to take a large studio or hall near Park Lane and there house my squadron of paintings, until after the war a large building is constructed for them in the rear of her house. She will pay the rent, furnish it, and I suppose supply a page boy or secretary: also a stage for Theatrical Performances, Lectures, etc.

It sounded like a new and improved Rebel Art Centre under his exclusive control.

The 'power of painting' included the completion of work commissioned by Mrs Turner in June 1914. About the time they began their affair, she asked him to decorate her drawing room at 33 Park Lane. During preliminary discussions he told her that he intended painting six wall panels for the room, but the details of these, together with the overall decorative scheme, Mrs Turner was to leave entirely to him. She agreed to pay him

£250 for his work and enclosed an initial cheque for £100 with her letter confirming the commission.

However, in the first week of the war, she informed him that she could not, after all, afford the 'complete set of furniture, rugs, lamps, etc.' that his designs would necessitate her buying. She had hoped to have 'a very unusual room' but, on reflection, decided to leave the walls bare and use her old furniture instead. She promised to pay him, by the end of September, the £150 balance for the commission. 'This seems only fair', she said. Three days later she sent him a cheque for £50.

Lewis may already have begun work on the six panels by this time. It was decided he should go ahead and complete them as they were to be paid for anyway. By the end of the year they were nearly finished and Mrs Turner apologised again for having to give up the Drawing Room scheme 'for the present', implying it might be taken up again when the war was over. She suggested that, in the meantime, he might wish to exhibit the panels somewhere. 'People ought to have a chance to see them', she said.

In January she paid him a further £15. It may have been then that she discussed with him the larger enterprise he told Pound about. Perhaps she intended the six pictures, originally designed as panels for her drawing room, to form the decorative focus of the projected 'large building . . . in the rear of her house'.

*

While the recrudescence of gonorrhoea prohibited the physical exertions of painting, let alone the half-mile walk from Percy Street to his studio, Lewis wrote three new opening chapters for his novel, as well as material for the next issue of *Blast*.* He also cast his editorial eye over other contributions. Some 'excellent bits of scholarly ribaldry' had come from T. S. Eliot. 'The Triumph of Bullshit' included the refrain 'For Christ's sake stick it up your ass', while each verse of 'The Ballad for Big Louise' ended with the lines: 'Put on your rough red drawers/And come to the Whore House Ball!' Lewis longed to publish them but, mindful of the enforced excision of even the mildly offensive lines from Pound's 'Fratres Minores' in the first issue, he was determined 'to have no "Words ending in -Uck, -Unt and -Ugger"'.

*

The opening of the second London Group show at the Goupil Gallery on 5

---

* He may also have written *The Ideal Giant* at this time – a play set in the Restaurant Gambetta, a thinly disguised Tour Eiffel complete with Austrian proprietor following his stomach about among the tables, 'playing with it like a large ball'.

March 1915 attracted a large crowd. The *New Witness* correspondent 'never saw so many folk assembled for a private view before, except at the annual academies'. It gave the lie to those who prophesied war would bring about a lessening of interest in the modern movement. On the contrary, *The New Witness* seemed to regard the London Group as providing essential light relief in desperate times. 'The public that interests itself in this kind of art is amused, tickled or shocked by the works it sees. It regards these [artists] as a new sort of clowns. It does not understand them or their work, nor does it want to.'

Jacob Epstein's towering *Rock Drill*, a second-hand quarrying machine, tripod-mounted and straddled by a robot-like white plaster figure, dominated the exhibition. Lewis exhibited two canvases, *Workshop* and the six foot by five grid-like composition in earth colours called *The Crowd*. According to the *Times* critic this was as far as Vorticist asceticism could possibly go. The anonymous correspondent even came near to making the suggestion, somewhat provocative in time of war, that Lewis and his colleagues, Wadsworth and Roberts, were unpatriotic:

> in our desire to relate them to something in the actual world, we can only call them Prussian in spirit. These painters seem to execute a kind of goose-step, where other artists are content to walk more or less naturally. Perhaps if the Junkers could be induced to take to art, instead of disturbing the peace of Europe, they would paint so and enjoy it.

Lewis was advised by friends 'that to call you a "Prussian" at the present juncture is done with intent to harm, to cast a cloud over the movement, if possible, and moreover that it is actionable'. This was not the last time in his life that Wyndham Lewis would find himself stigmatised with alleged sympathy for the Teutonic jackboot.

*

Evidence of the interruption wrought by his venereal disease in Lewis's output of oil paintings during the first half of 1915 may be gathered from the fact that, three months after the London Group show, he included the same two canvases in the Vorticist Exhibition at the Doré Gallery. On this occasion *The Crowd* was renamed *Democratic Composition*.

The Doré opening, on 10 June, must have been blighted by the news that the only sculptor represented in the exhibition, Henri Gaudier-Brzeska, had been killed in France five days before. P. G. Konody, referring to the loss in his *Observer* review, suggested it 'should disarm the anger which might otherwise be aroused in a good many people by the fact that the "Vorticists" continue their antics in times as serious and critical as the present'.

On the day of the private view, Mrs Turner sent Lewis a cheque for £35, bringing the amount paid for her six pictures to £200. Two of these had been included in the exhibition, catalogued as *Two Shafts – Man and Woman*, while the remaining four were still in Lewis's possession. Mrs Turner had closed up her Park Lane house and had not yet thought of anywhere they could be stored. She wrote from Dunkerque, where she was busy setting up and organising a mobile field hospital. Apologising for not sending the remaining £50 owing to him, she promised she would pay it when she could. 'Every penny I've got is going into my hospital', she told him.

The day after the private view, hearing that a second issue of *Blast* was due to appear, and assuming that her former business partner was financially solvent once more, Kate Lechmere issued Lewis with a writ to recover the sum of £97 she had lent him to launch the first issue. Lewis wrote to her in an injured tone: 'do you really intend to go on throwing mud which . . . must soil you at least as much as it dirties me? Is this quite the time to squabble sordidly in public?' While confessing to 'vagueness in business matters' he thought that £40 or £50 was nearer the amount she had lent him. Besides, 'the War has stopped art dead', he told her. As a result his finances were as precarious as ever and the debt irrecoverable:

I have no money at all . . . Short of the sale of a few tables and chairs, the most venomous proceedings on your part could have no effect.

It may have been the pressure brought to bear on him from Lechmere's writ that prompted the 'very extraordinary letter' he sent to Mrs Turner on 18 June and which she received in Dunkerque on the 23rd. It demanded immediate settlement of the £50 she owed him. Apart from that blunt message, its tone and contents can only be guessed at. 'I had no idea that you were capable of writing me such a letter', Mrs Turner replied.

She sent him a cheque by registered post. She was instructing her solicitor to collect the pictures and store them for her. She regretted that she would not be proceeding with her plan to rent the 'large studio or hall near Park Lane' in which to exhibit them. And she concluded: 'It's not worth your while being rude to me, you only lose a friend who might have some time been of service to you.'

Lewis had told Kate Lechmere that he was 'shortly going to the Front', and when his solicitor wrote to her solicitor on 22 June, he would have been portrayed as a man about to fight and possibly die for his country. As a result of his solicitor's letter, although judgement was signed against Lewis for £97, together with £4 8s. 6d. in costs, it was agreed 'that Miss Lechmere would not take steps to enforce the judgement until six months after the termination of the war.'*

Mrs Turner had suggested Lewis's rudeness lost him a friend who might have been of service. In early July, having received the balance of his money, he nevertheless wrote asking a service of her. Smoothing over the harshness of his former letter, he summarised and excused it in Music Hall terms: 'the poor artist (imaginary melodramatic figure) asked the rich woman (howls from the Gallery) for the settlement of an obligation a little forcibly.' He then outlined his case:

> I must join the Army. I have as little reason to be shot at once . . . as any artist in Europe, but have certain accomplishments (such as an unusual mastery of French) that might be of more use . . . than my trusty right arm, which, I flatter myself is rather a creative than a destructive limb.

Presumably thinking that the operation of her hospital scheme gave her a certain degree of influence in military circles, he wondered if she could pull strings on his behalf. 'Can you be of any use to me?' he asked her. 'Are you willing to be of any use to me?' He understood that interpreters got shot 'at once', and that a Second Lieutenant's commission in the infantry was 'a death warrant more or less'. He reasoned that his best chance of survival was as a private soldier but anticipated he 'should find the ennuis and fatigues of that intolerable'. On reflection, his ambitions lay in three areas, what he described as 'places of advantage': a commission in the Army Service Corps, a commission in the Howitzer Brigade and, lastly, the secret service. And, lest she still held his previous missive against him, he concluded: 'If you want to say anything disagreeable just don't answer the letter.'

Mrs Turner's reply, if any, has not survived.

*

Late in July the second issue of *Blast* was published. It had fewer pages than the first and was a dour companion to that brash tome of the previous year. With the harsh angularities of its cover design, black on off-white, it matched the gravity of its block-lettered subtitle: 'WAR NUMBER'.

Over half the contributions were by Lewis himself, including 'War Notes', 'Art Notes', a 'Review of Contemporary Art' and the first instalment

---

* According to Miss Lechmere, when she attempted to pursue the action in 1920, Lewis appeared in court, 'pleaded poverty and added that he had just returned from fighting for his country'. As a result the court took his part and Lechmere's suit failed.

of 'The Crowd Master', a fictionalised account of his train journey from Berwick-upon-Tweed to London during the mobilisation. There were poems by Eliot, Pound, Hueffer, Dismorr and Saunders.

There was also a statement, 'written from the Trenches', by Gaudier-Brzeska affirming the continuity of art and nature in war. It was followed by the black-bordered announcement of his death in action at Neuville St Vaast.

*

War prohibited Lewis from spending his customary summer vacation in France. In early August he went instead to stay with the Wadsworth family at High Greenwood House, near Hebden Bridge in Yorkshire. A childhood memory of Barbara Wadsworth suggests that the holiday got off to a bad start. He appeared in the kitchen doorway and the four-year-old exclaimed 'Oh! Here's dear fat old Wyndham Lewis come to visit us!' Lewis glowered at the child and, she claimed, caught the next train back to London. A photograph of Lewis in cloth cap, tweeds and walking boots, however, suggests his departure was not so precipitate, and his ruffled feelings sufficiently smoothed to allow him a spell of healthy exercise.

*

A 'Notice to the Public' following the Editorial excused *Blast*'s delayed appearance as 'due to the War chiefly' and to the Editor's (unspecified) recent illness. Subscribers were told that, since it was a publication run by painters who 'do their work first, and, since they must, write about it afterwards', *Blast* would not always appear on time. However, two further issues were confidently promised before January 1916.

This promise came close to being honoured. A letter postmarked Thursday 16 September informed Alick Schepeler that *Blast* would 'commence appearing' the following day and copies would reach her the following Thursday. Some time in October, Lewis wrote to Rutter: 'I am getting Blast no. 3 out in 6 weeks or so, on quite different lines again to the last: with several full size two page colour blocks'. But this did not appear and no further mention was made of it. The 'WAR NUMBER' was to be the last.

In the late summer of that year Lewis carried out what was to be his final interior decorating commission. It is not known how much Rudolph Stulik paid him for transforming the small first-floor dining room in the Restaurant de la Tour Eiffel, nor even if money ever changed hands. When

William Roberts painted three large panels in another part of the restaurant he was paid lavishly in free meals for a year. Lewis may have worked under a similar arrangement, perhaps being paid in cash and in kind. Stulik had an especially soft spot for his neighbour at 4 Percy Street. 'I vould do anyting for Mr Lewis', the Viennese proprietor was fond of saying.

With Helen Saunders acting as his assistant, Lewis had finished the room by the end of the year. Invitation cards were printed, on production of which the Vorticist Room could be viewed daily, from 11 in the morning until 6, for the last three weeks of January. The correspondent for *Colour* described it in the April 1916 issue:

> Gay Vorticist designs cover the walls, and call from the tablecloth. They are good in colour, and very decorative, although their meaning is not self-evident.

For years afterwards, the words 'Vorticist Paintings' set Stulik's establishment apart from other restaurants listed in Baedeker's handbook for *London and its Environs*. However, like the decorations in Lady Drogheda's dining room, like those in Hueffer's study at South Lodge – 'very violent and explosive' with accompanying red doors and skirting boards executed in November 1914 – and like the six panels designed for, but never installed in, Mary Borden Turner's drawing room, the designs of 'The Vorticist Room' in the Tour Eiffel have long since been dispersed or destroyed.

*

The publishing destiny of Lewis's *Tarr* was linked at this time with that of another first novel. Serialisation in *The Egoist* of James Joyce's *A Portrait of the Artist as a Young Man* ended in September 1915 and in early October Ezra Pound was trying to find a publisher to bring it out in book form. Responding to a remark by Lewis that the novels would be in competition, Pound decided not to make two rival claims on a publisher's attention at the same time and agreed to withhold Joyce's manuscript from John Lane until after *Tarr* had been submitted. Lane received Lewis's novel in late October or early November. His caution about publishing what he described as 'sexual disagreeableness' would have been redoubled by the criminal proceedings being brought against Methuen for D. H. Lawrence's *The Rainbow*. It was not surprising, then, that by late November he had rejected *Tarr*, on the advice of his reader, as being 'too strong a book'. The decision incensed Pound: 'God damn the fucking lot of 'em, readers, hog washers, etc.'

For most of December Lewis's novel remained in the hands of another publisher: Werner Laurie.

Pound outlined contingency plans should *Tarr* receive the same treatment there as it had from Lane. 'If Laurie rejects,' he told Lewis, 'you are to write to Miss H. S. Weaver . . . and make an appointment. I suggest that you call and read her the opening of the novel.'

Harriet Shaw Weaver, co-editor of *The Egoist*, meanwhile, was waiting to learn the fate of *A Portrait of the Artist as a Young Man*. If no other publisher could be found for it, she intended publishing Joyce's novel in book form under the imprint of the Egoist Press. If, however, it was placed elsewhere, Miss Weaver might consider publishing *Tarr* instead. And so a curious interdependence developed between the two novels, as Joyce's followed Lewis's from one publisher to another. If *Tarr* was rejected by Laurie, Joyce's novel might be accepted, which might in turn mean Miss Weaver would accept *Tarr*. If, on the other hand, Laurie rejected *A Portrait of the Artist as a Young Man*, it would be published by Miss Weaver and all Lewis could expect for his novel from that quarter was serialisation in *The Egoist*.

Werner Laurie rejected *Tarr* on 22 December. The reader's report, as Lewis recounted to Pound, said that the book 'dealt entirely with Germans, and English people who were not much better'. Whilst conceding it to be 'extremely "clever"', the report 'was a long and gloomy statement of antipathy'.

Following Pound's advice, Lewis went to see Miss Weaver at 11 o'clock on the morning of 30 December. The following day he reported:

> I read her the first 4 pages, and then left off, as I was sure she would not like it, and we were in an empty room under depressing conditions. I did not leave the MSS with her: I thought I must make some further move with it.

He concluded: 'I am afraid I may have bungled the Weaver business.'

Even when she had at last been given the opportunity of reading Part I of the manuscript for herself, Miss Weaver did not like Lewis's novel. 'I should class it as of the same family as Mr Bernard Shaw's plays', she told him:

> 'diabolically clever', yes, and very interesting, but *not* a work of art. The characters appear to me mechanical automatons, wound up in order to spout forth opinions, instead of breathing with life.

Despite her reservations she wished to publish an abridged, serialised version in *The Egoist*. By this stage Lane had rejected Joyce's novel and if Laurie followed suit, Miss Weaver was to publish *A Portrait of the Artist as a Young Man* herself. In the meantime she offered Lewis £50 for the serial rights, together with a promise that the type for the shortened *Tarr* would be kept set up 'so that it would be easy . . . afterwards to have it printed as a book (with the deleted portions added).'

With the fate of Joyce's novel still uncertain, Pound advised Lewis to accept Miss Weaver's offer: '£50 now and . . . the chance of getting another wad . . . when you publish in a volume.'

*

At the end of 1915 Lewis confided his economic state to Pound. He owed £7.10s. in back rent. He owed £10 to the Harlesden printer, £4 to a furniture man, £1 to his frame-maker and had sundry other debts amounting to a further £10. He was also at least £25 in arrears with maintenance payments: 'the upkeep of my son and heir etc.' as he put it.

Set against this he was hoping to receive £50 for his book, £10 for a cover design and £30 from Quinn for four drawings. The £90 would allow him to pay his debts and leave 'a little margin for [his] pocket'. Pound was also working to get more money from Quinn, advising him 'that THIS IS the time to buy a big picture . . . by Mr W.L.'

EIGHTEEN

'My dear, safe as a church'

By the middle of January 1916 Lewis had 'attested' – that is to say he had filled out a registration form declaring himself ready and willing to serve his country. He was still exploring every influential, first- and second-hand, contact he possessed for the most 'advantageous' branch of the service to apply for a commission.

At Alick Schepeler's suggestion he wrote to Major Robert Gregory, explaining he was willing to enlist for two or three months in the ranks so long as he could be assured of a commission eventually. He had mentioned 'two dependants' in his attestation form, he told the Major, and a wife was not among them. With such heavy responsibilities he could not 'with as free a mind as many men, take up a post of the utmost danger', he explained. 'My death might leave a nastier mess behind than any mess a shell could make of me.'

He enumerated his qualifications:

1. Prodigious command of French tongue.
2. Profound knowledge of French people.
3. No sentimentality about or particular fondness for French people.

by which he meant he would not allow an old woman to swindle the British government over the price of a cabbage 'because her language was so beautiful'.

4. Organising capacity.

He had after all 'organised the "Cubist" invasion of England without the loss of *a single Cube*!'

5. Rugby School.

He stressed especially his 'Public School Education' and pointed out in conclusion that he had described an ideal transport official in the Army Service Corps.

Another avenue of influence, probably suggested by Pound, was Maurice Bonham Carter, private secretary and son-in-law of the Prime Minister. He wrote from Downing Street that he was doing what he could to secure Lewis a commission in the Army Service Corps but that there was a long waiting list. He suggested that a job in the artillery would be easier to come by.

Meanwhile, Pound brought more pressure to bear on Quinn to buy 'a big picture' and in early March was able to report that the lawyer 'evidently intends to take Kermesse'. Lewis was delighted. 'Quinn is concentrated virtue', he beamed, and thanked Pound for his 'happy initiative in the matter'.

*

Following the advice of the Prime Minister's private secretary, Lewis renounced hopes of a commission in the Army Service Corps and enlisted in the Royal Garrison Artillery instead. When Ezra Pound mentioned his friend's branch of the service to Bonham Carter's wife one evening, the charming Violet Asquith exclaimed: 'What! *GARRISON* artillery!!, my dear, safe as a church.'

In January Lewis had expressed himself as willing to spend two or three months in the ranks if he could be assured a commission eventually. But he arrived at his first posting, in late March, with no such assurance. His rank was 'Gunner', his number 71050, and his address: Depot 1, R.G.A., Hut 20, Fort Burgoyne, Dover. His hut was on top of a cliff and the sound of the wind at night was 'antediluvian'.

He expected to remain in Dover for three weeks before being moved to Hull, Leith, Weymouth or elsewhere. Woolwich, of course, would have been ideal so far as proximity to London was concerned, but Woolwich was 'only for the heavy guns, and the siege ones'.

A fortnight later he was passing through Waterloo Station on his way to Weymouth and taking advantage of a charity bar staffed by Duchesses. 'I [ate] six pieces of bread and treacle with great relish', he told Pound. 'The Duchesses were very treacly too.' His first night in Dorset was spent in a YMCA hut where 'a man [was] making a shit of himself on the piano.'

He was soon shifted into another hut: Hut 61, R.G.A. Westham Training Unit, Weymouth. Once there, his primary consideration, like many another newly enlisted man's, was home leave. He needed to get back to London to see a dentist and also to work *Kermesse* into a suitable state for delivery to Quinn.

The big canvas that Fry praised in *The Nation* in 1912 had already been touched up when Bell described it the following year in the same periodical as 'altered and greatly improved'. Three years later Lewis believed it to be still too 'primitive', 'uncouth' and 'unfinished' to leave his hands. Pound had received and was holding a cheque for £70 of the £120 Quinn had agreed to pay for the painting but was under instructions not to let Lewis have it until after shipment had actually taken place. This was a shrewd and necessary precaution. Lewis was already overcomplicating the deal by making contingency plans involving immediate payment and deferred delivery:

> Should I come through the War safe and sound, I can . . . paint a hundred Kermesses . . . Quinn has nothing to fear: I will do him another Kermesse, and throw it in, to celebrate Peace . . . On the other hand, should I get killed or smashed up so that I *can't* paint any more Kermesses, he can have (1.) The Kermesse as it is, or (2.) As many more drawings as would, by their combined price, cover the money he had paid out.

Fortunately Lewis got his leave, finished the picture to his own and Pound's satisfaction, and it was duly shipped to the United States. A number of drawings by Lewis, as well as by his former colleagues of the Rebel Art Centre, went as well. Quinn was organising, at great personal expense, a Vorticist exhibition for the spring at the Montross Gallery in New York.

He paid out over £80 in freight, insurance, and framing costs only for the Montross Gallery to withdraw its offer of hosting the show. 'Exhibition of the Vorticists' eventually opened on 10 January 1917 in the Penguin Club at 8 East 15th Street. Seventy-five works were on show by Lewis, Etchells, Roberts, Dismorr, Saunders and Wadsworth. A note in the catalogue stated: 'Pictures marked with a star are loaned and are not for sale.' The lender was John Quinn himself. In September 1916 Pound had told Miss Saunders that the New York lawyer 'had about cleared up the whole show'. He had 'taken practically all the Lewis drawings' for £375. Lewis was represented by 46 works and an asterisk appeared alongside 37 of them. No asterisk appeared alongside catalogue number 13, *Kermesse*, the work Quinn is known to have paid £120 for earlier the previous year. Despite Lewis's efforts at touching up the painting during his weekend's leave from Westham Camp, Pound reported Quinn to be dissatisfied with it. The absence of an asterisk might mean that he was, in effect, offering it for resale at the Penguin Club.

The huge canvas, however, remained in Quinn's possession and only found a buyer in 1927, after his death, when it was knocked down at auction 'for a song'.

*

Lewis enjoyed swift promotion to NCO, his transition from Gunner to Bombardier being marked by a single chevron stripe. His subsequent progress however, was slow in spite of surprisingly benevolent superiors.

The Officer Commanding the Portland Defences, Colonel Inglis, was an amiable and apparently cultured man. Shortly after Lewis's arrival they discussed the Paris *Salon des Indépendants* as well as the prospects and procedure of applying for a commission. On another occasion, when Bombardier Lewis was called away from drilling his squad on the parade ground, the conversation concerned modern poetry:

> The Colonel . . . sent for me . . . to ask me what 'Imagisme' was. With my rifle at the slope I explained as best I could. But the Colonel said that I would never make him understand such things, and carrying my right hand smartly across the body, I placed it, palm downwards on the small of the butt: then cutting it smartly to the side, took a step to the rear, and turning rapidly about, moved back to continue the instruction of my squad.

Lewis asked Pound to send Colonel Inglis a copy of *Cathay*, so they would have something further to talk about and in the hope that his commission 'might ripen in [a] bed of Chinese interpretations'.

The Colonel's Adjutant, despite being 'half-cracked and very unreliable' was also 'well-disposed'. He told Lewis one morning 'that he took fancies to people' and on the strength of that did him 'an extremely good turn'. The nature of the 'good turn' Lewis did not reveal, but urged Pound to 'always have the Adjutant of the Portland Defences in [his] prayers'.

On the other hand, he believed his chances of being recommended for a commission were being crushed by a particularly implacable enemy. 'For Christ's sake *always* blast Captain Nind', Pound was told, 'whenever you are "blasting".' Captain H. J. Nind was Instructor of Gunnery, a broken-nosed veteran who, Lewis believed, was determined to go to any lengths to keep him in the ranks. He was convinced that Nind had tampered with his 'more positive marks' in a gunnery examination. 'Since he had to work for 20 years for his commission,' Lewis reasoned, 'he is resolved that no one else shall find an emergency short-cut by way of him.' There was also a story that the Captain's intransigence was due to his having a nephew serving in France whose own efforts to gain a commission had thus far not met with success. In the meantime Lewis was to be 'snubbed, harried and worn down' by this Nemesis only to have half his marks 'knocked off for "delivery" or some elusive thing' at the end of it all.

*

What he suspected to be a recurrence of 'clap' added to his anxieties. He confided in Pound and the poet agreed to consult a doctor on his friend's behalf, but not before gleefully indulging in some diagnosis of his own:

> I should be much inclined to doubt whether your trouble were the clapp, glleet or ghonnerrrreaa, but rather a natural secretion caused by the continual lucubration or friction or pricktion of the route or rut march. You should state whether same is accompanied by redness, soreness, irritation or whether it be a gentle deposit in the said longish foreskin of white gelatinous substance . . . You should . . . state WHEN you were last a prey to the gleetish activities, also your habits!!!!.

His 'habits' were those that might be expected of a bombardier garrisoned close to a sea port. There was a gap in the hedge of Westham Camp, through which unauthorised access to the town could be gained. Later he told of brothel visits in the company of a Sergeant Major and a Quartermaster, and of one in particular which ended in a police raid and the trio narrowly escaping arrest. It would not have been surprising if an infection had been contracted from some 'pub houri' on this or another occasion. Pound was unaware of his friend's adventures as he continued to offer reassurance in lieu of more expert medical opinion:

> Unless you notice a definite soreness or pain I don't think you need be in any way worried, and even a soreness, so that it be not pustulent, is not of vital import . . . [If] the discharge be perfectly clean and white and of jismatic appearance I think you can put it down to simple superabundance plus the friction of pedestrination.*

*

By June Lewis had come to the conclusion that ' "the Ranks" are a trap'. He regretted his haste to attest. 'I should have waited and said "Commission or nothing" ', he told his mother. 'Had I realised what I was in for I should certainly have done that.' Violet Asquith's airy opinion, relayed by Pound, can have offered scant comfort: 'If he's any good, he'll get recommended for promotion anyhow.'

Early in July he underwent medical inspection 'for Service Overseas'. Presumably no trace of his recent infection was found, and a few days later

---

* This letter, 68 in *Pound/Lewis*, was misdated 'June 1917' by Materer. Internal evidence suggests an earlier date of April or May 1916.

he was assigned to the 183 Siege Battery and told he would be moving from Weymouth. This settled matters so far as recommendation for a commission was concerned. He resolved to make fresh efforts for a cadetship once he was clear of Westham Camp and beyond Captain Nind's malign influence.

In the meantime he thought the 183 Siege 'a pleasant enough little battery' and the Sergeant in charge was of the opinion that he had acquitted himself better on the field than anyone else. He was given a small promotion bringing an extra fourpence-halfpenny a day, and in mid–July acquired short-lived celebrity on the camp. The *Daily Mirror*'s Rambler included a photograph in 'This Morning's Gossip'. The uniformed head and shoulders were identified as belonging to 'the well-known Vorticist artist and author', editor of 'that preciously peculiar publication' *Blast*. The Rambler told his readers:

> I hear that Mr Lewis is about to publish a series of articles showing how a vorticist views military life. The view should at least be original.

A superior remarked that, following his appearance in the press, 'Bdr. Lewis was drilling better than he had ever heard him before'. Despite this, Lewis was convinced he would remain a Bombardier 'to the end of the chapter'.

The Rambler was misinformed. No such series of articles was published.*

*

As he prepared to leave Westham Camp for Roffey Camp, Horsham, in Sussex at the beginning of August, Lewis appeared to have momentary second thoughts about becoming an officer. It is possible that news of the carnage wrought in July, the first month of the Somme campaign and the most costly in British lives of the entire war, brought about this uncertainty. 'The R.G.A. is not quite so "safe as church"', he told his mother:

> A man just back with shell-shock tells me that over a space of 6 months his battery . . . lost 5 officers killed, and the sixth wounded, arm amputated. The loss amongst officers in the Artillery seems higher than in the ranks . . . It is really difficult to know what to do about it. I shall probably be made full Bombardier soon, and get consequently 19/- a

---

* However, Lewis contemplated offering what he described as 'a more or less pot-boiling article on a military subject' to the *Daily Mail*. It was called 'The Bull Gun'. Published, with an introduction by Robert Edward Murray, in *Stand To! The Journal of the Western Front Association* (April 1991).

week, better than nothing . . . I am not sure that I shouldn't be better off
to stick where I am.

*

He was in Horsham for about ten days. The period was marked by a
weekend spent as Orderly Officer when he had to 'count the money in the
canteen, inspect the latrines, and blackguard a lot of abashed lads because of
their buttons'. He also encountered Field Marshal Sir John French. The
Commander-in-Chief of British Forces, while on a visit to Roffey Camp,
discovered Bombardier Lewis engaged in an artillery exercise, shook his
hand and thanked him.

He had hoped to make 'a fresh start' at gaining a commission, and it was
during his next posting, at Lydd in Kent, that this became a possibility. 'I
am progressing favourably in my military exercises, I think', he told Pound
shortly after arriving. 'I might even put in successfully for a commission.'
Matters were delayed by the absence of a Commanding Officer, and
application to 'the beshitten suet-faced little microbic Sub[altern] . . . at
present in his place' was out of the question. However, by September the
process was under way. A form passed from one London address to another
for signature: from Masterman of the Propaganda Department at Wellington House, it went to Violet Hunt, who forwarded it to Laurence Binyon.
The Deputy Keeper of Oriental Prints and Drawings at the British Museum
returned it, having verified good character, to Lewis at Lydd. The candidate
for cadetship had then to get the Education section of the form signed,
presumably by a more amenable Instructor of Gunnery than Captain Nind.

No letters survive from his period of officer training, but according to
Lewis's autobiographical account of 1937 he was sent first to the Field
Artillery Cadet School in Exeter where, as if to elevate him physically as
well as officially above the class of 'Other Ranks', he was taught to ride a
horse. 'I nearly lost my life in the riding school', he recalled:

Several people were killed while I was there, trying to ride. It was a
weekly – perhaps a daily – occurrence . . . There was one [horse] whose
tail I had to clean with a sponge (for I had to clean these disgusting beasts
as well as ride them) whose behaviour left me speechless and almost lost
me a leg. The same outrageous devil nearly broke my neck in the riding
school.

He would not have been the first avant-garde painter to be killed as a result
of a riding accident. The Futurist Umberto Boccioni, also training for the

artillery, fell from his mount during a cavalry exercise in August and died of his injuries.

Lewis escaped from what he called the 'inferno of horseflesh' and went on to No. 1 R.G.A. Officer's Cadet School at Trowbridge in Wiltshire. Here he successfully negotiated his exams, coming, by his own account, 'fifth from top' and, on Christmas Day 1916, gained the right to his single 'pip': the star on sleeve and shoulder, marking him out as a 2nd Lieutenant.

Whatever misgivings he had expressed to his mother about becoming an officer were, at least outwardly, dispelled. He bought himself 'two well-cut suits of old-gold khaki, in Saville Row, a cane, a revolver, and a sumptuous British Warm'. He had himself photographed: head and shoulders with upper lip curled over cigarette, flaming grenade prominent on lapel, gun carriage on cap, and full length, with the same pendulous cigarette, legs apart, his left hand thrust into jodhpur pocket, his right holding the cane as if about to slap it against a leather-cased calf.

NINETEEN

'You need sympathy, sympathy, sympathy'

On 22 May 1917 Lewis wrote to Pound from Cosham, near Southampton: 'Our advance party sails this afternoon, and we are standing by. Two days should see us pushing forward on what the *Daily Mail*, *Sphere*, *Morning Post* and *John Bull* describe as the Great Adventure . . . Au revoir. A bientôt!' They were not taking their guns. In the chaos of imminent embarkation no one seemed certain of what precisely they were being sent to do. Whether they were going as 'reinforcement to sadly depleted Trench Mortars', or to take over captured German guns, 2nd Lieutenant Lewis did not know. 'This is of course unsatisfactory.'

The next day he told Quinn: 'Going to war is a most complicated job for such an untidy man as myself. I am making a last frantic effort to adjust my affairs, and send a blast of military orderliness through my chaos of papers and interests.' He had compiled an inventory of his writings, paintings and drawings. Some drawings were to be found at Pound's flat and some at Helen Saunders's. A number of paintings, including those belonging to Miss Turner and the *Christopher Columbus* that was 'quite unfit for exhibition' and to be painted out by Miss Saunders, were in his mother's house at 43 Oxford Road, Ealing. In the event of a posthumous retrospective exhibition 'in which it was desired to get together all [his] things', there was a list of names including Quinn, Baker, Lechmere, Fry, John and Madame Strindberg, all of whom possessed paintings or drawings.

His literary legacy was to consist of five books: *Tarr*; a collection of already published essays and stories to be called *Our Wild Body*; his critical writings collected as *Kill John Bull with Art*; the play set in Stulik's restaurant, plus short fiction produced since the outbreak of war, to be called *Miss Godd and the Ideal Giant*; and *The Enemy of the Stars*, which might include fragments of a play written 15 years before, together with sonnets from that period selected by Sturge Moore and Pound. In addition, there was a possible sixth book called *The Bull Gun*, comprising 'sketches, stories etc. that I may find time to write at the Front'.

*

On 24 May the 330 Siege Battery, consisting of 6 officers and 154 other ranks, boarded the SS *Viper* at Southampton. The formal roll of officers noted in the Battery's War Diary included the name of 2nd Lieutenant P. Wyndham Lewis. The following day they arrived at Le Havre and the congenial limbo of Number 2 Rest Camp. For the next week 330 Siege Battery led 'a pleasant life in tents' and waited. On 3 June they received orders to proceed up the line.

At 2 o'clock the following morning they entrained at the Gare Maritime and arrived in Rouen at 6. From there motor lorries took them to the headquarters of the 69th Heavy Artillery Garrison near La Clytte. Here the Battery was split up into five detachments and seconded to other units. Lewis and an unspecified number of other ranks went as reinforcements to the 224 Siege Battery.

By 6 June he was in the firing line for the first time. 'Whizzing, banging, swishing and thudding completely surround me, and I almost jog up and down on my camp bed as though I were riding in a country wagon or a dilapidated taxi', he told Pound. 'I am, in short . . . in the midst of an unusually noisy battle.' Most of the noise came from their own 6-inch 26 hundredweight guns; 'the Germans are making a similar din a mile or so away!' he explained. He was about four miles southwest of the smashed town of Ypres, opposite the village of Wytschaete. Censorship, however, prohibited him from giving Pound the whereabouts of 'this unfortunate conflict'.

He wrote a reassuring letter to his mother:

> Many more people are wounded than killed. One of the officers of the Battery the day before yesterday got seventeen wounds: but all of them together did not amount to a mortal wound, or a permanently serious one. – Anyway it is all pure chance.

He promised to send her a field postcard two or three times a week to show he was still alive. 'If you do not hear for some days, however, do not be anxious. It will probably only mean that I have missed a post.' He also told her that at this part of the line gas shells came over practically every night. 'This necessitates sitting sometimes for two hours or more with gasmasks, and makes regular sleep out of the question.'

That same night he was slumbering soundly enough in his dugout when the shells came over. He told Pound that he was gassed in his sleep because the sentry had not realised he was there and omitted to wake him.

The morning of 7 June was a momentous one in the Ypres Salient. After two years of comparative calm there was to be a push forward by General Plumer's 2nd Army. This was the start of a major campaign: the 3rd Battle of Ypres. At 3.10 a.m., 19 enormous mines were simultaneously exploded in tunnels under the German front line at Messines Ridge. It was, at the time, the largest man-made explosion in history. The shock wave was felt in London. Over 12 miles to the south, in Lille, a University Professor of Geology sprang from his bed, convinced that an earthquake was in progress. Lewis, however, made no mention of the cataclysmic event either in his letters or in his memoirs, and it must be assumed that he slept through it. The explosion, huge as it was, did not make an unusual amount of noise because of the muffling effect of depth on the subterranean charges. All the same he must have been profoundly asleep indeed not to have been woken up by the shock wave.

He cannot have inhaled more than a whiff of the gas, because by about 11 a.m. he was able to visit an Observation Post on the Wytschaete Ridge. From there he watched as New Zealand troops attacked the village of Messines: 'an immense and smoky struggle . . . tanks advancing, cavalry . . . tanks hit, air fights – panorama of war, in fact'. He returned to his Battery and, in the late afternoon, set out in the 2nd Army's wake with his Company Commander to reconnoitre their new front line, gained a few hours before. It was an opportunity to see at first hand the effects of high explosive. They passed 'through the desolation of the Bosche concrete dugouts in a wilderness of charred spikes that was formerly a wood, everything . . . pits and gashes: dead Germans lying about like bloody waxworks.' Lewis picked up a copy of the *Vossische Zeitung* from one smashed enemy trench. He was to spend that evening reading the newspaper with the aid of his German dictionary.

The 2nd Lieutenant and his Company Commander stopped their exploration at the crest of Messines Ridge. By the end of the day the British front line had advanced in certain places more than two miles. At the close of his second day in action Lewis had seen a lot of war. 'I have been particularly lucky', he told Pound, 'in dropping into the midst of a very big attack.'

The attack had been successful and all was fairly peaceful on 8 June, 'like a quiet day in the country; no row, fine sun . . . a half hour's shooting, more calm.' If Miss Saunders could send him the first eight pages of his story, 'The Soldier of Humour', destined for publication in *The Little Review* later in the year, he thought he would have time to make alterations.

Ten days or so later he contracted trench fever. His face, neck and testicles became swollen, the condition being not unlike mumps. Also his tongue turned green.

By 24 June he was in the Casualty Clearing Station eight miles behind the front line at Bailleul. On the 28th he was taken further west to the 46th Stationary Hospital at Étaples, just south of Boulogne.

The first day of July found him in good spirits; 'the best of *jolliest* and *jauntiest* health and *Humour*'. He was considering a piece of writing for the theatre. Combative metaphors for the creative process and its effects upon an audience were drawn from his artillery experience. 'My head is swarming with dramatic fragments', he told Pound:

> if they could be integrated into an 8. inch Play, they would make a fine black fountain of dung and smoke in the midst of the Unseen Canaille, detailed charts of whose positions I have long been provided with!

A week later his condition had improved. 'My balls are smaller and less troublesome: I have less (or usually no) pain in my eyes. I am almost well.' He was anxious to hear the results of Quinn's negotiations with the New York publisher Knopf. Much depended upon a profitable US sale of *Tarr*. He felt that he had spoiled any chance of decent English sales by having it brought out piecemeal. 'Any people who had read a chapter or two in the *Egoist*, and got sick of the serial nuisance, will never read it as a book.'

Meanwhile, his old Battery, the 330, had been sent north, from the Salient to the Belgian coast, where they were on temporary attachment to the Navy and engaged in mounting 7-inch Naval Siege Guns. Preparations were under way for a projected offensive against the port of Zeebrugge, where the German U-boat force, the main menace to British shipping, was based. Lewis's servant wrote to him on 9 July with the news that there had been casualties. Gunner McMahon had been killed two days before and several others wounded. Gunner Coombe was severely wounded on the 10th and died on the 11th.

The day he received this letter, Lewis wrote again to Pound. He had now heard from Quinn and the negotiations with Knopf for *Tarr* were moving apace. Quinn expected that the war would continue for another three years and, evidently considering the possibility, if not likelihood, of Lewis being killed in action, urged him to appoint executors. The news of McMahon's death, and the prospect of an imminent return to his hard-pressed and lethally shelled Battery, made Lewis take the lawyer's advice seriously. Pound was the obvious candidate to execute his literary estate and he had already thought vaguely of asking Pound, Sturge Moore and Guy Baker 'to execute for my children, and keep an eye on my boy occasionally'. He now felt that a more precise arrangement ought to be made. 'I wonder if I should send you a legal document resembling a will', he asked Pound. 'I would rather execute your books than your children', Pound replied.

The July issue of *The Egoist* had arrived at Étaples. Lewis was irritated to read, in the current instalment of *Tarr*, during the duel scene between Soltyk and Kreisler:

> Soltyk, in rear of the others, struggled with his bile. He slipped into his mouth a sedative tablet, oxide of bromium and heroin.

It was a reminder of the speed with which certain parts of the novel had been written, and of the slapdash state of the typescript he had left with Pound. 'Now, here we have another of my bloody dummies. That is to say I wanted to specify the sedative tablet taken, and for the time being put down the above extraordinary concoction . . . Obviously before appearing in book form these things must be dealt with.' When *Tarr* was published in America the following year the sedative became 'oxide of bromium and aniseed'. Other 'dummies', reproduced by the English printer, had been appearing throughout the serialisation. They were mostly approximations of abusive German epithets he had no doubt heard shouted at him by Ida Vendel but had never seen written down.

On 17 July he was issued with a Transport Order for 'Un Officier, Armée Anglais' from Étaples to No. 8 Michelham Convalescent Home, Dieppe, where he was admitted two days later, 'convalescent, sick'. It was a large hotel converted into a nursing establishment. 'The food is plentiful, good, Hotel like', he told his mother.

He stayed for a month, his 'disease . . . oozing out of [him] in the rays of the sun', then, convalescence over, he returned to the front. It was a different front from the one he had left. 'I have come to a tedious spot', he told Pound:

> It is really extremely bad. The parapet of one of our guns was smashed last night. We were shelled and gassed all night: I had my respirator on for two solid hours. There is only one bright side to the picture: a good concrete dugout.

He had rejoined the 330 Siege Battery on 13 August. Prohibited from giving Pound his exact location, he passed on the information in a form that no enemy spy who might intercept the letter would understand. 'I am now not so far from the port where I did my Timon drawings one summer.' Dunkerque. The Battery position was in fact some 15 miles away from the French port, at Oost-Duinkerke, in Belgium, on an extensive stretch of sand dunes just west of Nieuwpoort. The officers' 'dugout' was the remains of a whitewashed cottage on the road that ran along the edge of the dunes. It had been earlier converted by the French into a virtually bomb-proof shelter. The thickness of the walls and roof had been more than trebled with a lining of concrete. This meant that it could withstand even a direct hit, and in the couple of weeks the officers of 330 Siege Battery had been in residence it had sustained several. Inside there was a dormitory, mess and kitchen.

It was the Battery cook who greeted Lewis when he arrived. 'You've come to a nice place, sir! They never stop shelling that road. You've come to a hot place. It's a little hell away from hell.'

Two days later on 15 August the concrete dugout sustained another direct hit while Lewis and his fellow officers were having lunch.

*

Back in London, Pound was preparing a publishable text of *Tarr* for dispatch to New York. His task was made difficult because parts of the original typescript, edited down for serialisation, had apparently gone astray at *The Egoist*'s printers in West Norwood. As a result he was forced to plug gaps with printed pages from the September 1916, February, April and June 1917 issues of *The Egoist*. By 17 August the textual collage was complete. 'I have got *Tarr* together, all together at last and Miss S[aunders] is going over the foreign expressions', he informed Lewis.

*

When you come to the end of a per - fect day,
And you sit a - lone with your thought,
While the chimes ring out with a car - ol gay,
For the joy the day has brought;
Do you think what the end of a per - fect day
Can mean to a ti - red heart,
When the sun goes down with a flam - ing ray,
And the dear friends have to part?

It was Sunday, 19 August and the voice of Alma Gluck sounded through the 'pitch-dark, dank and chuck-full' dugout on the Nieuwpoort road. Big shells howled over and exploded in the dunes beyond. Lewis had withdrawn as far from his brother officers and their music as the 12 by 8 foot mess would allow. 'There is one awful shadow over my existence here: and that is the too frightful incompatibility of my companions.' He was writing to Pound but the phonograph was an irritating distraction. The 20 or so recordings of popular songs 'they' had introduced into the cramped living quarters were the most recent horror of his wartime existence. A combination of Alma Gluck and continuous enemy bombardment was getting on his nerves.

He had been on duty from 4.30 until 8 a.m., and they had been hammered with 11-inch naval shells just before breakfast: 'craters big enough to put a horse and cart in'. The shelling had gone on all day. 'As you probably know,' he told Pound, 'a shell is most dangerous when it falls on top of your head. It is next most dangerous at from 200 to 400 or 500 yards – a big one that is. We get nothing but big ones.' But he professed not to mind the constant danger of maiming or death by shrapnel. 'In fact I am both glad and ashamed to say that I rather enjoy it.' His major bugbear was the company he was forced to keep.

Someone put another record on the turntable and lowered the needle to the spinning shellac. A sugary duet in waltz time from *The Firefly* crackled out:

> You need sym – pa - thy,
> Sym – pa - thy, sym – pa - thy.
>
> I'm just try - ing to be friend - ly and gen - tle
> But not sen - ti - men - tal;
> So if I should touch your hand,
> Don't mis - un - der - stand
> Its mean – ing:
> You must know
> I'm but show - ing sym – pa – thy

Lewis poured his accumulated bile for his companions into the letter: 'They've just put on "Sympathy"; may their next fart split up their backs, and asphyxiate them with the odour of their souls!' Later that night his gun pit was hit by three shells in succession:

> Well this is the end of a per - fect day.
> Near the end of a jour - ney too;
> But it leaves a thought that is big and strong,
> With a wish that is kind and true;
> For mem -'ry has paint - ed this per - fect day,
> With col - ours that nev - er will fade,
> And we find at the end of a per - fect day,
> The soul of a friend we've made.

The following day he was at Battery Headquarters and he continued his letter:

> As I left this morning from the distance I . . . had the satisfaction of seeing
> an 11″ shell fall in the middle of our gun positions.

When he got back from Headquarters he learned that shrapnel from the explosion he had observed with such equanimity had wounded Staff Sergeant Scotland and Sergeants Smith and Nobles. Smith, Lewis's Sergeant, died of his wounds the next day. Lewis had to write to his widow. He told her how popular her husband had been.

By the following Saturday, Pound had at last completed his assemblage of *Tarr*. Helen Saunders having finished correcting the 'furrin languidges', the parcel was dispatched to New York by registered post.

Meanwhile, Lewis's sleeping bag, hanging in the doorway to air, had been ripped through by fragments of a shell that landed five yards away. Their dugout had sustained its fifth direct hit and was being repaired. It was five days after his Sergeant had died. There was 'a little extra work', he reported. 'Otherwise humdrum.'

One of the coincidences of war brought an old rival as neighbour. Lewis discovered that T. E. Hulme was in the next battery. No visits or respects were paid. And it was there, in the dunes near Nieuwpoort, that the 'heavy philosopher' was blown to pieces:

> I did not see him hit, but everything short of that, for we could see their earthworks, and there was nothing in between to intercept the view. I watched from ours, his battery being punched full of deep craters, with large naval shells: and from the black fountains of earth that spouted up, in breathless succession, occasional debris hurtled around us as we looked on. I remember a splintered baulk of wood sailing over and striking the dugout at my back.

Lewis's account, written two decades later, was a fabrication. When Hulme was killed on 28 September 1917, Lewis was over 20 miles away, back in the Ypres Salient.

*

On 31 August the 330 Siege Battery moved south to billets at La Belle Vue near Wormhoudt. The following day they moved again to the Eecke area near to St Sylvestre Cappel. 'Before going to our new position (a bad one, they say)', Lewis wrote, 'we are billeted for 4 days in a pleasant country.'

Unfortunately the phonograph had sustained the journey from Nieuwpoort in full working order:

> I need sym – pa - thy,
> Sym – pa - thy, sym – pa - thy.

Tho' I'm try - ing to be prop - er and nice
I'm not made of ice;
And if my poor heart skips a beat
Each time we meet,
Don't blame me
Tho' I know
You're but show – ing sym – pa – thy.

'Should I ever in after life meet the man who composed that song,' he wrote to Alick Schepeler, 'I shall – the mere thought of what I shall do makes my flesh creep.'

He had a new Commanding Officer. Captain F.J.C. Hindson was a native of Hull. Lewis railed to Pound about 'the ways of the Army, in giving such unspeakable, foolish and dismal muck a Battery'. As he wrote, the CO was close by. He was stooped, balding and had a hanging crimson underlip.

There was nothing much to do that first week as they waited for their guns and stores to arrive from Calais, and when his request for leave of absence to get himself a restaurant meal was challenged for the third time, Lewis told Captain Hindson: 'I am in your Battery, not in your Sunday School.' The CO drummed his fingers for some minutes and blushed.

On 13 September their guns arrived and were installed on a stretch of road southwest of Ypres.

The Ordnance BL 6″ Mk 19 on travelling carriage Mk 7A, its official nomenclature, was a monstrous piece of field artillery. It weighed just over ten tons and was 27 feet long from the mouth of its barrel to the end of the gun carriage. With the barrel raised to its maximum elevation of 38 degrees it could hurl a 100-lb shrapnel round a distance of ten miles.

On 15 September, the biggest artillery bombardment yet employed in the war began. A total of over 4 million rounds were fired from the 3,000 British guns.

Lewis's Battery was a day late joining in. Sight gear for the 6-inch MK XIXs was received from base and fitted on the 15th. At noon the following day the four guns of 330 Siege Battery opened fire on the heavily fortified rubble of Zonnebeke.

There was still tension in the dugout. Surprisingly, following the retort about Sunday School, Captain Hindson was not unfavourably disposed to Lewis. But an argument with another officer had created an atmosphere of dogged attrition. 'We sit dead opposite each other in the Mess,' he reported, 'and . . . do not exchange conversation, or extend to each other the usual courtesies.' In order to get away from the battery for a while he was even prepared to volunteer for particularly dangerous jobs.

Consequently, he was Forward Observation Officer on top of a section of ridge 400 yards behind his own front line and some 600 yards from the Germans'. His position afforded him a vivid impression of the effect of artillery fire. 'I . . . had the extreme gratification of seeing, in the midst of our barrage, a large Bosche fly into the air as it seemed a few feet below me . . . I looked down into the German front line,' he told Pound, 'as you might into Church Street.'

It had been a two-hour walk from his own Battery to this Observation Post. On the way he saw further grisly evidence of enemy shelling. One recent Scottish corpse evoked the bizarre recollection of a picture he had once seen in the Louvre*: 'head blown off so that his neck, level with the collar of his tunic reminded you of sheep in butchers' shops, or a French Salon painting of a Moroccan headsman.'

Communicating with his Battery from this Observation Post he registered a barrage of shrapnel on the church at Zonnebeke. 'I was glad that it was a presumably empty ruin that I was guiding the bursts upon', he confessed. 'I am truly not sanguinary except when confronted by an imbecile; not, thank God, from lack of stomach. Too much sense. Alas, too much sense.'

Lewis's position was itself a target for the enemy's guns, and he and his party of signallers were shelled steadily for five hours before withdrawing.

At zero-hour, 5.40 a.m., on 20 September, the offensive for which the British bombardment had been devastating preparation was launched along a front of about 8 miles from Langemarck in the north to Hollebeke on the Ypres–Comines canal in the south. The guns of 330 Siege Battery fired for six hours in support of the 1st Anzac Corps' attack and capture of the western part of Polygon Wood. On the 26th, at 5.50 a.m., the second stage of the offensive began: the 4th and 5th Australian Divisions in conjunction with British formations captured the rest of Polygon Wood, and Zonnebeke. The total number of casualties sustained by the seven attacking divisions was 15,375.

*

Three days later Lewis wrote to Harriet Shaw Weaver. He thanked her for serialising his novel in *The Egoist* and supposed she had by then heard of its sale to Knopf. But he had been thinking: 'is *Tarr* complete? Is there not a page missing somewhere? If there is, and you remember which and where it is, will you be so good as to send me the two numbers of *The Egoist* *preceding*, and the two *succeeding* this hiatus . . . I might then be able to

* *Exécution sans jugement* . . . , 'Summary Execution under the Moorish Kings of Granada', by Henri Regnault (1843–71).

remedy it. – I have a recollection that it has something to do with the character Butcher.'

*

Between 30 September and 2 October the four MK XIX guns of 330 Siege Battery were moved to a new position two miles to the east, following the advancing British Front Line. Map reference I16c 2.6 was five hundred yards from the great *gigot*-shaped body of water that was Zillebeke Lake and just behind a place known as the Moated Grange. It was equidistant from a Hellfire Corner to the north and a Hellblast Corner to the south. On the same day that the relocation was completed a German aeroplane bombed the new position, and the Battery Diary for 2 October recorded 11 men wounded. Casualties included all but two of Lewis's detachment, including his Sergeant, the second in six weeks. 'I have lost, I am sorry to say, many a pleasant companion by this – Old Bill amongst them . . . He dreamt the night before that the whole detachment had been wiped out.' While fellow officers remained for the most part 'poisonous refuse', it was clear that Lewis's contempt did not extend to the other ranks. He sent the customary platitudes back to wives and mothers of the dead. 'They are perfectly easy to write, for the more crudely conventional the better. But it is a nasty official task.'

Whenever military duties allowed, he endeavoured to fill in the 'missing parts' of his novel. Miss Weaver had sent him the September 1916 and May 1917 issues of *The Egoist*, in which it seems the gaps had occurred. But it was a difficult task, 'like trying to remember the shape of a cloud'.*

Ten days after the air attack, Lewis's gun pit behind the Moated Grange was 'a melancholy place', the inadequately reinforced division 'crawling about like a mutilated insect'. He was still volunteering for dangerous excursions to observation posts, and he supplied Pound with a thumbnail sketch of himself engaged in such activity: 'a bulging figure covered with mud, with haversacks, field-glasses, etc. hanging round it, plodding through a spacious and sinister desert, at the head of a small party of signallers, loaded in their turn with coils of wire, lucas lamps, telephone-cases etc. – all suffused with mud.'

Around the middle of October he escaped these glutinous conditions for an evening, and had dinner in the town of Cassel, about 20 miles behind the lines. He recognised a familiar face at a neighbouring table. Below the face, a

---

* Whatever these mysterious 'missing parts' contained, Lewis did not succeed in recreating them.

Major's crown glistened on the shoulder. It was William Orpen: Slade Scholar, Associate of the Royal Academy and now an Official War Artist for the Department of Information. The year before he had been in the ranks, but a commission to paint pictures for his country brought him an officer's commission as well.

Despite having been placed upon the proscribed list in *Blast* only two years before, the Major was glad to see his old Slade contemporary. He proffered whisky got from Haig's mess, he said, that very morning. Lewis must have envied him his 'cushy' job, living in an excellent hotel miles from the mud and shrapnel, with occasional sketching trips into 'Hell'. Years later, Lewis recalled their conversation and how the Irish painter pronounced the word as 'Hail':

> 'It's hell isn't it? It must be hell!'
> 'It's Goya, it's Delacroix – all scooped out and very El Greco,' replied Lewis. 'But not hell.'
> 'Ah yes, it must be hell!'
> 'Hell sometimes for the infantry. But it's merely a stupid nightmare – it's not real.'
> 'Same thing!', retorted Orpen.

'Damn Orpen anyhow', Pound wrote when Lewis told him of the encounter.

The prospect of turning his painting talents to the war effort did not immediately occur to Lewis. He did, however, feel the need for some sort of change. Writing to Pound from the 46th Stationary Hospital in July, he had mentioned a transfer to Intelligence:

> I want to be in another Push or two. After that, there will be nothing to gain by remaining at the Front, practically nothing more to see or experience ... Life ... is only justifiable as a spectacle: the moment at which it becomes harrowing and stale, and no aesthetic purpose is any longer served, War would be better exchanged for Diplomacy, Intelligence!

He estimated this moment would arrive in about two and a half months time. 'That', he added, 'is giving myself a good number of opportunities of ending my existence.'

When he encountered Orpen at dinner a little over three months later, the moment was overdue. He wrote to Pound the following day listing jobs his knowledge of French, German and even Spanish qualified him for:

Railway Transport Officer . . . District Purchasing Officer, Prison Camps,
Deputy Assistant Provost Marshal, Intelligence jobs, and War Office jobs.

He did not mention the job of Official War Artist. And when he had dinner
with Orpen again a little later and was introduced to a young man called De
Trafford from Intelligence, it was on that branch of the Service that his
sights seemed to be set.

*

In between Lewis's two dinners in Cassel, on Thursday 18 October, some
two thousand copies of the current issue of *The Little Review* were delivered
as usual to the New York Post Office from Margaret C. Anderson's
headquarters at 24 West 16th Street, Manhattan.

Second-class postage had been paid and any second-class matter of a
dubious nature delivered to the Post Office was brought to the attention of
the Superintendent of second-class mail. So it was that Mr Frederick G.
Mulker came to read a story about a soldier and a village girl, called
'Cantleman's Spring Mate'. He thought that parts of it contravened section
211 of the United States Criminal Code and accordingly referred it to Mr
Thomas G. Patten, Postmaster of the City of New York. It was Patten's
assistant, Thomas F. Murphy, who wrote to the solicitor for the United
States Post Office in Washington, the Honorable William H. Lamar,
requesting a ruling. He enclosed a copy of the October *Little Review* and had
marked the following lines in the story's final paragraph:

> At their third meeting he brought her a ring. Her melting gratitude was
> immediately ligotted with strong arms, full of the contradictory and
> offending fire of the spring. On the warm earth consent flowed up into her
> body from all the veins of the landscape. The nightingale sang ceaselessly
> in the small wood at the top of the field where they lay. He grinned up
> towards it, and once more turned to the devouring of his mate. He felt
> that he was raiding the bowels of Nature; not fecundating the Aspasias of
> our flimsy flesh, or assuaging, or competing with, the nightingale.

The first sentence of Section 211 of the United States Criminal Code
comprised exactly 275 words. Even in the tide of ponderous legal
documentation* that was shortly to flow across the bench of the Southern
District Court of New York, section 211 was mercifully summarised as
follows:

---

* Case File no. 49537 National Archives and Records Office, Washington DC.

> Every obscene, lewd, or lascivious, and every filthy book, pamphlet . . .
> writing . . . or other publication of an indecent character . . . is hereby
> declared to be non-mailable matter and shall not be conveyed in the mails
> or delivered from any post-office or by any letter carrier.

Lewis had been well aware of the ease with which contemporary writing
could fall foul of such a statute: witness his 'naif determination to have no
"Words ending in -Uck, -Unt or -Ugger"' in the pages of *Blast*. He had
even toned down that last paragraph of 'Cantleman's Spring Mate' earlier in
the year, excising the lines:

> That night he spat out, in gushes of thick delicious rage, all the lust that
> had gathered in his body . . . He bore down on her as though he wished to
> mix her body into the soil, and pour his seed into a more methodless
> matter, the brown phalanges of floury land. As their bodies shook and
> melted together . . .

While the New York Postmaster's Office was awaiting Lamar's ruling,
Margaret Anderson had no idea that the October issue had been held up. It
was only when she received complaints from her subscribers* that she
went to the Post Office and was told that the matter could be taken up with
Mr Lamar.

It was at this point that John Quinn entered the affair. Representing Miss
Anderson he sent Lamar a four-page letter on 5 November, expressing his
professional opinion that Lewis's story did 'not come within gunshot of
violating the statute or any Federal statute'. He felt sure that, upon reading
it, Lamar would agree that 'there is nothing either lewd or lascivious or
indecent in it or anything that is calculated to corrupt the morals of any of
the readers of *The Little Review*.'

After due consideration, on 7 November, Lamar wrote to the New York
Postmaster, T. G. Patten:

> Referring to the October issue of *The Little Review* . . . I have to advise
> you that this issue of this publication is regarded as unmailable under
> Section 211 of the Criminal Code, Section 480 of the Postal laws and
> Regulations of 1913. You will please notify the publisher promptly of this
> ruling.

The following day Patten duly notified Miss Anderson. The two thousand
copies of the 'unmailable' October issue could be withdrawn from the

---

* Even Lewis himself, writing from a map reference somewhere in the Ypres Salient, remarked to
Pound: 'No Little Review this month yet.' (*P/L* 96).

Pennsylvania Terminal Station by any representative presenting authority to receive them.

On 20 November Miss Anderson instituted an action against the Postmaster of the City of New York and a subpoena was served on Thomas G. Patten. He was ordered 'to show cause why injunction should not be issued ... enjoining and restraining defendant, his agents, servants and employees, from treating the October issue of *The Little Review* as non-mailable matter.'

Letters passed from Patten to the Postmaster General in Washington, Mr A. S. Burleson, and from Burleson to Thomas W. Gregory, the Attorney General. Gregory then instructed the New York District Attorney, Francis G. Caffey, 'to protect the interests of the Government in this matter.'

The motion for injunction was argued before the Honorable Augustus Noble Hand on 26 November, John Quinn in support; Joseph A. Burdeau, Special Assistant US Attorney, in opposition.

Margaret Anderson stated in her affidavit that '"The Little Review" is not mailed to girls' grammar schools and does not cater to girls' seminaries, nor has it any day nurseries or children's schools on its lists.' It had, however, 'more than fifty public libraries on its books, both in the United States and Canada, who are holding bound volumes ... as a literary asset.'

On Tuesday, 4 December 1917, 'at 10.30 o'clock in the forenoon of said day, at the office of the Clerk of the United States District Court, Southern District of New York', the Honorable Augustus Noble Hand signed his pronouncement on the motion of complaint brought by Margaret C. Anderson against Thomas G. Patten: 'it is ORDERED, ADJUDGED and DECREED that the said motion be and the same hereby is in all respects denied.'

The effective suppression of 'Cantleman's Spring Mate' by the New York Post Office's decision to regard it as unmailable cannot in all fairness be regarded as a notable martyrdom of the Modern Movement. It is of interest primarily as being the only occasion on which a work by Wyndham Lewis was judged to be obscene. Over the next 20 years three of his books would be suppressed and the prospects of a fourth damaged by a circulating library boycott, but his name would never again be connected, in a court of law, with the words 'lewd', 'lascivious', 'filthy' or 'indecent'.

*

Lewis escaped from 'Hell' without a scratch. Late in October he received a telegram informing him that his mother was dangerously ill with pneumonia and he was granted compassionate leave.

Shortly before this he had a narrow escape. At 4.30 in the morning of 24 October a shrapnel burst in the dugout wounded 2nd Lieutenants Underhill and Dyne. Pound told Quinn: 'his life was only saved because he was taking some extra duty and the officers whom he relieved were sleeping where he might have been.'

Ten days later, on 6 November, the village of Passchendaele was taken by Canadian troops. But by the time the four-month-long 3rd Battle of Ypres had ground to its bloody and mud-caked conclusion with the attainment of this final objective, Lewis was safely back in London. He had been relieved to find, on his arrival, that his mother was out of danger. He took a room at the Dean Hotel in Oxford Street and began to take full advantage of his period of leave.

TWENTY

'Why not paint a picture instead?'

On Sunday night, 11 November 1917, as her train pulled out of Victoria Station, Sybil Hart-Davis was very happy, a little drunk, and experiencing increasing discomfort. 'Three glasses of port beat hard on the bladder', she wrote, 'que faire?'

She was on her way back to Norton Priory, her sister's house in Selsey near Chichester, and was already scribbling a note to Lewis, with whom she had spent the evening. 'Darling. How happy we were – Roses, roses all the way ... You were so perfect all the time.'

She wrote: 'I think I rather love you', and then crossed out 'rather'.

Blonde and blue-eyed, she was a little over 30 when she was introduced to the handsome 2nd Lieutenant, newly returned from France. Her husband, a Captain in the Royal Fusiliers, was still out there. Since her disastrous, loveless marriage to Richard Hart-Davis, when she was 17, Sybil had had a great many affairs, and her two children, Rupert and Deirdre, were later to delight in speculating as to the identity of their respective fathers. Her two closest female friends were Iris Tree and Nancy Cunard. Lewis was to have affairs with them both in the early Twenties.

But as 1917 came to an end, it was Sybil who evidently fascinated him. Nancy would remember him in Venice during the late summer of 1922, talking about her every day:

> There was no one like her, he said ... I listened to much praise of Sybil – a most unusual thing to hear from Lewis. He told me he had been very much in love with her indeed.

In the early months of their relationship, Sybil talked to Nancy about him too. She asked her friend what she thought of his looks and Nancy, who hardly knew him at that time, said she thought he looked like a 'bicycling plumber'. She was never quite sure why she thought this.

That Sunday night in November, 12 miles out of Victoria, the train stopped long enough for Sybil to void the port. 'All is well', she wrote. 'Relieved at Sutton.'

*

One of the projected books inventoried by Lewis before he boarded the SS *Viper* was published that month. *The Ideal Giant*, 'privately printed for the London office of the Little Review', was sold at fashionable Christmas bazaars. That it also contained a story which the United States Post Office deemed 'obscene, lewd, or lascivious' must have encouraged sales, as well as the lionisation of the 2nd Lieutenant himself. 'Lewis has been having a hell of a go socially', Pound reported to Quinn. 'No duchess without a copy of Cantelman [*sic*] and the Ideal Giant.' He was also said to be 'lunching with Asquith, Curzon and co., assisting inebriated viceroys, etc.' This was at Claridge's during a function given by Lady Cunard. He was the only guest in uniform, 'the only one of military age, or not of cabinet or viceregal rank'.

He had met Mr Asquith before the war, at Lady Ottoline Morrell's house in Bedford Square. On that occasion the conversation had been about modern painting, and the Prime Minister had appeared interested in the views espoused by the leader of the 'Great London Vortex'. As if his thoughts were seldom far from international affairs, he had at one point enquired of Lewis 'whether [he] was in touch with people of similar views in other countries'.

At Claridge's, three and a half years later, Lewis sensed the former Prime Minister was at a loss how to continue the acquaintanceship:

> 'What are you in?'
> 'The Artillery.'
> 'Ah, yes, the Artillery . . .'
> There was a pause.
> 'Been at the Front, or are you perhaps . . . ?'
> 'Yes, at the Front.'
> 'Ah, at the Front.'
> There was another pause.
> 'Just back from the Front?'
> 'Yes, just back.'
> 'From the *real* Front . . .'

The conversation languished and Asquith changed the subject. Lewis was aware he had lost a particularly talented son to the war.

He remembered Lord Curzon, former Viceroy of India, sitting alone on a sofa, his face distorted by a 'twisted grimace of painful, staring rumination'. Whether Curzon was one of the 'inebriated viceroys' Pound reported Lewis as assisting is not known.

*

Lewis claimed that it was Guy Baker who initiated his final escape from the front line. When his period of compassionate leave was over, Baker said to him: 'Why return to your battery? Listen. It's quite unnecessary. Why not paint a picture instead?' As Lewis told the story, it was Baker who bundled him into a taxi and insisted he visit P. G. Konody, then engaged in recruiting artists for the Canadian War Memorials Fund.

The scheme had been set up late the previous year by the future Lord Beaverbrook, Sir Max Aitken, Officer in Charge of Canadian War Records. Its purpose was to provide 'suitable Memorials in the form of Tablets, Oil Paintings etc., to the Canadian Heroes and Heroines in the war'. A Canadian War Memorial building was planned, but never built, to house the collection produced by over 40 commissioned painters. Among those eventually represented were several associates of Lewis: Roberts, Nevinson, Wadsworth, Bomberg, Gilman, Ginner and Augustus John.

Konody had been given a blessing in the 1914 issue of *Blast*, for his critical support in the pages of the *Observer*. If a third *Blast* had appeared after the war, the blessing would certainly have been repeated, if only for the enthusiastic welcome given to Lewis by the artistic adviser to the Canadian War Memorials Fund:

> Konody received me, almost literally, with open arms. When I asked him if he had among his artists an artillery-artist, to paint howitzers, he shouted NO! When I said I knew all about howitzers – how would it be for me to paint one – he screamed OF COURSE!!!

An interview with Aitken in Clifford Street, off Bond Street, confirmed the appointment and the Canadian War Records Office made application to the War Office in Whitehall for Lewis's secondment to the Canadian Army for the three-months duration of the commission. This process took considerable time.

Pound, ever mindful of his friend's safety, wrote to Quinn: 'I hope to God the thing goes through. His leave is up tomorrow, and it would be an excessive shame to have him blown up, during the interim between the application, and its being put into execution.' According to Lewis, through the good offices of Lady Cunard, his leave was extended four times to bridge this limbo. As a result, for six weeks or more 'I was in the society of Lady Cunard continuously', he recalled, 'and it was here that I had the opportunity of observing at first hand the less seamy side of the war.'

The salubrious interlude was interrupted briefly by one final, purely formal, risk to life and limb. He had to return to his Battery, somewhere in the muddy wastes around Ypres, report to his Commanding Officer, and be personally seconded by him to the Canadian Army. Captain Hindson duly signed the paper, Lewis saluted and went back to London.

At last he was instructed to return to France on Sunday, 30 December. He was to paint a picture of a Canadian Gun Pit on canvas twelve feet wide and of unspecified height, for which he would be paid, 'on completion and acceptance by the committee', the sum of £250.

On New Year's Day he wrote to Konody from a chateau at Lievins, near Lens: 'Arrived, installed and comfortable, incredibly comfortable. I have been shown the sights and put in touch with the requisite gunners . . . It is cold on this plateau . . . How I shall be able to hold a pencil, I don't quite know.' On his sightseeing tour he looked across fields to the town of Neuville St Vaast where Gaudier-Brzeska had been killed. He admitted to 'a dismal and angry feeling':

> The ground was covered with snow, nobody about, and my god, it did look a cheerless place to die in.'

A day or two later Augustus John arrived, dressed in a Major's uniform, and promptly slipped and fell in the snow outside the door to Canadian Corps Headquarters. Like Orpen he had been given lofty rank for the purposes of his Canadian War Memorials commission. Climatic conditions inspired his subject for the vast composition he had come to amass material for: *Canadians opposite Lens – Winter*.*

Lewis soon found 'a dandy gun pit' and began work. Following the heavy fighting of the previous April, the war had left Vimy Ridge behind. No guns fired on either side and when he informed Pound he was 'contending . . . with unfavourable conditions' he meant 'chiefly bad weather and scarcity of cars'. He enjoyed his three weeks. 'The Canadians display a great deal of hospitality', he reported to Konody. 'I like them very much.' He had also caroused with John, and on one occasion took a staff car closer to the Front Line than either man felt comfortable with. He went to Paris on Canadian War Records business and found it packed with Americans and with 'no signs of Art anywhere'.

By the end of January he was back in London, preparing to paint the biggest expanse of canvas he would ever attempt.

*

An article headed 'WYNDHAM WHISKERS' appeared in the weekly

---

* John completed a cartoon 12 feet high and 40 feet long, but the painting was never produced.

London Mail on 2 February. It referred to Lewis as one of 'the long-haired whiskered men at the Café Royal'. The anonymous journalist's sources combined accuracy and inaccuracy in about equal measure:

> he has gone to America, and ... written a short story which was instrumental in having the magazine in which it appeared suppressed.

A reference to his own magazine was predictably abusive:

> He produces a ridiculous periodical at uncertain intervals over here called 'Blast'. If you read it, you repeated its name if you were one of the unrighteous.

But it was the implication he had been sitting out the war in America that made the piece 'unpleasant and even libellous'. Pound suggested Lewis, Wadsworth and Baker should proceed, in uniform, to the paper's office without delay and demand an explanation of its editor. Wadsworth felt 'truculence should be the keynote of the interview' and that an apology for the piece ought to appear in the next issue. He also suggested 'perhaps a punch on the jaw for the journalist who wrote it, the bleeder, the bugger, the sod'.

It is unlikely this plan was put into action, because neither retraction nor apology appeared in any subsequent issue of the *London Mail*.

*

Still in Northern France sketching soldiers and ruined masonry, Major John wrote to Miss Schepeler:

> Have you seen anything of that tragic hero and consumer of tarts and mutton chops, Wyndham Lewis? He is, I think, in London, painting his gun-pit and striving to reduce his 'Vorticism' to the level of Canadian intelligibility – a hopeless task I fear.

Lewis had been initially seconded to the Canadian forces for three months, but covering a canvas 10 feet by 11 was a considerable task and the period he was 'loaned' for had to be extended by another four months. He was also, as John intimated, working under severe stylistic restrictions, although perhaps not so explicitly stated as those impressed on a Vorticist colleague when invited to participate in the scheme. 'I would be glad to know whether, providing you are given the necessary facilities and leave', Gunner William Roberts was asked:

you are prepared to paint the picture at your own risk, to be submitted for the approval of the committee. The reason for this request is that the Art Advisor informs us that he is not acquainted with your realistic work and Cubist work is inadmissible for the purpose.

In other words, if the painting was unsuitable the painter would not be paid.

Konody would have told Lewis what was required: a documentary record of his subject with few, if any, avant-garde flourishes. And Lewis worked 'like a galley slave' in a studio in Campden House Mews, to deliver what was expected of him.

Meanwhile, in April, he was approached by a second commissioning body, the organisation instrumental in sending William Orpen to visit and paint 'Hell': the Ministry of Information. Mr A. Yockney wrote to inform Lewis that, 'in connection with a scheme for utilising the artistic resources of the country for record purposes', it had been suggested that he 'be invited to paint a picture or pictures relating to the war'. Yockney had been instructed by his Committee to enquire how 2nd Lieutenant Lewis was 'situated in regard to [his] work and military obligations; and should the scheme mature, whether [he] would be disposed to enter into an arrangement with the Government'.

Lewis replied that he would be pleased to undertake the commission. He explained his commitments to the Canadian War Records Office but saw no reason why the 'paintings for the Canadian and Imperial Governments should not overlap'.

Soon after, Yockney's Committee met and agreed that Lewis was to paint a picture 125 inches long and 72 inches high. These were the dimensions of Paolo Uccello's *Battle of San Romano* in the National Gallery. It was, thought one of the Committee's artistic advisers, Robert Ross, 'a very charming size' for a war painting. Lewis was to be paid £300. This was £50 more than the sum he was being paid under the Canadian War Memorials Fund for painting a picture nearly twice as big.

*

In June, another volume of the literary legacy enumerated in Lewis's 1917 inventory was published by Alfred A. Knopf in New York. John Quinn was unable to give the American publication of *Tarr* his undivided attention because of an operation in early February to remove a rectal ulcer. He was still in hospital when the proofs of the novel were delivered to him for correction. A meticulous and conscientious man, he would have amended a profusion of typographical errors and other anomalies that eventually appeared in the Knopf edition. Instead, feeling weak after the operation, he divided the proofs between two friends who did not appear to earn the $50 each he paid them for the job.

In a letter to Miss Schepeler Lewis referred to 'the bad American *Tarr*' and assured her he had 'taken steps about that'. The 'steps' taken presumably ensured that the English edition, brought out by the Egoist Press three weeks after the American, was not riddled with errors as well.

Reviews of the novel were generally favourable, notably that by Rebecca West in *The Nation*, who, whilst conceding that the first impression was of 'a cleverish pastiche of Dostoevsky', went on to supply a puff that Lewis would quote in publicity material for the rest of his life:

> a beautiful and serious work of art that reminds us of Dostoevsky only because it too is inquisitive about the soul, and because it contains one figure of vast moral significance which is worthy to stand beside Stavrogin.

Other critics also noted the influence of Dostoevsky. In her box at the Theatre Royal, Drury Lane on 27 July, the last night of Sir Thomas Beecham's Summer Season of Grand Opera in English, Lady Cunard struggled to make herself heard over the crashing chords of *The Valkyrie*. She was attempting to introduce Lewis to the General commanding the American troops in England:

> the author of *Tarr* – a *novel*, General! Mr Lewis has been compared, General, to Dostoevsky! *The Times* says he has taken Dostoevsky for his model. Dostoevsky, General!

The American appeared impressed: 'Dostoevsky – Dostoevsky!' he said. 'And a very good model too!'

*

He had told Sybil Hart-Davis his Canadian painting would be finished by 21 June. This proved over-optimistic. In July, after six months and with his period of secondment nearing an end, he was visited by Captain Watkins of Canadian War Records and Sir Bertram Lima, who wished to inspect their investment. This viewing of the picture revealed that it needed a great deal more work. Captain Watkins applied for, and was granted, an extension of Lewis's secondment for a further four months, although expressing the hope to Yockney at Information that 'he will probably have completed the picture . . . well within that time.'

*

Lewis's affair with Sybil Hart-Davis foundered in suspicion and jealousy. At one point in the summer he wrote to tell her that their relationship was 'doomed' because of what he termed a 'new sentimental interest' that she was developing. She had no idea what he was referring to and called his letter 'unkind gibberish'. He was, she told him, 'a fiend . . . sent from Hell's lower intestine to plague [her]'.

For her part, she often mentioned the affair she suspected him of having with another blonde, Helen Saunders, whom she called 'the wild dandelion'. In the first months of their relationship she noted his absence from his hotel at an early hour of the morning and accused him of being 'not quite truthful'.

Incidentally, if Lewis did indeed have an affair with Helen Saunders at this time, he would have cause to regret it two years later.

In the main Sybil chided him for not writing to her. 'Is it wanton malice,' she asked, 'uncooked resentment or merely having nothing to say, that makes you refrain?' And she wrote of his cruelty and her hurt feelings in vivid physical terms:

> you can boast of having dealt out humiliation with a lavish hand. And you have possibly been of use to me – To be thrown, yet again, against the wall should bring a party to its senses. I feel wretched and quite unreasonably disappointed – But, believe me, even the shallowest of us suffer quite genuinely sometimes.

On more than one occasion the affair appeared to terminate, usually at Lewis's instigation, and after one emotional parting she resolved to trouble him no further. 'Remember the good chapters', she urged, 'for surely there were some.' Then, a reconciliation initiated, she would write again to her 'black angel', signing herself 'P', for 'Pet'.

Eventually they parted amicably. Sybil acquired a new lover but she and Lewis met socially from time to time. Writing to her son Rupert about one such encounter, she mentioned, in passing, the woman who had superseded her as the main emotional interest in Lewis's life: 'I dined with Lewis, a friend of his called Iris Barry who writes poetry and a married couple called Wadsworth (he camouflages ships).' Herbert Read described a visit to Lewis's flat in Great Tichfield Street – 'lots of stairs to go up, but a view and fresh air at the top and the jolliest suite of rooms: 1 bedroom, 1 sitting room, 1 bathroom, 1 kitchen sort of place (very small). But all very jolly and dainty.' He found the same dark-haired woman installed, apparently 'to pour out the tea'. Read did not catch her name but learned she was 'a young poetess who had not yet published'. He thought her 'quite a nice girl'.

She was born Frieda Crump – a name which encourages imaginative alternatives in adult life. Although in the main styling herself Iris Barry, she sometimes adopted the pseudonym Frieda Bark.

Towards the end of August, Lewis was away from the Great Titchfield Street flat for over a week and his neighbours had no forwarding address for his letters. According to Sybil Hart-Davis, he was in the northwest of England, either Liverpool or Blackpool. It is likely that he was in the company of Iris Barry and that it was during this 'Black or Liver poolian holiday' that the conception of their first child took place.

*

Guy Baker, writing from the Grand Pump Room Hotel in Bath, sent 'regards to Barry', at the same time bringing reminder of an earlier liaison. 'Be genial to Olive if you encounter her', he urged Lewis. 'She is terrify [sic] of you.'

The mother of Peter and Betty, both of whom were still being looked after in Norwood by Mrs Lewis and Mrs Prickett, worked in a hotel during the war, a prey to anxiety during Zeppelin raids and sustained by intermittent postal orders and surprisingly warm words from her former lover. Lewis had evidently forgiven her for the dose of 'clap' she had passed on to him in 1914, and a letter from Lydd in late 1916 or early 1917 addressed her by her pet name 'Dunk', concluding affectionately with 'Many kisses, little Dunkie'. Later, from France, she received less personalised missives: field postcards sent to her in Chichester Road, Paddington, simply dated and signed to show he was still alive.

On the face of it, in late 1918, there was no clear reason for Olive to be terrified of him.

*

When Yockney, accompanied by Muirhead Bone, art adviser to the Ministry of Information, visited the Campden House Mews studio on 24 September to view the huge Canadian canvas, it was probably, with the exception of the lower right corner, to all intents and purposes finished. Lewis would have been able to explain the precisely delineated details of the sighting gear on the 8″ howitzer under its canopy of camouflage netting, the ranks of high explosive shells, some with transit caps still fitted to their noses, others blue-tipped with the 'graze' fuses designed to detonate on glancing impact. The figures in the foreground, standing behind the shells or around the breech of the gun, seemed of secondary importance to the hardware. In the background was another canopied gun pit, ruins, and a clichéd column of soldiers wending, 'Tipperary' fashion, towards the blasted tree-spiked horizon.

Later he told Herbert Read:

> On looking at my Canadian painting today I came to the conclusion that Konody had succeeded in making me paint one of the dullest good pictures on earth. I have just done another painting in an afternoon which is at least 17 times as alive. What a nightmare this wicked war has been.

To John Quinn he could not even concede it 'good', although it attracted favourable comment at the Royal Academy's Exhibition of Canadian Pictures in January 1919: 'My painting . . . is not good,' he declared. 'Lots of people like it. I can only see in it what I *could* have made, and frankly hate the sight of it.' His contempt for *Canadian Gun Pit* was barely disguised by the final sentence of the description he wrote for the catalogue: 'It is an experiment of the painter's in a kind of painting not his own.'

Yockney and Bone, however, were impressed by what they had seen and, four days after the Armistice, a further extension of 2nd Lieutenant Lewis's leave from the Royal Garrison Artillery was requested of the War Office, to enable him to paint 'an important picture for the collection being formed by the Ministry of Information'.

*

By the end of the year Lewis had moved out of the Great Titchfield Street flat and, for the first half of 1919, had no settled address of his own in London. During this period he lived in Edward Wadsworth's place at 1A Gloucester Walk, off Church Street, Kensington.

TWENTY-ONE

'I'm thirty-seven till I pass the word round!'

In February 1919 probate was granted upon the estate of the late Charles Edward Lewis. The estranged husband of Anne Lewis had died at 6 o'clock in the morning of Saturday 23 November 1918, at 1844 North Bouvier Street, Philadelphia, Pennsylvania. He was 75 and the cause of death certified 'dilatation of heart'. Given that Anne never granted him a divorce following their separation in 1893, and given his bigamous marriage to Lillian Natalie Phipps in 1912, he was survived by two widows.

Response to Anne's enquiries showed that surviving members of her late husband's family were probably as ignorant of the dubious domestic arrangements of his later life as she was. A niece wrote to her from Oakville:

> you know I was quite a young girl, and he a travelling man whom we rarely saw, and while I never heard of any other marriage I would not swear to it.

In 1901, Charles had settled in Portland, Maine, with his companion Lillian Phipps, and Ethel Evelyn, aged about seven, whom he described as his daughter by his 'second wife, now deceased'. He acquired two adjacent houses in North Street and a property on Preble Street. Lillian bore him a son, Alexander, in about 1905. When he made a will in December 1911, Charles passed Alexander off as the issue, with Ethel, of his 'second wife, now deceased'. In the event of his death before the two children reached the age of 21, he appointed Lillian Phipps as guardian. Some time during the following six months he married Lillian and, in about 1915, moved with his family to the rented house in Philadelphia where he died.

He left personal property amounting to some $500 and real estate to the value of $12,000. To Ethel he bequeathed three violoncellos, two flutes, a large three-stone diamond ring and a smaller three-stone diamond ring. Alexander, 13 years old at his father's death, received two ruby rings, a silver watch, a gold English lever watch, two revolvers, two shotguns and a Winchester rifle. The three properties in Portland, together with 'household furniture, goods and effects' were to be divided equally between Ethel and Alexander.

There was only one other beneficiary mentioned in the will and, despite a significant untruth in his designation, the legacy was substantial:

> I give, devise and bequeath unto Percy W. Lewis, of London, England, my son born to me by my first wife from whom I was divorced many years ago, all the interest which I have in the house and grounds located at No. 23 Curzon Road, Southport, Lancashire, England . . . To have and to hold the same to him and his heirs and assigns forever.

Coincidentally, both Lewis and T. S. Eliot received word of their respective fathers' deaths on the same day: 8 January. As a result Eliot absented himself from a small gathering at Ezra Pound's triangular flat in Church Walk. Ben Hecht reported that Lewis attended, 'apologising for his seeming callousness with the fact that he had not seen his parent for some twenty years'.

When the property in Curzon Street, Southport, was sold in May the following year, it realised just under half the estimated value of Charles Edward Lewis's entire estate.

*

Lewis communicated a bustling sense of urgency in a letter to John Quinn:

> first of all, I must dash in straight away and get active, now the war is over. I must have a show of war paintings and drawings, here in London, now, and in a gallery with a big clientele and machinery of advertisement. I have exhibited nowhere during the war: I must do nothing but exhibit, write, work, during this year, if my health allows.

Unspecified ill health had dogged him in the last months of 1918 and he blamed that, together with 'war conditions generally' and also 'worry about [his] cursed Canadian canvas', for the fact that, by the start of the new year, he had got 'just enough completed, sound things for a show'.

In the wake of the Canadian War Memorials Exhibition at Burlington House, Lewis's one-man show, 'Guns', opened at the Goupil Gallery on Saturday 1 February. The best paintings and drawings to be seen there, he claimed, were 'about ten times as successful' as his monumental *Gun Pit*. Following the opening he told John Quinn that the show had been 'extremely well received by almost everybody' and he hoped for 'great things from this success in the coming year'. Before the private view Lewis put red spots alongside those he regarded as the ten best drawings, reserving them for the New York attorney. This proved presumptuous and, on seeing photographs of the ten, Quinn rejected all but three of Lewis's recommendations, agreeing to buy four others instead. Other purchasers included Lord Rothermere and Lady Tredegar.

'Every day fresh things are being sold', Lewis declared. But by the time the show closed a total of only 21 out of well over 50 works had attracted buyers.

*

It is estimated that the influenza pandemic that reached its peak during the winter of 1918–19 wiped out some 27 million people worldwide: well over three times as many as were killed in the Great War. John Quinn wrote from New York that 'one could not walk five blocks on the street without hearing the clanging of the ambulances taking people to hospital' and that 'there were too many funeral processions and hearses in evidence to make going around pleasant.' For the first time on record the quarterly death rate in England and Wales exceeded the birth rate.

Symptoms were fever, low pulse, pains in the eyes, ears, head and back and a feeling of dizziness. Pneumonia often followed. Around the middle of February Lewis came down with it. Helen Saunders enlisted the help of her sister Ethel, who had worked with the Voluntary Aid Detachment during the war, and she arranged for him to be admitted to hospital. The VAD nurse recalled, in later life, how she and her sister assisted the weak and feverish patient to the Endsleigh Palace Hospital for Officers off the Euston Road, and that he was 'very rude' and never thanked them for their trouble.

The influenza followed its customary course and developed into double pneumonia. For some weeks he had a dangerously high temperature. Then in March he was flat on his back but no longer at risk. His doctor told him he had 'staggered about a bit, but eventually rolled down the right side of the hill'.

Guy Baker, in another hospital, died of this postwar scourge.

*

Lewis stayed for another fortnight at the Endsleigh Palace Hospital, until about 20 March. From there he went to a convalescent home in Torquay. A month later he was still 'not yet in proper trim' and on his way 'from one seaside place to another': from Torquay to Aldeburgh in Suffolk. His route between these resorts took him to Birmingham, where Iris Barry, nearly eight months pregnant, was staying. Her mother lived in the suburb of Washwood Heath and Lewis wrote inviting her to visit them one afternoon.

Presumably anxious to avoid establishing too frank and close a relationship with Mrs Crump, he adopted one of Iris's pseudonyms for the occasion and signed the letter 'Percy Bark'.

By the middle of May he had continued his journey and was staying at 'The White Lion', Aldeburgh-on-Sea. He sent Iris two nightdresses and £8, promising to send more in a day or two. For her part, probably some time towards the end of that month, Iris moved into a nursing home in Edgbaston where, on 3 June, she gave birth to a son.

It can be safely assumed that Lewis was not present for this event. The following day he was attending an Officer's Dispersal Unit in London and having his Demobilisation Ration Book stamped. The address he entered on the Food Card issued him was the Coburg Court Hotel on Bayswater Road.

Iris called her son Robin. She registered the birth without divulging his father's name and, accordingly, no entry appeared in that category on the child's birth certificate.*

*

Later in June Yockney was pleased to hear Lewis had recovered sufficiently to make a start on his picture for the Ministry of Information, as he was keen to have the collection of commissioned paintings together by the autumn, in good time for an exhibition at Burlington House in the new year.

Lewis cannot have begun serious work on the picture until after 24 June, when he took over the tenancy of a flat and studio occupying the lower part of a house in Campden Hill Gardens, a cul-de-sac just south of Notting Hill Gate. It was a few minutes' walk from the studio in Campden House Mews where he had painted his Canadian picture the previous year.

In September, unaware of Lewis's current address, Yockney wrote to him at his former, temporary lodging at 1A Gloucester Walk, a house the Wadsworths had by that time vacated, leaving no one to forward the letter. In vain Lewis was informed that an illustrated catalogue for the Royal Academy exhibition was in preparation. 'How far advanced is your picture?' Yockney asked. 'Will it be complete within the next few weeks so that it can be photographed?' Receiving no reply, he sent a reminder in October to the same address.

Then, exasperated by Lewis's continued silence, on 16 October Yockney took the precaution of registering his next letter and charged it with a threat:

unless your picture is finished and delivered here by the 31st instant, or a

---

* Robin was cared for by his maternal grandmother, Annie Symes Crump, until the age of three or four, then placed in a private children's home at Woodford Green until the age of eleven. He was only made aware of the identity of his parents in adulthood.

reasonable excuse given before that date, it will be considered that the commission has lapsed. As Trustee for the Ministry of Information scheme, I am compelled to bring the transaction to a close.

Despite also being dispatched to 1A Gloucester Walk, this ultimatum actually reached Lewis at Campden Hill Gardens three days later. His nonchalant explanation that the previous letters had been 'marooned' at the old address did not explain how the latest one had reached him so easily. He assured Yockney that his picture would be complete by 31 October. This deadline had to compete with other activities.

Blast was to be revived. In August he had told Herbert Read that a publisher had been found and that his own contribution would be ready within a week or so. Following his months of illness and convalescence, Lewis was belatedly keeping to his promise made at the beginning of the year to 'dash in . . . and get active, now the war [was] over'.

One night, at Verrey's Restaurant in Regent Street, following a meal with Osbert, Sacheverell and Edith Sitwell, Lewis made a pencilled calculation on a matchbox. Then, with a yellowing cigarette stub clamped in his mouth and his left eye partially closed against the smoke drifting across it, he said: 'Remember! I'm thirty-seven till I pass the word round!' There was still a month or so to go before his birthday and he meant to extend his 37th year indefinitely beyond that date. Like many men who had been plucked out of the natural course of their lives by the war, he felt the need to make up for the time lost. In 1915 he had declared 'the War has stopped Art dead', and he now regarded 1914–18 as 'four years of the most vital period of his career . . . torn from his life'. It was not vanity that prompted him, from 1919 until his death, to deduct two, and as many as four, years from his age.

Edith Sitwell claimed to be so impressed by the seriousness of Lewis's injunction to her and her brothers that for a long time after, if a doctor examined her chest and commanded her to say 'Ninety-nine', she instinctively blurted out 'Thirty-seven'.

On the evening of Wednesday 22 October Lewis left off work on his Ministry of Information painting to give a public lecture at the Central Buildings in Westminster. It was one of a series organised by The Arts League of Service. Other speakers to the theme of 'Modern Tendencies in Art' were Eugene Goossens on 'Music', T. S. Eliot on 'Poetry', and Margaret Morris, who once performed barefoot at the 'Cave of the Golden Calf', on 'Dancing'. At 8.45 p.m. Lewis addressed the audience in the conference hall on the subject of 'Painting'. George Bernard Shaw was in the chair.

It was not a happy occasion. Lewis attempted to speak without notes and kept losing the thread of what he was saying. A report in *The Athenaeum* euphemistically referred to a 'repeated sectional incompleteness . . . , which produced an effect of incoherence, . . . possibly due to an inability or a reluctance on the part of Mr Lewis to keep his brain chained to a main issue.' Each time his discourse dried up he would mutter, 'and so on and so forth', while grasping for another thread to pursue. Years later, Lewis blamed the 'amiable buffoon G.B.S.' for playing to the audience and putting him off. Shaw's behaviour must indeed have been distracting. Kate Lechmere watched mesmerised as he put on 'four different pairs of spectacles in two hours'. During the discussion that followed the lecture, he kept referring to the speaker as 'Mr Wyndfield Lewis', and deplored 'the regrettable conditions of democratic society which force an artist to spend his time talking about his art'.

Lewis determined never to extemporise a lecture again.

*

The revival of Vorticism, promised in 1915 for 'the serious mission it [had] on the other side of World-War', never materialised. Nor did the third issue of *Blast*. Instead, Lewis's substantial contribution, *The Caliph's Design*, was brought out as a slim volume by the Egoist Press in marbled blue and white paper boards. The subtitle gave away its pedigree: *Architects! Where is your Vortex?* It was published on 31 October, the day Lewis had promised Yockney his painting.

Lewis's foreword to the catalogue of 'Guns' in February had begun:

The public, surprised at finding eyes and noses in this exhibition, will begin by the reflection that the artist has . . . abandoned those vexing diagrams by which he puzzled and annoyed.

The public might have been further refreshed and relieved to recognise the eyes and nose of a contemporary poet, in Lewis's larger than life-size portrait of *Ezra Pound Esq.*, exhibited at the Goupil Salon in November and praised to the skies by Frank Rutter in the *Sunday Times* as 'a great work by a great artist'. And a representational element formed at least a part of the 10 foot by 6 foot canvas called *A Battery Shelled* which he at last presented to Yockney for exhibition at the Royal Academy the following January.

Casting the eye from the left edge of the canvas to the right, as across a printed page, three figures are encountered first, realistic in that they do indeed have 'eyes and noses', and the one with a moustache recognisable as a likeness of Edward Wadsworth. They are cut off by the bottom edge of the canvas, as if standing just inside the picture, at one remove from the viewer. One of the men looks down at his pipe, another stares, as it were, out of the picture and the third looks towards the action: the battery under shellfire. It is not immediately clear that the scene occupying the majority of the composition is one of violent devastation, contemplated with apparent equanimity by onlookers from a neighbouring battery. As the eye continues its movement to the right, two more figures are seen, also cut off by the bottom edge of the canvas but smaller than the first three and intended to be further away. They are more stylised, less recognisable as individuals. And so the further to the right the eye travels, the more the picture's perspective increases. In the centre of the composition, the ploughed middle ground contains three figures, abstracted by distance, insect-like and mechanical. And as the eye moves further, on a rising diagonal toward the complex geometries of the background, men are barely distinguishable from the piles of shells and sheets of corrugated iron amongst which they struggle. Against the horizon explosions and plumes of smoke are strange, hard-edged, segmented structures like twisted pieces of metal or broken umbrellas.

A Battery Shelled would not have been accepted by the Canadian War Memorials Committee to whom 'Cubist work' was 'inadmissible'. But because Lewis had been allowed more freedom of expression for his second picture, the Ministry of Information received, in return for its £300, a more complex meditation on war than the *Canadian Gun Pit* could ever offer. By using the contrast between realistic and abstract form he had made an observation about the artilleryman's experience of fighting. Death and destruction occurred, for the most part, at long range and on map-referenced co-ordinates, and it was perhaps easy to forget that the distant spectacle involved any human tragedy at all.

TWENTY-TWO

'Most indubitably yours'

On 7 February 1920, fifteen months after the passing of her husband, Anne Stuart Lewis died of lobar pneumonia at home in 99 Oaklands Road, Hanwell. She was 61. Her son was with her and he registered the death two days later. Her estate was valued by Probate at £1,718 13s. 7d. She left £100, some clothes and furniture to her aunt and companion Frances Mary Prickett. The rest she bequeathed to her son.

Frances Prickett, now aged 78, also inherited custody of Lewis's two children by Olive Johnson: Peter, aged eight, and Betty, six.

*

At the end of March Lewis acknowledged himself a member of a group of painters for the last time in his life. 'Group X' exhibited only once, at the Mansard Gallery, 196 Tottenham Court Road. As spokesman of the group, Lewis wrote the catalogue foreword and a short piece in the *Evening News*. 'Why X?' he began rhetorically:

> Why is this group branded in that way? The reason is an aesthetic one, like the markings on the face of a savage. It signifies nothing more didactic than that, X, as a sign, pleases the members of this group.

It was, perhaps, not necessary to mention that the members of 'Group X' were ten in number. Five were former Vorticist colleagues: Dismorr, Etchells, Hamilton, Roberts, and Wadsworth. The rest comprised the sculptor Frank Dobson, Charles Ginner, E. McKnight Kauffer, and 'Jock' Turnbull, veteran of the Omega Workshops, to whom Winifred Gill once confided witnessing Lewis's unguarded posturings with a checked cap. Two facing pages of the catalogue were devoted to each of the ten, reproducing a drawing on the left and a self-portrait on the right, except for Lewis's two pages, which featured neither drawing nor self-portrait, only a list of the works he exhibited: seven self-portraits.

*

In June, probate of the late Mrs Lewis's will was granted to her son as sole executor. But it was to be another eight months before he succeeded in selling the unprofitable laundry business, and 'impossible', he claimed, 'to dispose of [it] at a reasonable price'. It is not known how much of the £1,718 13s. 7d. probate valuation of his mother's estate actually came to Lewis. However, the legacy from his other parent, the property at 23 Curzon Road, Southport, was sold for the considerable sum of £1,200. Mrs Prickett did not receive the £100 promised in her niece's will. Six years later, Lewis drew up a declaration and had her sign it:

> This is to say that since your mother's death you have supported me: and therefore the sum of money mentioned in your mother's will to be paid me in the event of your not otherwise assisting me has long ago been cancelled.

*

A telegram handed in to the Leicester Square Post Office at 3.35 in the afternoon of 1 June was testimony to the domestic arrangements prevailing at 83 Lansdowne Road, Lewis's current lodgings, just over three and a half miles away in Notting Hill:

PLEASE PREPARE CHOP EIGHT – LEWIS

On the back of the telegram Iris Barry itemised her shopping:

butter 1/4½d
potatoes 2/7½d
onions 4d
steak 2/9½d

She was doing her best to make him comfortable. And with some sacrifice. 'I have led a singular kind of life all the last year to try and fit in with your life', she told him two months later. 'I have no friends and no acquaintances and nothing at all either hobby or career or what not to "live" for except to "get on" with you.'

*

There was a notable absentee from the reunion of Vorticist colleagues at the Mansard Gallery under the brand of 'Group X'. Helen Saunders, she whom Sybil Hart-Davis had called 'the wild dandelion', because of her golden hair, was exhibiting disturbing signs of amorous obsession. She took to dogging Lewis in the street, demanding his attention and exhorting him to work.

Some time in January or February, while Lewis was still living at 20A Campden Hill Gardens, Helen's mother came from Oxford to discuss the problem of her daughter with him. After that meeting Helen continued to pester him with visits, letters and telegrams. The habit of secrecy with which he surrounded every successive dwelling-place and bolthole over the next two decades may have been established, at least partly, by this campaign of emotional persecution he felt himself to be a victim of in the first six months of 1920. When his lease at Campden Hill Gardens expired in March, he rented another studio at 37 Redcliffe Road. For a short period he was left in peace. Then, in late April or May, Jessica Dismorr had a breakdown, and Helen used this crisis in the life of a mutual friend as an excuse to seek out Lewis's new studio address and let him know. Thereafter she continued to write to him and pester him as before.

She begged to be allowed to live in his studio. She seems to have been, at one and the same time, pleading for release from his influence and lamenting the loss of it:

> You don't know what you are doing. You are killing me by mistake . . . If I have driven you away it is my death as a human soul because it is not possible for me to love any one else . . . I beg you not to drive me away from the discipline of your mind on my mind and body . . . What I begged release from was the awful sense that I was falling into involuntary bondage to some other mind . . . What I can't make you understand is that if you would let me be alone for a month I should be all right – but not if this other bodily life is forced on me . . . I am not fit to be alive just now . . . If it hadn't have been for my mother I should have killed myself last week . . . Please hear me this time – It is as if some one were beating me just over my heart.

What happened between Lewis and Helen Saunders to provoke these highly charged outpourings remains a mystery. But emerging from the tangle of her apparently contradictory desires is the suspicion that he had indeed seduced, and subsequently rejected, her:

> You have not let me grow up yet – I was on the way but because you did not believe in my affection something went wrong in the very centre of my life.

Whatever happened, the experience plunged her into a desperate schizoid state apparently polarising mind and body:

> I only want to be released from the idea of the other person . . . Don't let

me go into the mechanical body's life which I call the other person . . . I don't want the other life that is being forced on me – Don't turn me into a machine.

For a time she bombarded him with telegrams and letters postmarked 'Taynuilt'. It is not known what she was doing in this small village on the west coast of Scotland, but it must have been a comfort to Lewis that at least these irksome communications came from such a remote spot. But then she began travelling south. Lewis received another telegram, with a different postmark, announcing her arrival in London the following day and indicating her desire for a meeting. It was signed 'S.O.S.' At this point Lewis wrote to her mother:

> I don't want to distress you; and seeing that your daughter was for some time a very helpful and seemingly unselfish friend, I don't wish to take any steps that would shock or distress her in her present state. On the other hand, I cannot undertake indefinitely to support the persecution to which she has thought good to subject me for a year or more. You will see yourself that to have her perpetually turning up and ringing my bell, perpetually telegraphing and writing to me, is not a bearable situation.

The problem was eventually resolved. Mr Saunders wrote from Oxford to tell Lewis that, following an interview with her mother, Helen had promised not to see him, or communicate in any way, in the future.

*

As she prepared Lewis's steak and onions for 8 o'clock on the evening of 1 June 1920, Iris Barry was about six months into her second pregnancy. This time her condition seems to have been at Lewis's suggestion. 'I must remind you that last year you spoke of my having another child – yours – as a proof of good will and all that.' It appears that he had harboured suspicions regarding the paternity of Robin, now being cared for by Mrs Crump in Washwood Heath, suspicions not entirely allayed by Iris herself. On this occasion, however, she could assure him: 'I'm having another and most indubitably yours whatever stupidities you commit by conjuring up impossibilities to the contrary.'

By early August Iris was installed in the Nursing Institute at Mitcham in South London to await delivery. She spent the first part of her stay knitting Lewis brown woollen socks and sending meticulous timetable details. There were trains from Victoria at 3 and 4 o'clock, then 4.30, 5.22, 6.15 and 6.58.

If catching the train from Clapham Junction, two or three minutes were to be added to these times and the journey took less than half an hour.

Lewis visited her when his hunt for a new studio allowed him time, but going six miles into the southern suburbs remained tiresome. 'I am sorry I can't come and see you more often', he told her. 'The distance is very great, and you are awkward to get at.'

*

Although the postwar revival of *Blast* had been abandoned, Lewis was having discussions with the wealthy novelist Sydney Schiff, who wrote under the name of Stephen Hudson and the influence of Marcel Proust, about the launch of another journal – *The Tyro*. The sale of his father's house in Southport meant that Lewis was in a position to put £50 into the new enterprise, and Schiff offered the same. Harriet Shaw Weaver agreed to publish it but was unwilling to make any financial commitment.

Lewis's new patron had sound advice, necessary to anyone setting up a small magazine, about getting people to work for nothing. 'On the matter of paying contributors . . . we should adopt the principle that no one can receive payment until the new paper is in a position to pay them out of its own resources.' Schiff's connection with the paper was therefore to be kept secret. 'I have come into this thing to support you', he told Lewis, 'but as soon as certain [people] get wind of it they . . . would imagine that as I was in it they ought to be paid handsomely.'

When the Schiffs invited Lewis down to their summer place in Eastbourne for the weekend, Iris wished him 'best of luck with the powerful Semites'.

*

When his business affairs and studio search allowed him to make the journey out to Mitcham, Lewis's visits sometimes seemed a mixed blessing to Iris. 'We were both rather tired and wretched last night', she wrote to him after one ill-tempered visit, 'so it wasn't very satisfactory, tho' I was grateful enough to you for bothering to come, quite apart from being glad to see you.'

To spare her the stigma attached to an unmarried pregnancy, his letters would arrive at the Nursing Institute addressed to 'Mrs Lewis'.

She had optimistic plans for their future life together. Lewis's brown woollen socks had given her ideas for a thriving little business. 'I should begin in a very unambitious way by employing only one or two cheap cripples or people like that and . . . lay in a stock of sample work for people to order from – specially for Christmas. I should . . . teach knitting; and try to arrange with some firm of manufacturers making woollen underwear to be an agent for them, selling women's and children's vests etc. on commission. As I got more orders I should employ more knitters, and aim eventually at doing nothing but sell.' The business could be run from home, she went on, 'if we had two furnished rooms near wherever you have your next studio.' The enterprise was, she hastily assured him, dependent on one factor. 'Naturally all this is supposing we continue to see each other – which I certainly wish.'

An exquisite drawing shows Iris in what must have been a characteristic pose at this time: sunk in an armchair, her sharply pencilled features in profile, staring down in concentration at a complex knot of fingers and knitting needles. Lewis's views on the prospect of a cottage industry based upon knitted vests are not known.

She did not hear from him for some days and became preoccupied with how and where to dispose of the expected offspring. The cheapest place she had heard of was in Sudbury, near Harrow, describing itself as a 'Home for the Infants and Children of Gentlepeople'. It would charge 27/- a week to take the child off their hands, she explained, 'which is a lot but then you don't have to buy a pram.' She badly needed Lewis's advice and support: 'some place has to be found for it when I leave here, and I don't suppose you want to try and find anywhere even if you had time. What shall I do?'

His intermittent visits, and now the prolonged absence of a 'husband' from her bedside, was becoming a depressing embarrassment. 'Only do communicate with me,' she pleaded, 'I feel so very deserted when I don't know where you are, and it is so beastly being unmarried and nosey old crabs of women will come and be rude and horrid to me, I do so dread all that.'

She was evidently unaware, as she wrote this letter, that Lewis had already left London for a fortnight's holiday in France with T. S. Eliot.

*

Their first stop was Paris. Eliot had written to James Joyce before their departure, arranging to meet him on Sunday, 15 August. Ezra Pound had asked Eliot to deliver a package.

Those whom Lewis would later call the 'Men of 1914' – Eliot, Joyce, Pound and himself – were never, all four, in the same room at the same time. But that Sunday three of them were present in a red-curtained apartment at the Hôtel d'Elysée, staring at the brown paper parcel, mute representative of the fourth, lying on a gilt Second Empire table. Neither Lewis nor Eliot had any idea what Pound had entrusted them with. While Joyce struggled with the knots, Eliot sat impassive and Lewis adjusted his tie in a cracked mirror. Joyce had with him a 15-year-old youth over six foot tall, his son Giorgio, and they exchanged words in bad-tempered Italian. 'Give me a penknife!' snapped Joyce. 'I don't have a penknife!' snapped his son. Eliot at length proffered a pair of nail-scissors. The string was cut and the brown paper rolled back. 'Thereupon,' as Lewis gleefully recalled 17 years later, 'along with some nondescript garments for the trunk – there were no trousers I believe – a fairly presentable pair of *old brown shoes* stood revealed, in the centre of the bourgeois French table.'

An explanation of this embarrassing gift could be found in Joyce's correspondence with Pound from Trieste two months earlier. He had, he said, no clothes other than his son's cast-offs: a suit too narrow in the shoulders, boots two sizes too big. There was a postscript: 'This is a very poetical epistle. Do not imagine that it is a subtly worded request for second-hand clothing.' But Pound may subsequently have heard from Sylvia Beach about Joyce's visit to the Shakespeare & Co. bookshop in July wearing a pair of grubby tennis shoes. He could not have known that by 15 August, and this first meeting with Eliot and Lewis, the author of *Ulysses* had replaced the tennis shoes with a pair of elegant patent leather pumps.

Eliot had invited Joyce to join them for dinner but the novelist, smarting under the humiliation of Pound's misguided generosity, insisted upon taking them to a nearby restaurant and picking up all bills. Giorgio having been sent home with the old brown shoes, they were joined by the art critic of the *Petit Parisien*, the Belgian poet and novelist, Fritz Vanderpyl. Eliot commemorated the gathering, in a letter to Schiff, with a drawing of the four men under the puzzled gaze of a French waiter.

They left Paris the following day, intending to travel west to Vannes in Brittany. They reached Nantes by Wednesday 18 August and Lewis sent Iris a postcard and telegraphed that they would be in Vannes until the following Sunday.

The next day Iris wrote, poste restante, to Lewis in Vannes. She was now worried that the Home for the Infants and Children of Gentlefolk in Sudbury might find out that she was unmarried and refuse to accept the child. 'Ought I to tell them before or what?'

An 83-mile train journey of between three and four hours took Eliot and Lewis the last leg of their journey from Nantes to Vannes. But by the time they reached their destination the weather had turned cold and, rather than face the bleakness of the Breton coast in such conditions, they retreated to Saumur, a town some 85 miles back along the Loire valley from Nantes.

They stayed in the Hôtel Budan, first in Baedeker's alphabetical list, 'at the bridge, opposite the theatre'.

Iris's letter requesting advice about the Home for the Infants and Children of Gentlefolk arrived in Vannes after their departure.

A few days in Saumur was a time to recuperate from the rigours of travel and to write something more than a brief postcard or telegram. On Saturday the 21st, Lewis sent Iris an heroic if impressionistic account of the holiday thus far. Not having received her last two letters, he made no reference to her anxieties about the baby:

> I have been engaged in incessant Trek. I have risen at Six in the morning, have stood for 3 hours on end, 6 hours on one occasion, in corridors of crawling trains. I have crossed Gulfs, stopping at innumerable Islets, lain in the sun above beautiful Estuaries, driven in dusty carriages through the most divine villages.

Eliot took the opportunity to write to Sydney Schiff. 'W.L. has been sketching here and I have been roaming about . . . I have enjoyed Lewis's company very much, and have had a great many conversations with him – I do not know anyone more profitable to talk to.'

Their holiday idyll, however, was brought to a violent end when they hired bicycles for an excursion to Chinon, some 18 miles away.

It is possible that Lewis had not ridden a bicycle since July 1908, when his mother had cautioned him: 'be careful not to be run down by a motor on the road, nor to coast down long hills and get smashed . . . and you don't want to scorch on the bike as that is not good for your heart.'

They set off. After about 200 yards the chain flew off Lewis's machine. They stopped to fix it and continued. After another two or three hundred yards, travelling at a brisk pace, the fork over the front wheel broke. Lewis was thrown onto the pavement, sustaining a 'medium sized surface gash' to knee and hand.

Eliot managed to help the injured man to a bench outside an inn where brandy was reluctantly provided. Leaving Lewis there, his broken cycle beside him, Eliot mounted his own machine and peddled back to secure the hire of an open barouche for friend and bicycle. Back in Saumur, Lewis confronted the cycle shop proprietor, accusing him of renting out dangerously faulty equipment, while the proprietor, equally enraged, insisted the Englishman pay compensation for the damage caused. 'The dispute was terminated', Eliot recalled, 'in a hostile atmosphere, without any money changing hands.'

Leaving Eliot to explore the Gothic churches of Amboise, Loches and

Tours, Lewis returned to Paris alone. 'He believes that he has escaped lockjaw', Eliot reported to Pound.

A week later in the Hôtel du Quai Voltaire, he was daily anointing his wounds with ointment and complaining that he had lost 'what would have been a most useful day's work' at Chinon as a result of the accident. He had, however, renewed his acquaintanceship with Joyce and produced three portrait drawings in Indian ink of the bespectacled novelist. Joyce seems to have got on better with Lewis than he did with the reserved American. 'Your friend Mr Eliot' was how the Irishman referred to him in conversation with Lewis.

By this time Iris's letter had arrived in Paris, forwarded from Vannes:

> I can't decide whether to tell Nurse Thompson my position and get her to help but I think I shan't, because it's not the sort of thing people admire one for and I *hate* nastiness specially when I'm helpless!

Lewis told her not to confide in the nurse, that he would sort everything out when he returned. He did not know what day he would return, nor by which route, 'but soon,' he promised, 'a few days.' He seems to have been in no hurry to get back for the birth. 'I don't suppose you will void your foetus for several weeks yet.' As to finding a place for the 'foetus', he instructed her to 'make some temporary arrangements (in the neighbourhood)'. He would attend to permanent arrangements on his return.

He appeared to have second thoughts after posting the letter, because he accelerated his travel plans and dispatched a telegram the same day:

> BACK TOMORROW DONT WORRY WILL ARRANGE IMMEDI-
> ATELY MUCH LOVE WRITTEN – LEWIS

A letter awaited his return:

> This is just a note to greet you when you get back . . . I'm so sorry I've not gone to bed yet but I can't help it . . . I shall surely take to my bed this coming week, and we will spring into an autumn offensive of Little Men, Art, and knitting.

She did not have much longer to wait. The baby was born on 1 September. If Iris had been expecting another son she was disappointed. 'I want you to name the child', she told Lewis:

> she's a nice little female and may possibly transmit a few traits of intelligence into a cow-like world so you could take a little interest. I know

you don't like females but this one is bound to 'favour' you more than a male, and she'll like you better too: she won't like me! Is AUDREY too Shakespearean a name? Invent one, then.

The birth certificate of 'Maisie Wyndham' included the names of both parents: Percy Wyndham Lewis, 'journalist', and Iris Crump, of 'no occupation'.

TWENTY-THREE

Studios

Number 2, Alma Studios, at a rental of £125 per annum, a premium of £125 for fixtures and lease and a further £50 in rates and taxes on top of that, 'was at least twice as expensive as [he] could afford.' The building still stands. Studio 2 is a huge first-floor room with an enormous arched north-facing expanse of glass occupying nearly the entire wall and overlooking Stratford Road, off Earls Court Road. Entrance and stairs are around the corner in Radley Mews.

In addition to the rent, premium, rates and taxes, Lewis spent a further £35.14s. on essential studio furnishing:

matting	£3.10s.
adjustable drawing desk	£9.10s.
easel	£6.10s.
large mirror	£5.5s.
portfolio stand	£2.2s.
plan chest for drawings	£1
model's throne	£5
trestle table for paints	£2.2s.
studio table	15s.

He moved in on 7 October and Sydney Schiff lent assistance in the form of his servant, John Cook. 'You must tell him clearly what you want him to do', the man's master told Lewis. 'I shan't need him here till 7 o'clock and he can go tomorrow again if you find him any use.'

Lewis told the Income Tax authorities, for whose benefit the itemised list of expenses was prepared, that he began painting regularly in November, 'the settling in done with'.

He also claimed that, while attending to the sale of his mother's laundry business, finally disposed of in February:

my work as artist [was] so much interfered with that [I] could do very little of any use. Much ground [was] lost. [It] jeopardised my chances in my career as a painter and held up my work.

227

Be that as it may, by April 1921 he had succeeded in producing an impressive body of drawings and canvases for his exhibition at the Leicester Galleries.

Iris Barry figured in a number of the works, her thick dark eyebrows emphasised, often at the expense of her eyes. Lewis drew her frequently in a distinctive dress that especially appealed to him: very dark with a plain V-shaped neckline and long sleeves ending in two light bands at the cuffs. The skirt was a complex affair, incorporating an underskirt of the same material, hanging lower than the outer one and decorated with three broad bands matching the two on the cuffs. Sometimes she wore a wrapover waistcoat, fastening on the right, and sometimes a red tam o'shanter. But it was the heavy eyebrows, and stripes at wrist and calf, that most often serve to identify her.

A canvas, some three feet by five, showed the most impressive variation on the theme. Arising from the dark carapace of that familiar costume, her neck and impassive face were modelled in shades of blue steel, faceted like overlapping splinters of razor blade. The full lower lip was a startling blood-red crescent, while the dead irises of the eyes, under hooded metallic lids, were bright yellow. The folds of the sleeves lay in zigzag ridges, points and crests, highlighted dark green. Curled in the lap, the right hand was a shining prosthetic claw. Lower down, between the dual hems of the complex skirt, the curving parallel bands glowed bronze. An armchair, recognisable from other portraits of the time, seemed transformed and expanded to contain the monumental figure.

The title of the painting was in keeping with its sculptural formality. ' "Praxitella" is all you say it is,' he wrote to Jessica Dismorr. 'The reason I don't do more such work is that . . . one needs the courage of seventeen buffaloes to work . . . [in] the conditions we live under: . . . I only have the courage of about ten. But perhaps my herd will increase.'

Another sitter was the youngest daughter of Sir Herbert Beerbohm Tree, and niece to Max Beerbohm. When Iris Tree posed for Lewis her marriage to Curtis Moffat was about a year old. Her golden bobbed hair became an icon for a number of artists, including Vanessa Bell and Duncan Grant. When Jacob Epstein sculpted her in bronze, he left the face patinated but burnished the helmet of hair to a mirror-like shine. Lewis exhibited a number of drawings of her in April, together with a large portrait in oils.

It is not known when she and Lewis had an affair, nor how long it lasted. However, by the time his various painted and pencilled appraisals of her features appeared on the walls of the Leicester Galleries, she was referring to the liaison ruefully as a thing of the past:

We have never had any peace of mind, ripe tasty hours together Lewis, except those stolen from my domestic cupboard, leaving a skeleton there at that.*

When the show was being hung Max Beerbohm came into the gallery and Oliver Brown, the director, showed him around while Lewis hovered nearby. Beerbohm looked solemnly at the portrait of his niece languishing in a capacious armchair. Her knees were drawn up at a sharp angle and her elbow formed another sharp angle on the arm of the chair. Lewis asked him what he thought of it. 'It has its points', came the reply.

If Lewis's brief intimacy with Iris Tree had been unsatisfactory, her portrait lacked resolution as well. 'If I sell it in the show,' he told Quinn, 'I shall insist in any case on having another week's work on it. But I consider it inferior to most of the other things there.'

Apart from the portraits and figure studies that made up the bulk of the exhibition, five garishly coloured paintings contained outlandish grinning men with jagged hats, scalpel-bladed features and teeth like piano keys. 'A Tyro', Lewis explained in the *Daily Express*:

> is a new type of human animal like Harlequin or Punchinello – a new and sufficiently elastic form or 'mould' into which one can translate the satirical observations that are . . . awakened by one's race . . . The Tyro . . . is raw and undeveloped; his vitality is immense, but purposeless, and hence sometimes malignant. His keynote, however, is vacuity; he is an animated, but artificial puppet, a 'novice' to real life.

Adorned with ink renderings of these jarring creatures, the first issue of the new paper, *The Tyro*, appeared in time for the private view. Publication took place despite the fact that Lewis had withdrawn his £50 stake in the enterprise, pleading pressing financial considerations.

*

Square, white invitation cards were sent out:

* A number of letters from Iris Tree to Lewis, this one amongst them, were mistakenly ascribed to Iris Barry when first catalogued at Cornell.

TYROS AND PORTRAITS

Paintings and Drawings
by
WYNDHAM LEWIS

Messrs. Ernest Brown and Phillips request the
pleasure of your Company at the Private View
of the Exhibition on Saturday, 9th April.

THE LEICESTER GALLERIES
Leicester Square, London
10 till 6

The former Prime Minister, Mr Asquith, was among the first to arrive and
was presented with the first copy of *The Tyro*. On leaving he was heard to
say: 'This man is one of the finest draughtsmen we have!' The critic from
The Spectator appeared to agree but was correspondingly disparaging about
the paintings:

> The point might . . . be raised whether Mr Wyndham Lewis should ever
> use oil paint. It is a medium for which he seems to have little capacity and
> no sympathy, as may be seen in the large portrait of Miss Iris Tree. The
> first effect of a picture ought not to be to raise in our subconsciousness the
> complex of 'Wet Paint!' Really Mr Wyndham Lewis is a draughtsman,
> and his natural means of expression line.

The portrait did not sell, and Lewis eventually painted it out to reuse the
canvas.

Forty-five paintings and drawings were listed in the catalogue and 18 sold
during the exhibition's month-long run. There were also six ex-catalogue
works sold. This amounted to a total of £616 1s. When the Gallery's 33 per
cent commission had been deducted, Lewis would have received about
£413.

Edward Wadsworth, having just come into a substantial inheritance, bought *Praxitella* for £200 and Sydney Schiff spent a total of £100 on six works, including *Mr Wyndham Lewis as a Tyro*. When Richard Wyndham and his young wife visited the Schiffs with their nine-month-old baby, the infant was traumatised by this hatchet-hatted, leering self-portrait on its bright yellow background. Violet Schiff reported that he started screaming 'but kept on turning his head to look at it as though he were attracted but terrified'.

It was a reaction shared by some adults. Virginia Woolf wrote that her sister and Fry were sneaking glances at Lewis's new magazine: 'Roger and Nessa read him in shops, and won't buy him – which . . . proves that they fear him.'

'Tyros and Portraits' did not markedly improve Lewis's financial position. 2 Alma Studios was a considerable burden. 'I have to leave this studio at once,' he told Dismorr in April, 'and seek a cheaper one. But even then I don't see how I am going to get along with enough comfort to live.' But it would be another four months before he was finally forced out.

*

In an effort to sell work he went to Paris later that month, taking 60 copies of *The Tyro* with him. He renewed his acquaintanceship with Joyce, lectured him about Chinese art and told him that he found life in London very depressing.

'Had several uproarious allnight sittings (and dancings) with Lewis', Joyce reported to Frank Budgen, 'I like him.' They drank at the Bar Gitane near the Panthéon in the company of two local prostitutes who were kept supplied with drink but for the most part ignored. 'Remember you are the author of *The Ideal Giant*', Joyce reminded Lewis on one occasion when he overstepped decorous bounds with one of the women.

Lewis shocked the straitlaced Harriet Shaw Weaver by telling her that Joyce had drunk with him until dawn, had ended up dancing by himself, and had finally picked up the bar bill for the assembled company. Joyce still insisted upon paying for everything with money he could ill afford. Pride, moreover, was compounded with rivalry, as he invariably attempted to outdo Lewis in alcoholic consumption. But the author of *The Ideal Giant* was more than just a drinking rival.

'I'll never forget the feeling of water rushing round my arse during a thunderstorm in Paris', Lewis told Ruthven Todd at a party in the late 1930s, torrential rain falling outside. 'I was sitting in a gutter with Joyce. He was terrified of thunderstorms, you know? We were discussing the matter of our illegitimate children . . .' But at that moment Lewis was called away to talk to somebody else and Todd was left with only this tantalising opening of the anecdote. The story had evidently been told elsewhere because after the war, in St Elizabeth's Hospital, Washington DC, Ezra Pound recalled one further detail. It was a remark made on that stormy night which betrayed Joyce's insecurity in the company of other writers – an insecurity which may have accounted for his aloofness towards 'Mr Eliot' the previous summer. With the painter, however, he felt at ease, so long as Lewis restricted his activities to the medium of pencil or brush.

Sitting there in the rain with the water guttering around their boots and buttocks, Joyce had said to Lewis: 'You may paint this but I will write it.'

Lewis left Paris on the night of 30 May. 'My journey has been, from a business point of view, a complete failure', he told Iris Barry. However, when he wrote to Quinn a couple of days after his return, he seemed more optimistic. He intended taking a small cheap studio in London and 'a similar *pied-à-terre* in Paris'. He would then divide his time between the two, having a Paris dealer to take all the 'experimental stuff' that would not sell in London. Nothing came of this plan.

*

In July he prepared a statement of earnings and expenditure for the Income Tax Inspector. Because he had rented his studio in September 1920 he suggested taking September to September as his current year of work. 'We are now at July 20', he declared, 'and it is unlikely until next September that I shall sell any work, the Summer being a bad time.' His total studio expenses to date, at 'a rough estimate and certainly below the mark', amounted to £395.14s. His total income from painting and drawing came to £450, giving him a profit of £54.6s.

He had other expenses. Since his mother's death he had Mrs Prickett to support, together with Olive Johnson's two children who were now in her care. There was also 27/- a week to be found for Maisie's keep at the Home in Sudbury. He bought an outfit of clothes for Iris Barry, enabling her to secure a position at Bertry's of New Bond Street, purveyors of silk and woollen *haute couture*. This investment in her professional future was doubtless intended as a first step towards making her financially independent of him.

It should not be forgotten, however, that only the previous year Lewis had received a considerable amount of money from the sale of his father's property in Southport, not to mention the undisclosed sum he realised on the sale of his mother's business in February. What happened to this capital remains a mystery. It is difficult to believe that, even with twice the number of illegitimate children to support, he could have so efficiently exhausted his inheritance in such a short time. Be that as it may, in early August, no longer able to pay his rent, he was finally forced to leave Alma Studios. And even the ignominious removal of his furniture into storage was not without expense. 'The little margin that I expected to have went in moving', he told Barry. 'The men had to come three days running; lots of things had to be settled up of which I had kept no count.' For the time being homeless, he found temporary lodging with a friend, Bernard Rowland, at 16A Craven Road, Paddington.

*

At 8.30 one evening in mid-August Lewis made a delivery to a house on the eastern edge of Regent's Park. He left a note: 'I . . . paid call, but found you out. Left last parcel of effects asked for.'

It is not known precisely when he and Iris Barry separated, nor how long she had been living at 8 Stanhope Terrace when he dropped off the rest of her belongings. 'I wanted to see you', he told her, 'but I am afraid that will not be possible now, as I shall be off tomorrow or following day . . . I will try to send £2 during ensuing week.'

She was earning £3 a week at Bertry's but was still dependent on Lewis for the money she had to send each week to Sudbury. The invariable lateness of these payments, and the necessity of constant reminders, was to set the wrangling tone of their correspondence for many months to come. The news that he was leaving for 'a short holiday', naturally provoked accusations of extravagance which he was quick to refute. 'The fare 2nd class, via Ostend, to Berlin is £4.7.6,' he told her, 'about the same as it is to Cornwall.' Rocketing German inflation in the postwar period was also advantageous to the English tourist of modest means. In August 1921 the exchange rate of the mark was 350 to the pound. Before the war it had stood at 20. 'Therefore', he explained, 'once I get there I could not be in a cheaper place. So much for the costly appearance of my holiday.' He also reminded her that he was going to Berlin to try to sell work.

By late August he was stuck in Brussels, 'because of hitch in my money arrangements', he explained, and for a time thought he would be unable to continue his journey. He was exasperated, stranded as he was, that Iris's demands pursued him even there. 'Your letter has been forwarded to me', he replied:

I have enough money to take me to the place I propose going to, and back, and enough to buy an occasional cheap cigar, and that's all . . . You must absolutely cease to regard me as a portion of Providence.

And if she accused him of extravagance, he was prepared to retaliate in kind:

it came to my notice that you contemplate, in a week or two, a large addition to your wardrobe. I suggest that if you have such money to spend, you should first spend it in meeting the arrears for Sudbury.

He did not explain how her forthcoming expenditure had come to his notice, but he touched upon this ignoble theme some days later:

I repeat that the acquisition of handsome clothes hardly indicates the work house.

And he returned to it again on 1 September:

If I make some money in Berlin, I will send you some at once. I am taking you at your word as regards your situation, in spite of projected wardrobes, etc.

On the 2 September, after four days kicking his heels in 'this dull town', he managed to extricate himself from Brussels and travelled on to Berlin.

Lewis had been in correspondence with Herwarth Walden, editor of the Expressionist journal *Der Sturm*, and had even promised to let him have four pictures for an exhibition being organised in Paris in April. Whether he did, however, is uncertain, because his own show was running at the Leicester Galleries for the same month and he told Schiff he did not think he would have much left over worth sending. Establishing further contact with Walden, and perhaps negotiating an exhibition at his Sturm Galerie in the Potsdamerstrasse, was probably the main objective of this, Lewis's first visit to Berlin. On his arrival he was invited to tea and introduced to other artists. Ivan Puni, 'an ex-Communist, lately arrived from Petrograd', had a beautiful dark-haired wife who Lewis claimed 'could ogle a man until he was sick'. He also met Alexander Archipenko, the Russian sculptor: 'getting worse every day', Lewis thought, particularly repelled by 'a nasty thing of his' in Walden's possession.

He seemed not especially impressed with the great promoter of modern German art. 'Walden and his pictures', he reported to Violet Schiff, 'do not compare favourably, I think, with Paris dealers. As to the stuff he has all over his walls, it is like a rather dashing London Group show.' There was also a financial consideration. If the extraordinary German exchange rate favoured the tourist, 'any business dealings with Walden or another [were] out of the question for anyone coming from the West.' He was amiably received, however, and thought he might, later on, have an exhibition there.

Rowan Walker of the *Daily Express* may have suggested that Lewis write something about his visit for the paper. Lewis did not do so and seemed rather disappointed at not seeing half the fabled 'vice' of Berlin that Lord Beaverbrook had observed. It was to be another nine years before Lewis would succumb to 'journalistic inspiration' and write of the city's vice, and, more damagingly for his future reputation, its politics.

*

Three weeks later, having stopped off for a few days in Paris, he was back in London and searching for a cheap studio. Bernard Rowland's place at 16A Craven Road remained his temporary address for another two months. In mid-October he moved into a studio, the rental on which, at £75 per annum, was considerably less than he had paid for the splendid airy accommodation in Stratford Road. Lee Studio was an altogether more humble workplace. Virginia Woolf reported to Roger Fry: 'Lewis now paints in a shed behind a curtain – rites are gone through before you enter.'

A decade before, in 1911, the Engineer and Surveyor's Department of the Royal Borough of Kensington had granted planning permission to the painter John Brakewell ('Brake') Baldwin to have a temporary studio building erected in the long garden at the rear of his house, Number 6 Phillimore Terrace, in Allen Street. In order to give him the maximum working space possible, it was to be a tight fit. The plans allowed for a foot on one side, barely six inches on the other, separating it from the two party walls which stretched to the bottom of the garden.

Three weeks after the granting of planning permission, the temporary studio had been completed, inspected and allowed to be retained in the garden for three years. It was inspected again in July 1914 and found to be in good order and as originally constructed. It was therefore allowed to be retained for a further three years.

'Brake' Baldwin did not have the use of his studio for long. He died of a heart attack, at the age of 30, in 1915. Thereafter his widow made the three-yearly applications for retention. It was still 'in good order and as originally constructed' when Wyndham Lewis rented it from Mrs Baldwin in late 1921.

According to Edith Sitwell, the garden was 'an area of waste ground (rather like a deserted cemetery) haunted by hens scratching the ground and themselves and squawking desolately and phonetically.'

The studio was 17 feet wide, 29 feet long and 16 feet high. It was mounted on concrete blocks, roofed in patent 'Eternit' slates, and the exterior walls were clad in corrugated iron sheets. Inside, walls and ceiling were of tongue-and-groove planks. A ten-foot-square window rose from a point level with the top of the garden wall to the full height of the roof and faced across the other back gardens of Phillimore Terrace, in the direction of Kensington High Street. Panes of obscured glass ensured privacy and an even north light.

Because it cut off the top of the garden nearest the house from the bottom part with its high wall and back gate opening into Adam and Eve Mews, there were doors at either end of the studio allowing access from both directions. Lewis had exclusive use of the back gate and could come and go unobserved by his landlady. He would have kept the studio door facing Mrs Baldwin's house permanently locked from the inside.

In December he was able to move out of Rowland's flat and into a room at 5 Shaftesbury Villas in Allen Street. It was two minutes' walk from his studio in Adam and Eve Mews.

TWENTY-FOUR

Portraits

The year 1922 began well. Lewis signed a contract with Constable & Co. for a novel provisionally titled *The Life of a Tyro*, and was given an advance on royalties of £100. True, the novel was never delivered and eight years later he was forced to return the money with interest and legal costs, but in the first months of 1922, while he began work as a portrait painter in Adam and Eve Mews, the money must have come in useful for the time being.

Sydney Schiff had spoken of having a portrait of his wife painted in November when Lewis had just moved into his studio. In January a price was agreed upon. Schiff was to pay £30 for a study of Violet and £100 for the full-scale canvas to be produced later. In February, with the study under way, Schiff agreed to supply him with an advance of £20 on the portrait proper. In March the study was delivered, in a plain black frame, but Schiff was not entirely satisfied with it. Lewis was at pains to point out that this was 'not *in any sense*, [his] last word on the subject of Violet', that the face was 'sketched rather than painted' and the left hand had 'in any case at some time [to] be worked on and explained more'. And he went on:

> If Violet herself is not displeased with this first attempt, I shall welcome the further opportunity that the larger painting will afford me, of presenting you with something that will in a sense be *her*. – Do not therefore, psychologically bring *too* much to bear on this sketch.

When *The Tyro* first appeared in April 1921, its front page had promised: 'TO BE PRODUCED AT INTERVALS OF TWO OR THREE MONTHS'. On the second page there was a more cautious statement of intent:

> A paper run entirely by painters and writers, the appearance of the 'Tyro' will be spasmodic: that is, it will come out when sufficient material has accumulated to make up a new number; or when something of urgent interest hastens it into renewed and pointed utterance.

The second issue appeared over a year later in early March 1922. 'Between the first and second number', the Editor conceded:

> a longer time has elapsed than was intended; and no fixed date can be assigned, in any case, for its appearances. Roughly we aim at four numbers a year. But more, of a restricted size, may be produced; or the material may be made into a bulkier format, as in the present number, brought out less frequently.

Existing subscribers were told that the second issue was to be regarded as two numbers and that they could expect one further *Tyro* of whatever size for their 6/6d., inclusive of postage.

No further issues appeared.

*

Throughout April and May, Lewis was working on two major portraits in the corrugated-iron-bound studio beyond the high wall of Adam and Eve Mews. One sitter was the music critic Edwin Evans. The other was Edith Sitwell. The light was proving to be a problem, however, as he told Schiff: 'the days are too short; and often light-dark, light-dark, like a lighthouse lamp'.

He had begun painting Miss Sitwell in the last month or so of 1921, and by her own account she sat nearly every afternoon until the following June. She sat in the same armchair that Iris Barry had occupied for *Praxitella*, turned this time almost side-on to the artist. She wore a loose, emerald green jacket and a yellow skirt. Her face, as it eventually came to be presented on the canvas, was a pale, egg-like oval. The eyes were so heavily lidded as to appear closed and the long slender nose seemed designed to look down.

Some ten years later, having been, as she thought, pilloried in Lewis's gargantuan satire, *The Apes of God*, she wrote a memoir of her sittings. Its picture of Lewis's squalid working environment was perhaps partly coloured by revenge:

> The studio ... was very large, and the floor was crowded with old newspapers, books, drawings, housemaids' worries, pots, pans, kettles, a tea pot, tins of milk, and Mr. Lewis's discarded undergarments.

At times he seemed to take delight in unsettling his exquisitely bred sitter. 'D'you mind rats?' he asked her. 'Oh well, they're here all right. Night and day! Night and day!' Then, after a pause: 'I'll try to keep 'em off.'

Miss Sitwell never actually saw the rats but she heard 'a great deal of animation taking place among Mr Lewis's discarded shirts and drawings, which at times seemed to be absolutely whisking over the floor, in spite of all impediments.'

On one occasion she arrived to find him shaving.

'D'you mind waiting whilst I shave?' he asked her.

'Not at all', Miss Sitwell replied.

He sighed deeply.

'And *after* I've shaved, I mean *to wash my hands.*'

He sighed again.

'I suppose you do everything one after another, don't you? I mean you . . .'

He paused.

'. . . probably have a bath in the morning?'

Miss Sitwell said that she did.

'And after that, you probably . . .'

During each pause, Miss Sitwell remembered, he built a small edifice in the air with his hands as if attempting to communicate more than mere words.

'. . . brush your hair?'

Miss Sitwell agreed that she did.

'But before that you — brush your teeth?'

'Yes.'

He sighed again deeply.

'It's that damned Time! I seem to have so little Time for anything. Now sometimes I'll . . .

. . . wash my hands in the morning . . .

. . . and shave in the afternoon. At other times I'll . . .'

And in the middle of another pause he seemed to recollect his incomplete toilet:

'Well, I suppose I'd better get on with what I'm doing.'

Laundry was also a problem, as the tangle of soiled shirts and underclothes testified. Miss Sitwell remembered arriving one afternoon to find him dressed in an immaculately starched shirt but without a collar.

'D'you mind sitting to me in my evening shirt?' he asked.

'Not at all.'

'It's that damned laundress'.

If Miss Sitwell had heard rumours of his late mother's occupation she might not have been averse to inventing this particular snippet of conversation to bate him with, should her memoir ever appear in print.*

In May Lewis pronounced the portrait 'nearly finished: three more sittings should see it done as far as work from her is concerned'.

*

The stolid figure of Edwin Evans, dressed in a brown three-piece suit, sat bearded and extravagantly moustached in three-quarter profile. A Latin Quarter hat hung from a hefty walking stick propped between his knees. A group of composers, Arthur Bliss, Arnold Bax, Constant Lambert and Eugene Goossens, had commissioned the portrait in recognition of the *Daily Telegraph* critic's services to British contemporary music. They wished to present it to him during a dinner to be held in his honour in late June. At the beginning of the month Lewis was working on it in oppressive weather conditions. 'The most suffocating heat continues', he told Violet Schiff, 'my studio is an oven, the metal sides and roof cooking me every day.'

Work stopped, however, when it became apparent that Goossens and Bliss had not succeeded in raising the sum agreed on for the picture from subscribers. Years later Bliss could not remember how much Lewis had wanted, but a letter from Nancy Cunard, touching on his financial difficulties, linked the composer's name with the question: 'Whence £500?'

The presentation dinner was postponed for six months, from June until early in the New Year. This may have been because the painting was a long way from being finished, or it may have been to allow Goossens and Bliss more time to raise the shortfall in the painter's fee. In the meantime the canvas remained in Lewis's studio with the still unfinished portrait of Edith Sitwell.

*

Sydney Schiff had succeeded in interesting the Paris art dealer Léonce Rosenberg in Lewis's work and there was talk of an exhibition at his Galerie L'Effort Moderne, in autumn. While fully sensible of 'the importance of success in Paris . . . and the promises it [held] of greater freedom in work and development', Lewis seemed cautious. He claimed he was unable to 'set aside time to prepare a show for Paris', while at the same time proposing to show Rosenberg half a dozen drawings which he might, 'as an earnest of

---

* It did not appear in his lifetime. A letter from the solicitors Child & Child, dated 27 July 1931, strongly advised against publication on the grounds that it would render her liable to an action for damages by Lewis. She eventually incorporated much of the material from her memoir in a newspaper article: 'Hazards of Sitting for my Portrait', *Observer*, 27 November 1960.

goodwill, a sort of instalment', buy in advance, to ensure the show was financially beneficial to Lewis. Perhaps this caution might be better termed diffidence. Perhaps, offered the prospect of success in Paris, he was haunted by the possibility of *not* 'setting the Seine on fire' and of how damaging failure in Paris would be to his reputation.

Whatever reservations he had, Lewis mentioned his forthcoming Paris show to Charles Rutherston.* He also intended having another in London, simultaneously. But, lest nothing should come of these plans, he added darkly: 'This between ourselves.'

*

Early in July, Schiff paid Lewis £20 for a pencil drawing of his wife. Again Schiff was dissatisfied with it, just as he had been with the painted 'study' of Violet delivered in March. Lewis's defence of the drawing was almost identical with his defence of the study:

> As regards what you say about the drawing, it by no means exhausts what I *see* and think about Violet. I think it is like her and has many points as a drawing and a drawing of her. But I shall be eager to attack her again as you suggest, as often as she is willing to sit.

Eventually he took the drawing back, promising to find it a better frame. Instead, he sold it again. This may have been an oversight on Lewis's part, or else he reasoned that because Schiff had not been pleased with the pencilled rendition of his wife, he would not miss it. Either way, Schiff was later disconcerted to see the drawing hanging in the home of the critic O. R. Drey.

*

In August he was in Paris, probably with the intention of establishing personal contact with Léonce Rosenberg. Whether or not the autumn exhibition spoken of in April was still on offer, the art dealer's words, as Lewis later remembered them, certainly boded well for the future:

> Lewis, these things of yours are the only things being done in England today which would interest Paris. Give me some of these, as many as you like, and I will sell them for you.

* Brother to William Rothenstein. Like his other brother, Albert, Charles anglicized his name during the Great War. He bequeathed his collection of Wyndham Lewis paintings and drawings to the Manchester Art Gallery.

In the meantime, however, he was staying at the Hôtel de Varenne, and so short of money he was forced to write and ask Schiff for a further advance of £20 on the portrait of Violet. Schiff sent him the money and urged him to call on Marcel Proust, even promising to write to the Frenchman, suggesting he sit for a portrait drawing. There is no evidence that Lewis took advantage of this opportunity to meet the ailing author, who died only three months later.

He did, however, record his first meeting with another, more robust man of letters, when he called at Ezra Pound's apartment, 70 bis, rue Notre Dame des Champs:

> I rang the bell. A good deal of noise was to be heard but no one answered: therefore I pushed the door, which opened practically into the studio. A splendidly built young man, stripped to the waist, and with a torso of dazzling white, was standing not far from me. He was tall, handsome and serene, and was repelling with his boxing gloves a hectic assault of Ezra's. After a final swing at the dazzling solar plexus Pound fell back upon his settee. The young man was Hemingway.

Hemingway's account of this first meeting with Lewis was far less flattering:

> Wyndham Lewis wore a wide black hat . . . and was dressed like someone out of La Bohème. He had a face that reminded me of a frog, not a bullfrog but just any frog . . . and he watched superciliously while I slipped Ezra's left leads or blocked them with an open right glove. I wanted us to stop but Lewis insisted we go on . . . and I could see that . . . he was hoping to see Ezra hurt. Nothing happened. I never countered but kept Ezra moving after me, sticking out his left hand and throwing a few right hands, and then said we were through . . . We had a drink of something . . . I watched Lewis carefully without appearing to look at him, as you do when you are boxing, and I do not think I had ever seen a nastier looking man. Some people show evil as a great racehorse shows breeding. Lewis did not show evil; he just looked nasty. Walking home I tried to think what he reminded me of . . . I tried to break his face down and describe it but I could only get the eyes. Under the black hat, when I had first seen them, the eyes had been those of an unsuccessful rapist.

*

Back in London, on 27 September, Schiff paid Lewis a further £30 in advance for his wife's portrait. He also sent him an account, including precise dates and sums of money, of his outlay since the end of the previous year. There had been £25 on 8 December and another £25 a week later.

There was £10 on 10 January, £20 on 23 February, £20 sent to Paris on 16 August. He pointed out that all this, together with the final payment of £30, completed the sum of £130 originally agreed for the portrait and study. As yet, work on the portrait had not even begun.

Lewis acknowledged receipt of the last cheque on a postcard hastily scratched with an almost empty fountain pen. 'I will write you in morning more fully', he promised. 'I shall leave for Venice in a few days.' He was going to Italy for the first and only time in his life on the invitation of a current object of amorous interest.

Nancy Cunard had rented one floor of a 'rather exquisite', quiet house on a stretch of the Grand Canal for a month. The Casa Mainilla had two small terraces for him to choose from as outdoor studios. He would have his own room and be welcome any time until 20 October. 'Write to me there *and arrive*', she had told him.

A week into October he was still in London, lingering 'from day to day' in the hope of having enough drawings ready to give Léonce Rosenberg on his way through Paris. Since no subsequent reference to the proprietor of the Galerie L'Effort Moderne occurred in Lewis's correspondence, it may be assumed he did not succeed in his efforts and that further dealings, including the autumn exhibition and any possibility of 'setting the Seine on fire', came to nothing.*

*

He arrived in Venice on the morning of Friday 13 October 1922 wearing a 'squalid-looking tweed hat on the back of his head. Very dirty and untidy.' That was how he confronted Siegfried Sassoon on the same afternoon at Florian's, in the Piazza San Marco. 'Protruded his large unwholesome face at me with inquiring eyes (not quite certain whether it was me or not)', the poet wrote in his diary. 'As usual I felt quite ill at ease with him.' Over a decade later the memory was so vivid that Sassoon was able to draw the face on the flyleaf of his copy of *One Way Song*. With staring eyes, a three-day growth of bristles and the incongruous tweed hat, Lewis looked like a farmer fallen on evil days.

Ivor Novello was acting in a film being shot in front of the Ducal Palace. Sassoon fantasised that the disreputable-looking Lewis would murder him. 'I hope so', he wrote.

The season was over. 'Most of the heavy social stuff is no longer here', Lewis wrote to Violet Schiff. Pleasantly lodged, as Nancy had promised,

---

* As did the 'simultaneous' show in London, about which he had sworn Rutherston to secrecy.

there was 'every freedom, room to work and drinks'. The decadent atmosphere of Venice had a political charge to it now. Bologna had been taken over by the Fascists in May, Milan in early August, and Mussolini's march on Rome was only 12 days away. 'Autumn pederasts [were] everywhere, with a sprinkling of Fascisti.' There was little interaction between the homosexual 'Septembrists', or off-season tourists, and the blackshirts, he told Violet 'though I should have thought in many cases they were made for each other.'

He dined with the Sitwells, Osbert and Sacheverell, the first Sunday he was there and lunched with them on the Monday. Plagued by mosquitoes, he set to work drawing the two brothers before their departure for Rome the following Wednesday. He drew them seated together: Sacheverell, with legs crossed, took up the full height of the page, Osbert was further back, elbow resting on a round table, the suspicion of a plus-foured leg below. The pencil drawing was lightly gouached and squared off in preparation for a large double portrait oil he was never to produce.

On the following Saturday he was still hard at work producing drawings of Nancy and her friends. 'Yesterday I got a good drawing of M[ondino]'s sister', he reported, 'also 2 good starts of Nancy. Today Ruby [Peto] is coming. Tomorrow I shall finish Nancy and tackle M[ondino]. Lady C[unard] can be dealt with following day (Monday).'

And it was amongst these leisured tourists that he made one potentially lucrative friend: Richard Wyndham. 'Oh, he's the boy who's got Clouds,' Hugo Rumbold told Lewis. The tall, dimple-chinned young man had just inherited the large country house from his uncle, George Wyndham. Richard's wife, Violet, was the niece of Mrs Schiff, and it was their nine-month-old son who had been so terrified by Lewis's *Tyro* self-portrait. 'Dick' Wyndham was also an aspiring painter and Lewis gave him some lessons in draughtsmanship. 'I taught him how to sketch Venetian palaces,' he recalled, 'the fingers of one hand grasping the pencil and the fingers of the other grasping the nose' against the stench of the canals.

*

When the holiday was over Nancy and Lewis left the Casa Mainilla for the railway station at the same time, although not together. Two gondolas were needed. She sat in the first with one of her friends and Lewis had to follow in the second with her maid and luggage. Years after Nancy recalled he was so angry that he did not speak to her until they were halfway to Paris.

Perhaps the reconciliation aboard the Paris train went somewhat beyond verbal communication. Certainly one railway journey would become a fond memory for her. 'I wish I could see you more often,' she wrote to him a few months later, 'and as in Venice or rather as in the train that day.'

Her feelings for him were rather poetically stated in a letter she wrote on another train, to Scotland, in late December:

> Dear, dear, Lewis. I get warmed when I am with you – you are a sort of black sun, dark earth, rich and full of new things, potential harvests, always dark, plein de seve, oil, blood, bread and comfort (among other things) I cannot get a nearer word than Rich. I love you very much.

Lewis once told Kate Lechmere that Nancy's favourite mode of sexual congress with him was buggery. It was a practice he found distasteful and endeavoured to persuade her against.

It may have been sexual incompatibility that caused the break-up of their affair. It may have been her independence of spirit and way of life. It is difficult to imagine Nancy living a life 'all in one groove deliberately' for him as Iris Barry had done. Whatever his reasons, he eventually dragged himself away from her heady attractions:

> I . . . am thinking as I write 'I must see her tomorrow' . . . but I must write in spite of that to say that I do not wish to be involved any more, just now, in your ZEX-LIFE.

*

While he was in Venice, Lewis wrote to Violet Schiff promising that he would start work on her portrait when he returned to London in November. Work began in December and sittings continued well into the New Year.

*

Pagani's Restaurant in Great Portland Street was the venue for a dinner held on Sunday 21 January 1923. The company sat down to oysters, named after the facially hirsute guest of honour: 'Huîtres Royales Evans (Bearded)'. Three instigators of the dinner were represented elsewhere on the menu: 'Hors d'Oeuvre Bax', 'Petite Marmite Bliss' and 'Filets de Sole à la Goossens'.

Edwin Evans's portrait had been liberated for the evening from the cluttered garden studio in Adam and Eve Mews. Bliss and Goossens had collected it by taxi that afternoon and it was safely stored in Pagani's cloakroom until the moment of presentation. Apart from an item in the soup course, 'Crème Divine Wyndham Lewis', the painter himself was not in evidence.

The portrait was far from finished. The likeness of the critic, solidly enough modelled though it was, appeared to float against a thinly washed-in ground, the pencilled grid lines showing through. Only a patch of shadow under the chair served to anchor the figure to the canvas. Lewis had parted with it for the evening under protest, unwilling to have it judged in this unfinished state. Besides, he had still not been paid the balance of what was due to him, and insisted on the canvas being returned to his studio after the presentation for more work, pending further contributions from the subscribers.

For his part Evans was flattered by the gift and expressed himself very pleased with the portrait as it stood. Some time later, more money having been collected, but probably little extra paint applied, Lewis agreed to give Evans the canvas. Unfinished, it hung in his study until his death.

TWENTY-FIVE

'People are only friends in so much that they are of use to you'

Between the covers of a tiny *Sportsman's Engagement Book* for 1923, a two-and-a-half-month period of Lewis's life was minutely documented. Entries began with an appointment to meet P. G. Konody at noon on Thursday 17 May and ended with Lewis's departure for France on Saturday 28 July. Precise times, names and sometimes meeting places were painstakingly, often illegibly, noted down. Entries were crossed out and relocated. A meeting with Aldous Huxley at 44 Princes Gardens, in Knightsbridge, for instance, was postponed from Whit Monday to the following Friday. There were meetings with old friends from before the Great War: Frederick Etchells, Jessie Dismorr and Edward Wadsworth. He met Kate Lechmere, a friend again, and all forgiven, following her unsuccessful litigation, at the Royal Palace Hotel in Kensington High Street on 18 June. There was an appointment for dinner with Sickert at the Etoile on Thursday 24 May. Lady Cunard and Edward Marsh were to visit the studio the following day at 3. Violet Schiff was sitting for her portrait on 29 May, and on six other afternoons throughout June. A steady stream of ladies sat for portrait drawings: Betty Pollock, Elizabeth Lewis, Dorothy Warren, and, despite her husband's acrimonious dealings with the painter over the portrait of Edwin Evans, Mrs Goossens. Mrs Bridget Guinness was another sitter, 'a particularly handsome woman,' Lewis recalled, 'like a powdered eagle'.

Tuesday 22 May began with an art lesson from noon until 1 o'clock, when Sybil Hart-Davis brought her daughter to see him. Deirdre had started decorating her school exercise books with little drawings and Sybil thought she might benefit from tuition. Lewis equipped the 14-year-old with pencil and paper, placed a rose in a glass and told her to draw it. While he and Sybil talked, Deirdre produced nothing but 'a blur of erasures'. She was so discouraged by the experience that she never tried to draw anything again.

Later that day Lewis moved his domestic chattels from the furnished room at 5 Shaftesbury Villas into another furnished room at 61 Palace

Gardens Terrace. Nancy Cunard, informed of this, 'noted new and grandiloquent address'. Nancy was in London again and he met her for dinner at 8 o'clock on Sunday 27 May, a previous appointment being scratched out and MESSALINA, in Greek capitals, scrawled in its place. This was a few days after writing that he wished to extricate himself from her 'ZEX-LIFE', hence his private branding of her as the Emperor Claudius's notoriously promiscuous wife. Elsewhere in the diary, 'NAN' denoted such meetings, followed by a question mark. She could not always be relied upon. 'Forgive me angel please', she once wrote to him after missing an appointment, 'I am beginning to be appalled at my perpetual lateness.'

Throughout those three months one cryptic reference appeared in the *Sportsman's Engagement Book* more often than any other. Lewis met, or arranged to meet, someone named 'Ghos' on no less than 24 separate occasions. The four letters encoded a shadowy associate: a ghost lacking only the final 't' in his private designation. Usually a lower-case initial seemed to deny it even the status of a proper noun: 'ghos'. There were variations in the code: 'HOS' on 28 May at 7.30, evening meetings being generally the rule; 'goo' on 11 June; 'g' on the 18th; 'gh' on the 21st. For a meeting on 13 June the original four letters were transcribed into Greek as if to disguise them further.

Gladys Hoskins was born on 29 June 1900 in the southwest suburbs of London, at 23 Springfield Road, Teddington. She was the daughter of Harriet and Joseph Hoskins, a gardener. She had an elder sister, Adelaide, and a younger sister, who drowned in childhood. She also had three brothers. Ernest and Fred were both killed in the First World War; Willie died during the Second.

It is possible that Gladys had been married – when, to whom, and for how long, it is not known – and divorced, before she met Lewis.*

Less is objectively known about this woman, Lewis's future wife and his companion for over three decades, than about almost any other attachment of his life. The few details of her existence before meeting him, she herself revealed during interviews in the 1960s and 70s. She attended art school near Lewisham. She modelled hats in London and worked during the war in an airplane factory. At the factory she made the acquaintance of a life model, who, shortly after the Armistice, took her to a party in Fulham given by the painter Gerald Brockhurst. There she met Lewis for the first time, wearing his 2nd Lieutenant's uniform. He invited her to dinner the following evening.

* See below, p. 549.

Beyond that their relations are nearly a blank. None of the letters, postcards, telegrams that passed between them during the early 1920s until they began living together, and written communication became unnecessary, have survived. The correspondence that might have helped trace their relationship, as Lewis's relationships with others can be traced, must have been destroyed, probably by Gladys herself, after her husband's death.

It is likely that there was a hiatus between their first meeting and the beginning of a serious affair. The first identifiable drawings of Gladys are all dated 1922, the year after Lewis parted from Iris Barry. During the following year, if the period covered by the *Sportsman's Engagement Book* is a reliable sample, they met regularly.

Even after their marriage Lewis inscribed one of his books for her with a variant of the name used so often in the early days of their relationship: 'to my darling wife Geehos'. Later she adopted a middle name, Anne, absent from both birth and marriage certificates. Then the German wife of Meyrick Booth calling her 'frau Anna' resulted in 'Froanna', the name she would be known by to those of her husband's friends who became hers as well.

*

With his departure for France on Saturday 28 July, Lewis's use of the *Sportsman's Engagement Book* came to an end.

Part of this holiday he spent in the company of Dick Wyndham. In two undated letters written the following year, the younger painter referred to a conversation they had one night, outside a café, following a performance by a troupe of Circassian dancers. The precise whereabouts of this café are unclear, as one letter placed it in Toulon, the other over 200 miles away in Toulouse. However, the conversation remained clear in his memory. Lewis lectured the 27-year-old on his 'age snobbery' and told him he was a 'Narcissus' and probably a 'bugger'. Following these blandishments the conversation turned to friendship and Lewis made a remark that Dick was able to quote verbatim many months later. From that moment on 'a small devil of suspicion crept in,' he recalled, 'and has lurked in my brain ever since.' Lewis's remark, on the terrace of that café somewhere in the South of France, left a profound impression upon Dick Wyndham:

'People are only friends in so much that they are of use to you.'

*

One night in October, a tall, heavy-set figure might have been seen stealthily emerging from a back gate into Adam and Eve Mews. He carried a canvas nearly four feet wide and just under three feet high, the unfinished portrait of Edith Sitwell. He would have turned to his right and walked down towards the Congregational Chapel. Then he would have turned left, and left again, following the cobbled mews round until he passed through the high ornate archway and on to Kensington High Street. That route would have enabled him to avoid passing below Mrs Baldwin's windows on Allen Street. This might have been a consideration to be taken into account whilst absconding, with his studio rent unpaid, to set up his easel elsewhere.

From the Adam and Eve arch it was less than a mile's walk or taxi ride to his furnished room in Palace Gardens Terrace.

*

At the end of the year a financial lifeline was proffered him by a small circle of friends: the Wadsworths, the Dreys, Dick Wyndham and Robert Windeler. Each agreed to subscribe a sum of money to a joint fund which would pay Lewis a stipend of £16 at the beginning of each month for as long as he needed it. Fanny Wadsworth was the treasurer of this charitable enterprise. She drew the first cheque, had it countersigned by Anne Drey and dispatched it on 1 December.

To the subscribers it seemed a sensible arrangement. It would provide Lewis with a steady income, enabling him to finish writing what he described as his 'great book', undistracted by financial worries.

From the beginning Lewis was irritated by the joint fund. He would have preferred his friends to buy some of his unsold drawings instead of clubbing together to provide him with dole. Even in the first month of the fund's existence he was still hard up and offered Wadsworth the pick of his 'bankrupt stock', but Wadsworth honourably declined to take advantage of a fellow painter's straitened circumstances: 'I hope you will allow me to avail myself of your proposition but we will discuss that when your affairs are a little more settled.' In the meantime he enclosed £20, hoping it would 'be of some use'.

By the end of December Lewis had found another studio at 44 Holland Street, off Kensington Church Street and a quarter of a mile from Palace Gardens Terrace. It was sublet to him, at a rental of £5 a week, by the daughter of George Robey, 'The Prime Minister of Mirth', blessed by Lewis before the War.

*

According to Fanny Wadsworth payments of £16 from the joint fund were made to Lewis on 1 January and 1 February. Later in February he asked her for an advance on the March payment and she sent him £6 from her own account, paying him the balance of £10 on 1 March. In the middle of March he asked for the whole of the April payment in advance. She sent him £14, £2 having been deducted to partly balance a sum of £5 previously advanced by her husband.

It was on such officious monetary detail that the well-meaning charitable scheme was doomed to founder. Rarely did financial aid to Lewis come free from reciprocal hostility, and even the most generous of gestures were no guarantee that a benefactor might one day find himself castigated and spurned.

Quite independently of his contributions to the fund, Dick Wyndham had agreed to give Lewis 50 per cent of the profits from an exhibition he was having at the Goupil Gallery. He hoped that this share would amount to £60 or £70. It is true that Dick could afford to split his profits, as he did not have to paint to live. And he felt he owed Lewis a debt for assisting in his 'mental development', not to mention the lessons in draughtsmanship he had given him, although how far these extended beyond being taught to hold his pencil in one hand and his nose in the other is not known. Nevertheless, the offer seemed a particularly selfless one. But despite such generosity, or perhaps because of it, Lewis's relations with his benefactor were extremely prickly. When Dick neglected to keep an evening appointment at his Bedford Gardens studio, it was interpreted as a wealthy man's lack of consideration towards one less fortunate than himself. 'Although hard up', Lewis told him, 'I still find some things inconvenient.'

On another occasion, Lewis became suspicious about the company he was keeping and demanded a detailed account of his movements, the people he met and any conversations held in potentially hostile enemy camps that pertained to himself. Dick ingenuously obliged: 'One night I dined with the Wadsworths alone at their house. Twice I have been out to lunch, once to the Schiffs, once to Lady Colefax (where you were not mentioned). The rest of the time I have dined and lunched alone . . . and read Chekhov.'

One Sunday, Fanny Wadsworth took Lewis to task and pointed out the stupidity of his suspicions and of his seeking a quarrel with their mutual friend. She did not realise that henceforth she and her husband would be consigned to the ranks of Lewis's enemies.

PLEASE SEND MONEY BY WYNDHAMS SQUIBB TO 61 – LEWIS

Fanny received this telegram two days later, on 15 April. She was confused, as much by its peremptory tone as by its timing. She had sent Lewis his April cheque on 20 March at his 'special request' and the next payment was not due until 1 May.

She immediately telephoned Dick Wyndham and asked him to come over. She showed him the offending communication. She told him that Lewis was picking a quarrel with her. The telegram, it seems, was only the latest in a series of affronts and she cited the contents of a recent letter. There was also the occasion, at Dick's studio a fortnight before, when Lewis made a hasty withdrawal as the Wadsworths arrived, returning again as soon as they had left. 'On top of all this,' she complained, 'the telegram.' In the past he had communicated by telephone or letter 'to explain the pressing need of the moment and these matters [were] dealt with at sometimes quite short notice.' His reason for sending the telegram was clear: he did not wish to enter into personal relations with herself and Edward. She said that she did not want to have to manage the fund any longer and was 'jolly glad' to be going abroad in a few weeks time and able to hand over her onerous responsibility to Mrs Drey.

Dick met Lewis by chance in a restaurant that same evening and recounted the conversation.

Lewis in turn took offence, accusing Fanny of picking a quarrel with *him*. He accused her of dragging Dick, a third party, into the dispute, one 'accustomed from childhood to the most sheltered conditions', to whom 'the agitations of [Lewis's] life must seem often inexplicable'. She had 'made deliberate use of Dick's ignorance to disaffect and worry him'. She had, in short, endangered Lewis's friendship with his wealthy young protégé by placing him, Lewis, in the position of an ungrateful and quarrelsome person.

His telegram, it seems, was the result of a tortuous misunderstanding, quite at odds with Fanny's account.

He claimed to have made no such 'special request' for early payment of the April cheque. He had received it, on the contrary, with some surprise, 'but of course satisfaction, as this [was] a difficult time'. And he had 'naturally assumed' the middle and not the first of the month was henceforth to be regarded as pay day. All the subscribers, apart from Windeler, lived within a few minutes' walk of each other. Since Fanny would have had to go to the Dreys' house in Church Street for Anne's signature, and since she would have then been close to Dick's place in Bedford Gardens, Lewis had thought it would expedite delivery if Wyndham's manservant Squibb were instructed to take it round to 61 Palace Gardens Terrace, instead of it being sent to the studio in Holland Street that Lewis was not intending to visit that day. As for the peremptory tone of the message: 'a telegram is necessarily a curt means of communication, as it is an expensive way of communicating.'

The upshot of this bad-tempered exchange was Lewis's renunciation of his stipend. 'I am (only too naturally) sorry that it has to be done, but under the circumstances it would be intolerable to continue receiving it.'

He wrote to Dick enclosing a copy of his letter to Fanny. He also claimed a sizeable tranche of the half-share in Dick's Goupil Exhibition profits that had been promised him.

Dick was now in the uncomfortable position of standing between two warring factions. He did not want to break with the Wadsworths and at the same time wished to retain his friendship with Lewis. He expressed the opinion that Lewis's grand gesture in renouncing the fund was somewhat compromised by a simultaneous appeal for £30 from him. He had not received any of the Goupil money himself yet, and so the demand for so large an advance on the half-share came at an inconvenient time for him. However:

> Either I am a gullible fool, or else I am a sufficiently good judge of the human race to be justified in my great belief in you. You probably think the former – I like to think the latter, and am prepared to stake my judgement again, so enclose cheque.

*

Lewis's suspicions of his one-time patrons persisted. A year later when Pound sent him a £20 cheque for some drawings he wished to buy, Lewis accepted the money gratefully but had to be reassured that it came from Pound himself. 'You must not be offended if I am wrong', Lewis told him:

> but your letter left a doubt in my mind as to whether one or other of my wealthy friends, who some time ago left me in the lurch, were not using you to affect still to be 'helping' me. I should not like for a handful of silver to put myself . . . in that position . . . You will understand my desire to be fixed on the point of that not being a treacherous bounty.

Pound assured him that 'work or works of art ordered on 20 quid cheque are for personal consumption on the domestic hearth . . . and that the purchase of said works was instigated by NO outside pressure, suggestion or other occult or other influence.'

*

In the same month that friendship with the Wadsworths came to an end and that with Dick Wyndham was tried to breaking point, Sydney Schiff discovered that being a friend of Wyndham Lewis did not necessarily spare him from the sort of venom usually reserved for an enemy. In the April issue of Eliot's journal, *The Criterion*, was an extract from a satirical novel that would not appear in book form for another six years. The first of its eleven pages was headed:

THE APES OF GOD

By WYNDHAM LEWIS

EXTRACT FROM ENCYCLICAL ADDRESSED TO
DANIEL BOLEYN
BY MR. ZAGREUS.

It was an essay about the nature of the artistic communities of Paris and London since the war. It described how hordes of wealthy pseudo-artists were renting studios, which only they could afford, to 'daub and dabble' in to the exclusion of 'genuine painters' of greater talent and shallower pockets. Such pronouncements might have caused Dick Wyndham some disquiet: Dick Wyndham, whose name and address was listed in *Kelly's London Post Office Directory* under the Trades Category 'ARTISTS'; Dick Wyndham, the heir of 'Clouds'; Dick Wyndham, who had a large studio and a manservant called Squibb.

But it was not Dick Wyndham who took offence in April 1924. He would have to wait another six years before finding himself satirised in *The Apes of God* as Dick Whittingdon of the corkscrewing trousers, master of March Park and of his man Cubbs. And Dick Wyndham would retaliate with an advertisement in the agony column of *The Times* offering two large Lewis paintings for sale at insultingly low prices.

Instead it was Sydney Schiff whose eye lighted upon a sentence on page 306 of *The Criterion*. 'In a little artificial world of carefully fostered self-esteem I will show you a pseudo-Proust.' It was the use of his late idol's surname that made the connection plain to Schiff, and he was more hurt than angry at Lewis's evident appraisal. 'If I am to understand from what you wrote . . . that my work is included by you in the category of the Apes of God who "produce a little art themselves . . . but less than the 'real thing'"', then my work has failed so far as you are concerned and I regret it.'

*

On 1 May Lewis received what was to be his final cheque from the joint fund. It was accompanied by a conciliatory but frosty letter from Fanny:

> I . . . hope that you will put aside all personal quarrel or misunderstanding and to keep your part of the agreement by continuing to receive what has been subscribed.

Instead of £16, the cheque was made out for £13, the £3 balance of Lewis's outstanding debt to Edward Wadsworth having been deducted. Despite his earlier expressed intention of refusing any more funds from that quarter, Lewis accepted the money:

> I am so hard up that if the devil himself offered me anything from a half crown upwards I should have to accept it: and having got so far with my writing, I cannot jeopardise this . . . by being squeamish.

And he grumbled about her withholding the £3:

> I was anxiously expecting and counting on the £16 due under your scheme and your failure left an awkward gap (Dick luckily helping me).

He again told her that he did not wish the fund 'in its present form' to continue, nevertheless adding a pragmatic rider: 'If you sent it on June 1 and I were still penniless I should I suppose again have to take it.'

As epilogue to the shambles of the joint fund, another curt message deserves quotation even though it is, in all probability, apocryphal. The story of this other message comes at third hand. Geoffrey Grigson heard it from Hugh Gordon Porteus, and neither man had known Lewis at the time of the events in question. If Mrs Wadsworth had been offended at the peremptory tone of Lewis's telegram of 15 April, she would have been outraged at the words Porteus alleges were addressed to her when one monthly cheque failed to arrive on time. No telegraph operator in the country would have countenanced sending such a message, and Grigson was told it arrived in the lady's hands, written on the back of a postcard:

WHERE'S THE FUCKING STIPEND? LEWIS.

*

Luckily there was still another source of funding. In spite of that sneering appellation of 'pseudo-Proust' in *The Criterion*, Sydney Schiff's generosity continued. Between April and August he supplied Lewis with a total of £60.

He then gave him £20 on 29 August, another £20 on 17 September and a further £20 on 13 October. Schiff told him that he would supply more if it was needed but received an 'emphatic disclaimer' that this would be necessary. But when Lewis came down on him for more only a week later, Schiff told him that he could not comply. 'I cannot go on giving you money at this rate.' Lewis withdrew in wounded silence.

A few weeks later, Schiff tentatively resumed the correspondence. 'Where are we now with our relationship?' he asked. 'It seems to me that it was your move.' He soon received Lewis's icy reply: 'I realise that a game is being played, of course; but if you don't mind I will not join in.' The recent refusal of funds previously so generously lavished was the cause of offence:

> There was one move that you led me to expect that you intended . . . to make, which, when you failed to make it, put me in a fix . . . I am still experiencing the consequences of that piece of playfulness of yours.

The 'fix' referred to was probably a failure to keep up with rent payments. Early in October he told Eliot he had been forced to promise his landlady the £5 overdue on his room in Palace Gardens Terrace and that he had nothing to meet the £5 a week for his studio in Holland Street. Clearly, by mid-October this situation had become more critical, the house agent charged with collecting the studio rent more importunate. Then, when money he had regarded as half promised was, it seemed, capriciously withheld by his patron, he was threatened with a writ for possession.

Schiff attempted to restore peace with a proposition not unlike that which had precipitated Lewis's break with the Wadsworths earlier in the year:

> I now offer to give you £12 every four weeks . . . for six months . . . I shall not accept any drawings in exchange for this subsidy which I offer you as an earnest of my interest in the work you are doing, and from a desire to help you in so far as I can, to accomplish it. If, when these six months . . . have expired, you find yourself still engaged in unremunerative work, I shall, if my means permit, continue paying you £12 every four weeks until you inform me that you can dispense with it.

Angered by this further offer of 'dole' Lewis wrote back, demanding the finite sum of £40 which, he claimed, would enable him to finish his 'great book'. He also enclosed nine drawings, with the promise of a tenth to be sent later. Schiff assumed he was intended to choose four or five of these to cover the debt. The message was clear: if Schiff wanted to help the artist he should buy his work. Schiff replied, coolly pointing out that since 25 November 1920 until 13 October 1924 he had bought £712 worth of Lewis's work. This, he calculated, constituted spending at the rate of £14 16s. 8d. per month.

Furthermore, before agreeing to part with the £40 requested, Schiff wanted 'to clear up certain outstanding points'. He wished to know if it was Lewis's intention to finish and deliver a set of ten drawings, the 'Leviathan' series, he had paid £80 for the previous year and the portrait of his wife, begun three years before and for which he had also paid. Since nothing in Lewis's known graphic work answers to the group title 'Leviathan', it is likely that Schiff had paid for a sequence of drawings subsequently abandoned and lost. It is possible they were never even started.

As for the portrait of Violet Schiff, it would be another two years before this was delivered, unfinished, to her husband. One explanation for the abandonment of work on the canvas was that, in the early months of 1925, Lewis lost the struggle to retain his studio. Agents acting for 'The Prime Minister of Mirth's' daughter served an eviction order on him for non-payment of rent and he was duly turned out of 44 Holland Street.

TWENTY-SIX

'Concentrate on one book at a time'

Back in September 1922, Lewis had told Violet Schiff: 'I want to get a large section of my great book typed out in its roughest, earliest draught, so that I can slowly work on it through the next six months.' He presumably intended to differentiate this 'great book', a work of non-fiction, from two other books he was working on at the time.

One of these was the novel Constable's had contracted for earlier that year. *The Life of a Tyro* had a hero called Hoodopip, inhabitant of a twin world called O. It was intended as a satire on postwar England. The other book was to be a gigantic fiction about a schoolteacher. Provisionally entitled *Joint* or *Master Joint*, Lewis thought it could be published in seven separate volumes, or else in one abridged volume. It was, among other things, a parody of Joyce's *Ulysses*. By the end of 1924 these two books had proliferated. A novel called *Archie* followed the fortunes of a Jewish pupil at Joint's school and his relationship with his father in the East End of London. Another book, to be called *The Great Fish Jesus Christ*, was also planned.* *The Childermass* and *The Apes of God*, books that would not be published for another three and five years respectively, were at this early stage conceived of by Lewis as the two parts of a single novel. That made five different literary works that were progressing, more or less concurrently, during the early 1920s. And all this was in addition to the 'great book' itself.

By the end of January 1925, Lewis had been promising Eliot, 'for some months', that his 'principal book' would be ready for publication 'within a week or two'. The fact that there was indeed a 'principal book' must have come as a relief to Eliot, who had been concerned about the number of literary projects his friend seemed to be dividing his energies between. 'I have felt strongly', he told Lewis, 'that it would be in your own interest to concentrate on one book at a time and not plan eight or ten books at once.' At last, even as Eliot wrote these words, the manuscript pages of Lewis's 'principal book' were being collected together for submission to a publisher.

---

* None of these four works was ever completed beyond isolated chapters and fragments. Not even fragments survive of *The Great Fish Jesus Christ* and nothing, apart from the title, is known of it.

On Tuesday 3 February a large package lay on Alec Waugh's desk at the house of Chapman & Hall in Henrietta Street, Covent Garden. A covering letter introduced 'the complete mss. of the book, *The Man of the World*'. There were three pages at the beginning that Lewis had 'mislaid' and which he promised to post to Waugh the following day. There were also a few pages, 'four or five', missing from the end, and these were also to be posted on. But to all intents and purposes the manuscript was complete. Lewis told Pound it was 'longer than *War and Peace*, *Ulysses* and so on' and that it contained 500,000 words. This was probably a slight exaggeration. At roughly 700 words to a page, a manuscript of this length would have amounted to just over 700 pages. Instead, and allowing for the missing opening and concluding pages, Waugh was confronted that morning by a pile of single-spaced typescript consisting of foolscap sheets paginated from 4 to 506. The publisher might well have calculated with some alarm that *The Man of the World* would, if printed in its entirety, convert into a volume of well over 800 pages.

*

'Leave me alone for a bit.' Lewis had issued this injunction to Ezra Pound in July 1922, attempting to curb the latter's enthusiasm for promoting his friend's interests. With so many different books struggling for Lewis's creative attention, Pound's unauthorised negotiations with a Milanese gallery owner for an exhibition of his work, and playing *The Little Review* and *Two Worlds* off against one another in competition for publishing a 'Special Lewis Number', must have been a sore distraction. 'Let me alone for a little, that will be best', he therefore told Pound:

> You will have plenty to talk about before very long: and all your talkative, generous, burbling instincts be satisfied. Forget me for a year, say.

After nearly three years, in March 1925, Pound must have assumed the injunction against meddling had expired when he wrote to the secretary of the John Simon Guggenheim Memorial Foundation: 'Wyndham Lewis, I consider without exception the best possible "value" for your endowment, and the man most hampered by lack of funds at the moment.' He did not, however, mention this intervention to Lewis until later in the year.

*

It did not take Lewis long to realise that no publisher was going to accept the huge manuscript of *The Man of the World* as it stood. More to the point, and based on the experience of his approach to Alec Waugh, he knew that no publisher was going to give him the amount of money he felt was sufficient recompense for the time and effort he had put into this masterwork. Instead, he began splitting it up into more manageable sections for publication as a series of separate volumes. By the end of April he could report to Pound that his 'great book', like the projected epic, *Joint*, had been subdivided into seven.

He had, he thought, already found a publisher for one of the seven, an as yet unnamed book about 'the question of CLASS'. This publisher was Robert McAlmon, who ran a small firm called the Contact Publishing Company in Paris. Then there was a 100,000-word book 'about Shakespeare, principally'. The next, *Sub Persona Infantis*, dealt with the contemporary cult of youth. *The Shaman* was about homosexuality. There were two books of 100,000 words each called *The Politics of the Personality* and *The Politics of Philistia*. Finally, *The Strategy of Defeat* was to be a comparatively slim volume of 40,000 words.

On 20 May Lewis signed a contract with Grant Richards for the book on Shakespeare. 'The publisher's reader reported that it was the greatest book on Shakespeare in the English language', he told Pound. 'This excited the publisher very much, but convinced him at the same time that he would not sell very many copies.' Pound replied:

> If you have written an interesting book on Shakespeare it will be the *first* one on a damned uninteresting subject.

By the end of June Lewis had delivered the revised typescript, provisionally called *Shakespeare Unmasked*. However, *The Lion and the Fox*, subtitled *The Role of the Hero in the Plays of Shakespeare*, would not be published for almost a year and a half.

Meanwhile, his arrangement with Robert McAlmon having stalled, he told Pound that the book had been offered to Methuen as *The Critique of Class* and a contract had been signed.*

*

In June Pound was still making efforts on his friend's behalf, this time attempting to persuade Ernest Walsh to publish a special supplement on Lewis and reproduce several of his pictures in *This Quarter*. Lewis was now

---

* Either Lewis anticipated wrongly or this contract was subsequently cancelled. The material on class was eventually absorbed into *The Art of Being Ruled*, published by Chatto & Windus in 1926.

truly exasperated at Pound's well-intentioned intrusion into his affairs and told him so:

> I do not want a 'Lewis Number' or anything of that sort in *This Quarter* or *anywhere* else. Please note the following: because in the glorious days of Marinetti, Nevinson, machinery . . . , we were associated to some extent in publicity campaigns, that does not give you a mandate to interfere when you think fit . . . with my career.

Pound returned the letter, annotated with corrections of fact and with a typed addendum:

> I . . . hasten to assure you that I shall take no further steps whatever regarding any activity of yours until requested by you to do so. Good bye, and good luck.

Their correspondence lapsed for two months. It was resumed in September with a request from Lewis for a loan.

*

A visit to the London office of the American publishing firm Harper & Brothers in Great Russell Street on 23 July led to the first major delay in production of *The Lion and the Fox*. Harper's representatives told him that he would have to make several changes to his typescript before they would consider publishing it in New York. Lewis agreed to make cuts in parts I and II and to place part I, 'Shakespeare and Race', at the end of the book in the form of an Appendix. They also wanted him to reduce the number of quotations.

In the meantime he tried to squeeze a little more cash out of one publishing house or the other. 'In writing and research', he told Grant Richards, '*The Lion and the Fox* has taken up a very considerable time . . . I have stretched my resources to the utmost to get it done. If I undertook the suggested revisions could not you or Harpers make me some advance . . . to help me over the time I should have to devote to them?'

*

Lewis's resources were indeed stretched. As a result, his former mistress heard he was defaulting on maintenance payments for their son Peter. Olive had been married for the last three years to William Leslie Elstow, a painter, who had magnanimously agreed to adopt Lewis's daughter Betty. However

Peter, now 14 years old, was still being looked after by Mrs Prickett in Clapham. Mrs Prickett, it seems, had complained to Olive that she had received nothing from Lewis, 'lately or at any time', to assist her in the bringing up of his son. Lewis protested that, on the contrary, 'for a long time' he had supplied them with all his 'spare money', and that 'this crushing burden' was bringing him close to bankruptcy. He had, it was true, been unable to send anything a fortnight before but had just sent double the usual amount to make up for the lapse. In short, if Mrs Prickett said she had received nothing from him she was either not telling the truth or she was being robbed by her landlady, by the postman or by someone else 'who collars the letters'. He promised Olive he would go and visit the old lady to sort out the matter of the allegedly missing money. He was also considering a means of relieving himself of the 'crushing burden' of his son's maintenance by finding the boy work. At 14 Peter was, he supposed, 'old enough to get some sort of job'.

*

Harper had told Lewis that he might expect a possible US sale of *The Lion and the Fox* of ten thousand copies. But the prospect of such a lucrative transatlantic market appeared to be in question on 10 September when Grant Richards's secretary advised Lewis that he had already signed away his American rights to the book. This was technically true, as Richards now controlled American as well as British Empire rights. But Lewis evidently misunderstood this to mean that he would get nothing out of American sales. In fact, following standard publishing procedure at that time, the contract stated that royalties on the first American edition would be shared equally between Grant Richards and the author.

Nonetheless a protracted wrangle resulted in a codicil being added to the contract, stipulating that, while royalties on the first 5,000 sales in America would be shared by the author and his British publisher, royalties on US sales over and above 5,000 would be payable to the author in full.

In the event, Harper's real expectations of the US sales fell far short of the 10,000 they had promised Lewis, and this was reflected in the very cautious advance they paid him of $250. Their first printing was, in fact, of only 1,000 copies.

While still negotiating his American rights in mid-September, Lewis was dismayed to learn from Grant Richards that his book would not be published in England until after Christmas. 'It is of very great moment to me', he protested, 'that some work of mine should appear this autumn, and I want *The Lion and the Fox* to appear first and if possible to have a certain margin between it and the next.' He was even prepared to pay something from his slender American advance to oil the wheels of the presses:

> Is there no means, by sacrificing a not very large sum in the form of a bribe to the printers, to hasten the printing?

By early October, Charles Prentice at Chatto & Windus had accepted for publication the second great portion of *The Man of the World*. Remembering the complications of his agreement with Richards, Lewis chose to reserve the American rights to *The Art of Being Ruled*. His contract stated that he would receive, on publication, an advance on royalties of £50.

There was, between Lewis's delivery of his completed typescript to Chatto at the end of November, and publication of *The Art of Being Ruled* in March 1926, a gap of a little over three months. *The Lion and the Fox* had been delivered to Grant Richards in June, but five months later it had still not been printed. On 9 December Lewis lost patience:

> I am writing to you to propose that you should hand me back my manuscript and so enable me to make other and more satisfactory arrangements for its publication. To have my manuscript, over which I took so much trouble, worked at for so long and at considerable risk, for as you are aware I am a poor man – held up indefinitely by you ... is becoming intolerable. To have it published at all by your firm is, in consequence of the experiences I have had in the course of my transactions with you, extremely distasteful to me. I should be prepared to pay you a compensation for anything within reason you may compute as being due to you for time and expense in connection with it.

Relations with Grant Richards were not improved when the first 32 pages of proofs were delivered in mid-December and Lewis discovered that the printer had made unauthorised 'corrections' to his typescript. Eighty-seven 'unnecessary' capital letters had been substituted for the lower-case initials of such words as 'renaissance', 'shavian', 'newtonian', 'machiavellian', 'elizabethan', 'court', 'papal', 'king', etc. Lewis insisted they be changed back, and that he should not be charged for the changes. Grant Richards claimed that such eccentricities of capitalisation would hinder sales of the book, an argument Lewis dismissed as 'absurd'. If however the publisher was adamant on this issue, Lewis declared himself agreeable, if only to avoid offending the readers' nationalist sensibilities, to the capitalisation of such words as 'englishman', 'frenchman', 'german', 'english', 'russian' or 'chinese'.

*

If *The Lion and the Fox* might be loosely termed Shakespeare criticism, *The Art of Being Ruled* was a combination of sociology and political theory. Aspects of Western democratic society, Lewis argued, such as dress fashions, feminism, homosexuality, and the cult of youth, were being used to control and subjugate the public under the guise of giving it what it wanted and a spurious freedom to express itself. Into this 400-odd-page book had gone at least three of the seven parts into which *The Man of the World* had been split.

Throughout that year the book on Shakespeare, which was to have preceded *The Art of Being Ruled* in Lewis's scheme, remained stalled in mid-production north of the border at the Riverside Press in Edinburgh. Later it became apparent that the book was being held hostage by the Scottish printing firm against a large outstanding debt of Grant Richards & Co. For his part, Richards explained to Lewis that a printer's strike was partly responsible for the delay. A far more widespread stoppage would give him a further excuse some five weeks later.

Unable to extract a commitment for the speedy publication of his book, Lewis next took legal advice as to the viability of getting his manuscript returned and his contract with the publisher cancelled. The firm of Adshead, Gibbs & Fortescue wrote a letter threatening the publisher with litigation but, having also been advised of his shaky legal rights in the matter, Lewis instructed them to proceed no further and they charged him four guineas for their services.

*

In March he moved from his furnished room in Palace Gardens Terrace, across the Bayswater Road to a room at number 33 Ossington Street. This quiet plane-tree-lined street, just off the main thoroughfare, was to be the centre of his activities for the next five years.

*

The whole townland of London was up in arms and as silent as the grave and it was reported that in its eastern quarters, in the slum-wards such as Poplar, a Police-inspector and two Specials had been kicked to death and there were more and more violent riots in Hammersmith, where trams had been wrecked and street-rails torn up by the mob, and the Police stoned and injured: while it was confidently stated that in the North crowds had sacked the better quarters, in the big factory-towns, mines were flooded, mills were blazing, and the troops were firing with machine-guns upon the populace. The absence of newspapers fostered every report of disorder.

The General Strike of May 1926 was to form an ironic backdrop to the final section of *The Apes of God*. While the nine-day damp squib of a revolution brought London and the rest of the country to a standstill and the middle-class undergraduates and white-collar workers manned the trams, buses and trains to get London and the rest of the country moving again, and while the Prime Minister's calming words were read over the wireless: 'Keep steady! Remember that peace on earth comes to all men of goodwill', Lewis was in Paris. He was there, he told Charles Prentice, to finish writing *The Apes of God*, and when the strike was over he intended returning to London to arrange for the book's publication.* He hoped Prentice would take it for Chatto and, if so, that the current national paralysis would not prevent it from appearing early in the autumn. Writing on 11 May he assumed the strike would be finished 'in a couple of weeks', but on the following day the TUC capitulated and voted to return to work.

*

Before Lewis had left London the manager of Bumpus's in Oxford Street said he could tell his publisher that the bookshop would be happy to announce the titles of any of his forthcoming books along with *The Art of Being Ruled* which was selling very well indeed. And in Paris he was gratified to learn that Sylvia Beach's bookshop Shakespeare & Co. had actually sold out of it. However stocks were moving slower than these reports would seem to indicate, and by 23 May only 323 copies had been sold. Nevertheless, even this meagre trade had earned out Lewis's £50 advance on royalties. 'I am . . . extremely glad to hear', he wrote to Prentice the following month, 'that henceforth I shall benefit by the sales of my book, which I hope may keep up.' Thereafter he would get 15 per cent of the 18 shillings on every copy. But by the end of August only a further 182 had sold.

He promised the publisher he would soon be coming into his office in St Martin's Lane to discuss terms on *The Apes of God*. He could not say when this would be. As usual the book was taking longer to finish than he expected but, as he was anxious to deliver it in the autumn, he would 'hurry on its completion'. He was, perhaps, already drawing on the topical

---

* He had, by this time, abandoned the idea that *The Apes of God* should be published with *The Childermass* as one giant novel.

inspiration of the General Strike for the mock apocalypse of his closing pages.

*

Meanwhile, he was still trying to get *The Lion and the Fox* back from Grant Richards. In June, he again took legal advice and was again told he had 'no legal standing in the matter of recovery of [his] manuscript'. By this stage he was contemplating a means of avoiding the vicissitudes of conventional publishing altogether. He spoke to Audrey Waterhouse, wife of Sir Nicholas Waterhouse, about effectively spoiling the book for Grant Richards by polishing up the rough manuscript that was still in his possession and publishing it in instalments himself. He also thought of prefacing it with 'some remarks as to [his] reasons for bringing the book out in parts'. Sir Nicholas himself, however, persuaded him of the dangers in such a course of action. Grant Richards would be within his rights to bring legal action to bear under the terms of the original contract; added to which a writ for defamation could be served if Lewis's prefaced remarks were 'construed by Grant Richards as derogatory to their "good name" or bona-fides in the matter'.

The friendship and patronage of Sir Nicholas and Lady Waterhouse, dating from this time, was the one unexpected benefit to emerge from Lewis's acrimonious dealings with Richards. It was also one of the very few friendships in Lewis's life that were able to survive his one-sided financial obligation. Sir Nicholas, of the accounting firm Price, Waterhouse & Co., was to support Lewis through illness and financial crisis until the artist's death; thereafter ensuring his widow was provided for.

Lewis, for reasons that remain obscure, called Sir Nicholas, 'Docker' and Lady Audrey, 'Mauve' or 'Mov'. Sir Nicholas in turn called him 'Professor'.

Although a serialised version of *The Lion and the Fox*, with or without libellous prefatory remarks, was fraught with risk, Lewis's generalised talk of publishing his own books must have struck a chord with Lady Waterhouse and, in August, she made him a 'magnificent and disinterested, but otherwise unspecified present' towards the bringing of his ambitions to fruition. It appeared to take him by surprise. 'When I spoke to you of my plans', he told her:

> you, almost a stranger, were the last person that I thought of as likely to provide the necessary funds . . . but you have . . . far exceeded what I had fixed on as necessary for such an enterprise. You could not have acted with more kindness and generosity.

With Mauve's donation, and with a further £60 from her husband, Lewis was able to launch, early the following year, his third and last editorial adventure: *The Enemy*.

*

Late in September, James Joyce wrote to Harriet Shaw Weaver from Brussels where he was holidaying with his family: 'Lewis, it seems, has been to Paris and asked for the MS and is coming here as he wants to see me.' The manuscript was the draft, written that summer, of a section of 'Work in Progress' called 'The Muddest Thick that was ever Heard Dump'. Joyce let Lewis have it for publication in his new periodical.

*

By October the financial difficulties of Grant Richards & Co. had increased. Its bank had sent in the Official Receivers and the Riverside Press in Edinburgh, one of the principal creditors, was owed 'a very considerable amount' of money. It was for this reason that Grant Richards had been unable either to have *The Lion and the Fox* printed, or to have Lewis's manuscript released. Despite such embarrassment, he was still 'anxious to proceed with the publication of [the] book'.

*

As a new avenue of patronage opened in the Waterhouses, an earlier patron made one last attempt to receive a return on an old investment. In November Sydney Schiff asked Lewis for the portrait of his wife begun four years previously and still not finished. He told Lewis he did not even care that it was unfinished. He seemed wearied by the protracted transaction. 'Never again in my life shall I enter into a business relationship with any artist,' he told Lewis, 'least of all with you.' He did, however, soften this rather harsh, if justified, resolution with an assurance of continued good will. 'Least', he explained, 'because of my deep and lasting admiration and an underlying regard for you that are both unchangeable and must never be exposed to assault.'

Lewis surrendered the canvas. Many years later he described to J. R. Ackerley the slow and difficult process of painting a good portrait: 'building up the structure of the face, etc., putting in, making mistakes, painting out, and denied that one got quicker and more facile with practice.' He did not mention to Ackerley that, on occasion, surgery became necessary, as was the case with the portrait of Mrs Schiff. An oval scar can be seen in the surface of the canvas around the face. Lewis had cut out the overworked and evidently botched section and glued another piece of canvas onto the back in order to start again. If the face had been overworked, other areas were barely sketched in. The left hand in particular, as had been the case with the study he delivered to Schiff in March 1922, needed to be 'worked on and explained more'. He never signed the portrait and, seven years later, still intended to resume work on it. 'I hope', he promised in 1933, 'at my leisure, [to] do anything further to Violet's portrait that occurs to me when I next find myself in front of it.' He did not.

*

In January 1927 the firm of Grant Richards & Co. emerged sufficiently from its financial difficulties to publish *The Lion and the Fox*.

The first issue of *The Enemy: A Review of Art and Literature* was also to have come out in January, as indicated on its cover, 'but owing to miscalculation as to the time required to prepare it', a note inside explained, 'it is appearing in February instead.' Other numbers, 'uniform as regards format', were promised 'from time to time' during the year, 'longer or shorter according to circumstances'. It was published by The Arthur Press, a fictitious firm invented by the editor. Realising, after the first issue had been printed, that the 'Press' required an address, Lewis obtained permission from the lady running the Commercial School and Typewriting Offices that prepared copy for the magazine, to use hers. '113a, WEST-BOURNE GROVE, W.', was rubber-stamped in violet letters on each title page.

Most of its 200-odd pages consisted of a long essay by Lewis called 'The Revolutionary Simpleton'. It was an examination of what he called 'Time-notions', the time- and flux-obsessed philosophies of Henri Bergson, A. N. Whitehead and Samuel Alexander, and how they infused the Romanticism masquerading as Modernism of contemporary literature. Under scrutiny and attack for their adherence to such 'Time-notions' were Gertrude Stein, Ezra Pound, and another writer who had been led to expect somewhat different treatment from the pages of *The Enemy*.

If James Joyce had hoped to find there the first printing of 'The Muddest Thick that was ever Heard Dump', he was disappointed. Instead, chapter XVI of 'The Revolutionary Simpleton', and by far the longest chapter therein, was entitled 'An Analysis of the Mind of James Joyce'. Here Lewis memorably dismissed *Ulysses* as being:

like a gigantic victorian quilt or antimacassar. Or it is the voluminous curtain that fell, belated (with the alarming momentum of a ton or two of personally organised rubbish) upon the victorian scene. So rich was its delivery, its pent-up outpouring so vehement, that it will remain, eternally cathartic, a monument like a record diarrhoea. No one who looks *at* it will ever want to look *behind* it. It is the sardonic catafalque of the victorian world.

Of Joyce's current 'Work in Progress' he said little apart from calling it 'literary horseplay on the one side, and Steinesque child-play on the other'.

A short editorial intervention in this first issue of *The Enemy* was an article called 'What's in a namesake?' In it Lewis placed on record for the first time the distinction between himself and a man the *Daily Mail* referred to as 'the great English humorist, D. B. Wyndham Lewis'. Apart from indicating the confusion of identity and declaring that the writer responsible for the *Mail*'s column, 'At the Sign of the Blue Moon', was not, in his opinion, particularly humorous, this was as far as Lewis went in his public statement on the matter. Privately, however, he suspected this confusion to be the cause of his being hounded for repayment of debts in the mistaken belief that he had large 'journalistic resources' accruing from a highly paid column in the Rothermere press. Mistaken identity was to be a recurring joke and was to result in a great deal of misdirected mail for the rest of Lewis's life.

*

Dick Wyndham made a killing in New York on 9 February when the collection of the late John Quinn was put up for auction at the American Art Association. Henry McBride wrote in *The Dial*:

> The buyers in attendance ... displayed excellent judgement in their purchases and there were few real bargains – unless you call Mr Wyndham Lewis's things, which sold for trifling sums, bargains.

Dick Wyndham evidently regarded them as such. 'I succeeded in carrying back to England', he told the *Daily Sketch*, 'practically the whole of the Vorticist section for less than the cost of a case of American champagne.' In all he successfully bid for about 60 paintings and drawings. Of the 52 items by Lewis that came under the hammer, 24 were bought by his one-time friend. His hitherto modest Lewis collection was thereby enriched by 22 wartime and prewar drawings, and two huge canvases: the celebrated *Kermesse* of 1912, measuring almost nine feet square, and the 1914 *Plan of*

War, a little over eight feet high by nearly five feet wide. He gleefully informed the *Daily Sketch* what he had paid for the two paintings. It was a measure of how far even their strained friendship had deteriorated that he so readily divulged such information, inevitably harmful to Lewis's reputation. *Kermesse* and *Plan of War* were knocked down to him at auction for the dollar equivalent of £2 10s each, five pounds the pair.

'Trifling sums' indeed. 'The English Cubists', Henry McBride wrote, 'have not as yet obtained a footing in precarious New York.'

*

In April Charles Prentice accepted a bulky manuscript from Lewis, the first third of which consisted of 'The Revolutionary Simpleton'. The remaining two thirds was 'An Analysis of the Philosophy of Time'. The contract was signed in May and Lewis received an advance of £100. The nearly 500-page *Time and Western Man* was published in September. James Joyce, in playful retaliation for Lewis's treatment of him in 'The Revolutionary Simpleton', accorded the book dishonourable mention in *Finnegans Wake* as 'Spice and Westend Woman'.

Lewis received a more generous advance, of £150, for the comparatively modest proportions of *The Wild Body*, published later that year. This perhaps reflected Chatto's belief in the broader appeal of a volume of short stories. Some of these, like 'Beau Séjour', 'Bestre' and 'Brotcotnaz', were revisions of Lewis's earliest published works.

*

Both *The Lion and the Fox* and *The Art of Being Ruled* were published in America by Harper & Brothers. That summer, his first visit to the United States since childhood was, he said, 'mainly owing to my dissatisfaction, and my intention to place my interests in more active and intelligent hands. – I question if Harpers have made any effort at all to sell my *Lion and the Fox*.' During his fortnight or so in New York he found a new publisher, Harcourt, Brace & Company, willing to publish *Time and Western Man* and *The Wild Body*, and he also began writing a long essay that would fill the next issue of *The Enemy* at the end of September. He liked New York. He stayed at the Brevoort Hotel, 'a stone's throw from Washington Square', on the corner of 5th Avenue and 2nd Street, where a large room could be had for between two and three dollars a day. 'It has been very hot', he wrote to Prentice. 'The high buildings are very impressive, especially the later ones "hanging-gardens" style. The earlier ones are like particularly long-necked cathedrals or big english parish churches.'

He was still working on his essay, 'Paleface or "Love? What ho! Smelling Strangeness"', in mid-August on the boat home. It was an examination of the white 'inferiority complex' arising from romantic notions of race. Its primary targets were Sherwood Anderson's *Dark Laughter* and, lest it be suspected that this was an exclusively American 'complex', D. H. Lawrence's mystical broodings on the Hopi Indians in his *Mornings in Mexico*, published shortly before Lewis arrived in New York.

One American novel published the previous year was accorded high praise in 'Paleface'. This was Ernest Hemingway's satire on Sherwood Anderson, *The Torrents of Spring*.

Following its appearance in *The Enemy*, Prentice agreed to publish an expanded version of the essay and gave Lewis an advance of £100. Chatto eventually published *Paleface: The Philosophy of the 'Melting Pot'* in 1929. It was not published in the United States during Lewis's lifetime.

*

Towards the end of 1927 Lewis crossed the Channel in the teeth of an unusually severe gale. 'The boat lay on its side the greater part of the time,' he recalled, 'and as we arrived in France there were repeated earthquake shocks.' This was not an exaggeration. At 11 o'clock on the night of Saturday 19 November, earth tremors were felt across Normandy and Brittany. Reports came from Rennes, from Évreux, St Malo and Caen. Subterranean rumblings were heard in Le Mans and as far south as Tours. The shocks were anything up to a minute in duration, furniture shifted and crockery smashed.

In Paris he had lunch with Archibald MacLeish and Ernest Hemingway. This was Lewis's only other recorded encounter with the author of *The Torrents of Spring*, following that of 1922 when Hemingway was teaching Pound to box. Years later MacLeish could not remember what they talked about over lunch. His only recollection was what Hemingway said after they had taken their leave and the two Americans were walking home together.

The distinctly unfavourable impression of Lewis at their first meeting — as having the eyes of 'an unsuccessful rapist' — was written almost 40 years later. Hemingway's comment following the second meeting was both more immediate and enigmatic. Perhaps Lewis had been uncommunicative and defensive during the meal. Perhaps he had eaten in a fastidious way. As they crossed the Seine, Hemingway turned to MacLeish and said: 'Did you notice? He ate with his gloves on.'

Since neither man had actually seen gloves, 'the question', MacLeish recalled, 'became lurid and memorable.'

TWENTY-SEVEN

'Your output has become prolific'

Back in England the freak weather conditions of November continued into the New Year. 'There have been constant hurricanes here', Lewis wrote to John, wisely wintering at Martigues, in February:

> all the lobsters left the bed of the Channel and North Sea and came up onto the beaches for safety ... Then ... one morning when people got up ... and went out in the street ... they most of them fell down – there were five thousand accidents and many deaths. (This was a sheet of ice very thin and exceedingly slippery laid down on the pavements). The winds ... blew a man two miles in a bath chair ... and several people have been blown over and killed. A tidal wave came up the Thames ... from the North Sea at dead of night and drowned twenty people in cellars at Westminster and Putney ... They say the Magnetic Pole is changing its position.

There were in fact no more than 14 people drowned when the Thames overflowed its banks that night of 6 January 1928, and the disaster was caused by a fatal combination of an unusually high tide and a sudden and widespread thaw.

Lewis may not have been aware, when he wrote to John, of his personal, though far from mortal, stake in this catastrophe. When the river rose above the parapet at Millbank the cellars of the Tate Galley were flooded and a monumental gouache, owned by the Contemporary Art Society, showing three bigger than life-size, grinning versions of Kate Lechmere, called *Laughing Woman*, was destroyed. The large paper picture had been stored in the Tate basement, where the CAS had an office, following its return from a provincial tour in 1913. The last person known to have looked at it before the flood was St John Hutchinson, who visited Millbank in 1918 while selecting works for a CAS exhibition in Switzerland. *Laughing Woman* had been judged too big for the rather '*intime*' show in 'a smallish gallery' and was left in store.

The last seen of it on 6 January 1928 was 'a reddish expanse floating about on the surface of the muddy water'.

Many years later Ruthven Todd recalled Lewis enlarging on the story with a splendidly scurrilous anecdote which had James Bolivar Manson, the future Director of the Tate, deliberately pushing the picture under water. Manson had been secretary of the Camden Town Group in 1911, staunchest supporter of the reactionary faction represented by Lucien Pissarro, and certainly opposed to Lewis's inclusion in the Group's membership. While in all probability apocryphal, the anecdote was none the less vivid for being energetically acted out. 'Seizing a stick Lewis hopped around the imaginary edges of the waters, poking furiously at an imaginary painting floating on the top, and exclaiming gleefully, "Oh, that nasty Lewis! That nasty Lewis! This is the end of him. We won't see him again!"' Although the charge cannot be entirely taken seriously, Todd believed that 'all who knew the unspeakable Manson would agree . . . that he was more than capable of sinking a picture which happened to be in his charge merely because he disliked the painter.'

*

Between 9.15 and 9.30 on the evening of 21 January Lewis's voice was heard on the air waves for the first time. The programme was entitled:

Writers of Today: MR. WYNDHAM LEWIS
reading from his own Works.

The *Radio Times* helpfully differentiated the speaker from the *Daily Mail's* 'great English humorist', and warned his wireless audience that they might find themselves out of their depth:

> As an artist and philosopher, Mr Wyndham Lewis (not, by the way, to be confused with his namesake of the Sign of the Blue Moon) is as disconcertingly original as any in Europe. Neither his pictures nor his books are easy to understand, and listeners must be prepared to make some intellectual effort if they wish to get his meaning; a feat which those who have read 'Tarr', 'The Art of Being Governed' [*sic*], 'The Lion and the Fox', or 'Time and Western Man', will assure them is quite worthwhile.

Whether the audience was exposed to material from the three great components of *The Man of the World* during the 15-minute broadcast that Saturday evening, or whether Lewis chose instead to read selected passages from *Tarr* or from the recently published *Wild Body* stories, is not known. Whatever he read he seems to have been excited by the experience, and two days after his wireless debut he was still disarmingly eager for assessment of his performance. 'What a pity you didn't hear the whole of the reading', he wrote to Alick Schepeler:

> you could have told me better than anybody how it came through. That would have been so valuable, for I haven't the least idea what it came out like at the other end, except from what one friend of mine has told me, and that sounded too favourable, I thought. But I daresay it was awfully good. When [we] meet you must tell me what you thought of what you *did* hear, however.

*

On 3 February Lewis admitted to feeling 'a little screwed' despite having had 'nothing in particular to drink'. It was the intoxication of fatigue. He had just worked through the night in order to have his fourth manuscript for Chatto ready for delivery in the morning. The sleepless marathon was climax to several weeks' toil on this, his latest 'big book'.

The contract he signed with Chatto & Windus was for a work of fiction to be no shorter than 180,000 words. It was to be published in three sections. On signature of the contract and delivery of the first section Lewis received an advance on royalties of £200. He was to receive a further £200 advance on delivery of each of the two succeeding sections. No later than two years after the appearance of the third and final section, a composite edition of the entire epic work, *The Childermass*, was to be published in a single volume.

The action of the first section, delivered that Friday morning following a night without sleep, takes place in a an unreal landscape encountered after death. To the celestial north are distant mountains like 'a fringe of crystals'; to the infernal south, 'a mist that seems to thunder'; to the west, a red ridge of 'nummulitic limestone' separated from a broad river by a two-mile tract of land where a mass of post-mortem 'emigrants' is encamped either side of a road, awaiting admission to the great walled city across the water to the east. The official who judges them fit for admission is a hump-backed Punch-like figure known as the Bailiff. The city they aspire to may or may not be heaven.

A great deal of *The Childermass* is taken up with philosophical debate: the Bailiff, propounding the Romantic 'Time-notions' of Bergson, Whitehead and Alexander, clashes with the suppliants on whom he sits in judgement, notably Hyperides arguing the case for Classicism. Often it reads like a dramatised version of *Time and Western Man*, with the Bailiff jabbering away in the repetitive baby prose of Gertrude Stein or in the allusive verbiage of James Joyce. During this extended parody Lewis actually quoted from the portion of 'Work in Progress' Joyce himself, all unwittingly, had contributed to the first number of *The Enemy*.

*

Dick Wyndham had had no contact with Lewis for some years when, in April, a telegram reached him in Antibes. It had come to Lewis's attention that his former friend had lent several drawings acquired at the Quinn sale in New York of the previous year, together with *Plan of War* and *Kermesse*, for inclusion in a retrospective exhibition of the London Group to be held the following month.

Lewis's objections, of which his telegram was a necessarily curt manifestation, were expressed at greater length in a letter he wrote to the organiser of the show, Rupert Lee:

> My connection with the London Group ceased before the War and it was of short duration in any case. I ceased to belong to it because I did not wish any longer to associate myself with a society of artists with whose work I was not in sympathy. Under these circumstances to seek to advertise your retrospective exhibition by the inclusion of works of mine is extremely unjustifiable. But to do so with works that have never been exhibited nor offered for exhibition to your Group is doubly so.

He enclosed a 2/- postal order to cover Lee's expenses in sending an immediate telegram to the effect that the works had been removed from the exhibition.

The works were finally withdrawn on Dick Wyndham's instructions, wired to Lee from Antibes. On his return to England, Dick wrote to Lewis defending himself against the charge that he had bought *Kermesse* and *Plan of War* and agreed to exhibit them in an effort to harm the painter's reputation. He assured Lewis that he did not intend using his early works 'as a weapon, for reprisals, nor as subjects for childish "Tittle-tattle" '. The assurance nevertheless carried a malicious barb as he stated his actual reasons for buying the paintings. 'I consider them interesting works', he wrote, 'and cheap at 25/-, the price they were fetching in New York.'

Although confessing that, until his memory was jogged by the telegram, he 'had entirely forgotten [Lewis's] existence', being reminded of it, he took the opportunity to call for the settlement of an old score. Some years before, Dick had given him £100, for which he had been promised the manuscript of a book Lewis was working on at the time. This manuscript, he now claimed. Dick may have already been aware of the story about a drawing of

Violet Schiff, paid for by her husband, which Lewis sold again to someone else, because he added a rider to his claim:

> No doubt the M.S. of the book in question has already been sold at least once. But as I am told that your output has become prolific you can probably find some other M.S. that will suit me as well.

*

When David Garnett was lent a proof copy of *The Childermass* in May it was accompanied by the direst injunctions to secrecy. 'You will bear in mind', Lewis told him:

> my great anxiety lest any person except yourself should prematurely get a sight of this . . . I know I can rely on you to show it to no one but may I venture to suggest that should you have people staying with you in the house you should lock it up or hide it?

At the bottom of the page, written in red ink and inch high block capitals, were the words:

PLEASE SHOW TO NO ONE

A month before, Marie Meloney, editor of the *New York Herald Tribune*'s Sunday Magazine, had written to ask Lewis for an article to be called 'Modern Philosophy and Bunk' or for 'something on sign posts and posters'. She also asked if he could suggest 'some well-known writer' who could produce a 'personality sketch' of him. She thought that if these two pieces were published together, in the pages of the Sunday Magazine, they might help sales of the next book he had published in the United States.

It was for this reason that Lewis approached David Garnett and asked him to write the 'gossipy article of two thousand words' that Mrs Meloney was prepared to pay $100 for. And that he might better puff the forthcoming book, Lewis also lent him, 'with infinite precautions', page-proofs of *The Childermass*. Garnett found it, and 30 years later continued to find it, 'almost unreadable'. Diplomatically, he told Lewis there were 'very fine things in it' but that he did not like it 'as a whole':

> The parody of Joyce is a piece of virtuosity that seems out of place. And altogether there is too much Bailiff. I wish you could have compressed him. I like the first half best: many of the episodes are admirable.

277

Lewis was disconcerted by Garnett's unpromising initial verdict and considered paying him for his trouble and finding someone else, more sympathetic to his book, to write the article. What Garnett produced, however, was devoted mainly to a favourable exposition of Lewis's critical works. In the last three pages he addressed himself to the subject of Lewis as 'a creative writer' and declared him to be 'far too much preoccupied with ideas' to be 'a pure artist'. Nevertheless he found three or four hundred words of unequivocal praise at the end for *The Childermass*.

'It is popular, vulgar and totally inadequate', Garnett said of his article as he sent it, together with *The Childermass* proofs, to Lewis, 'but perhaps that is what the *Herald Tribune* want, though I don't suggest it is what you want. You are at complete liberty to suppress it.'

*

In June Lewis paid his second visit to New York. As before, the primary objective was to find himself a new American publisher. Harcourt, Brace & Co. were not 'pushing' his work sufficiently, he thought. His 'Time Book' was a case in point: published six months before, only 864 copies had been sold by the beginning of May.

'They should have sold 15,000 copies of *Time and Western Man*', Lewis complained to a friend of the critic Burton Rascoe. 'To whom?' the friend enquired. 'To the women of the women's clubs', answered Lewis, 'and to college students.'

'All of his profound investigations', Rascoe reported, 'have not robbed him of a certain naivety.'

He had displayed similar naivety the previous December when he demanded of Harcourt's representative, Montgomery Belgion, the dollar equivalent of £1,000 advance for the American rights on another 'big book', *The Apes of God*. Belgion frankly expounded to him the mathematics of publishing: that such a sum represented a 15 per cent royalty on nearly 14,000 copies of a $2.50 novel, and that no American publisher was going to risk such an outlay, 'or anything like it', on his book. Lewis was unconvinced and felt that Harcourt's considered his work 'neither good nor saleable'.

The Apes of God was not sold to an American publisher for another four years, but by the time he left New York in July he had made a deal with the firm of Covici-Friede to publish *The Childermass*.

Whatever reservations he may have had about David Garnett's article for the *New York Herald Tribune*, Lewis did not suppress it. He forwarded it to Mrs Meloney, and, during his stay in New York, he sent her an article of his own for publication alongside Garnett's 'personality sketch'. He requested payment before his departure. The title and precise subject of Lewis's article is not known but it was probably not called 'Modern Philosophy and Bunk', nor was it likely to have been 'something on sign posts and posters'. Instead he appears to have addressed himself to American society. This at least is the impression given by Mrs Meloney when she wrote to him requesting changes. 'It is possible', she advised him, 'that with your short stay in New York City your criticism and interpretation of one of the most complex nations in the world might be challenged.' A first draft of her letter had a harsher tone than the one she actually sent:

> until the sale of your books in this country has reached proportions which indicate a following and a wider acquaintance with your work, it would not be in your best interest to let your individual opinions and prejudices and personal experiences entirely dominate a philosophical discussion.

Responding to the more temperate request for changes, Lewis told her the article could not be altered but airily promised to write another more to her liking. Nothing, however, appeared under his name in the *New York Herald Tribune*'s Sunday Magazine. Mrs Meloney did not publish Garnett's 'personality sketch' either.

Burton Rascoe has left an account of Lewis in the thick of American society. The occasion was a Fourth of July garden party in Larchmont, north of New Rochelle, given by his new publisher Donald Friede. It was a few days before Lewis embarked for home:

> In Friede's garden, Lewis wore an enormous, broadbrimmed black hat, the crown of which was neither creased nor dented and he poised himself over his walking stick constantly like Millet's peasant over the handle of his hoe. He is quiet, soft-spoken and he wears a contemplative air that goes well with his costume. He is interested in American Indians and in totem poles and on his return to America this fall he is going to Canada in search of them. He was disconcerted when Isabel Paterson told him that the only totem poles in Canada were the property of the Canadian Pacific and the Canadian National Railway companies. He thought Mrs Paterson was pulling his leg.

Mrs Paterson's revelation can hardly be held responsible for Lewis's failure to return to America in the fall. His next visit would not be for another three and a half years.

*

On his return from New York, a month after the first section of *The Childermass* was published in London, Chatto gave him £100 advance on the second and third sections. They also agreed that, as he delivered each half-section of about 30,000 words, he would receive another £75 portion of the total advance.*

No further sections or indeed half-sections of *The Childermass* were delivered. It would be under a different overall title, under a different imprint and 28 years later, that sections two and three of Lewis's longest work of fiction would eventually be published. A fourth section would remain in unpublishable fragments at his death.

*

He was 'moving about a great deal' in August, writing to W. B. Yeats from Munich at the beginning of September, in gratitude for the poet's flattering endorsement of the first section of *The Childermass*: 'It is as powerful as 'Gulliver' and much more exciting to a modern mind ... There are moments in the first hundred pages that no writer of romance has surpassed.' With Yeats's permission, Lewis relayed the choicest remarks to his New York publishers, Covici-Friede, to promote their edition of the book in the United States.

It is likely that, in addition to Munich, he visited Berlin and explored for the first time the notoriously decadent night life he was to document two years later.

*

In March 1929 the third and final issue of *The Enemy* was published. Among the mass of advertising material at the beginning were two pages of extracts from English and American reviews of *Time and Western Man* and *The Wild Body* and a list of the six books Lewis had published since 1926. The list culminated in *Tarr*, 'entirely rewritten', and published by Chatto in a Phoenix Library edition the previous December. As if to prove that his first novel had been 'entirely rewritten' Lewis reproduced page 41 of the 1918 Knopf edition he had used for the revision, criss-crossed with arrowed lines, its margins crowded with ringed insertions and alterations.

Of possible interest to the house of Constable & Co. was an editorial note headed: '*Approximate publishing dates for Mr. Lewis's next books.*'

---

* It was also agreed that, should Lewis be prevented by his demise from completing *The Childermass*, Chatto & Windus were to have exclusive rights to the publication of a collection of his writings on painting, including *The Caliph's Design* and essays from *Blast* and *The Tyro*.

In answer to the 'many enquiries' he had received as to when *The Childermass* was to be completed, the publication date of *The Apes of God* and also of a book on 'Youth Movements' announced in *The Enemy* no. 2, Lewis offered a tentative timetable. *Paleface* was to be published first, in about a month or six weeks, by Chatto. This was to be followed 'at intervals of about a month or six weeks', by *The Apes of God*, and by *The Diabolical Principle*, printed in the current issue of *The Enemy*, to which would be added *The Dithyrambic Spectator*, first printed in *The Calendar of Modern Letters* in 1925.

Nowhere in this schedule of activities could Michael Sadleir of Constable discern any promise of the novel his firm had commissioned seven years previously. The publisher therefore began legal action against Lewis, either to enforce completion of *The Life of a Tyro* by a reasonable stated date, or else to secure the return of their advance of £100, 'together with interest thereon'.

Lewis pointed out that he had published no new work of fiction since 1922, apart from 'half of an epic', *The Childermass*. The reason for this, and for his consequent failure to fulfil the contract with Constable, was what he described as a 'revolution in [his] work' which drove him 'into a quite different type of production': the completion of *The Man of the World* and the breaking of it into so many separate publishable parts. When this disposal of his non-fiction assets was complete, he felt he would be 'better fitted to produce such things as "The Life of a Tyro"'. He intended to write the book for Constable, would do his best to finish it by the midsummer of 1930, but more than that he could not say. 'As to sending you a hundred pounds,' he told Constable's solicitors, 'I have not got that sum myself, I am a poor man. Mr Sadleir I am quite sure is aware of that distressing fact.'

Correspondence between Waterhouse & Co., Constable's legal representatives, and Withers & Co., acting for Lewis, continued for six months. Lewis was able to clear part of the debt by the end of August but was threatened with bankruptcy proceedings in October for recovery of the balance. Following further communication between the firms of Waterhouse and Withers, the remaining £50, together with 10 guineas in costs, was eventually paid, on Lewis's behalf. His benefactor, Sir Nicholas Waterhouse, had no connection, beyond a shared name, with the solicitors acting for Constable & Co. The contract for *The Life of a Tyro* was cancelled.

TWENTY-EIGHT

Peter London and Miss Mayfair 1924

In the late spring or early summer of 1929 Lewis was introduced to a 30-year-old former actress, best remembered for her performance in the small but showy role of Penelope Foxglove in Sir Kenneth Barnes's play *The Letter of the Law*. One critic had praised her portrayal of a flapper as epitomising 'Miss Mayfair 1924'. By 1929 Marjorie Firminger had given up the stage and was pursuing a career as fashion correspondent and popular novelist. She had a small maisonette in Glebe Place, Chelsea, and a lover, Sir Edward Morphy, who paid part of her rent and visited her on Wednesday evenings while Lady Morphy was visiting her own lover. Elliot Seabrooke, an actor and painter, had a studio above the maisonette and it was Seabrooke who invited Lewis round one evening. The ex-actress remembered a large black hat which he wore throughout the visit. She noticed his slightly crumpled dark double-breasted suit, pale shirt, conventional tie and his neatly laced shoes. She 'noticed his feet – on the small side – because after he had taken a few steps into the room he suddenly stopped and seemed to sway on them very slightly.'

He extended 'a pale well-shaped but slightly puffy hand' to her in greeting. 'He looked like someone who had spent his life indoors; there was an unhealthy tinge to his rather waxy looking face with its nice straight nose and large dark eyes.' The three sat down to talk, Lewis choosing a hard chair from which he leaned forward, long legs wide apart, elbows resting on knees and hands hanging down in between. He showed a flattering interest in Marjorie. He asked about her friends, the parties she went to, the 'great big chaps' of lesbians she knew. This was to be the basis of their relationship. She fed him gossip – 'chit' she called it – about the circles of 'bright young people' in which she moved. She and Lewis also had acquaintances in common, like Sydney Schiff, Edward Wadsworth and Dick Wyndham, so she could report back what was being said about him.

A thrilling atmosphere of darkness, drama and secrecy pervaded her first unaccompanied visit to one of Lewis's Bayswater boltholes. The previous November he had taken another room in Ossington Street. For a time he kept his books at number 33, and had 'a sort of studio' on the first floor of number 53. By July he had moved a lot of his books in there as well.

Marjorie had to ring the bell at number 53 more than once before the front door slowly opened. 'There wasn't much light in the narrow hall but his face showed pale under the floppy black hat. Then there was the pale proffered hand, the silent walk to the first floor and the turn to the right on the small landing into the smoke-filled stuffy little room, with its gas fire popping though it was quite a warm evening.'

His household accounts for that summer of 1929 show that he was feeding coins into the gas meter at the rate of 15 shillings a week. Loss of the body's ability to regulate heat can be a symptom of pituitary disorder. Sensitivity to cold, and the hothouse atmosphere of the rooms he inhabited, may have been early indications of the developing tumour below Lewis's brain.

'Once inside he shut the door firmly, remaining where he was.' She turned and faced him, taking a deep breath to steady herself, as she used to do in the wings waiting to make her entrance. 'At this his eyes opened wider behind their spectacles and he gave a tweak to the floppy black hat, making it curve down further still.' The theatrical gesture made her feel as if she really was back on the stage, Penelope Foxglove, 'Miss Mayfair 1924', once again.

'The room looked smaller than it was because it was so full, what with all the books and canvases dumped about, and the tables covered with papers and various tools. On the chimney piece were cuttings from newspapers . . . And hanging on one wall was a diagrammatic section of a man, showing his organs.' It was a gas-fired hermitage complete with *memento mori*. She looked out of the window onto the street, the opposite side of which was lined with plane trees. 'Rather convenient . . . as there was slightly less chance of being overlooked.' Marjorie had heard rumour of his secretive ways.

The chairs they sat in by the fire were comfortable, the guest's covered with sacking. They talked about her recent trip to Berlin, about the decadent night life she had sampled, and with which he appeared familiar from his last visit to that city the previous year. They discussed mutual friends like Alick Schepeler. 'Very *grande dame*, isn't she, Alick', said Lewis. 'Tries to be too bloody grand,' Marjorie agreed, giggling. 'This agreeing, this getting on together, was wonderful', she thought. And she gave him all the gossip she had about the 'bright young people' and the lesbians. One of the latter had a favourite expression and he was so amused by it that he kept nodding his head and repeating it to himself: 'Got him in the bed . . . Got him in the bed.'

Another of her acquaintances was Michael Bruce, author of a book of memoirs called *Sails and Saddles*. Lewis asked her if it was true he was a baronet and, when told it was, kept referring to him as 'Sir Mike'. He asked her to bring 'Sir Mike' to visit him some time. This was the seed for 'Sir Michael Kell-Imrie', central character of *Snooty Baronet*, a novel which, three years later, featured a particularly unflattering portrait of Marjorie herself: Val Ritter, a raddled gossip queen and pornographer whose favourite expression was 'Got him in the bed.'

That summer night in 1929, during her first entranced tête-à-tête with Lewis, he expressed surprise and mild outrage when she said that her lover, Sir Edward, was only paying part of the rent on her maisonette. '*People are there to be used*', he told her, stressing every word.

When it was time for her to leave, he walked her to the end of the street, hailed her a cab in the Bayswater Road and said: 'Now I must get back to the provinces.' His parting comment puzzled her, as it was no doubt intended to. So as Marjorie's taxi drove away, he did not return to the overheated room they had just left, nor to the other room he rented at 33 Ossington Street, ten doors away. Instead, he probably hailed another taxi and instructed the driver to take him north to what he called 'the provinces': 22 Tavistock Road was off the Portobello Road, between the Metropolitan Line stations of Ladbroke Grove and Westbourne Park.

He occupied a series of rooms in different houses. Interviewed in *Everyman*, amidst the clutter of 53 Ossington Street, a couple of years later he said:

> This is my office. Occasionally I work here, but not very often. I have a room in another house crammed full of books. I call that my library; there I do practically all my writing. Then I have a studio, an enormous shack of a place, in still another house, where I do my big paintings. That's not all! I have another room in a fourth house where I sleep. There's nothing but my bed in it.

Later that summer, he again invited Marjorie to his 'office', and this time she was to bring 'Sir Mike' along as well. The two men got on famously and the baronet told her later he thought Lewis was a 'jolly good chap'.

The next time Marjorie visited, Lewis suggested she bring him a lesbian.

*

As Montgomery Belgion had predicted, no publisher could be found, on either side of the Atlantic, prepared to pay Lewis an advance which, in his view, would adequately compensate him for the years of effort he had invested in completing *The Apes of God*. Accordingly, by September 1929, preparations were under way for private publication under the imprint of The Arthur Press. Lewis approached a titled lady who had expressed an interest in the venture, and asked her to lend the company £100. After consulting her accounts, Lady Frances Caroline Joan Moriarty, Viscountess Glenapp, found that she could indeed spare the cash.

*

Lewis's own household accounts for the last week of August and the first week of September that year give an impression of settled domesticity. Two people were spending money. Items listed under the heading 'W.L.' included: bread, newspapers, *Time* magazine, peaches, an anti-dandruff preparation called 'Nodan', skin ointment, 'Three Castles' cigarettes, matches and gin. Listed under the heading 'ghos' were: bacon, mushrooms, tomatoes, lettuce, potatoes, peas, haberdashery, two packs of washing soap, yeast, fish, milk, pie and ammonia.

Gladys Hoskins kept house, washed, cleaned and cooked at 22 Tavistock Road.

*

As requested, Marjorie brought one of her lesbian friends to Ossington Street at the end of October. They arrived very late in the evening by car — Heather Pilkington, somewhat the worse for drink, hammering the horn under Lewis's window. He had waited in for them, obviously keen to study the specimen his disciple had brought him. He led the way up the dark stairs, and when Miss Pilkington stumbled it was Marjorie, in the rear, who caught her. She marched into the small stuffy room with her ample bosom heaving under the severe coat and her short cropped fair hair ruffled. She refused to sit down but stood with her brogued feet wide apart, as if steadying herself.

'Why shouldn't I be a lesbian if I want to?' she demanded truculently.

The only words Marjorie Firminger could definitely remember Lewis uttering throughout the short visit were in response to that question.

'Why indeed?'

*

In the early hours of Tuesday, 7 January 1930, the Acorn Petrol Filling Station on the Kingston bypass in New Malden, South London, was burgled. When he arrived for work the manager found that a side window had been smashed and the contents of drawers scattered around the office. £113 worth of property, including an iron safe, £50 in notes and silver, two cheques, a portable wireless set, a 'Yost' typewriter, two electric torches and three keys, had been stolen.

Six weeks later, around midnight on Monday, 18 February, an old A.B.C. sports car came to a halt in London Road, Morden, and three young men got out. They walked about 75 yards to a garage, the North Holt Works. One of the men, Boulton, an ex-garage proprietor himself, forced out of business by the police for shady dealing, stayed in front where he could see anyone approaching the forecourt, while the other two went round the side to the works office. Robert Howard Rutter took a length of steel pipe from his overcoat pocket and used it to force a window. He climbed inside, lighting his way with an electric torch, and began passing cans of petrol out to his tall, dark-haired companion. At this point the previous owner of the garage, a Mr Bush, drove his car into the forecourt and Boulton, the lookout, made himself scarce. Bush went round the side and grabbed hold of the dark-haired youth who was leaning in through the window. He was joined by a Police Constable Mathews, whose suspicions had been aroused by the abandoned sports car nearby. Mathews kept hold of the one youth while Bush shone his torch through the window and found the other. Rutter was lying on the floor of the office, trying to hide under a counter. Both young men were arrested and charged with the theft of four two–gallon cans of petrol valued at £1 4s. 4d. Rutter's associate protested that it was 'a ridiculous charge' and gave his name as Peter London.

It was an alias probably adopted in panic by the young burglar, from the London Road where he was arrested. Although illegitimate he was entitled to his father's name: Lewis. He was known as Peter but had been registered at birth in Dieppe as Hoel. The son of Wyndham Lewis and Olive Johnson was now 18 years old.

Peter claimed to be a clerk, but he had been employed for only four or five months between leaving school at 14 and his arrest. Applications for chauffeuring work had been unsuccessful and he had received a number of summonses for minor offences, such as riding untaxed motorcycles without licence, silencer or reliable brakes. Mrs Prickett had paid the resultant fines out of the small income she received from Peter's father.

The youth was denied bail because he refused to give the police his home address. He was remanded in the 'Boys Section' of Wormwood Scrubs Prison as 'Peter London, of no fixed abode'. He also refused to give his fingerprints, but they were taken without his permission and found to match those at the scenes of over a dozen other recent burglaries, including the one at the Acorn Petrol Station on 7 January. Peter's refusal to divulge his home address to the police was doubtless connected with the contents of Mrs Prickett's coal shed at 5 Grove Road, Balham: 2 or 3 motorcycles, 2 or 3 pedal cycles, boxes of spare parts and accessories, many of them still in their wrappings, several gallons of petrol, a typewriter and a bunch of about 30 keys. Boulton's mother's house also contained motorcycles and spare parts belonging to Peter.

Peter's mother, now Mrs Olive Elstow, contacted Lewis on 6 March and pleaded with him to 'come forward' and help their wayward offspring. He immediately engaged a solicitor to take charge of the case. The following day a representative from the firm of Leonard Tubbs & Co. went with him to Balham to interview Mrs Prickett. On their way back to the solicitor's office in Moorgate, Lewis bought a copy of that week's *Clapham Observer*. His son's dubious portion of fame was chronicled on page 5 and headlined: 'Young Clerk's Downfall'.

*

Later that month Marjorie Firminger asked Lewis if he could spare the time to 'flick over' the typescript of a novel she had written. *Jam Today* had already been rejected by a number of London publishers on account of the lesbianism it contained, the possibility of its being libellous, or perhaps because 'it had no literary merit', she suggested. 'But they wouldn't know if it had', Lewis flattered her. He told her he would 'certainly look it over' and suggested she leave the typescript with him. On her next visit she noticed it lying on the floor. He said he had 'flicked it over' and wondered whether she would like him to send it to his American publisher, Donald Friede. He assured her that Friede would not consider it too outspoken. In fact she might even 'ginger it up a bit' for the American market. Marjorie promised to give him the typescript back in a day or two, 'complete with the gingering'.

Favours were being sought from a number of quarters that March. Iris Barry had also written a novel. She contacted Lewis with trepidation, uncertain of his address and mindful of their acrimonious break in the early Twenties. 'It is a bitter world', she wrote, 'and why you should do anything to temper it for me I don't really know. But I ask.' She asked him to glance at her book, and if there was anything he could say in its favour to say it, and perhaps do a drawing of her for the dust wrapper. His reply was noncommittal. 'So far the novel you speak of has not turned up', he told her. 'Yes, this is the address to which to send anything.'

*

Peter 'London' had spent nearly six weeks on remand in the Wormwood Scrubs borstal when his trial came up at Surrey Quarter Sessions on 1 April. By then his father had engaged another solicitor, Freke Palmer, 'one of the best criminal lawyers in London', Peter was assured. Lewis suggested that if the trial went their way and his son was not returned to prison, he should 'avoid joining up at the door of the court with undesirable Wimbledon friends'. Instead he was to go at once to the solicitor's office to meet his father and discuss how he might best find work and 'put all this behind [him]'.

Lewis was prepared to pay for Peter's defence, but for nothing else thereafter. On the morning of the trial Olive's husband, William Elstow, approached the probation officer and solicitor and expressed his willingness to offer Peter a home. The solicitor told him that if he did, Peter's natural father 'would not have anything whatever to do with the matter of the boy's future, financially or otherwise'. Elstow accepted this and, with it, full responsibility for Lewis's son on his release from custody. But Peter was to spend another seven weeks in the 'Boy's Section' of Wormwood Scrubs. The Chairman of the Surrey Quarter Sessions postponed sentence until 20 May so that the defendants 'should have a little more time to reflect on the serious nature of the offences they had committed'.

*

On 25 March Lewis had been the guest of A.J.A. Symons, author of *The Quest for Corvo*, at a formal dinner in the Savoy given by the 'Sette of Odde Volumes', a society of bibliophiles to which he belonged. Lewis had responded to the invitation with alacrity, promising 'to fly . . . upon swallow-tails and in a white tie – or a very pretty black one'. He also told Symons that his book, 'now a quarter of a million words long', would be ready 'in about 3 or 4 weeks'. He seemed particularly pleased with the size of *The Apes of God*. It was only on 1 April, the day of Peter's trial, that he had a chance to write to Symons again. He had 'been very much occupied for some days with a private matter', else he should have written before, to say how very much he had enjoyed the 'Sette of Odde Volumes' dinner and their subsequent conversation. He confirmed that he would be in London on 22 April and would be delighted to attend the next 'Odde Volumes' dinner that evening.

The 'private matter' taken care of for the time being, he was also able to deal with Iris Barry, who had by now overstepped the formal boundaries proper to estranged lovers:

> The endearments that you think fit to employ I confess disgust me . . .
> The lapse of so many years may have effaced from your memory the fact,
> but it has not effaced it from mine, that my acquaintance with you was of
> a most unpleasant nature . . . Your book is not, as you may guess, of any
> interest to me, and I am returning it to you.

Jam Today received more sympathetic treatment when Marjorie Firminger sent him the 'gingered up' typescript a couple of days later. On her next visit she noticed it was again lying on the floor of his 'office'. He told her he would be parcelling it up and sending it to Donald Friede in New York immediately.

TWENTY-NINE

Apes and Nazis

The Arthur Press's quarter-million-word, 625-page, doorstop production, *The Apes of God*, was published on 3 June 1930 in an edition limited to 750 signed and numbered copies. The huge tome weighed three pounds and three ounces and, by a numerical coincidence, it retailed at three pounds and three shillings.

The action of this immense novel follows the six-foot-tall, black-haired and exquisitely handsome 19-year-old poet Daniel Boleyn – Lewis's self-portrait of the artist as a young man – on a tour through London's bourgeois bohemia under the tutelage of a charismatic albino by the name of Horace Zagreus. Zagreus is, himself, under the sway of another character, Pierpoint, who never appears but whose pronouncements are delivered in the form of written encyclical, or lengthily 'broadcast' speech. While the utterances and opinions of the god-like Pierpoint can be ascribed to the author, it was generally assumed that the model for Zagreus was the notorious practical joker Horace de Vere Cole. A more obscure model was the architect, Freemason and mystic William Stirling, who befriended the 19-year-old Lewis nearly 30 years before and who committed suicide in his Adelphi flat.

The eponymous 'Apes' – prosperous amateur daubers and scribblers who aped the 'true' artist's vocation and, at the same time, made it impossible for him to earn a living by snapping up all the best studios for themselves at exorbitantly inflated rents – these were the targets of Lewis's not entirely dispassionate satire. Many of the people he had known, borrowed money from and grown to despise during the previous decade figured there, under the guise of one object of ridicule or another.

Edward and Fanny Wadsworth appeared as a 'rich mountebank marine painter' and, 'obese and smiling', his 'awful old bore of a wife'. In recognition of Wadsworth's war experience in the Naval Reserve, 'Richard and Jenny' are described in elaborate nautical imagery. Sydney and Violet Schiff were 'Lionel Kein', the 'pseudo-Proust', and his wife 'Isabel', effortlessly orchestrating her dinner guests, her 'brilliant handsome profile . . . like a large ornate knife at the head of the table'. Lewis's former sketching pupil, Dick Wyndham, was subjected to particularly personal mockery. An overgrown schoolboy with corkscrewing trousers and unco-ordinated blundering movements, Dick Wittingdon is the 'Ape-Flagellant' whose taste is for fast cars and whips. 'Dick' rents ten studios for himself to 'prevent ten geniuses from having a roof over their genius, and . . . keep them in small ill-lit rooms while he [sits] on . . . valuable workshops in solitary egotistical state'.

Finally Osbert, Sacheverell and Edith Sitwell were caricatured respect-ively as Osmund, Phoebus and Harriet Finnian Shaw, the family group of preposterous baby-talking middle-aged infants. Georgia, Sacheverell's Canadian wife, was a less easily recognisable model for Babs Kennson, the 'New Zealand jewess' eager to entrap Phoebus with 'the magic of her Maori money-bags' and holding 'all the trumps in her neat kosher fist'.

*

Some time in July Lewis arrived unexpectedly at Marjorie Firminger's maisonette and was shown in by the daily help. He was wearing a cloth cap, the peak of which he kept tweaking down over his eyes as he nervously glanced from side to side, uncomfortable that the cleaner was still in the flat. He appeared visibly to relax when he heard the front door slam behind her. He told Marjorie he was under attack from various quarters because of *The Apes of God* and he was having to prepare a manifesto to protect himself. Then he asked her 'very tentatively – shyly almost', if there were any possibility she might lend him £5 'to get a bit of typing done'. Delighted to be of service, she wrote him a cheque. She had never enjoyed writing a cheque more. There was a further embarrassed hiatus and then he asked her if it would be convenient for him to have cash instead.

'Of course,' she said, 'of course.' Unfortunately, he would have to wait for cash as she had no ready money and the banks were closed by that time of the afternoon.

'Never mind', Lewis said and told her he would come back in a couple of days to collect it.

*

The South African poet Roy Campbell, who had made a cameo appearance in *The Apes of God* as the libidinous Zulu Blades, wrote a favourable notice of the novel for the *New Statesman*. The literary editor Ellis Roberts rejected the review as being too favourable. 'I find you take a far more serious view of its merits than I can,' he told Campbell, 'and indeed take Mr Lewis altogether more seriously than I think is justifiable.' Campbell tore up the letter, then, realising its potential value as propaganda, he numbered the pieces and sent them to Lewis with a copy of his rejected review. These two documents were to form part of *Satire and Fiction*, the last publication to appear under the imprint of The Arthur Press, and for the typing of which Marjorie Firminger had been asked to contribute £5.

To offset Ellis Roberts's letter, printed in facsimile complete with jagged black horizontal tear marks, other letters, of enthusiastic endorsement, were included from Richard Aldington, Montgomery Belgion, J. D. Beresford, Meyrick Booth, Augustus John, H. G. Wells and W. B. Yeats. A two-page 'reader's report for an American publisher', written by Belgion, was presented as further evidence that the book should be taken seriously. Then there were eight pages containing extracts of reviews from *The Referee*, *The Sphere*, *The Spectator*, *Time and Tide*, *Everyman*, *Daily Telegraph*, *Daily News*, *Daily Mail*, *Times Literary Supplement*, *Evening News*, *Evening Standard*, *Weekly Sketch*, *Weekly Dispatch*, *Sunday Express*, *Western Mail*, *Yorkshire Post*, *Glasgow Herald*, *Weekend Review* and *Saturday Review*.

*

The generally favourable press reception of *The Apes of God* did not incline Chatto & Windus to undertake publishing another novel Lewis offered them of a similar character. *The Roaring Quean** seemed like a substantial splinter of the bigger book, a catalogue of other 'apes' that he had not found room for even in that capacious volume. Judging it only on an incomplete manuscript, it was 'one of the best things of its kind I have ever read', Prentice told Lewis:

> But the piece seems to us too risky for Chattos to do. Too many heads are cracked, and the result would be that the wounded would take it out of us . . . we don't feel we could face up to the whole cohort of the implicated.

Those 'implicated' in this satire of the book racket were Arnold Bennett, Virginia Woolf, Nancy Cunard, Gerald Gould, literature critic for the *Observer*, and Brian Howard, poet and fiction reviewer for the *New Statesman*, model for the eponymous 'Quean', Donald Butterboy.

The troublesome little novel, attended by mixtures of commendation and regret similar to that expressed by Prentice, was to pass through the offices of a number of other publishers over the next six years.

*

* Eventually published in 1973, as *The Roaring Quean*, by Secker & Warburg.

It was later in the year that those implicated in *The Apes of God* began a campaign of petty irritation. A novelty postcard reached Lewis from Nuremberg, showing a chubby baby wearing goggles and a beret. The sender had inked in a brim to the beret, emphasised the black rims of the goggles, drawn a pipe in the infant's hand and added a moustache. When the card was squeezed a mechanism inside emitted a whimpering cry. It was addressed to 'Percy Lewis esq.', and inscribed:

GREETINGS TO TARZAN FROM A GATHERING OF THE APES

Of all the victims of *The Apes of God*, Richard Wyndham was perhaps the most seriously offended by Lewis's satirical treatment of him. When the two men chanced to meet in a restaurant shortly after publication, Lewis reported with disingenuous understatement that the other 'did not seem friendly'. Only Richard Wyndham appended his real name to the Nuremberg novelty postcard. The other signatories were 'Phoebus', 'Jenny', 'Richard' and 'Babs Kennson'.

Then, in *The Times* personal column of 2 September, sandwiched between the notice of a vacancy for a public school boy on a farm in Southern Rhodesia and an advertisement for an ex-cavalrymen's association supplying messengers, clerks, semi-skilled and general labourers, the following offer appeared:

PERCY WYNDHAM LEWIS. – Two PAINTINGS for SALE, 9ft. by 7ft. and 6ft. by 4ft., £20 and £15; inspection. – Captain Wyndham, 77, Bedford gardens.

It was taken up the following morning in the *Daily Express*, under the headline: 'AN "AGONY" SURPRISE FOR CHELSEA'. The article pointed out that 'detailed specification of size, contrasted with the price, invites one to work out a simple little sum to show that you can buy a square foot of Wyndham Lewis painting for the trifling expenditure of 6s. 8d. or 7s.' The correspondent reported that he had visited the address given in the advertisement and been told that the pictures could be viewed 'only after arrangement with Captain Wyndham, whose present address is unknown, because he is travelling in France'.

Comment was invited from Lewis himself, who explained that the advertisement was one of many reactions he had received from people who believed they had been represented in *The Apes of God*. 'You would not believe', he told the reporter, 'the amount of abuse I have received by telephone and letter.' He denied that there was 'anything in the book in the least resembling Captain Richard Wyndham'.

This interesting development occurred too late to be reported in the body of *Satire and Fiction*, due for publication that month, but Lewis had the entire *Express* article printed as a flyer headed: 'A STOP-PRESS EXPLOSION'.

ENRAGED 'Ape of God,' believing that he caught sight of his own features in the crowded mirror of *The Apes of God*, sends up a cry of AGONY!

It is not known whether Richard Wyndham seriously intended disposing of *Kermesse* and *Plan of War* for such ludicrously low prices, or whether he was doing, in 1930, what two years before he had pleaded innocence of doing: using those early works 'as a weapon, for reprisals' against Lewis.

If, on his return from France, he did sell them, even for £15 and £20, he would have made a profit on the £5 he told the *Daily Sketch* he paid for them in New York. Neither painting has been seen again.

*

In the autumn of 1930 Lewis was preparing, with mounting frustration, to paint his first portrait since that of Violet Schiff. Towards the beginning of May he had been commissioned by Lord Glenapp to paint his wife's portrait for a fee of £300, to be paid on completion. Dress and pose were agreed upon: red lace, standing in three-quarter profile with left hand resting on hip, index and forefinger together pointing forward, ring and little finger curled back.

The Viscountess was initially enthusiastic, but her social commitments made it impossible for work to begin immediately. And in the ensuing months Lewis was unable to get her to stand still long enough for him to make a start. On 8 September she wrote from Scotland saying she did not know when she would be back in London. On 17 September she was still unable to let him know definitely when she could make herself available but hoped it would be the following week. Fortunately she had lent him her red lace dress, so he was able to carry out much of the work in her absence. Finally, on 1 October, his telegram intercepted her at the Piccadilly Hotel:

AM WORKING UPON DRESS TODAY CAN YOU SIT FOR HEAD TOMORROW MORNING TWELVE PLEASE TELEGRAPH DAY-LIGHT ESSENTIAL

This two-hour sitting at last produced a portrait sketch.

*

On 9 October 1930 the marriage took place at Paddington Registry Office of Percy Lewis, bachelor aged 44 years, and Gladys Hoskins, spinster aged 30 years. The groom gave his profession as 'architect' and that of his deceased father as 'captain in the Warwickshire regiment'. The witnesses were strangers. Wyndham Lewis later claimed that it was in an attempt to avoid press publicity that he omitted his distinctive middle name from the statement, pruned four years from his age and falsified both his own profession and his father's military background.

*

No further sittings with Lady Glenapp could be arranged, and by the third week in October Lewis had completed the picture without her. Later she told her husband that she never sat for him 'except for a few sketches'. This was portraiture without pain.

Lord and Lady Glenapp were in the final throes of a failed marriage which was to end in a swift Scottish divorce the following year. For the time being she was living at Cawston House near Rugby and he was occupying their London residence in Mayfair. There was little communication between husband and wife, and an air of vagueness prevailed when it came to viewing the portrait. Neither seemed to have the time. In November Lewis confessed to 'the very slightest pique' that the Viscountess had not yet been to see what he had done. Aware of his client's delicate matrimonial position he tactfully explored with her the procedure for disposing of the finished work and, more importantly, the question of who was going to pay for it:

> I have suggested to [your husband] that the picture should be sent to him at Culross Street or to you at Cawston, and have . . . informally sent him the bill, for £300. If however the arrangement should now be that you pay, I now informally send it to you!

His Lordship paid promptly, but deferred viewing his acquisition because of a sore throat.

Lady Glenapp was a little over 30 when Lewis painted her. She was a chronic insomniac and consequently dependent upon narcotics. The nearly full-length portrait shows her against a dark background, her hair bobbed and sculpted. The exotically patterned bodice and sleeve of the red dress, with which the painter had spent more time than with the lady herself, are finely worked. Her eyes are deeply and darkly ringed.

Lewis was keen to capitalise upon this, his first 'society portrait' for some time, by submitting it to the Royal Academy's Summer Exhibition the following April.

*

On 16 November he went to Germany. It was then that both Lord and Lady Glenapp began demanding to view the portrait. Telegrams were forwarded to him in Berlin.

The ostensible purpose of the trip was business: to find a publisher for a German edition of *The Apes of God*. This was not to be. 'The main reason', he was told by his German agent, was that 'the different characters of the book behind which English novelists and other well-known persons of the English Literature are hidden, might not be understood by the average German reader.' But it was not a wasted excursion. He was able to observe at first hand the beginnings of a major political phenomenon.

The German people had voted two months before, sending 107 National Socialists to the Reichstag. Adolf Hitler's crude appeal to the middle and working classes had attracted an increase in votes from 810,000 in 1928 to 6,409,600. His party had gained 17.5 per cent of the total vote, and was now second only to the Social Democratic Party's 21.9 per cent. The National Socialist German Workers' Party was no longer on the political fringe.

Lewis watched from a balcony of the Berlin Sportpalast, as Goebbels and Goering addressed a crowd of some twenty thousand people:

> In this gigantic assembly . . . there was something like the pressure of one immense, indignant thought – it was impossible to be present and not to be amazed at the passion engendered in all these men and women, and the millions of others of whom these were only a fraction, by the message of these stormy platform voices . . . Goebbels . . . was a tiny nervous figure, whose voice rose constantly to a scream.

By day Lewis read the newspapers for reports of the previous night's political street battles. After dark he toured Berlin's underbelly with a puritan's fascinated eye for the lush decadence of late Weimar democracy: 'night-circuses, *Negertanz* palaces, *nacktballeten*, flagellation-bars, and sad wells of super-masculine loneliness'. He relied upon the German press for his political research. As for the transvestites of the 'Eldorado' in Motzstrasse he saw and felt for himself the chin-stubble, and the cloth-covered wire cups, painted with red rosettes to represent nipples, scooped for his examination from under a low-cut evening dress.

He was back in London by the beginning of December. During the rest of that month, despite an attack of gastric flu just before Christmas, he wrote the first book-length study in any language of Adolf Hitler and the phenomenon of National Socialism.

*

Despite her demands for a viewing of the portrait while he was away, Lady Glenapp was now in no particular hurry to fit it in to her hectic and erratic social schedule. But one Sunday in mid-December she arrived unexpectedly at Ossington Street with a friend, Mrs O'Donnell. She was shown the picture and appeared pleased. That evening the two ladies insisted on accompanying Lewis and Augustus John to the Tour Eiffel in Percy Street. John was drunk, Lewis uncomfortable, and the ladies seemingly oblivious to any social embarrassment. Later Lewis escorted them back to Lady Glenapp's hotel in Weymouth Street, where she made a porter break open the drinks cupboard. She was evidently enjoying the estrangement from her husband and the Bohemian flirtation her acquaintance with Lewis offered. She commissioned a portrait drawing of herself as a birthday present for her lover, Captain Charles Douglas Beech. The following Thursday Lewis met her for lunch, which she insisted on paying for. 'I'm not a gold digger', she told him. Later that afternoon it proved too dark for the drawing to be done.

*

A year after she brought a rather drunk Heather Pilkington to visit Lewis, Marjorie Firminger's first and only novel, *Jam Today*, was published in Paris. Donald Friede had told her that, contrary to Lewis's advice, with the spicy details it could not be sold in the United States and without the details it would not sell. Its subject matter alone prohibited publication in London, earning it the invaluable selling point for the Paris market of being 'banned in Britain'. The novel contained a thinly disguised lesbian character, and Heather Pilkington was enraged. 'People are there to be used!' Lewis had told Marjorie, and she was thrilled to have shown herself so worthy a pupil. During the furious reception of her own book she reported to her mentor that Richard Wyndham had comforted Miss Pilkington, telling her that 'a much worse book' had been written about him.

Perhaps Wyndham – mercilessly lampooned in *The Apes of God* as the ridiculous Dick Whittingdon – now understood the wider significance of Lewis's chilling words, delivered across a café table in the South of France: 'People are only friends in so much that they are of use to you.'

Marjorie was yet to learn that she was not immune to such usage herself.

*

By 12 January 1931, Charles Prentice had read and accepted the Hitler book for Chatto, although he could not offer as large an advance for it as Lewis felt its topicality demanded. A 40,000-word book, even with illustrations, commanded a retail price of only six shillings, Prentice explained. A retail price of 7/6, on the other hand, 'would lay one open to the accusation of giving short weight, and would not help the book to gain a wide public.' On that basis Chatto could offer an advance of no more than £100.

Before publication, extracts appeared as a series of five articles in *Time and Tide* called 'Hitlerism – Man and Doctrine'. In the first, Lewis claimed to write as 'an exponent – not as a critic nor yet as an advocate – of German National Socialism'. A preliminary editorial note accompanied each weekly instalment:

> Whilst we do not find ourselves in agreement with Mr. Wyndham Lewis's attitudes towards the German National-Socialist Party and the political situation generally, the vivid picture of present-day Germany which he gives in this series of articles seems to us of such unusual interest that we do not hesitate to publish them.

Following the first two instalments, reactions began appearing in *Time and Tide*'s correspondence pages. Frederick A. Voigt, a *Manchester Guardian* journalist living in Berlin, declared that Lewis had been taken in by the Nazi press. He was accused of regurgitating *Der Angriff* and *Völkischer Beobachter* for his accounts of Communists helping the police to beat up brownshirts, and of brownshirts, armed only with their fists, pitted against Communist gangs armed to the teeth. Cicely Hamilton disputed Lewis's account of lurid decadence in the Wittenberg Platz. Claiming to have lived for several weeks just round the corner, she could not remember 'anything startling in the way of wickedness and vice'. The following week, Lewis's reply to his critics dismissed Voigt as a Communist partisan and Miss Hamilton as a kill-joy threatening to ruin Berlin's tourist trade.

Both Voigt and Hamilton retaliated in subsequent weeks, and a correspondent calling himself 'The Walrus' joined the debate, applauding *Time and Tide* for its enterprise in printing Lewis's views:

> I for one would rather enjoy such interludes in this time of depression than read the studied accuracies and judicial views of grave and normal persons like Mr Voigt, whose only merit is that they know what they are talking about, while Mr Wyndham Lewis demonstrably does not (as if that mattered!).

Some criticism came from the extreme Right, but only in matters of detail. The Honorary Secretary of the Kensington Fascist Group took issue with Lewis's assertion that Germany was a far greater nation than Italy. 'Fascism and Hitlerism', Mr W. J. Chambers protested:

> are two expressions of the same ideal . . . Should the day come when we in this country throw off our present demo-liberal system of government and adopt a policy of national organisation similar to that advocated by Mussolini and Hitler we shall find that it will not be a slavish imitation of one or other of these systems, but a synthesis of the two, an expression in the sphere of politics of the Anglo-Saxon soul, as Fascism expresses the Latin and Hitlerism the Teutonic.

*

By the end of January the volatile Lady Glenapp decided that she did not care for Lewis's representation of her after all. Her reasons are unclear. According to Lewis, she had expressed 'nothing but satisfaction with the work', had agreed to have it exhibited at the Royal Academy Summer Exhibition and consulted with him about a suitable frame. Then suddenly she began describing it as 'an example of extreme modern art' and proceeded 'to cover the picture with abuse'. Perhaps the heavily lidded, dark-rimmed eyes in the pale face displayed her neurotic insomnia too accurately for comfort. For his part, Lewis expressed himself as 'completely tired of the whole thing' and unwilling to exhibit the portrait at the RA or anywhere else.

Lord Glenapp made excuses for his wife, 'always a rather hasty tongued woman', and explained that she was suffering from an affliction of the ear and was 'a great deal in pain'. A frank allusion to her private affairs suggested there may have been other reasons for her erratic behaviour. 'I shudder to think', Glenapp told Lewis, 'what will happen to her if she is being advised as to the conduct of her life by Captain Beech, and taking his advice.'

It may have been on Beech's advice that, a few days later, Her Ladyship wrote to Lewis demanding the return of the £100 she had lent him in October 1929 to finance *The Apes of God*. If he was unable to repay it immediately she gave notice that she would require it in six months' time with interest. Meanwhile he was to send her a cheque for the interest and compound interest to date, by return of post.

*

Summoned to Ossington Street by telephone for 9.30 on a Sunday evening in early February, Marjorie Firminger arrived in her black suit, white shirt and stiff bow tie. Her outfit had 'a nice chap hint', as Lewis had commented approvingly the last time they had met.

'So you're going in for pornography in a big way, are you?' he asked as they settled themselves either side of the gas fire. *Jam Today* having been published just before Christmas in Paris, and duly banned in England, she had almost finished an even more daring book she thought of calling *After Thirty*. Lewis predicted that Europe would soon be flooded with 'finely bound volumes' of her work. He laughed at the euphemism and she was evidently expected to laugh as well. She felt a little put out at the way he talked about her work but let it pass. She did not regard the new book as pornographic but, since that was clearly the way Lewis liked to think of it, she did not attempt to persuade him otherwise. She even seemed to emphasise the racier elements when she gave him news of its development: 'I have just been describing an amusing fuck this afternoon', she told him on one occasion. She had no suspicion that such unguarded items of information were helping to develop the portrait of Valerie Ritter, whose 'expressions were quite unprintable, except in de luxe editions privately printed in Paris', that Lewis would unveil the following year.

He was in expansive mood that Sunday evening, his talk peppered with anecdotes about the Sitwells. At one point she laughed so much that she cried and could not find a handkerchief. Lewis went and fetched a piece of rag and she dabbed her eyes, 'enchanted to be sitting there in the smoke and the clutter and the dust, wondering where he had got the rag from, if he had torn it off a larger piece he used for cleaning his brushes. Was there a sink somewhere outside on the landing? And did Mrs. Lewis really live upstairs?' Having found him thus far so unguarded, she took the opportunity to ask about the story that he kept a wife up there who no one ever saw. Lewis's eyes narrowed beneath the brim of his hat. The atmosphere changed.

'Who said that?'

'Constant Lambert. The composer.'

'Lambert? LAMBERT? Yes, of course, Lambert!' and he deflected one piece of gossip with a side-swiping piece of his own.

'Lambert! Always pulling sheaves of invitations out of his pocket. By mistake, he says. But of course just to show how popular he is.'

She felt she had committed a *faux pas* as he got to his feet signalling that their interview was at an end. She stood also and they faced one another in silence. He was still looking at her suspiciously and she was beginning to flush when he suddenly asked if she would allow him to make a drawing of her. 'We'll call it jam to-day!' he said, and added that it could go on the cover of her next 'filthy book'. She was going to Paris to see a potential publisher for *After Thirty*, and if they could arrange a sitting soon she could have the drawing to take with her. She was of course delighted. Then he began to explain 'in a rather ponderous way, and with elaborate gesture' what he had in mind: 'the drawing must match the book in "abandon" . . . some lying-on-the-sofa sketch, naked or nearly so.'

It was the first time she was ever to contradict him, and he seemed slightly taken aback by her response. Such a drawing would be out of the question, she told him, and it would set entirely the wrong tone in publicity for the new book: 'The more "naked" my books the more prim should be my pictures.' He retreated: 'Of course,' he said, 'of course', and tried to pass off the 'abandoned' pose as not having been an entirely serious suggestion. She continued firmly that he must draw her fully clothed or not at all. Even the very becoming satin breeches she sometimes wore, and that Lewis had admired, would not do. 'Of course not,' he assured her, 'of *course* not.'

As usual he walked with her along Ossington Street to the Bayswater Road and, as they parted, promised to telephone and arrange the sitting.

Throughout Marjorie's rather breathless memoir there is an undercurrent of something that might have been sexual tension between them. His suggestion that she pose for him nude may have been a move towards seducing her, albeit a clumsy and risibly obvious one. On the other hand, she may have overreacted to a nudge and wink too far in their self-consciously 'liberated' conversation.

Lewis thought the meeting that evening sufficiently relevant to record in a makeshift journal: 'Saw M. Firminger for 2 hours at 9.30.' The other part of the entry, however, was dismissive: 'nothing of importance.'

He did not telephone to arrange the sitting and, despite a few letters attempting to lure him with promises of 'chit', she left for Paris without the drawing.

*

The period of time from first eyewitness impressions of the National Socialist movement in November 1930 to the appearance in the shops of Lewis's book on the subject was a little over four months. *Hitler* was published on 26 March 1931. The *Spectator* critic was more perceptive than perhaps he realised: 'The worst fault of the book is the inescapable feeling that Mr. Wyndham Lewis has thrown it all together in a few hectic afternoons of work. It is slapdash and often confused.' He conceded, however, that 'the slapdash and confused views . . . of an intelligent man are on the whole more preferable, in the case of a genuinely difficult subject such as the rise of the National Socialist Movement, to the most laborious and mature considerations of a dolt.'

Elsewhere, apart from unqualified praise from Hugh Gordon Porteus in *The Twentieth Century* and a favourable review in the *Times Literary Supplement*, critical response was lukewarm; at best the reviews gave Lewis credit for tackling a little-known subject in a racy and entertaining style. At worst it was dismissed by Clennell Wilkinson in *Everyman*:

> what do we find? It would hardly be unfair to answer 'Nothing.' Here is a mere 'write-up' of the Nazi case, entirely uncritical, vague and unsubstantial. It was positively a feat to fill so many pages and give so little information.

It was criticised for being biased, sloppily written, badly researched and inaccurate. But nowhere was it condemned as morally tainted. Supporting Fascism or National Socialism did not carry with it the stigma in 1931 that it would carry two years later. It did, however, attract some interesting new acquaintances.

Not long after the book was published, Lewis was visited by a man he described as 'the official representative of the Nazi party in London'. He was in fact the English correspondent for the National Socialist newspapers *Völkischer Beobachter* and *Der Angriff*. He was eventually expelled from England in November 1935 on the grounds that his activities were 'unrelated to those of bona fide journalism' – a Foreign Office euphemism for espionage. He was Dr Hans-Wilhelm Thost, 'pronounced toast', and he liked the book. 'He said it was not at all bad for an Englishman.' His only serious reservation concerned its analysis of the *Judenfrage*. Lewis did not take Hitler's anti-Semitism seriously. Far from regarding it as one of the pillars of National Socialist policy, he described the 'Jewish question' as 'a racial redherring' and, in a passage brimming with painful irony for the hindsighted, he had reassured his *Time and Tide* readers:

> Hitler *himself* . . . is, though not a man of compromise, yet not unreasonable, a violent or fanatical, man. I believe that, if he should come into power, he would discourage his followers from the reckless pursuit of any policy calculated to antagonise the rest of the European world. The Anglo-Saxon need not, I think, turn his back entirely upon Hitler because of this precious *Judenfrage*.

Lewis's visitor assured him he was wrong. 'If you do not understand the *Judenfrage*', Dr Thost declared, 'you have not understood Hitlerism. Without the Jewish question Hitlerism would not exist.'

The interview had its comic aspect. Dr Thost (or 'Herr Thost', as Lewis persisted in calling him) was preoccupied by a social dilemma. His father had been a friend of Lord Curzon, whose daughter was the first wife of Sir Oswald Mosley. Thost had a letter of introduction to Lady Cynthia but seemed embarrassed and reluctant to present it. 'But why not, Herr Thost?' Lewis pressed him for an explanation. It appeared that Lady Cynthia's Jewish ancestry was the obstacle. Lord Curzon had married Mary Victoria, the only daughter of a Chicago industrialist: Levi Zeigler Leiter. 'What a fearful obstacle-race life was', Lewis mused, 'for a member of the Nazi party, winding his way in and out of the family trees of his father's oldest friends.'

*

Thost was not the only Nazi to have reservations about Lewis's book. Reimer Hobbing Verlag, the Berlin firm who were preparing to publish a German translation, thought that the sales prospects would be much improved if one of the Party leaders were to write an introduction. But the translation appeared the following year without such an endorsement.

Articles in a weekly journal like *Time and Tide* are soon forgotten. But the same matter persists when expanded to over 200 pages in a book dustwrappered in swastikas. The threefold conjunction of Lewis's name with that of the German dictator and his crooked emblem has made of that hastily executed dustwrapper an incriminating exhibit. *Hitler* has done more lasting harm to Lewis's reputation than anything else he produced and, several decades after his death, that positive evaluation of National Socialism continues to be brandished against him. But an early damage assessment appears to have come from C. H. Brooks, his literary agent at A. M. Heath from 1931. 'These are long vendettas', Lewis wrote:

> A peculiar people, neither forgivers nor forgetters.
> All that I know is that my agents write
> 'Your Hitler Book has harmed you' – in a night,
> Somewhat like Byron – only I waken thus
> To find myself not famous but infamous.

Infamy did not come overnight. It came retrospectively as, two years later, the horrifying nature of the Nazi phenomenon began to be recognised in England.

303

THIRTY

Black-hatted in Barbary

Some time in March or early April Lewis phoned Marjorie Firminger to apologise for not having had time to do the drawing. He promised to phone her again soon to arrange a sitting.

Late the following afternoon the bell rang at 18 Glebe Place and, unannounced, Lewis was standing on her doorstep.

She was not at her best that day with an 'unusually painful dose of the curse', symptomatic of a condition for which she would require surgery the following year.

He came in and she remembered saying that she wished she had some gin to offer him. She had no news and felt tongue-tied and awkward. Then he briskly suggested getting down to the drawing.

'Oh no . . .'

'You don't want it?'

'Of course I do. But . . .'

'But what?'

She made excuses but did not tell him that she was in pain, that he had caught her in unbecoming clothes and quite unprepared to receive guests, let alone to sit for her portrait. She made excuses and Lewis looked relieved, as if he had not really wanted to start on the drawing and had mentioned it only out of politeness. He began talking of other things. Then he abruptly got up and said that if she did not want him to draw her he had better go. She protested that he had promised, the day before, to phone first to fix a time and that that was why she was not ready. He did not seem convinced.

'I'll write,' she told him as he left.

'That's it. You write.'

'A long letter.'

'Capital!'

*

At the end of April 1931, Chatto & Windus brought out their eighth Lewis title: *The Diabolical Principle and The Dithyrambic Spectator*, essays that had already appeared in *The Calendar of Modern Letters* and *The Enemy* in 1925 and 1929 respectively. A month before, Charles Prentice had accepted for publication what was to be the most troublesome of all the books by Lewis he handled during their seven-year association. Neither party appeared concerned that signing the contract for *Doom of Youth* on April Fool's Day might be regarded as tempting fate.

Also in April, and behind Prentice's back, Lewis signed a contract with Cassell & Co. for three books. For the first, *Snooty Baronet*, they agreed to an advance on royalties of £300: a third on signature, a third on delivery, and a third on publication. These were advantageous terms compared with the £100 Chatto had paid him for *Hitler* and the £150 they had just given him for *Doom of Youth*.

Cassell & Co. was a larger firm than Chatto, with offices in Toronto, Melbourne and Sydney. It was run by Neuman Flower, together with his son and fellow director Desmond, to whom Lewis had been introduced by A.J.A. Symons. The three-book agreement augured well for a fruitful collaboration and was not seriously marred even by an insensitive blunder at the outset. Although Lewis dealt almost exclusively with Desmond Flower throughout his association with the firm, it was Neuman Flower who wrote on 9 April, enclosing the contract for *Snooty Baronet* and addressing him as D. B. Wyndham Lewis.

*

With Cassell's initial hundred pounds and £150 from the firm of Nash & Grayson, who were bringing out a trade edition of *The Apes of God*, he travelled, by way of Dieppe, to Marseilles, from there by ferry to the port of Oran and thence to Morocco. His journey to North Africa was made more momentous by terminating his tenancy at Ossington Street. 'I sold my goods,' he wrote, ' "liquidated" my belongings . . . put in store my books . . . Thoroughly unanchored, all trim in the rear, ready for anything . . . unaccompanied, I set out.'

In fact he was accompanied by his wife,* although the seven *Everyman* articles and book that came out of their Moroccan journey made no mention of her. This was not surprising. No one he knew in London had any idea, beyond the vague rumours that Marjorie Firminger had heard, of his recent marriage. His public persona, 'The Enemy', was necessarily a solitary one. It was therefore unthinkable that he would chronicle the fact that he had embarked upon the North African adventure with anything so domestic as a

---

* She may even have accompanied him to Berlin the previous November. Their marriage in October was probably undertaken to avoid complications while travelling together.

spouse on his arm. The heroic first person singular was accordingly the favoured pronoun in *Filibusters in Barbary*.

That book is the only record of Mr and Mrs Lewis's itinerary. From Oran they took a train to Tlemcen, then to Oujda, which was as far as the passenger train went. From there, a six-hour journey by bus took them to Fez. They caught a train to Casablanca and then it was either six hours by rail or five and a half by road to 'the huge, red, windy metropolis of mud and sand' that was Marrakesh. Then they went south, 'rushing for four hundred miles up and down the sides of mountains in a mighty bus, and at last dropping with a dull roar into the ocean valley' of Agadir. This was to be their base for a month.

'The best time to visit Morocco', according to the 1933 *Cook's Traveller's Handbook*, 'is the late Autumn or Spring'. The summer is described as 'very hot', the months of July, August and September as 'particularly exacting'. Although not entirely impervious to the Moroccan sun, as he was to the popping gas fire in 53 Ossington Street, Lewis made few concessions to the scorching climate. Dressed in his customary wide-brimmed black hat and heavy navy blue serge suit, he cut an identical figure in Fez and Agadir to that which he cut in Bayswater.

Early in June, from the Grand Hotel in Fez, he wrote to Symons praising the climate and claiming that he was working on *Snooty Baronet*. He had 'brought it down to Africa', he said, 'to ripen it quicker so to speak'. He asked to be remembered to Desmond Flower. The Cassell director was to be assured that the novel was 'taking shape'.

His experience of the modern city of Casablanca was not congenial. Much of his time there was spent in 'attempting to undermine the colossal indifference of the French Postal personnel to the welfare of the Public'. This may be interpreted as 'indifference' to delays of mail sent poste restante to 'the Public' from London. There had been more entertainment in Fez, where Lewis was able to observe at close quarters the social interaction of a film crew on location: 'fifty dumb characters in search of an author dumb enough to concoct a plot and text for them (accompanied by the sharp-shooters of the mechanical staff) . . . vociferous and replete with a strident reality that was so thin as to stamp them anywhere as screen-folk – creatures that is of an art at one remove from the shadow-picture.' And later, in Marrakesh, Lewis and his wife were fellow guests at their hotel with an authentic 'Film magnifico'. Rex Ingram, Irish-born American actor and director, was in the declining years of his career and probably, at that time, working on the film *Love in Morocco*, his last of any significance.

About the third week in June they arrived at the port of Agadir, 'upon the edge of the Spanish Sahara', as Lewis rather expansively described it, 'baked by breaths from the Sudan, chilled by winds from the Atlantic'. From Fez he had reported to Flower that work on his book for Cassell was proceeding and that *Snooty Baronet* was even 'ripening' in those exotic surroundings. At Agadir, three weeks later, writing in what he described as a 'whitewashed cell', in a hotel run by an Italian ex-legionnaire, he told his other publisher, Prentice, that he was working on Chatto's eagerly awaited sequel to *The Childermass*. 'The country is most remarkable', he enthused, 'and the desert cities, humped antelopes, Berber brothels, etc. abound in suggestions of a sort favourable to the production of that major book.' He promised soon to 'have a section roughly filled in'. On the basis of this industry he extracted a further instalment of his advance from Chatto & Windus. 'Fifty pounds would be a quarter of the sum agreed per section as an advance on the completed Mss. of *The Childermass*. Thirty is all I immediately shall be needing. I leave it to you.' Prentice telegraphed him £30.

In Agadir Lewis encountered an English expatriate, whom he described as the 'unofficial British Consul' in the region. Major Thomas Girdwood MacFie ran an estate office, a farm and a motor bus business. His unwillingness to co-operate with Lewis's plans for exploring the wild country around Agadir resulted in his being ridiculed in *Filibusters in Barbary*. Although never referred to by name, the Major emerges from the pages with sufficient clarity for a libel action to be brought a couple of years later, during which extensive quotation from the chapter called 'The Filibuster of Tooting Beck' (*sic*), together with passing references in a chapter on gun-running, were made in substantiation of the claim.

Lewis and his wife eventually made forays into the area west of Agadir under the protection of the French army, and by the second week in July he could write to Naomi Mitchison* that he had:

> been to places, and broken bread with people, calculated to lay [D. H. Lawrence] out in a foaming ecstasy. At all events these folks are *the* Barbarians right enough, and they build the most magnificent castles, upon the tops of cyclopean rocks, in the heart of vast mountains. They have to be seen to be believed.

They were unable to go further into the 'Zone of Insecurity' than the fortress of Assads, where they dined with the local Sheikh. Beyond that, even French military protection would be lacking. Their itinerary, at least as far as *Filibusters in Barbary* is concerned, came to an end with Lewis thrilling to bloodcurdling tales, told by Antoine de Saint-Exupéry and other aviators, of the terra incognita to the south of Agadir, the Spanish Sahara or Rio de Oro.

* A recent friend, following her favourable review of *The Apes of God* in *Time and Tide*.

They left Agadir in late July, planning to go into the High Atlas before returning home. Some years later Lewis wrote admiringly of his wife that she had 'ridden all over the Atlas on a mule'. A blurred photograph survives, taken by a second-hand Kodak camera with a faulty shutter, of Mrs Lewis astride such an animal.

*

Marjorie Firminger remembered her final encounter with Wyndham Lewis with cinematic precision. As to the precise date she was unsure, but calculated it to be in or just before November 1931. As Lewis sailed for New York in the last week of October, the comedy of embarrassment must have been played out either earlier that month or in September following his return from Morocco.

He telephoned to ask if they could fix a time for him to 'come along and do that drawing' and arrived late in the afternoon of the appointed day. He was more or less on time and carried a large bulging portfolio. Opening the window to assure herself it was him, she hurried down two flights of stairs. Her racing heart left her flushed and speechless as she faced him over the threshold. She shook his proffered hand and led the way upstairs. He appeared disconcerted when they did not stop at the first floor but continued to ascend. She explained that the rooms she used to live in were now sublet to someone called 'Peggy' who claimed to have expectations of £10,000. Marjorie now occupied the floor above. 'Very nice to be on top of £10,000', he remarked.

He seemed impressed by the airy whitewashed room. At the far end there was a coal fire. The walls were decorated with reproductions of Lewis drawings: one from *The Enemy*, and the 'Victorian Savage' clipped from the previous July's *Time and Tide*. On her bookshelves *The Apes of God* took pride of place and there was a skull that Elliot Seabrooke had left her. Lewis said he liked the skull. She thought she noticed him looking at the door which she had left open and she went and closed it. She remembered walking back towards him and his seeming to look her up and down with approval.

He put his portfolio on a chair and sat down, suggesting they have a little chat before starting work. He asked her how things were going and she showed him a card from her publisher in Paris giving encouraging news about the marketing of *Jam Today*, which was soon to go into a cheap edition. He turned the card over, saw it was blank and then said that he must give her his new address. He asked if he should write it on the back of the card and she said 'Of course, of course', as he went over to sit at a small table by the divan. She watched his black-hatted profile as he produced a pencil and bent over the card writing carefully. He handed it to her and she laughed as she read:

PALL MALL SAFE DEPOSIT, CARLTON STREET, REGENT STREET, W.1.*

She possessed no other sample of his handwriting so clear.

He noticed the *Times Literary Supplement* lying on the divan. 'Anything in the Lit Supp?' he asked her and she felt happy and flattered because the question implied that he trusted her to know what was of interest and what was not. He mentioned Roy Campbell's new poem *The Georgiad*, about to be published, and told her it was first rate, that she must get hold of it and that it could stand alongside Pope's *Dunciad*.

Suddenly it was time to get down to work, and he asked her to sit in the high-backed chair by the fire. Quickly she settled herself, pulling the wide skirt of her black woollen dress down over her knees as she crossed them, shooting the cuffs of her pink and grey silk blouse out over her hands, resting them on the arms of the chair. 'A nice get-up', Lewis said as he sat on a pouffe opposite her on the other side of the fire and got out his drawing materials from the portfolio.

He worked in silence.

It seemed as if he had only executed a few desultory strokes on the paper when he got up and said that he had just remembered he must go round the corner to see someone about the sale of a drawing. She remembered him patting the portfolio as he said this. It was a nuisance but he was hard up and the drawing would probably fetch 60 or 70 pounds so it could not be helped. He did not envisage the transaction taking long and he promised he would be back soon to continue the drawing. 'On that you can absolutely rely', he said.

The suspicion that he was not coming back probably began to dawn long before she burst into tears and went to bed close on midnight.

Wong, her daily, woke her the following morning, bringing toast, coffee and the newspaper. She got up and put on a cardigan, then went back to bed. She was still upset and could eat nothing but she drank the strong coffee and lay there leafing through the newspaper. She heard the front door

---

* The secretive postal address caused amusement to others of Lewis's acquaintance. Reginald Pound, literary editor of the *Daily Express*, wrote in 1937: 'From the address he left, it appears he stresses his cave-man ideology by living in a safe-deposit.' (*Their Moods and Mine*, London, Chapman & Hall, 1937, p. 239.) When Lewis pointed out the hole in the wall in Carlton Street as his address to Rupert Grayson, the publisher observed: 'A big man like you must find it rather cramped in there.' Grayson recalled Lewis was not amused. (*Stand Fast, The Holy Ghost*, London, Tom Stacey, 1937, p. 132.)

bell ring but left it to the daily to deal with. Shortly after there was a knock at her door. Thinking it was Wong, she called: 'Come in', and Lewis entered, still wearing his large black hat and still carrying his bulging portfolio.

This time he did not shake hands. He behaved as if it had been only a matter of minutes since he had left to sell his drawings, instead of 12 hours. He seemed put out that she had gone to bed but was still eager to carry on with the drawing where they had left off. He crossed to the fireplace, the cold grate alone testifying to how long he had been away, and sat down on the pouffe to open his portfolio. Opposite him was the chair in which she had briefly posed the night before. Her underclothes now lay on the seat, her black dress and silk blouse were draped over the high back, and her stockings and high heels tangled on the floor underneath: the 'nice get-up' she had tearfully discarded late the previous night.

To sit for him again, as he evidently expected her to, she would have to get out of bed, undress and then dress again while he watched. This she could not do. She had read *The Apes of God* and knew how he could look at a human body and the cruelty and precision with which he could call it to mind. On the other hand to get out of bed and change at the far end of the room seemed, in the light of what she thought of as their frank and easygoing friendship, a little coy. She drew her cardigan across her chest and made no move to leave the bed.

Lewis appeared to take offence. Evidently she did not want him to complete the drawing. Worse still, by refusing to let him complete the drawing, she was denying him the opportunity to repay the £5 he still owed her for the typing of *Satire and Fiction*. Next thing she would be going around London, talking about him behind his back and telling everyone he owed her money. He wagged a finger at her and told her: 'It's in places like this that I have been consistently run down.'

For her part, Marjorie lay in bed unable to speak. She wanted to tell him that he had misjudged her and misinterpreted her unwillingness to sit. She had never regarded the £5 as a loan but more as a gift from one friend to another. She had regarded the drawing he proposed as being made in a similar friendly spirit. Never had she regarded the one as a payment for the other. But she said nothing.

He approached the bed and stood over her. Then he shook her hand: in parting, not greeting, and for the last time.

Even as she listened to him descending the stairs that morning in the September or October of 1931, and heard the street door closing behind him, she told herself that she could still clear up the dreadful misunderstanding with a letter.

In 1967, Mrs Marjorie McLean Hemming, as by then she had become, attempted to reconstruct the sporadic two-and-a-half-year acquaintanceship between herself and the man she had regarded at that time as a god. As the framework of her narrative, she referred to xeroxes of the 42 letters she had written him and which by then were part of the Wyndham Lewis Collection at Cornell University. The 113-page typescript she called 'No Quarter' remains unpublished and today lies in the same archive as her letters.

Of the 42 letters subscribed 'Marjorie' or 'M' preserved at Cornell, only one was written after Lewis stalked from her maisonette for the last time. There were others, poured forth in efforts at reconciliation that he, uncharacteristically, may have destroyed. 'Why are they missing from the collection?' Mrs Hemmings asked at the end of her memoir:

> So that there would be no trace of the wretched £5? Which I must have mentioned . . . to make clear . . . that I had never connected it with the drawing. And I expect I wrote other things that Lewis might not have wanted on record: when I thought I hadn't made something clear in one already posted I would hasten to try to do so in another, and the thought of what I might have said in them all makes me squirm. For though I could swear I wrote them in all seriousness and as an admirer, they may well have come out rather differently, and so be open in his suspicious eyes to misconstruction.

The last letter from her in the Cornell collection was written 31 May and misdated 1931. It was, in fact, written 1932 and contained the news that she was going to marry Francis Hemming. A cheerful letter, it left the door open for Lewis to give her a ring should he want 'an enemy chat'. It was written three and a half months before *Snooty Baronet* was published, when she realised what cruel use he had made of their meetings. She remembered reading it at a sitting. She was so upset that her future husband had to take the book away from her.

*

Lewis sailed for New York alone, arriving on 29 October.

Rupert Grayson, who was bringing out the first trade edition of *The Apes of God* and whose immense chin was to figure prominently in *Snooty Baronet,* was there at the same time and met Lewis at the Brevoort Hotel. They went on a tour of the speakeasies together and in one bar met up with a group of young American intellectuals. Here it became apparent that news of Lewis's recent publications had travelled but become somewhat garbled on the way. Grayson introduced him to them as the author of *The Apes of God*.

'*The Apes of God*!' one of the young men exclaimed excitedly, and held out his hand to shake Lewis's, 'then you must be Osbert Sitwell.'

He went to Washington for the weekend towards the end of November and stayed at the Mayflower Hotel, the most expensive in town, he claimed, but where a small room was affordable. He attended 'two or three functions'. He wanted to 'see all the fun of the fair' while he was about it. He wanted to go down to Virginia or North Carolina 'to have a look around'. He thought it a pity to be 'so near the South and not pop into it'. The cost was prohibitive, however. At one Washington function he met Alice Longworth, daughter of Theodore Roosevelt, and 'a *great girl*'. She showed him an article, recently published in the *Harvard Advocate*, about himself, Eliot and Joyce, written by her cousin, Joseph Alsop, then a student at Harvard. Lewis wrote to the young man and received an invitation to stay at his apartment in Cambridge, Massachusetts. The deep South would have to wait.

Alsop remembered him as 'a strange, but fascinating, man, who drank a good deal of gin'. This was in early December, towards the end of Lewis's stay in the United States, and he was short of money. Alsop arranged for him to meet people likely to commission a $100 portrait drawing. Later Lewis claimed to have been paid between $150 and $250 a time. Alsop's tutor, Theodore Spencer, sat for him, as did Mrs Spencer. There were drawings of Mrs Saltonstall and the future Mrs Archibald Alexander, Miss Jean Sears. It was a foretaste of the American patronage Lewis was to scrape by on a decade later, the next time he was stranded in North America with only the facility of his pencil to keep him solvent.

It was arranged for him to give a reading from *The Apes of God* at Theodore Pickman's house, and guests at the event were charged $2 a head. He also performed in the Senior Common Room at Harvard and was put up at the College's expense in the Continental Hotel, from whose windows, he learned later, he could have 'gazed into *Eliot's sister's* parlour'. Readings and portrait drawing gave him enough cash in hand to get back to New York, following a farewell dinner from his hosts. 'Boston is a good place', he concluded.

He returned to England on the SS *Berlin*, one of 14 passengers, and one of only four travelling Cabin Class. They reached Southampton on Christmas Day. The formal Christmas party photograph on board showed him louring at the back of a festive group gathered around the tree. He and Santa Claus were the only men not wearing evening dress.

THIRTY-ONE

'A roaming wild oat come to roost'

When Lewis and his wife returned from Morocco in August 1931 they transferred their domestic hearth from Tavistock Road to the martial-sounding 27 Ordnance Road* in St John's Wood. At about the same time their household was expanded by the addition of a small Sealyham terrier called 'Tut', 'Tutsi' or, latterly, 'Jo-Jo'.

It was not until May 1932 that Lewis acquired another 'office' or studio equivalent to 53 Ossington Street. 31 Percy Street was owned by a firm of manufacturing jewellers on the ground floor. It was on the opposite side to Lewis's wartime quarters at number 4, and nearer to Tottenham Court Road. The 'first floor back' of number 31 was sublet to him by a man called Love, whose congenial name remained on the bell throughout Lewis's occupancy. John Rothenstein recalled being entertained there:

> we . . . sat . . . in front of a red-hot iron stove, from whose angry rays we must have suffered painfully had we not been shielded by a yard-high range of cinders encircling the fearful source of heat.

Rupert Grayson described it as a 'sealed, locked, padlocked, bolted, enchained hideout . . . equipped rather than furnished with two well-screwed-up packing cases (for the occasional use of guest or model), an easel and a sinister black steel-braced trunk pressed into a shadowy corner of the room and, for greater security, clamped to the floor.' There was a second room but Grayson never saw inside. 'Only one thing was certain: it contained a utensil of sorts, because when [Lewis] disappeared therein one could hear the tinkle-tinkle one associates with a male person peeing into a tin can.' While engaged in this necessary activity he was able to keep a suspicious eye on his visitor through an ill-concealed spy-hole in the partition wall.

*

---

* Now Ordnance Hill.

In April Lewis showed *The Roaring Quean* to Desmond, Lord Harmsworth of Egham, nephew to the press baron, Lord Rothermere. Desmond Harmsworth was, for two years in the early Thirties, trying his own hand at publishing, but by May he had decided not to publish *The Roaring Quean*. Unlike Charles Prentice two years earlier, Harmsworth did not seem worried about courting libel action. His main concern was the £200 advance Lewis was demanding for the novel.

Despite this setback Lewis's publishing output in 1932 was remarkable. Including *Doom of Youth* from Chatto in June, his books appeared under four different British imprints. Harmsworth, although baulking at *The Roaring Quean*, produced an illustrated and revised edition of *Enemy of the Stars* in May and a portfolio of prints, *Thirty Personalities and a Self-Portrait*, in September. Rupert Grayson brought out *Filibusters in Barbary* in June and Cassell published the first in their three-book agreement, *Snooty Baronet*, in September.

At Chatto & Windus, Charles Prentice was enraged by this proliferation. His blustering letter of 21 June marked the beginning of a bitter dispute that continued into the following year:

> We are amazed to hear ... that Grayson & Grayson are publishing immediately a book by you on Morocco, and to see the announcement that Desmond Harmsworth is publishing almost at once your 'Enemy of the Stars' ... I note, too, that ... Harmsworth is under agreement to publish several other books by you, and we are also told that you have a contract with a third publisher for a novel.

What rankled was Lewis's failure to deliver the second and third sections of *The Childermass*, contracted for in 1928. Adding insult to injury, Lewis was publishing with Grayson his account of the Moroccan trip which had been partly subsidised by Chatto in the belief that he was getting down to work on the overdue sequel in the 'whitewashed cell' in Agadir. Also, according to their 1928 contract, Lewis had agreed not to publish any other work elsewhere until *The Childermass* was completed, without giving Chatto the first option. Lewis was quick to remind Prentice of the recent options they had declined to take up:

> was I to go on offering your firm for ever Roaring Queens and Apes of God – only to have them turned down on the score that they would be offensive to your Bloomsbury friends.

Ironically, the book that Chatto were about to publish would land them in just the sort of trouble Prentice had been guarding against when he turned down *The Roaring Quean. Doom of Youth* was the ninth Lewis title Chatto & Windus published. It was also, unsurprisingly, the last.

Chatto had initial qualms about Lewis's treatment of the novelist Michael Arlen in the latter part of the book. 'We speak with no precise knowledge of the working of the law of libel', they told Lewis:

> but we are inclined to think that the effect of calling him 'this dismal asiatic caricature of a *rastaqouère*'* and 'this tawdry gentleman who has filched the christian name of an archangel' would be to send him hot-foot to his solicitor.

Lewis was persuaded to tone down these and other references, and minor changes were made in proof. 'I am awfully sorry to bother you with these things', said Prentice, 'but clearly there is no point in putting one's head into the noose.' But when the book came out at the end of June, offence was taken in altogether different quarters.

*

For an intensive period of six weeks in June and July, Lewis was engaged in head-hunting for his portfolio *Thirty Personalities and a Self-Portrait*. Personalities from the publishing, literary and art world duly rang the bell marked 'Love' in Percy Street and sat for him in the Spartan 'first floor back'. The portfolio's publisher, Desmond Harmsworth, was one of these and he recalled Lewis's working method:

> The studio . . . was just a room (no skylight). For portraiture he had all shutters closed except one small square of light which shone painfully on the sitter facing it, Lewis having his back to the light.

When Harmsworth's uncle, Lord Rothermere, pleaded weak eyes, Lewis reversed their positions and worked facing into the light himself. With Harmsworth's wife he produced one of the most striking drawings of the set, his attention focused upon the complex arrangement of her clasped hands. He drew his other publisher, Desmond Flower, his wife Margaret, and his father. He added a brown wash to the drawing of Neuman Flower and was offended when the sitter protested: 'You make me look like the Aga Khan!'

There were 'personalities' from other professional fields. Noel Coward's head was a small slanting oval placed in the middle of the page, while Edith Evans posed with her right elbow raised, as if holding her hand behind her

---

* The pejorative French epithet translates as 'flashy wog' (Collins-Robert).

head. Wing Commander Orlebar wore a flying cap, and goggles pushed up on his forehead. The surgeon Ivor Back dressed in theatre gown and rubber gloves.

Augustus John made himself available only once and Lewis worked hastily against time on his 'proud and mettlesome sitter'. He admitted to William Rothenstein that the portraits were 'all . . . not equally good'.

*

Towards the end of July Lewis telephoned the novelist Stella Benson, another 'personality', in a state of panic to cancel her sitting. Miss Benson noted down what he said and transcribed it verbatim in her diary:

> I can't meet you to-day – I must get away – I must get right away at once . . . There is diphtheria in my house – I am quite sure I shall catch it if I stay. It is a fearful disease. Outrageous that I should be turned out of my house by a disease. Absolutely outrageous. But it is no use – if I stay in this house I shall catch it and die – I have had three libel cases on my hands this week – and it has been terrible – terrible – I am so nervously weakened that I shall certainly die if I catch diphtheria – and in this . . . state I am really almost certain to catch it.

It was an echo of his mother's panic in Lamy's Hotel, Amherst, Nova Scotia, on New Year's Day 1883 when he was less than two months old. Anne Lewis's concerns on that occasion were for her baby. Fifty years later, at 27 Ordnance Road, if Lewis had fears for anyone else's well-being, his wife's perhaps, he did not express them. It was 'very odd', Miss Benson thought, 'in these days of understatement and indifference – to meet a man who is really so important to himself – and is not afraid to say so.'

One puzzling reference in Lewis's terrified outburst over the telephone was to the 'three libel cases' he had on his hands that week. It is possible that Stella Benson misheard him. It is certainly possible that he was exaggerating. He was at this time dealing with only two actions for libel. Both were connected to *Doom of Youth*, published the previous month.

*

On 20 July a letter from the firm of Gisborne & Co., solicitors representing the actor and writer Godfrey Winn, was delivered by hand to Chatto & Windus:

> Mr Winn's publishers, his literary agents and a number of other persons

316

have called Mr Winn's attention to . . . the chapter . . . headed 'Winn and
Waugh' . . . A number of the statements made in the chapter are . . . in
the worst possible taste and are obviously meant to convey to the public
that Mr Winn is a young gentleman who has little or no ability as an
author and is not a serious artist but is merely commercialising his youth
and is able to earn money by that method and not by reason of his ability
as a writer.

The letter concluded with a demand that the book be immediately
withdrawn from circulation and 'a full and adequate apology' published.

Two days later Chatto's solicitors, Walker, Martineau & Co., agreed that
references to Winn as a 'hack' and 'a salaried revolutionary agent' were
indeed libellous. They proposed that Lewis amend the pages on which these
insinuations had been made and that they be reprinted and pasted in to
copies of the book withdrawn from sale and those still in the publisher's
warehouse. Winn's solicitors replied that nothing less than the removal of
the entire chapter would satisfy their client.

On 25 July Alec Waugh, just back from a fortnight in the South of
France, called to see his agent. He was told that Godfrey Winn was anxious
to meet him because they had both been libelled and he hoped that Waugh
would join him in instituting proceedings.

Alec Waugh, whose best-selling account of his schooldays, *The Loom of
Youth*, Lewis had parodied in his own title, claimed later that under normal
circumstances he would not have taken action. He was, however, in
belligerent mood:

> My visit to the South of France had been an unofficial honeymoon with
> the lady, Joan Chirnside, whom I was to marry in October. [She] was an
> Australian, accustomed to rather tough horseback riding men. I fancied
> that she thought that I was rather flabby. I was anxious to prove to her
> that I was not.

Two days after Waugh's visit to his agent, a letter from the firm of
Rubenstein, Nash & Co. was delivered to Chatto & Windus by hand and
marked 'Important':

> We are instructed to call upon you unconditionally and immediately to
> withdraw the book from circulation . . . and to publish a full and
> unqualified apology to Mr Waugh in terms approved by us in the NEW
> STATESMAN and NATION, THE OBSERVER, THE SUNDAY
> TIMES and THE TIMES LITERARY SUPPLEMENT.

Three days later Lewis ran into J. B. Priestley, a 'personality' who had already sat for his portrait in frowning double-chinned profile, and whose only connection with the case was that he shared the services of the same literary agent as Alec Waugh. Priestley told Lewis that Waugh's action was being initiated because of an imputation that he was a homosexual. Lewis was appalled that he should hear such details of the case at third hand and immediately suspected Charles Prentice, and Chatto's solicitors, of deliberately keeping him and his legal representatives in the dark for their own obscure reasons. Writing to complain to his own solicitors, he added in passing that Priestley disagreed that there was anything libellous in the book and that Lewis had merely described Waugh as suffering from 'infantilism'. Waugh, however, newly engaged to his Antipodian fiancée, was particularly stung by what he interpreted as a systematic demolition of his masculinity. One passage in particular seemed designed to place him in an unsatisfactory light for a future wife accustomed to tough Australian men:

> I should say that all the feminine, maternal attributes were excessively developed in him, and of course (Mr Waugh being a man) were thwarted. They relieve themselves . . . by means of . . . incessant literary compositions about small boys with sooty faces and bulging pockets . . . I do not wish to be offensive to Mr. Waugh, but I think . . . that there is something of an obsessional nature at work: and I do think that psycho-analysis would reveal the fact that motherhood in its most opulent form was what Mr Waugh had been destined for by nature, and that a cruel fate had in some way interfered, and so unhappily he became a man.

Over ten chapters further on, page 206 contained the words: 'the homosexual is, of course, an imitation-woman'. This, taken in conjunction with what had gone before, was sufficient for Waugh's solicitors to file a Statement of Claim:

> The said words meant and/or were understood to mean that the Plaintiff was a contemptible man, and that as an author and novelist he was so lacking in versatility that he could not write on any topic save public school boys and/or that the Plaintiff was sexually perverted.

While the legal machinery attendant on both these cases slowly ground into action on behalf of the plaintiffs, Messrs Winn and Waugh, the defendants were engaged in the early stages of a litigious battle of their own. Chatto & Windus were attempting to extract from Lewis the £150 they had paid him in 1928 for the second and third sections of *The Childermass*. Legal action had not at this stage been formally begun but the two sides were communicating through their solicitors.

At the end of July Lewis's legal representative from Barnes & Butler attended a conference to discuss a defence against Waugh's action. Also present were Charles Prentice, his partner from Chatto, Harold Raymond, and their solicitors Walker, Martineau & Co. Mr Barnes saw an opportunity of at least gaining some leeway for his client 'in connection with the Childermass matter'. He asked the publishers if Lewis could be given 'say another year', either to fulfil his contractual obligations or to pay back the money. 'I am sorry to say', Mr Barnes reported to Lewis, 'while Mr Prentice and Mr Raymond were extremely nice, I completely failed.' This smiling intransigence, coupled with Chatto's apparent concealment from him of the grounds for Waugh's action, made Lewis suspect a hostile cabal:

> Can we entirely rule out the fact that Raymond and Prentice are members of the same club as Waugh, and know him?

It would seem that at this point Lewis imagined that his own publishers were conspiring to engineer a lawsuit against themselves in order to damage him.

*

Following the diphtheria scare at 27 Ordnance Road, Stella Benson sat for her portrait drawing in the 'filthy back room (only by courtesy a studio) off the Tottenham Court Road':

> All the time he was drawing me he wore his hat and sat crouched over a swivelling easel; I had to keep my eyes fixed on a point just above his head, but I could see his teeth gleaming in his writhing mouth, as he talked of all his cruel experience of men and women . . . there really is something rather wistful in the look of this stout glowering snub-nosed man – sitting hunched on a too small camp stool, describing, without the slightest smile or irony, his position as the cynosure of all wickedness . . . He lives a curiously darkened life, continually assuring both others and himself that he is naturally a simple, gentle and pacific man, forced into the atmosphere of battle by other people. All his friends turn on him, he says – all business men try to cheat him . . . he is obsessed with the wickedness – active wickedness – of everyone except himself.

*

At 10.30 in the morning of Tuesday 16 August, in the Chambers of Mr

319

Justice Goddard, a request by Waugh's legal representatives for an interim injunction prohibiting further publication of the book was refused. His Lordship ruled that the remarks about homosexuals on page 206 'could not apply to the Plaintiff'.

Despite this initial victory, Chatto & Windus, on the advice of their lawyers, decided to withdraw the book. They had limited protection against liability for libel damages and their insurers had objected to further publication. They had also received letters from booksellers, informed by Waugh of the impending action, who did not feel inclined to sell any more copies until the matter had been disposed of. Anyone selling the book could be sued for 'publication of a libel' along with the publishers themselves.

Effective suppression of one book on 'Youth-politics' did not prevent Lewis from bringing out another. In the first paragraph of *The Old Gang and the New Gang*, published by Desmond Harmsworth, the following January, Lewis offered its 62 pages as the only extant work dealing with this field of criticism, until he had 'succeeded in rescuing [the larger book] from occultation'.

*

In September the Lewises holidayed in South-East France, staying at the Hôtel Bonnard in Pont-en-Royans, near Grenoble. On the way they had visited Berlin. A translation, by Max Sylge, of Lewis's Hitler book had been published earlier in the year as *Hitler und sein Werk*. Lewis visited the offices of its publisher, Reimer Hobbing, and was received by 'a peculiarly uncivil cripple of the name of Schmidt'. Herr Schmidt told him that his book had been shown to Hitler and Goebbels and it had displeased them:

> I displeased Herr Schmidt as well, that was obvious. The Nazis and the German people seemed to displease him even more. As I found Herr Schmidt exceedingly unattractive, that seemed to be okay all round.

*

On his return to London, Lewis was summoned to the offices of Cassell & Co. for an urgent conference. Neuman Flower informed him that their two best fiction-buying customers, the circulating libraries of Boots and Smiths, had judged *Snooty Baronet* to be 'a coarse and unprincipled book' and had 'banned it in the most unpleasant and effective of all ways' by taking only 25 copies each. Overall sales were thereby halved and the publisher could not even promote interest in the book elsewhere by advertising it as 'banned'.

Flower went on to say that if Lewis was to be paid the generous advances on his next two books for Cassell as stipulated in their contract, 'those books must be of such a character as to pass the Library censors of Messrs. Boot and Smith.'

Lewis argued that it had been the 'outspoken' qualities of his fiction that originally determined Flower and his son to take him on. Desmond Flower had even described him as 'the writer destined to succeed D. H. Lawrence upon the English scene' and, while Lewis did not exactly relish the parallel, he pointed out its potentially commercial value:

> Half the popular success of D. H. Lawrence . . . was due to the constant banning of his books, and the exhilarating spectacle of his battle with the antiquated and unreal prejudices of the puritanic conscience and the prurient bellowing of the embattled Grundys.

Now he was concerned about the implications of the circulating library ban on his next two books for Cassell, and particularly worried that Neuman Flower was contemplating a reduction in his advances.

A few days after this unpleasant discussion, Lewis noticed that Cassell had stopped advertising his book ten days following its publication. 'How strange it is', he told Flower, 'that I should have two books suppressed within the space of two months, and both by publishers! . . . you have as effectively killed *Snooty Baronet* as Chatto's killed *Doom of Youth*.' Then, in the complex fabric of the London book trade, he began to see conspiratorial patterns that might explain Cassell's changed attitude:

> As Mr Alec Waugh is one of your regular 'authors', a great personal friend of your son's, I realised that if he persisted in his ridiculous action against me, it would make it awkward for me in my new capacity of a 'Cassell author'. And I cannot help feeling very strongly, from all the signs, that you have been enlisted in this author's quarrel upon the other side.

Pressure from Chatto for the return of their money increased and Lewis believed his 'whole career [was] in some sort at stake.' On 6 October Prentice wrote him a letter containing the threat of action which, if put into effect, Lewis's lawyers assured him, might constitute a criminal libel:

> We understand that it is open to us to inform your other publishers – and indeed all publishers, if we want to – of your contract with us to give us the first option of any other work of yours before you finish 'The Childermass'; and that we can apply for an injunction restraining them

from publishing any book, contracted for with you, that has not been offered to us first.

He was in imminent danger of an effective blacklist.

*

On the same day that Prentice dispatched his threat to destroy Lewis's literary career, the Lefevre Gallery in King Street was opening Lewis's first major showing of graphic work for over a decade. 'Thirty Personalities' was well received by critics, although the correspondent of *The Times* found fault with the relationship between paper and portrait: 'the paper is artistically irrelevant as if the heads were intended to be cut out. They are firmly modelled in relief towards the spectator, but they have no implied backs to them.'

Desmond Harmsworth had published the series in good-quality reproduction in a shiny black portfolio, signed and limited to 200 copies, and priced at two guineas, before the exhibition opened.

*

The tangle of litigation already surrounding Lewis was made denser in early October by claims from the former Lady Glenapp's solicitors to get back money she had put into the Arthur Press in 1929. When he borrowed the hundred pounds, Lewis suggested that 'details could be arranged by lawyers'. Two years later the accumulation of interest and compound interest ensured that arrangements were still in the hands of lawyers. A couple of days after the Lefevre Gallery opening Barnes & Butler received a letter from Burton, Yeates & Hart to the effect that if they did not receive a remittance for the balance due by the middle of the following week they would 'proceed by way of a Judgement Summons'.

Mr Barnes wrote to Lewis asking for 'say £10' and promising to gain 'a further extension of time'.

Lewis had already repaid £100, and all that remained outstanding was the interest. Since her divorce in 1931 and her recent marriage to Captain Beech, the lady seemed determined to extract every last penny of the debt.

*

On Monday 24 October a postcard was delivered, addressed to 'Percy Wyndham Lewis Esq., 31 Percy Street, Tottenham Court Rd'. Each 'Percy' was underlined. It had been sent from Beaconsfield, Buckinghamshire, by the 7 o'clock post the previous evening. There was no message in the space designated 'Communication'. On the front was a photograph of two moustached men wearing ulsters and with their large floppy hats pulled down over their eyes. At the bottom were the words: 'So there are two of you.'

Osbert Sitwell had found the photograph at Renishaw and, struck by the resemblance of the 1890s actors to Lewis, had had it made into postcards. 'Every day that man gets one of these postcards', Edith gloated to a friend, 'either from London, or from the country in England, or from Paris.' One of them was delivered smeared with blood. Edith had pricked her big toe and written 'RACHE', German for 'vengeance', across the picture.

Edith also sent telegrams, or had them sent from Calais, inspired by Lewis's flirtation with German politics and intended to inflame his paranoia:

PERCY WYNDHAM LEWIS 31 PERCY STREET ACHTUNG NICHT HINAUSLEHNEN UNIFORMED COMMISSAR MAN DUE STOP BETTER WIRELESS HELP LAST NIGHT TOO LATE LOVE EIN FREUND SIGNED LEWIS WYNDHAM 21 PERCY STREET

This persecution provided bizarre accompaniment to the solicitor's letters which were arriving with increasing regularity. Lewis's position was further strained by demands from his own hard-working solicitors, Barnes & Butler, as their costs spiralled. On 7 November they asked him for £75.

With creditors on all sides, by mid-November Lewis was also about to be sued by Mr V. Tenney, His Majesty's Inspector of Taxes.

*

On 16 November Walker, Martineau & Co. finally went into action on behalf of their clients, Chatto & Windus, and served Lewis with a portentous document:

GEORGE THE FIFTH by the Grace of God of Great Britain, Ireland and the British Dominions beyond the Seas King, Defender of the Faith . . . We command you, that within eight days after the service of this writ on you, inclusive of the day of such service, you do cause an appearance to be entered for you in an action at the suit of Chatto & Windus and take note that in default of your so doing, the plaintiff may proceed therein and judgement may be given in your absence . . . The Plaintiff's claim is for damages for the Defendants' breach of a contract in writing . . .

Alternatively for the return of money paid for a consideration which has wholly failed.

When Lewis wrote to Barnes & Butler a few days later he was in belligerent good humour. 'I hope that the forensic arms forged in your office will prevail against the inferior equipment, and the less just cause, of our opponents. The war chest I am busily engaged in filling.'

However, in the space of five days, on 25 November, Lewis had transferred his complicated business to the firm of Powell, Skues & Graham Smith. What caused the breakdown of confidence is unclear, but it may have been Mr Butler's continued chafing as costs mounted and remained unpaid. When a messenger from his new solicitors arrived at their offices to collect Lewis's documents, Barnes & Butler refused to surrender them until his cheque for £45, settling their charges to date, had cleared.

*

It was in late November, when pressure generated by the Waugh and Chatto actions was reaching critical pitch, when the Inland Revenue and the former Lady Glenapp's solicitors were clamouring for settlement, that he became ill. The legal and pathological pressures were coincidental. 'A bug walked from my intestine into my bladder', he explained, 'and then planted an ulcer in an old venereal scar.'

The bladder inflammation of cystitis was probably caused by stagnant and infected urine dammed behind a stricture or narrowing of the urethra. The scar tissue that exacerbated the obstruction dated back to his negligently treated gonorrhoea during the first months of the war. It was, as Symons put it, 'a roaming wild oat come to roost'.

Just before Christmas another telegram arrived at 31 Percy Street:

ACHTUNG NICHT HINAUSLEHNEN THE BEAR DANCES

Lewis was not there to receive it. Early in December he had entered a private nursing home, the first of a series of such establishments that would count him as inmate over the next four years.

The Marchioness of Cholmondeley, whose features had been included among his *Thirty Personalities*, was a diligent visitor. On one occasion she brought him a sweater and on another, concerned that the institutional food might not be sufficiently nourishing, she instructed her cook to produce something for the invalid. The *crème de volaille* was not a success. Sight of the thick creamy soup with white lumps of chicken breast breaking its surface made him think of the organs of unborn cattle. Nauseated, he instructed Lady Cholmondeley to take it away with her.

Notwithstanding his rejection of such dietary supplements, the inflammation cleared up and by 3 January he was once more at large. His 'bigwig' specialist told him that he was over the worst and, provided he could take two or three weeks complete rest, no complications were to be expected. Docker sent £25 as an 'economical barrage' to carry him over this recuperative period. Lady Cholmondeley continued concerned. She would feel happier, she told him, if she were certain that the 'bigwig' specialist was really up-to-date. 'These things have gone ahead so rapidly of late that one wants to get the opinion of a doctor who keeps *au courant* of all discoveries abroad and in England.' She was convinced he would have to go to Paris for the best opinion.

Whether or not the 'bigwig' had been correct in his judgement that the patient was 'over the worst', Lady Cholmondeley's anxieties were soon confirmed. Lewis had left the sterile environment of the first nursing home prematurely, and by mid-January he was admitted to a second. Influenza had caused a renewed flaring of cystitis and until 21 February his address would be the Porchester Square Nursing Home in Paddington.

THIRTY-TWO

'Definitely something abnormal about her'

Among the visitors to 'Thirty Personalities' at the Lefevre Gallery during the previous October had been the wife of a Professor of Physics. She wrote to Lewis early in February, while he was still in Porchester Square, asking what he would charge to produce a similar pencil portrait of her husband to those in the exhibition. The curious relationship that developed over the following three years, between the artist, the Professor and the Professor's wife, was ample testimony to the loyalty and generosity Lewis could command from men, and the devotion, bordering upon clinical obsession, he could still inspire in women.

Mary Priestley Russ had been brought up in Leeds, where her unmarried sister, Dorothy Priestley, 'Dodo' to the family, still lived and practised as a physician and surgeon. Mary had contracted tuberculosis in 1928 and remained a semi-invalid for the rest of her life, functioning, according to her youngest son, on not much more than a quarter of a lung. She had time on her hands to read and keep abreast of current artistic trends. The founder of a small pacifist group called 'Women Against War' (WAW), year after year on Armistice Day she could be seen at the Cenotaph in Whitehall flanked by a pathetically dwindling membership. She was in her early forties when she made contact with Lewis and commissioned the drawing of her husband.

Sidney Russ held the Barnato Joel Chair of Physics at Middlesex Hospital, specialising in the field of medical applications for radium. In 1931 he had been appointed CBE for services to medical science.

*

After a bedridden month suffering from what he called his 'complicated flu attack' he was 'still in the clutches of the doctors' and about to submit to an electrical treatment aimed at curing his urethral problems. Diathermy, or thermo-penetration, consisted of a high-frequency current, oscillating at about a million times per second, being passed through the inflamed area of the body. Because the oscillations were so rapid the patient experienced no pain. The body formed a resistance to the current which increased the internal heat of the part being treated in much the same way as a modern microwave oven cooks meat. The idea was that the rush of blood to the inflamed area that this caused would quickly bring the infection under control.

While he waited for the course of thermo-penetration to begin, on 13 February at another nursing home in Beaumont Street, Marylebone, about a mile and a half away, Frances Caroline Joan Beech, former wife of Viscount Glenapp, died aged 34. An inquest heard that death had been caused by a combination of the sedatives medinol, paraldehyde, nebutol and potassium bromide, together with the possible complication of about 32 times the recommended dose of sal volatile, a stimulant. In extreme mental distress and desperately craving sleep she had been known to swallow anything that came to hand, including large quantities of scent. A verdict of death due to misadventure by narcotic drugs was brought in. Suicide was discounted.

*

Lewis's treatment started later that week. There was something familiar about the doctor in his crisp white drill jacket and protective dark glasses who was tending the diathermic apparatus. It may have been the glasses, or perhaps the frivolous little goatee beard, or that his face appeared crescent-shaped in profile, and with a prominent brow and jaw.

'You remind me of James Joyce', Lewis told him.

It must have been a sublimely surreal moment when he recognised the features of his one-time drinking companion standing behind the controls of a contraption designed to gently cook his private parts, as if in revenge for *Time and Western Man*.

'James Joyce?' The doctor blinked and looked uncomfortable and puzzled. 'I am afraid that conveys nothing to me.'

*

Meanwhile Lady Cholmondeley had been to Paris and consulted a Doctor Robert Wallich in the rue de Monceau who believed that the root of Lewis's condition might lie in the prostate gland. Best results, she was told, were to be obtained from 'very skilful massage', together with diathermy, and only three or four masseurs in Paris were capable of the tricky procedure.

By late February Lewis was preparing to leave the Porchester Square Nursing Home en route to Paris and waiting for a blizzard to pass before travelling. Lady Cholmondeley had agreed to pay his medical expenses when he got there. With the hoped-for improvement in the weather he set out, and by 2 March he was in the rue de Monceau consulting Doctor Wallich.

By mid-March he was back in London, having decided against the Gallic course of treatment because the hotels and restaurants had been prohibitively expensive. He complained, besides, that he had found himself in the hands of 'a rather alarming quack', but it is not clear whether this referred to Dr Wallich, one of the three or four Parisian masseurs Lady Cholmondeley had mentioned, or some other sinister medical man. He supplied no details, but later it became clear that professional clumsiness had exacerbated the initial problem of gonorrhoeal scarring. It was a common enough hazard: a catheter passed inside the penis in an attempt to widen the stricture might stray from its course, piercing the urethral wall and wounding the surrounding tissue.

'I regard my Paris experience as a particularly dangerous episode', he told Violet Schiff, 'I am glad not to have stopped there.'

But the damage was done. The importunate thrust of the catheter, if such it was, caused a diverticulum or cul-de-sac above and off to one side of the stricture; a sump for stagnant urine which, in time, ulcerated, creating a site of recurring infection that would incapacitate him every ten to twelve months for the next three years.

*

The Professor of Physics began sitting for his portrait soon after Lewis's return. Russ was a man of science, very much at ease in his own professional world yet disarmingly enthusiastic about the less familiar world he entered at 31 Percy Street. 'My attitude towards many things of the present day', he told Lewis early in their acquaintanceship, 'is coloured by the splendid failures of Art and the ghastly successes of Science.' The sittings developed into friendship.

Lewis visited the Russes at their Gower Street flat and lent them copies of his books. But the Professor's wife, who had initiated the friendship, soon became a source of acute embarrassment to both men.

While he was working on her husband's portrait, and shortly after, Lewis, by his own account, met Mary on only a few occasions. At one such meeting she disconcertingly informed him that she had arrived at a sudden realisation, while reading *The Apes of God*, that she could never become a Catholic. She even showed him the page and line that had led her to that conviction. From this he concluded that 'there was definitely something abnormal about her.'

The portrait drawing finished, paid for, and delivered and his books returned, Mary feared she might not see him again and was concerned he should not forget her. This at least was her explanation of the story she sent him and which began an eccentric and increasingly one-sided correspondence:

> There was once an old woman who lived in the country . . . Among her treasures was a canary in a cage and though the bird sang, its song was more the spiral of a curlew than that of a canary. The old dame was fond of gardening too and one day she found some seeds in a lovely coloured packet. She set them and they grew into the best flowers she had ever had. Not content with this bit of good luck . . . the silly old thing . . . took it into her head that she would like to thank the person who had collected them and put them into that particular packet . . . and one day without telling anyone she took the bird cage and as much luggage as she could carry and set off for a railway station . . . There was nobody about so she dumped the cage and the baggage on the narrow platform and sat down on the luggage to wait . . . But not a soul came in sight. Month came in, month went out and not even a luggage train clanked along those rails and as the years went by the old woman got too stiff to move, even if she had wanted to. The bird changed into a wooden bird and stopped singing. One summer day, as she was sitting gazing vacantly at a blue sky . . . suddenly . . . without the slightest warning of any sort down . . . came a book. A book out of the sky! . . . The light was too bright for her rheumy old eyes . . . and all she could see was a queer mercuryish figure with a book in one hand . . . The queer figure said 'I'll take that letter for you.' That was it of course! The letter, it was still on her knees . . . The queer figure had a kind voice which emboldened her, for . . . she said . . . 'To think such a lonely lost passenger, should have after all such a messenger.' Poor soul, even the messenger was charitable enough to think as he flew away. As for the old woman: for some earthly or unearthly reason she began to cry . . . till her bones melted and . . . she came unstiff again. Up she got at last and . . . trudged off down the road towards home cheerfully. But the strangest thing: would you believe it was . . .

She coyly withheld this 'strangest thing', leaving the end of the story hanging tantalisingly in the air: 'no I won't tell you that I think', she told him.

The message Lewis was presumably intended to read in the curious muddled little fable was that his books had sown seeds in the mind of this middle-aged woman and that even the most indirect contact with him had had a transcendent effect upon her life. The 'strangest thing', that she could not bring herself to admit to him, nor perhaps even to herself, may have been that after years of marriage and the nurturing of three children, she was experiencing erotic stirrings for a man she hardly knew.

*

By the end of March, the solicitors, Powell, Skues & Graham Smith, had negotiated a compromise with Walker, Martineau & Co., designed to resolve the case of Chatto & Windus vs. Lewis. It was agreed that if Chatto returned to Lewis rights to *The Caliph's Design* and other writings on art, held by them since 1928 as surety for their advance on sections two and three of *The Childermass*, and if he in turn could dispose of the former book to another publisher, Chatto were to receive £130 from the proceeds of the sale, together with their legal costs.

*

Lewis claimed that the German translation of *Hitler* had been suppressed when the Nazis came to power. If this were so, then it might be regarded as a vindication of the book. However, even Lewis admitted that it had not met with disfavour because the views expressed therein were particularly critical of the new regime. 'Goebbels's eye lighted on my Hitler book,' he wrote, 'still being sold in Berlin bookshops. This much-too-fair and disgustingly non-partisan volume continued to offend his harsh little eye.'

Nor was it destroyed by Nazi zealots in a spectacular conflagration like that of 10 May 1933 when the works of Thomas Mann, Stefan Zweig, Erich Maria Remarque, Jack London, H. G. Wells, Gide, Zola, Proust and thousands more went up in smoke. By comparison, the destruction of *Hitler und sein Werk* was banal:

> [The publishers] wrote to ask me if I objected to its being made into pulp – what was left of the edition. They pointed out that the situation had changed, the Nazis were in power, there was no longer any point in circulating my book. I replied that I had no objection to its returning to pulp. And pulp it accordingly became.

*

Although not actually pulped until March 1934, *Doom of Youth* had been unavailable in London bookshops for eight months. It had still not been found to be libellous of anybody, and all that was being sought on all sides, it seemed, was a face-saving form of words. On the same Wednesday that books were burning in Berlin, Lewis wrote to Graham Smith with instructions to throw in the towel, but as belligerently as possible. He was still not in the best of health. Four days before he had had 'a slight recrudescence of a cystitis' but it was 'beating a retreat'.

He denied the charge of libel against Waugh, 'the nonsense about "homosexuality"', but proposed that, in any future edition of *Doom of Youth*, chapter 7 in its entirety should be withdrawn. He made this offer ON CONDITION (twice underlined) 'that Waugh on his side categorically withdraws the "homosexual" charge, and states, in writing, that upon further consideration he sees that he was mistaken.' This last was eventually translated into a form of words agreeable to Mr Rubenstein's client and it was duly stated that: 'Mr Waugh unreservedly accepts Mr Wyndham Lewis's assurance that he did not intend to make any personal reflection against him.'

But Rubenstein's letter agreeing terms only served to confirm Lewis's suspicions of connivance between Waugh and Chatto & Windus:

> In view of the friendly relationship between our client and your co-defendants and for no other reason, our client generously agrees to forgo his claim for damages.

The action was formally discontinued in court on the morning of 1 June. All parties paid their own costs. Lewis's barrister, Richard Mitchison, in view of his wife Naomi's friendship with the defendant, instructed his clerk not to submit an account for the fee.

Three weeks later, Graham Smith told him that, in view of Waugh's action being discontinued, it was confidently expected that Godfrey Winn would 'drop the whole matter' as well. At the same time Walker, Martineau & Co. sent in their bill for costs arising from the Chatto settlement. Smith had estimated these would be about £30. They came instead to £45.

As one legal action ended another was slowly grinding on, and at the end of June Burton, Yeats & Hart, the late Mrs Beech's solicitors, were still trying to prosecute what remained of Lewis's three-year-old debt on behalf of her estate. 'Our instructions will not permit us to allow payment of the balance due to stand over any longer, and . . . unless the balance is paid by Wednesday next . . . we must proceed.' It must have seemed to Lewis as though his creditors were pursuing him from beyond the grave.

*

In the House of Commons on 11 May, the Labour MP Mr Frederick Seymour Cocks asked the Home Secretary if he had any information about the presence in London of two prominent members of the German National

Socialist movement: Herr Thost and Herr Rosenberg. The day before, Alfred Rosenberg had placed a large wreath, with prominent swastika, on the cenotaph in Whitehall. James Edward Sears, prospective Parliamentary candidate for southwest St Pancras and chairman of the Aylsham Branch of the British Legion, had removed it. He was charged with theft and, since the wreath had later to be retrieved from the Thames by the River Police, wilful damage. He was fined £2. The wreath, valued at £5, had been laid at the cenotaph by Herr Rosenberg on behalf of the German Führer. Mr Seymour Cocks was concerned about the likelihood of further 'incidents' and urged the Home Secretary to inform Rosenberg 'that we prefer his room to his company'.

On the same day in Berlin the British Ambassador, Sir Horace Rumbold, had an interview with the Führer. Hitler was enraged by the lenient sentence the English court had imposed on the desecrator of his wreath. Sir Horace informed him that there had been an unmistakable swing in English public opinion, based upon British concepts of freedom of the individual and consideration for other races.

The following day Mr Seymour Cocks's concern proved to have been well founded when a wax effigy was defaced at Madame Tussaud's. Red paint was poured over the head of the figure and ran down into the eyes and over the face, collar, tie, and uniform. A placard was hung around its neck: 'Hitler, the Mass Murderer'. Damage to the Nazi uniform was estimated to be about £10. Three men and a woman were arrested.

That day a leader in *The Spectator* commented on the spate of protest and appeared to confirm Sir Horace Rumbold's assertion:

> Herr Hitler's unofficial foreign secretary [Rosenberg] has been in London this week sounding British opinion regarding Germany. He can have had little difficulty reaching a conclusion. Rarely has this nation been more nearly of one mind on anything than it has been in reprobation of the excesses that have marked the political upheaval which Adolf Hitler has inspired.

It was probably about this time that people started spitting at Lewis's book. Although it was now two years old, following recent events in Germany *Hitler* was on prominent display in the window of Zwemmer's bookshop in the Charing Cross Road. It had acquired a belated topicality, and several times a day a shop assistant was sent out with a sponge to wipe saliva from the plate glass.

Lewis told Ernst Hanfstängl about what he assumed to be a demonstration of Communist disapproval.

American on his mother's side and Harvard-educated, Hanfstängl was

Hitler's Foreign Press Officer and intimate friend since 1922. He was a witty and entertaining companion and also an accomplished pianist, accustomed to giving nocturnal, private command performances when summoned to soothe his Führer after a tiring day. He was six foot four inches tall and so everyone called him 'Putzi', Bavarian dialect for 'little fellow'. He was in London about the same time as Rosenberg. There seem to have been a lot of Nazis in London that spring. Foreign opinion of the German regime was being energetically canvassed. Putzi had met Diana and Unity Mitford and promised them tickets to the party rally at Nuremberg. He also said he could arrange an audience with the Führer himself if the ladies would refrain from using lipstick for the occasion. He was also introduced to Lewis. Like Dr Thost, Putzi was impatient with Lewis's failure to fully appreciate the importance of the *Judenfrage*. When he heard the story about bookshop windows drenched in 'Red spittle', the gangling Nazi 'sprang up with a great "Ach Gott!" rushed to the other extremity of the room and back, in elephantine agitation . . . shaking an out-size fist in the direction of the Charing Cross Road. "Why do you call them Communists?" he roared. "Why don't you call them *Jews*!" '

*

Lewis and his wife moved from Ordnance Road in June to a pair of rooms and a kitchen at 21 Chilworth Road, Paddington. 'My secret address', he wrote to Geoffrey Grigson, 'do not leave this letter on your table.'

*

In late July Lewis entered into an agreement with the Leicester Galleries to produce work for a major painting exhibition in February of the following year. His last showing of paintings had been 'Tyros and Portraits' at the same gallery in 1921. The directors, Cecil Philips and Oliver Brown, advanced him £140 on delivery of the ten canvases he had already completed, together with ten drawings. These would be held as security. Brown suggested that the exhibition should consist of 'two or at the most, three large paintings out of a collection of twenty five . . . and a panel of selected drawings would be desirable in the interests of small collectors.' The gallery's commission on sales would be 33⅓ per cent. 'In the very unlikely event of the sum advanced not being recovered by sales, we should be entitled to take in settlement any of the paintings and drawings at 50% less than the agreed selling prices.' Brown and Philips also agreed to advance him a further £60 spread over the six months to February 1934.

The Leicester Galleries exhibition was considerably delayed and eventually opened over four years later in December 1937. The sum advanced in the interim was not recovered by sales.

*

Mary Russ visited him at 31 Percy Street to look at his paintings and to talk. She found it difficult to talk to him, she said, especially about things that mattered and that she needed to talk about: herself, her husband, her marriage. 'Talking nearly always involves dragging other people in', she wrote to him after one visit, 'I detest disloyalty and I don't know how to tell you a lot of things without seeming that to you, which I can't bear.' Later on, in letters he no longer replied to, she carried on trying to explain: 'ever since I was married . . . the real me went away I don't know where – anyway very far and I thought forever.'

Throughout July and August London baked in a record-breaking heatwave. Temperatures soared to 90 degrees Fahrenheit and drought threatened. In this pressurised atmosphere Mary developed a strange delusion. She wrote to Lewis in the middle of the night from the Gower Street flat:

> What has happened to you? All day yesterday I got it into my head you might be wandering about under Bedford Square! and the grids had got stuck in the heat so that you couldn't come up if you wanted to. I even went to look but there was no sign of you, only hot pavements and the dark heavy . . . tall trees and in their shade a few waifish orange tiger lilies, petals mostly on the ground.

And she had something else to tell him:

> . . . important – when can I come?

*

By September 1933 Lewis had still not returned Chatto's money and his old publishers were annoyed as news reached them of his continuing productivity. Another letter fluttered from solicitor to solicitor:

> In the Autumn Lists of Publishers there is a notice of a new book called 'One-Way Song' by Mr. Wyndham Lewis published by Faber & Faber at 7/6d with a special signed edition at £2.2.0. This has led our clients to enquire of us today what is the position in this matter and we have had to

334

inform them that no reply of any kind has been received to our letter to you of the 11th ultimo. You will realise that our clients are naturally very dissatisfied at this continued inattention on your client's part to his obligations to them . . . You will realise . . . that our clients cannot consent to be ignored in this way.

For some time before its publication in November, friends had been aware of Lewis's new excursion into satiric verse. He had read parts of it to Geoffrey Grigson over glasses of *crème de menthe* at a corner table in Frascati's and complained that Eliot had insisted he alter the line 'I belch, I brawl, I stink', to 'I belch, I brawl, I drink.' Hugh Gordon Porteus and, bizarrely, a flock of bleating sheep were audience to a reading of the entire typescript one afternoon in Kensington Gardens.

Apart from Eliot's punctilious objection to the word 'stink', rather surprising from the author of 'The Triumph of Bullshit' and 'The Ballad of Big Louise', Lewis was prevailed upon by Frank Morley of Faber to delete one entire canto from the middle poem of the sequence 'If so the man you are'. Morley clearly felt that, although the firm of Chatto & Windus was not mentioned by name in Canto XX, scurrilous references to 'A firm with whom I have some slight connection' might prove actionable. Lewis agreed to omit the offending 30-line section and sent Faber a telegram reading, 'Delete that canto Enemy', which was reproduced in its place.

Shortly after *One Way Song* was published, Herbert Read encountered Lewis by the ticket machine of Piccadilly tube station:

'I didn't know you wrote verse, Lewis.'
'I never knew it was so damned easy, Read.'

*

On Saturday morning, 18 November, Sidney Russ slipped a note under the door of 31 Percy Street. He was anxious to talk to Lewis and suggested a lunchtime rendezvous on Monday at Pagani's. In view of the increasingly eccentric letters he had been receiving from Mary Russ, Lewis cannot have been surprised at the 'matter of some importance' the Professor wished to discuss with him: that his domestic life was in crisis, his wife had 'chucked his ring back at him', had absconded and was naming Lewis as the object of her infatuation.

Lewis was sympathetic, but told Russ that the attraction was entirely on his wife's side and, shortly afterwards, in a letter Russ would later quote to his wife in an attempt to make her see reason:

you would I think be well advised to insist firmly upon the fact that she is
ill.

Having made the break, Mary stayed for a time with her sister in Leeds,
'Dodo' maintaining a frosty silence of disapproval at her leaving her
husband. It may have been during this strained interval that she sent Lewis
a single sheet of her sister's headed writing paper, blank except for twelve
meticulous lines of dots:

. . . .
... .
. . ..
. ...

. . ..
... .
. . . .
. . . .

. . . .
. . ..
... .
.. . .

It was a poem: each dot a letter, groups of dots forming words. There were
four lines of dots to a stanza; three stanzas; a poem encoded by her and
which only a recipient in psychic communion, perhaps, might decipher.
Lewis could not.

*

By 11 December 1933 Lewis was negotiating the outstanding rent on his
studio with Mr Clapham of Walter & Frederick Clapham, Manufacturing
Jewellers and landlords of 31 Percy Street: 'The rent for the last year', he
argued, 'was in excess a little of what would be the normal rent in this
difficult period for such premises.' He proposed that the £30 he owed be
reduced to £24, of which he would pay £6 immediately and the rest in
monthly instalments. He offered to remove his property from the room
there and then or else wait until Mr Clapham had got another tenant.

He planned to rent another studio after Christmas on his return from 'a
rapid trip around the European capitals'. Perhaps owing to his delicate
negotiations with the landlord and special pleadings over the rent, he was

anxious that no one should know he was leaving the country just at that time. 'Do not mention that I am going to Paris', he cautioned Richard Aldington.

*

Just before Christmas a solicitor's letter arrived at 4 bis rue Diderot, St-Germain-en-Laye, France, addressed to D. B. Wyndham Lewis Esq:

> We send you herewith copy of a letter we have today sent to Messrs Grayson & Grayson, Publishers of your Book called *Filibusters in Barbary* . . . It is manifest from a careful perusal of this book that it is permeated with libel matter of a most serious character concerning our Client, and we shall be glad to hear from you not later than next Wednesday morning what proposition you have put forward to compensate our client on a liberal basis before proceedings are instituted.

It was an easy enough mistake to make. The author of *Filibusters in Barbary* did not have a listing in *Who's Who* but his namesake did, and even that indispensable directory of notables was sometimes confused over which Wyndham Lewis was which. Soames, Edwards & Jones had consulted the 1932 edition of *Who's Who* to find out the defendant's address. In it the author of *A London Farrago*, *At the Sign of the Blue Moon* and *On Straw and Other Conceits* was credited also with *The Apes of God* and *Hitler*.

A week after the startled *Daily Mail* columnist had received the letter, Soames, Edwards & Jones had realised their mistake and a copy finally reached the person for whom it was intended via the Pall Mall Forwarding Company. It was, however, still addressed to D. B. Wyndham Lewis Esq.

Enclosed was a three-page letter which included extensive quotation from a chapter called 'The Filibuster of Tooting Beck' [*sic*] which Soames, Edwards & Jones maintained referred to their client Major Thomas Girdwood MacFie. The excerpts quoted referred to one of the British expatriates of Agadir as a 'middle-aged middle-class Bulldog Drummond of an ex-temporary Major . . . a house-agent of a peculiarly moroccan order'. The Major had recognised a libellous description of himself and instructed his solicitors to act against D. B. Wyndham Lewis Esq., the publishers Grayson & Grayson Ltd and the printers Kemp Hall Press Ltd.

Shortly thereafter Rupert Grayson sent the following distress signal to the 'Wyndham Lewis' most concerned:

> IMPORTANT . . . The man MacFie . . . is making lots of trouble. Can you give us the low down on him. We don't expect to get financial

assistance out of you but can you help us with information. He has issued his writ . . . S.O.S.

Grayson was being magnanimous. Under the contract for *Filibusters in Barbary* publisher and author were each liable to pay half of the costs which might arise 'where any matter contained in the said work shall be held to constitute a libel upon a person to whom it shall appear the author did not intend to refer'. Grayson was giving Lewis the benefit of the doubt as to whether he did or did not intend to refer to MacFie.

*

Lewis arrived in Berlin on the last night of 1933. It seemed as if the whole city was out of doors, celebrating in the snow. Once again he did the rounds of the publishing houses, thinking no doubt to spark interest in translation rights to his latest books. But New Year optimism seemed to be lacking in the book trade. There were no new publishers in Germany and the old ones were 'sulking in their tents, turning up their eyes in pious horror, quite resolved . . . to do nothing until the good old days return'. This mood was not surprising in view of the stranglehold that Dr Goebbels had placed on every aspect of the arts. In particular, no book could be published until it had first been submitted to the Propaganda Ministry for approval.

*

Lewis claimed that his gross income for the tax year which ended 5 April 1934 was £315. This comprised £150 advance from Cassell's for *Men Without Art*, £50 advance from Faber & Faber for *One Way Song*, £15 for a lecture in Oxford entitled 'Art in a Machine Age' and £100 advance from the Leicester Gallery 'in view of picture-exhibition, not yet held'. The true figure received from the gallery was in fact £200. His expenses came to £214 8s. There was £62 8s. studio rent and furnishing, £30 painting materials, £28 typing costs and writing materials, £24 for a work room, £35 travel expenses and £35 for books and periodicals. His net income for that year, taking into account the full advance from the Leicester Galleries, amounted to £200 12s.

The studio which accounted for £62 8s. in rent and furnishings was in Stratford Road, on the opposite side to the salubrious first-floor workspace he had rented in Alma Studios in 1921. Late in January, just back from Berlin, he summoned Grigson, 'and if he is free perhaps Stephen Spender'. The street entrance was impressive. A high gated arch surmounted by scrolled and florid plaques, 'Scarsdale Studios' flanked by emblems of

338

Painting and Sculpture, led through to a less impressive courtyard. Grigson and Spender, invited for 9.15 on Wednesday 7 February, found studio number 5 on the right with 'LEWIS' pinned to the door. 'No electric light inside. No furniture except three armchairs. Candles. Whiskey and glasses on a packing case. An easel in the background.' Lewis appeared harassed. The studio was damp.

*

When the case of MacFie against Wyndham Lewis and Others came before Mr Justice Acton on 23 February, MacFie's barrister clarified the confusion of identity in his opening remarks:

> The Defendants, Grayson & Grayson Ltd., are the Publishers and the Kemp Hall Press Ltd. are the printers of a book entitled Filibusters in Barbary by a Mr Wyndham Lewis, not, I understand, Mr D. B. Wyndham Lewis.

He briefly summarised the libel.

> In the Book there are descriptions which are capable of being understood to refer to Mr MacFie, and which were so understood, and they are in fact so grossly defamatory of him and hold him up to the greatest ridicule. It accuses him of defying the French Authorities and activities such as engaging in contraband traffic and smuggling arms and such like.

He went on to inform Mr Justice Acton that the publishers and printers of the libel had already agreed a settlement of £250 damages and 50 guineas costs, together with an apology to be made in court by their barrister. As well as making 'pecuniary compensation' to the plaintiff, the publishers had withdrawn the book from circulation.

The principal defendant himself was not present, nor was he represented. A 'notice of discontinuance' had been served on Lewis, which meant that MacFie's solicitors effectively dropped all claims against him. He escaped the proceedings without having to contribute to the compensation and costs. He did not apologise for the libel. All he had received from British publication of his book was an initial advance of £150, and now it had been withdrawn before any royalties could be earned.*

---

* Four months after *Filibusters in Barbary* was withdrawn and pulped, Grayson & Grayson tried to get some of their money back by siphoning off Lewis's profits from an earlier book: 'regarding royalties on *The Apes of God* and, as you know so well, the very heavy loss we were put to in connection with *Filibusters in Barbary*, we are holding the Royalties on *The Apes of God* in the hope that you are willing to help in this matter by kindly allowing these to be set off against the damages paid.' Lewis's reply has not been preserved.

*

Two days after the hearing Lewis began passing blood in his urine. He was admitted to the York Place Nursing Home in Baker Street at one in the morning and by 27 February was steeling himself for an operation. He was 52 years old. He explained his plight to Sir Nicholas Waterhouse in a note to be delivered in the event of his death under the knife:

> tonight the surgeon . . . thinks that it may be necessary to slit a little hole in the walls of my bladder to pull out a dried clot of blood. So just in case anything went wrong, I send you this, asking you to settle up immediate medical fees . . . and to look after in any way you are able or it occurs to you, my very much loved wife, Gladys Anne (who, in that unhappy event would send you this.)

THIRTY-THREE

The princess and the juggler

On the same day that the surgeon, Mr Millin, was considering whether or not to open Lewis's lower abdomen, the Professor of Physics at Middlesex Hospital wrote the artist an agitated letter. His wife's mental state was causing concern. 'Mrs Russ is threatened with delusional insanity and somehow or other we have got to save her.' He wanted Lewis to send a letter, in his own handwriting or else she would not believe it, assuring her that he felt nothing for her. 'It will be kind to be cruel', he added, 'it would be worse than useless to mince matters.'

Mary Russ was being cared for by the patient staff of the Tweedale Nursing Home, Tunbridge Wells. She made Lewis bookmarkers and wrote him letters late into the night:

> It's 4 o'clock and very quite; the only noise a sort of far off cawing – like ghost rooks . . . Every now and then a door opens or shuts and I can hear low talking; then quiet again.

She wrote him little poems – pieces of 'sugar' she called them – craving attention, begging for a response:

> Send me some roses or – some mignonette
> And all this bitterness will fade, forget
> Where I have failed you: if I have I have:
> Remember only all the love I gave.
> Send me some roses or – some mignonette.

And when no response came she hallucinated one:

> Such a queer thing happened here the other night – the rug in front of the french window was covered in roses! . . . every time I heard a noise in the night and I looked up some more came in! Somebody sending them in in shovelsful!

*

The note to Docker went undelivered. In March, Lewis was recuperating from the operation and writing to Richard Aldington about his surgical adventure:

> [It] enabled the surgeon to look with the naked eye into my bladder . . . the first man ever to do that! – and at last I know what has been the matter with me for a year and 4 months. It is not a malignant growth, I am glad to be able to tell you, or anything cancerous or tubercular; but internal varicose veins . . . – not at all pleasant, as you may guess, and the cauterising and cutting of them is going to be no joke.

An interval would have to elapse to allow him to recover from the blood loss before 'cauterising and cutting' could proceed. In the meantime, fearful that his creditors might get wind he was incapacitated and lay siege to his sick bed, he implored Aldington to maintain the usual secrecy:

> Please keep this address very dark – I am rather helpless at the moment and can only afford to let friends know my whereabouts – above all no duns!

Midway through March he was operated on again and the 'varicose veins' were cut and cauterised. Three days later, Professor Russ, still eager to gain Lewis's assistance in dealing with his wife, wrote heartily: 'They tell me you are doing well. Good.'

The patient replied: 'I cannot guess what reports you received . . . but all I do know is that I feel exceedingly ill.'

Lewis later became convinced he had been wilfully neglected by the surgeon who carried out this second operation. The neglect came as a result, he alleged, of an unpaid bill. Although Millin conducted the first exploratory operation in February the major remedial surgery in March was performed by a house surgeon. When Lewis received the bill he discovered that he was expected to pay for the work of more than one pair of hands. Even Russ was surprised. 'The pathologist yes', he agreed, 'but the idea of the house surgeon and the secretary getting a fee is quite new to me.' Since Lewis had originally contracted with Millin for his services, Russ told him, the surgeon had no right to employ someone else. His advice was to ignore the bill.

*

On Friday 30 March 1934 Ernest Hemingway and his wife called at Sylvia Beach's bookshop at 12 rue de l'Odéon. While the two women chatted,

Hemingway sat down to read the latest issue of *Life and Letters*. It contained a 13-page article by Wyndham Lewis called 'The Dumb Ox: A Study of Ernest Hemingway'. Despite the seemingly insulting title, the article began favourably enough with the statement: 'Ernest Hemingway is a considerable artist in prose fiction.'

The first signal Miss Beach received that Lewis's assessment displeased Hemingway was a loud snort. His face swelled and became purple. He threw *Life and Letters* on the floor, clenched his fists and looked for something to hit. A large bunch of red tulips stood in a vase on a table used to display modern fiction. The flowers had been a birthday present to Miss Beach, and Hemingway now started punching them. When he had decapitated the blooms he swiped at the vase, which overturned, flooded the table and smashed to the floor. Among the books lying in a puddle of water was Virginia Woolf's *Mrs Dalloway*. The two women mopped up while Hemingway sat down and silently wrote out a cheque for 1,500F before departing with his sodden purchases. The actual flood damage cost 1,000F and Miss Beach refunded the balance a couple of days later.

It was probably at the fifth page of 'The Dumb Ox' that Hemingway interrupted his reading to demolish the tulips. Lewis here embarked on an analysis of the American's prose style:

> He has suffered an overmastering influence, which cuts his work off from any other, except that of his mistress (for his master has been a mistress!). So much is this the case that their destinies (his and that of the person who so hypnotised him with her repeating habits and her faux-naif prattle) are for ever interlocked . . . But there it is: if you ask yourself how you would be able to tell a page of Hemingway, if it were unexpectedly placed before you, you would be compelled to answer, Because it would be like Miss Stein! And if you were asked how you would know it was not by Miss Stein, you would say, Because it would probably be about prize-fighting, war, or the bull-ring, and Miss Stein does not write about war, boxing or bullfighting!

'The Dumb Ox' formed the first chapter of Lewis's tenth book of the 1930s. *Men Without Art* was published in October 1934, its title a parody of Hemingway's book of stories about soldiers, pugilists and toreadors: *Men Without Women*.

*

Lewis left the York Place Nursing Home in the third week of April. By the beginning of May he was suggesting to Grigson, himself recently convalescent, that they lunch together at Frascati's:

> to celebrate on your side a recovery from alcoholic excesses but three weeks old; on my side, a recovery from excesses of a different order and of much longer ago than that!

But celebration was premature, recovery far from complete. Russ took advice from W. L. Webb-Johnson, 'no trifler', Lewis was assured, and 'not a man to beat about the bush'. The diagnosis, based upon the information Russ gave him, was not heartening. Although unable to give a definitive judgement without examining the patient, the consultant feared that unless he submitted to a further operation, the problems inherited from those long-ago excesses would inevitably recur. If Lewis had taken Russ's advice and allowed himself to be examined by Webb-Johnson, the shortcomings of his second operation might have been identified and a further two years of physical misery avoided. His response to the prospect of a third 'ordeal-by-the-knife', however, was to leave well alone.

*

The rent on a workroom must have proved too great a burden during his illness and he was forced to abandon number 5 Scarsdale Studios before he had even settled in. Until September his only work space would be the small back bedroom at Chilworth Street. He wrote on a pad on his knee, with his papers and books laid out on the bed and his inkpot by his side on a stool.

*

Early in June, Lady Cholmondely suggested an evening's entertainment to brighten up his convalescence. She had secured him a ticket for Oswald Mosley's 'circus' on the 7th. Her brother and a friend were going and they proposed having a light supper of 'zakuskis' at Her Ladyship's home around 7.15, leaving for Olympia at 7.40.

It is unlikely that Lewis took advantage of his ticket to the British Union of Fascists rally. Had he done so, then reference to this infamous event would certainly have been made in one or other of the books he published in the latter half of the 1930s. As it was, he would have had to rely upon accounts at second hand, such as that of Naomi Mitchison, a left-wing observer, who found herself surrounded by Mosleyite sympathisers. They bayed and hooted as blackshirted stewards beat up hecklers and threw them down flights of steps. Women protesters were grabbed and bundled out of the hall with their arms knotted behind their backs. Mrs Mitchison rather courageously entered into debate with one of the Mosleyites:

'You call yourself a gentleman ... do you like this sort of thing?'
He turned round. 'Yes, I do, I am enjoying myself! Do you want some of it yourself? Blackshirts! Here is another of them, turn her out!'
'How can you enjoy seeing people being hurt? I was a nurse during the war.'
'Yes, and I was an officer!'

She noticed that the stewards could be divided into two distinct classes: 'toughs', possessed of the nearest she had ever seen to the 'criminal face', and 'nice, blond, romantic-looking boys, not much over twenty ... able to worship a leader.' Fortunately for her, the two blackshirts summoned by the ex-officer turned out to be of the latter sort and she was left unmolested.

She found political arguments with Lewis rather trying too. She apologised on one occasion for becoming upset when he responded to her experience at Olympia by badgering her with counter-evidence of Communist brutality. 'If you want to talk about who interrupted who's meetings', she told him:

you must give me notice so that I can produce figures! ... One knows there are bloody people on both sides, and whether there are a few hundred more or less in London ... in one kind of shirt or another, doesn't matter an awful lot.

There was another female acquaintance of Lewis's who almost certainly did not attend the rally in Earl's Court that night, despite the fact that she had, like the 'romantic-looking boys', fallen under Sir Oswald Mosley's spell. Discharged from the Tweedale Nursing Home in Tunbridge Wells, Mary Russ was in Coniston throughout June, but a single-page fragment of a letter shows that she had become a member of the British Union of Fascists:

it's big enough to take in everything. I do hope I'm not following an illusion – it seems *now* to be the one thing that I have wanted to be in all my life. Something that's not material, something to aim at and somebody really worth following and admiration.

She complained that her sister in Leeds had disapproved of her 'silly little WAW' and that now she had joined the BUF, 'Dodo' had 'not said one

345

word or taken the tiniest bit of interest.' Extremist politics, so much more glamorous than Women Against War, was clearly filling a gap in her life:

'Dodo . . . knows how hard I've tried . . . but O Lewis I am so lonely.

*

Lewis had met Mosley for the first time the previous year – Mrs Mitchison having arranged an appointment – and thought him 'a good fellow'. During 1934 their association was an excuse for cloak-and-dagger theatricals. 'Wyndham Lewis used to come to see me in most conspiratorial fashion', Sir Oswald recalled, 'at dead of night with his coat collar turned up. He suggested that he was in fear of assassination, but the unkind said he was avoiding his creditors.' Lewis produced an ink portrait drawing of Mosley in blackshirt uniform, beetle-browed and prognathous. About the same time he made a companion drawing of Sir Stafford Cripps, Labour Member of Parliament, Communist sympathiser and co-founder of the Socialist League, wearing steel-rimmed spectacles and a frosty curl to the lip. 'The Governess and the Gorilla', Mosley commented when he saw the two portraits. Lewis seemed displeased. 'I found him agreeable but touchy', the Fascist leader remembered.

The drawings were published, facing one another across a two-page spread of the *London Mercury*, in October 1934. 'Two Dictators' was the caption.

*

Six months after leaving the York Place Nursing Home, Lewis was still being pressed for settlement of his outstanding bill. Eventually Russ helped out. 'I hate to think of you labouring to meet the fee of any surgeon. I am venturing to enclose a small contribution.'

But Russ's 'small contribution' was not, after all, used to pay the house surgeon who, Lewis believed, deliberately neglected his defaulting patient. 'I have suffered in the most awful way for that neglect', he wrote two years later. 'A few weeks of intensive treatment at the right moment . . . and I . . . should not have wasted a year of my life and endured every kind of anxiety and physical misery.'

In his letter thanking Russ for the cheque, he added 'please come round and see me some evening in my new flat (of which I am rather proud) . . . We shall be alone and can have a good talk.' The new address was 121 Gloucester Terrace, just around the corner from Chilworth Street, where his wife still kept house and where he ate and slept. For the first time since having to abandon 5 Scarsdale Studios he had a small workroom. It measured 13½ feet by 10½ and cost one hundred pounds a year.

*

Mary Russ was still writing to him. Sometimes her letters rambled over a dozen pages. Lacking both salutation and signature they were sections of a seamless monologue interrupted only by postage. Sometimes, desperate and agonised by some imagined slight, they were short:

> Cruel devil. It wasn't even clever to mesmerise even for a few years a thing so moth eaten and already hurt. Anyone could have done it if they had tried as hard as you did. Cruel devil.

She seemed under no illusions about the value he placed upon her outpourings. 'I'm sending you . . . all this rubbish. After all it's your own fault and you must suffer it – you can burn it easily enough unread if you'd rather.' But he kept everything, sometimes typing out the shorter notes as if preserving evidence:

> Coming to see you tomorrow I can't bear it any longer. *Don't* let the door be locked. Its thousands and thousands of years since then. I shall be there soon after 5 . . . If you are busy at that minute I can wait. Only *don't* let the door be locked.

The envelope was postmarked 'Leeds 13 August' and 'London 14 August' and delivered to the long-abandoned studio in Percy Street. It was forwarded to Lewis's solicitors in Essex Street and from thence to the Pall Mall Safe Deposit with a final postmark of 20 September.

If she did come to visit him in Percy Street that Tuesday afternoon in mid-August, following her train journey from Leeds, she would have got no response from the bell marked 'Love'. The door would, after all, have been locked. It might have been then, in that London street off Tottenham Court Road, that she saw the bird scarers.

Since first meeting Lewis she had experienced the pleasures and pains of hopeless infatuation. 'I thought my body was dead,' she once wrote to him:

> it ought to be I suppose and yet just last night . . . I woke. The window places were light grey though the room dark; the moon behind the clouds I suppose; hidden anyway. A light cool breeze came in on my face and

before I realised anything clearly, you were with me. O Lewis yes. I
thought all that was part of life – to be endured – but last night, last night.

But the paranoiac suspicion that he was mocking her, having locked the door
to 31 Percy Street against her, 'turned heaven into hell' and everyday reality
became a nightmare:

Every pane of glass in that hateful street had a thing like they hang in
gardens to frighten birds away: a tin cat's face with glass eyes and grinning
and every single one of them was you or so like you I couldn't tell the
difference.

*

The idea of a collaborative book was first discussed by Lewis and Naomi
Mitchison in May. 'If we did do it', she told him, 'I should think the best
thing would be for you to do the pictures and me to write the fairy story
around them.' Some time later she suggested a title and theme:

Au dela de cette Limite, or Beyond this Limit, like in the metros – tickets,
you remember, aren't [valid], and there might be a story in the place
beyond where one's ideas don't hold.

They worked at the book throughout the autumn. It was an amicable
collaboration despite ideological polarity. At one point her writing stalled:

I find the next bit difficult, mostly because it should, in the scheme I have
in mind, be political, but it obviously can't be in this collaboration,
because you and I have definitely opposed ideas. This can't be helped, and
you are a sufficiently great man to be what you please, but it's no good
pretending that we can touch on all subjects so I have to get round it
somehow.

She recalled that they worked with the enthusiasm of children. 'It was the
greatest fun . . . I think it was my idea to start with but it developed jointly.
I did the writing and he did the pictures but he came more and more into
the story as we went on.' Sometimes the pictures followed the writing,
sometimes the writing the pictures. The story evolved as a metaphor of their
collaboration:

There were two main characters, Phoebe who is me, is usually drawn in a
wide-skirted, unfashionable, not to say highbrow dress which I used to
wear at the time with a handkerchief knotted over my head . . . The ticket

348

collector, who is also Hermes the guide of souls becomes increasingly clearly a self-portrait.

At the end, the narrative complete and the ticket collector bidding her farewell, Phoebe grasps him by the lapels: 'No! . . . We've worked together . . . You can't leave me like this! I won't let you go.'

There was a difference of opinion at this point, as to how the book should finish. Mitchison held out for her favoured ending: the peaceful, seemingly endless descent by lift to the Kingdom of the Dead. Lewis, on the other hand, had favoured an explosive climax with the lift and everyone in it being inexplicably blasted to pieces.

*

In November, while completing the series of thirty Indian ink illustrations to *Beyond This Limit*, Lewis was asked to collaborate on another fairy story:

Once upon a time there was a poor though very gifted juggler. Now he used to go just where he willed, generally with laughter in his heart, but frequently with scorn upon his lips, and gave his exhibitions of skill for he had his daily bread to earn. One day a Princess happened to pass when he was in the middle of one of his juggling acts and she felt fascinated for this was something the Princess had never seen before, though she had often read about such performances . . . Now the Princess was married, though her husband was not in fact a prince at all, but spent his time over things which she wasn't very much interested in, though he seemed very much wrapt up in them. And one day her husband looked up from his work expecting to find the Princess in the garden where she much delighted to be. But to his surprise and concern she could not be found . . . As a matter of fact she was looking on at the juggler once more, still more fascinated than before and in fact she could not get the glitter out of her eyes, so light and bright were the gems which he tossed into the air. And now the juggler himself noticed the Princess among his audience. Previously he had not seen her, for good jugglers have no eyes for their audience only an ear for their applause. But something shining about the Princess brought her into the ambit of the juggler's vision . . . And on that day when he had finished a particularly brilliant act of juggling . . . he sought her and spoke certain words to her and an even lovelier light shone in her eyes than had ever shone there before. And on that same day her husband found her in the garden transplanting some lilies that had long wanted just that bit of attention from her and the children when they saw her wondered where she had been but like children they soon gave up wondering and were quite content to listen to her ghost stories as of yore.

Professor Russ arrived at Chilworth Street with a family friend on the evening of 13 November. Hester Gorst was a QC's wife, a dilettante painter and writer. After chatting for a while about pictures and books Russ blurted out the purpose of their mission. A 'psychological experiment' was proposed, 'to be clothed in symbolic language', in an attempt to bring Mrs Russ to her senses. If the object of Mary's obsession would consent to, as it were, enter the romantic world of that obsession and send her the Professor's concocted fable of Princess and Juggler as if it were his own, the estranged wife might be persuaded to return to her family. Mrs Gorst thought that the situation should be handled 'as if one were dealing with a child'.

Lewis felt he had been trapped into an acutely embarrassing position, being already financially obligated to Russ. He also bridled at the figure he cut in the Professor's fairy story. 'Of course I am poor', he told him, 'although as little a music hall comedian as you are the Prince of Wales – and after two years of illness, culminating in a major operation, very poor, instead of just poor.' But it was the suspicion that Russ was calling in favours for his generosity that particularly distressed and humiliated him. 'Had I realised that what I took to be your disinterested help was in some way a bribe for services of the nature you have divulged tonight, I should never, however hard up, have accepted them.' He was also mistrustful about the efficacy of the 'psychological experiment' itself:

> You say that your wife should be treated as a child, under the circumstances: well, if you show weakness where a child is concerned, and invariably fall in with its whims, is it not likely to ask more and more for what is so easily obtained? Is there ever any end to the demands of a spoilt child – and those who are suffering from delusions of any sort are notoriously apt to plot to contrive that things shall conform to their delusions. If, however, you are persuaded that everything, even psycho-analysis, should be tried, would it not be better to consult some not-too-bogus practitioner of that science, rather than resort to amateur intervention?

With or without Lewis's 'amateur intervention', about two weeks later a tentative reconciliation was effected between the Professor and his wife. This did not mark the end of Mary's obsessive interest in Lewis, however. As late as July of the following year she was still pestering him with letters.

Later she haunted his sleep and the dream was recorded on canvas. In 1936 he began work on a painting which now exists only in ghostly photographic monochrome. A robed figure stands with three smaller figures to either side and behind. In the background, in the top left corner of the canvas, a jumble of spherical and ovoid forms that might be other figures spill from a shadowy opening. The upper right corner looks as if it has been ripped away like part of a painted backdrop, leaving a jagged tear line and revealing beyond a single-masted sailboat tossed between turbulent sea and sky. Through this jagged hole, as if from one world to another, a bird flies away. One of the small foreground figures turns its head to look after the bird and holds another bird cradled between hands and forearms. Across the lower third of the picture shreds of mist pass in front of the figures. The three attendants possess the familiar ball heads of other compositions of the period, but the leftward-tilted face of the central figure, revealed by a hand drawing aside its cowl, and gazing directly out of the picture, is something more than a cipher.

The canvas was exhibited at the Leicester Galleries in December 1937 and Lewis explained, in the catalogue foreword, how it came to be painted:

> the Departure of a Princess from Chaos is the outcome of a dream. I dreamed that a Princess, whose particularly graceful person is often present in the pages of our newspapers, was moving through a misty scene, apparently about to depart from it, and with her were three figures, one of which was releasing a pigeon. This dream, with differences, was repeated, and it was so vivid that, having it in my mind's eye as plainly as if it were present to me, I painted it. As to the resemblance of the figure in the canvas to the princess in question . . . the likeness is not material, and I have seen nothing but press pictures of my dream 'model'.

The 'graceful person' referred to was the Greek-born Princess Marina, who had married Prince George, becoming Duchess of Kent in September 1934.

It is entirely credible that a dream was the genesis of the painting; it is equally possible that at one level at least of Lewis's unconscious mind, the ubiquitous Duchess of Kent was his 'dream model'. But a photograph of Mary Russ, with her baby daughter on the beach at Walberswick in the early 1920s, a little over a decade before Lewis met her, bears an astonishing resemblance to the 'Princess' in the painting. Faces do not change fundamentally in ten years and the line of cheek, chin and jaw is unmistakable. Sidney Russ's 'Princess' emerging from the chaos of her 'delusional insanity', surrounded perhaps by her children, inspired both recurring dream and subsequent canvas. Some time after it was exhibited, Lewis painted out the picture.

Another painting, *The Room that Mary lives in,** shows an interior

---

* Completed and dated 1949, exhibited at the Redfern Gallery that year but almost certainly begun much earlier. *The Room that Mary Lives in* (30″ × 20″) was until 5 June 1992 in the possession of the Vermilion County Museum Society, Illinois. It was auctioned at Christie's but failed to fetch its reserve.

cluttered with the strange abstract forms commonly found in Lewis's imaginative compositions of the 1930s. In the middle ground sits a female figure dressed in a turquoise gown decorated with black wedges. The style is similar to a figure he drew for *Beyond This Limit*. The featureless head inclines to the left at an angle echoing the heads of two ball-jointed lay figures sitting side by side in the background as if keeping the central figure under surveillance. On her left, in the centre of a small round table, stands a bowl of red and white flowers, 'some roses or some mignonettes'. Among the abstract shapes that loom from the dark recesses of the interior, a glowing spot of the same bright red as the flowers forms the boss of a round medieval shield. The autumnal tones of the background range from dark umber through brick red to brilliant yellow ochre; this last slashed through by a vertical, silvery wedge of the palest blue and white which exactly bisects the upper third of the composition: an opening to the light beyond the room. Continuing the analogy of shield and fairy-tale princess, this might be a tall lancet castle window. Or, perhaps, an escape route similar to the 'tear' in the *Departure of a Princess from Chaos*. At the feet of the female figure is a pool of light, a sketchily painted chaotic swirl of letters and crumpled paper.

Even without knowledge of Mary Russ's breakdown, her haunted existence, loneliness and compulsive letter-writing, Naomi Mitchison thought the picture terrifying: 'at least to me; I have plenty of nightmares of my own.'

*

His 'Princess' returned, Professor Russ's domestic life approached normality. There were still rows: once she called him a 'rhinoceros headed idiot', and on another occasion actually thumped him. But life went on much as before, with the healthy difference that she now shouted 'rhinoceros headed idiot' at him instead of only thinking it, which did not keep the peace, her husband observed philosophically, but at least it cleared the air.

Lewis kept a large sheaf of Mary's letters but eventually surrendered, at her husband's request, a package of papers, including two exercise books, that she had sent him from the Lake District. Professor Russ received the 'Coniston papers' in late February 1935. It is not known what the two exercise books contained, and Russ took measures to ensure that it never would be known. 'Thank you for your letter and separate packet', he wrote to Lewis, 'the latter has been consigned to the flames already.'

The rest of Mary's letters remained in Lewis's possession until his death. They were not among the first collection of manuscripts that his widow sold to Cornell University in 1960. Nor were they included in the final batch of papers gathered together by Omar S. Pound on behalf of the Wyndham Lewis Memorial Trust and dispatched to Cornell when Mrs Lewis was admitted to a nursing home in 1977, a year and a half before her death. In the shambles of her Torquay flat, Mr Pound glanced briefly at the often unsigned, inadequately paginated ramblings that remained as evidence of Mary Russ's pathetic infatuation. He decided that, whether or not these outpourings were of the remotest interest to the future generations of scholars who would trawl that archive in upstate New York for insights into Wyndham Lewis's contribution to 20th-century art and literature, for the time being at least they were 'nobody else's damned business'. He placed them among the small pile of sensitive, potentially embarrassing or otherwise unclassifiable material to which public access would be denied for the foreseeable future. That cache of papers was then placed in the care of the Trust's solicitors where, in the battered black metal deeds box, they remain to this day.

*

On 13 December 1934, Professor Russ paid Lewis £26.5.0 for the 30 original ink drawings illustrating Naomi Mitchison's modern fairy story *Beyond This Limit*, published by Jonathan Cape in the spring of the following year.

THIRTY-FOUR

'Anything but a Jubilee year'

1935 began well. In January it seemed as if Lewis's five-year-old manuscript of *The Roaring Quean* was finally to be published. Unaccountably retitled *Foul Play's a Jewel*, it was accepted by Wren Howard of Jonathan Cape on terms considerably less extravagant than the £200 Lewis had demanded of Desmond Harmsworth in 1932 for this problematic little satire on the book trade. It had already been rejected by several publishers:

> in the nature of things the *small* publisher would be afraid of publishing it for fear of offending his big colleagues, and . . . the big publisher would hardly feel very genial about it. [Jonathan Cape] on the other hand, were one of the 2 or 3 publishers in London who still stuck to a high standard of publishing, and so might do it . . . Such a book, going to the 'fiction-critic' for review, could not be expected to meet with a very cordial reception; the popular libraries could not be expected to coo over it; so its publishers could not be expected to pay anything to speak of for it.

It was on the basis of such reasoning that Lewis accepted Cape's offer: a modest advance of £30, to be paid on the day of publication.

The manuscript was still unfinished and Wren Howard suggested that an extra 10,000 words would add 'a little more substance'.

Lewis was also struggling with his third book for Cassell: *False Bottoms*. He had recommended writing the novel the previous October, having settled in to his workroom in Gloucester Terrace. 'I had not had a day's holiday since my operation', he told Desmond Flower:

> so was not perhaps as fresh as I might be, but full time work began. It was my hope that I should be able to take up and complete, in intervals of the drudgery of articles, the novel for you. But that has been far more difficult than I had supposed.

Flower was magnanimous. 'I will not trouble you unduly in the matter of the novel, but know that we can rely upon you to let us have it as soon as it is possible for you to do so.'

On the other hand, by March Wren Howard was becoming mildly restive about the Cape novel, which had now reverted to its original title. He wanted to know an exact date for delivery of the complete manuscript of *The Roaring Quean* before making plans for its publication.

By the end of April, work on *False Bottoms* was going well. Selected friends were favoured with bulletins and occasional readings. The book's progress was enthusiastically charted by Russ:

> it is nothing less than splendid news that you are glorying in a burst of work with people not bothering you – you already whet the appetite about what is going to be in the pot.

At ten o'clock on the night of 30 April, Lewis's clipped nasal voice was broadcast on the BBC's National Programme. The talk was the fifth in a series of thirteen called *Freedom*. 'You were very good,' Professor Russ told him:

> But why so short? I don't think you took more than 18 minutes. I expected 30. However, that's over and you will have the freedom to turn to what interests you more, because after all you can't be very creative on the wireless.

Previous speakers had been Sir Ernest Benn, J. L. Garvin, The Right Honourable Herbert Morrison and J. A. Spender. The 13 talks, 'which were considered too valuable to be allowed to fade away on the ether', were published in a single volume by George Allen & Unwin the following year.

Work continued on *False Bottoms*. 'I can only say that I have been very glad to see your star brighten week after week', Russ enthused. 'And when you say you are at work I can hear an anvil ringing.'

On 21 June he was on the wireless again, this time in a series called *Among the British Islanders*. Eminent speakers were asked to give an account of some aspect of British life from the perspective of a visitor from Mars. 'Art and Literature: A Martian reviews our books' was the penultimate lecture of seven. Under the comic pseudonym G. R. Schjelderup, Lewis gently satirised George Bernard Shaw, H. G. Wells, D. H. Lawrence, and James Joyce:

> I bought his latest masterpiece the other day . . . it was completely incomprehensible. I showed it to the waiter at my hotel. He assured me that he could not understand a single line of it. I asked him if it was English, and he said no . . . I asked him if he thought it might be Irish: and he said that he did not know any Irish, but that it might be that.

'Your stuff was really very good on the wireless tonight', Russ congratulated him. 'Hitting the nail on the head every time.'

*

July was suffocatingly humid and the Lewises' living quarters in Chilworth Street were far from satisfactory 'When it rains the water pours into the top floor of this accursed maisonette', he complained. Perhaps as a result of these swampy conditions, he fell ill again. 'I am . . . laid on my back by a chill which has taken the form of a mild cystitis' he told an Inland Revenue official in explanation for his failure to submit tax returns for 1932. 'In a few days . . . I shall be in full working order again.'

His prognosis was optimistic however. This recurrence of urethral infection was to put him out of action for the best part of three months.

Professor Russ introduced him to a new medical man: Dr Ian McPherson, 'a sound fellow', and assured him he was in 'competent and scrupulous hands'. He urged him 'to quell that spirit of damn-it-all-ness, get into and out of the hands of reliable medicos as soon as possible and then a holiday.' Russ even promised him financial assistance towards a recuperative trip to Germany when he felt better. When ready for such assistance Lewis was to wire a coded message which would appear to concern hospital business:

REQUEST FOR RADON SUSTAINED MIDDLESEX

The Professor's wife was still apt to intercept any undisguised communication from Lewis.

*

On the afternoon of Wednesday 28 August he entered St Peter's Hospital for Stone and other Urinary Diseases, in Henrietta Street, Covent Garden. It was 'a first class nuisance' but there was 'no help for it.' He was assured there would no question of his having to undergo an operation and that his stay in St Peter's was for the greater convenience of the treatment:

> As I have the infection, the treatment has to be gone about more cautiously, and I have to be where I can receive more constant professional attention than would otherwise be the case. Alas, it is of critical importance that I should have the curative process – made necessary by long neglect – speeded up.

Mr Andrews, his surgeon, estimated the treatment would take about a week. Lewis wrote to Russ the day he was admitted, asking him to visit. 'I am a little nervous about being in a hospital, I confess.'

Russ sent him roses and promised to visit the following week. But by the time he rang the hospital on Sunday to see how he was, 'the bird had flown.' Lewis had discharged himself.

*

By mid-September he seemed fully recovered. There was no sign of the infection and, following a further visit to his surgeon, he anticipated the remainder of the treatment would be of a fairly routine nature. Russ, after paying his children's school fees and consulting his accounts, found he had a small balance which he was willing to share: he sent Lewis a cheque for £25. 'I hope you won't think this an excess of meanness on my part, but I do also get hard up sometimes.' He was also able, the following month, to put a minor portrait commission Lewis's way. 'It might not interest you frightfully', he told him, 'but it would certainly mean a few guineas.'

His sister-in-law, Dr Priestley, wished to present portrait drawings of two former headmistresses as a gift to Leeds Girls High School. One was a woman of 73 with 'a live, mobile face', the other was 60, 'good featured, infinitely more difficult to catch'.

It would still be necessary to conduct the transaction in absolute secrecy to avoid pursuit by Mrs Russ. 'Madame might get news from her sister as to where the sitters were going to', Russ cautioned:

> in fact if she were very keen on finding out she might go to the sitters themselves – but there are ways of circumventing. You could meet sitters at their London hotel and take them to [the] studio and [she] would not know where they were – all sorts of ways will suggest themselves to you I expect.

Whatever methods finally suggested themselves for smuggling the two elderly ladies into Lewis's presence – at an 'address to be kept in the strictest confidence', they had been told – portrait drawings of Miss Helena Powell and Miss Low were completed by the end of the year.

Lewis was probably not told about the aftermath: how 'Dodo' and Mrs Kirk, the then head mistress, presented the drawings at a meeting of the school governors and how the governors carped and criticised and eventually sent for Miss Harwood the art mistress to give an opinion. Professor Russ's daughter, who remembers the story, has no idea why Miss

Harwood advised them not to accept Dr Priestley's gift, 'but that was her advice and they took it.'*

*

That year the nation celebrated King George V's quarter-century on the throne. In a letter to Lewis in December, referring to the artist's three months of poor health, Professor Russ commented ruefully: 'Well, 1935 has been anything but a Jubilee year for you, and so I wish you better luck in 1936.' The year to come, however, was to be considerably less of a Jubilee even than the last.

*

Desmond Flower had received the manuscript of *False Bottoms* in November. Following the loss of profits occasioned by the circulating library embargo on *Snooty Baronet* three years before, Cassell & Co. were anxious to avoid giving costly offence to Smiths and Boots again. Accordingly Lewis's typescript was subjected to an in-house vetting and he was asked to alter anything that might cause problems. To begin with, the overly suggestive title *False Bottoms* was dispensed with and it became instead *The Revenge for Love*. When completely confident that the novel would not offend, Flower submitted it to Mr Richardson, the reader from Boots.

*

By the middle of April Lewis had finished a political book for Jonathan Cape. Called *Bourgeois-Bolshevism and World War* at this stage, it would be published in June as *Left Wings Over Europe*. The typescript of *The Roaring Quean* was also finished for Cape.

Meanwhile Cassell & Co. were holding up production of *The Revenge for Love* until the Boots representative had passed it as suitable for the circulating library readership. Desmond Flower was anxiously awaiting Mr Richardson's report. 'The . . . avoidance of any difficulty with Boots', he told Lewis, 'has always been . . . regarded as one of our first cares.' But when the report arrived it was 'extremely unfavourable' and unless further changes were made the book would be condemned to the same fate as *Snooty Baronet*, its sales effectively halved. Without telling the author about the reader's report, Flower passed the typescript to the man who had originally

* Dr Priestley and Mrs Kirk kept one each. The portrait of Miss Helena Powell now belongs to Leeds City Art Gallery. That of Miss Low is still privately owned by the Russ family.

introduced Lewis to the firm of Cassell, in the hope that he might be able to suggest changes.

So on the morning of 6 May Lewis was startled to receive a note from A.J.A. Symons congratulating him upon the novel, which he had just finished reading. 'It was with mixed feelings that I received your . . . letter', Lewis replied, 'great satisfaction to learn that you should have approved of my Mss., but less satisfaction to find that its journey to the printing-works was apparently as far off as ever.' He was dismayed at the hint, contained in Symons's second paragraph, that further alterations were to be demanded of him. There were 'one or two points' that Symons would like to talk over, and could he 'spare the time to come in for a glass of Sherry and half an hour's discussion?'

Lewis was particularly stung that he had been kept in the dark about Richardson's report and refused to discuss changes with Cassell's intermediary. The relationship with his publisher, embarked on with such optimism five years before, was rapidly souring. Everyone concerned was dissatisfied. Lewis claimed to have had 'nothing but disappointment and difficulties' from the firm, Desmond Flower felt that the association had 'been attended by nothing but disagreement', while his father seemed anxious to be rid of the new novel altogether. 'I think it is the whole note of the book which is wrong for Cassell's', he told Lewis, with evident embarrassment:

> Put plainly, I do not think it is any good to you or to Cassell's for the book to come out from this House, because I do not think it is a book Cassell's would do well with. As you know, certain publishers do well with certain types of books, and not with others.

*

At the end of May Lewis sold his Edith Sitwell portrait to the Leicester Galleries for £50. It had been abandoned in 1923 with the head complete, the coat largely finished and the legs in position. He had taken it up again some time in 1935, providing its background of formalised books, and pale blue and dark to light shaded grey panels. The coat was completed and the brightly coloured sleeves covering the forearms painted. In what might have been a vindictive slight upon an old enemy, the sitter's delicate and highly prized hands, the only part of her anatomy of which she was truly proud, were noticeably absent from the composition.

At 121 Gloucester Terrace he painted in a room, not a studio, with the canvas propped up on a chair. He was preparing as best he could for the long overdue Leicester Galleries show. But by early July he was working in increasing physical discomfort.

The cause of the problem was once again related to the diverticulum in the urethral wall inflicted three years before by a clumsily applied catheter. As urine seeped in and stagnated behind the stricture, this diverticulum had become the site of periodic infections ever since. The last, treated at St Peter's Hospital, under Mr Andrews, had been 12 months before. But now the condition had become exacerbated and Mr Millin prepared him for an exploratory operation, at All Saints Hospital in Lambeth, involving 'the necessary dilatation of the stricture and enlarging of the opening of the diverticulum . . . combining this with the X-ray'. The urinary tract, with all its natural and unnatural crevices and detours, was to be flooded with dye for the X-ray. It required two or three days in hospital at the most and Millin booked him a room from 7 July.

What showed on the X-ray would have been a roughly Y-shaped line of dye marking the track of the urethra itself and the blind branch of the diverticulum leading off it. The neck of the diverticulum had narrowed with scar tissue to such a degree that the morbid growth of necrotic tissue, produced by the infection, and its expanding reservoir of pus, had become sealed in the cul-de-sac. Denied a passage back into the urethra, it would follow the line of least resistance: burrowing down through the fatty tissue to the perineum, emerging, if unchecked, just behind the scrotum.

Lewis had been sitting upon an abscess Millin described as 'the size of a duck's egg'. He was advised that, if it were to burst, it would certainly kill him.

*

In June, Jonathan Cape had published *Left Wings Over Europe*, having 'pulled every available string' to get it favourably reviewed. With a pre-publication subscription of 500 copies, the book promised to do reasonably well. Included in a list of the author's books printed opposite the title page was: 'THE ROARING QUEAN (in preparation)'.

On 22 July Neuman Flower saw an opportunity to rid Cassell of the troublesome *Revenge for Love*. 'I see that you have published a book with Jonathan Cape', he wrote to Lewis:

I am wondering, therefore, whether you feel you could agree to Cape taking over the novel we have . . . This is only a suggestion on my part with a view to a friendly solution which shall be as satisfactory to yourself as ourselves.

*

360

Draining the abscess was a simple operation but as Lewis could not, on this occasion, afford a private room he was forced to endure the democracy of a crowded general ward and the grim nocturnal eavesdroppings upon other diseased lives and deaths. 'I still can hear the soft thudding rush of the night nurses,' he wrote in 1950:

> when certain signs appraised them of the approaching end. For some reason it was preferred that death should occur in another ward, reserved for the purpose. The patient would be hurriedly wheeled out to die. Though I saw death often enough as a soldier, that was the only occasion on which I heard the authentic death-rattle.

The name and location of the institution is not known. 'Somewhere in hospital land', he wrote at the top of a letter to Eliot on Friday 31 July. The previous Monday he had again submitted to the knife. 'Operated on . . . satisfactorily I think', the bulletin continued. 'My diverticulum is no more. I feel very fine indeed, but am of course in rather low water for the present.' The surgeon told Mrs Lewis that it was remarkable her husband had survived the physical strains of the last three years. 'He must be very strong', he told her.

Removal of the abscess left a fistula 3 millimetres in diameter in the perineal region between anus and scrotum. It would be referred to in the pathologist's post-mortem report twenty years later.* 'The scrotum', Lewis wrote to Grigson when once more at large again:

> and the surrounding areas is a part of the body to which my attention has been repeatedly called of late. Hang on to your balls . . . whatever happens! Even if not in constant use, they are essential to the equipment of any self-respecting freebooter.

*

In the middle of August Rupert Hart-Davis, the son of Sybil Hart-Davis, and Wren Howard's fellow director at Jonathan Cape, sent Lewis proofs of *The Roaring Queen*. He was puzzled by the change of spelling:

> When we first had the beginning of the MS you spelt it Quean, but I see that you have now changed it to Queen. I can't help preferring the former, but if you think the latter is better we will, of course, leave it at that.

---

* Also noted there was the fact that his prostate gland had been removed, probably at the same time as the abscess.

But towards the end of the month, as he read his own set of proofs, Hart-Davis was beginning to have more serious doubts than about the variant spelling of a slang term for effeminate homosexual. One particular sentence raised concerns that the conjunction of the Russian secret police with a similar-sounding name to Victor Gollancz would be too easily recognised as representing the left-wing publisher whose professional connection with Gerald Gould, chief novel-critic on the *Observer*, was equally well known. The sentence ran:

> There is Geoffrey Bell who is reader for *Hector Gollywog and Ogpu*, who in his capacity of novel-critic of the *Sunday Messenger* writes the most glowing accounts of the books that reach him as critic from the firm to which he belongs, as reader.

It was, thought Hart-Davis, 'highly amusing' but 'a bit too near the real thing'. He asked Lewis to modify the sentence to something 'no less amusing, but less libellous'. The author's reputation for attracting writs was clearly causing alarm bells to ring in the house of Jonathan Cape.

*

On 30 September Lewis finally confronted Neuman Flower's proposal of offering *The Revenge for Love* to his other publisher. He pointed out that, having already drawn attention to the book by announcing it in their spring list and then having it vetted by Boots, Cassell had made it a less than attractive prospect for any other publisher, 'the entire book-trade having been frightened in advance'. He was determined to hold them to their side of the contract. 'And I have no intention of allowing you to suppress my book by indefinitely delaying its publication', he told Flower. 'I contracted to write the book and you contracted to publish it.'

Early in October *The Revenge for Love* was at last on its way to the printers. Among the 60 or so textual alterations Lewis had been forced to make by Cassell and the straitlaced Mr Richardson were: 'breasts' to 'bosom', 'bastard' to 'devil', 'bugger off!' to 'Go to Hell!', 'naked' to 'unclothed', 'come-to-bed eyes' to 'eyes', 'sex' to 'lust', 'bloody neck' to 'neck' and 'passing the maid's flurried bottom' to 'passing the simpering maid'.

By early October, *Left Wings Over Europe* had slowly but steadily sold 1,531 copies, leaving Lewis a credit balance with Jonathan Cape of £9.6.8. The book had been reprinted in late August and the list of the author's works printed opposite the title page altered in one respect: 'THE

ROARING QUEEN (in preparation)'. Then, on 19 October, a bombshell arrived from Wren Howard:

> we submitted a set of proofs . . . to our solicitor and asked him to advise us in the matter of possible libels. After reading it he sent us a report which we have since consulted him about verbally and in great detail. I am exceedingly sorry to have to report that the final conclusion come to by our solicitor is that he must advise us not to publish the book.

It was not a case in which judicious cuts and alterations would be of any avail: 'the possible libels . . . were so far-reaching as to make it impossible for them to be removed without completely destroying the book.'

Lewis's protestations that his novel dealt with 'the "Bloomsbury" principle' and that there was 'no caricature of any *individual* "Bloomsbury"', his assertions that the directors of Jonathan Cape had known the nature of the book when they accepted it, and his demands for precise clarification of the nature of the alleged libels, went on throughout November.

At the beginning of December, Wren Howard attempted to draw the matter to a close:

> I am afraid that it will not help matters to continue this correspondence.

THIRTY-FIVE

The Black Principle

In *Left Wings Over Europe*, Lewis offered a parable of the state of Europe midway through the fourth decade of the 20th century:

> The political landscape, if we were to look down upon it from a passing airship, would appear somewhat as follows. Our bird's-eye view would show us a very considerable plain, on which ninety per cent of mankind passed their lives in a highly unpolitical manner . . . Situated at either extremity of this very extensive plain we should remark two little ranges of rugged hills, in which two . . . races of hillmen dwell, both bursting with political consciousness . . . We should learn, if we inquired, that the 'black' mountaineers on our right were called fascists, and the 'red' mountaineers on our left were called communists. Both . . . had established . . . a very reprehensible form of government . . . and the popularly-elected mayors of the various important townships of the lowlands feared and disliked both heartily. But of the two they disliked the 'black' highlanders much more than they did the 'red': because, whereas the reds announced it as their intention quite simply to abolish the governments of the plain altogether as soon as they got the chance (which the governments in question regarded as absurd and impossible), the other lot expressed themselves as determined to put an end to the corruption of these happy-go-lucky regimes, and to rule on similar (though better) lines in their stead. This appeared to the plainsmen's political leaders as a much more ungentlemanly point of view. From our coign of vantage . . . we should notice signs of considerable excitement everywhere beneath us, both on the plain and in the hills above . . . From what we heard we should gather . . . that a decisive struggle had started between the red principle and the black principle for the mastery of the plain. And it would . . . appear . . . that the rulers of the plain were compacting with the reds . . . against their so-called 'totalitarian' adversaries. – But the anti-red mountaineers, on their side . . . were hastily arming themselves too . . . determined to *save the plain*, from what they described as 'the Red Menace'. A great and universal conflict was well under way: that would be as far as we should be able, from such an altitude, and in the face of issues so obscure, to unravel the matter.

In the same year that he composed this fable to show why the Conservative democracy of England favoured Soviet Russia against Nazi Germany, he propped a two foot by four canvas on a chair in his workroom at 121 Gloucester Terrace and painted a picture which he called *Red and Black Principle*. The two gladiatorially garbed figures, standing amicably shoulder to shoulder and both painted in shades of red, appear to contradict the opposing elements of the title. Black shapes loom behind the figures. By the side of one can be seen the bundled rods of the *fasces*, by the side of the other, a sickle. If the figures are representative of polarised political ideals, there seems confusingly little to differentiate them.

However, the dustwrapper design of another political book by Lewis, of April 1937, showed the two identical figures locked in conflict with daggers raised, emblems of hammer and sickle and swastika discernible amongst the struggling feet. The book was called *Count Your Dead: They Are Alive!* Concerned largely with the Spanish Civil War, it favoured General Franco as 'an ordinary, old-fashioned anti-monarchical Spanish *liberal*':

> no more a Fascist than you are, but a Catholic soldier who didn't like seeing priests and nuns killed ... didn't want to see all his friends murdered for no better reason than that they all went to mass and to the more expensive cafés and usually were able to scrape enough money together to have a haircut and a shave.

Against the propaganda of the Left Lewis pitted the propaganda of the Right. He saw the Spanish conflict as a rehearsal for a far greater upheaval and the book was subtitled 'A New War in the Making?' The previous year's *Left Wings Over Europe* had been subtitled: 'How to Make a War about Nothing.'

If Lewis came down on the side of the Black Principle as opposed to the Red, it was in the belief that his country's squaring up to Germany and tacit support for Russia, with the complicity of a left-wing intellectual orthodoxy, was hastening on another major European conflict. It was to avoid war that he mounted his campaign of hastily written political pot-boilers. The anti-war books were, by his own admission, 'futile performances – ill-judged, redundant, harmful of course to [him] personally, and of no value to anybody else'. A question mark at the end of this dismissive list raised a momentary prospect of qualified defence, but he concluded: 'Certainly they were in the main just that.'

The admission was made over a decade later when the war he recognised 'in the making' had run its course and a volume of autobiography, subtitled 'narrative of my career up-to-date', called for an explanation of his 1930s political stance.

In January 1937, the cover of *The British Union Quarterly*, formerly the *Fascist Quarterly*, carried Lewis's name alongside those of Ezra Pound, Roy Campbell, and the leader of the Norwegian National Socialist Party, Vidkun Quisling. Lewis's article made no claim to balance. In fact the author declared at the outset that he would not avail himself of the *Quarterly*'s editorial offer, to criticise, if he felt disposed, 'the Fascist Principle'. Balance, in the climate of opinion in which he was writing, was already so firmly weighted in favour of the Red Principle that he concluded with a paean of praise for the Black. It revealed a more deep-rooted sympathy for the Right, based upon economics, than that which he later acknowledged:

> a word to the Fascist at large. You stand to-day where Socialism stood yesterday – for the Poor against the Rich. You do not stand against Property; you are reproached for that, but you should in fact be congratulated upon it . . . You as a Fascist stand for the small trader against the chain-store; for the peasant against the usurer; for the nation, great or small, against the super-state, for personal business against Big Business; for the craftsman against the middleman; for all that prospers by individual effort and creative toil, against all that prospers in the abstract air of High Finance or of the theoretic ballyhoo of Internationalism.

*

In February 1937, in a letter to Oliver Brown at the Leicester Galleries, Lewis reviewed his achievement, during the previous year, as a painter:

> I am encouraged to think that the time spent in painting was well spent. Very various paintings – the 'Cubist Museum', the 'Siege of Barcelona', and a good many more – represent a considerable output . . . I think it compares very favourably with what most English artists I know of get through in the year. I cannot conjure up enough modesty to feel that, in quality, it ranks below the productions of my $\frac{1}{2}$ dozen most eminent fellow painters.

What concerned him most was a lack of official recognition:

> In the many institutions for the encouragement of art in this country – such as the Contemporary Art Society, the numerous public galleries in London and the provinces – I am unrepresented.

The CAS, of course, had lost the large gouache of three grinning studies of Kate Lechmere when the Tate Gallery cellars flooded in 1928. The only works in a public collection, he claimed, were the drawings left to

Manchester by Charles Rutherston. He had either forgotten about the drawings left to the Victoria and Albert Museum by Captain Guy Baker, or else he felt it would spoil his thesis of neglect if he were to mention them:

> Many little known and relatively undistinguished artists find a lucrative haven for their pictures in public galleries. It is that I am completely unrepresented, that is the point I am labouring. It is against that zero that I lift up my not inconsiderable voice.

And it was the word 'lucrative' that touched on the nub of his complaint: while the Manchester Art Gallery and the Victoria and Albert had been bequeathed examples of his work, no public collection to date had actually gone so far as to buy anything from him.

The Leicester Galleries had already half a show of Wyndham Lewis in their cellars: '12 paintings and masses of drawings'. Lewis's problem was to get the other half painted in time for an exhibition at the end of the year. 'I should like a portrait or two', he told William Rothenstein, 'I can do them awfully well. Quite traditional – no square jaws and green eyes!'*

*

In March, Lovat Dickson Limited submitted the proofs of Lewis's latest political book to their solicitors to be read for libel. By coincidence, they took advice from the same legal firm as did Jonathan Cape. Accordingly it was Mr Rubenstein, of Rubenstein, Nash & Co., the solicitor who had advised Wren Howard against publishing *The Roaring Queen*, who was now asked to pronounce upon *Count Your Dead: They Are Alive!* On page 345 Mr Rubenstein noticed a passage about debts incurred from the Great War:

> Then the Jews were awfully good to us, and Lloyd George says we promised them to clear Palestine of the Arabs for them as a reward for their financial accommodation.

Although not of a libellous nature, it was somewhat dubious and Mr Rubenstein took the liberty, in his report, of saying so:

> The statement attributed to Lloyd George is presumably another invention of the author's, but I expect he is used to this.

---

* By the end of the year when the Leicester Galleries show opened, he had managed to get 'the other half' painted. 24 canvases were exhibited. There were two oil portraits: one of the artist's wife and the other of Anne Bowes Lyon.

When he read the report Lewis was furious. Not content with single-handedly wrecking the publication prospects of his last book, it seemed that Rubenstein was attempting to undermine his future prospects by questioning his integrity as a writer. 'I can see no excuse', he thundered to Lovat Dickson:

> for the gratuitous offensiveness in which he has thought proper to indulge, . . . this sort of thing, if allowed to continue with impunity must affect my reputation and livelihood . . . On Monday I am seeing my lawyer. Protect myself I must.

And, on the same day, as if reminded to take up the cudgels again upon the other matter, already six months old, of *The Roaring Queen*, he wrote to Wren Howard: 'Oblige me by telling me what exactly it is in my book that Rubenstein objected to?'*

Perhaps wisely, Lewis took no further action against a firm of solicitors skilled in the laws of libel. *Count Your Dead: They Are Alive!* was published at the end of April, with the reference to Lloyd George intact. And following hard on the heels of one book about Spain came another: Cassell brought out *The Revenge for Love* in May.

Although appearing at the height of the Spanish Civil War, the novel had been written during the period of political turmoil preceding it, and completed and delivered to the publishers a full six months before Franco's rebellion against the Republican government sparked off the conflict. Set against a background of gunrunning over the Spanish border, of Communist agents and art forgery, it was, in particular, a withering satire on Bloomsbury 'parlour pinks'. Because of the timing of its publication, and the polarised climate of political opinion in which it was at last appearing, Lewis was afraid that his anti-Communist satire would attract harsh criticism. He was even concerned that Cassell, out of spite perhaps at the trouble it had already caused them, would not do their best in marketing it. He appealed to Desmond Flower not to visit his displeasure upon the book and 'to forget its politics' if he found them displeasing. His novel was being published 'under auspices of the most black and disheartening kind', he claimed:

> And yet as I was reading my proofs I realised that the book that is thus about to be contemptuously flung upon the market is probably the best complete work of fiction I have written; and . . . that it will be considered one of the best books in English to appear during the current 12 months.

---

* 'I am sorry the position is unclear to you', Wren Howard replied. 'The advice we received was to the effect that the restricted range of the *motif* coupled with the essentially allusive treatment of the subject matter of your book rendered it inherently dangerous from the point of view of libel.'

*

In July 1937 Lewis and his wife moved into temporary quarters at 10, Sussex Gardens, and thence, in October, to an address they would occupy off and on for the rest of their life together. It could be difficult for visitors to find. From the Olde Swan public house at the top of Church Street it was about ten yards to the right along Notting Hill Gate that an archway at number 29 penetrated the frontage between Timothy Whites hardware shop and the Primrose Tea Rooms. The discreet name-plate divulged Kensington Gardens Studios. Lewis told one prospective visitor that there was a bell at street level, with his name on it, that the bell did not work and that he was perfectly content with this arrangement. A narrow covered passage, white-tiled like the entrance to a public lavatory, led to the rear of the block, emerging into the open air close to the junction of two sidestreets: West Mall and Rabbit Row. To the left, draughty stone steps zigzagged up the outside to the top of the building. Landing succeeded landing, draped in pegged-out washing and with scuffed chalk hopscotch grids underfoot. At the second storey another dark, narrow passage plunged back into the fabric of the building and after some twists and turns the door to Studio A was reached. The tenant's name appeared on a piece of card to one side, typed downwards, one visitor noticed, 'as if to be more difficult'. The bell provoked a shuffling response, the door opened and the hatted and piped figure appeared very large in the cramped entrance. A short flight of stairs rose sharply left just inside, and this made opening the door in the confined space rather awkward. To greet his visitor Lewis had to swivel round suddenly into view from behind the opening door like a theatrically contrived piece of clockwork.

Entrance to the Lewises' living quarters lay directly opposite the front door, but guests would not be invited there until some years later. Instead they were ushered up the short flight of stairs to the studio with a huge, north-facing skylight running its entire length. It was a spacious room, scrupulously tidy, and inadequately heated by a gas fire installed by the previous tenant 'without the expert assistance of the gas company'. At one end, beyond a partition, was a small kitchen with a window overlooking Notting Hill Gate. Here, a guest remembered, Lewis would set a kettle on the stove for tea. The kettle, 'by a device novel at the time, would put forth a vigorous whistle when ready.' The tea would be served at a low square table. There must have been a kitchen downstairs in the living quarters as well, because Julian Symons recalled Lewis thumping on the floor with a stick, and, following an answering thump from below, collecting a tray of tea and bread and butter from the bottom of the studio stairs.

*

Between their removal to Sussex Gardens and their occupation of 29A Notting Hill Gate, Lewis and his wife toured three European capitals: Warsaw, Berlin and Paris.

They arrived in Poland on 31 July. Lewis's reasons for wishing to visit this country are mysterious. Mrs Lewis recalled that, when they were in Warsaw, she had wanted to see the Black Madonna of Krakow, but her husband was content 'just sitting around cafés' and so they did not go. Apart from a memorable descriptive passage in a book published a year and a half later, nothing is known of the visit. On the last day of their stay they went sightseeing. 'I felt I had seen very little of the outlying parts of the city,' Lewis wrote:

> so I engaged a droshky. We made a tour of churches and palaces, or drew up in front of them, looked and passed on. Then at length the driver, speaking over his shoulder, announced: '*Maintenant, messieurs et m'dames, nous nous approchons du Ghetto.*' In this ex-czarist barouche, its seat a long way above the street-level, we charged into the Ghetto, the driver cracking his whip. Its crack had a strangely knout-like inflection. Aged crones, spitting out curses, scuttled to one side: old kaftaned cripples hobbled out of the path of this rattling Gentile juggernaut. The driver relished this part of the sightseeing more than I did. He pointed his whip and proffered obscure information. He slowed up to inform us of the proportion of Jews to Gentiles in Poland. I gathered it was ten Jews to one Pole. If anyone is desirous of forming an opinion upon the Jewish Problem they should visit the Ghetto in Warsaw. This inferno continued for miles upon miles: or so it seemed . . . The percentage of diseased, deformed, and generally infirm persons is what strikes one most: that and the inexpressible squalor.

They crossed the border into Germany on 12 August. On this visit, by his own account, Lewis declined a very momentous meeting indeed:

> When . . . I informed an English admirer of Herr Hitler that I was going to Germany he wrote me to say that it had been arranged that I should see the Führer. That, however, I had no desire to do, and I told him so. I passed through Germany *en touriste*, as I have always done.

He did not divulge the name of this 'English admirer of Herr Hitler', and the letter offering an audience with the German Führer has not survived. One possible candidate for the shadowy intermediary was a man who once sat down to eat with Lewis, Lovat Dickson and Sir Oswald Mosley. The lunch took place at Mosley's flat in Ebury Street, and Dickson recalled the fourth member of the party: a small man with a long scar curving back from the right corner of his mouth.

William Joyce is said to have received his disfigurement at the hands of Communists in Lambeth during the 1924 by-election campaign. A razor was put into his mouth and a flick of the wrist opened his cheek to the earlobe. He was to become an infamous figure during the ensuing war, broadcasting from Berlin, giving 'aid and comfort' to the enemy, and popularly known, and reviled, as 'Lord Haw-Haw'. Dickson claimed that Lewis introduced him to Mosley and Joyce, who were keen for him to publish their work. The meal was served by heel-clicking blackshirts who raised their arms in 45-degree salute on entering or leaving the room. Lovat Dickson died in 1987 and his story cannot be verified. His is the only testimony to establish a dangerous link between a man who flirted with National Socialism and one who was hanged for his activities on its behalf. Joyce destroyed all his papers before he was arrested, and any evidence of friendship between himself and Lewis would have been destroyed along with them. No letters from William Joyce to Lewis have survived either, but the trial of Lord Haw-Haw and his execution for High Treason in January 1946 would have led anyone acquainted with him to judiciously weed out potentially incriminating correspondence from their private papers.

In Berlin Mr and Mrs Lewis stayed in a hotel off the Kurfürstendamm. They noticed the miserably run-down Jewish-owned shops, the window of one in particular, beneath the name 'ISRAEL', displaying 'deplorably outmoded' women's dresses, 'crumpled, and one or two actually hung upside down'. In November 1938, such already demoralised establishments would be put out of business permanently in a State-condoned orgy of looting and splintered glass: *Kristallnacht*.

Lewis had last visited Berlin in January 1934, only six months after Hitler assumed absolute power in Germany. Three and a half years later he was able to cast an eye over the trappings of the Third Reich fully fledged:

> I watched . . . a party of Black Guards falling in, and marching off down the Wilhelmstrasse. I noted the ascetic, the monkish appearance of their pale faces under the black casques, and the clock-like solemnity of their movements, with the violent kick of the goose-step that leads off the quick march!

It was not a happy visit. 'We left . . . very quickly', Mrs Lewis remembered, 'because we found it very uncomfortable, or Wyndham did at least.' And a letter from his literary agent at A. M. Heath, shortly after they returned to London, commiserated: 'I am so sorry you had such a trying time in Germany.'

*

Publication of Lewis's latest book in October was attended by bitter dealings with one of the directors of Eyre & Spottiswoode, Douglas Jerrold. In response to Jerrold's objection that too much space had been devoted to James Joyce, T. S. Eliot and Ezra Pound in his autobiography, *Blasting and Bombardiering*, Lewis wrote to him as follows:

> in all arts and sciences there are a few men, a very few, whose views on each other's work are of substantial and enduring importance . . . which will not be allowed to vanish, which will be quoted and reprinted for the sake of a percipience that is rare. Conversely, there is a large number of others who play a humble though not necessarily dishonourable part in dissemination, and whose views are of only commercial importance. If you are not able to grasp this distinction . . . you would be better employed in the grocery trade.

Not for the first time he developed the suspicion that a publisher was deliberately sabotaging his work by not bothering to market it enthusiastically. This arose from Jerrold's fatalistic remarks, doubtless intended to comfort the author, about the disappointing sales of his own autobiography, *Georgian Adventure*, published by Collins earlier the same year. According to Lewis, the director of Eyre & Spottiswoode was 'an embittered "author" turned publisher, who had invented for his own consolation the dogma that "no good book can sell", and had pursued his calling with so much languor that in effect his dogma could be guaranteed to justify itself.'

*

It was partly to mark the forthcoming exhibition at the Leicester Galleries, that A.J.A. Symons' younger brother Julian published a special Wyndham Lewis number of the small magazine he edited, *Twentieth Century Verse*. The project had had Lewis's blessing and all contributions had been submitted to him for approval before being included. With the single exception of an outright attack on Lewis by the American critic Kenneth Burke, all the material submitted was used.

The November/December double issue of *Twentieth Century Verse* included a review of the Leicester Galleries exhibition by T. W. Earp, an evaluation of Lewis 'The Novelist' and 'A Note on One Way Song' by A.J.A. and Julian Symons respectively, a review of *Blasting and Bombardiering* by Constant Lambert and an article by Eliot on *The Lion and the Fox*. Other contributors were: G.W. Stonier, Gilbert Armitage, E.W.F. Tomlin,

Ruthven Todd, D. S. Savage, Keidrych Rhys, Glyn Jones, Rex Warner, Gavin Ewart, John Beevers and H. B. Mallalieu.

The collection was prefaced by a letter to the Editor from Lewis himself:

What a quantity of friends 'The Enemy' has nowadays! I am a little abashed. No company, this, for a public enemy. I am very much afraid that you have compromised me!

Privately he told Symons: 'the Double Number . . . will remain for me one of the milestones in my life as an artist.'

Another friend was unimpressed. 'What a curiously anti-feminist publication . . . this is', Naomi Mitchison complained to him:

Presenting a picture of Wyndham Lewis walking over the prostrate bodies of Virginia Woolf and Gertrude Stein – It would have looked better to have one woman contributor anyhow, and if they hadn't been a set of adolescents they would have seen that . . . One gets so sick of all these young men. It obviously isn't your fault, but fuck and bugger the bastards who make you look to me and other women what I'm quite sure you aren't.

*

So recent was some of the work that one large canvas had to be hung when the paint was still wet. A 16-page catalogue, with a foreword by Lewis, accompanied the show:

> It is . . . the function of the artist to translate experience, pleasant and unpleasant, into formal terms. In the latter case, as what we experience in life is not all pleasant, and the most terrible experience, even, is often the most compelling, the result is a tragic picture, as often as not . . . And many of these pictures belong to the tragic art.

The 24 canvases had all been completed during the five years of intermittent illness since December 1932 and the titles of three pictures explicitly reflected that context: *The Invalid*, *The Mud Clinic* and *The Tank in the Clinic*.

A schematised figure, *The Invalid*, was painted in warm shades of yellow and zigzagged diagonally across the earth-toned geometries and dazzling white of the background, its face framed in a dark trapezium. A companion figure, partially concealed behind the patient, slightly inclined its oval head.

Elsewhere, the specifics of sickroom and the hospital experience had undergone more radical transmutation. In the compartmentalised abstraction of *The Mud Clinic* sat billiard-ball headed mannequins. Others lay prone or supine, each with a vacuous, full-lipped grin. All but the blindfolded patient at the bottom stared with round, vacant eyes.

A sinister form of treatment seemed to occupy the upper half of *The Tank in the Clinic*; featureless brown and beige bodies crammed passively down into an ultramarine precipitate. Below the tank, to the right, a fork-legged stretcher-case protruded from a storage drawer. Occupying the centre foreground, three figures studied something bulbous on a tall pedestal. In another context they might be art critics examining a piece of modern sculpture: a cubist rendering of a mandolin perhaps. But in this clinical nightmare the object raised to such grail-like significance was the humble receptacle of a sick man's urine, a bottle designed to rest on its side in the bed without spilling. To the left a couple of women were partnered in a *Totentanz* by tall, bony wraiths. On the extreme left of the phantasmagoric scene stood a smaller figure, in dark glasses, wearing a red dressing gown, the lapels trimmed with brown, and with a blue cord round the waist: a portrait of the artist as inmate of the clinic. The painting was otherwise unsigned.

Elsewhere, images of a post-mortem existence recalled the infernal world described in *The Childermass* a decade earlier. Figures waited in limbo for obscure judgement: *Group of Suppliants*, *Group of Three Veiled Figures*, *Queue of the Dead* and *One of the Stations of the Dead*.

Forming a spectacular centrepiece was the five-foot-high figurative epic that was still wet when hung: *Inferno*. Lewis described it in his catalogue foreword:

> In this composition (an inverted T, a vertical red panel, and a horizontal grey panel), a world of shapes locked in eternal conflict is superimposed upon a world of shapes, prone in the relaxations of an uneasy sensuality which is also eternal.

Blazing red figures gushed through a white open door, flung back against a background of hospital green. Below, a tangle of emaciated mannequins, the familiar round heads grinning with crescents of bared teeth. In the centre, the back of a flesh-toned figure with curly blond hair relieved the bald, ashen monotony of the mass grave.

In contrast to these horrors, another 'recent painting' was a tender portrait of a woman, in pale blues, her hands clasped and looking wistfully to the left in three-quarter profile. *Portrait of the Artist's Wife* was Lewis's first public acknowledgement of Gladys's existence.

After the private view Lewis was taken by A.J.A. Symons and his brother to Wheeler's seafood restaurant in Old Compton Street. The founder of the Gourmet Club was noticeably pained to see his guest vigorously salting and peppering his oysters. Lewis was delighted at the gourmet's dismay 'and thumped his thigh with pleasure', Julian Symons recalled.

*

The morning after the private view, a report in *The Times* listed an impressive couple of dozen titled notables as having been in attendance. It may have been this publicity and the imagined prosperity conferred upon the artist by his obviously well-heeled guests that attracted attention to him from an unwelcome quarter. The day after *The Times* report was published, a short note from an address in Wimbledon was posted care of the Leicester Galleries:

> Dear Mr Lewis, I would like to have a word with you, at your convenience, on a matter which I consider concerns you vitally.

It was signed 'Anne Cumiskey', a lady acting as intermediary for a third party. A fortnight later, when Lewis had not responded to the first advance, a second came direct to his home address. This time the intermediary had been dispensed with and the message was couched in the style of blackmail:

> Would you please write me by return of post and arrange a suitable time

for meeting me – I suggest Saturday morning about 11.00 am or Friday. If I do not hear by Friday morning I will come to the Leicester Galleries and make myself known – not as in the past, using discretion for your benefit. Yours sincerely Peter.

Lewis's son by Olive Johnson had just turned 26 years old. A good six feet tall, and with the dark good looks inherited from his father, he would not have gone unnoticed in the Leicester Galleries. It is not clear what substance lay in his veiled threat, but it cannot be denied that a young man from south of the river visiting a West End gallery and claiming to be the painter's illegitimate son would have caused, at the very least, some measure of embarrassment.

Lewis instructed his solicitors to deal with the matter and drafted the letter they were to send. It would appear that this was not Peter's first approach, and that Lewis had paid him off on at least one former occasion:

Our client . . . has asked us to write to you (in reply to your letter threatening to make trouble for him in some way at the Leicester Galleries) to remind you of your promise [some time ago] not to interfere with him any more if he found the money you then needed. He hopes that you will abandon the idea of extracting money from him indefinitely, and understand that you have no claim on him of any sort.

*

Peter would have been sadly mistaken in the belief that the Leicester Galleries show had made his father a profitable target for extortion. Notwithstanding the Lords, Ladies and Knights of the Realm assembled at the private view, by the end of the first week only a single painting had sold, *One of the Stations of the Dead* – and that to a friend, Naomi Mitchison, for £105. With only a fortnight left for the exhibition to run, Stephen Spender asked Lewis's permission to organise a letter to the press. Permission was granted and the following statement appeared in *The Times* on 16 December 1937:

Many years have passed since the strange mind of Wyndham Lewis began to invigorate English painting and letters. Mr Lewis is now holding his first exhibition since 1921, and it seems to us an appropriate time to suggest that Lewis's deep and original art should be publicly recognised. Social change has made it inevitable that in these days the place and duties of the private patron should be handed over in a large degree to the public galleries; and those rarer artists whose vision and energy are too great to be confined in small or decorative pieces must depend more and more on the wide discernment of the galleries. We believe Wyndham Lewis to be such an artist, ... and we hope that the opportunity of acquiring a representative work by him for the national collection will not be overlooked.

Twenty names appeared underneath: Henry Moore, Eric Gill, Paul Nash, Mark Gertler, Edmund Dulac, Edward Wadsworth, P. H. Jowett, Randolph Schwabe, John Piper, Serge Chermayeff, Raymond McGrath, Arthur Bliss, Michael Sadler, W. H. Auden, Herbert Read, Lady Rhondda, Rebecca West, Naomi Mitchison, Stephen Spender and Geoffrey Grigson. It was Grigson who had written the letter and collected the names.

Wadsworth's support suggests that their acrimonious dealings of the early 1920s had been forgiven, if not forgotten. The only person approached who refused to append his signature was Walter Sickert.

The signatories' hopes were fulfilled. It may even have been as a result of this timely intervention that the Tate Gallery purchased item number 50 in the catalogue, *Red Scene*, for £84.

*

When the Leicester Galleries exhibition closed on 24 December, only six drawings and five canvases had been sold, for a total of £423 3s. The Gallery's 33⅓ per cent commission was subtracted, leaving £282 2s. Framing costs of £60 8s. reduced it further, and the £221 13s. 3d. that remained was swallowed up in a labyrinthine debt of £418 to the Leicester Galleries that had accumulated, in the form of occasional advances on the exhibition, since 1933. A balance of £196 6s. 9d. on this debt was still outstanding. So the Gallery retained seven canvases with a catalogue value of £365 8s., for half price, as they were entitled to do. These included *Siege of Barcelona*, *The Inca (with birds)* and *Tank in the Clinic*. Brown and Philips also exchanged the portrait of Ann Lyon, which they had already purchased for £40, for *Portrait of the Artist's Wife*, at half price, £52 10s. The balance of £12 10s. from that exchange finally settled the debt.

Although the exhibition was far from being a financial success for Lewis, it may not have given this impression to creditors and other parties eager to extract money from him. Apart from Peter, at least one other old score soon emerged from the past for settlement.

Rupert Grayson, Lewis's co-defendant against Major MacFie back in 1934, began an action for libel on his own account in January 1938. The letter from Gordon, Dadds & Co. referred to matters defamatory to their client in Lewis's novel *Snooty Baronet*.* Because the book had been

---

* Grayson believed, quite rightly, that he had been the model for the absurd, large-chinned 'Humph'.

published five years before Grayson allegedly discovered himself to be libelled, the belatedness of the claim required explanation:

> For some time past various friends and acquaintances of our Client have been informing him that he is referred to in the book in question, but it was not until recently that he was told of the serious imputations which have been made.

It is difficult to believe that Grayson would have neglected to read for himself a novel in which he had been told he figured. It is also difficult to believe he would have neglected reading it for five years. It is much easier to believe, however, that he took action when he judged that the supposed proceeds of a prestigious exhibition had made Lewis worth suing.

Whatever his motives, or his sense of timing, Grayson did not pursue his claim beyond this exploratory sally.

THIRTY-SIX

'X'

During the first half of March Lewis was fully occupied painting a large portrait of T. S. Eliot. Dressed in a dark business suit and tie, the poet sat with his hands crossed over the bottom buttons of his waistcoat, his elbows resting on the curved wooden arms of the chair. The broad chair back had a slight upward curve behind his head, seeming to accentuate the droop of his shoulders. He stared at a point to the lower left of the painter's easel. In later years, Lewis would tell people that he always left a bottle of scotch by the chair leg for Eliot to drink while he was sitting. The anecdote would end with Lewis making 'a little thing' about having to remember to leave the bottle out of the painting.

Because of Eliot's busy work schedule at Faber & Faber, sittings had to take place between 8.30 in the evening and midnight, sometimes later.

During the day Lewis worked on the portrait without the sitter. He needed to have it finished by the last week in March if it was going to be considered for inclusion in the 170th Summer Exhibition at the Royal Academy.

*

At 10 o'clock on the morning of Monday 28 March the 14 members of the Selection Committee met in Gallery III, the largest space Burlington House had to offer. They sat in a shallow arc, the President occupying a winged armchair in the middle. In front of the President was a small round table covered, as tradition dictated, with a green baize cloth on which lay a snuffbox and three large brass letters mounted on turned wooden handles: 'A', 'D' and 'X'.

The first painting was carried to a point opposite the President's table by two white-aproned labourers and rested upright on a squat four-legged stool. A square cushion protected the lower edge of the picture frame and prevented it slipping. Beneath the cushion, the stool had a circular top mounted on an axle, enabling the picture to be turned to face Committee members at either end of the arc. There were also castors fitted to the legs so

379

that stool and picture could, when necessary, be moved in for closer scrutiny.

The foreman of the labourers stood just behind the picture and watched for the President's signal. After a brisk show of hands the President raised one of the letters and the foreman wrote 'A', 'D' or 'X' on the back of the canvas with a piece of chalk.

The chalking of an 'A' was a rare event. A work was only 'accepted' by the Selection Committee when there was a unanimous vote in its favour. 'D' signified 'doubtful' and meant that the work had prompted two or more hands to be raised in its favour and would be looked at again when the Hanging Committee, consisting of nine out of the original fourteen, met the following week. The Hanging Committee would exhibit all works that members had sent in, together with any works by non-members that were chalked with an 'A'. It would also endeavour to exhibit as many 'doubtful' works as possible. Some would eventually be designated 'doubtful – not hung', due to lack of space, and the creators of such works might derive a crumb of comfort therefrom. 'X', raised by the President and duly chalked by the foreman, denied the artist even that dubious honour: 'Rejected'.

It can be assumed that a 'rejected' work would not have had a single vote in its favour, because there was an informal rule: if one hand were raised in defence, another would second it to make a verdict of 'doubtful'.

No record of works submitted for consideration is ever preserved apart from statistics in the Academy's annual report. 11,221 works by non-members arrived at the rear entrance of Burlington House between 25 and 29 March 1938. 9,156 of these were consigned to oblivion by the Selection Committee between 28 and 31 March. Eleven were 'accepted'. Of the remaining 2,054, chalked 'doubtful', that came before the Hanging Committee between 5 and 14 April, 1,266 were exhibited. 777 were 'doubtful – not hung'.

Among the buff-coloured notifications of rejection sent out in the third week of April was one for Wyndham Lewis.

Sir William Llewellyn, in the last year of his Presidency, had raised the brass 'X' and the foreman had scrawled a stigmatic cross on the back of *Portrait of T. S. Eliot*.

On Thursday 21 April the news broke in the *Daily Telegraph and Morning Post*:

ROYAL ACADEMY SURPRISE. WORK BY WYNDHAM LEWIS REJECTED

Readers were given a brief description of the spurned painting:

a seated figure, slightly over life-size, with a screen of decorative design in the background. Although the artist is a leader of the more advanced section of the contemporary British school, the Ingres-like proficiency of draughtsmanship which the portrait displays is entirely of academic standard.

The purchase of *Red Scene* by the Tate Gallery three months before was offered as evidence of the artist's importance.

Lewis himself was interviewed and his comments appeared in a number of papers the following day. He seems to have enjoyed turning quotable phrases for the journalists. 'I am voicing the opinion of fellow-artists', he told the *Daily Mail*, 'when I say that the Royal Academy is – if you think this is suitable language – a "foul institution".' The *Daily Herald* ran the headline:

ACADEMY CALLED A 'FILTH BAZAAR'

In contrast with the spleen he was venting, Lewis was reported as speaking 'in a quiet, gentle voice . . . "The Royal Academy is a disgusting bazaar in which every sort of filth is accumulated every year." '

The *Daily Telegraph and Morning Post* correspondent contented himself with quoting a more measured line of abuse:

I personally think the Academy does not know what art is. There should be ten competent men on the Selection Committee. Nothing short of radical transformation can possibly do any good. Their selections are all alike – last century impressionism, or coloured photographs which they call portraits. They always select what they think will please the most stupid person. It would be interesting to hear their side of the question, why they rejected my picture, and then ask the opinions of a few impartial judges . . . This was the first time I sent a picture. Its rejection shows that the Academy is prejudiced against present day art.

On the Saturday morning an anonymous Committee member's reply was printed:

I do not know what Mr Lewis means by present-day art. Art is art in whatever period. It is well known that the Academy is looking anxiously for good modern art. There is so much bad art about. However, we are not here to exhibit experiments, but achievements.

As to why the portrait was rejected, the Committee member observed simply that 'it was not so good as others that were passed.'

In the meantime, the subject of the portrait himself wrote to Lewis expressing relief at the Selection Committee's decision:

> I am glad to think that a portrait of myself should not appear in an exhibition of the Royal Academy, and I certainly have no desire, now, that my portrait should be painted by any painter whose portrait of me would be accepted by the Royal Academy.

The story would probably not have remained newsworthy into the following week had it not been for a protest from within the Academy's own ranks. The RA's Annual Report for 1938 contained a brief summary of the affair and its outcome:

> the Council received with regret a letter from Mr A. E. John resigning his Membership owing to the rejection by the Selection Committee of a portrait of Mr T. S. Eliot by Mr Wyndham Lewis. As John had informed the President that he could not alter his decision, the resignation was accepted.

Augustus John, made an Associate in 1921 and Academician in 1928, had written to Lewis on Saturday 23 April: 'I read yesterday of the rejection of your picture ... This is the limit and I resign with gratitude to you for affording me so good a reason.' On the same day he wrote to Llewellyn:

> Dear President, After the crowning ineptitude of the rejection of Wyndham Lewis's picture I feel it is impossible for me to remain longer a member of the R.A. and I am writing to [the Secretary] tendering my resignation. With many personal regrets I remain etc.

Efforts were made at dissuasion but a telegram on the Monday showed him adamant:

VERY SORRY GOING AWAY CANNOT ALTER DECISION – JOHN

The Star interviewed him by telephone for Monday's Late Special: 'I very much regret to make a sensation,' John was quoted as saying:

> but it cannot be helped. Nothing that Mr Wyndham Lewis paints is negligible, or to be condemned lightly. I strongly disagree with the rejection. I think it is an inept act on the part of the Academy. A picture by a person of Mr Lewis's eminence should have been unquestionably exhibited.

Lewis happily stirred the controversy further when *The Star* reporter approached him for a response:

> For a long time I think, Mr John has chafed at Royal Academy action – or inaction, rather . . . I have never discussed this with [him]. I have avoided the subject of the Academy as an indelicate – I might say indecent – subject, a disreputable association that he would prefer to forget. For obviously, Mr John is the only important artist inside the Academy. All the others are outside it. This cannot have been a very comfortable position for him . . . It was indeed a case of a Triton among the minnows or of a lion among the guinea pigs. This resignation . . . should be a mortal blow to the Royal Academy – if it is possible for one to use the expression 'mortal blow' with reference to a corpse.

The gloating diatribe continued in the *Evening Standard*:

> The Royal Academy can now be seen in all its gigantic platitude without a single name behind which to shelter. The name of Augustus John was its dazzling alibi. That has been removed. There is no true artist in England who will not be profoundly grateful to Mr John.

The Academy was still not acknowledging the crisis on the following day when an official was invited to comment. 'All we know is what we have read.'

To keep the story running, Lewis was appointed by *The Star* as its art critic for a single assignment. Furnished with a press pass he was able to infiltrate the 'sinister institution' in Burlington House and attend the private view on Friday 29 April. He was photographed in the courtyard, his back to the main entrance, feet apart and Peterson pipe gripped between his teeth, looking mightily pleased with himself. And his presence did not go unnoticed inside the building. 'Mr Wyndham Lewis was there for all to see,' wrote the *Daily Mail* critic:

> massive and inescapable, his huge and dusty felt hat looming in doorways and before gilt frames, his audible comments on various well hung works drawing a crowd of delighted eavesdroppers . . . and the sisters, cousins and aunts of the Academy revolved round him at a polite distance, inquisitive and embarrassed.

He was accompanied on this critical swathe by Hannen Swaffer, art correspondent of the *Daily Herald*. 'There is not one here that I would hang on my walls', he told Swaffer at one point. 'I came with an open mind.'

As critic of *The Star* he made his own selection of the works on view. He proved himself far more rigorous than the Committee that had voted down his portrait of Eliot, and a damningly small number of paintings were listed for approval:

> I have not shirked my duty as a critic. I have gone through the Royal Academy exhibits with a fine-comb, from gallery to gallery, taking them picture by picture. I find that there are thirty-two exhibits all told, which I can gaze upon without a sensation of uneasiness or without a feeling of the utter vanity of human life. Out of 1,587 exhibits, I am able to pass 32 as fit.

He pointed out that even the 32 were not masterpieces: there was a Lavery 'reminiscent of Sargent in one of his slick and glittering Venetian interiors'; there was a 'goodish' Wilson Steer; there was *The Gathering Storm* by E. Leslie Budham, 'an agreeable travel advert – "Go to sunny Cornwall for your holidays."' In order to make the number up to 50 he was prepared to include half a dozen drawings, five of the best official portraits and, as a final makeweight, seven or so by Alfred Munnings. 'They would all go comfortably into Gallery one. The remaining Galleries could be used as dance halls; as reading and rest rooms; lecture rooms, or ice rinks.' He also thought that the bar laid on for the private view should be made a permanent fixture. 'I could never have written this [article] without the timely refreshment offered me by the R.A.'

The review was accompanied by a reproduction of the painting that had excited sufficient comment to be dubbed by the press 'Picture of the Year'. Needless to say this monumental and topical treatment of summary execution by firing squad, called *In their own Home (Spain's Agony of Civil War 1936–1938)* by Russell Flint RA, was not included in Lewis's selection of 32:

> Gallery Two contains . . . a genuine atrocity . . . Since it has a political, and, therefore, serious subject matter, it is all the more unfortunate that it should, with its studio-peasants posed against a wall, fail in moving the spectator to indignation at the 'Desastres de la Guerra', because of the so much more obvious disaster it records in the mere matter of technical tact.

Flint was the only member of the 1938 Selection Committee whose work was singled out by *The Star* critic for especial malevolence.

'What I Think of the R.A.' appeared on Saturday 30 April. That evening the Academy held its Annual Banquet. Huddersfield Town had lost 1–0 to Preston North End in the FA Cup Final at the Empire Stadium in Wembley and northern soccer supporters joined the crowds in Piccadilly to watch the dignitaries arrive at Burlington House. A guard of honour of the Artists Rifles was inspected in the courtyard by the Earl of Athlone. The guests included the Belgian, Chilean, Chinese, French, Japanese, Portuguese, Soviet and Turkish Ambassadors, the High Commissioners for Canada, South Africa and Eire. There were representatives of the Church, the Armed Services and the Government.

The Prime Minister responded when Sir William Llewellyn toasted 'His Majesty's Ministers' and it was clear that the controversies of the previous ten days had not escaped Neville Chamberlain's notice:

> You can imagine . . . what a relief it is to be able to turn away from the hurly-burly of the House of Commons and enter into the tranquil atmosphere of art, where such things as resignations are unknown . . .

There was laughter at the ponderous irony.

> . . . where artists, like little birds in their nests, agree. If there was any suspicion of this enviable harmony being in danger of being disturbed, I should like you to remember that the Government is still pledged to a policy of non-intervention.

There was more laughter at this. It was a good joke. Only two days before, the Prime Minister had maintained his government's policy of non-intervention and rejected M. Daladier's call for joint Anglo–French action against the German threat to Czechoslovakia.

At 9.45 on that Saturday evening, had he switched on the wireless and tuned to the BBC's National Programme, Lewis would have heard Mr Winston Churchill MP, direct from Burlington House, propose a toast to 'The Royal Academy of Art'. He would have heard that institution warmly approved for the orthodoxy he so despised – an orthodoxy he must have been well aware of when he delivered his portrait of T. S. Eliot to the Burlington Gardens back entrance in March. He would have heard those who challenged that orthodoxy dismissed by Churchill as 'highmettled palfreys prancing and pawing, sniffing, snorting, foaming, and occasionally kicking, and shying at every puddle they see'. He would have heard the complacent laughter from assembled guests and Academicians. He would have heard the future Honorary Academician Extraordinary go on to speak in sonorous tones of 'tradition' and 'innovation' and he might have been amused or insulted, with equal justification, by a veiled reference to himself as a fledgling of the Arts:

> The country possesses in the Royal Academy an institution of wealth and

385

power for the purpose of encouraging the arts of painting and sculpture
... The function of such an institution ... is to hold a middle course
between tradition and innovation. Without tradition art is a flock of sheep
without a shepherd. Without innovation it is a corpse. Innovation, of
course, involves experiment. Experiments may or may not be fruitful ...
There are many opportunities and many places for experimental artists to
try their wings – and it is not until the results of their experiments have
won a certain measure of acceptance from the general agreement of
qualified judges that the Royal Academy can be expected to give them its
countenance.

Following the clapping and cheers, and the President's reply, the broadcast
from Burlington House came to an end at 10.15 and the BBC Theatre
Orchestra took over that evening's wireless entertainment.

The Art Establishment had closed its ranks against disturbing outside
influences. The ten-day sensation of the 'Rejected Portrait' was over bar the
grumbling of a letter or two to *The Times*. Lewis made a belated reply the
following Wednesday but it was clear which side had won:

The 'controversy' regarding the Royal Academy has been decorously
interred ... by oratory at a public banquet ... Even the most resounding
denunciations poured forth by mere artists, however famous, will just roll
like water off the back of the proverbial duck, so long as next minute an
eminent ex-Minister of State can be found to turn on the ... romantic
Parliamentary rhetoric.

*

The year had started with the portrait of one American poet. It ended with
the portrait of another. When Olivia Shakespear fell ill in early October, a
telegram brought her son-in-law, Ezra Pound, from holiday in Venice. By
the time he reached London she was dead, and he stayed on through
November to settle her affairs. He also presented himself at 29A Notting
Hill Gate to be painted. He 'swaggered in, coat-tails flying, a malacca
cane out of the 'nineties aslant beneath his arm, the lion's head from the
Scandinavian north-west thrown back. There was no conversation. He flung
himself at full length into [Lewis's] best chair ... closed his eyes and was
motionless.'

'And now, mon, fire away!' the great Scottish historian Thomas Carlyle
is said to have grunted at Whistler in 1872, as he took up the pose for the
portrait called *Arrangement in Grey and Black No. 2*. Pound may have had
this anecdote in mind as he settled himself into the armchair:

'Go to it Wyndham!' he gruffled without opening his eyes, as soon as his mane of as yet entirely ungrizzled hair had adjusted itself to the cushioned chair-top.

During that first sitting Pound did not move for two hours, nor did he sleep. But as work progressed the relaxed pose caused him to doze off occasionally, and measures had to be taken to keep him alert. Ruthven Todd remembered being telephoned by Lewis:

Are you free this afternoon? Good. I'm painting a portrait, and he *will* fall asleep, and I need to have someone to irritate him. Come about two.

Todd was disappointed in Pound. He had wanted to talk about the structure of *The Cantos* but was treated instead to a lecture on economics and a eulogy of Mussolini's Italy which included the assertion, apparently made without a trace of irony, 'At least the trains run to time.'

Pound's collapsed pose dictated the disposition of canvas to easel and ensured that he be presented to the world 'landscape' instead of 'portrait'. It also suggested the simple geometry of the composition. An imaginary line taken along the ridge of Pound's nose, extending forwards to the bottom left corner and backwards to the upper right, divided the oblong picture surface in half. Apart from a small section of forehead and hair, the poet's likeness was confined below this diagonal.

By the time the sitter returned to Italy at the beginning of December, work was sufficiently advanced to excite enthusiastic comment from visitors to Lewis's studio. Lord Carlow thought it his best portrait to date. Hugh Gordon Porteus and Michael Cullis, collectively 'the portcullises', were impressed, and E.W.F. Tomlin and his wife 'tittered approval'. Lewis himself assured Pound: 'It is *very* good.'

But there was an obvious and fundamental problem about the composition that he explained by diagram in a letter that followed Pound to Rapallo. The diagonally split rectangle consisted of two equal right-angled triangles. The cross-hatched lower triangle showed the half of canvas occupied by the picture's subject. The upper triangle, what Pound called 'that thaaar north west corner', contained only a question mark.

During the 1930s, Lewis had developed a repertoire of solutions to such spatial problems.

The portrait of Mrs T. J. Honeyman, painted 1936–7, is roughly composed as a reversed 'L' shape: chair back, head and torso are vertical and slightly off centre, chair arm and crossed leg horizontal. In such an arrangement, something always has to be found to occupy the open part of the 'L'. To the left of Mrs Honeyman, between chair back and draped chair arm, is something that can best be described as an abstract doodle. Brightly coloured and fantastic, its sole purpose is to fill an otherwise empty space.

In the centrally aligned vertical composition of the Eliot portrait there are two spaces, to right and left, filled with coloured arabesques, although the area behind the sitter's head was left uncharacteristically blank.

Rarely does a subject dominate the rectangle sufficiently to make such space-fillers redundant. Even in the 1938 portrait of John McLeod, whose spectacularly long legs seem folded up in a violent and vain attempt to cram everything in, there was still a small area to the right of the head that Lewis thought necessary to plug with the picture of a kasbah.

But in no other composition was Lewis faced with such a dauntingly large area as that which yawned above the restful slanting figure of Pound. Clearly something more than a colourful abstract flourish was required. And, powerful as the portrait was, there was a risk that whatever was put into that triangular expanse of canvas might detract from it. By February the problem had been solved. Lewis decided that the leonine head was strong enough to fight its own battle for attention against a *nature morte*, taking up over half the total width of the canvas.

On top of the low round writing table, with its still lower round shelf, lay a clutter of studio properties familiar from other portraits of the time: the heavy bulbous glass ashtray, the ornamental rectangular plate with scalloped edges decorated with 'Sailor's Farewell',* and a sheaf of newspapers. Three Gothic letters from the *Manchester Guardian*'s masthead are visible at a fold. The only unfamiliar object is a blue and white piece of porcelain chinoiserie.

'Tonight', Lewis told Pound on 10 March, 'by rotary photogravure your image will be stamped out one million eight hundred thousand times.' This mechanical proliferation was preparation for an issue of *Picture Post* two weeks hence. Pound's portrait was reproduced in colour, part of a display of nine plates illustrating John Rothenstein's article on Lewis: 'Great British Masters – 26'. Augustus John had been the subject of 'Great British Masters – 25' and John Nash would be the 27th the following week.

The caption in *Picture Post* described it as 'only just finished', but the painting was not, in fact, quite complete. Lewis had yet to paint the planes which were to break up and help differentiate the background: the dark brown section of floor boards and gradated grey wall to the left, the double row of nail heads defining the wash of pale green and ochre to the right as an area of painted canvas.

---

* Sweet, oh Sweet is that Sensation,
  Where two hearts in union meet:
  But the pain of Separation,
  Mingles bitter with the Sweet.

But even when the painter set it aside as complete, a roughness remained. Of the poet's clothes, only the loose Byronic collar has any linear definition. The jacket, tie and waistcoat are barely differentiated in a black, cloudlike billow, thinly and raggedly painted with patches of untouched canvas showing through it. The amorphous body, sloping up from the lower left, has the effect of focusing attention on the precisely modelled head, jammed into the top right corner.

John Rothenstein, appointed Director of the Tate only the year before, had watched the portrait of Pound develop 'with growing admiration' and, although regarding it as 'lacking quite the force and precision of a drawing of the same subject made some eighteen years before', promised Lewis that he would bring it before the next Trustees' committee meeting with a view to buying it for the gallery.

THIRTY-SEVEN

'I want to escape from this economic inferno'

Deprived of its contemporary resonance and context, irony can have an all too short shelf-life. Its meaning can become distorted, even offensive. This was the case with Lewis's analysis of anti-Semitism which appeared on 21 March 1939. It was slated by the *British Union Quarterly* and highly praised by the *Jewish Chronicle*. When published, its title was intended, and recognised, as a parody of Gustaff Renier's best-selling humorous study of national stereotypes: *The English: Are They Human?* Sixty years later, Renier's book forgotten, Wyndham Lewis's book is condemned, unread, on the basis of its title alone: *The Jews Are They Human?*

The *British Union Quarterly* reviewer argued that the question of whether or not Jews were human was irrelevant. Just as, in 1931, Lewis was accused by Dr Thost of the *Völkischer Beobachter* of not understanding the *Judenfrage* and dismissing it as a 'racial red herring', he was now criticised for taking an individualist view of the problem. 'No one', declared the anonymous correspondent whose initials were A.R.T.:

> is going to deny that individual Jews can be both intelligent and interesting; but the problem convulsing the modern world is not that of the individual Jew, but of the collective Jew – the Jewish race.

Lewis was compared unfavourably with Hilaire Belloc, 'as great an intellectual giant', in the opinion of A.R.T., who had pointed out in the early 1920s the folly of ignoring the Jews' 'racial peculiarity'. But both 'intellectual giants' were found wanting when compared with the leader of the British Union of Fascists:

> We prefer Belloc to Lewis, and Mosley to both, because he is prepared to take the lead in that inevitable segregation of the Jewish People, which Belloc had not the intellectual courage to advocate.

The conclusion of Lewis's book was quoted with some gratification, on the other hand, by the *Jewish Chronicle* reviewer:

The 'Jewish Problem' is not inherent in the nature of the Jewish people, but in the character of the Christian nations, and in their attitude towards the Jews . . . We must make up for the doings of the so-called 'Christians' of yesterday – who degraded the Jew, and then mocked him for being degraded. We must give all people of Jewish race a new deal among us. Let us for Heaven's sake make an end of this silly nightmare once and for all, and turn our backs upon this dark chapter of our history.

*

Early in 1939, Lewis was approached, probably for the last time, by his son Peter. The tone of the letter was respectful and conciliatory. He hoped his father would consider him 'less of a nuisance than on the last occasion' they met. Peter was 'in employment' and had married a pretty young woman called Vera Hall on 29 December 1938. The marriage certificate gave his profession as 'Fruit Salesman'. Earlier that year Vera had even spoken to Lewis on her fiancé's behalf, but the purpose and substance of the discussion is not known. Peter now wanted very much to see his father and 'have a chat'. As if to allay any anxieties this prospect might cause, he added: 'no recriminations'.

No details of the reconciliatory meeting between father and son, if indeed it took place, have survived.

*

In mid-April, as tension in Europe increased following the German occupation of Czechoslovakia, and Neville Chamberlain's pledge to defend Poland made war more likely, negotiations with the Tate Gallery over the sale of the Pound portrait were, 'owing to the crisis', temporarily stalled. The Trustees' meeting that was to have decided the matter on 18 April was held over for another month. 'Help!' Lewis wrote to Pound. 'Things have become like a madhouse here . . . *Everywhere* it is the same thing; a complete paralysis. The shops are not renewing their stocks (of needles and thread, blind-cords and whistling kettles) because they have to pay cash.'

*

In May, Laidlaw & Laidlaw published a collection of 'Mr Wyndham Lewis's major utterances on the art of Painting'. It was called *Wyndham Lewis The Artist*. The previous year's portrait of T. S. Eliot figured in the dust wrapper design and the controversy of its rejection by the Royal

391

Academy provided the book's alliterative subtitle: 'From "Blast" to Burlington House'.

Later that month Lewis made his first and only appearance in the infant medium of television. On Tuesday 23 May, at 9.40 in the evening, households in the Greater London area fortunate enough to possess television receivers could have witnessed a 40-minute discussion on contemporary art, broadcast from Alexandra Palace.

Geoffrey Grigson and Wyndham Lewis spoke 'for Modern Art' against two Royal Academicians speaking 'for the Traditionalists': architect Sir Reginald Blomfield and muralist Alfred Kingsley Lawrence. The discussion was chaired by Sir William Rothenstein, 'perched above . . . to see fair play, like a little owl on the table,' Grigson remembered, 'who blinked slowly as owls do.'

Each of the four speakers had chosen two works representative of his 'Modern' or 'Traditional' taste. Statements in defence of his own choice and in denunciation of his opponent's had been prepared in advance. Lewis was pitted against Blomfield, Grigson against Lawrence. Although the discussion was broadcast as it happened, the participants were put through their paces in rehearsal before the great Emitron Cameras began to roll.

'Wyndham Lewis came in looking like a bull spruced for a show', the journalist Hubert Nicholson recalled:

His big face sweated, his thin copper-wire hairs had been brushed back in parallel lines over his blunt head which was going bald. He wore a rough dark green suit flecked with white, a blue-and-white tie and horn-rimmed spectacles behind which he blinked furiously. He looked formidable, but he roared like a sucking dove. He hummed and ha-ed, seemed unable to open his lips freely when speaking and gave . . . a painful impression of stage fright. So much so, that the producer, Mrs Mary Adams, concealed during the rehearsal in a glass loft and speaking down through a terrific loud-speaker, begged him to read his notes, of which he had a large sheaf written in a big round hand.

The audience, apart from Hubert Nicholson and others actually present in the studio that evening, was limited. The number of flickering cathode tubes able to receive the Alexandra Palace signal at that time was around 20,000. The discussion would have had a much wider circulation in the pages of *The Listener*. Here, if any of the stammering inarticulacy of stage-fright remained in Lewis's performance after rehearsal and into the live broadcast, it was edited out in transcription.

Following Rothenstein's introduction it fell to Lewis to open the debate.

He had selected 'a little at hazard' his 'standard revolutionary picture', a still life by Braque:

> What can I find to say in a few words that will enable this modest little scribble to stand up against the succulent turkeys with which you are about to be regaled by Sir Reginald Blomfield?

He used the word 'scribble', with its connotation of handwriting, intentionally:

> A clumsy signature often has more style than a copybook one impeccably executed, so this ramshackle note in oils – for it is only a note – has more style about it than it would have if that dish of fruit were less wobbly – that knife more suggestive of a steel utensil.

When Sir Reginald replied for 'the Traditionalists', he took issue with Braque's wobbly vase and with the jug in the foreground that did not sit properly upon its base. He had chosen another still life, Frank Brangwyn's *Poulterer's Shop*, incidentally pointing out to the viewers that, contrary to what Mr Lewis had said, the bird in the picture was not a turkey but a swan 'hung up with a lot of fruit and vegetables'.

Lewis in turn dismissed the Brangwyn as looking 'like an advertisement from a Victorian cookery book'. Of all the speakers that night, he was the only one who attempted to inject a little irreverent, if heavy-handed, humour into the rather po-faced proceedings. Paradoxically, this may have been due to the fact that nervousness prevented him straying from his written script, prepared jokes and all. 'What Lenin is doing in the background I cannot determine', he said at one point, referring to the balder-headed of two figures on the right of Brangwyn's picture:

> but he is probably up to no good. If I am not mistaken, he is garrotting the poulterer, as I suppose the second figure to be, preparatory to confiscating this unnecessarily lavish display of all the good things in life.

And he followed this observation by suggesting that the vegetables 'would render many of our unemployed delirious with hunger, taken in conjunction with the resplendent poultry.' But for all that, he could not see in the picture 'any of the sensitiveness to shape, that high organisation of form which gives the Chinese and Japanese artists, for instance, so great an advantage over the artists of the West, and which makes the dry little assemblage of roughly scribbled objects in the Braque so much more satisfactory.'

Lawrence chose a rather dull mural by Monnington, Grigson countered with a geometrical composition by De Chirico, featuring two *petit beurre* biscuits. His next offering was *Face of a Market Place* by Paul Klee, to which Lawrence responded with a painting of Loch Lomond by his fellow Academician Sir David Cameron.

When Sir Reginald Blomfield proffered his second choice, the photograph of a piece of sculpture appeared in front of the camera: Hamo Thornycroft's statue of Cromwell in the wide ditch between Parliament Square and Westminster Hall. 'There he is', said Sir Reginald:

> standing in his great riding boots with his right hand on his sword and his left hand clasping the Bible to him. Whatever you may think of Cromwell, he was a great hearted man, and he raised the power and prestige of England to a point which she did not reach again until after the Battle of Waterloo. In my opinion that most impressive figure shows how a sculptor ought to approach his subject.

Lewis began his reply by saying that Thornycroft was a 'photographer in stone' and 'hardly worthy of the name of artist at all'.

At this point Sir Reginald interrupted, hastening to correct his opponent as he had done over the swan a quarter of an hour earlier: 'Excuse me, Mr Lewis,' he said, 'but the figure of Cromwell is not stone but bronze.'

Either Lewis did not hear the interjection, or he refused to be diverted from his script. He introduced a stone figure by Henry Moore 'to banish . . . that totally unplastic pedestrian piece of hard, imitational chopping of Thornycroft's . . . unworthy to be in the Alexandra Palace at the same time as it.'

Sir Reginald did not choose to challenge him on the inappropriateness of the word 'chopping' for a bronze statue. Instead he obligingly conformed to his 'Traditionalist' role by expressing 'disgust and contempt' for the work of Moore and his fellow moderns:

> When I look at these polished and rounded lumps of stone they might mean to me either a woman with no clothes on or they might mean a suet dumpling.

*

When the meeting of the Tate Gallery's Trustees, postponed in April, was finally held on 16 May, it was agreed that the *Portrait of Ezra Pound* be purchased from the artist for £100.

By June their latest acquisition was on display to the public next door to the Whistler room, where its spatial harmonies might have been compared with those of *Arrangement in Grey and Black No. 2*, on loan from Glasgow. Lewis told Pound's father about the close proximity of his son's portrait to Thomas Carlyle's, as if he were inviting such comparison.

He might also have compared the modest sum the Tate trustees agreed to pay him, to the princely one thousand guineas that Whistler had demanded and received from the Glasgow corporation coffers nearly fifty years before.

Nevertheless, he professed himself grateful to the new Director for exercising influence in his favour. ' "Dr John" has done me a very great service', he wrote to Sir William Rothenstein. 'I am quite sure if it had not been for his . . . sympathetic awareness that no one else in that mandarin world would have bestirred themselves from their sluggish groove of unintelligent patronage.'

In fact the knockdown price he was paid for the portrait rankled with him for years afterwards. 'I have a natural dislike of being patronised by sleek gentlemen for whom the fine arts is a fine lucrative official assignment', he told 'Dr John' Rothenstein in 1943:

> I don't like that, in fact it makes me feel a little sick: also always receiving my hundred pounds . . . where others are far more highly rewarded for what is grotesquely bad – I am through with that hundred pounds business too.

To make matters worse the Tate Trustees, their bargain secured, made him wait for his money. Despite the Director's special request for prompt remittance, by 23 June he had still not been paid. 'Where public funds are concerned,' Lewis wrote to Rothenstein:

> the custodians of those public monies . . . should . . . bear in mind the very great hardships of the times in which we live, and not emulate the casualness of the great in settling their debts to the tradesman.

Whether in response to this appeal or incidental to it, the cheque for £100 was sent out to him three days later.

Meanwhile he slaved over other portraits in a stifling heatwave. With only one tiny window that he could open for air, 'a submarine-like atmosphere in its toxic oppressiveness' prevailed under the plate glass of his studio roof.

There were a number of works in progress.

Lord Carlow sat at his ease, an upward curl to one side of the mouth, jacket opulently double-breasted and a sharp vertical crease to the crossed trouser leg. The hands lay in his lap, fingers interlaced and thumbs steepled. *Portrait of a Smiling Gentleman* was another £100 picture.

A portrait of Julian Symons was embarked upon with even lower financial expectation. Lewis offered to paint the editor of *Twentieth Century Verse* and was told he could not afford to pay for it. 'Have you got £10?' Lewis asked. 'You have? Very well, then.' Work began but, perhaps because the monetary incentive was lacking, the portrait was not completed for another decade.

Miss Josephine Plummer worked for the Drama Department of the BBC and was introduced to Lewis by E.W.F. Tomlin, who thought her long face and sharply cut profile would be of interest to him. Perhaps because of the heat, she wore a short-sleeved blouse for the sittings, open at the neck. While he worked, Lewis told her he was relying on the money from this and other portrait commissions to finance a visit to the United States. He had been considering such an expedition for some time.

*

The 1939 World's Fair had opened in New York on 30 April. In the British Pavilion, an exhibition of Contemporary British Art comprised 283 oils, watercolours, drawings and prints. It represented the work of 57 artists and included pictures by J. D. Innes, Ambrose McEvoy, Sickert, Wilson Steer, Augustus John and Muirhead Bone. According to *The Times*, 48 of the 57 were living artists and the remaining 9, although dead, were 'said to have influenced the modern movement'. About 30 of the paintings were the work of Sickert, Steer or John. Lewis, who was not mentioned in *The Times* report, was represented by only one: *The Surrender of Barcelona.**

Back in December, while still contemplating a blank triangle of canvas, he had told Pound:

> I shall I hope be dropping over to the New World . . . The New York Exhibition opens in 5 months time. By March 1st I should be ready to quit work. I shall then have a lot of paintings ready.

His plan was to put on a show of his recent work at a New York gallery, thereby taking advantage of the overflow of interest from the British Pavilion exhibition. From there his ambitions lay to the north and west in a concerted head-hunting campaign:

> My idea is to . . . visit Boston, Chicago and so on, attempting to knock down *sitters* here and there and make 'contacts'. I should not mind being in America for some months.

* It was first exhibited – at the Leicester Galleries in 1937 – as *The Siege of Barcelona*. The painting was reproduced in *Wyndham Lewis the Artist*, published in March 1939, as *The Surrender of Barcelona*, only four months after the Spanish city fell to General Franco's forces.

Nothing came of Lewis's plan to have an exhibition of recent paintings in New York. He and his wife eventually crossed the Atlantic in September. Their stay was to be considerably more than a matter of 'some months'.

*

Following Miss Plummer's last sitting, Tomlin telephoned Lewis to ask how it had gone. 'She never brought the boodle', was the mournful reply. According to Tomlin, Lewis never spoke of the fee or the payment for a portrait. It was always 'the boodle'. Miss Plummer, like the Tate trustees, had clearly not borne in mind the 'very great hardships of the time'.

Nor, unfortunately, had his bank manager. Lewis paid the Tate's £100 into the bank in the last week of June, but the following Monday, when he tried to cash a cheque on his chronically overdrawn account, he was told that 'the political situation is of so very serious a nature as to compel them radically to restrict credit.' Also, a letter was pushed across the counter to him announcing a change of policy regarding his account. He was asked to reduce his overdraft by £25. 'It is precisely that type of action', he complained:

> which makes it so difficult for people placed as I am to earn that surplus which would make it possible to liquidate an overdraft. To say that it is the worst possible moment to ask me to find such a surplus is an understatement.

When he got home he wrote to Naomi Mitchison in somewhat less measured terms:

> What a filthy period we live in. My bank has stopped down on my credit with a bang again ... Every business crook can get credit from these institutions to enable him to carry on his 'work', but not such people as I. Or if they are given a little credit it is stopped suddenly on the grounds that war is likely at any moment! I want to escape from this economic inferno.

He asked her if she would commission him to do three or four drawings of her family for £30 and signed himself 'the beggar of Notting Hill Gate'.

The previous year he had painted Mrs Mitchison's portrait and produced drawings of her youngest son Avrion. The child had been fascinated by inverted pudding basins on the floor of Lewis's studio, especially when told there was a mouse trapped under each of them. Neither he nor his mother ever found out if this was true. A pencil and wash sketch of Valentine

397

Mitchison aged five or six, signed and dated 1939, together with drawings of Denis and Murdoch, her teenage brothers, suggest that the 'beggar of Notting Hill Gate' was allowed to execute his emergency £30 commission.

*

On the Monday in early July that his bank chose to take so unyielding an attitude to Lewis's financial difficulties, a little boy with a talent for draughtsmanship wrote to him from 39 Elm Tree Road, St John's Wood. The letter, comprising two short sentences, provides a glimpse of Lewis in a rather unlikely role. A day or so before, he had judged and presented prizes for an Open Art Competition at the 13th Annual Children's Garden Party in aid of the Duchess of York Maternity Clinic. Proof of this somewhat uncharacteristic departure has survived in the brief letter from St John's Wood, and on the flyleaf of a book awarded to another child and 'presented by Wyndham Lewis as 1st Prize for Portraits by 8 to 10 year olds'. The bizarre image of a large, black-hatted figure on a stage in the sunshine, stooping to shake little hands, is irresistibly brought to mind. The winner of the 1st Prize for Portraits by eight- to ten-year-olds walked away proudly with Compton Mackenzie's *Santa Claus in Summer*. It is not known what the little boy from St John's Wood received his prize for, nor the title of the book he was awarded. All that remains is the polite letter to the gentleman who had given it to him:

Dear Mr Lewis
Thank you for
Judging the drawings.
I won the prize and I
Like the poems inside the
book.
Love from
David.

*

In August a young bearded man arrived in London from Toronto. He wore a Daks suit and orange shirt and brought with him an unpublished first novel that he was anxious Lewis should read. 'I ... sent him the manuscript', the young man recalled, 'which I had finished that I might do just that: send it to him.' The hero-worshipping young Canadian's name was John Reid. His novel was called *There Was a Tree*.

A day or so after posting his manuscript, the telephone rang and a voice like 'some catarrhal Indian colonel' announced itself as that of Wyndham Lewis. Although the flat where Reid was staying lay only five minutes' walk from Kensington Gardens Studios, meticulous directions were given.

Reid found his way, the following afternoon, to the far end of the dark corridor, knocked on the door and waited while a small dog barked on the other side. There were sounds of a scuffle, a whimper, a bolt being drawn, and Lewis appeared in legendary broad-brimmed black hat. Reid thought that Lewis convinced himself at their first meeting, quite incorrectly, that his visitor disliked dogs.

Upstairs in the studio they drank gin and bitters and Lewis told stories about Augustus John. He said he would write an introduction to *There Was a Tree* and offered to introduce Reid to Robert Hale, who had published Lewis's *The Mysterious Mr Bull* the previous November. He confided to Pound that, although it was 'rather a good book . . . about a small Canadian town', he did not think any publisher would touch it because it featured 'little girls undoing little boys fly buttons'. Lying in an untidy heap at one side of his chair, Reid's manuscript had distracted Lewis from working on his own book, a neat white pile on the other. Provisionally entitled *The Jingo God* up to a month before, it was nearing completion as *The Hitler Cult and How It Will End*.

On the eve of the Second World War, the book was a belated revision of his ideas about the man he had referred to as a 'man of peace' less than a decade before. The same eyewitness impressions recorded then were now subtly altered by hindsight. Sitting in the balcony of the Berlin Sportpalast, in November 1930, Lewis had heard Goebbels and Goering speak. The fervour of the audience had gained his respect, even his admiration, certainly his tacit approval.

Nine years later, the event was recalled as a far more ugly phenomenon. A peppering of emotive vocabulary transformed the rally into a fearsome spectacle:

> it was like being at a boxing match. The atmosphere was breathless and fierce, the crowd a boxing-match crowd . . . From the sea of people . . . rose a surge of hoarse applause, sinking to a sultry murmur while it strained its ears for fresh incitements to riot, then suddenly ascending to a scream of hate. I shall always remember the giant rustling and breathing of this mastodon, in the intervals of pandemonium – of this Berlin mob, the New Proletariat in its first months of epileptic life.

*

In the heat of the furore surrounding the Royal Academy's rejection of

Lewis's portrait of T. S. Eliot, he told the *Daily Telegraph*: 'The picture is being bought by public subscription for a large national collection and will eventually be hung in one of the national collections in America.' There was nothing, beyond wishful thinking, to support this claim. But by the end of 1939 the portrait had indeed found a place in a collection, that of the Durban Municipal Art Gallery in South Africa. An anonymous donor supplied the necessary asking price of £200 and the purchase was confirmed by wire on the last day of August. The sale was providential, affording Lewis 'time to turn around and make [his] arrangements' during the following couple of months. On 2 September he left England, with his wife and their dog, and sailed for Canada.

*

Later he claimed to have booked berths for Quebec three months in advance. This was untrue. The stretching of chronology absolved him from a possible charge that he fled his country just as war was declared. Less than a month before, he had still not finalised his travelling plans. 'I hope to get out of here very soon,' he told Pound on 10 August, 'will let you know when.'

So it can only have been three weeks in advance at the most that he booked berths on the *Duchess of York* sailing 1 September. However, because his wife was superstitious about travelling on a Friday, he changed the booking to the *Empress of Britain* that would sail the following day. He had to pay a supplementary charge for berths aboard this much larger ship. John Reid had sailed as a third-class passenger on the *Empress* the previous week. Lewis and his wife followed in a degree of comfort, midway between third and second: Tourist Class.

They sailed from Southampton the day after the Wehrmacht and Luftwaffe swept into Poland. 'Everything was blacked out and battened down', Lewis wrote in a quasi-fictitious memoir the following year. 'As we left we must have looked like a floating coffin.' There was a brief stop to pick up more passengers on the other side of the Channel:

> Indescribable scenes of frantic exodus at Cherbourg. Crowds of rich young men, escaping out of Europe with beautiful women or else with other (beautiful) young men. British, Swiss, French predominate. Aimless bundles of frightened women charged on board with medieval faces, as if escaping from the powers of darkness.

At 11 o'clock the following morning, 3 September, the British ultimatum to Germany to withdraw from Poland expired. An hour later the Prime

Minister, Neville Chamberlain, announced to Parliament and then to the nation that Britain was at war with Germany.

That night three torpedoes from the German submarine U30 exploded into a blacked-out passenger ship 288 miles west of Ireland. At one minute to 9 o'clock the radio station at Malin Head received a distress signal from the SS *Athenia* foundering 56 degrees 44 minutes North, 14 degrees 05 minutes West. Survivors were picked up by the Norwegian tanker *Knut Nelson* and other ships that answered the mayday call, but not before 112 passengers had drowned.

Lewis and his wife meanwhile, on board the *Empress of Britain*, were about a hundred miles away from this, the first attack on shipping of the war.*

Notices were posted throughout the ship. Passengers were instructed to wear their lifebelts at all times and wherever they went. 'They even were to be worn on the lavatory seat', Lewis wrote. 'The first time I wore my lifebelt on the lavatory seat I felt rather absurd. I was glad no one could see me.' After a few days the more reckless passengers began to neglect such precautions. It was reasoned that 'at least the same submarine could no longer be a threat . . . seeing that these little vessels are extremely slow; and seeing also that the sea was exceedingly rough.' Grinning snapshots of Lewis, hand to hat against the wind, standing on deck with his wife and in the company of fellow passengers, show this more relaxed regime: lifebelts still very much in evidence but held like hand luggage, slung over the shoulder or draped across a forearm.

The *Empress of Britain* zigzagged north to avoid the U-boat peril:

> The sea got rougher and rougher, and the temperature colder and colder . . . We had cut off our radio and were holding no communication with the outside world. We were just seeking safety among the ice-floes; and now, all our portholes and saloon-windows blacked out, and our decks hemmed in with canvas, to make us invisible to an external enemy, we were all by ourselves, in an icy sea, plunging along at top speed in the general direction of the Northwest Passage.

The captain and crew, Lewis, his wife and the rest of the passengers could not have known that they had what amounted to a pledge of safe conduct from Adolf Hitler himself, as of midnight on 4 September. Conscious that the sinking of the *Athenia* amounted to another *Lusitania* in terms of adverse

---

* Lewis claimed that his wife's insistence on changing their booking from the *Duchess of York* to the *Empress of Britain* saved their lives because passengers from the *Duchess of York* had been transferred at short notice to the *Athenia*.

propaganda, the German leader sent an urgent order that passenger ships should not be attacked until further notice.

The *Empress of Britain* would remain unharmed until 28 October the following year when, a less discriminating policy being followed by the U-boat fleet, it became the largest Allied passenger vessel sunk by the Germans throughout the war. But for the time being it was plain sailing and, in spite of the evasive diversion close to Greenland, the *Empress* added only one day to her schedule and arrived in Quebec on 8 September.

THIRTY-EIGHT

'How would I live out here without portraits to paint?'

They travelled on to Toronto, where they stayed in the palatial King Edward Hotel for a week. Lewis wrote from there to a friend with the news that he had secured three portrait commissions. This proved an unduly optimistic projection and only one, a portrait of the President of the University of Buffalo, was to materialise.

On 13 September Lewis and his wife met John Reid for tea at Muirhead's, a modern chromium-clad establishment their young friend thought would be to Lewis's taste. Lewis said it was 'like an operating theatre'. There was an uncomfortable moment when Reid told him that a Toronto bookstore was selling off its unwanted copies of *Apes, Japes and Hitlerism*, John Gawsworth's little book about him, published in 1932, for a nickel. It was a first inkling that he might be undervalued in Canada. Reid later believed that by bringing the fate of Gawsworth's book to his attention he became, in Lewis's eyes, 'part of the plot to render him unacceptable'.

But apart from that frisson, Lewis was on good and genial form at Muirhead's. He regaled the young man with anecdotes of their recent adventure, the zigzagging manoeuvres to avoid U-boats and the unwelcome encounters with fellow passengers in the bars. He was already honing his material.

The Lewises' Atlantic crossing, their movements in Canada and the United States, the people they encountered and the places they visited until about midway through the following year can be tracked in *America, I Presume*, the book Howell, Soskin & Co. published in August 1940.

The narrator is a caricatured Englishman, complete with monocle. Lewis adopted the Indian Army background of one of his maternal forebears, although not Lieutenant Henry Benson Stuart's rank, for the blimpish Major Archibald Corcoran. Gladys, on the other hand, was cast as a female version of Lewis himself. Corcoran's wife is an American-born novelist. And with a nod in the direction of Gladys's preferred reading matter, and borrowing the Christian name of that genre's foremost exponent, Agatha Morgan is a writer of detective stories.

Buffalo, where they moved on 15 September, passes as Nineveh, NY: 'queen of the up-state cities, and . . . the tenth largest in the United States'. They stayed first at the Buffalo Hotel, one of the Statler chain, then at the Stuyvesant: 'A House of Homes' its proudest boast. In between they had a brief excursion to the home of Charles D. Abbott.

Abbott was director of the Lockwood Memorial Library at the University of Buffalo, and Lewis had met him in London the year before. He was largely responsible for Lewis's first portrait commission in the United States. 'An awful nice feller', Major Corcoran says of Abbott, thinly disguised as Harry Whitaker. 'A real white man with a jolly decent little wife.' He had been a Rhodes Scholar in the Twenties and was 'still very much Oxford':

> He holds his head high, and stares meditatively in your face. He scans the world about him with an arrogant competence. Whether the slothfulness of his gait and expression is a hangover of the leisure of the Oxford colleges, or just the laziness of the American I cannot decide. He is the sleepiest looking live wire I have ever met, but that he is a live-wire is beyond any manner of doubt . . . A little of the spirit of Cecil Rhodes has got into this indolent American. He is sort of empire-building for Ninevah.

Abbott's academic imperialism took the form of building up the Lockwood Memorial Library's archive of 20th-century literary manuscripts. This was the project that had brought him to London and into Lewis's ken in 1938.

Charles Abbott had another tenuous and, at the same time, potentially embarrassing connection with Lewis. His brother, John Abbott, was married to Lewis's former mistress, Iris Barry. In the late Forties when Stephen Spender passed through Buffalo on a lecture tour, he stayed with Charles Abbott. He remembered being shown a copy of *America, I Presume*, with a key in the back to the true identities of all its characters. Abbott also told Spender that while Lewis was in Buffalo he tried to blackmail him on the subject of his brother's marriage. The wider Abbott family, it seemed, had no idea that John's wife had two illegitimate children. 'It would be to your interest', Lewis is alleged to have told Charles Abbott, 'if I did not publicise the fact that those children were mine.' He even suggested that certain sums of money be placed in a bank account to ensure his continued silence. Spender was not certain how serious Lewis had been in making the suggestion, nor how seriously Abbott had received it.

The Lewises had not been in Buffalo for long when Abbott invited them to Gratwick Highlands for a few days. This was the sprawling run-down country estate, in the Genesee Valley, 50 miles east of the city, where he lived with his 'jolly decent little wife' and child. Theresa Abbott came from a wealthy family that had lost all but Gratwick Highlands in the Depression. Her brother Bill Gratwick lived on the farm with his family, raising Dorset sheep and cultivating tree peony hybrids, while Theresa and Charles occupied the old coach-house. Lewis, his wife and dog stayed in the main house, 'baroque and rustic . . . a massive wooden villa the lines . . . as beautiful as a Chinese junk', with Theresa's mother whose palatial home had once been tended by a staff of between 20 and 30. The bankrupt's widow appears in Lewis's book as Mrs Persons:

> She possessed the glorious white hair American women acquire to grow old gracefully . . . Large and prominent eyes of velvet black, fastening on one with a cynical benevolence, proved Mrs Persons an intelligence that would have to be reckoned with in any drawingroom.

The Lewises' quarters on the first floor were luxurious enough but, because the pumps did not work, there was no hot water. Their hostess only lived there during the summer months, returning to Buffalo in the early fall before the lack of a furnace rendered the place uninhabitable.

*

In late September Lewis began work on the portrait of Chancellor Samuel P. Capen, President of Buffalo University. It was 'a big thing', he wrote to Iris Barry in New York, and 'it occupies me very fully.' The canvas was over six feet high and a little under three feet wide, and both Capen and his wife appeared pleased with the work in progress. Sitter and painter got on well together. When John Reid came from Toronto to visit during the Canadian Thanksgiving weekend, Lewis showed him the unfinished canvas. 'I am trying to make it as academic as possible and still keep it a work of art', he explained.

The commission was being paid for by Thomas B. Lockwood, a prominent Buffalo lawyer who had endowed the Lockwood Memorial Library where Charles Abbott conducted his empire-building. Lockwood had paid $500 up front 'after the minimum of parley' and a further $500 was due on completion.

Having used his influence to secure Lewis the commission, Charles Abbott left town on library business and was away until late December. Before going he assured the Lewises they would be in great demand on the Buffalo cocktail party circuit. But by mid-October invitations were proving scarce. Following the down-payment on the portrait, Lewis claimed to have seen or heard nothing more of Lockwood 'or indeed anybody else'. This was disappointing because it was only by moving among such people, canapé in one hand and martini in the other, that there was any likelihood of further portrait commissions.

There are few clues as to why he was not more of a success in Buffalo society. Abbott heard on his return that there had been 'minor troubles' with Thomas Lockwood. But whatever they were, Abbott told Lewis, they had not 'hung on with Tom, who wrote of you and of the picture with great appreciation'. However, when John Rothenstein arrived in early December he heard complaints that Lewis had offended even those people who did extend social invitations, ensuring that they were not repeated. When she asked him to dinner, one lady told Rothenstein, Lewis insisted on seeing her guest list before he accepted. He had, it seemed, made a number of enemies.

For instance, he saw little of the Washburns after Mrs Washburn was discouraging about his search for studio space. Ruth Washburn may have been stating a simple fact of life when she gave him the benefit of her local knowledge that there were no studios available in Buffalo, but Lewis evidently suspected her of being maliciously unhelpful, and eventually found himself a room on North Street, two blocks from the Stuyvesant Hotel, without her help.

But it was her husband that Lewis came to regard as his principal enemy. Gordon Bailey Washburn was director of the Albright Art Gallery and, according to Lewis, 'considered . . . anything that happened in the City of Buffalo in the field of the Fine Arts should happen through his agency.' If this were the case it was inevitable he should deeply resent the go-getting Abbott's snatching of the Capen commission for his man. Lewis must have reasoned that if there was a concerted campaign to deny him social recognition and withhold cocktail party invitations, Gordon Washburn must have been behind it. Despite this chilliness from the art establishment, Lewis still believed that if the Capen portrait was a success it would lead to further work in the city and that 'something Buffalonian may come along'.

Nothing else did. Marshall McLuhan heard the rest of the story from Lewis three years later:

> You can divine what ensued: you know how bored people are in a provincial city and how intrigue is necessary to them. I found myself in the middle of a gang war and was the protégé of the weaker gang. For result, my portrait, although greatly liked by the sitter . . . was attacked and belittled . . . as soon as it was on view – and indeed before anyone had seen it.

Chancellor Capen himself told Lewis that the hostile faction derided it as looking 'like a poster'.

Real or imaginary as these conflicts between rival cultural power bases might have been, Lewis could still conveniently blame such political considerations for his failure to win more portrait commissions. And a stranger wandering across this battle ground might have got a different impression of the conflict depending upon which of the protagonists he spoke to. John Rothenstein, for instance, heard the complaints of 'the friendly Director of the Albright Art Gallery'. Lewis had told Washburn that he felt snubbed and that his presence in Buffalo was not being 'officially recognised' by the Albright. As a consequence it was Lewis who refused to allow his portrait of Capen to be exhibited there.

Official recognition of a sort was granted when an audience gathered in the large ivy-clad Italianate building at 595 Delaware Avenue to hear him speak. The bulletin of the Twentieth Century Club had apprised its membership of his credentials: 'Wyndham Lewis, painter, poet, novelist and pamphleteer, leader of the Vorticist movement in England – to which T. S. Eliot, Ezra Pound and Hulme belonged. Author of "Tarr", also of "Revenge for Love" and "Time and Western Man".' On Wednesday 15 November, 'Mr Lewis will speak on Intellect and Character in the Arts.' The lecture was to be followed by a 'Thanksgiving Luncheon'.

It was the only speaking engagement Lewis had in Buffalo during the whole of a two-and-a-half month stay. Nevertheless, when Rothenstein lectured the following month it was 'apparent from the number of questions asked about him that the presence of Lewis was provoking the liveliest interest.'

When Lewis requested an endorsement from the Twentieth Century Club he approached the member who had probably been most active in inviting him. Significantly, this was one of the faction favourably disposed to Chancellor Capen's portrait. Mrs Grace Capen told him that, while her club did not give official endorsements to speakers, she was prepared to answer any prospective enquiries herself.

*

The *Buffalo Courier-Express* of Wednesday 29 November reported that the portrait of Samuel P. Capen had been formally presented to the University of Buffalo the day before at the annual meeting of the University Council. It is clear from the press photograph of the Chancellor, standing alongside his slightly larger than life size 'brilliantly-executed likeness', that more work was still to be done on it. The lower right corner was still lacking Lewis's customary space-filling fantasia of patterned drapery, and also the pile of books which any academic subject must traditionally expect to find at his elbow.

When he had written to Rothenstein, on 17 November, Lewis and his wife were expecting to leave for New York some time around the 25th. But departure was postponed by continued work on the portrait and by an invitation from Toronto. Since his visit to Buffalo the month before, John Reid had been busy on Lewis's behalf and, through an intermediary, arranged for him to meet a potential source of further commissions, the President of Canada Packers, J. Stanley McLean. Gladys remained in Buffalo as Lewis left on this short head-hunting expedition. Before going he must have surrendered the Capen portrait to the University on the understanding that it be returned to him for finishing after the Council meeting.

On the same day people in Buffalo got their first sight of the portrait in the bleary newsprint of the *Courier-Express*, and its detractors were able to attack it before it was even properly finished, Lewis was at the University of Toronto, signing the visitor's book in Hart House, guest of the English Warden. It was J. Burgon Bickersteth's custom to invite celebrities to dinner and show them the facilities of which he was so proud. Three days before Lewis, John Rothenstein had been so honoured. The great three-storey pseudo-Gothic pile of Hart House had been opened on Armistice Day 1919 and was now 20 years old. A social and recreational centre of the University, and open to undergraduates of all faculties, it contains restaurants, bars, library, cinema, theatre, swimming pool, rifle range, gymnasium, and even a raked indoor running track on the first floor. Membership was, and remained until the 1970s, exclusively male. Lewis was given a comprehensive tour of the place and devoted an entire chapter of *America, I Presume* to it. Major Corcoran is conducted at a punishingly strenuous pace around Brunswick Hall by its enthusiastic Warden, Brandleboyes. He is shown everything, not 'let off a single clothes closet or private lavatory'.

Much of the journey is at basement or sub-basement level in a labyrinth of overheated passages and chambers through which Brandleboyes, Virgil-like, guides his monocled Dante. Like 'a couple of invisible interlopers' they are largely ignored by the young men who cross their path.

Shown the art collection, built gradually over a number of years with judicious purchases of contemporary Canadian work, the narrator admits:

I hate pictures and I'm not ashamed to say it . . . However, one is obliged to look at the beastly things. People disburse good hard cash for them and expect you to look at them.

Through the Philistine consciousness of the Major, Lewis held Bickersteth's domain up to gentle, and sometimes abrasive, ridicule. The mural decorations of the small chapel, for instance, had been recently completed by the Canadian painter William Ogilvie:

> More pictures! . . . hundreds of horrid little angels, all with the same face, like strings of quintuplets. Like that Johnny Blake, that kind of thing. Spooky and ugly. Hope I don't go to heaven if it looks like that.

Such comments, when published the following year, may have prepared a somewhat cooler reception in certain quarters for Lewis's return to Toronto in November 1940, than that accorded him in November 1939. And to those same quarters his innuendo-laden presentation of the all-male community and its well-respected Warden would have seemed offensive if not libellous.

At an early point on their tour, Brandleboyes and Corcoran look down on two brightly lit arenas that must have been squash courts, to see:

> a blaze of athletic flesh . . . two pairs of dazzlingly naked young gentlemen, with the bulging breasts with birdsnests in the middle, and bulbous calves, obtained by those who muscle around after balls . . . They wore only a piece of tape round the waist and a dangling twisted rag in front.

Brandleboyes whispers to Corcoran: 'We don't allow women in here! It wouldn't do.' And as one young giant turns, attention focuses as through a zoom lens, upon a single detail: 'a tape trickling down the cleft of his buttocks'. In the sweaty atmosphere of barely suppressed homo-eroticism, Corcoran finds his mind running on unaccustomed lines, among images of gladiatorial combat and voluptuous slaughter:

> of swords plunged into those heaving shining bodies: of those eyes rolled up in death, as vanquished they sank upon the sand of the circus. How much better than bulls! . . . a boy bleeding to death in the arena.

After viewing other completely naked young men sporting in the swimming pool, the Major remarks: 'What a place for Socrates!' and the Warden lays a hand on his arm: 'I'm glad you like all this, Corcoran.'

When he returned to Toronto the following year, two months after the publication of *America, I Presume*, Lewis was at pains to assure a friend that no offence had been intended:

> I feel that if the [Warden] . . . realised how impressed I was – for I can say with my hand on my heart that I do not believe another such educational, or recreative, wonder is to be found anywhere on this earth, and that it is a tremendous feat to have built up that hive of collegiate activity – he would not mind the burlesque form my admiration took.

He did, however, realise that the chapter might have caused offence but concluded: 'No great harm seems to have been done, fortunately.'

Bickersteth was not available for comment when the book was published. He had returned to England in June on temporary leave from his Wardenship and was doing his bit as a member of the Home Guard in Canterbury. Over 20 years later, following his retirement, he was interviewed at great length for a history of Hart House and his copious reminiscences were recorded. Nowhere in the conversation, or at least in that part of the conversation transcribed and published in 1969, was any mention made of Wyndham Lewis, his visit, or of his 'hymn of praise, couched in burlesque form'.

Lewis on the other hand probably dined out on the experience for some time. The day after signing his name in the Hart House visitors' book, he gave John Reid a full account. They were in the back of a taxi cab on their way to the York Club, on the corner of Bloor and St George, for a dinner hosted by J. S. McLean. The story, Reid recalled, was a lot funnier than the version in *America, I Presume*, 'where he had time and the necessity to falsify it.'

Gathered at dinner to meet Lewis that St Andrew's Night were eight of the most cultivated men in Toronto. McLean himself was one of the city's most prominent art collectors, and a year later this meat-packing millionaire would provide Lewis with commissions for two portraits and bring influence to bear on the commissioning of another: a portrait of himself paid for by his employees.

Douglas M. Duncan was proprietor of the Picture Loan Society, a generous patron of Canadian art and regular source of emergency folding assistance to Lewis in the difficult years following his return to Toronto.

Barker Fairley taught German Literature at the University, but was also a critic and talented amateur painter. He represented a potentially invaluable entrée to the city's academic community.

Terence W. MacDermot was Master of a prestigious private boys' school: Upper Canada College. He had been instrumental, with John Reid, in arranging for Lewis to meet McLean.

Eric Arthur was an architect and architectural historian.

Lastly, the three most important contemporary Canadian painters were there: A. Y. Jackson, Charles F. Comfort and Carl Schaefer. Jackson in particular was to prove a generous friend, and Lewis would have seen Comfort's striking portrait of Schaefer the day before, hanging above the library fireplace at Hart House.

After dinner they all drove out to the McLean estate. Russia had invaded Finland and, that day, reports were coming in that Helsinki was being bombed. The well-lubricated gaiety might have been slightly subdued, but Lewis was still the life and soul of the party. Everything must have seemed possible to him that night. He was in good and influential company and there must have been talk of portrait commissions over dinner. MacDermot had a friend and colleague in Montreal who would want his portrait painting. He also knew people in the legal profession and a couple of months later passed on the news that the Law Society of Upper Canada wished to commission a Chief Justice's likeness. But all that could wait. He was on his way first to see what conquests New York had to offer, and it is not altogether surprising that he was in ebullient mood when he left late that night. Reid remembers him in the snow outside the McLean house, 'displaying his newly-acquired boxer's victory shake of clasped hands above his head'.

The following day he returned to Buffalo. He was still in great good humour on 6 December when he sent a note to John Rothenstein, who had just arrived and was staying around the corner from the Stuyvesant. He even gave the newcomer advice on American pronunciation: 'ring me at GRANT 8020. Remember to say "Grant" not "Grarnt" or they won't understand you.'

Rothenstein visited later the same day. The studio on North Street had been given up and Lewis was putting finishing touches to the Capen portrait in his hotel room. The visitor thought it 'not among his best' but did not say so. 'I think you know my wife', Lewis said. Rothenstein did not, although he recognised Gladys from the portrait, *Froanna*, he had seen at the Beaux Arts Gallery, in London, the previous June. This was the first time Lewis had introduced her to him or even mentioned her existence.

Conversation was dominated by the events in Europe and in particular Russia's Finnish adventure. Lewis was still struggling to come to terms with the Nazi–Soviet Pact and its implications. 'The revelation of the opportunism of forces he had assumed to be consistently antithetical had shocked him', Rothenstein recalled. As they spoke, Lewis's new book on Nazism, *The Hitler Cult*, was being published in London, and he knew that its argument was skewed by events before it could even reach the bookshops.

There was also talk of the Buffalo hostilities, and Lewis seemed amused by the 'widespread local consternation' his presence appeared to have provoked.

A few days later, leaving the now definitively completed portrait of Chancellor Samuel P. Capen to the defence or derision of whichever Buffalo faction emerged in the ascendant, Lewis and his wife boarded the train for New York.

Abbott got back to town after their departure and did not see the portrait until early January. 'I was taken completely off my feet', he gushed to Lewis the following day:

> Really, you know, it's a brilliant job . . . I knew you could do it, and knew you would do it; and now I am inclined to crow in the face of the doubters.

The less enthusiastic Rothenstein remembered something Lewis had said in his Stuyvesant Hotel room, with the six-foot canvas, nearly finished, standing in the background: 'If there's one thing more than another that I'm afraid of, it is that America will come into the war and lose her new-found cultural interests, including the commissioning of portraits. After all,' he said, 'how would I live out here without portraits to paint?'

THIRTY-NINE

'This tough city'

When Lewis and his wife booked into the Winthrop Hotel on the corner of Lexington and 47th in the second week of December 1939, the 'grim, abstract metropolis' of New York City was in thrall to two powerful cultural icons: Santa Claus and Pablo Picasso.

'It is a spectacle. It is immense', the *New York Times* correspondent wrote of the 360-odd oils, sculptures, watercolours and lithographs that made up the Museum of Modern Art's Picasso Retrospective that had opened a month before. It had been well trumpeted in advance by the furriers Bergdorf and Goodman, who were entrusted with a number of the oils and displayed them in their windows on 5th Avenue at 58th Street. 'WE ARE PROUD TO EXHIBIT OUR FURS WITH SEVEN GREAT PICASSOS', crowed the advertising campaign. *Nude in Grey* and *Bone Forms Against the Sky* could be viewed through the plate glass amongst Chinchilla, Russian Sable, Ermine and Mink, the latter 'supple and magnificent in this notable Mink year'. John Rothenstein described the 'extraordinary scenes' when the MOMA exhibition opened and the public clamoured to expose themselves to the avant-garde:

It was the first occasion on which I had seen paintings induce a near-riot mentality. A vast crowd seethed and jostled in all but hopeless attempts to get near the exhibits. People were desperately fighting their way; girls with torn dresses and tears in their eyes were wandering lost in the concourse.

Iris Barry, who had 'a rather pleasant job' at MOMA, 'more or less under the Rockefeller wing – doing things about movies', told Lewis that the gallery was 'crowded beyond belief, people even queueing up outside to get in, and it [was] quite impossible to see anything seriously'.

While he was still in Buffalo Lewis had been commissioned by John Crowe Ransom of the *Kenyon Review* to write an article on the show. The magazine paid $5 for a page of between 350 and 400 words – 'not enough' Ransom admitted – and the deadline for the Spring issue was 10 February. Lewis submitted a 6,000-word antidote to the Picasso fever, calling him 'a protean jack-in-the-box among painters: a painter who deserves our admiration and attention certainly, but who should not be allowed to develop into a stultifying obsession, as he threatens to do in the United States.' He was, Lewis declared, 'an interpreter rather than a creator – a great critic and "taster", rather than a man who wants to make something new'.

Among the first people Lewis contacted on reaching New York was the publisher James Laughlin IV. Pound had told him the head of New Directions Books had rich relatives. 'Pittsburgh steel is in the background', he thought, and 'his ma and especially aunt need portraits.' Henry Eliot was not sure whether it was 'Pittsburgh glass' or 'Chicago steel' but he 'has money and knows people with money'. Lewis assured Laughlin that his prices were reasonable and his painting style inoffensive:

> I will take any mug that offers, without insulting it, or experimenting with its facial items. (No billiardballs for eyes, postiche noses or cauliflower ears! Such a job as Durer or Bellini would have done, were they alive today.)

However, he did not succeed in gaining a commission from either Laughlin or any of his relatives.

At the house of the architect Philip Johnson, Lewis met Geoffrey Stone, a young critic who was to be a source of emergency handouts when life in New York began to get difficult. Stone invited him to visit 'Sheepfold', the farm where he lived in Bethlehem, Connecticut, to do a portrait drawing and stay for the New Year festivities. Lewis accepted on condition the invitation be extended to his wife and dog. 'The ideal time would be 4 or 5 days, for several sittings would be desirable.' He told Stone that a pencil and wash drawing would cost $150.

Lewis arrived in Bethlehem during Christmas week bearing all the tackle of his trade, but otherwise unaccompanied. After a couple of days he announced that he had wanted to look the place over before fetching his wife. Then he went back to New York and returned with Gladys and Jo-Jo in time for New Year's Eve. They stayed for ten days.

Lewis had difficulty achieving a likeness of the squarely handsome Geoffrey Stone. He made several attempts and eventually handed over two for the reduced price of $250 the pair. He was not entirely satisfied with either of them.

He drew Stone's wife a year later in severe profile, pose and features reminiscent of Baldovinetti's *Portrait of a Lady in Yellow* at the National Gallery in London. This quattrocento Florentine quotation in snowclad New England may have been a gesture towards Dora Stone's Italian parentage. She found Lewis charming and, apart from behaving 'quite hysterically fearful if one tried to seat him in a restaurant with his back to the public', very much at his ease in congenial company:

> I think the most endearing quality . . . which to me, seemed to prove him a splendid fellow, was his intense interest in everyone and everything around him. He never talked about himself but managed to draw everyone else out. For instance, my husband, being very reserved and mostly silent was inspired by Lewis to speak out and his wit had us all in paroxysms of laughter – Lewis being the most appreciative.

Paradoxically, this inspirational influence did not extend to Mrs Lewis, who 'rarely opened her mouth', according to Dora Stone. 'Lewis so overshadowed her that she seemed not to be there.'

*

By 9 January 1940 they were back in New York, staying this time at the Tuscany Hotel at 120 East 39th Street. Rothenstein was in town at the same time and he and Lewis went out together. Lewis was in boisterous spirits, Rothenstein recalled, and sang lustily in the taxi that conveyed them from restaurant to café. This was the only occasion he ever heard Lewis sing.

They talked of hatreds and literary expression. Lewis claimed he felt no rancour towards individuals but only towards ideas, systems and institutions. Rothenstein challenged this assertion, pointing to the way, in his writings, Lewis skinned individuals alive who personified neither institutions, systems nor ideas. He also pointed out that Lewis needed individuals and not abstractions to satisfy his impulse to rancour. Lewis conceded a point here: 'But even were it possible, should one suppress hatreds?' Rothenstein believed that one should come to terms with hatred, expelling it from the system, but that the man of conscience should direct his hatred towards legitimate targets. Lewis replied:

> But you know, we're all of us ridiculous and wide open to attack to anyone with sharp eyes and the opportunity of using them. You say that one ought to get one's hatreds out of one's system legitimately. The most effective means of ridding my own system of a quantity of putrescent matter would be to write a book on Roger Fry: he personifies as much as anybody what I dislike most about the art world, and I've always disliked the man himself. And if ever I make enough money to be able to afford to disregard the uproar it would raise, I'll write it.

Then he added: 'You wouldn't care to collaborate, would you? I suppose as an official it would be difficult for you to serve up quite such strong meat as that book would be.'

*

On the afternoon of 26 January he was in Harvard to speak on 'Satire and Contemporary Poetry', invited by Theodore Spencer, whom he had met on his last visit eight years before. Among his audience was I. A. Richards's wife Dorothy. A fortnight later she wrote to a friend: 'Wyndham Lewis came and read a lecture or rather muttered a few minutes before reading great slabs of his very limp one way song. Undergraduates were nearly all laughing at him before he'd finished. But perhaps that is the fate of all idols.'

The lacklustre impression he made upon Mrs Richards is surprising if the performance of sections from *One Way Song* recorded during the visit is anything to go by. Writers are not always the best readers of their work, but Lewis acquitted himself well, rattling over the complexities of diction like a train over points and sounding every one of the consonants with which his verse bristled.

*

Back in New York, on 1 February he had a meeting with the publishing firm of Howell, Soskin & Co. on East 45th Street, and attempted to interest them in the American rights for *The Hitler Cult*. William Soskin wrote a fortnight later expressing the discouraging view that, even with a specially written introduction, it would not 'overcome the chronic American boredom with the subject of Hitler that has set in'. On the other hand he had higher hopes for another type of book from Lewis:

> It occurs to me that you have been in America long enough, and attentively enough to have a book churning in you on the subject. As you know, the natives here are suckers . . . for British observation. Wouldn't you like to consider something of the sort for the Fall?

As if no sooner said than done, Lewis was sent a contract on 1 March and by mid-April Soskin had a manuscript for *America, I Presume*.

There was another book 'churning' which did not so readily find an American market. Five days after his initial meeting with William Soskin, Lewis lunched with Louis P. Birk, vice-president of Modern Age Books Inc., to whom he gave the opening section of a novel. When complete, this was eventually to be published, although not in America during Lewis's lifetime, as *The Vulgar Streak*. It had been promised for some time.

A contract was signed with the London publisher Robert Hale for the novel, provisionally entitled *Men at Bay*, in September 1937. The action of the first part is set in Venice during the Munich Crisis of September 1938 and was written before the Lewises left England. A later section, concerned with counterfeiting money, was researched in March 1939 when Lewis visited the 'Black Museum' at Scotland Yard to obtain 'technical dope' on the subject. The novel's protagonist is Vincent Penhale, a young man of apparently privileged background who is, in fact, a child of the Poplar slums of East London. A self-made Eliza Doolittle, he has so convincingly altered his accent and mannerisms and invented his public school education, that he passes comfortably among members of a class far above his own. Funds to carry off the deception are acquired from passing counterfeit money.

Modern Age Books Inc. considered the opening section of *The Vulgar Streak* for a week before returning it to its author. Birk and his colleagues believed the novel to be 'too deeply orientated toward European taste to have a strong enough appeal for the average American reader'. However, it was hoped that Lewis would approach them again with 'a novel of a more general topic than the theme of the war or pre-war period'.

This was not the last time Lewis would be told that his writing needed to be tailored to an American readership. Selden Rodman at *Common Sense* even went so far as to return him a commissioned article on the World's Fair as being 'too obviously "dashed off"'. Rodman apologised for 'the necessarily small fee' they had offered him but added caustically: 'even when we don't pay anything we expect, and get, the author's best.'

One of those who would reiterate such advice in the coming months was John Jermain Slocum, junior partner, shareholder and secretary of a new firm of literary agents, Russell & Volkening, on 5th Avenue. During the first quarter of 1940, even before the agency was fully in operation, and having only an office, stenographer and contract of incorporation, but as yet no furniture or telephone, Lewis was meeting Slocum regularly.

An appointments book records his activities throughout February and March until the second week of April, when torn-out pages preclude further investigation. There were eleven meetings with Slocum, one with E. E. Cummings at the urging of Pound, a renewal of acquaintance with Ben Hecht at the Jack and Charlie Club on West 52nd, a lunch in the Faculty Club with Professor Donald Lemen Clark, and an informal supper given by the Professor's wife in the Lewises' honour, to which Peter Jack and other writers and artists were invited. Lewis was also to be seen at the apartment and gallery of Alfred Stieglitz, photographer, picture dealer, and husband of the painter Georgia O'Keeffe.

On the evening of 14 February, at Columbia University, while a blizzard engulfed the city, he gave a lecture, written the day before, on the subject 'Should American Art Differ from European Art'. Afterwards, a member of his audience, Israel Citkowitz, a 31-year-old music teacher and composer, told Lewis that he had recently been the subject of 'a political storm' in New York. The young man's sister, Rebecca Citkowitz, had written a favourable notice of *The Revenge for Love* for the left-wing periodical *Partisan Review* and it had been returned to her as unsuitable. Again she had submitted it and again it had been returned. Submitting it a third time and demanding an explanation she received a letter from the editor to the effect that her glowing appraisal of a novel portraying Communist activists in so negative a light was inadmissible to the *Partisan Review*'s pages and that 'if [the protagonist] Percy Hardcaster was *her* idea of a communist it was not *his*.' It was an obvious parallel with the rejection of Roy Campbell's review of *The Apes of God* by the *New Statesman*. The single difference was that Citkowitz's piece had not been spiked for the alleged personal spite of an editor whose friends he had offended, but on political grounds.

For that thrice rejected article in defence of his work, Lewis greeted her warmly when they met, later calling her his best friend in New York: 'a Russian Jewish young woman who writes – physically a Virginia Woolf of the Bronx, shrinking, and by turns mildly bold.'

*

On 13 March the Lewises moved from the Tuscany Hotel into apartment E5, 81 Irving Place, Gramercy Park, 'a quite pleasant little place formerly occupied by Thornton Wilder'. It would be recalled nostalgically from the austerity of postwar London as being just round the corner from Esposito's on Third Avenue where 'melons and things' could be bought. Despite having it only on a three-month lease, Lewis ordered headed writing paper from a local printer a week after moving in, giving the address a confident air of permanence for business purposes.

He was, however, already harbouring the suspicion that his prospects in New York were not of the best. 'In the four months since my arrival,' he told Alfred H. Barr of the Museum of Modern Art, 'great stagnation has attended my presence here.' He had hopes of Barr, as one who could 'sponsor [him] with the intelligent rich'. In June 1938, during an exhibition of Lewis's work at the Beaux Arts Gallery in London, hastily put together to capitalise on the publicity from the 'rejected portrait' uproar, Barr had bought the oil study of T. S. Eliot on behalf of a Mrs Resor. Now the director of MOMA attempted to use his influence to secure Lewis a commission to paint that lady's husband and others of 'the intelligent rich'. Nothing came of Barr's efforts. Even the well-connected Mrs Florence Lamont, patron of the arts, and married to a director of the Carnegie Corporation, had been discouraging about the possibility of portrait commissions. The war was on everyone's mind, she told Lewis, to the exclusion of all other considerations.

During the year he spent in New York, the only tangible prospect of lucratively exercising his brush came from north of the border. Terence MacDermot, one of the men who had feted Lewis at the York Club in Toronto on St Andrew's Night, wrote with news that the Law Society of Upper Canada wanted a portrait of the Chief Justice of Ontario. MacDermot told the Society's treasurer, D. L. McCarthy, that Lewis was known to charge between $2,000 and $3,000 for a portrait, but would probably accept less. MacCarthy was confident he could persuade the finance committee to pay $2,000. Lewis was 'the coming portrait painter of the day', he assured Goldwyn Larrett Smith KC, the committee's chairman:

> I have made the most searching enquiries . . . and everybody tells me that if we can get a Wyndham Lewis . . . we are extremely lucky.

The chairman was not impressed, however:

> I have no doubt but that Mr Lewis is all that you say he is as a portrait painter but I do not think the Society can afford to pay his price even if the portrait could be obtained for $2,000 . . . I do not think we should spend more than $500 . . . After all, what we want is a likeness and not a work of art.

*

In May, Lewis and Gladys paid their second visit to Gratwick Highlands to stay with the Abbott family. He was fascinated by this decadent relic of financial ruin and his description, in the book published later that year, tipped over into purple melancholy:

> Nothing . . . had been touched since the Depression hit these gardens like a typhoon . . . In a tennis court a torn and rain-soiled net drooped. In a hollow garden hidden with large trees, an extinct fountain at its centre, fragments of statues and bits of pediments lay submerged in prairie-grass, where the wilds were coming again. A high walled kitchen-garden . . . was

an expanse of vegetation to which it is impossible to give a name. What happens if fruit is not picked, if potatoes and turnips are not removed from the soil where they grew, if cabbages and dockleaves and a hundred other varieties of parasite and waste product all sprout on each other's backs, had happened here.

The eastern side of the gardens afforded a view out across the Genesee Valley, and 30 miles due south, on the opposite side of the river and still just within the boundary line of Livingston County, lay the village of Nunda. The local people pronounced it 'Nunday' and 'Nunday' was how Lewis remembered hearing of it as a child.

Eighty years before, old Shebuel Lewis had arrived here from a log cabin 20 miles away in Caneadea, Alleghany County. He brought with him his wife and sons and six-year-old daughter Mary who, in 1893, would be so 'grieved and astonished' when her brother 'Char' absconded from her New York home with a pretty English housemaid. Mary's two youngest brothers, Henry and Julius, were 11 and 9 when the family settled in Nunda, while Albert, Charles and George ranged from 13 to 19.

Charles Edward Lewis's son made a pilgrimage to the place his father had spoken of as home. Charles Abbott drove him there. They stood on Stone Quarry Hill to the south of the village and looked down towards the gorges and falls of the Genesee. It was a paradise for Fenimore Cooper-inspired childhood where the Lewis boys had 'emulated Leatherstocking, and hunted woodchuck with catapults'. At the foot of the hill was the house and the 'tract or parcel of land' that old Shebuel, Lewis's grandfather, had purchased in 1859. Locally it was known as 'Cedar Place' because of the trees that once lined the long walk from highway to house.

Family legend had it that Charles returned here from West Point and announced his intention of joining the Confederacy but was dissuaded by family pressure and enlisted in the Union Army instead. Standing on the wooded hill overlooking Nunda, his son believed that it was as much the place as the people that had tipped the balance in favour of his joining the Northern cause: 'once he had gone to Nunda, he was lost to the South.' And one of Charles's brothers wrote in 1900 of the emotional power and pull of the name alone, 20 years after leaving, when Nunda was only an occasional railroad stop en route to other destinations:

It is the most genial halt on the line. Then it is we are partially aroused from our listless indifferent state by the shock produced in a sudden cessation of the infernal vibration, and are brought full out of our lethargy by the porter shouting in stentorian tones, 'Nunda! Nunda! Twenty minutes for refreshments!' – 'Nunda!' we exclaim involuntarily. 'Why

Nunda is home!' And there is a tremulousness in the voice – for this is not home-in-law but in-nature. Not the teasing invention of a later fancy, but the original and indisputable heritage of early love.

'The peace of the Genesee', Lewis told Iris Barry on his return to New York, 'was the most unreal thing [he had] ever experienced.'

*

In mid-June, their lease up on the apartment in Gramercy Park, they moved into the Hotel Brevoort and thence, in July, to a house at the far end of Long Island for August, September and half of October. This holiday accommodation, a hundred miles away from 'the pluperfect hell' that was New York in summer, came rent-free, courtesy of John Jermain Slocum. Representative of the fledgling firm of Russell & Volkening, Inc., Slocum was, by this time, Lewis's exclusive American literary agent.

It was in the Jermain House, Main Street, Sag Harbor, that he settled down to finish writing *The Vulgar Streak* – W. W. Norton & Co. having returned to him the first third, professing themselves 'too much in a doubting Thomas mood to plump for the manuscript at this stage'.

While awaiting completion of this book, Slocum was attempting to place short pieces of journalism for his new client and impressing upon him that, although the contents of *Esquire* magazine might appear 'slick and superficial', the handling of such material had to be anything but, requiring finishing 'to a fine bright polish'. Accordingly, his agent returned to Lewis an article entitled 'American Citizenship is a Rite, not a Passport', feeling it to be 'a little hasty, a little slap-dash'. Slocum also thought the piece was inadequately researched:

> It doesn't seem to me you have taken the trouble to find out why we have certain restrictions on citizenship, which the British don't need, as it has been many generations since any great numbers of foreign nationals desired to become British citizens.

Lewis had also, it seemed, misjudged the feelings of his potential readership:

> Above all else it seems foolish . . . to lay yourself open to the charge of rank ingratitude. That you can find no good word to say for [the] immigration system of the country that harbors you, while your chosen foster country goes up in smoke. At a moment like this it is possible to jest about the difficulties and nuisances connected with citizenship, but only from a sympathetic point of view.

The 'difficulties and nuisances' connected with alien status had been exercising Lewis considerably. He and his wife had already, three months before, applied for and been granted an extension of their temporary stay in the United States, until 9 September. This expiry date approaching, in August Lewis attempted to establish his American citizenship. Section 1993 of the Revised Statutes of the United States appeared to favour the claim, even if his possibly spurious declaration, that he was born on a yacht in Canadian waters, had been true:

> All children . . . born out of the limits and jurisdiction of the United States, whose fathers were . . . at the time of their birth citizens thereof, are declared to be citizens of the United States.

His claim was disqualified, however, by the first paragraph of Section 2 of the Act of 2 March 1907:

> That any American citizen shall be deemed to have expatriated himself when he has . . . taken an oath of allegiance to any foreign state.

The Department of State so deemed that Lewis had forfeited his citizenship when he swore allegiance to King and Country on entering military service for the British Empire in 1916. Accordingly it was as aliens that Lewis and his wife continued 'to have [their] fingers and toes inked and impressed upon printed forms and a lot of other clownishness', in order to remain in the United States a further two months.

By September *The Vulgar Streak* was finished and being considered by the firm of Howell, Soskin & Co., who had brought out *America, I Presume* the month before. By the beginning of October they had decided not to publish the novel and Lewis was forced to borrow first $225 and then a further $50 from John Slocum. Taking into account $100 lent to him previously, Lewis was now in debt to his agent to the tune of $375. Slocum drew up a note for his client to sign, agreeing that $100 would come from any advance on *The Vulgar Streak* when it was eventually disposed of, and the remainder from a number of short stories Russell & Volkening were trying to place. Lewis had been under the impression that the $100 had been a personal loan having nothing to do with his and Slocum's professional relationship. He insisted that a clause be inserted to the effect that $100 be forfeit from the novel's advance only if that advance amounted to $500 or over. As always, when made overly aware of a financial obligation, Lewis took offence and made a note of the transactions conducted in the offices of Russell & Volkening 1 and 2 October. He 'resented very much the offensive and high handed way this operation was carried through by Mr Slocum.' He never repaid the money.

From Howell, Soskin & Co., *The Vulgar Streak* went to Duell, Sloan & Pearce, who held on to it for much of October. Initial verbal reactions were favourable. He had done a 'magnificent job', they told him, and it was 'the best book [he had] written'. Nevertheless, towards the end of the month, they too declined to publish it on the grounds that it was 'too critical of England'. Slocum then passed the manuscript to Doubleday, Doran & Co.

'There is . . . no "criticism of England" involved in this book', Lewis told his agent, 'not of *England*, but of something that handicaps England intellectually. In so far as the theme may be detached from the pure storytelling, the educational system of the English Middle Class as organised by Dr Arnold in the last century comes under fire.' In short the book was critical of English 'social snobbery (the bane of the Arnold system)' rather than of England itself.

*

The Lewises left Sag Harbor on 21 October and spent the final weeks before their enforced move to Canada back at the Hotel Brevoort. After four months of rent-free accommodation, the high cost of a week of New York living hit hard, so that when *The Vulgar Streak* was rejected for a second time Lewis's spirits plummeted. It was particularly aggravating that he had incurred extra expense awaiting Duell, Sloan & Pearce's fruitless decision. On 27 October he wrote a number of desperate letters. He wrote to Frank Morley at Harcourt & Brace asking for $50. He wrote to Iris Barry requesting $50 but, on second thoughts, asked her for $100 as an advance on some drawings she was enjoined to sell to Barr at the Museum of Modern Art. He wrote to James Johnson Sweeney asking for $35 to cover his rent at the Brevoort.

Sweeney, a lecturer at the Institute of Fine Arts, had recently received a letter from an old friend of Lewis's, living in the so-called 'free zone' of France, some 12 miles from Vichy. Three months before his death, James Joyce was trying to move his family to the safety of neutral Zurich. The situation was complicated by the need to get German permission, and American Red Cross co-operation, for the transport of his daughter from her sanatorium in the 'unfree zone' at St Nazaire. Financial problems exacerbated the predicament: his French bank account had been seized by Pétain's government and he was unable to get money transferred from London.

Despite these extremities, as Sweeney read him the letter, Lewis found himself envying Joyce:

> so much nearer the centre of his world and of mine: with so many more friends than I have too, within some sort of reach. I feel as if I were in some stony desert, full of shadows in human form. I have never imagined the likes of it, in my worst nightmares.

The frustrations of his year in New York City were epitomised by Sisyphean journeys, pedestrian or by public transport, 'according to whether [he] had the dime or not for the bus', from the Brevoort Hotel, north on that main commercial artery, 5th Avenue, to petition Barr at MOMA, or beyond that, his agents, Russell & Volkening, and back again. 'I never thought I should hate a *street*', he told Frank Morley, 'but I know and abominate every building in Fifth Avenue.' A block further on from the Brevoort Hotel, 5th Avenue ended at Washington Square, dominated by Stanford White's 80-foot-high triumphal arch, built in 1892 to commemorate the inauguration of George Washington's presidency. This 'wretched little Arc de Triomphe' became the focus of Lewis's jaundiced attention again and again as he returned on foot or by bus from thwarted money-making expeditions, watching the top of the arch 'appear over the edge of the hill at 34th Street [and] slowly increase in size as [he] marched or rumbled towards it.'

Late in 1939 he had lunched with Frank Morley. He remembered his companion saying something about 'this tough city'. After the nightmare of finding himself near penniless on 5th Avenue, he understood just how tough it was.

With the help of handouts from a number of quarters, the Lewises limped from the United States on 9 November and spent two nights in Montreal. No business could be conducted because the city was effectively closed down for Armistice Day, but opportunity was taken to seek out a well-heeled cousin, President of Lewis, Apedaile & Hanson, in his office at the Lewis Building on St John Street. Later an important benefactor of McGill University, Gordon Lewis acknowledged the visit with a superficially friendly letter, but offered nothing in the way of assistance to his impoverished cousin Percy:

> I am sorry not to have seen more of you when you stopped over here . . . However, I'm so glad we were able to have the nice little chat we had together. With best regards, 'Cheerio'.

*

By 13 November Lewis and his wife were in Toronto. It was just two weeks short of a year since he had left, following that heady St Andrew's Night when, lionised and flushed with alcohol, he had stood in the snow outside the McLean estate and bade the company farewell, shaking his clasped hands above his head.

His hopes for New York had come to nothing, and a fitting coda to this dispiriting year followed him to Toronto, care of Thomas Cook & Sons. Slocum was returning his short stories. They had already done the rounds of *Harper's Bazaar*, *Esquire*, *The New Yorker*, *Atlantic Monthly*, *Town & Country* and *Story Magazine*. 'I do not feel that the short story is your medium', his agent opined, and pressed home the point by enclosing some editors' comments on a separate sheet of paper:

'doesn't add up to enough . . . Sorry.'
'beyond us and out of our field . . . much too complicated for our simple pages.'
'darned entertaining, but we just can't see these in the magazine.'
'Both these pieces are terribly dreary.'

If Lewis felt the work of an Englishman was received with hostility in New York, it was ironic that his novel had been rejected for precisely opposite reasons. Later came the typescript of *The Vulgar Streak*, rejected by Doubleday, Doran & Co. on the grounds that it was too critical of England during a time when America was 'being almost unctuously polite to Sassenachs'.

Lewis gave up hoping that Slocum would find the novel a publisher and left responsibility for this in the hands of Iris Barry.

*

In retreat from United States Immigration regulations and with nowhere else to go, Lewis put a brave face on his exile to the local press. 'Wyndham Lewis, painter and author . . . is in Toronto today', the *Star* reported. 'So much does he like the city that he is going to rent an apartment. He revealed he had come to Canada to paint snow.'

The Lewises' new address was 559 Sherbourne Street. Apartment 11A, in the rear annexe of the Tudor Hotel, comprised one large room, kitchen and bathroom. It cost '14 bucks a week', he told Stone, 'which is cheap at least.' But John Reid said it was 'seedy and as expensive as others that would have given more comfort'. Initially regarded as 'an interim dwelling', it was to be the Lewises' home for the next two and a half years. The City Planning Board's Neighbourhood Classification of 1944 would officially designate the area between Yonge and Parliament, which included Sherbourne, as 'declining'.

FORTY

'Attendance upon the great ones of this bloody earth!'

Canada appeared to offer everything New York had withheld, and by December Lewis had several irons in the fire. A trip to Ottawa yielded the promise of three wireless broadcasts, albeit badly paid at $30 apiece. H. O. McCurry, the Director of the National Gallery of Canada, invited him to lecture on 'The Importance of the Visual Arts', and also suggested he produce 'five portrait drawings of prominent army and navy personalities' that the Gallery would purchase for $125 each. He was in a position to make about $700 that side of Christmas from Ottawa alone.

In Toronto he hoped to sell 'a pamphlet' to Lorne Pierce at the Ryerson Press for an advance of about $50. And there were prospects of more substantial rewards from another source. He and Gladys were to have dinner with 'one of Toronto's bigwigs'. Canada seemed, he told Stone, a land of opportunity. He was shrewd enough to realise, however, that as well as being ready to seize opportunities, it was often just as important to remain calm and patient 'while this or that opportunity is pruned down and secured to one'. To be able to exercise this degree of sangfroid he needed a little working capital to ensure he did not give an impression of financial desperation to his future patrons:

> It is fearfully important that during the next two weeks I should not appear hard-up or have to ask for advances . . . I feel that what happens between now and Christmas will decide the whole of my life for some time – for the duration of the war.

Inevitably, at the heart of the two–page letter to Stone was a request for money. Long communications from Lewis, outlining his glowing prospects, were often assurances that not only past debts, but those advanced to meet pressing present needs, would be swiftly repaid.

*

At a quarter to eight on the evening of Thursday 12 December, 'Wyndham Lewis – novelist, painter, journalist and lecturer' spoke from Toronto on the national network of the Canadian Broadcasting Corporation. The announcer accurately introduced the speaker as 'Canadian born' but, perhaps relying too literally on the title of his 1937 autobiography, added that he 'served in the last war as bombardier'. Recent purchases by the Tate Gallery in London, as well as his *Canadian Gun Pit* in the National Gallery at Ottawa, were enlisted to establish Lewis's credentials as a painter whose works were 'sought after by collectors'. The subject of his 15-minute talk was 'Can Democracy be Defined?':

> Good evening! In speaking for the first time to a Canadian radio-audience, I feel just as the first pioneers must have done in the presence of the virgin forest – except that all the indians are 'good indians' – all are white; all miraculously speak my own native tongue; all have names beginning with *Mac*!*

Most of the ensuing discourse on the superiority of Anglo-Saxon democracy over Prussian totalitarianism found its way into the 'pamphlet' the Ryerson Press were to publish at the end of June: *Anglosaxony: A League that Works.*

*

The local 'bigwig' he mentioned to Geoffrey Stone was one of those Canadians with a Scottish prefix to their name: J. Stanley McLean. The date of the dinner was 15 December. The following day Lewis was able to acknowledge an airmailed cheque from Stone in Bethlehem, Connecticut, with the news that he had just clinched a $500 portrait commission without having to ask for an advance.

Work 'on the portrait of a rich young lady' began immediately in the little studio he rented for $12 a month at 22 Grenville Street, a short walk from the Tudor Hotel, and Lewis developed a routine of rising at 7 o'clock in the morning. McLean's daughter Mary was much preoccupied with preparations to become Mrs Douglas Stewart, and the earliness of the sittings suggests that they had to be fitted in to her already busy schedule. The painting was intended by her father as a wedding present.

This was the first of three commissions to come Lewis's way from the head of Canada Packers. One was a portrait of McLean himself, which his grateful employees were to pay for by subscription. He also wanted a

---

* Another radio talk, 'Address to French Canada', was delivered in French. It called on the English- and French-speaking peoples of Canada to unite, as those in Europe were doing, against a common enemy. The subject of Lewis's third CBC talk, and whether it was even broadcast, is not known.

portrait of Lisa, the wife of his friend Robert James Sainsbury, head of the great grocery chain back in London.

The elegant Mrs Sainsbury fared better under Lewis's brush than did Mary McLean.

*

'I work like a helot and march up and down to my studio in blizzards', he told Stone in early January. 1941 was opening with great prospects of success. But eleven months later, at the beginning of December, he had just seven cents in his pocket. He had enough money for a stamp or enough for a telephone call but not enough for both.

Lewis failed in Toronto against what initially seemed very favourable odds.

In spite of the early morning regime of sittings, McLean's wedding present to his daughter remained unfinished when Mary and her new husband departed for Vancouver. Thereafter work proceeded from a photograph. He was aware of how important this portrait was to his future prospects. 'If it is liked', he told Stone, 'it must lead to other work.' It is surprising, then, that he turned out something almost guaranteed not to satisfy. It was unflattering and ineptly drawn to the point of clumsy caricature. The enormous limpid eyes might have found favour with a sentimentally inclined sitter, despite the vacuous quality they gave the oval face, but the nose between them was an affront: long, sharply ridged and flaring out at the nostrils like a toy trumpet. Beneath the plain neckline of the plain mauve dress the square, frumpy expanse of mannish chest was framed by pipelike forearms and sketchily modelled crossed hands. Below the waist the pose was awkward and unconvincing, the left knee bent at far too acute an angle, the lower leg tucked up and disappearing underneath her.

Mary admitted to disliking Lewis and thought he disliked her. A. Y. Jackson believed that the portrait reflected their mutual animosity.

Perhaps anticipating an unfavourable reaction to his work, Lewis appeared unwilling for it to be seen, and it had still not been surrendered when his second commission was formally unveiled at noon on Saturday 19 April. The portrait of Mary's father was shown off to family, friends and the employees of Canada Packers in the convention room of the firm's Welfare Building in West Toronto. The occasion was reported, and the picture described, in the *Toronto Star*:

The portrait is a harmony in blue, green and brown, and is a subtle study

429

in strong shades cleverly balanced. Dressed in a blue business suit, the industrialist sits in front of a palebluish-green background.

In the upper right of the composition was a section of *Mining Town*, a painting of Cobalt, Ontario, by A. Y. Jackson. This, said the *Star* correspondent, symbolised Mr McLean's interest in art, while the books at his right elbow 'stand for the sitter's wide reading'. The artist gave a short speech:

> In my portrait I have said – more concisely and precisely – than it is possible to say in words – what I think of the very distinguished man who is President of this company. It has been a great privilege to have been selected to record, in this way, the personality of a great business leader, who appears destined to play an increasingly important part in the life of this young and vigorous nation. As an artist, I can say that I regard myself as extremely fortunate to have had so interesting a subject to paint, and also a man like Mr McLean, has found time, in the midst of a strenuous business career, to give his attention to cultural matters, and especially to the particular arts that I practice. – All in all, the painting of this portrait has been for me a great and pleasurable experience.

That evening Mary and Douglas Stewart drove him to the studio he was now using in Severn Street, to view her father's belated wedding gift. But by the time the car drew up in front of the studio building, Lewis seems to have changed his mind about allowing the picture to be seen. Probably making a show of searching his pockets, he said that he was sorry, but unfortunately he had forgotten to bring his keys. The Stewarts had the distinct impression that he was lying.

Later, following considerable pressure from the family, he delivered the portrait to the McLean estate. Mrs McLean thought it made her daughter look like a horse and refused to give it houseroom. Lewis took it away with him. Mary herself would not see it until the late 1950s, after the painter's death.

The portrait of Mary's father did not find favour with the employees of Canada Packers who had commissioned it. It was eventually taken off its stretcher, rolled up and stayed in storage until an exhibition of Lewis's Canadian pictures brought it back into the light in 1992.

*

Lewis's few days 'among the civil servants and statesmen' of the Canadian capital in November 1940 had yielded more opportunities than he could at that time take advantage of, and he realised he would have to return. 'You have to *keep on* seeing these people', he told Stone. 'The machine set up there, for running Canada, contains a number of quite agreeable persons and is the ideal place for a portraitist.' He believed he had, with the support of H. O. McCurry at the National Gallery of Canada, a great deal of business to conduct in Ottawa. He had heard that accommodation was scarce and proposed establishing a base two hours away by train, making weekly visits to the capital to paint portraits. Accordingly, in mid-May, Lewis and his wife left the Tudor Hotel for the time being and, Ottawa being 'inconveniently full', took a very small two-room apartment in Montreal at 430 Prince Arthur Street West.

During his first weekly trip he stayed at the Chateau Laurier Hotel, Ottawa, and wrote to Gladys about his round of social engagements:

> All this tiresome business *has* to be done. Probably at lunch I shall have no opportunity of talking about portraits: so have to do that at six o'clock drinks. Doing business is always long-winded . . . people give you a job or do you a good business turn because they like you 'round' – like talking to you and so on: not because they like your work. – Wastes a lot of time, but can't be helped!

That first expedition proved futile, as did subsequent forays. In fact, Lewis's projected portraiture campaign 'among the civil servants and statesmen' appears to have failed entirely. Nothing even came of the 'five portrait drawings of prominent army and navy personalities' which McCurry had promised to arrange for him.

The rental on the Montreal apartment was due to expire on 15 July, but by the end of June Lewis and his wife were back in Toronto at the Tudor Hotel.

*

'I think they're really afraid of you.'

The young poet Douglas LePan blurted out these words one September afternoon while he sat in a room at 86A Isabella Street, the little place Lewis was by then renting as a studio. LePan remembered it as being surprisingly unlike a traditional artist's studio: 'it was a bed-sitting room . . . in a boarding-house or apartment hotel; and it was suitably, and oh! so tastefully, fitted out with crocheted doilies on the tables, and crocheted anti-macassars on the chairs, and potted plants by the windows overlooking the street.' Lewis wore a flat-crowned, flat-brimmed black felt hat throughout the sittings. They would have tea and Lewis would get to work on the portrait drawing.

He had been asking LePan about the University of Toronto, where he had been an undergraduate and his father the Superintendent of Buildings and Grounds. Lewis had been speculating about the reasons why he had not been offered work at the University and why the academic establishment had apparently not recognised his presence in Toronto over the past year. The young man's words came in response to such ruminations: 'I think they're really afraid of you.'

In June, writing from Montreal with suggestions as to where unprejudiced reviews of *Anglosaxony: A League that Works* might be courted, and warnings against allowing it to fall into the hands of unsympathetic University professors, Lewis confided to Lorne Pierce at the Ryerson Press:

> I did not exactly hit it off with the intellectuals of Toronto . . . Actually *some* people were very rude to myself and wife while I was there, so I regard it . . . as a rather alarming place.

However, some time during the first half of the year an attempt had been made to introduce Lewis and his wife to the City's academic community. With possibilities of lucrative portrait commissions and other forms of employment, acceptance here would have made a great difference to their quality of life over the next two and a half years. Barker Fairley, painter, and Professor of German, one of that small group who had dined in his honour on St Andrew's Night 1939, invited Lewis to dinner to meet some of his University colleagues. This preliminary encounter seems to have been satisfactory. Shortly afterwards it was arranged that Mrs Lewis should accompany him to Professor E. J. Pratt's house so that 'the various womenfolk would be able to make each other's acquaintance'. This was a larger gathering to which the Lewises were driven in the writer Morley Callaghan's car.

Two years later the party still loomed so large in Lewis's memory as to form the main bone of contention in a two-page letter to the Professor of German, by then saluted icily as 'Mr Fairley'.

Details of what happened chez Pratt are sketchy. At some point in the evening Lewis became aware that 'something was amiss'. His wife was being troubled by a woman who insisted on 'regaling her with obscene stories and limericks'. Callaghan's wife had made several attempts to rescue her but was unsuccessful. Eventually the aid of Professor Bower's wife was enlisted and the woman was driven off. Both Mrs Lewis and Mrs Callaghan were upset by the incident and it dominated conversation in the car going home.

This deeply felt but factually skeletal version is the only record of the occasion that exists, but it is difficult to resist the suspicion that there was more to the embarrassments of the evening than the unwelcome attentions of a dirty-minded bore. That in itself would not explain why, following the Pratt party, no faculty member or wife made further contact with the Lewises. As the whole point of the gathering had been to make them better acquainted with University staff and their families, the neglect could only by interpreted by the indignant Lewis as 'pointed rudeness'.

Some details missing from his version of events might have accounted for the ostracisation. He did not, for instance, identify the 'female ruffian', nor her standing, influential or otherwise, in the community. And he did not mention how he and his wife behaved after the alleged insult.

Whatever else happened that night, barriers subsequently shot up between the two residents of the Tudor Hotel and the University of Toronto. Professor Fairley claimed that, when he next encountered Lewis, he was 'deliberately and without provocation . . . boorishly insulted'.

*

'I think they're really afraid of you.'
LePan regretted the opinion as soon as it was uttered:

> My remark gave him too much satisfaction. I could see him rolling it over on his tongue with relish behind his prominent, ravaged teeth, and his eyes glinting with unholy joy as he thought of it and savoured it.

The academic community might indeed have been nervous about Lewis. After all, his talents as a satirist had already found a target in one of their number: the well-respected warden of Hart House, Burgon Bickersteth.

But there were other reasons Lewis might have found himself shunned. Like the lady who could not take the hint that her limericks and stories were causing offence, Lewis himself seemed, on occasion, unskilled at gauging the sympathies of his audience.

An unwholesome picture of him in this insensitive mode, rampaging in Toronto society, comes, undulled by 40 intervening years, from LePan's memoirs. It was a hot July evening following his return from Montreal, during a dinner party at the house of Mrs R. J. Sainsbury. Lewis, resplendent in a bright scarlet silk cummerbund, dominated the conversation:

> I remember in particular a long malicious account he gave of a well-known Toronto figure, of which the unmistakable implication throughout was that he was homosexual. The whole recital was as replete as it could be

with bad faith. Not only was the main point made by innuendo and implication rather than by anything said directly; but there was also the further implication that . . . the locals, poor clods – would be shocked to the core while the narrator with all his cosmopolitan sophistication would be quite unaffected. The truth was, however, that all those in the company knew very well what were the sexual inclinations of the figure in question – I doubt whether they were often acted out – and accepted them, so that the effect intended . . . fell noticeably flat. It was all rather meretricious, and sad . . . I looked down at my plate demurely like all the others and dutifully helped to turn the conversation in a different direction when the time came . . . But the question did cross my mind, I remember: Who among us is really being the most provincial tonight?

The 'well-known Toronto figure' was Douglas Duncan, another one of the St Andrew's Night dinner companions, proprietor of the Picture Loan Society, and a man who was a willing source of handouts to Lewis throughout this, his 'Tudor period'.

*

It was probably soon after Professor Pratt's party that Lewis began harbouring serious suspicions about John Reid. The rudeness visited upon him and his wife, so the reasoning went, resulted from somebody maligning them. Reid was the only person in Toronto to have known the Lewises, however briefly, in London before the war. It was assumed therefore that any stories spread about them, from that other world and time, must have originated with him.

Relations with the young Canadian had been distant since Christmas. 'Don't think that I'm trying to avoid you', Lewis told him when they ran into one another on the street. Reid had suspected no such thing until it was mentioned. He was as sensitive to real or imagined slights as his mentor. That Lewis was indeed avoiding him became increasingly apparent. Phoned several times, he was too busy to arrange a meeting. Sometimes he would answer the telephone briskly and then affect a 'sleepy' voice, when he heard who was on the line, in order to cut the conversation as short as possible.

Eventually, in February, the young disciple called unannounced at the Tudor Hotel and found Mrs Lewis cutting out material for a black dress. He had brought cakes and she told him he could wait for her husband, who was expected shortly. Lewis arrived complaining about the cold and immediately suggested a walk to the Grenville Street studio. Outside, however, he turned north instead of south and on the windswept corner of Church and Bloor, confronted Reid:

'Frankly, we don't think you're trustworthy.'

Reid did not immediately understand.

'We think you go around telling harmful stories about us.'

Lewis also accused him of using and exploiting his friends.

'You can't be loyal to your friends; you don't know how to be friends.'

Reid was too shocked to reply. Later he became physically ill as a result of the incident. He vomited. He was able to quote to Lewis, five months later, the prescription number, 116950, of the 'nerve medicine' he got from MacMillan's pharmacy while recovering from that confrontation.

At the end of the month Lewis phoned as if nothing had happened and asked Reid to sell him his copy of *The Lion and the Fox*. Reid agreed to let him have it at the price he had paid and Lewis took the book, promising payment in a few days. Reid was short of money and pawned his typewriter while he waited. He phoned Lewis and was told he would get in touch in 48 hours. Reid pawned his watch. Three weeks later, on 22 March, Reid phoned again and Lewis arranged to meet him, again on the corner of Church and Bloor, in a quarter of an hour. He also wanted to buy the young man's copy of Hugh Gordon Porteus's *Discursive Exposition* and to borrow the dust jacket of *The Apes of God*.

Reid did not have the bus fare but made the one-and-a-half-mile walk to the rendezvous in 20 minutes. Lewis kept him waiting in the wind for another 20 minutes. When he arrived he gave Reid the money he owed to date and thrust a receipt into his hands to sign:

Received from Wyndham Lewis the sum of four dollars and eighty five cents in payment for one copy of The Lion and the Fox.

It was another hurtful sign for Reid, if one were needed, that he was not trusted.

*

Late in August Lewis cabled a Harley Street ophthalmologist. The unpunctuated staccato prose style of such communications gave the 57-word message a tone of rising panic:

GLASSES YOU PRESCRIBED MISLAID IN PACKING VISITED

435

TORONTO DOCTOR HE INFORMS ME NERVE LEFT EYE ATROPHIED RIGHT EYE TEN PER CENT UNDER NORMAL SUSPECTS GLAUCOMA GIVES ME SIX MONTHS TO LOSE SIGHT UNLESS USE DROPS CALLED PILOCARPINE WHAT FROM KNOWLEDGE CASE DO YOU ADVISE IS PILOCARPINE SOUND YOU WILL REMEMBER YOU SUSPECTED LEFT EYE HAD SUSTAINED INJURY

The Toronto doctor, 'one of the most highly esteemed specialists', had, it was true, hazarded glaucoma as a tentative diagnosis only. In order to be sure he needed to apply a pressure test to the eyeball which would require anaesthetic. Lewis declined the test on the grounds that he had work to do the following day, but partly, perhaps, from fear of a final, irrefutable proven diagnosis. He pushed away the unthinkable:

> I do not believe that I have glaucoma ... if my eyes go I go too. Loathsome as the world is, I do like to see it. That sort of blackout I could not live in.

He visited another Toronto doctor, 'to check up on the first.' The second opinion was more reassuring. He did not have glaucoma. The condition of his eyes could instead be directly traceable to the decayed ruins that were Lewis's teeth.

Affleck Greeves, the Harley Street ophthalmologist, sent a cable on 29 August stating that he had detected no signs of glaucoma when examining Lewis's eyes two years before. On the other hand he could not rule out an onset of the condition during the interval and advised him to follow the Toronto doctor's advice. But this, along with the second doctor's categorical assurance that he did not have glaucoma, was enough to incline Lewis, 'not entirely on account of ostrich-like optimism', towards the hypothesis that his teeth, 'a septic centre of the first order', were in all probability the cause of his failing left eye.

These considerations were, as he told Iris Barry, largely academic in his present financial position:

> it has almost ruined me seeing these eye-doctors and getting the glasses they prescribed. As to having my teeth attended to, that is, as things stand, a complete impossibility ... I can never make money enough to have a margin for expenditure on doctor or dentist. It is all I can do to buy tooth-paste.

Writing to Stone early in September he did not confide the frightening condition of his eyes. He nevertheless produced a bleak picture:

Things have come to an awful pass here: if I don't do something to break out of the net, I shall end my days in a Toronto flophouse.

*

One way out of the net lay some 900 miles northeast of Toronto, in Bathurst, New Brunswick. It was here that the President of Algoma Steel, Sir James Dunn, was convalescing from a coronary thrombosis under the watchful eye of his secretary, soon to be wife, Miss Marcia Christoforides.

Back in May, Sir James had seen and admired Lewis's portrait of J. S. McLean and had written, holding out a tentative promise:

If I can see my way to afford (in these days when taxes take everything) having a portrait painted I will ask you to do it.

Lewis assured the millionaire he could offer a bargain:

I am satisfied with much more modest sums than an artist is accustomed to expect in England. I am not so well known on this side of the water as the other. To be specific, I will paint a portrait for anything from 700 to 1000 dollars.

But before Dunn could take advantage of these knockdown rates he fell ill and was henceforth in the care of his secretary.

Lewis renewed the campaign in early August, and Miss Christoforides told him that Sir James was considering employing him, not only as a portrait painter, but also to execute a poster design for Algoma Steel. If Dunn had been in any doubt about Lewis's financial plight following the offer of a portrait for $700–1000, such doubts would have been dispelled by his next letter:

There is a wolf at the door, which has to be kept away. If very soon I don't shoo it away, it will devour me. I do not have to tell you how, even in his home town, an artist is always apt to have a wolf on his doorstep. But we are in Canada – in the midst of an economic blizzard.

He may have been aware that Sir James had kept the wolf from Sickert's door during the Thirties by giving him the much-needed commission for a series of 12 portraits of friends.

Miss Christoforides suggested Lewis visit the ailing magnate at Camp Dunn, his sprawling country place outside Bathurst, New Brunswick. And he was given the tantalising impression that a number of other portraits would be required. There would be one of Dunn himself if he was well enough to sit. There would be one of the Managing Director of Algoma Steel, a Mr Thomas Rahilly, who was expected at Camp Dunn while Lewis was to be there. Another high-ranking but as yet unspecified executive was to be tackled, as was, finally, no less a personage than the Premier of Ontario, the Honourable Mitchell Frederick Hepburn. This last portrait would be a gift to the province. Hepburn had been very useful to Sir James in the past. He had oiled the wheels of the controversial bid to take over Algoma Steel in 1934, and in 1939 had provided the firm with a government subsidy.

By 10 September Lewis was awaiting the green light. 'Whenever I receive telegram I shall begin getting ready', he told Miss Christoforides. 'Within 48 hours I could start.' She had warned him about the inclement weather in New Brunswick and he assured her that he was prepared:

> though I am no pioneer, and if polar storms bear down, I shall keep pretty near the hot water pipes!

If all went according to plan, the trip promised a profitable end to the 'economic blizzard' howling around his ears in Toronto.

By 21 September Lewis was back from Bathurst with his canvas untouched. The Managing Director of Algoma Steel, Mr Rahilly, had not, after all, arrived at Camp Dunn. Sir James himself was there, but with a doctor in attendance and under the solicitous eye of Miss Christoforides. There was some discussion about Lewis painting her in a winged collar and with her hair in a pigtail tied with ribbon, but this project did not get further than discussion.

The woods had been peaceful and there was a small lake nearby where he strolled, waiting to see if Dunn would be found strong enough to sit. After a day or so the doctor decided he was not. 'He is trying to run before he can walk', Miss Christoforides reported. Sir James would not be fit enough for another month. But in the meantime the Honourable Mitchell Hepburn was in Toronto and could be painted immediately. In a month's time Lewis was to return to Bathurst to tackle Sir James and, no doubt, Miss Christoforides. 'Of course I greatly regretted being snatched away from the delightful task of transferring to canvas your image', he told her. 'Still we can take that up at a more propitious moment.'

When he got back to Toronto he was optimistic about what still seemed an upturn in his fortunes. 'My next portrait is of a *very* big shot. If I am not assassinated by the local portrait-painters', he told Stone, 'it should put me on the map.'

438

Conscious that he needed to pin his 'big shot' down as quickly as possible before the political concerns of Ontario carried him away, Lewis telephoned Hepburn the weekend he got back. He left a message but his call was not returned. On the Monday he delivered a letter by hand:

> Here I am, and shall hold myself in readiness to start work. May I add that I regard it as a great honour that I should have been chosen to do your portrait, and am greatly looking forward to the experience.

Unfortunately, although Miss Christoforides had told Lewis he was to paint the Prime Minister, she appears to have neglected to inform the Prime Minister himself. A rather frosty response reached the Tudor Hotel from Hepburn's office:

> I am directed by the Prime Minister to acknowledge your letter of recent date. Mr Hepburn left yesterday for New York and on his return at the end of the week will have to go to Ottawa for conferences with the Federal Government. I do not know just when any arrangements could be made along the lines you suggest.

Shortly after his return from Bathurst, as it became clear that painting a Prime Minister's portrait would not be as straightforward as he had at first thought and as he realised that the campaign to get commissions might have to start again from scratch, he went to see Lorne Pierce in his office at the Ryerson Press. He told Pierce he wanted to do a drawing of him. It would not, he explained, cost anything but might be used to get other commissions. Pierce was a busy man and unable to spare the time to pose formally. However Lewis was welcome to try to capture a likeness while he worked at his desk. Lewis produced a large sheet of paper, pinned it to a board and began to draw. After a while he suddenly tore the paper from the board, crumpled and dropped it into the waste-paper basket. Then he left the office without a word, slamming the door behind him. A couple of days after this he returned, walked into the office without knocking, settled himself in a chair near to Pierce and began again. A day or so later he came back and completed the drawing. He finally delivered the delicate pastel, signed and dated on blue paper, to Pierce on 8 October with meticulous instructions as to its preservation:

> These drawings in pastel chalks require extremely careful handling . . . Consequently, I am leaving you the drawing pinned to a drawing board and suggest you do not allow the drawing to leave the board until it is framed or mounted. If you are not having it framed at once, but only

mounted, then I advise very strongly that you have a cellophane face fixed on it . . . It is my experience that the frameworker is none too careful – he is quite apt to leave the drawing face up on a work-bench; other things may be placed on top of it, and so it gets rubbed. So I have blocked out a warning notice and pinned it to the top of the drawing-board . . . All this may sound fussy, but there is a bloom to these pastel-surfaces which it is easy to lose.

Nothing meanwhile had come, or was to come, of the commissions discussed at Camp Dunn. Lewis did not paint the Honourable Mitchell Hepburn. Neither did he paint Sir James Dunn and his Managing Director Mr Rahilly. And, finally, he never painted the beautiful, wing-collared and pigtailed features of Miss Marcia Christoforides, who had stage-managed the entire futile exercise and who was to marry her employer the following year.

The pursuit of these potentially lucrative commissions had not been a waste, merely, of his time. It had actually cost him money. Apart from canvas, paints and travelling expenses, 'I have spent a hell of a lot . . . on making myself respectable', he complained to Stone, 'a new suit, and all other requisites of attire for personal attendance upon the great ones of this bloody earth!'

*

When he was in New York 18 months before, he had talked of the prospect of portrait commissions to Mrs Florence Lamont. She had been pessimistic, telling him that war was on everyone's mind, to the exclusion of all other considerations. She had been right, he now told her. 'The portraitist must lay aside his brush.'

A fortnight after he had arrived at this conclusion there was a brief, tantalising addendum to his dealings with the Canadian powerful. It was as inconclusive as anything that had gone before.

On Thursday 9 October he received a telephone call from a Miss Pritchett at the Parliament Building. She introduced herself as secretary to the Speaker and asked Lewis if she and Mr Hepburn's secretary might visit his studio and look at his pictures. He explained that he had no studio at present and only possessed photographs of his pictures. Nevertheless the two women still wanted to meet him. He wondered whether he might visit them at the Parliament Building instead, and Miss Pritchett agreed, suggesting the following Wednesday at noon. Lewis was a little uncertain as to the wider purpose of the meeting and asked if it was to have anything to do with arrangements to paint Mr Hepburn. Miss Pritchett replied: 'Yes, or somebody else.' He got the impression that this 'somebody else' might turn out to be the Speaker. She told him, on the other hand, that Mr Hepburn was difficult to fix in one place for very long and Lewis agreed that in such a time of pressing national emergency it would be difficult for him to sit for his portrait. Miss Pritchett said that all the same he ought to be painted, however busy he was, and then his portrait could hang in the Parliament Building along with the other Prime Ministers. Lewis said he would telephone her on Wednesday to confirm their noon appointment, and replaced the receiver believing, once more, that there was light at the end of the tunnel.

For all the benefit that came to him from these arrangements, they might just as well have been part of an elaborate hoax. And the most malicious hoaxer could not have raised more radiant expectations than Miss Pritchett innocently did with her telephone call that Thursday. 'She implied there would be other portraits,' Lewis wrote excitedly to Pierce half an hour later, 'she wasn't specific.'

He immediately set about preparing for the meeting. He gathered photographs of his recent portrait work: *J. S. McLean*, *Chancellor Capen* and perhaps *T. S. Eliot*. He also needed to borrow the portrait drawings he had produced of LePan and get back the drawing of Pierce he had delivered with such detailed instructions for its welfare only the day before. And he had to borrow $30 from Pierce, no doubt to supply him with requisites for further attendance upon 'the great ones of this bloody earth'.

There is, however, no more evidence of meetings with Parliament Building staff, relating to plans for painting Speaker, Prime Minister or indeed anybody else, high or low, in Toronto society. And no explanation offered or offers itself as to why such bright prospects came to nothing.

FORTY-ONE

'Some modest perch out of the storm'

'The portraitist must lay aside his brush', he had told Mrs Florence Lamont, and it was to this lady that he now turned for help in a fresh search for gainful employment: 'something taking with it a regular salary however small, and some time on the side to do my own work'.

In Ottawa the previous June he had met the brother of a man who, it appeared, was in the fortunate position of combining a painting career with economic security. André Biéler was resident artist at Kingston University, Ontario. 'This appointment', Lewis was given to understand, 'recalled scholastic medieval habits. The "resident-artist" was given a studio: in some universities he taught and lectured: in some he was generally on tap but gave no lectures.' However arranged, it seemed 'an ideal shelter for an artist blown about and economically battered by war'.

Through Mrs Lamont's husband, a Carnegie director, Lewis's case was presented to Charles Dollard, assistant to the President of the Corporation, who explained how the Resident Artist Plan worked: 'painters, sculptors, muralists etc., are enabled to spend a year or two on a college campus to the end that the non-professional student of art may be stimulated to a greater interest in creative work.' If the Carnegie Corporation were to receive a proposal from a suitable college in the United States or Canada, requesting Lewis's services, it would be given careful consideration.

All Lewis had to do was find a College President willing to make such a proposal. The campaign to achieve this simple end would exercise him for a considerable length of time.

He enlisted the aid of a man he had met over dinner at a Paris restaurant in the company of Ernest Hemingway. Archibald MacLeish, poet and librarian of Congress, and his colleague, R. D. Jameson, began canvassing likely colleges on his behalf. Alfred Barr at MOMA also agreed to help.

Although the Carnegie Corporation was prepared to consider funding his appointment to a college in Canada, Lewis was convinced that his chances of finding such a position lay exclusively south of the border. Canada, he told Jameson, had only three or four major colleges, each in its own way unsuitable. Without mentioning his personal feud with the University of Toronto he pointed out that, because it depended upon government grants, it was 'an ultra conservative institution possessing a big staff of fine art "experts"' already. Montreal's McGill University was 'reactionary to a redoubtable extent' he had been informed, and 'no person of independent outlook can breathe within its precincts'. The University of Vancouver was 'inimical to all forms of art, good or bad'. The only institution of any apparent worth was Queen's College in Kingston, Ontario, and they already possessed, in André Biéler, a resident artist. Lewis concluded that Canada was 'no alternative for the vast and diverse United States'.

At the beginning of November MacLeish reported a first bite from a private academic institution linked with the United Methodist Church. Paul Douglas, President of the American University in Washington DC, was interested in having a resident artist assigned there. 'It will really be a great thing if this comes off', Lewis wrote to McLeish. 'I can't tell you how beholden I am to you for so expeditiously finding for me the very thing I wanted.'

It would not be the last time in the coming months that the very thing he wanted was to be dangled just out of reach before being withdrawn.

Sensibly, other approaches were being made at the same time. Alfred Barr had received an encouraging reply from another college President, and Jameson had been in touch with Joseph Brewer, President of a small liberal arts college in Olivet, Michigan. This avenue seemed particularly hopeful because Lewis had actually met Brewer, 'a very charming fellow', some years before.

*

On Saturday, 29 November he wrote to Barry. He had been waiting for a letter containing money from her all week. 'I shall have to borrow a few dollars to carry me over the weekend', he told her. The prospect of sales of his drawings through Douglas Duncan's Picture Loan Society were favourable but could not be speeded up, and the weekend threatened to be particularly lean because Duncan was away in Preston and the 'few dollars' from him were not forthcoming.

By the morning of Monday, 1 December, he had precisely seven cents to his name. All he could do was wait for Duncan to get back to town. Of the seven cents in his pocket, five were needed for the phone call to his benefactor when he returned. All this, he explained to Barry on the Tuesday, was why he had had to delay sending his letter to her. He could not afford to buy the stamp.

*

Meanwhile he was still waiting to hear from Paul Douglas about the prospects for his appointment to the American University in Washington DC. It was nearly a month since first contact had been made. 'So far no signal has reached me', he told MacLeish, 'and I am beginning anxiously to speculate whether there is really life after all upon that distant planet.'

During the first week in December, news came from Jameson that the deal had fallen through. Lewis blamed the Japanese bombing of the American Pacific fleet at Pearl Harbor:

> I was just about to get an appointment in the States when, the very week in which it was all being settled, bang – bang – bang! went the filthy little descendants of Hokusai: and my appointment went up in smoke.

While it was true that colleges throughout the USA were eventually forced to cut back on expenditure as student rolls fell to recruitment in the armed services, it is difficult to credit the events of 7 December 1941, the day President Roosevelt declared would 'live in infamy', with having so immediate and dramatic an effect upon Lewis's chances of a job. Indeed, the American University appointment had evaporated three days before the Japanese attack.

Lewis was assured that other Universities were still interested in having him: Annapolis, near Washington, was a possibility. And Olivet was still in play. He urged Jameson that if nothing could be found 'near the centre of things', he had no objection to California or Maryland.

*

Barry wrote enclosing a money order and explaining that she had been bed-ridden for the previous week following a fall from an automobile. She was still trying to find a publisher for *The Vulgar Streak* and hinted at some renewal of interest. Lewis replied that he was sorry to learn of her concussion but 'overjoyed to hear that very soon there would be some news of the novel'. Things had looked up for him since the lean weekend:

> A sale of a drawing has at last occurred. I have paid my debts – that is to say my rent here up to Monday last and ten dollars to my friend [Douglas Duncan]. That does not leave much but it eases things, which were again very desperate.

But, on second thoughts, between draft and fair copy, he decided not to include this piece of qualified good news. As an experienced sponger he knew better than to tell Barry of even modest sums gained through his own industry. If she had known about the sale she might not have made such an effort to scrape together the money she was now regularly sending him.

A fortnight later, as Christmas loomed and another two weeks' rent fell due, he again included the good news in his rough draft, along with the prospect of another sale. But this was also cut from the straightforward request for rent money that Barry actually received.

Arising from the gratifying sales were new social contacts, 'new friends' as he told Pierce the Sunday before Christmas. It was all 'very agreeable' and a little party was being thrown for Gladys and himself that evening. Unfortunately, it seems not to have been entirely successful. Just as the ice-breaking gathering at Professor Pratt's house earlier in the year had mysteriously soured relations and stored lingering resentment against the entire Toronto academic establishment, so the only record of the 'little party' given by his new friends was an enigmatic outpouring of bile to Barry in a letter that was never sent:

> one of those ill disposed people who possess an evil talent for thinking up quite useless people to introduce one to – when one is in such distress that inhuman treatment is more likely than at other times to constitute the last straw, frivolously added, that breaks the camel's back – one of those harpies has caused me to waste a lot of time over such an ingeniously contrived futility.

And he was having second thoughts about the Olivet College appointment. It was small and might not meet the Carnegie specification of a 'good college'. Also the climate was forbidding, though 'in such times as these, a hurricane or two of mere wind or a phenomenal snowfall is a small matter.' But just after Christmas even the bleak prospect of Michigan began to recede. Joseph Brewer wrote suggesting he come to Olivet for a probationary week. Lewis was at a loss to understand why Brewer should make this a requirement. 'As a matter of fact', he wrote to Jameson, 'the necessity for getting acquainted is not apparent, seeing that about twelve years ago, when Mr Brewer was a publisher in New York, I spent some hours with him at his apartment, and so we are personally known to each other.'

The possibility did not occur to him that this might have been why Brewer suggested a trial period. Instead he considered the damage that might be done to him if the probationary week went badly:

Were I, for argument's sake sent back here ... as unsatisfactory, my prospects would not have improved as the result of this experiment.

And in the draft of his letter to Jameson he thought better of, and cancelled, an elaboration of the possible consequences:

I might theoretically go from college to college and the presidents of some might write to the Carnegie Corporation and say 'We are very sorry, but Mr Lewis has been here for a week and we find we don't want him among us any longer. His work is lousy, he drinks, and we don't like his face.'

Lewis replied to Brewer in friendly fashion declining the offer and saying that his physician had 'very strongly recommended a less severe climate altogether than that prevailing in ... Michigan'. As it happened, this excuse proved unnecessary. Olivet College already employed a resident artist and the Carnegie Corporation would not fund a second. Lewis was astonished that Brewer had made no mention of the incumbent and felt he had wasted everybody's time. 'After all a poor girl always tries to find out if the gentleman she is proposing to wed already has a wife.'

*

With the new year a new name began to appear in his correspondence, a name to which hopes were to be pinned for the next couple of months.

Dexter Keezer was the President of yet another private liberal arts institution: Reed College, Portland, Oregon. As early as 5 January he was being mentioned by Jameson as a strong possibility, and at the end of the month a letter came from Oregon: subject to Carnegie approval Mr Lewis would get his appointment as resident artist. Lewis wrote eagerly by return of post that he greatly appreciated the warmth accorded McLeish and Jameson's proposal that he be invited to pass a year or so on the Reed campus:

As to the proximity of Portland, Oregon to the present battlefields of the Pacific, you do not need to reassure me. I spent a considerable period during the last war as a soldier dodging bombs, shells and bullets, and if a Japanese bomb found me out upon the quiet campus of Reed College ... then certainly my name would be on it in very large letters indeed.

In case Keezer were in any doubt about how the Resident Artist Plan worked, Lewis quoted Dollard's letter of the previous October: 'painters, sculptors, muralists, etc., are enabled to spend a year or two on a college

446

campus to the end that the non-professional student of art may be stimulated to a greater interest in creative work.'

And with a disarming enthusiasm he outlined his own estimation of the resident artist's role: he would be a quite extraordinary educational asset to Reed College:

> To have an artist actually producing on the spot, in the concrete, paintings and drawings day by day, so that the process may in a certain sort be watched, is one of the best ways of bringing to life the interests of the college student in the visual world and the arts which interpret it. By conversation and advice the resident artist ... can stimulate and encourage those who are gifted in those directions, better perhaps than a lecturer.

And, lest Keezer be under the impression that this resident artist were not capable of imparting academic rigour as well as stimulation and encouragement to the students:

> on the other hand I should be quite prepared to lecture too ... I am luckily able to express myself coherently, which is more than most artists are. – I could be at stated times accessible in my studio. I could map out a course of lectures. In short I could direct my energies into whatever channel was considered the most profitable ... I should certainly want to do something more active than just 'residing'.

Lewis waited a fortnight for a reply. After three weeks he wrote to Jameson asking if he had heard anything from Keezer. 'I know time is needed to complete such an arrangement.' Keezer would first have to apply to the Carnegie Corporation. 'Then of course Oregon is a devil of a long way by mail from New York.' And the Carnegie committee would have to consider the application. While he was writing to Jameson a thought struck him that there might be another reason for Keezer's silence. Heavily cancelled from the rough draft, the thought was put out of his letter if not out of his mind:

> I see there is a great annual educational conference taking place at San Francisco. I hope all my college presidents will not get together ... and loosen my hold on Oregon!

The paranoiac fantasy that Paul Douglas from Washington and Joseph Brewer from Michigan might be talking about him to Keezer in some San Francisco ante-room was not shared with Jameson.

Having waited a month he wrote again to Keezer asking if there was any news from Carnegie. There was no response, so he turned in desperation

447

and with some trepidation to Charles Dollard of the Carnegie Corporation, apologising for the 'highly unorthodox' practice of writing to him directly. Dollard's reply, when it came, was a crushing disappointment. In the middle of discussions with Carnegie about appointing Lewis, Dexter Keezer had left Reed College and taken a government post in Washington at the Office of Price Administration. Dollard was not encouraging about future prospects. He anticipated that the pouring of young manpower into the armed forces would seal the fate of the Resident Artist Scheme. 'All the colleges are faced with the necessity of reducing budgets in anticipation of further decline in enrolment, and . . . most of them could ill afford even the modest contribution which the resident artist experiment involves.'

As efforts were made in the United States Congress to reduce the draft age to 19, Lewis reasoned that it would only be male student enrolment that would be in decline. With a dogged persistence, admirable in the face of so many disappointments, for a time he pursued the possibility of gaining an appointment at a college for women. Smith College, Massachusetts, was canvassed, as was the Sarah Lawrence College in Bronxville, New York. But he was clutching at straws. Every door in the collegiate system of the United States seemed slammed in his face. North of the border the prospect was even bleaker:

> Educational jobs are quite impossible to find because the teaching profession in Canada is undernourished and there is a hungry home guard, jealously vigilant, mounted before every job – even the college janitors.

Only one narrow avenue might still remain open, and he wrote to Leonard Brockington to explore the possibility of work in the Canadian government. He was at pains to point out how low his sights were set:

> I am not an ambitieux . . . I want to climb nowhere, except onto some modest perch out of the storm . . . Some ill-paid, half-time, job would be the ideal, in which I was left half my time free for my usual work, of writing and painting.

For a time it looked as though he might get a job in the Censorship Department but even that finally fell through.

At the end of April he seemed finally to be beaten. 'Already my life here is unbelievably difficult and my wife nearly crazed with worry', he told Sweeney:

> All along I have recognised that millions of people everywhere are

448

suffering in the most terrible way – that my misfortune is merely typical of a universal misery. For my wife's sake even more than for my own (for I feel responsible for what is happening to her) I have incessantly exerted myself to find some solution. I am still doing so. There is no stone that has not been turned over. But all I can say is that . . . I can see no prospect of relief. If I did not have a hotel which providentially does not seem to mind about the payment of rent we should be on the streets . . . I refer to this as my 'Tudor Period' – and these are indeed 'spacious' days.

The Tudor Hotel had by then been their home for a year and a half. Apartment 11A was about 25 feet long by 12 feet wide – 'about' being the only word of approximation in the microscopically detailed account Lewis gave of it in the fictional record of their Toronto experience, *Self Condemned*. It may have been difficult to pace out the dimensions with absolute precision, because some six feet of the apartment's length were occupied by bathroom and kitchenette. But during the months Lewis and his wife spent inside their apartment, those dimensions must have been paced more than once to arrive at even the approximation.

The place was lit by six windows shrouded in green mosquito netting during the summer. During the winter thick ice covered the inside of the panes, which only a sponge of hot water could clear. A patina of cooking grease and nicotine was thereby also rinsed away, even though the ice almost immediately reformed. The industrial grime on the outside of the glass was never washed off. Three of the windows formed a bay, and Lewis pictured himself to friends in England, crouching here and staring out over the line of backyards north between Sherbourne and Bleecker Street.

From this window they could see, 120 yards away, the backyard of the Carload Grocetaria at 599 Sherbourne. When there was a meat shortage in Toronto, Lewis and his wife could spot the arrival of delivery trucks at the rear, the carcasses being carried in at the side door, and they could phone the manager to reserve a small joint before it was all sold.

'It isn't poverty', says René Harding in *Self Condemned*. 'That is the worst of it. I am rich – in a city where people die every day from undernourishment . . . The fat from our food collects in the bottom of the oven. If we scraped it out and ate it on our bread, that would be hard times.'

'These are hard times', his wife Hester replies. 'Different from the poverty of the rag-picker, but in some ways worse.'

Lewis and his wife, like their fictional counterparts, had food and they had shelter, albeit freezing cold in the daytime and stiflingly overheated at night. They had cigarettes to chain-smoke and occasional gin. And towards the end of 1942 they even had a wireless which brought them the wisecracking solace of Jack Benny and Rochester every Sunday evening at 7 o'clock. This was a highlight of their week. Lewis relished the half-hour, even noting down Benny's humorous asides the better to remember them:

'I have to watch this guy! He's dynamite!'

or:

'I have to watch that boy. He's making a monkey of me!'

And when, too mean to buy himself a pair of slippers, Benny's staff gave him a single one for Christmas:

'Well I'll be darned – a bedroom slipper! Now I'll be able to hop over and close the window at night!'

Theirs was not abject poverty. Nevertheless there was a three-month period when Gladys was unable to leave the apartment because she had no serviceable shoes. In *Self Condemned* money from a New York friend frees Hester from the same predicament, enabling her to buy a new pair. 'She cried a little. It was like a cripple recovering the use of her legs.'

In June, following this interval of bare-footed purdah, Gladys applied for work at a tarpaulin-sewing factory. Admitting to no previous experience of handling power machinery she was unsuccessful. She would need to be in her early twenties, they told her, to be taken on without such experience.

Beyond the walls of apartment 11A the other denizens of the Tudor Hotel were engaged and preoccupied with their own lives. Lewis had to complain to Harry Dix Rogers, the manager, about nocturnal activities in the apartment above. He and his wife had, he said, been woken at a quarter to three in the morning when their neighbours arrived home and tramped around overhead. The morning before this they had been disturbed at a quarter to six. Lewis pointed out that unless he slept from 1 o'clock until 8, he could not work during the daytime. The manager's wife was petitioned and asked to persuade these people to keep quiet between those hours. 'I should like to say between 12 and 8', he told her, 'but I do not wish to be unreasonable.'

In the apartment below, there was an even more turbulent regime. Here lived a man who beat up his wife every night. Finally he attempted to throttle her and she left him. Thereafter he beat up his friends or they beat him up, Lewis was not sure. Next door but one along the corridor from apartment 11A was an arena of further routine violence. A Canadian Indian beat up his small German wife at night and sometimes during the day as well. The German screamed a great deal but was thought to derive pleasure from her abusive treatment. Lewis once overheard Mr Rogers intervene in one of their disputes: 'A gentleman', he told the Indian, 'does not call a lady a bitch.'

The only apartment from which no unruly noise issued day or night was occupied by a lesbian drug addict.

FORTY-TWO

'He is a well-known British artist – not a knight'

At the end of May 1942 a bulky missive arrived from the west:

> Dear Mr Lewis, to do honour to a passionate regard for language but not for mere virtuosity, to a concern less for words in themselves than for their meanings, and to let the style of this letter develop straightforwardly out of the intellectual quality directing the purpose rather than to counterfeit the speech of the intellect by a dainty verbalism; and then to attain precisely the requisite posture for addressing you, to squat rather than lunge like your fate rushing from its auger-hole to seize you; all this places me in a predicament which, little as I wish to dramatise it gratuitously for you, is loaded form with high and sanely-spirited satisfaction or with fierce dismay, the choice swaying precariously on my as yet untested capacity to meet the demands of your judgement.

Picking his way through this tortuous first sentence, Lewis might have been reminded of the convoluted prose in which, as a young man over 30 years before, he had corresponded with Augustus John. It may have been the reason he continued reading. At least this letter was typed, and not in the cramped illegible hand that John had had to contend with. And there was always a possibility that something lay buried in this mass of verbiage that would be of benefit and succour.

At the bottom of the third page, preliminaries over, the author arrived at his reason for writing. Lewis would have experienced a slight pang of disappointment at the words:

> I have written a play in fact, and am looking for some not too impossible way of asking you . . . to read it.

The letter concluded, after another seven pages, with a curious benediction:

> from all cults, societies, juntas, squads, brotherhoods, sisterhoods,

colleges, universities, councils, conclaves, committees and conventicles; fleets, flotillas and squadrons; gangs, tank-brigades, commandoes and panzer-divisions of poets, parcel-poets, poeticoes, poetaccioes, and from all mechanists, mystics, moralists, metaphysicists and mathematicians, and all other spawn of the life-force and monsters of the flux, Good Mercury defend you.

The signatory was a young man of 23 calling himself David Kahma, his address, Room 8, 817 Granville Street, Vancouver, British Columbia, and the title of his play, in blank verse, *Arbiter Rex*.

Kahma had been his mother's maiden name, the 'h' to be sounded, a velar fricative, as the 'ch' in 'Loch Lomond'. A Finnish emigrant, she had married an Irishman called McCaughie in Canada, given birth to David in July 1919 and died in December of the same year. Brought up by his father, David adopted the maternal family name on reaching majority. However, Lewis was asked to reply, and a self-addressed envelope had been enclosed for the purpose, using the young man's paternal surname. This was to avoid confusing the postal service because he had thus far neglected to make the change from McCaughie to Kahma by deed poll.

Throughout the six-month correspondence that followed, letters arrived from Vancouver signed 'David Kahma', while replies were dispatched from Toronto with the salutation 'Dear Mr McCaughie'.

There was barely time to read the first communication, let alone digest it or respond, before the second arrived. This was clearly intended to quicken the pulse. A two-inch-long, heavily inked black arrow rose in a steep diagonal, drawing attention to the upper-case message across the top of the page:

THIS LETTER DEALS WITH ECONOMIC PROPOSALS OF EXCEPTIONAL URGENCY, SO I WOULD BE MOST GRATEFUL IF YOU WOULD READ IT AT ONCE.

The sentence would have impressed itself upon Lewis's consciousness even without the big black arrow. Kahma had money: 'private means' that he wished to employ 'in a very definite manner'. With an economy of words that may have caused him difficulty, he outlined his plans:

1. To continue my present work in moderate comfort, with as much security as I can muster.
2. Not to monopolise that comfort and security.

He intended bestowing grants to support 'anyone concerned with the

English language as an instrument for the communication of Meaning . . . anyone whose instinctive tendency is to move from flux to terra firma.' Anyone engaged in 'serious writing' along the Classical lines approved in *Men Without Art*, the book Kahma had adopted as his critical benchmark, would qualify. Lewis himself was to advise on the most likely candidates. Kahma planned to spend a total of $30,000 in the first year and between $35,000 and $40,000 each year thereafter. Lewis would receive an 'Advisor's Grant' in the form of an unconditional lifetime annuity of between $4,000 and $5,000 starting on 31 December 1942.

These details were not all outlined in Kahma's second letter, nor even in the four-page 'Prospectus' that followed it. They emerged over the following months as more letters came from the west, over 30 of them, raising hopes, so far as the Lewises were concerned, of near fabulous degrees of wealth and security.

*

A week before Mrs Lewis made her unsuccessful application to work in the tarpaulin factory, the 84th meeting of the War Artists Advisory Committee, under the chairmanship of Sir Kenneth Clark, convened at the National Gallery in London on 10 June 1942. The following item was minuted:

> Mr Eric Kennington had reported that Mr Lewis was now in Canada . . . and would like a commission to paint war subjects. Agreed that he should be so commissioned subject to it being possible to make the necessary payments to him in Canada. The Secretary to investigate.

At the 85th meeting, held seven days later, the results of Mr Dickie's investigations were duly minuted:

> Any fees which might be recommended to be paid to this artist for work he would do in Canada would be subject to the Exchange Control of the Bank of England. This would probably mean that such payments would be required to be made in Mr Lewis's London account, there to remain until the end of the war. Agreed that the Chairman discuss the problem with Mr Vincent Massey [the Canadian High Commissioner in London]. He would mention the possibility of Mr Lewis being employed to make records for Canada to be paid out of Canadian funds.

The 90th meeting of the Committee was held on 22 July, and Sir Kenneth Clark raised the issue of Wyndham Lewis once again:

The Chairman informed the Committee that he was in touch with Mr Vincent Massey and that he hoped it would prove possible to obtain at any rate temporary employment for this artist as a Canadian War Artist. It was clear that employment as an English War Artist would involve serious difficulties in the payments.

By 30 July, Vincent Massey had wired Ottawa to ask if the authorities there could arrange for Canadian dollar payments to be made to Wyndham Lewis, while corresponding payments were to be made in sterling by the Ministry of Information to Canada House.

Memoranda fluttered to and fro throughout August, and by the beginning of September a way had been found for Lewis to receive the necessary funds in Canada. In the course of a lengthy correspondence with Sir Kenneth Clark on the finer points of payment, Lewis questioned the allotment of expenses and 'maintenance' during the period of the commission: '£1 a day for an absence from home of 24 hours and a day allowance of 6/3d for an absence from home of more than 10 hours.' Lewis pointed out to Sir Kenneth:

> I am constantly, alas, 'away from home', which is in London, and rent for which still has to be met by me. So that 'maintenance' provision would apply, I assume, to the Tudor Hotel.

Eventually, he was offered an overall payment of £300: a fee of £200 for the work and £1 a day in 'maintenance' for one hundred days, the period of the commission.

*

His home at 29A Notting Hill Gate had been preoccupying him of late. Concerned about his belongings in the abandoned flat and studio, he had written to his landlord's agents, Swain & Company, in July, apologising for having left London without paying his rent and 'so unceremoniously dashing off'. He explained his present predicament and urged patience. 'Be easy in your mind', he told them, 'as to the ultimate payment of the rent.'

Messrs Swain & Company replied by air mail, the matter being urgent. His tenancy was due to expire in September, leaving arrears of rent to the tune of £390. There was also another £50 owing for damage to the property resulting from a burst water pipe. Lewis was requested to make arrangements for the immediate settlement of these debts. This done, Swains would be prepared to help in any way they could in the removal and safe storage of his goods.

Replying in mid-September, Lewis ignored the alarming arrears of rent and challenged, instead, the assumption that he and his wife were liable for the £50 in flood damage:

> Before leaving we turned the little wheel just inside the front door, thereby shutting off the water. Consequently I think you must be mistaken in attributing a burst water pipe to us.

*

At the end of November Lewis wrote to the office of the High Commissioner for the United Kingdom in Ottawa:

> As I am not clear as to whom I should address myself first, I am writing to acquaint you with the commission I have received, and would be obliged for any information you can give me. I shall not be starting work quite at once.

A week later the letter landed on the desk of Mr Eliot Warburton, who wrote to Mr R. B. Pugh at the Dominions Office in London for guidance. Evidently presuming a degree of eminence for an artist invited by HM Government to record Canada's war effort for posterity, Warburton enquired of Pugh: 'Am I right in thinking that he is a knight?' Without waiting for confirmation or denial he wrote with all due deference to 'Sir Wyndham Lewis' the same day and told him enquiries were being made.

The envelope must have raised eyebrows as it passed among the staff of the Tudor Hotel, and the management might have been excused for wondering why so lofty a personage in his own country should be consistently behind in his rent. Lewis was amused. 'I may of course have been knighted in my absence,' he said, 'but I hardly think I should not have heard about it.'

Meanwhile Mr Pugh at the Dominions Office sought guidance from Mr G. G. Vincent of the Empire Division and Vincent suggested that Warburton reply to Lewis and offer all necessary information and facilities for the carrying out of his commission. 'He is a well-known British artist,' Pugh was told, '*not* a knight.'

*

Some time towards the end of 1942 Lewis was on a train returning to

Toronto.* He was alone, sprawled in the end seat of the carriage where the conductor usually sat. Shortly after the train left Brockville, Charles Comfort was moving down the swaying coach when he spotted the solitary brooding figure. Comfort had been another of Lewis's dinner companions on St Andrew's Night 1939. He was now in uniform and preparing to depart the following week to start work in Europe as an official war artist. He stopped and greeted Lewis.

'What do you want? Bugger off and leave me alone!' Lewis growled.

Comfort understood him to be in a particularly nasty mood.

'Just a minute', said Comfort, 'I wouldn't dream of interrupting your ugly reveries. I'm leaving for England in a few days and I shall report your characteristic behaviour to Mr Massey and Sir Kenneth.'

Having thrown out this rather childish threat, Comfort swayed back to his seat. Sixty miles or so further along the line the train stopped at Belleville to take on coal and Lewis came to sit with him. He apologised for his rudeness and explained that he had been feeling resentful about a failed interview in Ottawa.

The abrupt switch from brooding hostility to ingratiation at the mere mention of Vincent Massey and Sir Kenneth Clark suggests how desperate Lewis must have been at this time to curry favour with anyone who might put in a good word for him in London.

If Lewis had been mentally reviewing the year 1942 as he sat slumped in the guard's seat on the Ottawa to Toronto train, then it was little wonder that his mood was gloomy and bad-tempered.

His efforts to find gainful employment through the Carnegie Resident Artist Programme had proved to be a time-consuming catalogue of disappointment. Hopes had been raised, practically by the month, only to be dashed with a seeming arbitrariness that must have begun to look like malign conspiracy. Even the most far-fetched promises of salvation from Vancouver had been given a seriousness of consideration born of desperation. But Kahma had turned out to be, what Lewis had in all probability suspected from the beginning, an amiable enough, but ultimately insubstantial, purveyor of dreams.

1942 had been an even worse year than 1940. 'In New York I latterly worked on a margin of two bucks,' he wrote to Louis MacNeice, 'here as a rule I am a buck and a half off the gutter or flophouse.'

And the chimerical 600 dollars for two boat tickets continued to elude him. 'I have never had six hundred cents to spare, much less the six hundred dollars', he told Mr Palmer, secretary of the War Artists Advisory

* He had apparently been to Ottawa on business. It may have had something to do with his Ministry of Information commission. It was almost certainly to do with the acquisition of much-needed funds and, just as certainly, the expedition had been unsatisfactory.

Committee. 'But I think of stealing a small motor-boat, and making a dash for it in the Spring. If you hear I have landed in Iceland, you will understand.'

1943, while not promising so dramatic an escape from their Canadian exile, at least saw the jaws of the trap widen sufficiently to enable the Lewises to get free of Toronto.

*

In the late summer of 1942 Lewis had been approached by Father J. Stanley Murphy from Windsor, Ontario, to take part in the Ninth Annual 'Christian Culture Series' of the Assumption College Lecture League. He was to give one public lecture in Windsor and, to make the journey worth his while, another across the Ambassador Bridge, at Marygrove College, Lansing, Michigan. The fee was to be $100 for the first and $75 for the second, but Father Murphy held out the strong possibility that there would be more lecturing work to come.

Just before he was driven from Assumption College to the Vanity Theatre in Ouellette Avenue, Windsor, on the evening of Sunday 7 February, a speck of cinder lodged in Lewis's eye. Father Murphy recalled him being practically hysterical with panic. It seemed an exaggerated reaction to such an everyday discomfort, but it must have provided a stark reminder of the vulnerability of his eyesight, which for the last six months had been, according to one medical authority, under virtual sentence of extinction.

The impediment was speedily removed by Sister St Desmond, Assumption College's infirmarian, but his vision was temporarily affected and, in what seemed a precursive rehearsal of the blindness that would encroach over the next decade, he had to be led onto the platform to speak. Father Murphy remembered the following remark, as the speaker paused to scrutinise his hand-corrected typescript:

I cannot seem to make out what I have written here: seems like islands of light and dark.

His audience at the Vanity Theatre for the 'Christian Culture Series' lecture, 'Religion and the Artist', might have assumed the words 'islands of light and dark' to be part of the text that he was having difficulty deciphering. But nowhere in his discourse on Georges Rouault did this phrase or anything like it appear. 'Islands of light and darkness' was a literal description of what he saw in the immediate aftermath of that temporary blindness. Ten years later, in *Self Condemned*, and derived from far more

458

costly personal experience, there is another description of the fragmentation of the visual field:

> he saw in front of him something like a large black hole in the landscape whichever way he turned his head.

The day after the lecture, as he travelled to Lansing to speak on 'Modernism in Art' at Marygrove College, J. D. Grant wrote from the University of Toronto inviting him to address the Graduate English Club. It may have been coincidental that a thawing of the Toronto academic establishment's frosty relations with him should occur at the precise moment he was being warmly welcomed elsewhere. Or it may have been that news of his lecturing engagements had spread, persuading the Chairman of the Graduate English Club to extend an invitation from his own organisation.

Whatever prompted the building of this diplomatic bridge, Lewis had little hesitation in burning it down when he got back to Toronto. Out poured two and a half years of blistering resentment. He could not help feeling indignation at this so tardy recognition of his presence in the neighbourhood of the University. Quite apart from the obscure and mysterious insults the Lewises had sustained at Professor Pratt's ill-fated ice-breaking party, the University's neglect had made any future relationship impossible:

> I think that the students are intelligent enough to realise that the occultation of my presence here for so long signifies some official disapproval, and this would impair the authority of anything I had to say. I should be embarrassed – and then I do not propose to expose myself to the chances of further insults.

He wrote all this to Barker Fairley, who must have been surprised to receive the three-page letter as he had had nothing to do with either J. D. Grant or the Graduate English Club invitation. But Fairley was the only member of an impersonal academic establishment that Lewis had had any face-to-face dealings with. The Professor of German, therefore, addressed as 'Mr Fairley', became the logical, and most easily targetable, recipient of his spleen.

To J. D. Grant, Chairman of the Graduate English Club, on the other hand, he merely replied that he was too uncertain about his future presence in Toronto to accept speaking engagements.

With the strong possibility of further work in Windsor, he could afford to turn a principled back on the University of Toronto. On the same day that he was writing to 'Mr Fairley' and by extension Fairley's colleagues, Father Murphy was writing with the news that the strong possibility had hardened into a formal offer of employment. Lewis was to teach Summer School at Assumption College from 28 June to 8 August and then from 24 September to June 1944. It amounted to ten months' work at a monthly salary of $200.

Lewis intended visiting Ottawa during the week beginning 15 February, and had arranged to meet High Commissioner Malcolm MacDonald to discuss plans for carrying out his War Artists Advisory Committee commission. But a domestic upheaval of particularly spectacular proportions overtook his plans.

*

Early the previous year Lewis had written to Stone about the suffocating atmosphere in the Tudor Hotel:

> intolerably overheated nights (*why* when they invented hot water pipes did they not arrange for some gadget to make you turn them off – or when they provided such a gadget, why did they so fix them that they *never* work?)

He had written to Docker about the harsh Toronto winter at the end of January:

> As I write I can see through the window icicles four feet long suspended from the eaves of a nearby house. The other day a man was killed by one, it shot down and pierced his skull . . . So icicles are things to be reckoned with in these parts; and on the whole it is the ice, and not the snow. I walk with short and cissie steps across the glistening surface as I go to the drugstore at the corner, my eyes streaming with water and my ears on fire with the cold.

And it was an awesome confluence of elements – fire, ice and water – that formed, a fortnight after he wrote to Docker and a week after he returned from Windsor, the single major punctuation mark in the Lewises' two-and-a-half-year stay in Toronto.

On the Sunday night of 14 February, at 11 o'clock, it was 13 degrees below zero. The temperature dropped at the rate of about a degree every hour until, at 8 o'clock on the Monday morning, it reached 21 degrees below. Shortly before 10 o'clock, the manager of the Tudor Hotel, Harry Dix Rogers, noticed smoke coming from the door leading to the furnace room and went down to investigate. From the stairs he heard a crackling noise and saw flames climbing the wall. He ran back up and raised the alarm.

The Lewises were having breakfast in their apartment in the annexe at the rear. Lewis told the *Daily Star*:

> It was about 10.15. I heard people rushing around the corridor. I went into the hall. It was full of smoke. Rogers . . . told me there was a little fire down in the cellar. He said it wouldn't come into the back. That's the annexe. Mr Rogers said we'd better get out. I pulled my trousers over my pyjamas and got out. I didn't even get my typewriter. My wife and I went down into the back furnace room. Mrs Rogers told me it was the soft coal in the furnace which started the fire. A man in the furnace room said it started in the beverage-room partition. When I went back to the hotel a little while later to get something out, I couldn't get near it. The place was a mass of flames.

The fire spread rapidly through the two floors of the main building. Window panes exploded in the heat, flinging shards of glass 30 feet across Sherbourne Street. Firemen with their rubber coats frozen stiff as boards fought the intense blaze. Icicles hung from their eyebrows and their moustaches froze. Many suffered nosebleeds due to the cold.

'The greatest personal loss was suffered by the English novelist and painter Wyndham Lewis', the *Daily Star* reported. Lewis told the correspondent he had lost two large portraits, of Lisa Sainsbury and J. S. McLean's daughter Mary, hundreds of drawings and smaller paintings and two unfinished manuscripts, a novel and a study of the origins of American liberties:

> There were also dozens of books I borrowed from the Toronto public library.

Lewis exaggerated his losses. Neither portrait came to any harm. The fire never reached apartment 11A.

That the Tudor Hotel should burn in such freezing conditions was not coincidental. The Toronto Fire Service had never been so hard-pressed as it was on this exceptionally cold morning. There were 57 fires in that 12-hour period, many of them originating in furnaces dangerously overheated in desperate attempts to combat the intense cold.

The Lewises moved to the Selby Hotel on the other side of Sherbourne for one night, and then further down the street to the St Regis for another three, but on the 19th they moved back to the Tudor Hotel annexe and something approaching normality resumed. 'The main building is no longer there,' he told MacDonald, 'but "Tudor Hotel" is, for the present, still my address.' In fact the address had changed from 559 Sherbourne to 354 Bleecker Street, the annexe being accessible from the rear only. Winds blew through the waterlogged shell of the main building at the front, and both Lewis and his wife had colds, but he expected to get to Ottawa during the following week. The High Commissioner had suggested Mrs Lewis join them for lunch at 'Earnscliffe', the official residence, on 26 February. MacDonald's sister was to be their hostess and Mr McCurry, director of the Canadian National Gallery, had been invited as well.

On the 25th, while packing, Gladys fainted. Lewis wired MacDonald:

VERY MUCH REGRET HAVE AGAIN TO POSTPONE JOURNEY AS A RESULT OF EXPOSURE DURING FIRE MY WIFE CONTRACTED CHILL NEW SYMPTOMS WORRY ME AND MUST STOP HERE

The following day they both had flu, but Lewis was still optimistic about visiting MacDonald: 'the moment I am alright again, and I feel it is possible to leave my wife alone in this blackened, windy residence! – I shall set out.'

FORTY-THREE

'We consider the artist not
a very responsible person'

He reached Ottawa, alone, during the second week in March. He was entertained by Malcolm MacDonald and his sister and introduced to Mr Rielle Thomson of the Department of Munitions and Supply, with whom he discussed potential subjects for his painting commission.

Thomson thought it might be possible to gain him access to International Nickel, over two hundred miles north of Toronto, in Sudbury. There was also an Aluminium Company at Arvida, six hundred miles to the northeast, in Quebec, with a gigantic hydro-electric plant close by that he would find interesting. Copper-mining at Noranda and a company producing metallic magnesium at Renfrew were also suggested. Through Thomson, Lewis was put in touch with the publicity manager of Canadian Industries Limited of Montreal. The nondescript name disguised a sinister network of death-dealing factories. In the explosives plant at Nobel, Ontario, for instance, Lewis could witness the nitration of wood pulp into gun-cotton and cordite. Twenty-five miles outside Toronto, near Oshawa, was the shell-filling plant at Pickering. Here publicity manager C.P.C. Downman promised scenes of interest, 'perhaps in the actual pouring of TNT into shells as well as the monorail equipment for carrying loaded shells through to the paint spray booths'.

Sir Kenneth Clark had written, on the day of the Tudor fire, agreeing to pay Lewis £150 at the beginning of the commission and the remaining £150 when it was completed. On 5 April he received his reply by telegram:

PLEASE HAVE ADVANCE CABLED IMMEDIATELY – LEWIS

The Committee's decision to pay half the money in advance had not been referred to the Finance Department of the Ministry of Information, and Mr Trenaman, the Ministry's accountant, was not happy about it. He referred the matter to his colleague Mr Dowden, who in turn referred it to the head of the Finance Department, Mr Parker.

463

Mr Parker thought that the arrangement committing the Ministry of Information to advance payment of money was 'unsatisfactory'. In his memorandum to Mr Dowden, Mr Parker expressed the underlying fear of all concerned:

> I do not know whether Wyndham Lewis is reliable or not, but some would not be, and we are committed to paying money belonging to the Country for something which the Country may not get.

Nevertheless, the Ministry of Information paid £150 to the Canadian High Commissioner's office in London and requested him to arrange with the Department of External Affairs in Ottawa for transferral of credit in Canadian currency to Lewis.

As early as 13 April, Malcolm MacDonald had assured Lewis that arrangements to send him the initial £150 of his money were 'in train'.

However, due to 'an unfortunate mechanical delay in the transmission of . . . funds' the cheque for Canadian dollars did not reach the Office of the High Commissioner for the United Kingdom until 15 June. This was precisely two months after Lewis's telegram to Clark.

By the time the 'advance' arrived, Lewis claimed to have nearly finished the commission. He had been unable to carry out an ambitious series of drawings covering the wide-ranging activities of Canada's war effort because 'it was economically impossible, owing to the delays, to embark on a program of travel.' He laid the blame for his thwarted creative endeavours on the grinding slowness of bureaucracy and the 'cryptic taciturnity . . . and . . . phenomenal and pointed unalacrity' of Sir Kenneth Clark. But the late arrival of his advance had little or no material effect on his ability to carry out his drawing programme. Between 15 April and 27 May, on Malcolm MacDonald's instructions, Lewis was able to tap the High Commissioner's Office for payments of $200, $150, and two more of $100 each. A further payment of $114.50 on 9 June brought the total to $644.50, the precise equivalent, converted at $4.43 to the pound, of the delayed £150 advance from London. These payments began only ten days after Lewis sent his cable.

In fact he visited a number of factories in late March, Mr Thomson's letters of introduction smoothing his path wherever he went. He was made welcome. One factory manager took him to lunch 'at a sort of country club' and offered him 'a most delicious dry sherry and an imported Chateau Margaux'. The factories themselves disclosed other wonders – 'wildly interesting', he told MacDonald. He visited a glass factory and described 'a great tank like monster they have christened "Winnie" which bears down upon the furnace, puts a great claw inside, and draws out in its clutch the white hot jar of molten glass.' But even the influential Mr Thomson could not gain him access to the nickel mines at Sudbury. The management was averse to visitors because of recent accidents to sightseers.

Finally, he settled on the Anaconda American Brass Foundry, not far outside Toronto, as the focus of his attention. Having made a preliminary visit in January, it was not until early April that he began serious work there, producing drawings for his commissioned composition. 'I believe I can put my hands on the money to buy the canvas', he told Kennington at the end of March:

> and I can get free transport to the factory. Wish me luck! – it is a lulu as they say here: a most rugged subject, full of the apparatus of industry, which by screeching and roaring stages becomes in due course the apparatus of war.

In the casting shop he was confronted by 'a busy scene in a factory, with all the contraptions that pertain to such a scene . . . the casts into which the molten metal is run, for instance, or the hoods which are swung over the furnaces to catch as much of the smoke and fumes as possible and pass them up into the shoots.' Much of what he saw was indistinct – 'there was a great deal of smoke and steam, and not a great deal of light.' As if to compensate for the poor visibility, he focused upon details:

> I discovered (from the superintendent) the meaning of a certain cleft shape in the hoods. It turned out to be an extra bit they had added on, because the original hood was not large enough.

When one shift came to an end and before the next started, he managed to get close enough to the hood to make a detailed drawing just in case he should need to use that particular feature.

He claimed to have sketched in that 'demonic casting shop' for six weeks, out of the allotted hundred days for which his maintenance was supposed to last, and to have produced somewhere in the region of a hundred preparatory drawings, 'quite unsaleable since they [were] in the first place very dirty and . . . nothing but notes of how . . . things work, their relative proportions and positions'. He got on well with Edward J. Beatie and his colleague J. S. Vanderploeg in the managerial quarters, while on the shop floor he was regarded with some scepticism:

> The men thought I had been sent there to think up safety-devices, and believed that my account of myself, as an artist engaged on an oil-painting, was baloney.

*

Lewis and Gladys made preparations to leave Toronto for Windsor. By 24 April a house had been found for July and August at a rent of $50 a month. Mrs Hettie Hagarty was a school teacher and would be away for the summer. Lewis told her that he and his wife would move into 424 Tecumseh Road between 25 and 28 June.

At the end of May, responding to threatening letters from London, Lewis was still attempting to placate Swain & Company and persuade them against disposing of his goods at 29A Notting Hill Gate to clear his rent arrears:

> Have patience and don't put them up for auction. – Many things you'd only get a few shillings for but replacing would cost lots of money. The books are tools of my trade, collected over a period of years and as to the things pertaining to my other trade in the studio upstairs, they would fetch very little.

He was, he explained, stranded in Canada and could not return to London while hostilities continued even if he could afford the fare:

> I have my wife here and have not wished to take cattle boat back; nor for that matter will the captains of slow and vulnerable ships accept women . . . as passengers.

*

On 16 June Lewis wrote to MacDonald with the news that his picture for the Ministry of Information would be finished by Monday the 21st at the latest, leaving him the five days until Friday the 25th to prepare to take up his teaching post in Windsor:

> My picture is 45″ by 33″ showing the furnaces of a strip mill or casting shop. The faces of the work men are as black as those of Commando personnel, and if I have succeeded in conveying a tenth part of the drama of the scene, then my picture should not be an inconsiderable contribution to the collection of War Records.

He was however unwilling to surrender the picture immediately, wanting to take it with him to Windsor, and, perhaps, do some further work on it.

*

466

'There is nothing pretentious about it', Mrs Hagarty had told him. 'It is just our home.' The school where she taught did not close until 29 June, and this meant that she would not be vacating the house for some days after the Lewises' arrival. She also had a friend staying until the 29th. 'However your bedroom will be all ready and we can just share the rest of the house until I move', she told Lewis. 'If you provide yourself with linens everything else will be to hand.'

But shortly after their arrival in Windsor alternative accommodation had to be found. It is not clear what went wrong at 424 Tecumseh Road, but the Lewises evidently found it impossible to cohabit with Mrs Hagarty and her friend even for the short period they were to overlap. 'The Tecumseh place was hopeless,' Lewis declared, 'and after a few days there, crouching in a small bedroom, we fled to a hotel. I believe the woman was demented.'

*

On 26 June Mr Pugh from the Dominions Office telephoned Mr Trenaman at the Finance Department of the Ministry of Information to say that a cable had arrived from His Majesty's High Commission in Canada to the effect that Lewis had finished his painting and was now applying for the £150 balance of his fee. Trenaman wrote to his colleague, Mr Dowden, suggesting that it was now for the War Artists Advisory Committee to say whether they recommended payment of the balance without seeing the picture. Trenaman displayed the deep mistrust of any conscientious official asked to dispense large sums of money in circumstances for which there was no readily discernible precedent. Dowden discussed the matter with Sir Kenneth Clark, who was quite prepared for the payment to proceed before delivery of the picture. 'He points out', Dowden told Trenaman, 'that the Committee could not very well reject it!'

On 17 July Lewis received the cheque for $664 and 50 cents from the High Commissioner's Office in Ottawa.

He was by this time heavily involved in lecturing on 'The Philosophical Roots of Modern Art and Literature'. For 50 minutes a day, five days a week, he held forth on a range of books from *War and Peace* to *Of Mice and Men*. The reading and preparation for this series took up far more time than he had expected. Lectures on Tolstoy, on Hegel, on democracy and the effects of modern technology and modern communication, left him no time to work on his Anaconda painting.

By mid-July the Lewises were installed in a basement on Ellis Street East. They had been lucky to find it so soon after their flight from Mrs Hagarty. Lewis claimed 'he had simply stood on a street corner, asking passers-by the possible whereabouts of a space for himself and his wife until he found this apartment.' 2 Royal Apartments was sublet to them by Mrs Delores Sills until 1 October at a rental of $30 a month.

Towards the end of his lecture series, Lewis received a letter from a young Canadian lecturer at St Louis University. Alerted to Lewis's presence in Windsor by his mother, who had attended the Vanity Theatre lecture, Herbert Marshall McLuhan – future communications theorist and guru – requested an audience:

> If you are not too busy or too exhausted by our heat, there is nothing I should more enjoy than a chat with you.

McLuhan arrived at the Royal Apartments in the company of an Italian American colleague from St Louis, Felix Giovanelli. Father Murphy was present in the Lewises' apartment that evening. Lewis was extremely happy to be holding court, and the two young academics hung on his every word. Father Murphy remembered one incident:

> Lewis, in the middle of a long explanation, left the room for a moment to Giovanelli, McLuhan and myself. When he returned, he hesitated to recapture the train of thought. We were all interested. Dr Giovanelli beckoned, respectfully: 'Please continue your paragraph!'

*

In response to a letter from Lewis expressing anxiety about his books and manuscripts in the abandoned Notting Hill Gate flat, Swain & Company wrote on 27 August with grave news:

> We have recently effected an entrance . . . in order to deal with some water leakage to find that the carpets and rugs have been largely disintegrated, apparently by mice.

The books Lewis was concerned about, however, seemed intact. Swain & Company were surprised he should have displayed such disquiet at this time because, for the previous year or two, his possessions had been of apparently little interest to him. Once again they returned to the issue of what was owed them:

> We think we should have some definite understanding that the arrears of rent will be paid.

*

During a brief period of respite from teaching and lecture preparation, Lewis rented 'an excellent small studio' at 938 Ouellette Avenue and resumed work on his painting. Mr Vanderploeg, from the Anaconda Foundry, was planning to visit Windsor and Lewis had to make excuses for not allowing him a sight of it. 'Alas . . . the picture must remain incognito for at least two weeks', he told him:

> There are times when the outside world must not see a picture, just as there are stages of a woman's toilet when it is fatal for her to be seen. But . . . in September, I shall be going with it to Ottawa, and my promise stands that yours shall be the first eye to see it.

In fact the picture was giving him trouble and instead of comparing it to a delicate stage in a woman's toilet, the analogy of wholesale cosmetic surgery would have been closer to the truth.

Meanwhile, nearly five hundred miles southwest, preparations were under way to bring him to St Louis, Missouri. McLuhan and Giovanelli visited Charles Nagel, acting director of the City Art Museum at Forest Park, with the suggestion that Lewis be invited to lecture there in February of the following year. The engagement would coincide with an exhibition of contemporary American painting and carry with it a fee of $150. McLuhan was confident that another lecture could be lined up, 'probably a big affair sponsored by the Junior League which should bring . . . at least $500.' He and Giovanelli were also planning to line up portrait commissions. St Louis, it seemed, was a town of bargain hunters, 'but if one person with a reputation for shrewdness can be persuaded to sit, then the rest will flock along.' Vladimir Golschmann, conductor of the St Louis Symphony Orchestra, was a possibility. Also, Mayor Becker had recently been killed in a plane crash and McLuhan and Giovanelli had begun negotiations with the dead man's friend, 'a hard-headed, ignorant Irish lawyer' by the name of Leaky, for Lewis to paint a portrait from photographs for the City Hall. The press had been alerted and were lined up ready to give Lewis's visit 'real attention'.

*

In mid-September, during a lull between the end of Summer School and the 12 Heywood Broun Memorial lectures that would occupy him from early November until the week before Christmas, Lewis managed to do more work in his studio. 'I have turned to my Anaconda painting again', he

469

told MacDonald, 'and I think greatly improved it. I have wanted it to be one of the best of my things, and that it has become, if I am not mistaken.'

When the Department of Information's Finance Division authorised payment of the balance of Lewis's money in July, before the War Artists Advisory Committee had seen the Anaconda picture, they did so against their customary procedures. This 'departure from regularity' would be a weight upon the mind of one particular member of the Finance Division for the next year and a half.

Mr Trenaman wrote to Mr Gregory, the secretary of the Committee, on 22 September: 'Has Mr Wyndham Lewis's picture been received yet please?' The following day Mr Gregory replied:

> I have got into touch with Mr Pugh of the Dominions office who is seeing what can be done to expedite the receipt of the picture.

Mr Pugh then wrote to Mr Costley-White at the Office of the High Commissioner in Ottawa asking him to contact Lewis, to take delivery of the painting or drawings, have them safely packed and sent through the diplomatic bag to Mr Gregory at the National Gallery in London:

> The War Artists people do not know whether in fact Mr. Lewis has produced one painting or several drawings. In any case, however, his work should not be bulky since even if it is a painting it can be dismantled and rolled into a metal tube.

*

In October, their lease on Mrs Sills' basement having expired, Lewis and Gladys moved into a first-floor apartment. Sandwich Street West runs along the Windsor waterfront and the apartment at 1805 had a large window opening on the west, offering a view of the skyscrapers of Detroit and of the Ambassador Bridge connecting the two cities. The move, however, 'was accompanied by difficulties with the other tenants, wasting a great deal of time.'

In the close-knit apartment block community they did not like strangers, and there was gossip about Lewis being a Nazi spy. The local butcher was once heard to mutter: 'Father Murphy has brought some pretty suspicious persons to Assumption College.'

The real or imagined slanderous campaign originated with insinuations made by Mr Kibble, the janitor of 1805 Sandwich Street West, Mr Kibble's wife and a family called McCarthy. It is not clear what was said but it may have been to the effect that the thick-set Englishman and the wife he sometimes called 'Frau Anna' had sympathies for a country with whom Great Britain and its Dominions were at war. Certainly Father Murphy suggested a degree of 'war psychosis'. Whatever was said, Lewis took the matter seriously enough to pay a visit to the local Police Chief and was told his best course would be to engage a lawyer. A King's Council by the name of Kenning was engaged and he immediately set down a barrage of letters to the other tenants warning them against making further slanderous allegations.

The janitor's son, Sidney Kibble, leapt to his parents' defence and instructed his own lawyer to write to Lewis's:

> I am instructed by Mr Kibble that he has no knowledge whatsoever of any slanderous statements made about Mr Lewis or Mrs Lewis and would appreciate very much your clients giving him the source of their information.

The second part of the letter hinted at other intriguing background details to the dispute:

> [Mr Kibble] states further that the conduct of Mrs Lewis on at least one occasion in the past has been very objectionable. In fact, I am instructed that Mrs Lewis assaulted Mr Kibble's mother without any provocation whatsoever.

The English intruders were warned against making further trouble and put firmly in their place:

> This letter is to state that if there is any recurrence of this conduct on the part of Mr Lewis or his wife and unless Mr and Mrs Lewis in future keep to such part of the building in which they reside as is necessary for the proper enjoyment by them of such rights as they may have in the building, or if there is any recurrence of objectionable conduct, appropriate action will be taken.

A copy was sent, at Mr Kibble's instruction, to the Lewises. The lawyer's covering note contained the sentence, made more peremptory by its lack of a concluding question mark: 'Would you kindly be governed accordingly.'

They retreated with as much dignity as they could muster. 'I have followed the advice you gave me,' Lewis told Mr Kenning:

> to 'drop' the matter, at least temporarily. If I decide to take it up and bring it home to these people (and ordinary human justice seems to demand that such persons should not be suffered to gang up in this way

471

with impunity against a stranger simply because he is a stranger and pays more rent than they do) I should go about the matter quite differently.

The injunction to keep to their own part of the building was easily complied with:

> The topography of the house is such . . . that we luckily do not in the ordinary way see the Kibble and McCarthy faction at all. We have our private door. The slum is upstairs, where all the housewives gossip at their doors.

*

At the end of November he gave a lecture at the Detroit Institute of Arts: 'The Cultural Melting Pot'. He expressed the belief that:

> the day of closed systems, of watertight group-consciousness, are at an end. With television tomorrow causing us to be physically present (in our living room, with one of its walls a screen for long distance projections) at contemporaneous happenings all over the earth: with the vast development in the immediate future of airtravel, which will abolish distance, and strangeness: with the cultural standardisation which has already resulted, and must in the future increasingly result, from this – with all these and many other technological devices expanding our horizons and making a nonsense of the old-fashioned partitions and locked doors of our earthly habitat . . . national or nationalist . . . cultures must disappear.

Lewis told McLuhan that he got tight in the restaurant before the lecture and 'it really was delivered.'

The big $500 lecture in St Louis, on the other hand, had not materialised and nothing more was to be heard of it. Instead, Lewis was invited to speak at the Wednesday Club – 'a snooty affair' – for $100. It was reasoned that his interests would be well served, and the chances of portrait commissions increased, by his appearance at this affluent women's club. McLuhan had done such a good promotional job that Mrs Knight, the club's President, had taken the time and trouble to look Lewis up in the Public Library and decided he was 'really stuff' and 'undiscovered' as well. 'Personalities in the world of modern art and letters' was the title provisionally agreed upon for the lecture. McLuhan told him:

> frankly they want anecdotes about 'Long-haired people I have known.' You can please them completely, simply by making it a chat about familiar names – Yeats, Joyce, Eliot, Picasso, Augustus John, T. E. Lawrence etc.

Let it embrace more than one field. A musician wouldn't be amiss. The more your own life is seen to be merged in all theirs the more thrilled they will be.

At one point Mrs Knight asked about the speaker: 'What sort of personal appearance does he make?' 'Oh, a duke at least', McLuhan replied. 'That really settled it', he reported to Lewis. 'You can't be too Bond Streetish for these people.' The speaker accordingly went out and got himself fitted for a new suit. The material was dark blue with a submerged stripe. 'I think it will be a lulu', he told McLuhan, using his currently favoured Americanism.

*

In mid-November the War Artists Advisory Committee had heard nothing of Lewis's picture for nearly two months and, at Mr Gregory's prompting, Mr Pugh sent a reminder to Mr Costley-White in Ottawa:

The . . . Committee is growing a little troubled at not having received Lewis's work, for which they have now paid. Could you do anything to persuade him to deliver the goods or failing that let us know what has happened to him?

The reply, in Costley-White's absence, came from O. L. Williams, who informed Pugh that the artist had at last contacted the High Commissioner's Office. He had been seeking expert advice, but thought it unwise to roll a thickly painted canvas for transportation in a metal tube as Mr Pugh had suggested. Lewis had assumed that delivery of the picture could wait:

What I was hoping was that since the end of the war cannot be so very far distant, the delivery of my picture in London would not be expected until then. Indeed I took this for granted.

Mr Gregory consulted Sir Kenneth Clark and the chairman of the War Artists Advisory Committee told him delivery could not wait until hostilities had ceased. Mr Gregory then wrote to Mr Pugh, who wrote to Mr Williams with the following suggestion regarding the picture: 'If it can't be rolled then it had better be sent in a crate.'

Meanwhile, Lewis had again written to Williams, who reported to Pugh:

He maintains his objection in principle to shipping the picture to the United Kingdom before the end of the war. On the one hand he states that all expert advice points to the impossibility of rolling up the painting into a small space for transmission by air and, on the other hand, he takes the view that the risk of loss by enemy action ought to preclude its being sent by sea.

On the last day of 1943, Mr Trenaman expressed his disquiet in a memorandum to Mr Gregory: 'Finance Division is not a little concerned at the non-delivery of the picture.' He pointed out that full payment had been made six months before. As for Lewis's expressed concern about the threat to his work posed by the U-boat fleet, 'consideration of any risks in connection with its transport is a matter for the Ministry and not for Mr Wyndham Lewis.'

At Trenaman's urging, Mr Gregory again wrote to Mr Pugh at the Dominions Office, calling for renewed rigour:

> I do think that we ought to take a really firm attitude . . . My Committee feel that as the picture has been paid for the picture is now our property and it is for us to decide whether it ought to be sent over during the war or not.

And Mr Gregory, secretary of the War Artists Advisory Committee, added the following:

> For your private information I may say, and this is confidential, we consider the artist not a very responsible person in his negotiations . . . and I feel there is grave risk if we do not get the picture sent over now the future would be too uncertain.

FORTY-FOUR

'I fear that we have simply been swindled'

The temptation to accept your incredibly generous offer . . . is very great . . . I don't know what to say about it. I feel we shouldn't, or rather I know we shouldn't.

The Giovanellis had offered to vacate their apartment, leaving Lewis and his wife the run of it for the duration of their stay in St Louis. And now Lewis expressed a hitherto unacknowledged, if only half serious, tendency towards vegetarianism as he playfully wrestled with his conscience:

I know I shouldn't eat a mutton chop, since it involves the murder of a helpless and rather charming, if foolish, animal, and as to pheasants and partridges! I do all these things, never making up my mind to take the great step, and confine my depredations to the vegetable kingdom. So now I cannot make up my mind. My wife who is far more brutal than I am (though sharing my compunctions regarding 'livestock' and game) is delighted at the idea of turning you out. – I don't know what to do.

Such tender feeling towards dumb creatures and their suffering must have been sharpened over the Christmas holiday with the invasion of Mrs Lewis's beloved dog by a malign abdominal growth. In another letter to Giovanelli, a fortnight later, Lewis paid Jo-Jo a moving tribute. And he could not resist coupling this miniature domestic tragedy with the last four wretched years he felt he had suffered at the hands of faceless enemies:

We are on the grim side just now. The death of our hirsute gremlin has left an ugly gap. You will understand that people never forgive you for possessing more of anything than themselves – more reputation is a sore offence: and if you put yourself in their power they can make you tolerably uncomfortable. By coming to Canada – in the middle of a worldwar – I did that. And my wife has had to pay as well as myself. So this small creature, which stood for all that was benevolent in the universe, sweetened the bitter medicine for her. Like the spirit of a simpler and saner time, this fragment of primitive life confided his destiny to her, and went through all the black days beside us. She feels she has been wanting in some care – for why should this growth in his side, almost as big as his head, have gone undetected? – Such are the reflections that beset her. Whereas I am just another human being – by no means a well of primitive *joie-de-vivre*: so not much comfort!

*

With the New Year, McLuhan recruited a powerful ally to his campaign promoting Lewis's visit. Edna Gellhorn was not a wealthy woman, but her influence was formidable. She was 'the public lady number one of St Louis'. She was also Ernest Hemingway's current mother-in-law. Lewis was to produce a chalk drawing of her for the risibly token fee of $40, on the understanding that word would spread that she had commissioned it for a larger but undisclosed sum. This was expected to result in a flood of wealthy friends prepared to pay $200–500 for something similar. McLuhan reasoned that, because Mrs Gellhorn knew she was getting a bargain, she would be all the more eager to enhance it by ensuring others paid the full price.

Almost as influential, and another prime target for this unashamedly cynical publicity machine, was the conductor of the St Louis Symphony Orchestra, Vladimir Golschmann, 'recognised connoisseur and picture bargain-hunter'. McLuhan suggested he be charged a knockdown $150 for a drawing in order that photographs of him sitting for it might appear in the press.

And there were still hopes of securing a commission to paint the late Mayor Becker. If Lewis were to produce a study of the deceased from photographs before leaving Windsor, it would benefit the cause immensely. McLuhan's breathless enthusiasm then spun off into hyperbole:

> to have your Becker sketch with you when you arrive would be like riding into St. Louis on a charger . . . It would become a case of the Emperor's new clothes among the public here. Nobody would dare to expose himself by raising a sceptical note when such a signal compliment had been paid their king by a world-famous painter . . . It would become a matter of local pride to boost the drawing. It would be talked of as much here as the Eliot was in London, and would probably be reproduced in many other cities.

*

Meanwhile, in Windsor, Lewis was writing Malcolm MacDonald a three-page progress report on the Ministry of Information commission and endeavouring to explain why it was still unfinished. From the beginning, he had been aware that there were two ways of approaching so complicated a scene as the Anaconda casting shop:

> One could be described as the 'impressionistic' approach. That would entail no great accuracy of detail. Even the purposes of the various objects need not be studied . . . I started with the 'impressionistic' approach in mind . . . and . . . my aim was to paint an impression rather than what Cézanne called '*quelque chose de solide et durable comme l'art des musées.*'

It was this 'impression' that Lewis had almost completed after three months of work around the middle of June 1943, just before he left Toronto for Windsor.

At that time there did not seem to be a great deal of pressure on him. So far as he knew, the Ministry of Information were in no particular hurry for their picture, so he decided to keep it by him in case 'some supplementary work on it might suggest itself after a lapse of a few weeks'.

When, in mid-September, he had an opportunity to work on the picture again, he began to make use of the sketches he had produced in the casting shop. The technique thereby shifted from an 'impressionistic' approach to a 'more solid and detailed one . . . more in harmony with [his] own tastes and manner of work'. What followed inevitably pulled the painting back from a state in which it could be delivered to his employers. As one detail of the composition was picked out from smoke-blurred impressionism, another needed to be brought out to match it: 'one part after another took body and bristled with factual stuff. So that at last it all [had] to be brought in to a far more solid pattern.'

The result of this tinkering was that, by January 1944, the picture was further from completion than it had been the previous June. He now promised MacDonald that the picture would be finished in six months' time. 'All this additional work', he pointed out, 'is a gift I make, in time and labour, to the august purchaser; and it is time I am obliged to steal from other things.'

He did not tell the High Commissioner that he was shortly to leave Windsor to pursue portrait commissions in the United States.

*

A letter had just arrived from McLuhan concerning preparations for his lecture to the ladies of the Wednesday Club. 'Personalities in the World of Modern Art and Letters' had been the original title, but now the President, concerned that her members might think the subject matter a little too highbrow, wanted to make it clear that the talk would be as gossipy as possible. She stopped short of 'Long-haired people I have known', but McLuhan's irony had not been entirely wide of the mark. 'Latest title suggested by Mrs Knight', he told Lewis, ' "Famous people I have put in my books and on canvas", God help us!'

*

In February the implacable Trenaman wrote to Gregory enquiring what was the current position with regard to the picture and asking him to make another approach to the Dominions Office. Mr Gregory wearily renewed his correspondence with Mr Pugh:

> My Finance Division is worrying me about the Wyndham Lewis painting again . . . Perhaps you would be good enough to make another effort to obtain the picture.

And Pugh wrote to Williams, his style rendered terse by repetition: 'My letter of 20th January about Wyndham Lewis' painting. Is there any more news?'

*

Excitement mounted in St Louis. According to Giovanelli, Mrs Gellhorn had browbeaten three of her smart friends into commissioning drawings:

> everything is snowballing, the machine is in motion, the 'right' people are talking and thinking about you, the publicity set up is all mounted and Mac's seeming Quixotic optimism is justified, my pessimism discredited.

But on 1 February, even the irrepressible McLuhan felt nervous:

> Will this Bergsonian flux gell when you arrive? Will all these eggs I've been sitting on these past weeks hatch the moment you appear in the papers?

That morning he had had an irritating telephone conversation with a Mrs Sayman, who told him she had deferred making a decision about commissioning a portrait until she had consulted her English son-in-law, an assistant naval attaché in Washington DC, Lieutenant P. Otway-Smithers RNVR. What Otway-Smithers had to say about the painter was to have decided the matter. But since Otway-Smithers had never heard of Wyndham Lewis, Mrs Sayman concluded he must be a nobody. McLuhan was annoyed that 'a little snot of that type should travel so far to spoil good work here'.

But if Mrs Sayman's son-in-law had damaged Lewis's prospects, the views of Edna Gellhorn's son-in-law did him nothing but good.

Mrs Gellhorn carried weight on a committee which was planning to commission a portrait of the Emeritus Professor of Physiology at the Washington University Medical School, Dr Joseph Erlanger. His work on the differentiated functions and electrical potential of single nerve fibres would win him a share of the Nobel Prize for Medicine later in the year. If Mrs Gellhorn had any doubts about putting Lewis's name forward for the job, they were dispelled when she sought the advice of her daughter's husband. Ernest Hemingway gave Lewis a glowing endorsement and urged her to do everything she could for him. The *Life and Letters* article, 'The Dumb Ox', which provoked Hemingway's tulip-thrashing tantrum in Sylvia Beach's Paris book store a decade earlier, had apparently left no hard feelings.

As the time of the Lewises' arrival got closer, Giovanelli was having doubts about the suitability of his apartment. He and McLuhan were now convinced that if Lewis was to get portrait commissions from the 'right' people, then nothing less than a suite at the Park Plaza Hotel would do. Everyone they spoke to agreed – 'If he wants to make any impression here he must put on a front.' A deal had been struck with Mr Jones, the assistant manager of the Park Plaza, that Lewis be given $10 a night accommodation for $5. And in terms more appropriate to the hiring of an exclusive call-girl's services than a portrait painter's, McLuhan suggested that the assistant manager 'might discreetly inform his millionaire clients that he had an "in" with Mr W. Lewis and might be able to get a job done for them. Not much hope of course. But just a chance that Lewis might relent for $5000.' Mr Jones, needless to say, was promised 10 per cent of whatever his discreet solicitations netted.

With all of McLuhan's and Giovanelli's meticulous arrangements in place, deals made and Mrs Gellhorn's handling of the people prepared to put out big money for paintings, Lewis and his wife arrived in St Louis on 15 February.

Greatly against his will, Lewis claimed later, they stayed for the first week at 'that palatial and fantastically expensive home of the local plutocracy', the Park Plaza Hotel.

*

Mrs Gellhorn's reception on the early evening of 16 February was necessarily exclusive, her house being of modest scale. But it was a lavish affair. She spent $100 entertaining about 15 guests who could 'well afford to be painted'. In St Louis it was understood that anyone attending such a party was a prospective client. 'There is no hypocrisy in the air at all', Lewis was assured.

Vladimir Golschmann was there, and Lewis spoke to him in French, haltingly at first, Margaret Giovanelli remembered, but then fluently. It was as if, in conversation with the conductor, he became a European once more. But in spite of this cosmopolitan exchange of pleasantries, Golschmann declined to commission a portrait.

However, John Brett Robey, British Vice-Consul of St Louis, commissioned a portrait of his wife, Betty. When Mrs Gellhorn introduced him to her guest of honour, Robey said he was aware that there were two Wyndham Lewises, made it clear he realised which one he was speaking to and, in passing, made a slanderous comment about the painter's namesake D. B. Wyndham Lewis. John Brett Robey's inconsequential remarks on this occasion would be recalled seven months later when Lewis's dignity was nettled by a carelessly addressed envelope.

If there was a correlation between attendance at Mrs Gellhorn's reception and subsequent commissions, then other guests that evening would have included: Erma Stix, wife of the President of Rice-Stix Dry Goods Company, Importers, Manufacturers and Wholesale Distributors; Isidor Loeb, Emeritus Dean of the School of Business and Public Administration, Washington University; Mrs Evarets Graham with her son and daughter-in-law, the psychologist Frances Graham; Edgar Curtis Taylor, headmaster of the Taylor School on North Central Avenue; and Carl and Gerty Cori, distinguished biochemists and future Nobel Prize winners.

Dr Carl F. Cori was chairman of the committee at Washington University School of Medicine charged with commissioning the portrait of Joseph Erlanger.

The day after the reception, McLuhan told his mother that everybody of note had been there. 'There is nothing that can be done for Lewis that hasn't been done. Something is going to click soon. Something big for him. A little time is needed.'

On Friday 18 February at 8.15 he addressed The Wednesday Club of St Louis on the subject 'Famous People I have put on Canvas and in Books'.

McLuhan gave him an introduction and then Lewis rose to speak. Beginning with a short digression about his accent, he told the audience that he had also been invited to speak at a local school. A production of a George Bernard Shaw play was in rehearsal and those taking part were anxious to hear a genuine English accent. Owing to the briefness of his stay a visit to the school could not be scheduled, but he understood that a number of the young performers had been encouraged to come and listen to his lectures:

> Under these circumstances I must be careful to stick to purely English locutions. The American idiom is catching. The other day I caught myself saying golly, for instance. I must be careful not to talk like that!

He paused for laughter.

Enlarging on his theme, he recounted the experience of recording excerpts from *One Way Song* at Harvard in 1940. 'When they played it back to me', he declared, 'I was astonished to find how English it sounded.' He had also listened to recordings of Auden and MacNeice and they sounded the same. E.E. Cummings, on the other hand, sounded much better. 'He sang more.' From this he concluded that the staccato English accent was entirely suitable for everyday usage – asking somebody to 'pass the salt', for instance, or for ordering mashed potato and spinach. But for literature 'the singing accents are the best.' And he suggested that the students might be better advised to perform their Shaw play with an Irish accent.

This led him smoothly to the first 'famous' name to be dropped in front of the Wednesday Club ladies and their guests: William Butler Yeats. And he gave a spirited impression of the legendary poet reciting 'The Wanderings of Usheen':

> Arl the words that I utter
> And arl the songs that I wroite,
> Must spread out their wings untoiring
> And never rest in their floight.

Here he paused again, perhaps for applause, before turning to his present assignment:

> What my young friend Marshall McLuhan (not to be confused with Marshal STALIN) meant by the words 'people that Mr Lewis has put into his books' I do not know.

He had indeed, he said, 'written about certain people'. He dropped a hail of names for his audience to be going on with: Joyce, Eliot, Hemingway, the Sitwells, Gertrude Stein, and so on. And he whetted the Wednesday Club ladies' appetites for the gossipy morsels to come:

> Now most of the amusing things I could tell you about these famous people are of course UNPRINTABLE – UNMENTIONABLE . . . If

here and there – ever so cautiously – I say too much, it is in the interests of my very human audience.

How many 'unprintable' or 'unmentionable' things he imparted is not known. According to his surviving notes the lecture drew heavily upon anecdotal material already published in *Blasting and Bombardiering*.

*

Three days later, Monday 21 February, he fulfilled his only other speaking engagement in St Louis, at the City Art Museum. It was ostensibly the same lecture he had given at the Detroit Institute of Arts in November, 'The Cultural Melting Pot'. And it is possible that the state of alcoholic intoxication that he claimed had enhanced his delivery on that occasion was even more pronounced the second time. Charles Nagel remembered the performance as a clumsy shambles:

> the lecture was held in one of the largest galleries. It was . . . hot and the acoustics far from ideal. Nevertheless, and giving Mr Lewis every allowance, my recollection is, I'm sorry to say, of nothing he said but of the nightmare way he said it: starting, interrupting himself, reading parts of his typed talk to himself, then balling them up and throwing them aside – it was just something to be endured until it ground to a halt finally!

Nagel concealed his disappointment with a single sentence of faint praise when he sent Lewis the Museum's cheque for $150 a few days later: 'I enjoyed particularly your analysis of the relation of nature to art and your remarks on the inevitable limitations of abstract painting.' Nagel's comment suggests that gin might not have been the only factor responsible for the mumbled incoherence of Lewis's discourse. He seems to have attempted, unsuccessfully, to combine two lectures: 'The Cultural Melting Pot' and 'Nature and the Abstract: a discussion of abstract art and the superior potency of Nature'.

But if his performance on the lecture platform had been less than inspirational, he had evidently succeeded in making a good impression on Carl F. Cori at Edna Gellhorn's reception, because by the end of February the chairman of the Medical School portrait committee had offered him $1,000 to paint Dr Joseph Erlanger.

'I was lured down here by the promise of big money', he told Malcolm MacDonald some months later. 'The latter has not been forthcoming.' While he admitted that enough portrait work had come his way to keep him going, it is true that the fees he commanded in St Louis fell far short of the figures of $200–500 for a drawing and $5,000 for an oil that McLuhan had mentioned during the previous months.

Lewis and his wife maintained the expensive front of the Park Plaza only long enough to impress prospective patrons. After a week they moved to less luxurious, and at $25 a week, less expensive quarters at the Park View Hotel.

Declaring himself to be the 'banker' of Lewis's 'camp', Felix Giovanelli supplied him with $100 to settle the Park Plaza bill. Three months later Lewis claimed to have had no idea whence 'these "fighting funds" and necessary expenses came.' The discovery that he was expected to pay the money back and was personally liable to Giovanelli for the debt soured their relationship for a time.

In March they moved from the Park View to The Coronado, where they stayed for three weeks.

*

The Lewises' continued residence in the United States necessitated a monthly return to Canadian soil and renewal of their visitors' visas. On the first of these round-trips to Windsor Lewis took with him a letter of application from Marshall McLuhan to Father Murphy.

Although a Canadian citizen, McLuhan was subject to the American draft and could be called up to serve his adopted country at any time. If he waited to be drafted in the United States, he could only return to Canada on condition he join the Canadian Forces. If, on the other hand, he took a job in Canada before the US Draft Board turned its attentions to him, he hoped to avoid serving in either army.

Lewis was delighted to endorse his application to teach at Assumption College. However, some time after the post was secured and the McLuhan family settled in Windsor later in the year, relations changed. 'He accused me of vile intrigues against him in Windsor', McLuhan recalled. 'I had inveigled him down to St Louis and then shot up here to steal his job.'

*

Back in St Louis by mid–March, Lewis rented a second floor, northwest-facing studio above Hildebrand's Artistic Framing at 4967 Maryland Avenue. Here he began his portrait work.

The recently married Frances Graham sat for a $100 chalk drawing. The large room was freezing cold, so she lent Lewis an electric fire for the duration of the sittings. The fact that Mrs Graham was a psychologist impressed him and he plied her with questions, trying to get her talking about case histories. She believed he intentionally prolonged the sittings, sometimes laying down his chalks and talking for three-quarters of an hour at a stretch. Another chalk drawing, of Dean Isidor Loeb, brought him $150.

Towards the end of March Lewis accepted the Giovanellis' offer to give up their home. He and Gladys moved out of the Coronado Hotel and into 312 Convent Garden Apartments on Taylor Street, while Giovanelli and his wife 'took a room and began eating out'. McLuhan was present when the handover was effected:

> How well I remember Lewis seated in that apartment the first day, dramatically announcing to Gio and myself that wherever he went he split up old friendships.

That same day Lewis noticed *Hitler* on the bookshelf. It was McLuhan's copy, recently lent to Giovanelli. He became agitated about possible misinterpretation, anxiously asking whether Giovanelli's wife Margaret had read it and what she had thought of it. 'There is a passage or two which has rather upset her, because read out of context,' Giovanelli told him, 'but I assure you that she is over that, and finds what she has read of it of great interest and as prophetic as I have found it.' Lewis was not comforted by this. 'I must explain the whole matter to her', he replied. To spare him further anxiety, Giovanelli hid the 15-year-old embarrassment behind a row of books on the top shelf. Some time later, when Giovanelli moved back into the apartment, he looked for the volume and found that Lewis had taken it away with him.

*

Through April and May 1944 Lewis worked on two oil portraits concurrently: one a 70-year-old Professor of Physiology, the other a teenage chorister.

Joseph Erlanger sits to one side of a cathode-ray oscillograph and the tangled workings of apparatus designed to analyse the twitching of a bullfrog's sciatic nerve. A number of laboratory visits were scheduled so that Lewis could sketch the equipment so closely associated with the work for which the Nobel Prize was to be awarded in December. Erlanger holds in his hands a sequence of five photographs showing the spiky configurations recorded by the amplified action of electrically stimulated nerve fibres upon a horizontal electron beam across the oscillograph's fluorescent screen.

Young Jimmie Taylor, the headmaster's son, stands three-quarters on in a short white surplice, apparently singing from a bound anthem. In the background are the altar rail and Caen stone reredos of Christ Church Cathedral, St Louis. A 'choir boy with the whole of Winchester Cathedral behind him' was how Lewis described the portrait, and this was close to being true: the Christ Church reredos was a copy of the altar screen at Winchester with the slight variation of a carving of the Nativity substituted for the row of saints immediately above the altar. Lewis went by taxi to sketch in the Cathedral during the last week of April and the first week of May, and the carved stone thatch of the Nativity stable, proof of this diligent pursuit of accuracy, is visible just above the top edge of the anthem cover that Jimmie Taylor is holding.

*

The Lewises stayed in the Giovanelli apartment for only a fortnight. Their departure was acrimonious, the reasons unclear. McLuhan was reminded of Lewis's remark about splitting up old friendships when he became the confidant of whispered complaints – 'Gio had begun making nasty remarks about wanting back his apartment. Gio had insulted Mrs Lewis's cooking and ridiculed Lewis's toothless or worse than toothless condition.' When McLuhan tried to reassure him as to Giovanelli's continued good will, Lewis snapped back: 'So, you like him more than you like me?'

*

Lewis and his wife lived temporarily at his studio above Hildebrand's Artistic Framing, before moving into the $20-a-week Fairmount Hotel, further down Maryland Avenue at number 4907.

Spring had arrived and they might have been seen at the St Louis Zoo. Lewis described to Pauline Bondy, a friend in Windsor, the 'scratching, bellowing, growling and whistling to mark the advent of the exciting season'. They still felt the cold, however. 'We prowl about in our thick Canadian overcoats like a pair of exotics', he said. 'Only the bears understand us!' And he wrote to Mrs Graham asking if he might keep her electric fire in his studio for a week or two longer.

*

Two months had passed since Mr Trenaman's last memorandum to Mr Gregory, but on 12 April he returned to the worrisome bone of contention:

> we do not appear to be any nearer to obtaining possession of the picture
> . . . than when we first started on this quest.

He suggested that the War Artists Advisory Committee should decide what course of action might be taken. When, on 3 May, the 154th meeting moved that Sir Kenneth Clark 'should try and get this picture through Mr Vincent Massey', the Canadian High Commissioner in London, Trenaman responded with his shortest memorandum on the subject to date: 'Noted with satisfaction!' But satisfaction was short-lived.

Clark seemed an unwilling participant in this extended wrangle, and when Gregory prodded him with a reminder of his promise to contact Vincent Massey there was an exasperated reply: 'Yes, but what am I to say?' And in view of the fact that the war was expected to be over before long, he questioned the worth of 'taking a great deal of trouble to get the picture a few months sooner'.

*

Meanwhile, from Ottawa, Malcolm MacDonald was gently attempting to gauge from Lewis the rate of progress. 'As the War Artists Advisory Committee . . . have been asking about your picture, I am wondering whether there is anything further which you could tell me?'

Lewis explained that the 'big money' he had been lured to the United States for had not materialised. There was a possibility, how good he could not say, that more portrait commissions might be offered him in St Louis. In that case he could devote the two hot months of summer to his own work and complete the picture. If the commissions were not forthcoming he would teach another Summer School course at Assumption College. This work, although poorly paid, would allow him the spare time to finish the painting.

In either eventuality the picture would not be ready before the end of August. He was 'extremely distressed at not being able to send . . . a more satisfactory reply'. It was 'a case of force majeure'.

MacDonald dictated a reply on 20 April. Having to respond to repeated enquiries from the War Artists Advisory Committee, he explained that he was sending it copies of their recent correspondence. He concluded in genial fashion that he was sorry Lewis had been having a difficult time and hoped circumstances would improve. He was soon to realise what a diplomatic

486

minefield corresponding with Lewis could be. When his secretary typed the letter she began with the salutation 'Dear Mr Wyndham Lewis'. MacDonald signed it and either failed to notice, or failed to appreciate, the offence that the prefix 'Mr' might cause. Back came the reply:

Dear Mr MacDonald. Your letter informing me of the despatch of correspondence to London duly reached me. The formal mode of address and forbidding tone is of course a reproof. I am sorry you adopted it for I have done nothing to deserve it.

And his self-righteous offence extended further, to the Chairman of the War Artists Advisory Committee himself:

I have perhaps the right to demand a modicum of understanding, or at least not to be additionally harassed on account of what I have done to further the arts in England. To badger and attack me through the Dominions Office, as Clark is doing, will not I believe in retrospect look attractive.

*

At the end of May the Lewises moved from the Fairmount Hotel into a rooming house on Washington Boulevard. At $13 a week it was the cheapest rented accommodation they had occupied in St Louis so far. 'The . . . place is averse to visitors,' Giovanelli was told, 'and not suitable for same anyway.'

Two months after moving out of the Convent Garden apartment, Lewis's relations with Giovanelli were still frosty. Realisation that the $100 used to settle the Park Plaza bill in February was not a gift but a loan, and that he was personally in Giovanelli's debt, did not improve matters. With McLuhan about to take up his new teaching post in Windsor, Lewis felt he was being abandoned to confront alone that fearsome creature, the importunate creditor.

For his part Giovanelli was willing to cancel the debt, and succeeded in allaying Lewis's mistrust by disarming and continued generosity:

Feel free to make such modest calls on my financial help as may be necessary. I get no particular satisfaction out of yielding up money, even to you, but there is something in me – I suppose it to be an amalgam of ineradicable affection, high respect for your achievements, and, of all things, a feeling of responsibility for your physical welfare – which impels me to want to be a source of financial availability to you. I can never help you in any big undertakings, but, unless you are foolishly suspicious of my motives, I can help you against economic pin-pricks. You can make what you want of this letter. Permit me to advise you, however, to take it as literally as possible; there are no catches, no booby traps, no hidden meanings.

*

Pressed once more by Finance Division for a resolution to the deadlock of Wyndham Lewis and his painting, Mr Gregory sent a memorandum to Mr Trenaman:

In view of . . . the signs of the war soon terminating, had not this matter better be left till after the war?

But Mr Trenaman proved, as ever, dogged in his pursuit of what had been paid for:

I fear that it is not within the competence of Finance Division to agree to waive delivery of the picture until after the war as you propose, and unless the Advisory Committee wish to take any further action in order to induce Mr Wyndham Lewis to hand it over I shall be obliged to refer the matter to higher authority in the Ministry.

*

Lewis had been warned that the summer heat in St Louis would be ferocious. There was no need for Mrs Graham's electric fire now, as his studio was immediately under the baking roof and there were 'two large sun-smitten windows' making the atmosphere inside almost intolerable. In addition, by the middle of June he was having difficulty with Jimmie Taylor. 'One hour's sitting', he told the chorister's father:

or even a half hour during which my sitter is relatively still would be more valuable than three hours spent with a sitter constantly in motion – and you know enough about boys of thirteen to realise that they cannot be relied on . . . to accommodate themselves to the task of sitting still on a summers day.

He wondered if the boy might be accompanied, for two one-hour sittings, by someone who could ensure complete immobility.

There was also a financial consideration. The Taylor family was shortly to leave for their summer holiday. 'I do not relish being obliged to stress this', he told Jimmy's father, 'but the war conditions make it imperative for me to receive the final payment of three hundred dollars before you go.'

Lewis and his wife were also preparing to leave for Windsor. But before their departure, Lewis secured another portrait commission that would ensure his return in the fall. Mrs Stix wanted a portrait of herself for which she was prepared to pay $500 in advance and a further $500 on completion.

Also awaiting his attention in September was an unfinished portrait of the British Vice Consul's wife, Mrs Robey, and the portrait of Jimmie Taylor, for which the balance, despite Lewis's urgent request, was still to be paid.

Lewis drew up his accounts. During the five months in St Louis, he had made $250 from lectures and $2,750 from portrait commissions, a round total of $3,000. But with money still to be paid him by Mrs Stix and the Taylor family, the total he had actually received amounted to $2,100. He had spent $696 on accommodation in St Louis, $300 in train fares, $170 on artists' materials and $100 on incidental expenses. With $200 in rent for the apartment in Windsor, total expenditure came to $1,466.

When expenditure was subtracted from income, Lewis calculated that profits amounted to approximately $30 a week for two people to eat, drink and smoke. 'So the position is as it has been all along during this ghastly period of my life: no surplus, unremitting anxiety.'

The Lewises caught the train for Detroit on Monday 17 July, arriving at Wabash Station at 10.30 that night. They were met by a car from Assumption College and driven to the Sandwich Street West apartment, which their friend Pauline Bondy had looked after in their absence. Despite Miss Bondy's care, all of their mail, not forwarded to St Louis, had been lost.

*

At noon, the day after his return, Lewis gave the first in a series of six classes at Assumption College: 'The A.B.C. of the Visual Arts'. He envisaged a 'measure of practical demonstration' and instructed students to provide themselves with 'an inexpensive drawing-pad and a couple of pencils'. How far practice was balanced or overwhelmed by theory is not known, but Father Murphy, who, with McLuhan, sat in on most of the classes, recalled a heated debate between Lewis and one of the lay professors, which had evidently developed into abstruse realms. McLuhan leaned over to Murphy and whispered: 'They're both on the same side.' And weeks later, the lay professor said to Murphy: 'I am sorry that I did not understand him at the time; he was perfectly right.'

After three weeks, his teaching commitments over, he painted furiously for a further five. His Anaconda picture, however, remained untouched.

The commission to produce portraits of former Assumption College

Presidents had been mooted by Father Murphy in March. At that time the figure of 14 paintings of Basilian Fathers Superior was mentioned, but subsequently a round dozen was agreed upon.* There had been resistance to the project from the current President. Father Guinan, according to Murphy, would have been content to entrust the memorialising of his predecessors to 'some "ham-and-egger" of an artist in Toronto or Detroit to do such a job for around $400–$500 and make the paintings look like photographs.' In the face of such 'ham-and-egg' competition, Lewis offered Assumption College his rock-bottom rate:

> I am prepared to do a painting a week for 45 dollars . . . Therefore if I work for 12 weeks and got 540 dollars for what I did it would be approximately what you would pay the Detroit or Toronto artist.

Although four of his subjects were still alive, he worked from small monochrome photographs, most of them taken from the College's Diamond Jubilee Yearbook: *The Basilides.*

His original estimate of being able to execute a picture a week had been made on the understanding that he would have three months to do the job: the whole of May and June; then, following his Summer School course, a further five weeks until the fall. But, having delayed his return to Windsor until the last possible moment before the start of classes, and as he was planning to return to St Louis in September, his work schedule had to be drastically telescoped. He painted in the apartment at the rate of two Basilian Fathers a week. At times the commission must have seemed like a cottage industry, with Mrs Lewis recruited to share the work.

At the end of the third week of August he was ahead of schedule. 'The little job . . . proceeds apace', he told A. Swinton Paterson, the British Consul in St Louis. 'I have 8 out of 10 phizzes on canvas. It is not entirely an unamusing occupation.'

*

Following Trenaman's threat to refer the matter of the Anaconda picture to a higher authority in the Ministry, Sir Kenneth Clark wrote to Malcolm MacDonald. The High Commissioner had after all established something of a personal rapport with the man causing such a bureaucratic tangle in the Ministry of Information. MacDonald was asked to bring his influence to bear. Mr Gregory expressed an optimism he probably did not feel: 'I hope this will fetch the picture', he told Trenaman.

* Only ten were produced.

*

Towards the end of August Lewis's attention was distracted briefly from the drudgery of his work on the Basilian Fathers by a dispute with a local laundry. Of a parcel of washing collected three weeks before, only bedclothes, towels, tablecloth and napkins, what was called the 'flat wash', had been returned. The Puritan Laundry, 'name of evil association', had lost two summer dresses in grey cotton and leaf print, a pair of woman's pyjamas, two white slips, ten handkerchiefs, two of Lewis's white shirts and four pairs of his underpants: two in white cotton, one in blue cotton and one 'aertex'. According to the carefully itemised inventory Lewis left among his papers to be eagerly seized upon by future biographers, the replacement value of the loss amounted to $39.50. He asked advice of Father Murphy, incidentally mentioning a loss of $50:

> If you know a lawyer personally who would do something about it, for a modest fee, we might recover something. Otherwise it seems we just have to submit to this thievishness and go about our business. Our pardonable anger is extreme.

*

They were planning to leave for St Louis on 7 September, but delayed their departure to receive a visitor. The Honourable Paul Martin, Parliamentary Assistant to the Minister of Labour and soon to be Secretary of State for Canada, wished to discuss the possibility of Lewis painting his wife Eleanor. Other painters to whom he had proposed the commission had, he said, demanded nothing less than a thousand dollars. If Lewis was prepared to do the job 'for some unspecified sum short of one thousand', Martin promised to line up several people in Windsor who had money and could afford to pay more. Lewis was of course familiar with the economics of such an arrangement. It was not unlike the deal McLuhan had struck with Edna Gellhorn at the beginning of the year: a chalk portrait at a token $40 in exchange for the brow-beating of her wealthy friends in St Louis. And not surprisingly, the same agency was responsible for the Eleanor Martin portrait commission. It was McLuhan who 'got the job for Lewis', urging the future Secretary of State to catch the painter before his departure for St Louis and suggesting he might get the portrait at a bargain price if he was prepared to recruit more sitters.

This piece of business concluded, and the promise of work lined up to bring him back to Windsor before the end of the year, Lewis and his wife gave up their apartment.

He was still working on the tenth Basilian 'phizz', that of Father William G. Rogers, an hour before the priests arrived in the Assumption College car to drive him and his wife to the station. He scarcely had time to paint in the buttons on Father Rogers's jacket.

*

In St Louis they moved back into their less than salubrious $13 a week accommodation on Washington Boulevard. There was no telephone but anyone wishing to make contact could phone Hildebrand's Artistic Framing on Maryland and leave a message, or Lee Hildebrand would call Lewis down from his studio on the second floor. 4967 Maryland was also used as a tolerably secure postal address, as Lewis was concerned about the safety of his mail at the rooming house.

He had expected to start work immediately on Mrs Stix's portrait, but she was in Cape Cod. In need of a further advance from her, Lewis had to write instead to McLuhan. 'A pox on Stix', came the reply from Windsor, and shortly thereafter the arrangement of a $40 loan.

McLuhan had to get the money from his mother in Battle Creek, and to save time she sent the $40 directly to Lewis with a note presenting it as 'a loan for two weeks as requested by my son'. Knowing how quick Lewis was to take offence, McLuhan wrote, hastily excusing his mother's 'distressing' way of putting the matter and urging him to overlook 'the "two week" phrase' as being 'quite irrelevant and unfortunate'. Lewis showed himself magnanimous. 'The phrase you refer to is unobjectionable', he replied. 'Please do not chide Battle Creek for that.'

Awaiting Mrs Stix's return, he busied himself with the portrait of young Jimmie Taylor against the pseudo-Winchester backdrop. He expected to have this finished by 30 September, when the balance of $300 from the boy's father would be due.

And it was on the last day of September that John Brett Robey, British Vice Consul in St Louis, wrote suggesting Lewis finish the portrait of his wife Betty, begun in the summer. Lewis was furious when he caught sight of the envelope:

Your method of addressing me – namely 'Mr D. B. Wyndham Lewis' – I find gratuitously offensive. I might attribute this to ignorance . . . were it not for one thing. I refer to your words of greeting, upon being introduced to Dr McLuhan and myself at Mrs Gellhorn's reception – the party given to welcome me to St Louis. In announcing on that occasion your consciousness of the existence of two Wyndham Lewises, you indulged in a definition which I think describes my namesake as little as myself. As to the official propriety of that I wish to say nothing at this time. This note concerns merely a small matter of studied discourtesy – though, may I suggest it is not with impunity that you can indulge in the libel to which, in passing, I referred.

This was the letter he drafted to Mr Robey. Then, perhaps because he had not yet been paid for the portrait, he judiciously muted his indignation:

Dear Mr Robey. I am not, as you are aware, Mr Dominic Bevan Wyndham Lewis; I shall work a little more upon your wife's portrait as you suggest.

*

Two months after Sir Kenneth Clark wrote to Malcolm MacDonald enlisting support in the delivery of Lewis's painting, no reply had been received from the High Commissioner's office. Trenaman brought this fact to Mr Gregory's attention on 10 October and told him that the Finance Division would 'draw the file in another month's time'.

*

Following Mrs Stix's return from Cape Cod, the task of getting her image onto ten square feet of canvas proceeded very slowly. The portrait gave him 'untold trouble'. The precise nature of the trouble was not specified, but by late October the portrait was far from finished and, to make matters worse, Mrs Stix was bored. The 60-year-old wife of the dry-goods tycoon was finding the process of portraiture tiresome, as sitting succeeded sitting and she was not even allowed to see the work in progress. Lewis was dismayed by this development, clearly envisaging the $500 still due to him being snatched away on the impatient whim of a capricious 'bored' woman. 'If you are "bored" with your portrait, as you express it, I am not', he told her:

However it is discouraging and even alarming . . . if every time you see your patron she declares she is bored with what she has commissioned you to do . . . Now I want you to tell me with frankness what you want; for were you to inform me that you did not wish me to continue with my work it would be extremely unjust, but if you allowed me to go ahead and complete the picture, and then anything went wrong, it would be for me a catastrophe.

A month later on 22 November he had precisely six dollars and fifty cents in his pocket. The Thanksgiving weekend loomed and he borrowed $35 from Gerty Cori, tiding him over until Mrs Stix's portrait was handed over on the Monday in exchange for his $500. The portrait was 'really a good one', he told Dr Cori:

> and I am anxious not to spoil the effect by showing it prematurely . . . Poor woman, she has no idea what kind of an image I am making of her, so it is I suppose natural she should be nervous. She will I believe be pleasantly surprised.

After Mrs Stix's portrait had been delivered and her curiosity and anxiety allayed, he was to 'have a breathless week painting against the clock a boy of seven', in the once again refrigerated conditions of his studio, before he and his wife could leave St Louis for Windsor. The seven-year-old was Carl and Gerty Cori's son Tom.

*

When Trenaman drew out the file of correspondence relating to Wyndham Lewis and the War Artists Advisory Committee's picture on 7 November, he had few hopes of further development. A memorandum was sent to Gregory: 'I assume that no reply has been received to Sir Kenneth Clark's letter.' When this assumption was confirmed by Gregory two days later, Trenaman referred the matter to the 'higher authority in the Ministry' he had mentioned four months before. Accompanied by extracts from War Artists Advisory Committee minutes from June 1942 to May 1944 and copies of the related correspondence, Mr Trenaman's report to Mr W. G. Crossley began: 'This is an unfortunate case.' Three paragraphs dealt with the history of the affair: the commissioning of work, the initial payment of £150 in advance, payment of the balance when the picture had allegedly been completed and the subsequent deadlock over delivery. Trenaman was concerned that if the matter was left as it stood there was a 'risk of the picture being overlooked altogether after the war'. He concluded that there was little hope of resolution to the problem from further application to either the Dominions Office or the High Commissioner:

> and if we write to the artist direct . . . he will probably not reply to our letter at all or deliver another lecture on art.

Between Trenaman's report and Crossley's response, Mr Gregory received dispiriting but hardly unexpected news from Sir Kenneth Clark. Malcolm MacDonald had written to Lewis about the painting in August but, aware of how 'very temperamental' he was, had 'thought it wise to allow things to ride for a while rather than appear to hustle him.' He had written again in October, again without response. Now, in late November, MacDonald told Clark:

> I am afraid . . . that despite friendly words from my side he now regards me as being in the enemy camp. What a difficult fellow!

Passing this letter on to the Secretary of the War Artists Advisory Committee, Clark wrote at the top of it: 'Mr Gregory, I fear that we have simply been swindled.'

Four days before he and his wife left St Louis for Windsor, Lewis wrote to Malcolm MacDonald. He was concerned to correct a misapprehension on the part of Sir Kenneth Clark and the rest of the War Artists Advisory Committee. Although he had initially experienced misgivings about his painting of the Anaconda casting shop braving the U-boat-infested waters of the Atlantic, this was not his present reason for withholding the picture:

> I literally have not had time to work on it. Certainly moving of large canvases across oceans during a world war is an idea that does not recommend itself to me, but that is not at this moment what we have to talk about.

MacDonald sent Clark a copy of Lewis's letter and concluded: 'the War Artists Advisory Committee will have to wait for Wyndham Lewis to send them his picture in his own good time.'

Mr Gregory passed the correspondence to Mr Trenaman on 29 December with the comment: 'I am afraid it is a sad story'. Mr Trenaman passed it on to Mr Crossley, who was inclined to agree. Crossley noted Clark's fears that they had been swindled. 'It certainly is beginning to look like that', he told Trenaman:

> but I do not see that either the War Artists Advisory Committee or the Ministry [of Information] can take any further measures which would be likely to remedy the position, and I should be sorry to waste much more of the time of important people on a matter of this sort.

Mr Trenaman's superior in the Finance Division then absolved him of bureaucratic responsibility and outlined a procedure that would allow him to wash his hands of the whole sorry business:

> I should like you to ask Mr Gregory to arrange, as a matter of record, for

the inclusion in the minutes of an early meeting of the Committee of a statement to the effect that the Ministry regards the position with dissatisfaction, which it understands the Committee to share;

Reading through the typed memorandum, prior to having it dispatched, Mr Crossley took up his fountain pen and inserted the word 'much' between the words 'with' and 'dissatisfaction'. The memorandum continued:

subject to any suggestion which the Committee may be able to make, the Ministry feels that there would be little or no advantage in taking further measures at the moment; and that the Ministry would propose to let the matter stand for six months and then to ask the Committee to make a further effort, through such channels as may then seem most likely to be effective, to obtain possession of the picture. Should this further attempt fail, then the Ministry would find it necessary to report the matter fully to the Treasury.

This portion of Crossley's memorandum was marked by Trenaman and sent to Mr Gregory for inclusion in the minutes of the next meeting of the War Artists Advisory Committee. This meeting was held on 17 January. The following day Mr Gregory informed Mr Trenaman that 'a paragraph on the lines laid down by Mr Crossley' had been duly minuted. Mr Trenaman then wrote his final words on the matter:

Mr Gregory, noted. Thank you! Trenaman, Finance, 19.1.45.

With that, responsibility for the unfinished painting of the Anaconda casting shop passed from Mr Trenaman's shoulders for ever. It was not to become the concern of Finance Division again until the war was over.

FORTY-FIVE

'Smile up to your ears!'

'Although people in St Louis wished me to stop there,' Lewis told Paul Martin, 'I risked it and came back ... to Windsor.' Arriving on 16 December 1944, he and Gladys stayed first at the Hotel Norton-Palmer and then in room 612 of the Prince Edward at $5 a night. The principal reason for their return was the commission to paint Mrs Martin for a still unspecified fee, and her husband's promise of more lucrative commissions once the portrait was in a sufficiently advanced state to show prospective patrons.

Lewis began work as soon as he arrived. A preliminary sketch shows 'Nelly' Martin sitting in the corner of a sofa, 'intimate, domesticated', her body upright, legs stretched along the seat to the left. For this she wore a beige suit. The right-angled composition of the pose gave the drawing its title: *3 o'clock*. But something closer to 6 o'clock was eventually decided on. The painting shows her to be so frontally posed, her legs completely concealed by a deep blue ball gown, that at first glance she seems to be standing. Only the bundle of interlaced fingers resting on the promontory of dark dress material enveloping a crossed knee shows her to be seated. Otherwise she does not appear to make contact with the yellow upholstered armchair behind her.

At Mrs Martin's suggestion, they had tried out the same pose with her wearing the beige suit, but Lewis was not satisfied. 'It does not seem to me that you pass over from intimacy into formality with the beige suit', he explained. The choice, between 'intimacy and formality', between 3 o'clock and 6 o'clock, was left to her husband. Lewis pointed out that since she had such 'a beautifully shaped head', he himself favoured the more exacting frontal pose, 'the head erect instead of in a relaxed position'.

'Smile up to your ears!' Lewis told her. The red cupid's bow lips tilted slightly at the corners, the blue eyes widened and stared straight ahead, the interlaced fingers probably tightened. She hated the sittings and had the feeling that Lewis was trying to shock her delicate, 25-year-old sensibilities. She remembered him telling her that Lady Cunard's daughter had a black man for a lover. As he talked, her attention was involuntarily drawn to his long yellow equine teeth.

When Paul Martin left Windsor for Ottawa en route for England, he had done nothing about getting Lewis further commissions. It was better to wait, he said, until Nelly's portrait was sufficiently advanced to show. Lewis was disconcerted when he discovered Martin was going away. Admittedly the portrait was not yet ready to be shown, but it very soon would be. In the meantime, his failure to find an apartment made unavoidable an expensive stay at the King Edward Hotel. The fee for the commission had been 'left fluid', and the ill-defined financial arrangements created inevitable misunderstanding. If Martin was under the impression that a cheque for $150, dispatched on 8 January during the hour before the Ottawa train departed, covered 'the balance owing', and so settled the matter, he was to be convinced otherwise over the following month and a half.

That Monday, Lewis was expecting a visit from his patron, and waited in his King Edward Hotel room for him all day. Phoning Martin's office, he discovered the MP was actually in the same building. The implication was clear:

> I was very upset when on the last day you avoided me – for your secretary told me you were in the hotel 'with the Minister', and you could I take it have spared ten minutes to see me, seeing I was only a few yards away.

In fact Martin had been fully occupied, 'the Minister of Labour being on hand, and . . . having to superintend, as it were, his visit'. Added to which, he explained, 'there was the necessity, precious to me, . . . of wanting to spend some time alone with my wife.'

The Parliamentary Assistant's meeting with his Minister was a final briefing for the 94th Session of the International Labour Office's Governing Body to be held from 25 to 31 January at the Ministry of Labour and National Service in London. Paul Martin was attending as his government's representative and as Chairman of the Committee on Constitutional Questions dealing with relations between the ILO and the system of world security proposed in the final months of the war to preserve the forthcoming peace, the United Nations Organisation.

Such statesmanlike activity would prove an inevitable distraction and prevent him from fulfilling the promises he had made to find subjects for Lewis's brush in Windsor.

Martin had originally mentioned three such possible portrait commissions. A painting from photographs of his secretary's brother, an airman recently killed in action, came to nothing. This left a 'Dodge millionairess' and a 'Windsor businessman'.

As his patron's absence abroad lengthened and as Mrs Martin's portrait had long since reached a point at which it could be shown, Lewis became restive. He sounded out Mrs Martin, mentioning the prospective portrait of the 'Dodge millionairess' in passing. Mrs Martin appeared uncomfortable. Lewis persisted:

> Whenever I referred to that she seemed very reserved, seeming anything but sanguine. At last she definitely was so discouraging that I wrote that off.

This left 'the Windsor businessman' as the sole remaining prospect, 'the third of the original trio, and never as much in the foreground as the other two'.

*

In the meantime Daphne Hein, secretary of the Windsor Art Association, had invited him to speak at a members' tea in the Willistead Manor Gallery, held to coincide with an exhibition of three contemporary women painters from Montreal: Prudence Heward, Anne Savage and Ethel Seath. The event was to take place on Sunday afternoon, 4 February, and Lewis was to be paid a fee. Details of the exhibition and of the tea were reported the week before in the *Windsor Star*, where the speaker was referred to as 'D. B. Wyndham Lewis, distinguished English artist and writer'. The day before the members' tea a longer article, including a photograph, attempted to correct the mistake. He was, the *Windsor Star* assured its readers, 'completely different from D. B. Wyndham Lewis, the humorous essayist, who is not related to him'. There were other mistakes. He was 'born in England in 1886'. He edited *Blast* 'for years after the war'. Finally, 'in 1932, his portrait of Augustus John was rejected by the Royal Academy.' It was not, however, the harmless mangling of a press release that gave rise to trouble and led to the members of the Windsor Art Association waiting in vain for their speaker the following day. Instead, it was a section of the article in which the local reporter had got his facts more or less correct that embarrassed Lewis and caused him to cancel the engagement. In the second paragraph he was described as 'editor of the *Blast*, a magazine publishing the works of many well-known writers, including Ezra Pound.'

Since his indictment for treason by a Federal Grand Jury in Washington DC on 26 July 1943, the author of *The Cantos* had become a potentially dangerous man to be associated with. Following the attack on Pearl Harbor and America's entry into the war against the Axis Powers, he had continued broadcasting on Rome Radio, thereby 'adhering' to his country's enemies and 'giving them Aid and Comfort'. There was a strong likelihood that, when the war was over and the time came for such scores to be settled, Ezra Pound would hang.

Lewis was horrified at a 40-year-old association with an indicted traitor being publicised in a small community naturally mistrustful of strangers and in wartime positively xenophobic. He and his wife had already been the target of gossip and insinuations whispered from door to door by the Kibble and McCarthy families on the upper landing of the Sandwich Street West apartment building the previous winter.

Lewis set about tracing the source of the press release. The most likely candidate for blame was a man who had been a cause of irritation and veiled resentment for some time. Whether or not he was responsible, it nevertheless served as an excuse for Lewis to rid himself of an irksome acquaintance.

Marshall McLuhan claimed never to have known the reason for the letter Lewis sent him on 4 February. It began 'Dear Mr McLuhan', a formal salutation announcing the young Canadian's consignment to the ranks of 'enemy' for the next eight years. 'In a small community,' he went on, 'where everybody knows everybody else, and one is an outsider, intrigues of the most moronic kind are bound to blow up.' Here the shades of Kibble and McCarthy reared in the memory. 'You', he accused McLuhan, 'appear to have been at the centre of this one.' That was the only point in the letter offering a hint as to the nature of the offence with which he was charging his erstwhile friend. Thereafter it was concerned with generalities and long-festered grudges:

> I neither care much for you nor for the way you behave towards those you are the 'friend' of and 'admire'. I am ashamed to say you inveigled me down to St. Louis. You came up here to avoid the draft. We changed places. But I returned 2 months ago to this city . . . and do not want or intend to be interfered with . . . I send you this as a preliminary warning off, and I hope you will take it to heart.

This was the letter McLuhan received. There was another, longer version written the same day but not sent, detailing past slights: McLuhan leaving his wife in the car when he came to visit; McLuhan holding a drinks party on the same evening as Lewis's and poaching his guests; McLuhan making a fool of him in front of a visiting academic. Only in the first line of this draft was reference made to the current crisis:

> You have made it impossible for me to give my lecture.

*

Paul Martin had given his assurance that he 'would and indeed *must* be back' from London by 30 January at the latest. Since the International Labour Office Conference began on the 25th and ended on the 31st, this schedule proved unrealistic, and it was not until the second week of February that his arrival in Montreal was reported by the Windsor press. Lewis phoned his office and was told that the MP would be home on the 16th or 17th. By this time the portrait of his wife was close to completion. In a peevish letter greeting Martin on his return, Lewis mentioned the 'difficult conditions' under which the work had been done, confessed himself 'surprised' he had received no word of explanation or reassurance at the prolonged absence of one he had relied upon to secure him further commissions and, finally, implored him to get in touch as soon as possible. The 'difficult conditions' referred to were presumably Lewis's lack of a studio and the necessity of living and painting in room 612 of the Prince Edward Hotel. Martin seems to have lost little time in coming to see the portrait. The day after he got back to town, he and his wife stood with Lewis in front of the five-foot-high canvas. The meeting, that Sunday afternoon, was tense. Lewis got the impression that Martin resented his still being in Windsor. While Mrs Martin 'impulsively expressed her delight' when she saw what Lewis had done, her husband 'did not utter a word during a half hour examination of the picture.'

The interview must have started amicably enough, with the two men arranging to meet the following day to visit a Detroit framemaker. However, their subsequent conversation led to Lewis sending a terse note the same evening cancelling the excursion. Probably, later in the afternoon, Lewis had demanded more money: money in addition to the $150 Martin had paid him as 'the balance owing' in January; money in addition to the undisclosed sums Mrs Martin recalled giving him while her husband was away.

Lewis's rationale appears to have been simple. He had agreed to paint Mrs Martin at a reduced fee in order to gain other commissions which her husband had promised to secure for him. However, since Martin's absence had prevented him from fulfilling his side of the bargain, the original fee for his wife's portrait was to be increased as compensation to the painter for loss of earnings:

> under these circumstances the least I can agree to is 750 dollars. With that
> I shall be out of pocket.

*

On Monday 12 March he was in Chatham, about 25 miles east of Windsor, to speak at the Ranklin Hotel on 'The Problem of Beauty'. The invitation had come from one of his former students at Assumption College, Dan Taylor, who now ran a bookshop in town and sponsored the series of 'Chatham Lectures' of which Lewis's was to be the first.

Dan Taylor recalls that, when he was studying at Assumption, a bootlegger's son paid fellow students $5 a month for the use of their ration books. Taylor himself, although he could have used the money, passed his liquor coupons to Lewis, who exchanged them for gin. It may have been in recognition of these past favours that Lewis agreed to lecture for a fee of only $35 and his return railway fare. About 125 people paid to attend and the event appears to have been a great success. Taylor himself recalled nothing of the talk, having been in a state of considerable anxiety all afternoon about his speaker. Lewis started drinking gin at 2 o'clock and kept at it steadily until it was time for him to speak at 8.30:

> His method of drinking was to break a hole in an orange, and squeeze two drops of juice into a tumbler of gin which he then drank slowly.

It did not appear to affect his performance, Taylor recalled:

> it was not one of his worst lectures. I had heard him give worse, as well as better, at Windsor.

*

Three days later, on 16 March, he crossed the river from Windsor to lunch with a Detroit collector, Charles E. Feinberg. Lewis had phoned him, mentioning Augustus John's name, and they arranged to meet in the Book-Cadillac Hotel. Mr Feinberg brought along one of John's etchings of the youthful Lewis, intending to have it inscribed over lunch. But he retained unpleasant memories of the encounter:

> At first he spoke of England and pleasantries. He was looking for commissions for portrait drawings. I agreed to help him. I don't remember the turn of the conversation or what turned him on the Jews, but his remarks angered me. I told him that as a Jew, I considered his remarks offensive. He started to splutter, but I quickly got up from the table, paid the cheque for the lunch, excused myself and left . . . That was my only contact with him. Years later, I mentioned the incident to Augustus John and his only remark was, 'He was a bloody fool'.

When he left the restaurant Feinberg had not shown the John etching to Lewis nor had it inscribed.

*

With the portrait of Mrs Martin finished, but acrimoniously delivered unsigned in view of the shortfall in his fee, there was nothing to keep Lewis in Windsor apart from a smattering of minor commissions.

He produced a portrait drawing of William R. Valentiner, Director of the Detroit Institute of Arts – 'very successful' in the sitter's estimation – and another, 'which . . . did not come out very well', of the Assistant Director, Edgar Richardson. There were also two chalk studies of John Stoughton Newberry, Honorary Curator of the Department of Prints and Drawings.

In late April or early May, Valentiner was responsible for getting Lewis his last sitter in the Detroit area. The 28-year-old Henry Ford II commissioned a drawing of his wife Anne. Lewis undertook it in the familiar but fading hope that an example set by the future Ford Motor Company President would encourage others and generate more work. When the coloured chalk portrait was finished the Fords invited Lewis and his wife to a small gathering of friends assembled to view it. But any hopes that the rendering of Anne Ford would lead to further commissions, clinched over cocktails, were disappointed.

What happened at the viewing remains a mystery, but Lewis's patience seems to have snapped at this point. 'It was a complete failure', he told Richardson the next morning. 'Nothing could be more so. There is nothing to do but get out – go somewhere.' The war in Europe was over and if he and his wife could get to the State Capital, the British High Commissioner would look after them until sufficient funds were raised to get them back to England. Richardson agreed to help. 'I had a hard time finding enough money to pay the Lewises' train fare to Ottawa', he recalled. 'I know Lewis thought I should have found more but I had to put in all I could afford myself to make up what I gave him.'

Their move from Windsor to Ottawa more than halved the distance to Quebec and embarkation home but offered little in the way of paid employment. Lewis estimated that they needed about $725 or £182 to get them, with their 'long baggage train of crates and boxes', to London. But there was still no means 'to make anything over and above that needed to pay hotel bill . . . and satisfy hunger and very moderate thirst.'

Malcolm MacDonald helped out with a loan of $150 and engineered the few meagre commissions that allowed the Lewises to survive those last two months in Canada. But something more was needed to raise the boat fare.

At the end of June MacDonald approached Sir Kenneth Clark with a proposition. It was a proposition which, given the recent history of Lewis's relations with Clark and the Committee he chaired, was surely doomed to failure. The approach was made through Sir Eric Machtig at the Dominions Office, who was asked to pass to Clark the following message:

> Wyndham Lewis ... would like to get back to England, and wonders whether you and your colleagues on [the] War Artists Committee would be willing to commission him to do some pastel or oil portraits for war records. If you are, I suggest that the best arrangement would be for you to authorise me to pay to Lewis the dollars required for passage money and expenses ... It would be deducted from the amount that you eventually paid him for the portraits. It would allow him and his wife to leave for Britain by an early boat.

As intermediary in Lewis's evasive dealings with the Ministry of Information over the previous two years, MacDonald must have known this was a hopeless cause. His message ended with a vain inducement: 'Lewis would bring with him the picture about which we have had earlier correspondence.'

For his part, Clark must have felt surprised that there was, after all, a picture to be delivered, having entertained suspicions for some time that Lewis had not even begun work on it. But not surprisingly Clark declined MacDonald's proposition: 'I do not think I can go to the Finance Division for more money to be paid to Lewis in advance.'

MacDonald now realised that, if Lewis and his wife were ever to get back to England, he himself would have to lend them the passage money.

On 7 August he cabled Sir Eric Machtig another message to be passed to Clark:

WYNDHAM LEWIS HAS SAILED FOR THE UNITED KING-
DOM ON S.S. STRATHEDEN

Owing to luggage restrictions he did not take the Anaconda painting with him. MacDonald agreed to have it shipped to him at the expense of His Majesty's Government, whose property it now was.

The SS *Stratheden* sailed from Quebec on 2 August and eight days later docked in Liverpool. It was 10 August. Atomic bombs had devastated two Japanese cities during the Atlantic crossing and the world was at peace.

*

Lewis and his wife knew of the creeping dilapidation of their home, through water damage from a burst pipe in 1942 and, by 1943, the devouring of rugs and carpets by mice. On their arrival they discovered the property had also suffered from enemy action during the Blitz. The greatest havoc was upstairs in the studio: 'the glass roof . . . had been shattered . . . Although the glass had been replaced, everything was in indescribable confusion. Someone had emptied on the floor cases in which Mss etc. had been stored and a mass of stuff of all kinds had been rained on. The bodies of birds attested to the length of time [the] studio had only half a roof.'

They had been away for nearly six years. Lewis was a couple of months short of his 63rd birthday. Downstairs in the flat he picked up the dusty telephone receiver from its cradle on the window sill and found that the line was dead.

*

In August 1943 Lewis had vowed to John Rothenstein: 'I will not ever return to my hand-to-mouth existence in London. I have a great horror of it.' However, he came back to a city where 'only millionaires can breathe . . . with freedom', where nearly everyone was hard up and where rationing was to keep life at a near wartime level of austerity for the next nine years. But on the whole he preferred being hard up in London to being hard up in Toronto. Even the routine swindling seemed congenial by comparison. As one who had not used English currency for six years, Lewis fell particular prey to this:

> The number of times I have given shop assistants half a crown and got change for a two shilling piece: they seem to know I'm green, but my God they might be Canadians!

Under rationing they did not go hungry, although he found that he missed the American T-bone steaks. What seemed a more serious problem was the shortage of alcohol. Eliot was invited to dinner:

> All I can offer is hot soup and cold fowl and alas beer – unless you can tell me where I can get some gin.

But cheerless came the Possum's reply:

> Hot soup and cold fowl would be very acceptable, but I am not allowed beer or wine and my means of getting gin are limited to about a bottle every six weeks or so.

With the end of war, the political climate of Great Britain had abruptly and, so far as the former Prime Minister Winston Churchill was concerned, ungratefully changed. Following the July General Election, Lewis was 'devoutly thankful to learn the Tories had not got in'. This at least was what he told Naomi Mitchison, whose husband had taken his seat on the government benches as Labour MP for Kettering:

> In orderly progression let us hope all necessary measures of nationalisation will be carried through, and exploitation of the people (us and the rest) be made impossible. Capitalism is rampant as never before ... And my landlord – or his agent – is the ugliest capitalist of the lot. It is difficult to see why the Government does not go for my landlord.

In the months that followed the bleak homecoming to 29A Notting Hill Gate, debts, accumulated over the war years, clamoured for settlement.

When Lewis and his wife left London in September 1939 the rent was about £33 per quarter, with 'all Rates, Taxes and Assessments in respect of the premises' paid by Lord Francis Manners, his landlord. When that tenancy agreement expired on 28 September 1942, rent arrears stood at around £390. But thereafter, without a tenancy agreement and with the premises still occupied by his possessions, Lewis became liable both for rent and for the annual Council Rate of around £75 per annum. By the end of September 1945, therefore, arrears of rent amounted to £780 and Kensington Borough Council were demanding £228 6s. 3d. worth of Rates for the past three years.

Lewis was suspicious that the Rating Authority seemed so accurately informed of the expiry date of his tenancy agreement. This intelligence could only have been gleaned from his landlord's agents, Swain and Company, whose Mr Saunders was coincidentally a Kensington Borough Councillor. Lewis drew his own conclusions:

> I am tightly held in the jaws of the Rating Authorities and my obscene landlord ... They are evidently cutting up my body between them.

He protested that he had written to Swains 'on two occasions' from Canada, instructing them to store his belongings and rent the property to someone else. Instead, everything was left where it was and the studio remained unlet. Swains may have considered that, with so great a proportion of its roof consisting of plate glass, it would have been difficult to find anyone foolhardy enough to rent the place while London was undergoing the nightly hazards of a German blitzkrieg.

Either Swains agreed that their claim for the three years' rent following

28 September 1942 was unjustified or they took Lewis at his word that he was quite incapable of finding that amount of money 'or anything like it'. They agreed to halve their claim. Then, following a further exchange of views during which Mr Saunders apparently lost patience, 'was extremely uncivil', and refused to discuss the matter further, Lewis, discouraged from any more dealings with his landlord's agents, wrote instead directly to Lord Francis Manners himself. He wondered if His Lordship would be prepared to accept 'a cash down payment of one hundred pounds, against the £400 odd owing'.

He agreed to settle his debt to the Rating Authority with monthly payments of £15, although on occasion even this arrangement proved unmanageable and they were asked to content themselves with £10 for the time being.

Meanwhile, he was annoyed to learn that before his telephone could be reconnected the Post Office were demanding a £36 rental for the six years their instrument had been 'sitting quietly, half buried in dust' on the window sill.

*

In October, the painter Allan Gwynne-Jones was making final preparations for an exhibition of portraits he was organising for the Arts Council at Wildenstein's Gallery in New Bond Street. The show was in two sections: 82 large photographs illustrated aspects of the art of portraiture in Europe from Graeco-Roman painting up to Whistler's *Miss Alexander* and English portraiture of the Twentieth Century, represented by works borrowed from public and private collections or from the artists themselves. 'When disappointed in obtaining a picture I wished for,' Gwynne-Jones wrote in the catalogue foreword, 'I . . . tried to fill the gap with another painting by the same artist.' He mentioned Lewis's portrait of Edith Sitwell, acquired by the Tate Gallery in 1943, and currently touring the provinces with an exhibition of wartime acquisitions, as one of the pictures he was unable to borrow.

His alternative choice had been promised by the Tate Trustees late the previous year. It was delivered to the Wildenstein Gallery in time for the opening in early November 1945. However, it was Lewis himself who raised an objection to this picture being exhibited. 'As to the portrait of Ezra Pound,' he told Gwynne Jones in late October:

I can see how attractive this might prove from the macabre point of view: a kind of Madame Tussaud exhibit. It is not mine, but as far as I am concerned, I should not choose this particular moment to show it . . . Pound will at any moment now be tried for his life. Far be it from me to suppose that a man who broadcasts from an enemy capital at a time of war can expect anything else. But I have known Pound for a very long time and I do not like the idea of helping to put him on show.

A concern for his own interests may not have been entirely absent from his thoughts as he expressed this unwillingness to have the portrait shown. As in Windsor the previous February, Lewis may have believed that association with an indicted traitor could do him harm, and even compromise his chances of re-establishing himself in the London art world. Any relationship with Pound, even that of artist to sitter, might have recalled his own ill-advised defence of an infamous political system and the damaged reputation he hoped had been left behind on the other side of World War.

Another event which may have brought such matters to the forefront of his mind was the trial of William Joyce, once a fellow guest at Sir Oswald Mosley's dinner table in the 1930s, for doing in Berlin what Pound was accused of doing in Rome. Sentence of death on the man known as 'Lord Haw-Haw', handed down in Courtroom no. 1 of the Old Bailey only a month before Lewis's letter to Gwynne-Jones, was an eloquent expression of the postwar mood of the country.

Since the portrait was the Tate Gallery's property and the Trustees had agreed to lend it to the Arts Council, Lewis's veto need not have been taken into account. Gwynne-Jones, however, respected his wishes and the picture was returned to Millbank. Lewis invited him to his studio to choose a substitute and it was the long-legged portrait of John McLeod that went into the exhibition for sale at £250, so late an addition that it was not listed in the catalogue.*

*

On 9 November Miss W. M. Dodd, Senior Executive Officer in the Finance Division of the Ministry of Information, wrote to Mr Gregory of the War Artists Advisory Committee 'regarding Mr Wyndham Lewis and his picture on which £300 from official funds has been expended although the picture has not been forthcoming.' It was a matter she had inherited from her predecessor Mr Trenaman, now promoted to Chief Accountant of the Division. 'We trust we may be able to avoid suing Mr Wyndham Lewis,' she told Gregory, 'but unless the picture is produced or the money

---

* Leaving aside his scruples regarding the Pound portrait, the substitution of *John McLeod*, being Lewis's property, meant that he would benefit in the event of its being sold.

advanced for it is returned to H.M. Government this course may be necessary.'

The unfinished Anaconda picture had been crated and shipped to Lewis, care of the London Depot of the Canadian National Express, at the end of August. On 28 November, at the 195th meeting of the WAAC, it was agreed that Mr Gregory and Mr Jowett visit Lewis at his studio to see the picture.

*

Long after grudging settlement of the disputed £36 rental, Lewis's telephone had still not been reconnected due, the Post Office informed him, to a 'shortage of labour'. The arrangement of business and social engagements necessitated his tramping down several flights of stone steps to the street. At 12.40 in the afternoon of 29 November, an image of the changed face of postwar London might have been seen in Notting Hill Gate – Wyndham Lewis, his large frame muffled against the cold and surmounted by a broad-brimmed black hat, squeezed into a red public telephone box attempting to make contact with Augustus John, besieged the while by a truculent queue of impatient housewives at his back.

His friend's telephone rang unanswered and Lewis doggedly mounted the stairs home again to write him a letter: 'To telephone is not easy', he told John.

With the onset of winter a combination of coal shortages and industrial action by the Gas, Light and Coke Company workers brought such a reduction in gas pressure that the fire in Lewis's studio was no sooner lit than it popped out. Unable to paint in these arctic conditions, he sat downstairs in the flat keeping his left foot warm against the feeble gas vouchsafed him and keeping his right foot warm with an electric heater. Over hot soup and cold fowl, Eliot told him he was forced to use a similar combination of inadequate heat sources in his own furnished flat nearby.

*

Mr Gregory and Mr Jowett 'with much trembling' readied themselves for their visit to view the Anaconda painting at 3.30 in the afternoon of 7 December, only to have their expedition to Notting Hill forestalled by a telegram on the 6th:

SORRY MUST BE NEXT WEEK ANY AFTERNOON AFTER TUESDAY – WYNDHAM LEWIS

Further arrangements were made and notice given that the deputation would visit the following Thursday at 3.45, but on this occasion the two men were told by Mrs Lewis that her husband was not at home. They went away promising to return the following day at 3.30. Apologies were profuse, Lewis claiming he had mistaken the day and blaming himself for allowing Mr Gregory and his companion 'to make a journey for nothing'. As for their visit the following day, he told Gregory by note that evening: 'You may depend upon my being here.'

*

On Saturday 29 December 1945, his seventh wedding anniversary, Peter Lewis died of lymphatic cancer in Westminster Hospital. He was 34 and left a widow, Vera, and a five-year-old daughter.

Official documentation of the last decade of his life charted a varied career. 'Fruit salesman' at the time of his marriage, he was a 'commercial traveller' in 1940 when Margot Angela was born and the occupation listed on his death certificate was 'aircraft manufacturer'.

Peter's mother, Olive Elstow, née Johnson, survived him and attended Vera's second wedding, to an RAF flying officer, at All Saints, Kingston-on-Thames two years later. A photograph shows Olive on this occasion, striding towards the church, ribboned limousine reflected in a shop window. The strong broad face of 'Mamie', drawn by her lover in pencil and wash 36 years earlier, was still recognisable, the hairstyle unchanged.

There is no evidence that Lewis was informed of Peter's death. A little over 11 years later he expired in the same hospital as his son.

*

With the New Year, concern and responsibility for Lewis's Anaconda painting passed from the War Artists Advisory Committee at the National Gallery to a former Bedlam on Lambeth Road: The Imperial War Museum. All the works paid for by the Ministry of Information were stored here before being dispersed to other London and provincial galleries. On 30 January, the Art Sub-Committee agreed that a letter be sent to Lewis asking him to bring his painting to the Museum. This, presumably, was intended to establish if indeed a painting actually existed, for despite Lewis's assurances to Gregory and Jowett that he would be at home to receive them on 14 December, neither man had thus far succeeded in seeing it.

FORTY-SIX

Merulius lacrymans

In February 1946 Lewis told Geoffrey Grigson, with only a slight degree of exaggeration, that for five months he had been sitting in his chair, drawing board on his knee, writing. He had seen no one:

> My book is finished, thank goodness, and next Tuesday we are going out to dinner for the first time . . . and I shall be able to be more sociable again.

Why it had taken him so long is not clear, because the book consisted largely of recycled material from his Assumption College lectures and an article called 'The Cosmic Uniform of Peace' that he had posted to the *Sewanee Review* just before catching the boat train to Quebec. He found a publisher for *America and Cosmic Man* in September, only a month after his return. Editions Poetry London was run by the maverick Sinhalese poet and Fitzrovian character James Meary Tambimuttu. An imprint for non-commercial books of modern verse and prose, Editions Poetry London, like Tambimuttu's bi-monthly journal *Poetry London*, was subsidised by the publishing firm of Nicholson & Watson.

As it turned out, Lewis's sense of urgency regarding the completion of *America and Cosmic Man* was misplaced. Completed in January 1946, his first postwar book was not finally published until July 1948.

*

Only one man had actually been allowed to see the Anaconda painting when, in March, a new champion took up the challenge of persuading Lewis to part with it. Ernest Blaikley, Keeper of Pictures at the Imperial War Museum, began the report of his experiences with a brief account of the failure and partial success of his predecessors:

> Mr Gregory and Mr Jowett had separately and together visited Mr Lewis but without obtaining satisfactory results. Mr Gregory had, however, [subsequently] succeeded in seeing the picture.

Blaikley himself made two unsuccessful attempts to meet Lewis and then, on 22 March, he lay in wait and managed to ambush the artist on his doorstep as he returned from a shopping expedition. 'After a very long conversation in the passage outside his flat,' Blaikley recalled, 'he agreed to show me the painting.' Lewis explained that it was still not finished because he was unable to heat his studio. 'If the Government wants the picture', he declared, 'the Government ought to supply fuel.' But after further discussion Lewis promised to deliver it personally to the Imperial War Museum at 10 o'clock on Monday 25 March. Blaikley assured him that after the Committee members had viewed it later that day, the picture would be returned for him to finish.

Blaikley must have been greatly pleased with himself when he returned to Lambeth Road but, just to ensure there be no misunderstanding, he wrote to Lewis reiterating day, date and time for delivery of the canvas and even included directions to the Museum for the taxi-driver: 'near the Lambeth Baths. Big building with dome and portico, standing back from the road.' On Monday morning he was handed a telegram:

HAVE FLU COLD UNFORTUNATELY BUT ANY DAY AFTER WEDNESDAY SAY YOU CAN BRING ANYONE HERE BY APPOINTMENT – WYNDHAM LEWIS

Blaikley gave the Committee 'an account . . . of the position of affairs' and explained why the picture was not yet available for their scrutiny. He also informed Lewis that he would call to collect it on the following Thursday at about 10 o'clock in the morning:

On Thursday, 28th, therefore, I made another call in the morning and once more had a very long (and friendly) talk with Mr Lewis. I could not, however, persuade him to let me bring the picture away with me. He said he wished to work on it over the weekend, but if I called on Monday, 1st April, I should have it without fail.

Despite expectations on such a date of further hoax, trick and foolery, the intrepid Blaikley once more set out for Notting Hill, and this time his efforts were crowned with success. The canvas was handed to him without further prevarication, and as he got it safely down to the street and into a taxi he must have been a contented man. Settling himself for the ride back to Lambeth he might have reflected on his recent dealings with the painter, and how the job of Keeper of Pictures could on occasion be so much akin to that of diplomat:

Throughout these visits I could not help observing that Mr Lewis showed an extreme sensitiveness to any suggestion that he was being compelled to do anything. He is perverse and obstinate and it would almost seem that in order to obtain results one must ask for the direct opposite of what is required! Our relations were, however, almost cordial and our talk ranged over a large number of subjects, interspersed with reminiscences and autobiographical notes – always returning to the matter in hand.

In three days' time the Committee was to meet, and Blaikley spread word that the picture, albeit unfinished, could now at last be shown to them. 'Everyone so far is very pleased,' he told Lewis, 'especially the Financial Experts who are likely to have a firework display in your honour.'

On 4 April the Committee expressed its satisfaction, although whether at the picture itself, or the fact that a picture of requisite size and subject had actually been delivered, is open to question. Over the previous three years there were members who must have entertained doubts that Lewis had ever even laid brush to canvas for his £300.

The formality of the inspection over and the Ministry of Information apprised of its delivery, Lewis asked for the return of the picture. 'The weather is fine,' he told Blaikley, 'and I should be able to work on it.' With the fine spring weather he was indeed planning to begin painting again. But he was preparing to paint a portrait for ready money instead of further tormenting the tired expanse of overworked canvas for which he had already long since been paid.

Having been forced to paint portraits to survive in Canada and the USA, Lewis claimed to have grown heartily sick of the human face and made a vow that if he ever escaped from that treadmill he would never paint it again. The resolution was short-lived. In April, Duncan MacDonald, Director of the Lefevre Gallery, brought Nigel Tangye to see him.

The commission seems to have been clinched with a casualness verging on the perfunctory just as the two men were leaving. Perhaps it was because Lewis had grown accustomed to hard-headed financial wranglings in America that he found the interview disconcerting and immediately wrote to Duncan MacDonald to make sure all was well:

> The matter of the portrait came to a head so suddenly that I find myself starting work on wednesday, and I do not know whether the necessary financial arrangements have been made or not. Did you on your way to the station talk to Tangye about it? Is that all settled?

The fee was £400, 'and the sitter young and handsome (no problems with double chins)'. Tangye was 37, air correspondent of *The Times* and an Auxiliary Air Force officer during the war. He had married his third wife in

1939, the English actress Anne Todd, currently enjoying great celebrity as star of the 1945 film *The Seventh Veil*.

The first week would be spent drawing and making decisions on pose and dimensions before ordering the canvas. Painting would begin in May, but in the meantime the privations of postwar austerity appeared to include a national shortage of those indispensable tools of the painter's trade: 'hogs'.

Addressing himself to the War Artists Advisory Committee on 29 April, Lewis was unaware that the long overdue inspection of his painting three weeks before had been among that body's final items of outstanding business, and that it had now ceased to function. Accordingly, his letter was passed to Ernest Blaikley to deal with. As he read further, Blaikley's face may have cracked into a wry smile at the sheer brass-necked audacity:

> As you know, my war-picture still requires working on. Since this is surely work of a national character and of great importance, I think I should be given some brushes.

As hogshair brushes were currently unobtainable, he suggested that perhaps a chit made out in his favour by the Committee 'would secure this essential equipment'. He also implied that no further work could be done on the picture without an endowment of that nature. 'Such brushes as I brought with me from America', he said, 'are all worn down to mere stumps.'

Blaikley suggested that, as the picture was destined for the Tate Gallery, Dr John Rothenstein 'might be able to work the oracle'. Failing that, Blaikley himself could supply ten pre-First World War hogshair brushes. 'Do you use flat or round, or both? Probably mine won't suit you – but they might be better than nothing. You see how eager I am to help you!'

Lewis was delighted. 'But can you spare these priceless things? If you really can, I most gladly accept them, and will pay you a fantastic price for them.' Only five of the ten were of any use to him, however, and even these were not of the smaller variety he most needed. Such as they were, he kept them, promising to send Blaikley a cheque as soon as he had ascertained their approximate value. Needless to say, Blaikley heard no more of this.

Fortunately, Lewis was able to find a further source, and with the delivery from Dott, Aitken & Sons in Edinburgh of 4 'hogs' for 7/7d. and a pound's worth of the smoothest canvas they had, he was ready to start work.

For the first five sittings he had Tangye wear his Auxiliary Air Force uniform, but then decided on a more relaxed outfit of yellow cardigan, open-necked shirt and cravat. He sat with legs crossed and with a writing pad and fountain pen held on his knee. To the right of the armchair Lewis incorporated the familiar round double-tiered table and a property book with a long trailing marker. For background he copied the green patterned hanging from Hans Holbein's *Ambassadors* in the National Gallery.

A temporary workroom was rented for the purpose, Lewis's long abandoned studio, despite the fine weather, being still unfit for use. Tangye remembered a house somewhere near the north end of the Earl's Court Road. 'It was not like a studio, but a room an artist might use *en passant.*' The sittings took place in the afternoon, confirmed by the prominent dial of the watch on the sitter's left wrist, painted with hands at 3 o'clock. He recalled the experience as strangely restful considering the tense concentration that seemed to accompany the work. 'Sittings were tranquil, to the soothing accompaniment of pent-up breath released through the nose.'

*

In mid-July Lewis signed a contract for a volume of autobiography. He agreed to deliver to Messrs Hutchinson & Co. Ltd a complete typescript of not less than 90,000 words, not later than 31 October 1946. At Lewis's request 'October' was crossed out and the delivery date set back by one month. The book, provisionally entitled *Story of a Career*, was promised for the anomalous 31 November.

*

Meanwhile, by 21 July the portrait of Nigel Tangye was all but finished apart from a slight reshaping of one of the trouser legs. Tangye and his wife were leaving for the United States, their destination, Los Angeles. The cancelled draft of a letter suggests Lewis considered entrusting them with an errand:

> When you reach Hollywood, see Walt Disney. Tell him what a fine portrait I have done of you . . . Say I shall before long be revisiting the USA and if two portraits could be lined up (don't forget the expression 'lined up', it is what they say) I would like to visit Hollywood . . . I have a boundless admiration for Disney . . . Most people in Hollywood are not artists, as you know. But Disney is a great artist. – See?

The economic miseries and frustrations of wartime exile seemed to have been erased from his memory and, bringing analogy of fires and frying pans to mind, Lewis now regarded America as a viable alternative to London.

'The food problem here is indescribable,' he told the editor of *The Sewanee Review*, 'and drink is even worse. Gin, which is seventeen dollars a bottle, is going to be scarcer yet, and of course, dearer. So what we are getting is prohibition only without speakeasies.' Nevertheless he seemed to have discovered a reliable source of alcohol, and enjoyed making use of the old bootlegging term for this useful member of the community: 'my blind pig'.

When Tangye reached New York, mindful of the British 'hog' shortage he sent back brushes. Lewis wrote to thank him and, although not pursuing the subject of Walt Disney, still seemed fascinated by Hollywood:

> Do, when you get there tell me – off the record – what you think of it, what the social life is like – whether it is all acting and nothing else.

It is not known whether the creator of Mickey Mouse ever became aware of Lewis's admiration or ambitions to visit Los Angeles.

*

Close work on details of the Tangye portrait may have served to draw Lewis's reluctant attention to his failing eyesight. In mid-August he was examined by Dr McPherson, who hoped to send his patient a container for a faecal specimen in the following few days. As with so many other necessities at that time, there was a shortage of such containers 'and one cannot get new ones made', McPherson confided.

Precisely what he expected an examination of Lewis's stool might reveal is unclear, but McPherson was clearly throwing the net wide in his investigation. If the ocular degeneration was traceable to some form of systemic sepsis, then the faeces must have seemed as promising an area of enquiry as any other. Once the nature of the infection had been ascertained, an 'inoculatory treatment' might follow.

Lewis trusted McPherson, but while claiming to have full confidence in the general diagnosis of his condition, he appeared to disagree as to the likely source of the toxins. He seemed to derive comfort from the belief that it was his rotting teeth that were causing his sight to fail. That after all had been the opinion of the Toronto ophthalmologist consulted five years earlier, and it had been a far less alarming diagnosis, on that occasion, than glaucoma.

But while believing the trouble lay in the jagged, yellowing 'frightful state' of his teeth, he seemed reluctant to have that trouble eradicated. It was not, as might have been suspected, an entirely economic consideration. Only the previous month he had paid his Austrian dentist 24 guineas for constructing a dental plate and two artificial teeth to fill a gap at the front of his mouth. Just before that 'masterly operation' had commenced, he held Dr Weinsberg back from wholesale demolition.

And in early September, having taken delivery of a recycled container for his faecal sample, Lewis continued to vacillate: 'It seems to me', he told McPherson:

> that before undertaking an inoculatory treatment I should clear up the most probable centre of infection in my teeth ... But that I cannot do until I see a clear space ahead. Consequently it would not be fair to you to start you off upon an analysis of the faeces and then do nothing about it: for by the time I was ready for the treatment an entirely new set of bacillic enemies might have invaded my system; or ... the extraction of the abscessed teeth may improve matters sufficiently so that I shall not need a treatment for the present. The best thing for me to do is to return the bottle empty and await developments.

*

During November, the focus of Lewis's attention was a hole in the inside surface of his right leg. It was 'a slightly indented red area the size of a two shilling piece ... one inch above the ankle bone'.

After a bout of flu he had gone out one morning for the first time in nine days, and crossed the street to buy a newspaper. He had almost reached the opposite kerb of that notoriously bottlenecked section of Notting Hill Gate in front of Kensington Gardens Studios, when a motorcycle 'moving ... at a speed greatly exceeding the rest of the traffic' overtook a car on the inside and hit him. The motorcycle 'slewed away, up on the pavement' and did not stop. Lewis seemed not greatly the worse for the collision. 'I walked off, dusting myself indignantly.' Apart from the injured leg manifesting 'a little soreness' when he walked, he had a sprained right thumb and forefinger. 'For a couple of days [he] could not lift a full glass of water without discomfort.' The hand soon returned to a normal state in which he could lift with impunity, but the throbbing in his leg became worse. His doctor's only advice was to sit with the limb stretched out across two dining chairs, a hot water bottle laid over the injury. So long as he followed this advice there was neither swelling nor pain but the healing process took time. He watched as the pink ring of new skin gradually gave way to blue as it encroached on the slowly shrinking pit of the wound.

Immobilised in his chair he continued to work on the autobiography which, despite his best efforts, was not going to be ready for delivery by the end of November. At one point he scribbled a note and dispatched Gladys to the 'blind pig' for essential supplies:

Any Nicholson's Gin?
Asked my wife to show
you this, for identification
purposes. – Be in next
week (bad leg)
    Wyndham Lewis.

He wrote his telephone number on the reverse of the paper should the black marketeer demand further verification.

*

Invalidity coincided for a time with the further disruption of major plumbing work. Occasional leakage from the Lewises' bathroom had been damaging the ceiling of the flat below for some time. The plumber, believing he knew where the trouble originated, disconnected the bath, deposited it in the middle of the living room and began work, back in the bathroom, replacing the waste pipe. 'Charlie . . . spent practically the whole winter with us', Gladys recalled. Lewis, who thought his head reminiscent of a 15th-century French king, had long conversations with the plumber and even incorporated him, disguised under the name 'Harry', in the book he was writing for Hutchinson:

> He tells me of his day-long diarrhoea earlier in the week: I am a casualty of the bottleneck of Notting Hill Gate, hence – I tell him – my recumbent position. We talk of wounds, . . . of house drains, of diarrhoea.

For some time, the bath lay in the living room. 'We were expecting daily to have the toilet deposited in the same place,' Mrs Lewis said, 'however Charlie . . . had pity on us and desisted.'

Charlie might have solved the problem had he put them to this additional inconvenience. Three years later, another plumber discovered that leakage into the lower flat had in fact been coming from the toilet pan all along.

*

1947 began, characteristically for Lewis, with a financial crisis. The last quarter's rent, due on 25 December, was needed. 'I must take desperate measures', he wrote to Duncan MacDonald at the Lefevre Gallery, on New Year's Day, 'as the situation is this time really desperate.' The picture dealer was leaving for Brighton in a few days, and when he got back Lewis had a painting to show him. He felt sure MacDonald would regard it as saleable

518

and was prepared to let him have it for any reasonable offer he cared to make. If MacDonald did not want it then Lewis would paint him something else. But more immediate alleviation was called for. 'Will you meanwhile do me this favour: either, (1) send me a cheque for £30 which can be regarded as a personal debt, or . . . (2) telephone your bank manager and guarantee me £30 until your return?'

Economic considerations may have necessitated a delay in pursuing the causes of his failing sight. Affleck Greeves, his ophthalmologist, wrote in ominous terms to remind him: 'I . . . advise you not to delay further investigations, as I think the matter is of some urgency.'

*

Temperatures fell to minus 16 degrees Fahrenheit and the freezing weather continued into March. 'Worst winter on record', Lewis told Giovanelli:

> all the pipes are on the outside of the houses; the moment it freezes you get no water. Then it thaws and they burst . . . There were icicles in our kitchen. There were three inundations from the cistern on the roof: we were nearly drowned in our beds.

And the appalling weather was exacerbated by fuel shortages. Under the Fuel and Lighting (Coal) Order of 1941, a householder's ration of coke, anthracite or dry steam coal was a maximum of 40 cwt for the year, of which not more than 20 cwt (1 ton) was to be supplied each six-month period from May to October or November to April. Consumers who relied entirely on coal for cooking or who had special needs might apply to the local Fuel Overseer for additional supplies.

Lewis had invested in 'a beautiful great big "Essa" stove' for his studio, together with the ton of anthracite he was entitled to. But the anthracite turned out to be made up of 50 per cent inferior coal and the meagre ration was eaten up by this 'miniature furnace' at an alarming rate. In addition, the stove radiated heat for about a distance of two yards, '4 yards from it you are as cold as you are in the street', he complained.

*

In February, Lewis revisited an old haunt. The establishment at number 1 Percy Street had undergone many changes since he lived alongside it 30 years or so ago. The Restaurant de la Tour Eiffel had changed hands in 1938 and Rudolf Stulik, once magnanimous and insistent that he 'vould to anyting for Mr Lewis', had died in obscurity. Lewis's wall panels commissioned by the plump Viennese for the first-floor dining room, and which so distinguished the premises from others in interwar Baedekers, had disappeared, nobody knew where. Even the name of the place had changed.

At the barely recognisable 'White Tower' Lewis met Anna Kallin from the BBC to discuss a broadcast for the Third Programme. He was to be the fifth speaker in a series called 'The Crisis'. V. S. Pritchett, Herbert Read, Elizabeth Bowen and Graham Greene had already spoken on consecutive Sundays 'about the book . . . which produced a crisis in their lives'. Herbert Read, who had described the impact two works by Friedrich Nietzsche had had upon his 19-year-old mind, joined Kallin and Lewis for lunch. Discussing Lewis's contribution, the restaurant in which they sat must have been conducive to reminiscence, if only of what had been and was no longer.

Searching backwards into his young life, as he described it, 'to identify some really decisive experience' that constituted the crisis through which he became what he was, Lewis went further than Stulik's Eiffel Tower, and London on the brink of the Great War. In Paris when the century was even younger, he found not one, but a wall of books: 'the creative literature of Russia'. Paris, he claimed, was for him 'partly the creation of these books'.

The talk was composed, recorded and, on 16 March, broadcast during the 20-minute interval between Acts I and II of Mozart's *Die Entführung aus dem Serail*. 'I now realise', the speaker concluded:

> if I had not had Chekhov in my pocket I should not have enjoyed my aperitif at the 'Lilas' so much or the beautiful dusty trees. It was really as a character in Tolstoy – I remember now – that I visited the *bal musette*. And the hero of the first novel I wrote reminded a very perceptive critic of Stavrogin. In view of all this I think we may really say that the first time, moving down the *Rue des Ecoles*, I arrived at my particular bookshop opposite the 'Montagne' to find a book by Faguet, and took away *Letters from the Underworld* as well, crisis was at hand.

The 'Crisis' talk had been a timely commission, its script sliding, with minimal revision, as 'Chapter XXVII: The Puritans of the Steppes', into the bulky typescript he submitted, more than three months overdue, to Hutchinson & Co. Delivered at the end of March or beginning of April, and now entitled *Ascent of Parnassus*, the book was some 20,000 words longer than the 90,000 contracted for the previous July.

Lewis now had two books in production.

Publication of *America and Cosmic Man* had been attended by difficulties since the time in May 1946 when the first set of page-proofs were inadvertently interleaved with a bundle of old newspapers and left out for the binmen, an oversight for which Lewis, uncharacteristically, had taken full responsibility. Thereafter, his relations with Tambimuttu, Editions Poetry London and its parent company Nicholson & Watson had deteriorated as one delay led to another and the book became the subject of heated correspondence and potential legal action. More than a year after its completion, *America and Cosmic Man* was now held up in a log-jam of books competing with one another for publication, against a national paper shortage. The troublesome little pot-boiler was to appear in July of the following year, about two years later than planned.

His volume of autobiography for Hutchinson, however, was not published for over three and a half years.

*

By the end of April, Lewis's doctor and ophthalmologist were both concerned that further delay in diagnosing his failing sight would result in irreparable damage. 'Time is passing and I have not heard from you regarding the investigations', McPherson wrote to him on 1 May:

> As Mr Greeves rightly says, the degree of possible recovery of the good eye is dependent on the speed with which we relieve the optic nerve. If you are not ready to enter a nursing home, at least let us get the x-rays done and your name put on the waiting list of a hospital.

Reference to relieving the optic nerve suggests McPherson, with or without faecal divination, had already discounted systemic sepsis as a cause and had begun to suspect some sinister form of intra-cranial pressure.

*

Meanwhile, Lewis was endeavouring to relieve himself of contractual obligations entered into with Editions Poetry London on 21 February 1946 for a novel to be called *Chateau Rex*, an account of the gradual dissipation of a middle-class hotel during wartime in a thinly disguised Toronto. Mr Mitchell, Lewis's solicitor from the firm Clifford-Turner & Co., gave it as his opinion that 'since the happy relationship . . . fundamental to a successful collaboration between author and publisher, [was] utterly lacking in the present case,' it would be in the best interests of both parties 'if the agreement in question were terminated by mutual consent.' The solicitor cited 'pressure of other work and . . . difficulties . . . experienced over the last year in regard to *America and Cosmic Man*' as having affected Lewis to the extent that he had been unable to devote any attention to *Chateau Rex* and could not 'undertake to consider it further within any foreseeable period'. Lewis was prepared to return the £150 originally advanced him, upon hearing that termination of the agreement was acceptable to the publishers.

By 27 May, Tambimuttu had written to Lewis's solicitors agreeing to revoke the contract on repayment of the £150 advance, plus interest on that sum at the rate of 10 per cent per annum.

Freed from contractual obligations to Editions Poetry London for *Chateau Rex*, Lewis next contracted with Hutchinson to deliver them the same novel under another title: *The Victory of Albert Temple*. He was paid £225 in advance of royalties, a clear profit of £75 on the previous transaction.

*

In September a *Times Literary Supplement* review of a collected edition of William Gerhardie made repeated and favourable reference to *Tarr*, 'described by its author as "the first book of its epoch in England"'. Lewis protested on the letters page that this description was not his own but probably the paraphrase of a 1918 notice of his book. He wished to make it quite clear that the phrase 'first book of its epoch in England' was not, as implied, an outburst of boastfulness on his part. Reviews in the *TLS* were always anonymous, and the reviewer replied anonymously to the letters page, politely referring Lewis to the preface of the 1928 edition of his novel, which began:

> Published ten years ago, *Tarr*, my first book, in a sense the first book of an epoch in England.

The following week Lewis closed the correspondence with an apology for having thrown doubt upon the reviewer's accuracy.

As such exchanges go it was of little importance, but it gave Alan Pryce-Jones, the new literary editor of the *TLS*, an excuse to invite Lewis to lunch at the Travellers' Club and persuade him to become a contributor. Also invited was the author of the Gerhardie review and admirer of *Tarr*, Anthony Powell.

Lewis described Pryce-Jones as a 'kind of tory pansy', part of 'a little high tory group . . . who have grown far more snobbish, since all those things upon which social snobbery feeds are so much harder to come by in a bankrupt and socialist England.' He was as little impressed by them as he was by the places they frequented. 'The "Travellers" is today a shadow of itself, as are all the Clubs. Almost anyone can belong to "Whites" who can pay the fees.' Lewis's impressions of Anthony Powell, his fellow guest at Pryce-Jones's luncheon table, are not recorded. Powell's impressions of Lewis, however, were of a man ill at ease in the Travellers'. 'Big, toothy, awkward in manner, Lewis behaved with an uneasy mixture of nervousness and hauteur. In his white shirt and dark suit he looked like a caricature of an American senator or businessman . . . From time to time in the course of the meal Lewis swallowed what were presumably digestive tablets.'

Pryce-Jones's hopes for the lunch were fulfilled when Lewis agreed to write for the *TLS*, and some time later a copy of *No Voice is Wholly Lost: Writers and Thinkers in War and Peace* by Harry Slochower was sent to him for review.

*

It was some time in late October that Lewis stretched out his arm in the dark, feeling for the light switch, and buried his finger in the wood of a door. Elsewhere in the flat he found a window that wobbled in its frame and, leaning there nonchalantly, noticed his fingernails sink into the windowsill.

Merulius lacrymans flourishes in a moist but not wet environment, a temperature of below 80 degrees Fahrenheit, still air and a plentiful supply of food. Under these conditions wood will be found enveloped in thick, luxuriant drifts of white silky fibre. The fungus derives part of its name, *lacrymans*, weeping, from its ability to create water through chemical reaction with the wood, and this gives rise to the characteristic droplets of moisture that cover its surface. In a dark cellar they glisten like tears when a torch beam is played across them. Strands, sometimes as thick as pencils, take water from the moist wood under attack to drier wood elsewhere which would not otherwise be vulnerable to infection. These vein-like rhizomorphs can pass through plaster, brickwork and masonry as they forage for healthy wood for the organism to feed on. *Merulius lacrymans* extracts cellulose from timber leaving it cracked, friable and considerably reduced in weight. It is the desiccated state of the decayed wood that gives the condition its popular name: dry rot.

The Lewises were told that the rot in their building had originated in a Christian Science Reading Room at number 25. *Merulius lacrymans* was no respecter of party walls. It was quite capable of insinuating itself through the fabric of Timothy Whites & Taylors Ltd at number 27 before reaching a perfect environment for further growth at number 29.

The war had created laboratory conditions for the spread of the fungus. Dwellings like 29A Notting Hill Gate were left empty and unheated, bomb-damaged roofs allowed rain to penetrate, and in many buildings the airbricks that would have created ventilation were sealed as a precaution against enemy gas attack.

Workmen were already busy in the other flats below Studio A, and the noisy regime would begin early every morning. In order to get sufficient sleep Lewis had to retire early at night, a time he normally devoted to letter writing. The result was that his work routine was severely disrupted. By 15 November the workmen had reached the flat below, hacking through plaster and burning out the infected wood with their blowlamps. A hole had been opened in the floor of the room where Lewis was writing and the atmosphere was becoming intolerable; 'they . . . are wafting as much of the blow-pipe fumes as possible up through the hole. I open the windows. But it is cold, so I compromise.' He fled to the National Gallery.

It was not long before the surgery of crowbar and cauterising blowlamp began in the Lewises' flat. The ceiling of the little entrance hall had been ripped out and the lavatory was a shambles. At the end of November they were told that the beam supporting the roof and taking the weight of the huge studio window had to be removed and replaced. 'While this and other operations are proceeding', he told David Kahma, 'we shall live downstairs: then when they start on downstairs . . . we move up (or this order may be reversed).'

The order was reversed, and as they took refuge under the rotten studio roof, wholesale mayhem continued below.

FORTY-SEVEN

'In the absence of proof of malice'

1948 began, as 1947 had begun, with another quarter's rent due and another appeal for money. Lewis was, he told Docker, still paying off rates arrears to the London County Council, had parted with 10 guineas thence a couple of days before, and now needed £38 for his landlord. He deeply regretted having to ask his friend for the sum. 'I am appalled at my situation.' It was 4 January and only the day before, John Rothenstein had let fall a piece of information that gave rise to bitter thoughts as Lewis composed his begging letter to Docker:

> Mr Beddington Behrens has refunded the Tate Gallery the £350 they paid him for my Sitwell portrait – saying that as he only paid me £50 for that picture he thinks he ought not to keep the money!

He wondered why Behrens had not thought fit to pay the money to him instead.*

A little over a week later, Docker received a further desperate appeal. Lewis's landlord had given him until the following Saturday, four days, to find his quarter's rent, due 25 December:

> I have not the money. Were it Saturday week I should have the money; not this Saturday . . . I am terrified.

That same day he lunched again with Alan Pryce-Jones amidst the

---

* The story is more complicated. Lewis was paid £50 for the picture in May 1936, by Messrs Phillips and Brown, directors of the Leicester Galleries. Two months later they sold it to Behrens for £350. In 1943 Rothenstein persuaded Behrens to sell the picture to the Tate Gallery and Behrens offered it at the price he had paid seven years before. But on being told the Tate Trustees had 'fearfully little money', he let them have it for £250. Then in July 1947 Behrens wrote to Rothenstein explaining he had always felt uncomfortable at the Tate having had to buy the picture when most other works from his collection had either been given on loan or donated. With the letter he enclosed a cheque for £350. It had evidently slipped his mind that the Trustees had only paid him £250 in the first place. It must also have slipped the collective mind of the Trustees, because they warmly accepted Behrens's generosity and relabelled the portrait as a gift. It was a further two years before the overpayment was noticed and the Deputy Keeper, Norman Reid, was asked to send Behrens a cheque for £100. The last item of correspondence on the subject is a note from Behrens thanking Reid for his letter, but politely pointing out that he had neglected to enclose the cheque.

splendours of the Travellers' Club. Looking around at the careless prosperity of those about him he had to keep shaking himself to remember he was in an inflationary country, that his rent money had gone in the purchase of goods, overpriced and weighted down with taxes, and also that the suit he was wearing, making him look, to Anthony Powell, like an American senator or businessman, was in all probability the last he would ever be able to afford.

Letters to friends in the United States were a constant litany of the sordid details of postwar austerity:

> We now get no eggs at all, or at most one apiece every month . . . The ingredients of the bread is said by medical men to be actually injurious to health and is so dry and gritty as to be disagreeable to eat . . . The water is now so heavily chlorinated it is almost undrinkable. When the taste of the chlorine wears off, you taste the sewage, which is worse . . . sometimes for a short while the water tastes quite normal again . . . garbage has ceased momentarily to flow into it, or they have run out of chlorine.

While Lewis sat in his studio writing this to Geoffrey Stone on 15 January, a ten-day upheaval was about to interrupt both domestic life and letter. The carpenter and his men had finished their activities in the flat below and now announced their intention of carrying the rot-eradication campaign upstairs. 'Everything had thereupon to be moved *down*. Everything got lost . . . in a whirlpool of furniture and food and blowlamps and typewriters.' Things became relatively calm again on 25 January and Lewis was able to resume his catalogue of complaint, now on behalf of Gladys:

> as is the case with all women . . . here, except Princess Elizabeth,* she has to think from morning to night of food, coupons, coal, chars, 'purchase tax' and such things. We both hate the 'purchase tax' more than we have ever hated anything. Next to that we loathe an expression which our conquerors never cease to employ. It is this: 'Too much money chasing too few goods'.

Geoffrey Stone responded by sending lipstick and six packets of Pillsbury's Roll Mix. This last immediately produced 'a dazzlingly white loaf of bread', Lewis told the man in Bethlehem, 'about the finest present I can imagine, being a great bread-eater: that and the butter to put on it, of which we happily possess as much as we need at present.'

It was soon to become illegal for persons in the United Kingdom to

---

* Voted £40,000 per annum by Parliament the previous December.

purchase from overseas parcels containing rationed foods. Unsolicited gifts, however, might still be received with only the warmest gratitude tendered in exchange.

*

In February, preparations were under way for '40 Years of Modern Art' in the basement of the Academy Hall Cinema at 163 Oxford Street. The exhibition was to be the first project of the Institute of Contemporary Art and intended to raise funds for that fledgling organisation, 'co-ordinating', as Herbert Read put it, 'the emulative efforts of a thousand other centres', whereby 'a wholly new aspect would be given to our life and civilisation.' Selected mainly from private collections, the works on view were largely unfamiliar to the general public. There were paintings by Picasso, Matisse, Rouault, Braque, Chagall, Derain, Dufy, Juan Gris, Modigliani, Bonnard and Vuillard. The large British section included pictures by Sickert, John, Duncan Grant, Frances Hodgkins, Paul Nash, Matthew Smith, Sutherland, Pasmore and Lewis.

One morning, a week before the show opened, Lewis called at the Academy Hall. Herbert Read had already written to ask where the Committee might find examples of his work from before the First World War, the earliest of the four decades under review in the exhibition. Lewis had made it clear that he did not look with favour on the overexposure of his youthful experimentation and the comparative neglect of his more recent work:

> To speak frankly, I have come to object a great deal at seeing myself consistently mis-represented in mixed exhibitions, by people who affect not to know what I have done for the past thirty years or so.

And it was with some urgency that he asked Read to keep him informed. 'If you have obtained anything of mine . . . please be so good as to tell me what.' But before Read could reply, Lewis lost patience and went to Oxford Street to see for himself.

Read was not at the Academy Hall that morning but someone else was on hand to show Lewis the painting the Committee had selected for their show. It was not, after all, from the period before the First World War. To his 'infinite disgust' he found that his contribution to the art of painting in the first half of the 20th century was to be represented by the angular, grimacing caricature with bilious background that had so terrified Dick Wyndham's nine-month-old baby in 1921: *Portrait of Mr W.L. as a Tyro*. It was a piece of work he now dismissed as 'posterish'.

He sensed conspiracy and blamed the Committee. Neither Roland Penrose, the chairman, nor Watson were 'great fans' of his, and E. L. T. Mesens was 'in the employ of one of them'. Of the remaining two members Herbert Read, who might have been predisposed in Lewis's favour, was 'never at committee meetings'. It followed that a hostile majority had determined he should be represented by an inferior painting.

Lewis left the Academy Hall and walked to Zwemmer's Gallery in Charing Cross Road, the nearest place he knew where an alternative to the 'posterish tyro' might be found. He walked out of Zwemmer's with 'an excellent painting' under his arm, the 1937 *Red Portrait* of his wife, and this he loaded into a taxi and delivered to the Academy Hall. After lunch he sent a telegram to the ICA Committee:

INDIGNANTLY PROTEST AT PROPOSED EXHIBIT AS REP-RESENTING MY CONTRIBUTION TO CONTEMPORARY ART HAVE SUPPLIED WHAT I SUGGEST AS SUBSTITUTE

The following day he wrote to Read:

Should [the Committee] think the 'red portrait' . . . is too good and would advertise me too much, there is this alternative. Still abolishing the posterish 'tyro' (which is essential) one can substitute a drawing, also at Zwemmers (which I would if necessary fetch and deliver). It is 'modernist' – I am sure you would like it. You will observe the trouble I am taking. Over a small matter, do you say? No, because this is one of a number of small matters. And it is one too many.

In fact there was one 'small matter' more.

Five days after taking action against what he perceived to be a malicious interpretation of his contribution to contemporary painting, he took up cudgels in another quarter to defend his prose style against editorial mangling.

Alan Pryce-Jones had sent him galley proofs for his *TLS* review of the Slochower book on 3 February, but it was not until the evening of the 9th that Lewis found the time to read them, along with Pryce-Jones's covering note: 'I hope you will not be too much shocked by the changes I have made here and there. They have only one object in view – to make your article fit easily into our normal scheme of anonymity.' Lewis's original had contained a number of first-person singular references that would be rendered meaningless in an unsigned review.

Lewis's response, thought Anthony Powell, was 'expressed in scarcely sane terms'. First he threatened immediate legal action against the *TLS* if

Pryce-Jones's 'spiteful joke' was pushed so far as to print what he had 'fooled about with' of Lewis's text. He had stopped reading on the second page of the galley proofs 'when it became clearer at almost every line', that the editor's intention was to be 'very offensive'. He then went on to delineate three of Pryce-Jones's 'transformations' with a withering, homophobic sarcasm:

> I had, however, read enough to admire . . . the femininely placed very, 'on the very title page' . . . : to note how infinitely more elegant the word 'comprise' is than the word 'is' . . . : and to mark your really radical improvement of one of my unworthy sentences, from which emerged your masterly 'emphatically an archipelago'. This fills me with awe: obviously those two words were brought into the world to coalesce – 'emphatically an archipelago' – but they awaited your fairy wand to effect the graceful conjunction.

Powell, who heard only Pryce-Jones's side of the argument, drew his own conclusions. 'The impression . . . that all was not well with the balance of Lewis's mind could not be avoided.'

The article, with or without Pryce-Jones's 'transformations', was not published.

As for the painting hanging in the basement of the Academy Hall Cinema and representing Lewis's contribution to '40 Years of Modern Art', it is not known whether the 'posterish tyro' was removed and replaced by something more to his liking. The despised *Tyro* certainly remained listed, however, below a Fernand Léger, in the alphabetically arranged catalogue:

> 48. Lewis, Wyndham. Born: England 1884. Lives: London. Self Portrait, c.1920 Oil lent by Mrs Violet Schiff.

*

Between his intervention at the Academy Hall Cinema and his outburst to Pryce-Jones, Lewis received news from his solicitor of a small but significant legal victory. Responsibility had at last been accepted for the two-year delay in the publication of *America and Cosmic Man*. Something in the region of £150 damages and legal costs had been wrung from the firm of Nicholson & Watson. 'It is a triumph', Lewis wrote to his solicitor Mr Mitchell. 'I am tremendously grateful.' Thereafter, in all his dealings with the firm, Lewis acted with his 'big lawyer' at his elbow. Three months later he was able to boast that Mr Roberts, the managing director of Nicholson & Watson, 'always keeps appointments and seems terrified of me'.

In mid-June the publication of *America and Cosmic Man* was announced in the *New Statesman* and the *Sunday Times*. Lewis told Mr Mitchell it would be out on the 21st and he promised to inscribe his legal champion's copy with a glowing endorsement:

> in my dedication I shall speak only of your powers ... to make publishers perform like circus horses, and eat out of the author's hand.

But, due to an error on one of the pages, the book remained stalled at the printers. When his three author's copies were finally delivered on 1 July the book seemed to Lewis an abomination of austerity publishing. It was, he raged to Roberts, 'an all time low in book production ... The paper is cheaper than the poorest paper used in "mystery story" books or cheap novels.'

He had been warned that limitations on the choice of paper size necessitated a somewhat smaller format than was ideal for such a book: something below demy octavo and above crown octavo, resulting in an untrimmed page of between $8\frac{3}{4}''$ and $7\frac{1}{2}''$ from top to bottom. 'In the event it turns out to be a crown – $7\frac{1}{2}''$ by $5''$ – the size of the smallest popular book, or of a reprint.' The type, however, had been set to fit a demy octavo page:

> Consequently there is hardly any margin, and at the bottom of the page the last line is very nearly on top of the paper edge. At the beginning of the book the ink is pale and wan. Later on it gets quite strong and black. You must among other things be economising on ink. Shall I speak of the hideous green cloth cover with red lettering on the spine? No. It was the cheapest line they had and you said okay.

His only positive words were for the 'quite good jacket', and then only because it 'decently' concealed the atrocious binding. But even this faintest of praise was muted by an observation that the jacket had been 'chopped down and mutilated'. The jacket, like the typesetting, had been designed to fit a larger format.

Lewis's mood cannot have been improved by a raging toothache. 'Left side of my face is in uproar', he complained to Giovanelli. 'I am in pain.'

*

It may have been that year, on 23 August, that Constant Lambert dragged the artist and writer Michael Ayrton to the 'rather dispiriting public bar of Notting Hill Gate Underground Railway Station' to catch a glimpse of

Lewis. It was Lambert's birthday and he told Ayrton that on a previous 23 August he had had the rare privilege at that location of hearing Lewis sing a mournful popular ballad:

> I'm a broken-hearted Milkman, in grief I'm array'd.
> Through keeping of the company of a young servant maid:
> Who lived on board wages, the house to keep clean,
> In a gentleman's fam'ly near Paddington Green.
> Oh! she was as beautiful as a Butterfly, and as proud as a Queen,
> Was pretty little Polly Perkins of Paddington Green.

Lambert did not mention whether all seven verses of the song had been rendered.

Late that night, Lambert and Ayrton arrived at the 'grim and forbidding edifice' and found it empty but for two figures standing at either end of the long bar. One was an orchestral conductor who had deserted from the army during the war and was still technically on the run. The other figure was Lewis, with customary large black hat pulled down over his eyes:

> No one spoke and the only sound was that of trains groaning and roaring beneath our feet. Without seeing us and without singing a note, Lewis turned and strode out into the night.

Derek Stanford went to the same establishment in search of Lewis and discovered him sitting on a stool at the bar and wearing a black patch over one eye. 'Mr Wyndham Lewis, I believe.' Lewis swung round and told Stanford he was mistaken, identifying himself instead as 'Captain Brown'.

*

By 10 September Doubleday, Doran & Co. of New York were expressing keen interest in publishing a US edition of *America and Cosmic Man*. Felix Giovanelli, now teaching Romance Languages at New York University, was brokering the deal, fanned by Lewis's 'enraptured' gratitude.

Meanwhile in London, with the exception of one column-inch, albeit of praise, by John Betjeman in the *Daily Herald*, the book had been critically ignored. 'It is a watertight boycott', Lewis told a friend. He claimed that Nicholson & Watson had delayed distribution for six weeks, bringing the book out finally in August, during the summer 'holiday-blackout', when it would be most likely to go unnoticed.

Before *America and Cosmic Man* was finally released to the reading public and to what Lewis regarded as a less than sympathetic critical cabal, he had written the following for a book that would be published four years later:

> that cross, smart, shallow, excitable animal . . . is still with us everywhere, entrenched in broadcasting, art-racketeering, the literary reviews, and even the most stately of the daily and weekly press. Which is just too bad for those upon his black list (a list at least twenty years old). May the Lord have mercy upon those books of mine which fall into his hands.

When *The Writer and the Absolute* appeared in mid-1952, these lines carried a footnote. It meant little or nothing to his readers but was indicative of how firmly he believed that the eventual publication date of *America and Cosmic Man*, the Friday of the August Bank Holiday weekend, was far from coincidental:

> It will interest the literary historian of the future to know that these lines were written at least six months before a significant date in publishing history – and in the annals of conspiracy and boycott: namely July 30, 1948.

In New York the sale of the book to Doubleday was settled and awaited only signing of the contract. The $750 advance, $250 less than the 'regulation "thousand berries"' he told Giovanelli had been customary eight years before, was of less importance than the prospects for further books. John Sargent of Doubleday reported enthusiastic preliminary responses from bookshops, and this augured well for commercial success and better terms in future.

Then on 30 September Lewis received word from Giovanelli that his English publisher had entered into communication with Doubleday informing them that US rights to *America and Cosmic Man* belonged to Nicholson & Watson.

Lewis flew into a rage. Nicholson & Watson did not own the American rights, he told Giovanelli. In fact they barely merited the definition 'publishers'. As for the managing director, Mr Roberts – 'remember his name', Lewis enjoined, as if marking him out as target for special retribution in the future – he was nothing more than 'an ex-shopsteward of a very large printing works'. Inventive epithets for Mr Roberts followed, ranging from 'double-crossing little rat' to 'unspeakable lying homunculus' and back to 'bubble-headed rat'.

This crisis coincided with the arrival of a food parcel from America containing bread mix and luxury. He tore it open 'in a nightmare'. The bread was baked and 'devoured . . . in a feverish dream'. He poured maple syrup over a *compote* of pears, muttering how delicious it was and racking his brains the while for a means of tackling his 'tiny enemy'.

He telephoned Nicholson & Watson, but succeeded only in speaking to Roberts's secretary. That unfortunate woman told him the managing director was flying to New York on 10 October and would be speaking to Doubleday while he was there. She was roundly cursed for this information and ordered to tell her master 'he would find himself in a court of law before very long.' Roberts returned his call the same day and protested innocence. Doubleday had written informing him of their desire to publish *America and Cosmic Man*. Roberts had replied: 'That's fine', and sent over a copy of the book. 'No, of course the rights are yours', he assured Lewis. 'I was not muscling in!' And he promised to cable Doubleday early the following day to make that absolutely clear.

The same morning that Roberts cabled to this effect, 1 October, the 'watertight boycott' of *America and Cosmic Man* was breached by a three-and-a-half-column notice in *The Times Literary Supplement*. It was not of the sort that would encourage sales. The anonymous reviewer pointed out half a dozen inaccuracies or dubious points of interpretation and declared: 'Mr Wyndham Lewis very clearly does not know enough American history to justify him in the generalisations of which he is fond.' Even grammar and prose style were criticised.

Lewis believed that sheltering under the anonymity which the *TLS* gave its reviewers was no less a figure than Alan Pryce-Jones himself. Still smarting from the treatment his own review received under Pryce-Jones's editorial pencil, a passage such as that beginning, 'We do not wish to be too particular or pedantic', must have touched a raw nerve indeed:

> it is really necessary to make a protest against the English in which this book is written. It must be a long time since a single volume contained so many sentences that are innocent of verbs. Nor are the objections to the author's sentences merely grammatical. They are peppered with obscure conversational asides and qualifications which make it extremely difficult, and sometimes impossible to follow his meaning.

'I cannot write, it appears', Lewis protested to Giovanelli. 'Well, I cannot certainly do that if the boneless pansy fluency of Mr P-J is to be our canon.'

*

Meanwhile, despite Mr Roberts's assurance that Nicholson & Watson had no intention of 'muscling in' on arrangements with Doubleday to publish *America and Cosmic Man*, Lewis still believed he was being 'doublecrossed'.

On the eve of Roberts's departure for New York, he was prepared for the worst and already laying plans for legal action. 'Now, if the deal falls through', he told Giovanelli:

> and clearly it will be the result of Mr Roberts intervention if it does – . . . do your damnedest to get hold of text of . . . letters and cables to Doubledays and . . . carefully note . . . anything Sargent transmits orally. This will be valuable. Indeed without it I have no evidence.

He confided paranoiac suspicions of a wider conspiracy, hatched perhaps by a Sitwell, a Clark, or some other shadowy enemy intent on sabotaging his livelihood:

> There is one thing that must not be lost sight of, fantastic as it may seem. Mr Roberts may be acting for a third party. I have realised all along that there might well be a Mr X., or a Sir X.X., in the background.

*

In fact the Sitwells, Osbert and Edith, were occupying his thoughts at this time as a rather unlikely source of profit. They had recently arrived in the United States at the start of a lecture tour and Giovanelli was being encouraged to shadow them:

> If Osbert performs in New York, try and be present. If he libels me I can get from the English courts a fat slice out of his fat annual income.

Since his friend could not realistically be expected to eavesdrop on every public and private function the Sitwells attended, Lewis instructed him to engage the services of a press-clipping agency and order cuttings for the name 'Wyndham Lewis'. This he hoped would secure him the text of any defamatory statements made by either Sitwell during the course of their stay, and 'shake money out of them if they are careless'.

*

On 13 October anxieties about the managing director of Nicholson & Watson 'muscling in' on the US publication of *America and Cosmic Man* were finally allayed by the arrival of a four-word cable from Giovanelli:

CONTRACT CONCLUDED ROBERTS EXCLUDED.

*

Lewis soon discovered that the author of the hostile *TLS* review was not Pryce-Jones after all, but Raymond Mortimer. 'That Bloomsbury gentleman', he recalled, 'wrote 10 or 12 years ago somewhere that Mr Lewis should not paint. Now he writes that Mr Lewis cannot write.' Members of the 'little high tory group' frequenting the Travellers' Club, Mortimer and Pryce-Jones were friends. They were therefore, Mortimer as writer, Pryce-Jones as publisher, interchangeable as enemies and equally responsible for the attack on Lewis's reputation and livelihood.

A fortnight after the review appeared, his retaliation occupied a substantial section of 'Letters to the Editor'. With ponderous mockery he suggested the reviewer 'give himself a little longer in the [British] Museum Reading Room'. Point by point he defended the 'inaccuracies' in his book with supporting quotations from higher authorities. It was another three weeks before Lewis's letter was brought to the reviewer's attention and received a response. Anonymously, Mortimer defended his criticisms, point by point, and concluded:

> Mr Wyndham Lewis is in fact wrong in all his contentions. Even if he had been right in all of them it would not have affected my general verdict on his book.

These were to be the last words the *TLS* published on the subject.

When Lewis submitted a reply, criticising the paper for not sending his book for review to an authority in the field and serving up instead the 'fake-"scholarly", and the pseudoexpert', Pryce-Jones informed him it could not be printed as the correspondence page of the next issue was already set up in type. Lewis threatened litigation if this arena remained closed to him. 'Obviously I cannot afford to allow you to attack me with impunity', he told Pryce-Jones:

> If you do not print my letter in your next issue I shall put the whole business in the hands of my lawyer.

The letter was not printed in the next, nor in subsequent issues. A month later, in belated response to the original article and with his jaw swollen by a large abscess 'playing ugly tunes on [his] nervous system', Lewis attended a conference at the Lincoln's Inn chambers of King's Council Mr G. Gardiner, accompanied by his solicitor and solicitor's clerk. He returned to Notting Hill Gate having been given a useful, if discouraging and rather expensive, lesson in the workings of the law of libel.

His solicitors presented their bill for professional charges. For attendance on their client and 'advising as to proceedings being taken in respect of the defamatory matter contained in the ... article', for 'perusing and considering papers', for 'preparing lengthy Case to Counsel to advise and instructing Counsel to advise in conference' and for attending with their client at conference with Counsel, Clifford-Turner & Co. claimed ten guineas. The fee of Mr G. Gardiner KC for his advice, 'that in the absence of proof of malice, no proceedings should be commenced', came to a further £21 15s.

'It appears I can be attacked with impunity and with obvious malice, provided I am not personally maligned', he told David Kahma.

*

At the same time the Sitwells were costing him dear. Services of the American press-clipping agency Giovanelli had engaged were far more expensive than Lewis had expected, and neither Osbert nor his sister had as yet made any public pronouncement for which he could sue them. 'If that great fat bum doesn't utter a good hot libel', he railed, 'I will never pay any attention to him again.'

Evelyn Waugh was in New York at the same time. 'The Sitwells were rampaging about ... cutting a terrific splash', he wrote home. 'Every magazine has six pages of photographs of them headed "The Fabulous Sitwells" ... Goodness how they are enjoying it.' Giovanelli sent Lewis press clippings of their triumphant progress. A photograph in *Life* magazine showed a party given in their honour at the Gotham Book Mart. Lewis described them:

> surrounded by all the dolly vardens – pansies or whatever you call them ... The British pansy-poet, Auden, was there, perched on a ladder ... [Charles] Henri Ford squatted on the floor, Osbert (his hair permanently waved) with a sullen frowning, frustrate uneasy smirk. Edith is the only dignified girl there.

It is difficult to believe that a degree of envy was not mixed with the scorn. The Sitwells' lionisation in New York, a city in which he had experienced such miserable and impecunious defeat nine years before, must have been especially galling. At the same time, their success encouraged his own plans for an American lecture tour in the new year.

In September he told Giovanelli he would be reaching New York 'shortly after Christmas' and at the beginning of November he was planning to arrive 'late January or February'. Giovanelli visited the Colston Leigh

Lecture Bureau in New York and was told that a tour needed to be planned from eight to twelve months in advance, but in December, undeterred, Lewis still intended to make the trip if he had '2 or 3 odd lectures . . . in or near New York', to be arranged, if possible, for March. The further setting back of his departure was occasioned by plans for a retrospective exhibition at the Redfern Gallery in Cork Street. A fortnight later he told Giovanelli the show was to open on 30 March. This of course would further delay his arrival in America.

FORTY-EIGHT

'A great artist's dental plate'

The year 1949 began with a flurry of overdue tasks:

> Why had I not handed in the Index! ... Where the hell was that bookjacket! Didn't I know it was the deadline for that article!

The deadline was from J. R. Ackerley at *The Listener* calling for his views on the Chantry Bequest: paintings and sculpture from successive Royal Academy Summer Exhibitions, purchased through a fund set up in 1897 by Sir Francis Chantry and presented, year by year, to the Tate Gallery as 'works of the highest merit ... that can be obtained ... in Great Britain'. Published on 13 January, the article was occasioned by the Chantry Collection's return to Burlington House, on loan from the Tate, for a temporary exhibition. Lewis concluded that the Academy should keep the 'ghastly junk', even suggesting 'the galleries on the right as you go through the turnstile' should be reserved for it. 'The spring exhibition of the R.A. would be a trifle smaller', he observed, 'but still would be all-too-large.'

He had been reviewing current exhibitions, 'Round the London Galleries' in *The Listener*, regularly for two years and would continue to do so for another two.

The index for his second volume of autobiography, now called *Rude Assignment*, had been 'a very tough job, discovering the christian name of Marat, or whether Epictetus was just that or more, and how many ts and ns and ms people have in their names'. The urgency was rather premature, since the book was not published until November of the following year.

He designed the lettering for *Rude Assignment*'s dust jacket that first week of January, but the drawing, later signed and dated '1950' to coincide with publication, had probably been produced in the late 1920s. It showed a straddled figure holding palette and brushes, the head a confused amalgamation of forms in which a prominent nose can be discerned and, complementary to the painter's tools, a monstrous eye. When it was originally executed it prefigured the cartoon drawn by 'Trier' for Lewis's *Lilliput* article of July 1939, 'The Life of an Artist': a tiny figure painting at an easel, the smocked torso surmounted by a single gigantic veined eyeball with an upper lid and lashes giving it a fringe of 'hair'.

Both images were shortly to acquire belated, but cruelly ironic, significance.

*

The BBC wrote to D. B. Wyndham Lewis requesting his permission to read 'The Song of the Militant Romance', the second section of *One-Way Song*, on 14 January. By the time the Corporation's copyright department discovered they had written to the wrong man the broadcast date was close. They managed to contact the real Wyndham Lewis with only a day to spare, and he granted his permission by telephone call and telegram on 13 January.

For a reading of the 104-line poem he would receive a fee of 11 guineas. Clearly embarrassed by the mistaken identity, Miss Layton of the copyright department hastened to reassure him:

> Acknowledgement to the title of the work and your name as author will, of course, be made at the time of broadcasting.

Next evening preparations got under way for the 10.30 reading. The monocled producer was E. J. King-Bull. 'Can't make head or tail of this stuff', he told Julian Symons who was to present the programme. 'Hope the reader can understand some of it.' The reader, still suffering from a smashed arm and cracked ribs sustained from falling off a bicycle the month before, was Dylan Thomas. Symons had been a little nervous about meeting Thomas. Only the previous week his radio talk, 'The Romantic Reaction in Modern Poetry', had attacked George Barker, Edith Sitwell and Dylan Thomas as 'windy rhetoricians whose vague wild words concealed the socially reactionary nature of their work'. Fears of physical retaliation allayed by sight of the poet's arm in a sling, Symons asked if he was familiar with 'The Song of the Militant Romance'. Thomas replied with a glazed look that belied the fact he was stone cold sober: 'Great man Lewis, great man.' Symons recalled that, familiar with it or not, he read the piece remarkably well.

Symons's broadcast prompted the re-establishment of contact. 'Have you a few hours free?' Lewis asked him. He was needed for completion of the portrait started in 1939 before the world changed. It was in fact finished, all but the jacket. 'I walked once more down the white-tiled passage', Symons remembered, and the door was opened by the same man in the same black hat . . . As I sat up in the studio and Lewis, discarding his black hat for a green eyeshade, went on with the portrait that had been begun when I was slimmer and more optimistic; as I listened to his thick, rather nasal voice denouncing Cripps, . . . telling me that builders, and butchers and bakers were not what they had been; as I watched the mice come out and scamper round the large iron stove that warmed the room, gambolling almost under Lewis's feet, my head drooped and once or twice I fell into a light sleep. From this Lewis wakened me courteously, by dropping a heavy book on the floor, or by the suggestion that we should have a cup of tea.

Instead of banging on the floor with a stick to summon refreshment, as had been his practice before the War, he invited his sitter downstairs, 'the ever-closed door was opened' and Symons was at last introduced to Mrs Lewis and found her 'charming, cultured and friendly'.

Domestic arrangements at 29A Kensington Gardens Studios, as they stood in January 1949 at least, were detailed in a text that was to have accompanied publication of *America and Cosmic Man* in the United States: 'The Vita of Wyndham Lewis'. From this is learnt that a charwoman called Mrs Montgomery was employed, that the Lewises took seven morning papers, and relied heavily upon friends in America and Canada to alleviate the rigours of postwar rationing.

From Giovanelli came Cuban and Los Angeles honey, jam that was so much better than the turnip-supplemented concoction obtainable in England, wedges of ham, butter and Carolina rice that was brown but cooked white and swelled to twice its size.

Eugene Nash, formerly of St Louis and living in Monroe, Louisiana, 'a paper-manufacturer in a big way', sent icing sugar, evaporated milk, Oolong tea, maple syrup and, most essentially, Pillsbury's Hot Roll Mix.

'Mister Lewis!' Nash had often asked while they were in St Louis. 'Will you do my portrait for a hundred dollars? Next month I shall have the money.' In August 1948, the painter had come to an arrangement with the paper manufacturer. If he would undertake to send over a dozen cartons of Pillsbury's Hot Roll Mix each month, after three months, and thirty-six cartons of Mix, Lewis would give him 'a beautiful drawing'.

The first consignment arrived at the beginning of September. Mindful of the ruinous expense of smoking in Britain, Nash dropped three packs of cigarettes into the parcel. Lewis vehemently proscribed such friendly but misguided gestures in the future, fearing that the whole parcel would be impounded at the port of entry, the cigarettes smoked by Customs men, the bread eaten and he himself heavily fined.

The second consignment, with maple syrup substituted for smokes, reached him in October. It went almost unappreciated by Lewis amid the preoccupation and rage attending Mr Roberts's threatened interference in his Doubleday negotiations.

'Relays of bread mix' continued to arrive from Monroe, Louisiana, for much of the following year, and Lewis referred to the matter a month or so after the November consignment arrived, concluding the deal and completing payment for the 'beautiful drawing'. He promised to put it aside and 'not allow it to be engulfed in the exhibition'.

But it was not Nash, the paper manufacturer, who supplied Lewis with stationery. From Kahma in Vancouver this came, 'papers, matte and glossed, thick and thin . . . Some of it . . . literally untearable', also 'very welcome, though unnecessarily expensive' note-pads, paper clips and good strong envelopes. By the end of 1949 Lewis had received so much paper that a buff form was sent him by HM Customs & Excise, 'who affect to believe', he told Kahma, 'that your parcel of stationery is merchandise which you ship me for sale in England – presumably I run a stationery business. Curse them.'

Kahma also sent soap, and hair rinse for Mrs Lewis. 'If we are both of us not clean and sweet-smelling', their benefactor was told, 'it is through no fault of yours!' And of course there were regular shipments of foodstuffs: butter, tinned jam, corned beef, ham, tongue and China tea. There was cake, pudding and brandy butter at Christmas. The parcel arriving on 13 January disclosed a pineapple that made a compote for rice pudding, cheese, devoured by the Lewises before they even had to claim their week's ration, and boned chicken which provided a curry.

*

In May 1949 a man in a dark blue business suit stood in a Cork Street gallery looking at the painting of a man in a large hat. The only other figure in the room was a man in a large hat who was looking closely at the painting of a man in a dark blue business suit. Mr T. S. Eliot and Mr Wyndham Lewis scrutinised each other at one remove.

The Redfern Gallery consisted of three exhibition rooms at street level and a number of tiny exhibition spaces and offices in the brick-ceilinged basement where customers could leaf through canvases stacked ten deep against the walls. A month or so before Michael Ayrton witnessed Eliot and Lewis studying one another's painted images, another painter, Patrick Heron, wandered downstairs, turned the corner at the bottom and looked to his right. Wyndham Lewis was visible through a doorway, sitting in a room not much wider than the doorway itself. His right elbow rested on a low table, he was wearing overcoat and hat, smoking a du Maurier cigarette and seemed to fill the tiny room. He had evidently been looking in the direction of the stairs to see who was coming down, because as the younger man turned he found his gaze locked onto that of Lewis. 'Heron!' His memory was impressive. It was only the second time they had met, the first being on the stairs in the same gallery. Lewis now launched himself into a fascinating and wide-ranging monologue. After a time he stopped. 'Forgive this homily', he said. 'I have just come from painting T. S. Eliot, the poet, you know.' Heron could not resist it. 'He is not a very good sitter, is he?' This was not in fact true. Heron had found Eliot to be an ideal sitter two years before. But he could not resist letting Lewis know that he was not the only one to have painted 'the greatest poet in the world'. Lewis exploded. 'Are *you* painting him? He's kept that very dark from me!'

Lewis had begun work on his second portrait of Eliot in early February. The first of the sittings coincided with freezing weather, necessitating applications to the local Fuel Overseer and 'form filling galore', to secure coal in excess of his ration for the studio stove.

'The Nobel Prize and Sweden has freshened him up', Lewis reported to Nash, when Eliot had been sitting for a month, 'but he still becomes drowsy when immobilised in one position and his bottom "goes to sleep".' The poet had returned from Stockholm with greatly enhanced value as a portrait subject, and picture dealers would shortly be beating a path to Lewis's door for anything from his hand of the 1948 Prize-winner:

Two drawings of Eliot I sold to a dealer . . . *he* sold within 24 hours . . .
An American dealer named Schwarz . . . has written to say that he wants anything I have of Eliot.

There seems to have been a boom in pictures of highbrow poets, the Possum's honour perhaps validating modernism, because Schwarz was also interested in Pound: 'saleable now, whereas only 9 months ago he would not touch E.P.' Lewis even thought it might be necessary 'to fake up some Ezra studies' because he had hardly anything left.

He told J. R. Ackerley that Eliot's portrait was done in only 12 sittings, sometimes of four hours at a stretch. Over lunch at the White Tower, the *Listener*'s literary editor heard of 'the slowness and difficulty of making a good portrait – . . . building up the structure of the face, . . . putting in, making mistakes, painting out'. Speed and facility did not come with practice; 'if one got quicker one was probably painting worse.' The discourse made a great impression upon Ackerley and he recorded it in his diary. Included in the entry was an account of how unsettling an experience sitting a table's width from Wyndham Lewis could be:

An uncomfortable man, with such ugly horse-like teeth and a gaze which seems not to lift to one's own eyes, to be reluctant to rise quite up to them, a sort of curved glance which, instead of striking levelly at one, gives the impression of dropping as it leaves his own eyes and rising nearer one, unexpectedly, yet never quite to meet one's own. Like the handshakes of schizophrenics, I thought, who can't decide whether to or not, hold out their hands and then withdraw them from one's responsive action.

What Lewis did not mention, as he appeared unable to meet or focus on his companion's eyes, was that his sight had now deteriorated to such an extent that he had had to leave his easel frequently and peer closely at Eliot's face from a distance of inches, 'to see exactly how the hair sprouted out of the forehead, and how the curl of the nostril wound up into the dark interior of the nose.' His sight was still adequate at this stage. But he had to move very close to the forms he was studying.

*

The Redfern exhibition was to open on 5 May, and a week before Lewis was still frantically painting. On 29 April he thought he still had three days to get work finished, but then there was a telephone message: 'they hang *tomorrow*', he told Kahma, 'Eliot's hair still to be painted.'

The hair got painted, and it must still have been wet when the portrait was hung at the gallery. The burnt umber and burnt sienna Lewis squeezed out onto his palette to complete the head, during those few days at the end of April and the beginning of May, was possibly the last paint he ever applied to canvas.*

*

Following the opening he went to Paris, but was back by 9 May with a broken tooth, one of two that served to anchor his dental plate. This necessitated an appointment with his Viennese dentist on 11 May and persuading Dr Weinsberg to construct a new plate which would take account of the altered toothscape. Weinsberg favoured extraction:

> Mr Lewis! Were it just anybody, I should not worry at all. Why should I? If they preferred to injure their health by refusing to part with their bad teeth, that would be all the same to me! But in you I am interested. I know you are a great artist.

* Some months later he started a portrait of Stella Newton but abandoned it.

He knew his patient to be so because he had read it in the *Daily Telegraph* only two days before. T. W. Earp had written comparing the Redfern exhibition with a display of Old Masters at the National Gallery. It was, he said, possible to view Lewis's work after the treasures of the Munich *Pinakothek* without a sense of anticlimax:

> Few others of to-day's painters would survive the test. Lewis, the most original of contemporaries, yet follows the way of the masters.

'You are a great artist', Weinsberg told him. 'That is why I tell you. Those two teeth ought to come out.'

Lewis wrote to Earp thanking him for the review. 'Your article will get me a great artist's dental plate instead of the average man's.'

Elsewhere critics inevitably referred back to the Vorticist Movement of over 30 years before. Eric Newton, writing in *The Listener*, felt his work to be more convincing 'now than it was then' and, in a phrase that would have given Dr Weinsberg further critical ammunition for the extraction of teeth, submitted: 'that if this can happen then he is a great artist.'

'One knows', wrote Patrick Heron in his review for the *New Statesman and Nation*, 'that he is a man of some sort of genius.' It was something Eliot had told him during a walk through Welwyn Woods. The young painter had asked what he thought of Lewis while the poet was negotiating a large puddle in the path. 'A man of undoubted genius', Eliot said, carefully manoeuvring what must have been sparkling, impeccably laced shoes along the muddy verge, 'but genius for what precisely it would be remarkably difficult to say.'

*

Lewis complained to Augustus John that he had 'not so far made a cent' from the Redfern exhibition:

> It is like being dead and watching a dealer making money out of one. One would, if it happened when one was dead, undoubtedly 'turn in one's grave.' I, alive, do a bit of *turning*!

By 19 May, the Gallery had sold 'ten thousand dollars worth of stuff', he told Kahma. 'Alas, only a small proportion of the exhibits are my property'. But he did entertain hopes that *The Times* notice, that had praised the likeness of T. S. Eliot as 'far more exact than that of the ordinary commercial portrait', would help to sell one of the few works that were his exclusive property. And it was with this in mind that, on 17 June, he took his canvas to the Tate Gallery and had it carried to John Rothenstein's office.

Rothenstein clearly felt the portrait marked a falling off. Prefacing his remarks with the words 'I know you will not like this', a day or so later he told Lewis that in his opinion the sheaf of galley proofs to the sitter's right was the best thing in it. This curate-like appreciation of the good part of an otherwise indifferent egg was a diplomatic ploy Lewis had come to recognise. When he sent the Tate Gallery director a photograph of his portrait of another Nobel Prizewinner, Dr Erlanger, Rothenstein 'wrote back to say how good the *hands* were'. Rothenstein's low opinion of what was to prove Lewis's last painting was presumably shared by his colleagues. Just as the first portrait of Eliot was rejected by a committee at Burlington House in 1938, eleven years later a committee on Millbank rejected the second.

At 2.30 pm on Thursday 23 June, the Board of Trustees of the Tate Gallery met to deliberate on possible acquisitions. The Honourable Sir Jasper Ridley was in the chair, presiding over William Coldstream, Lord Harlech, Lord Jowitt, John Piper, Sir Donald Somervell and Charles Wheeler. Rothenstein as Director and the Deputy Keeper of the Tate, Norman Reid, were also present. A decision was duly minuted:

> The Board declined 'Portrait of T. S. Eliot' (oil) by Wyndham Lewis offered by the artist for £250.

Lewis consoled himself with a whiff of conspiracy:

> When I learned . . . who were the committeemen, I saw that no other outcome would be possible. For practically all of them are . . . friends of Sir Kenneth Clark, that great organiser of mediocrity, who has packed it in order to control it as he controls almost everything else in English art of the forties to make *quite certain* that the second rate will be on top.

It seemed all too obvious that Clark, 'on whom Fry's mantle is supposed to have fallen', should harbour beneath that mantle a 35-year-old stiletto of Bloomsbury vendetta. Even now, separated from the Ideal Home controversy by two world wars, Lewis still believed that, due to the quarrel with Fry, his career continued blighted 'by a sneer of hatred, or by a sly Bloomsbury *sniff*'. When Rothenstein tried to convince him to the contrary, telling him that during the course of wide-ranging conversations over a number of years he had never heard Sir Kenneth Clark speak adversely of him either as man or as artist, Lewis affected momentary deafness.

The Art Gallery in Durban, South Africa, rescued the first Eliot portrait from undignified rejection and brushed away the stigma of the chalked cross on its back. The second portrait likewise found hanging space within a very short interval of its being spurned by the Tate Trustees.

The Fellows of Magdalene College, Cambridge, wished to obtain a portrait of Eliot. Since the eminent Honorary Fellow was expected not only to sit, but also to pay for the painting, Eliot believed his own preference in the choice of painter could not be disregarded. He had already given Lewis's portrait a hearty testimonial in the pages of *Time* magazine:

> I shall not turn in my grave if, after I am settled in the cemetery this portrait is the image that will come into people's minds when my name is mentioned. It seems to me also a good picture, as well as a good portrait; and if it were the portrait not of myself, but of someone whose features I could contemplate with more tenderness, I think I could live with it.

Eliot informed I. A. Richards of his choice. Richards, himself a Magdalene Fellow, was spending his customary summer vacation from Harvard in London. He visited Lewis to view the work on 8 July, and on the same day wrote to reassure the Master of Magdalene:

> Wyndham Lewis might suggest puzzling cubes and slices and such and the awful job of having to explain it to visitors. But this is a most calm and masterly likeness, with the essentials of a magnificent presence simply offered.

He urged that a place be found for it in the Combination Room, where its predominating blues would go very well with the new Chinese carpet.

The picture had been priced at £375 when it was at the Redfern. This was intended to take into account the Gallery's 33⅓ per cent commission. It was offered to the Tate reduced by a third and, at the same price, £250, to Eliot himself.

When Eliot sent him the cheque it was drawn out for £300. 'What was the significance of the additional £50?' Lewis asked. 'If a slip of the pen, tant pis, it all went into my bank! You will no doubt inform me if it was an error.' Eliot replied that it was no error and that he had merely wished to pay something closer approximating to the true value of the work.

It was eventually hung, not in the blue-carpeted Combination Room but on the staircase to one side of the main refectory, 'perfectly placed to keep it from being seen,' Eliot told a friend some years later, 'poorly lighted and . . . no place where you can get far enough away . . . to see it properly.'

*

'People are only friends in so much that they are of use to you,' Lewis had pronounced to Dick Wyndham sitting outside a café in the South of France on a summer night in 1923. His advice to Marjorie Firminger, each word carefully stressed, some time later was similar: *'People are there to be used.'* Both erstwhile friends discovered to their cost the painful significance of his remarks. Rarely did Lewis act in anybody's exclusive interest but his own. His generosity towards a 26-year-old black painter from Georgetown, British Guyana, therefore, was noteworthy. In his capacity as art critic for *The Listener*, Lewis was supportive of new talent, giving early boosts to the careers of Colquhoun, MacBryde, Bacon, Vaughan, Pasmore and Ceri Richards. But the help he gave Denis Williams went beyond weekly critical puffs.

Williams had spent a year studying art in London on a British Council scholarship, upon the expiry of which he worked for two years as a clerk in the Colonial Ministry. In July 1949 he was sharing an exhibition at the Berkeley Gallery in Davies Street with the Ghanaian painter Kofi Antubam, 'the son of a paramount chief of the Gold Coast', as dull, thought Lewis, as Williams was bright. 'Mr Williams . . . possesses most remarkable gifts', he told his readers in *The Listener*:

> Collectors would be well-advised to have a look at these pictures. I wish that some could be bought.

He invited the young man to his studio and, hearing about his background, thought it 'abominable for the British Council to give him one years lift, and then drop him'. Williams would be returning to Guyana the following week and intended visiting New York on the way. Lewis dashed off an immediate letter to Alfred Barr at the Museum of Modern Art, commending Williams as 'a young man of very unusual talent' and asking him to give any advice or encouragement he felt able to. Giovanelli was also recruited to do what he could: 'assist him re any charitable organisation to help visiting Negroes of the student type. That sort of thing.'

When Williams reached New York he found Giovanelli 'urbane and charming, but . . . less than optimistic . . . , for racial reasons, of [his] contemplating a career in New York.' At the Museum of Modern Art his work was thought to be immature and over-influenced by the Cuban painter Wilfredo Lam. Finding New York an alienating environment in which to paint, Williams abandoned the idea of making it a permanent base and continued his journey to Georgetown.

Lewis, meanwhile, was making enquiries of the Foreign Office, in the event that Williams might wish to return and settle in London. He learned that the policy laid down by the Colonial Administration could be summed up in one phrase: 'to educate here for use in the Colonies.' It seemed that a Nigerian would be trained as a doctor in London to practise in Nigeria, while a native of British Guyana was brought to study in London 'so that he may go back and promote Culture in British Guyana'.

Lewis regarded this policy as plainly absurd in the case of an artist, and criminal in the case of an artist of such obvious talent. 'Guyana is no place in which to be a painter', he believed.

There may have been more to Lewis's support for Denis Williams than that of an older artist for a talented young protégé. It was perhaps the sympathy of one former alien for another. He had spent six years on the American continent as an impecunious and, at times, less than welcome immigrant. While the experience of a white Englishman in the USA and Canada bore scant comparison with the experience of a black Guyanan in late 1940s London, Lewis was nevertheless empathetic to the economic disadvantages of an outsider. 'Negroes are in such a weak position that, like other people in weak positions, they must often be very hard-up.'

While he was unable to offer financial assistance when Williams returned to London the following year, he did all he could to make it possible for the young man to earn a living.

*

That August Geoffrey Stone and his wife visited England. Lewis met them at the airline office and took them to the Palace Court Hotel where he had reserved them a room. On their last night in London the Stones dined in the Notting Hill flat and afterwards sat talking in the studio above.

Something was said which irrevocably blighted their friendship.

The conversation turned to Roman Catholicism. Dora Stone had been raised a Catholic and Geoffrey had recently converted. On that occasion Lewis expressed wholehearted approval of the step he had taken. 'If one is going to be anything the "old religion" is the only one', he declared. When Mrs Lewis revealed that she herself had considered joining the Catholic Church, Dora Stone said she would be delighted to sponsor her and act as Godmother. The atmosphere in the studio froze and the following morning, when the Stones called again at the flat to say goodbye, Lewis opened the door but neglected to invite them in. He seemed bad-tempered. Geoffrey Stone put it down to a hangover and the flat being still untidy from the night before.

'It was my enthusiasm at the idea of Mrs Lewis becoming Catholic that annoyed Lewis,' Dora said later, 'and my husband pointed out afterwards that it was tactless of me, as it would have meant her leaving Lewis. She had been married before.' Mrs Stone's account is noteworthy as comprising the only known piece of evidence suggesting Gladys was a divorcee. If true, it would explain Lewis's disquiet. Because the Catholic Church does not recognise divorce, Gladys would not have been free, in the eyes of Rome, from the marriage to her first husband, when she married her second. Had she converted to Catholicism, her 19-year union with Lewis would have been null and void and had she professed herself bound by the Church's laws, she would have been morally obliged to part from him.

Lewis never communicated with their former hosts in Bethlehem again and when Stone sent a copy of his book on Herman Melville later that year it was not even acknowledged.

*

In September, Colston Leigh wrote to inform Lewis that his firm was now ready to begin preparations for a lecture tour in the fall and winter of 1950–51. Lewis handed the letter to his literary agent A. P. Watt and instructed him to negotiate a deal. Watt in turn passed the matter to his agency's representative in New York: Willis Kingsley Wing was to confer directly with Leigh.

A two-month silence ensued. Then, in December, Wing informed Watt that Colston Leigh was no longer prepared to undertake arrangements for the lecture tour. When Lewis angrily demanded an explanation he was told that the firm was experiencing a delayed reaction following the boom wartime years when 'people were lecture and book minded', when 'forums sprang up . . . in communities which normally would not have considered a speaker' and when 'colleges were extremely lavish with fees for visiting lecturers.'

The climate had changed abruptly since the previous year when Colston Leigh had presented the Sitwells to an enthusiastic America. Edith and Osbert seem to have ridden the last wave of enthusiasm with their tour.

By contrast, during 1949 it was found that 'many of the forums have folded . . . the colleges are . . . back on a normal schedule and spending very little for visiting lecturers because . . . the students will not attend the lectures.' Colston Leigh felt that, while Lewis's name was known in certain circles in the USA, it was not a name 'known to the "man in the street"' and at the present time 'the only kind of a speaker who can get an audience is a name that will "draw".' If Leigh had any views on the comparative drawing power of the name 'Sitwell' over that of 'Lewis', he tactfully did not express them.

In addition to public apathy towards anything but a name that would draw, there was a great deal of anti-British feeling in the country. In short, it was doubtful that an American lecture tour by Wyndham Lewis could even meet his expenses.

Lewis chose to disregard Leigh's explanation and levelled the blame instead at the agent and the agent's New York representative. If Mr Watt and Mr Wing had not, as he at first suspected, sold Colston Leigh another author or authoress in his place, they had certainly been negligent in pursuing their client's interests. 'You were inaccessible by telephone,' he told Watt:

> laconic in response to my anxious pressure; the autumn months drifted by and at the end of it without any warning I found my lecture tour had evaporated.

*

The news that Colston Leigh had abandoned plans for the tour coincided with a renewal of more serious anxiety. 'I have practically been driven mad with one thing and another', he told a friend on 21 December, 'my eyes particularly.'

On 27 December, following the 'loathsome holiday' of Christmas, he wrote to Kahma:

> Tomorrow life begins again, and with it eyes have the spotlight. My myopia is relatively slight: there is nothing visibly wrong with the eyes, but it is said that the optic nerve is being injured by some toxin. So remove the poison is the cry. I tremble to think what steps may be taken to expel the toxin. But no operation is contemplated, thank heaven.

The next day he reported to a Dr W. H. Coldwell in Welbeck Street, Cavendish Square, where ten radiographs covering his upper and lower jaw were taken. The year 1950 was to begin with an oblique assault on whatever was affecting the optic nerve and the cause was to be sought, not behind, but below the eyes. 'I shall be unpleasantly occupied after Christmas', he told Kahma.

The dental radiograph taken on 28 December and presented to ophthalmic surgeon Robert Lindsay-Rea two days later showed 'generalised *very* severe infective changes in both jaws involving all the existing teeth and the retained roots'. There were multiple root abscesses. Bone degeneration was so severe that two incisors, two premolars and four molars hung in the tooth sockets literally by their root tips. 'All the other teeth show severe alveolar absorption with periodontal and periapical infection with considerable surrounding bone infection.'

That an explanation for his failing vision might seriously be found in his mouth had first been suggested back in 1941, the second and least frightening of the medical opinions canvassed in Toronto. As the first diagnosis of glaucoma had raised the stark prognosis of blindness within six months it was not surprising that he had then clung to dental decay as the lesser evil, admitting to Frank Morley 'my teeth are not unlikely to rank as a septic centre of the first order.'

Wholesale extraction, it was now hoped, would tackle the optic problem root and branch. Maximum bleeding would be encouraged in order to expel the toxins.

'The doctors are urgent: if some toxin is not removed I lose my sight,' he told Docker on January 13. 'Monday they start pumping in penicillin. Two days later starts the pulling out of lots of teeth . . . Pray for me.' The same day he made and signed what was to be his last will and testament, leaving all his property of whatever nature and wheresoever situate to his wife Gladys, and appointing her his sole executrix.

FORTY-NINE

'Nothing is visible, there is no pain, no disagreeable sensations'

St Vincent's Clinic was a small Catholic nursing establishment in Ladbroke Terrace, off Notting Hill Gate, a short distance away to the west. In the first phase of the campaign against the toxins, Lewis was there for six days at the end of January, having all the teeth removed from his upper jaw. All went well apart from a curious incident that did little to allay his deep suspicion of the medical profession. Mr Hopkins, the anaesthetist, who was supposed to have administered the gas, failed to turn up, the Matron having forgotten to telephone him beforehand. After considerable disturbance which Lewis, already on the operating table, was too sedated to be aware of, his GP, Dr Fant, knocked him out with a shot of Pentothal and the operation proceeded. Dr Weinsberg let slip this information 'as a great joke' a week or so after Lewis left the Clinic. Far from being amused, Lewis regarded it as a piece of gross professional impropriety and arrived home from his dentist extremely upset. Gladys tried to calm him down:

'Well, what else could Fant do? Surely it was better for him to do that than postponing things for another day.'

Lewis rounded on her:

'Oh I know. If you'd found out you wouldn't have told me!'

She agreed:

'I certainly shouldn't have. You know time is of the essence and for such a small thing I'm sure Fant is quite experienced enough to administer an anaesthetic.'

Details of this exchange are taken from a fragmentary narrative Mrs Lewis compiled of their relations with Dr John Fant, covering the period when full knowledge of the seriousness of her husband's condition began to dawn. The apparently mundane encounters and conversations detailed in these notes acquired sinister, nightmarish qualities as she loaded paranoiac significance upon them. Following the conversation about Fant's anaesthetic intervention she commented: 'After a time [Lewis] began to feel better, especially as I became the victim.'

Her sense of being persecuted by a malicious and obscurely vengeful general practitioner began late one Saturday afternoon in February when he arrived at the flat to give Lewis the first in a course of injections. This was, presumably, the 'inoculatory treatment' Dr McPherson had recommended in 1946. Fant appeared quite friendly to Mrs Lewis at first, but she did not respond. Her husband had been particularly bad-tempered of late and she 'felt more like crying than laughing'. Fant seemed to take umbrage at her lack of response and, from that point on, during the course of injections, he appeared sulky and taciturn whenever they met. 'Insults', she claimed, 'started to rain on my head from my age to what sort of soap I used.'

The doctor was expected to complete the course on 24 February, and that afternoon they waited for him and listened to the election results on the wireless as the Labour Party maintained power with a drastically reduced majority of 17 seats. The telephone rang. 'Is that Mr Wyndham Lewis's?' It was Fant's secretary, 'all fluttery', saying the doctor had been delayed but would call at 8 that evening. Lewis went and turned off the gas under the kettle. Fant did not arrive at 8. At 9.30 they gave him up. 'So ended the injections.'

Doctor Fant's secretary was soon to become another major figure in Mrs Lewis's phantasmagoria. The delusional implication seemed to be that Fant and his secretary were involved in an illicit sexual intrigue, and that the doctor's supposedly offensive attitude towards Mrs Lewis was due to her being an unwilling accessory or witness.

The following week, she accompanied her husband back to St Vincent's Clinic where he was to have his lower teeth removed. She sensed an atmosphere among the staff – 'very chilly indeed' – due, perhaps, to unease about the irregularity of the first mass extraction having been conducted with no qualified anaesthetist in attendance. The Matron referred to her as 'Mr Lewis's watchdog'.

Returning home alone, she did some needlework then turned on the Light Programme at 9.30 to listen to Wilfred Pickles in 'Have a Go!' About a quarter to ten the telephone rang. It was Fant's secretary. Her first thought was that Lewis had been taken ill at the clinic. The secretary spoke in what Gladys called 'her grand-one-sentence-shop-girl voice':

'I am phoning from Dr Fant's house. He said he was going round to see Mr Wyndham Lewis and I want to get hold of him.'

'Mr Wyndham Lewis is in a nursing home.'

'Oh I didn't know th-a-a-a-t!'

Then the caller seemed to lose control of herself.

'He can't do that to me!' she shouted down the line. This was followed by mumbling and gasping 'like some drunken old street woman'. Mrs Lewis noted no details of the fit of temper apart from calling it a 'filthy display dragging me head first into affairs that were no concern of mine'. There was a pause as the secretary appeared to be waiting for her to say something. Mrs Lewis said: 'Oh I don't know', and put the receiver down.

The excavations to Lewis's lower jaw were comparatively straightforward, and he had to spend only two nights in the clinic this time. 'All noxious teeth have now been removed', he told Kahma. What remained was to hope for, and monitor, any improvement in his sight.

When Mr Hopkins, the errant anaesthetist from his first operation, now presented his bill for two attendances instead of one, Lewis was outraged. Sending him a cheque for five guineas of the ten guineas demanded, he also dashed off an angry letter to Dr Fant. 'This involves a brand of professional ethics of which I have had no experience hitherto', he complained, accusing Fant, by implication, of colluding in the unethical behaviour.

When Fant telephoned in response, 'Lewis told him off and he positively cringed when he apologised.' Gladys felt a mixture of sympathy and contempt for him. 'Why didn't he take up a better attitude?' she wondered. 'W[yndham] would have respected him much more.' Having complained about Hopkins's bill, Lewis now demanded that Fant send in his own. Fant promised to do so but, perhaps in trepidation, claimed only seven guineas for his professional services, instead of the 20 guineas Lewis had been expecting. He telephoned Fant to complain, this time, uncharacteristically, at being undercharged. When a more realistic bill arrived for 17 guineas, he paid it immediately, although Mrs Lewis still felt it was rather low.

It was about a week later that the most mysterious of the incidents feeding her paranoia occurred. It was late afternoon and her husband had just finished telephoning Fant to demand a receipt for the 17 guineas. She was preparing for a bath when there was a knock at the door. She opened it to find a young woman in the passageway. Gladys recognised the voice, a 'grand-one-sentence-shop-girl voice':

'I am a photographic model looking for work,' she said, 'are these photographic studios?'

'No', Mrs Lewis found herself replying. 'Artists' studios and my husband is doing no work at present.'

'I see.'

And Dr Fant's 'so called secretary' picked up her attaché case and went away. Gladys was 'extremely upset at this . . . especially at seeing what a low creature she was.'

When Lewis asked who was at the door, she decided to keep quiet about the curious encounter:

'Oh, a girl who said she was a photographic model looking for work.'

*

It soon became clear that the wholesale extraction of teeth had been in vain and that an explanation for his failing sight would have to be found elsewhere.

One possible cause was eliminated after blood was taken for a Wassermann Test. The test, for syphilis, proved negative.

In the ensuing months Lewis ran the gamut of medical opinion, both in London and abroad. Everybody seemed to know of a good eye man and he went from one recommended specialist to another. He passed through a bewildering series of consulting rooms and was introduced to surgeons, neurologists, ophthalmologists and radiologists. It was a professional breed of extravagant nomenclature. Lewis's Viennese dentist suggested Miklos Klein in Upper Wimpole Street. Agnes Bedford favoured Charles Leonard Gimblett, down the road from Klein in Devonshire Place. Gimblett in turn recommended a neurologist: Dr Swithin Pinder Meadows.

A year later even David Kahma would be consulting a specialist, by the more homely name of Appleby, on Lewis's behalf on the other side of the world in Vancouver.

During a hectic interview, Gimblett favoured surgery:

'Put up a fight for it, man!' he said.

And when Gladys agreed that he should take the risk, Lewis turned on her:

'Yes, I know you want me dead so you can marry again.'

'If you think that after the disastrous results of marriage to you, I would risk anything of the sort', she snapped back, 'you must be mad!'

*

The deterioration of his eyesight was graphically represented to him on 24 March when Mr Rupert Strathmore Scott, Consultant Surgeon at the Royal London Ophthalmic Hospital, charted his visual fields with a Perimeter.

With his head perfectly still, one eye covered and the other eye as close as possible to a vertical spindle at one end of the apparatus, the patient was asked to focus his attention on a fixed point at the other end. From that fixed point a graduated arc of metal curved up and over to a position directly above the vertical spindle in front of the patient's eye. The eye was thus positioned at the centre of a circle, of which the metal curve formed part.

From above his eye and from beyond his field of vision, a small round index marker was moved slowly down the graduated arc until he became peripherally aware of it. At that point he signalled to the operator of the test,

555

either verbally or by tapping the table with hand or pencil. As he signalled, a chart of concentric circles, divided into 24 segments and printed on a square of thin cardboard, was pricked by a stylus. This recorded the angle between eye and index mark, and hence the upper limit of his visual field.

The graduated arc was then rotated 15 degrees from the vertical, the index mark moved until Lewis signalled, and the stylus pricked the cardboard of the chart again. This process was repeated until the arc had rotated 360 degrees and the square of card with its concentric circles, not unlike a fairground rifle-range target, was punctured by 24 small holes.

The irregular area enclosed by the line of holes represented his field of vision: the extent of visual perception possible with that one eye looking straight ahead. Even patients suffering from serious ocular defects may not be aware of interruptions to the visual field, having become accustomed to compensate for blind spots with slight movements of the head and eyes. The results of a Perimeter test may surprise such patients.

In Lewis's case, it was not the area of chart mapping his visual field that would have concerned him, so much as the unmapped areas representing that perceptual *terra incognita* where the index marker had moved again and again through the full 90 degrees of the graduated arc without his seeing it. These areas of chart, darkly hatched by Rupert Scott's fountain pen, showed the field of his right eye sharply split down the middle and with the entire temporal half obliterated. As for the field of his left eye, only a small island in the lower nasal quadrant remained clear in the waste of shading.

On 27 March Scott referred him to Dr Meadows, physician to outpatients at the National Hospital for Nervous Diseases in Queen Square, the same neurologist Gimblett had recommended. Meadows examined him four days later. The precise nature of deterioration to the visual fields shown in Scott's Perimeter charts suggested a chiasmal lesion. As to what had caused the damage, Meadows noticed, during his physical examination of the patient, clear signs of pituitary dysfunction: smooth skin, hairless chest and diminished hair in the armpits. 'He probably has a chromophobe adenoma of the pituitary gland,' he told Scott, 'and I am arranging for him to have an X-ray of his skull. Alternatively he might have a suprasellar meningioma.'

Meadows arranged an appointment for Lewis with his colleague in Queen Square, the radiologist Dr James William Douglas Bull, who was to take the cranial radiograph. Before they started Lewis asked if it was a very expensive process, and Dr Bull replied that it would cost him six guineas and that many people considered this too expensive. Lewis said that he thought it a reasonable charge.

Midway through the first week of April, Dr Meadows had the cranial radiograph in front of him.

Lewis's head appeared as a grey speckled dome. A large black capital 'R' in the lower left corner of the radiograph indicated the direction X-ray bombardment had come from. A tangle of milky white strands at the bottom and to the right represented the bony intricacies of cranium floor and facial structure. Isolated from this white evidence of bone, and clearly visible against the grey expanse of soft tissue behind the eyes, Meadows found what he was looking for – the curved sliver of white, like the newest of moons, showed an abnormal presence of bone *above* the base of the skull. A much smaller reversed crescent appeared a little over four centimetres to the right of the first. Together they formed the partial outline of a large ovoidal mass rising out of the sella turcica. As well as making visible that which would not otherwise have registered on the radiograph, the partial calcification of the mass showed it to be of considerable age.

On Good Friday, Dr Fant arrived at 29A Notting Hill Gate carrying a human skull. Meadows had just communicated his findings and Fant had telephoned Lewis to ask if he might come round. Lewis consulted Gladys.

'As far as I am concerned he can', she said.

'My wife is needleworking,' Lewis spoke into the receiver, 'but she says you can come.'

They rushed round clearing away writing and sewing materials. Lewis washed and shaved. Gladys changed into a black dress. The doctor arrived while she was out of the room combing her hair. When she entered, Fant got up from his chair and turned his back on her, as if she had no business being there:

> I was by this time getting thoroughly used to his insults but what was getting me down was [Lewis] pretending not to see them. Saying he is not observant is one thing, but he must see some of the things that happen.

Given what Fant was about to explain to them, it was not surprising that Lewis might remain oblivious to things happening outside his central field of vision.

Fant used the skull he had brought to explain Meadows's findings. He would probably have pointed to the little depression, known as the sella turcica, that the neurologist said was considerably enlarged and then, raising his finger, traced the approximate location of the phantom body the X-ray showed looming above it. Finally he would have pointed to the area behind the jagged orbits of the skull to where the optic chiasma was being crushed. Perhaps interpreting Fant's brusque manner as an attempt to spare his wife's feelings, Lewis told him that neither of them was frightened of skulls. 'She has been to Art School', he added. Fant grinned.

Later on he demonstrated to her how surgeons performed a prefrontal lobotomy, what he called 'an operation for people with strong wills'. He told her a small electric saw was slipped through the skull: 'zzzz – snap – all over!'

As he was preparing to leave, he explained to Lewis what the Wassermann Test had been for.

'Of course they were trying to take your character away.'

'Who?' said Lewis.

'When you were having your blood-test. It was to see if you had syphilis.'

'I have had most things,' Lewis said, 'but syphilis is one thing I haven't had.'

'When I was in Medical School,' Fant replied, 'we were told that if an Archbishop came to see us it was the first thing we must suspect him of having.'

Gladys found the barrack-room tenor of the conversation repulsive. The doctor left his *memento mori* behind.

*

Lewis sometimes displayed an extraordinary psychological detachment from his condition. The day after Fant's demonstration of what was happening inside his skull, he calmly wrote to Dr Bull challenging his fee for the radiographs which had yielded such disturbing information:

> You will recall that I asked you before we began whether it was very expensive. You told me it was 6 guineas. When you said that many people considered 6 guineas too much I did not conceal my view that 6 guineas was a reasonable charge. I did not say I regarded it as too little. The enclosed bill is however for 7 guineas: a mistake I assume.

*

Medical opinion was divided as to the advisability of a surgical operation. While the belligerent Gimblett urged him to 'put up a fight for it', the more circumspect Lindsay-Rea counselled against surgery and placed his faith in deep X-ray therapy. Meanwhile Dr Meadows was insistent that Lewis come into the National Hospital for Nervous Diseases in order to get a neurosurgical opinion. Lewis was unwilling to go into this or any other hospital, and by mid-April he had telephoned Meadows and asked for his radiographs to be returned.

Rupert Scott was disappointed he had lost faith in the neurologist, 'one of the best authorities in [this] type of case', but respected Lewis's wishes for a further opinion. 'Were I in your place', he told him, 'I should do the same.'

> You feel well and are able to continue with your writing. I cannot say for how long you will be able to do so; perhaps the vision of your right eye may remain as it is for some time yet, a few years in fact. It is . . . impossible to give a prognosis. If an operation be considered possible it would be a very hazardous one with risk to life. Should it be undertaken with success it could not restore what vision you have lost, but would, I trust, preserve what you have.

On the same Saturday that Scott offered this admirably balanced analysis of his prospects, Lewis telephoned Dr Fant's office around noon to ask if he had received the radiographs back from Meadows. The secretary told him Fant was not there. She seemed distraught. First she said the X-rays had arrived, then that they had not. Eventually she said she did not know. When Lewis put the telephone down he said:

'She is getting completely impossible. Vaguer and vaguer. I can't stand her affectedness.'

Then he went out to buy meat. As soon as he had gone Fant telephoned. Mrs Lewis claimed she knew he would. She told him her husband had gone out.

'I know, I know', he replied. He told her that Meadows's letter had arrived but not the report and X-rays. Gladys remarked, sarcastically, that to put an X-ray in an envelope would tax most people's resources to the limit. Fant asked how Lewis was getting on and she replied that he was 'running round in circles getting the money', making plans to extend the increasingly expensive canvassing of medical opinion abroad. Then Fant said:

'It's not too late, Mrs Lewis.'

She did not remember precisely how she replied to this 'very unusual remark', but she did recall, in her account of the conversation: 'I suddenly knew what he meant!' There was a silence. She said, 'Goodbye.' He did not answer and she put the telephone receiver down.

Fant presumably meant that it was 'not too late' to do something about her husband's condition, but the sinister significance with which Gladys loaded the remark must remain a mystery.

She went out shopping and was crossing Kensington Church Street when she heard the sound of gears being mangled as a car came to a violent stop about ten yards away. She turned to see Fant behind the wheel and, occupying the passenger seat, his secretary. She hurried on across the road feeling extremely upset.

Back at home, after tea, Lewis said he was tired and went to lie down in the bedroom. She sat brooding. 'I . . . felt if I did not stop all this nonsense I should be ill . . . I was determined that I was not going to have any more humiliation.'

At about a quarter to nine she made a telephone call:

'Hello.'

'Is that Dr Fant?'

'Yes.'

'Dr John Fant?'

Impatiently:

'Yes.'

'This is Mrs Lewis speaking.'

'Which Mrs Lewis?'

She was silent. It was so like what she had expected to happen. 'Every step one takes one knows just what is going to be said and done.' He repeated his question, louder this time:

'Which Mrs Lewis?'

'Mrs Wyndham Lewis.'

'Oh!' Fant almost shouted as if calling for someone's attention. And then very slowly and deliberately: 'Mrs – Wyndham – Lewis!'

There was a slight pause. Then she said:

'Why are you deliberately trying to humiliate me, Dr Fant?'

She thought she heard a slight gasp on the other end of the line.

'I don't know what you mean, Mrs Lewis.'

'I'm not sure that I do either,' she replied.

And she replaced the receiver.

Afterwards she felt relieved and free as if she had faced something and it was now over. She ran upstairs, through the studio to the kitchen to cook. As a result of all this they dined late that night.

The following day, when Lewis came down from the studio for lunch, she told him how much better she felt. He asked what she meant and she told him what she had done the previous evening. She saw his lips twitch as if suppressing a laugh. He took Fant's side and she vigorously defended herself. As she was talking, she thought she heard Fant saying: 'I didn't mean to do you any harm, Mrs Lewis.' Greatly disturbed by what she regarded as 'thought transference', and especially by the formality of the 'Mrs Lewis', she found it all 'so odd and unusual'.

Fant's next visit to the flat was a short time later, having just received Meadows's report and the X-rays. He appeared to be in a bad mood when he arrived. There were a few strained exchanges with Lewis during which he mentioned gin fizzes. Gladys asked him how a gin fizz was made and Fant snapped: 'Oh I don't know!' After that she kept quiet. Conversation between the two men was desultory, the atmosphere tense. Eventually Gladys picked up cigarettes and matches and prepared to leave the room. Then Lewis asked her to look for a book. She could not remember ever having seen it – *The Psychology of the Brain* or perhaps *The Physiology of the Brain* – but she dutifully crossed the room to find it. She was surprised when Fant offered to help, and followed her. They stood together in front of the bookshelves. He pointed out Jung's *Psychology of the Unconscious* to her but said nothing. He appeared to be gritting his teeth as they scoured the spines. All this time she had the strangest impression that he wanted to violently knock her to the floor and she was amused to find herself wondering whether she would be angry if he did. Instead, he suddenly bent down and stuck his backside in her face. At this point Lewis came over to join them and Fant quickly changed his posture, bending his knees and sinking down on his haunches. Gladys said: 'I think I'll go upstairs and see if it's there', and her husband said: 'I should if I were you.' When she came back down from the studio the men had resumed their seats. She sat with them smoking but taking no part in the conversation. At one point she dropped her cigarette on the front of her blouse and Fant said something about people 'being over-emotional'.

Fant told Lewis that he often felt like giving a patient five pounds just to go away rather than take his one pound and have to treat him. Just before leaving he said that he had often thought of writing a book about his patients. He slapped the table fiercely: 'They would not recognise themselves if I put them in a book!'

Gladys believed that it was on this day that Fant decided he was going to get his own back on Lewis. She also knew that he was going to do it through her. After he had gone she told her husband so.

*

Lewis took his X-rays to Dr Cecil Charles Worster-Drought, Neurologist at the Royal Cancer Hospital in Fulham Road, who made an appointment for him with the Director of the Radiotherapy Department there for 3 o'clock on Thursday 4 May.

It is not known whether this meeting with Professor David Waldron Smithers, author of 'X-Ray Treatment of Malignant Tumours in the Region of the Eyes' in the *British Journal of Ophthalmology*, actually took place. If it did, the consultation cannot have proved satisfactory because, shortly after, Lindsay-Rea arranged for him to see the eminent Dr Russell John Reynolds, CBE, MB, BS, FRCP, DMRE, FFR, Physician in charge at the Department of Radiology and Electrotherapy, Charing Cross Hospital and Honorary Adviser in Radiology to the Ministry of Pensions.

Lewis, however, was not to submit himself to deep X-ray treatment under Dr Reynolds's care for another four months.

Determined to explore every avenue of relevant opinion, he went to Switzerland early in June. He had mentioned to Giovanelli at the beginning of the year that such an expedition might be necessary and, when he consulted Worster-Drought, had asked whether he should have another cranial radiograph taken while he was there. Lewis seemed convinced that Swiss technology could produce a sharper image of his head and its contents than was possible in London. Perhaps he even entertained a faint hope that the evidence of intracranial tumour, upon which Meadows had based his diagnosis, might turn out to be no more than a flaw on the X-ray plate.

In spite of Worster-Drought's response that it was to Sweden he should have to go for the best X-ray photography, and indeed for the greatest advances in deep X-ray therapy, Lewis made his preparations for Switzerland. Dr Fant came to the flat to append his signature to a passport application form, the favour customarily asked of family doctor, clergyman and Justice of the Peace alike. This was the occasion for yet another psychological duel with Gladys. 'At twelve promptly he came in', she recalled:

> I knew before he came it was going to be an ordeal. So much so I simply could not do my hair. He was now going to complete his insult . . . I could not look but only stand and wait. He said, in the soft voice he has when he is preparing his insults, with a slight sigh: 'Hallo Mrs Lewis.' I said 'Hallo.'

Gladys was never quite sure how much her husband was aware of these offensive undercurrents, so obvious to her, so blatant and so threatening. She was convinced Lewis knew something was happening because he always gave Fant the lead. A sinister complicity seemed to prevail over the mundane exchange on this occasion:

> W[yndham] said 'Well how did you enjoy your holiday?' This was it! [Fant] gave a warm intimate laugh, staring at me saying, 'It was the most exciting time I've ever had in my life.'

Just what, if anything, was meant by this, or how she interpreted it, is impossible to say. The way he stared at her while answering her husband's

562

question suggested some sort of innuendo, and she reacted as she might have done had the doctor suddenly exposed himself:

> My head turned automatically as if he had slapped my face. I then to my consternation flushed. But I then was able to look up. It was done and over. As I lifted my head, my eyes glanced across his. He was looking his malicious look. I loathed him. He seemed just like a fat bloated spider. I have never in my whole life disliked and scorned anyone so much. He is the lowest of louts!

*

Lewis's five days in Zurich yielded little more than a dispiriting reiteration of information and advice he had already received: 'If you do not receive surgical treatment you will go blind.' Professor Doctor Marc Amsler, 'the star Swiss eye-doctor', said that his condition could be helped with deep X-ray therapy but warned him that 'there were different ways of doing this and it was very important to get it done the right way.'

Meanwhile, Worster-Drought, unaware of the expedition to Zurich, telephoned Dr Russell Reynolds to find out how Lewis was responding to the deep X-ray treatment he assumed was in progress at Charing Cross. He was surprised and disturbed to learn that the treatment had not even begun. 'It might be of course, that you are taking a holiday first', he wrote to Lewis, 'but it is really essential for you to start as soon as possible.'

But when he got back to London he was still unwilling to begin the treatment. Despite having originally referred him to a British radiologist, Lindsay-Rea seemed now to favour Scandinavian consultation. 'The best thing you can do, to avoid [an] operation,' he urged, 'is to go to Sweden.' Lewis interpreted this as a lack of confidence in Reynolds:

> As the X-ray specialist in London to whom I was going had been found for me by the eye-doctor . . . who says Sweden is a much better bet . . . the conclusion seems obvious. His opinion of X-ray work in England cannot be very high.

Eliot had lent £200 to get him to Switzerland. Application was now made at the same source for further subsidy to Stockholm:

> On enquiry I find that all the sea-transport . . . is booked up until mid-August. As it is dangerous to wait, I must go by land. It is extremely expensive – but I can see nothing for it – either I fool around here and

waste time and money or manage to get there somehow, and live there for six weeks. The fares alone will cost £150.

He asked Eliot to guarantee him, at his bank, a further £200 and allow him to reduce it 'a bit at a time' as soon as the treatment was over. 'It is of course maddening that I have to waste all this money', he concluded, 'but I have given a good deal of time and care to sifting the evidence.' The following words were crossed out of the letter:

what I have is practically inoperable – or an operation is a desperate measure only and there is no alternative.

Lindsay-Rea wrote to Dr Granströmm at the Karolinska Institute in Stockholm, asking him to guide Lewis to the best radiographer there, and concluded: 'the more heads we have in this matter, the better for him.' Alas, if this had been so then the combined heads of the 20 or so medical men consulted by Lewis or on his behalf that year would have made him a healthy man indeed.

Lewis and his wife travelled north to Newcastle, embarking on a ship called *Jupiter*, which reached Bergen on 12 July. They crossed Norway and into Sweden, arriving at the Hotel Continental in Stockholm on the 15th. Ten days later, consultations completed, they sailed for Tilbury aboard the *Saga* from the port of Göteborg. 'The Swedish visit like the Swiss visit was a visit to doctors,' he told a friend,

not a tour to mountains and fjords. Nothing is visible, there is no pain, no disagreeable sensations. But my condition is extremely unsatisfactory. I just tell you this and let us speak no more about it.

Back in London, from 28 August to 11 September, he finally submitted to deep X-ray therapy under the care of Dr Russell Reynolds.

There were to have been six sessions, but after four or five Lewis was alarmed to find that the deterioration of his vision was rapidly accelerating instead of being arrested and refused to continue. 'The X-ray treatment appears to have set me back – not to have advanced me', he told Docker:

My GP informs me that in a text-book on the subject it is said that sometimes X-ray treatment produces a liquid (discharge?) which temporarily impairs the sight. On the other hand my eye-doctor [Lindsay-Rea] assures me that in all his experience he has never known X-ray to be responsible for such a reaction. But there is no question that [in the period during which I was treated] my sight worsened . . . – Naturally I am alarmed: although of course it may be only a temporary decline. My confidence in my eye-doctor is a little shaken.

Two years later the blind man received a letter from Messrs Stook-Vaughan, Webster & Co., representing Dr Russell Reynolds, and threatening legal action if £12 15s., being the balance of his fee for six X-ray therapy treatments, was not forthcoming. Lewis wrote to the doctor asking whether a final settlement of half the sum, £6 7s. 6d., would be acceptable, in view of the fact that the course of treatment, so unsuccessful as to be injurious rather than therapeutic, had not been completed, and that the blindness which ensued had done little to improve his financial position.

Following the setback with deep X-ray therapy, he told Docker he intended consulting a couple more specialists in order to bolster his shaken confidence in Lindsay-Rea. He confided to Meyrick Booth on 8 October that 'death, total blindness, paralysis or insanity' had already been offered him as possible consequences of surgery. Two days later the eminent neurosurgeon Sir Hugh Cairns, Nuffield Professor of Surgery at the Radcliffe Infirmary, Oxford, limited the prospect to '*death* only – not the other things'. Cairns did his best to persuade him to scrape along as best he could in view of his age. Lewis replied that he would not make a very good blind man 'or even a hopelessly myopic one'.

*

On 23 November, some four and a half years after the contract for it was drawn up and three and a half years after submission of the completed manuscript, Hutchinson published *Rude Assignment*. It was subtitled 'A narrative of my career up-to-date'. The startling 20-year-old bifurcated figure on the dust jacket, palette bristling with brushes, and the single, large artist's eye goggling from the side of the head was a mockery that cannot have escaped Lewis, well aware as he now was that the nerves communicating impressions from his retina to his brain were approaching a condition of terminal atrophy.

*

Despite the awesome preoccupations with which he was struggling at this time he was able to give Denis Williams important practical assistance. The young painter had returned to London from Georgetown, British Guyana, in May, and after about six months of intensive painting had made contact again.

Williams recalled Lewis inviting him to bring some of the new canvases to his studio and, sensing his protégé was hard up, even providing the taxi fare. He seemed genuinely to like the work and set about bringing it to the attention of certain key people, notably Henry Moore and, in hectoring terms, Herbert Read:

> as you did not mention Denis Williams, I assume you have not seen his paintings. Committeeman! The British Council has been helpful with regard to this young Negro, but if he is to survive he must be found a job. Because of colour this presents great difficulties. It is a pity that all this talent should be lost for no better reason than that its possessor's skin is controversial. I understand, for instance, that it is going to be exceedingly difficult to find a school prepared to engage a Negro teacher. As his dealer says, Williams could not live on his work as an artist. At this juncture, Committeeman Read, your vigorous action might be decisive.

After a month, with or without Read's assistance, Lewis managed to secure Williams a teaching job at the Central School of Arts and Crafts in Southampton Row, together with a visiting tutorship at the Slade School. He also arranged a choice of two London galleries prepared to offer an immediate one-man exhibition. Because of the scale on which Williams was now working, the larger was selected: Gimpel Fils in Duke Street, W1. Nevertheless, as Lewis pointed out in *The Listener* on 7 December, the place looked congested and seemed as if likely to burst at any moment under pressure from 'pictures the size of a pantechnicon'.

He began his article, the penultimate art notice he was ever to contribute, with the words:

> I do not wish to be guilty of what is called overpraising (as if an artist could be overpraised), but I consider Denis Williams a young man of very remarkable talent.

Following a detailed and generously effusive description and discussion of the paintings he concluded: 'No one interested in what is being done in London today should fail to see them.'

*

On 20 December 1950 Mrs Lewis visited Dr Fant to complain of his treatment of her. Instead of treating her as a sick woman, he lectured her. A week later Lewis himself went to see Fant, but the doctor was unable – 'that is to say . . . unwilling' – to take any action to make matters better.

Then, in early January, Lewis wrote to Fant, recapitulating the events of the previous year: the fraudulent anaesthetist's bill, the strange telephone call from the doctor's secretary while Lewis was in St Vincent's Clinic, the even stranger visit by that young woman posing as a photographic model and Fant's slighting and discourteous behaviour towards his wife. He concluded that if the doctor did not apologise in writing both for himself and his secretary to Lewis's solicitor, he would 'be obliged to forward this letter with a covering note to the relevant medical authorities'.

The draft of this communication, which may or may not have been sent, covered 25 pages. It was written in a large hand at the rate of some ten or twelve lines to a page.

FIFTY

'The Tapewriter' and 'The Biro'

On 18 January 1951 J. R. Ackerley had a meeting with his art correspondent. Lewis informed him that he could make no further comment upon exhibitions of contemporary painting for *The Listener* because he was rapidly becoming blind. Ackerley was stunned. 'You were so wonderfully good in the way you gave me your tragic news', he wrote two days later:

> that you enabled me to get easily through an interview distressing to us both. When I left your cool presence I felt wretched beyond words.

Significantly, Lewis's last exhibition review for *The Listener*, published that same day, concentrated as much upon the aural and sensual as upon the visual. The critic seemed to be preparing himself for the final blackout when touch and hearing would have compensatory importance. A collection of Alexander Calder mobiles was on show in New Bond Street:

> The Lefevre Gallery is full of a soft tinkling suggestive of an Indian temple: the air is full of the movement of large and small, black, red, and yellow metallic leaves. They are the airiest things imaginable. If they touch your head or leg they gently recoil.

*

Lewis was unable to keep an appointment in Paris with a Doctor Payenneville, on 16 January, due to an alarming domestic crisis. Only terse reference was made to it in a letter to Kahma:

> My wife is suffering a breakdown in health, received drugs, acted drunk, caused fire.

She must have injured herself at the same time because, over the next four weeks, she had a course of ten physiotherapy sessions costing a total of 5 guineas.

Lewis managed to get to Paris at the end of January to keep his appointment, although with little hope of success:

'It is much too late . . . I fear. One year ago would have been the time to know of a treatment. But one can never hear of these things until too late.

By 4 February he was back. 'Doctor I am afraid not much use'.

*

Agnes Bedford, the accompanist and piano teacher who collaborated with Ezra Pound on sundry musical ventures in the 1920s, had been a friend of Lewis during the same period. In 1921 he addressed her as 'Miss Bedford' when gently chiding her for encouraging Pound in the purchase of a bassoon. In his *Sportsman's Engagement Book* of 1923, she appeared as 'Agg' or 'Aggy BED'. Lewis admitted that 'there had been talk of his marrying her (in the late Twenties) but he had decided against it.' During 1930, in the course of sporadic diary entries, she was referred to, for reasons that remain a mystery, as 'Twin'. Their liaison ended with Lewis's marriage to Gladys Hoskins in October of the same year. Severance of the connection was commemorated on a page of chronological notes for 1930, written in Lewis's hand: an arrow pointed between the months of September and November, labelled 'Cease to see Twin'.

Twenty years later Agnes Bedford, still enigmatically known as 'Twin' to both Lewis and his wife, re-entered their lives.

Nursing her mother outside London during the war, her musical career had languished. When arthritis clawed and crippled her hands, it was abandoned. After the war she lived alone in a cramped Belgravia mews cottage with a bright blue front door approached, by way of a broad arch, from Lyall Street.

With the onset of his blindness and the strain beginning to tell on his wife, 44 Eaton Mews North now became Lewis's office and principal workplace. Because he could no longer see to read, everything had to be read to him. Agnes Bedford remembered reading George Orwell novels aloud so that he could pass judgement on them in Part IV of *The Writer and the Absolute*, and reading from Arnold Toynbee's multi-volume work, *A Study of History*, to make convincing the discussions in the early part of the 'long novel' he was writing. She recalled his extraordinary powers of absorbing and retaining what was read to him and that he rarely asked her to make note of a particular point, ever confident that he would remember what he heard. She helped with his correspondence, writing letters to his dictation.

Her devotion to Lewis lightened the workload of his wife at the same time as it created a tension born of rivalry between the two women. 'Twin' became another object of suspicion for Gladys's paranoia. A journal entry in March recorded: 'Twin came', and asked: 'Is she malicious?' A week later Gladys, convinced her husband was having an affair with the other woman, confided as much to her friend, Elsie Hirst:

> Told her about Lewis and Twin, and said I was going to a lawyer.

*

During his distressing interview with Ackerley in January, Lewis had discussed making a statement in *The Listener*, announcing his retirement from art criticism. The statement, when ultimately framed, Lewis declared, 'must be very carefully worded'. In April, prior to the more public explanation of his plight, Lewis began breaking the news to friends. 'Plenty of writers go mad', he told Porteus, 'but surprisingly few become blind. It is incredibly malignant to visit this on me, at the same time a visual artist. But there you are, what can you expect.'

Stella Newton came to visit, and afterwards made him a present of the latest thing in the field of writing implements. 'Thanks for . . . making us known to the Biro,' Gladys wrote to her:

> and for sending us a specimen . . . It is a great success . . . Wyndham when you had gone made minute enquiries about the colours of your garments. Thinks of purchasing telescopic spectacles, which might enable him to see.

'What a hellish thing, isn't there anything to be done?' Naomi Mitchison demanded by return of post when she received Lewis's letter. 'My goodness, you haven't deserved that.' And yet she found a crumb of comfort in the bleak prognosis. 'I don't think it will hurt your writing, indeed one may now get the latter part of the Childermass.'

As if in response, a week after Mrs Mitchison expressed this hope, Geoffrey Bridson, a young BBC producer, wrote to Lewis with a proposal to adapt his 23-year-old epic of the afterlife as a radio play for the Third Programme. This was the beginning of a four-year project which enabled Lewis to complete the second and third parts that Chatto & Windus, almost a quarter of a century before, had rashly promised for the autumn of 1928.

*

The Listener carried an article on 10 May, explaining why no art criticism had appeared from his pen for four months. Designed to take readers by surprise, it began in the safe and prosaic realm, for the English, of recent weather conditions. What a deplorable winter it had been, consistently cold and dank from start to finish and with a constant, blue-grey veil of moisture reducing buildings, traffic, people, to blurred silhouettes. The page-long piece was the 'carefully worded' statement Lewis had mentioned to Ackerley in January. It was called 'The Sea-Mists of the Winter'.

In the third paragraph he abruptly abandoned the conceit. 'The truth is that there was no mist', he announced. 'The mist was in my eyes: there was no sea-mist in nature.'

> What, in brief is my problem, is that the optic nerves, at their chiasma, or crossing, are pressed upon by something with the pleasing name of cranial pharyngeoma. It is therefore a more implacable order of misfortune than if I had a jolly little cataract.

He had told Naomi Mitchison that the importunate mass destroying his sight had 'a beautiful name'. It was not, however, a pharyngeoma, but Lewis could not have known this. Only after his death, the top of his skull removed and brain longitudinally bisected, would Meadows's initial diagnosis be confirmed by a less beautiful name: chromophobe adenoma.

In *The Listener* he described his day-to-day, often comic, experience of near blindness; standing on the pavement and hailing private cars and small vans as taxi-cabs or, having secured a cab, trying to enter the body of the vehicle at two or three places instead of through the space produced by the opened door. When friends visited in the evening he saw them 'fragmentarily, obliquely, and spasmodically'. His central vision obliterated, he could no longer see anything directly in front of him:

> But an awareness of the bodily presence is always there, and as one turns one's head hither and thither, glimpses constantly recur, delivering to one's fading eye-sight a piece of old so-and-so's waistcoat or bald head, or dear Janet's protruding nose. These token odds and ends of personality are really just as good as seeing them whole, and their voices have an added significance.

Even this impressionistic perception, he anticipated, would be gradually denied him from week to week until what he termed 'the absolute blackout.' A decade earlier, in wartime Toronto, the prognosis of total blindness had been just one medical opinion, to be discounted or superseded by another more optimistic. Even so, he had faced the prospect before shutting off his mind to it. 'If my eyes go I go too', he had said. 'Loathsome as the world is, I do like to *see* it. *That* sort of blackout I could not live in.' Now, with a unanimity of medical opinion closing off comforting options, he could approach the 'absolute black-out' with comparative equanimity:

> Pushed into an unlighted room, the door banged and locked for ever, I shall then have to light a lamp of aggressive voltage in my mind to keep at bay the night.

He explained that his work as a writer would continue with the aid of a dictaphone. A month later, such a machine was purchased with the aid of a £100 grant from the Royal Literary Fund, secured for him through the good offices and influence of Alan Pryce-Jones. The editor of the *Times Literary Supplement* apparently harboured no ill will towards the man who had taken such vituperative exception to his editorial interventions three years before. With the publication of 'The Sea-Mists of the Winter' it was time for old scores to be forgotten and bridges built.

Lewis seemed perfectly resigned to his fate as a writer. Indeed, many American authors, he had heard, even when sharp-sighted, preferred the dictaphone to the pen or typewriter. Anticipating his readers' question: 'And as an artist, what about that?' Lewis deftly turned aside from acceptable, even predictable, self-pity, with a particularly barbed statement:

> Ah, sir, as to the artist in England, I have often thought that it would solve a great many problems if English painters were born blind.

Because they were second-rate; or in order to spare them the pain of having their work rejected; as a last piece of trenchant art criticism; or as a bitter swipe at the hostile critical fraternity that he felt had made his own working life so great a struggle – this might have left an unpleasant taste in the mouth, had it not been immediately followed by the last paragraph:

> And finally, which is the main reason for this unseemly autobiographical outburst, my articles on contemporary art exhibitions necessarily end, for I can no longer see a picture.

Much could be forgiven a man in his predicament, even the wishing of congenital disability upon his fellows.

It was a perfectly judged performance, hitting just the right note between seriousness and humour. One reader wrote to tell him he had actually succeeded in making her laugh, and Patrick Heron figured in *The Listener*'s correspondence page, calling it:

a brilliant, witty, even a gay article; and the evocation of the sensations of failing sight was shatteringly powerful.

Stephen Spender met Augustus John in the street. Both men had read 'The Sea-Mists of the Winter'. Spender said how terribly sad it was that Lewis should have gone blind. 'Yes,' said John, 'I've just written to tell him on no account to give up his art criticism.' Spender thought the remark very amusing, the notion of a blind man passing judgements on the visual arts being demonstrably absurd. But John had actually made a half-serious point in his letter:

> I really don't see why you should discontinue your art criticism. You can't go so far wrong even if you do it in bed. You can always . . . discover fresh talent and demolish stale. The names can be invented; likewise the pictures if you are tired of the old ones.

Kate Lechmere waited six months after reading the article to make contact. She reminded him how he had flapped his new check-lined coat at her in 1914, 'beating your wings like an old raven and remarking how unobservant women were!' And with nostalgic warmth she recalled how she had hardened to his honorary title: 'Bloody bitch!'

Memories returned from further back when his old Slade contemporary Herman Hildesheim, now Hubert Hilton, wrote to tell him of the oil portrait he still had from their student days:

> I made you look rather Byronic and why not? . . . I think you were seeing visions and were ready to stand firmly for what you believed.

And from further back still, a name he barely recollected: Kerrison Preston, who had known him at Rugby. Lewis replied in elegiac vein:

> Since the days when you and I were snub-nosed brats . . . a lot of dirty water has flowed under Westminster Bridge, a good many wars have been fought, pictures painted, babies born.

The article brought him letters from total strangers. A Miss Vanner, 33 years old, wrote to ask him whether his condition was the same as hers and wondered should she have an operation or not. His reply was a model of kindness, setting out for her the considerations he himself had had to take account of over the previous year and offering her the names of 'the three best neuro-surgeons in England'.

A man called Hicks urged him, since orthodox medicine had failed, to consult one of several 'healers' who had had 'outstanding success in the treatment of all kinds of intractable cases'. Mrs Margaret Lyon of the Psychic Healing Centre in Glasgow and Harry Edwards of Shere, near Guildford, Surrey, were two of the most outstanding. Mr Hicks was nearly 70, claimed not to be a crank, apart from doting on pictures and practising painting. He had no religious convictions and no wish to interfere with Lewis's own, if any.

A man from the BBC wrote addressing him as D. B. Wyndham Lewis and asking his permission to broadcast a recording of 'The Sea-Mists of the Winter' on the German Service. Lewis sent a telegram granting permission and the man from the BBC wrote back, thanking Mr D. B. Wyndham Lewis and enclosing a cheque for £3.

Finally, *The Listener* article became a source of inspiration for listeners to the Home Service's early morning weekday religious broadcast, 'Lift Up Your Hearts!', when the Reverend William Evans quoted some lines from it during one of his five-minute talks in late July.

*

Domestic tensions belied the stoic serenity of the face he turned to the public. Five days after 'The Sea-Mists of the Winter' appeared, while letters of condolence and support poured in from friends and strangers alike, his wife was preparing to get as far away as she could from him and the amorphous conspiracy she sensed was closing around her. She was going to visit Hedwig and Meyrick Booth in County Cork. 'As to when I shall return and where I do not know. It depends on how quickly I get well.' Her letter, typed but probably not delivered to Elsie Hirst, gnawed over the previous year's grievances. There had, it seems, been another disturbing incident involving Fant's secretary in January:

> a telephone call to tell me they knew what doctor I was going [to] and why. People do not disguise their voices very well on the telephone.

She promised wide-ranging but unspecified retaliatory action:

> I shall . . . go to a lawyer and start a full scale investigation into the events . . . which led up to my illness . . . There have been too many malicious things happening and the insults I have had to bear in the last year have been too much . . . However everything is now going to be brought out into the open and sanified. I will not go through life to be maligned and degraded by evil people. That I will not stand.

She had reached the Booths by 18 May.

Lewis meanwhile went to stay with Agnes. Gladys was aware of this, had actually anticipated it, writing along the edge of a page of her notes the previous March:

> Lewis is manoeuvring me into position to go & stay at Twins I know. Sweet as chocolate cream.

However uncertain Gladys's plans were for returning, Lewis's were straightforward. He would be in Ireland from 26 May to 2 June, he told Dorothy Richards. 'After that my address will be 44 Eaton Mews North, Lyall St.' He supplied a telephone number, Sloane 7008, and expressed the hope Mrs Richards and her husband would call on him during their visit to London in June. It was not clear whether he expected to be moving into Eaton Mews North in the company of his wife.

How aware he was of her state of mind at this time, it is difficult to judge. If Gladys's letter to Elsie Hirst seemed to cast doubt over their future relations, no such shadow was evident in the letter he laboriously drafted for Agnes to type on 18 May:

> My dear Froanna. I was so glad you arrived without mishap, and that Hedi and Meyrick's farm is the dream-come-true sort of place. I am so looking forward to seeing it, you, and them.

He would be joining her when Geoffrey Bridson, who was adapting *The Childermass*, had delivered the script at the end of the following week and he signed the letter 'All love and blessings. W.L.'

Meanwhile, Gladys wrote again to 'Hirstie', announcing her intention of returning to Notting Hill Gate and seeking legal advice. 'However long the proceedings take I shall go on with this until it is completely clear and open what all this means.' Fant's secretary's 'uncalled for performance' on the telephone a year ago the previous March, the same young woman's appearance on their doorstep pretending to be a photographic model looking for work, the January telephone call, imperfectly disguised and threatening, were, she believed, all intended 'to cover up for these people's grotesque relationship'. The 'considerable mental distress' all this had inflicted on her had resulted in a deterioration, 'to a remarkable degree', of her marriage. Given that it coincided with the onset of Lewis's blindness, this was 'unparalleled brutality', she declared, 'worthy of Belsen.'

And she even suspected the 'filthy intrigue' went further back still, implicating Terence Millin, who operated on her husband in 1934:

Surely eighteen years of illness was sufficient for one man to impose upon another without causing further injury?

Lewis set out for Ireland on 26 May. To lessen the tribulations of blind-man's-buff that unaccompanied travel had now become, he was escorted by Ezra Pound's son. On the train through South Wales to catch the Cork ferry from Fishguard, they shared a compartment with an elderly clergyman. Lewis was entertained by the young student of Eastern languages engaging this worthy in heated debate and declaiming verses at him from the Koran in Persian.

'What kind of hat is she wearing?'

Omar Pound remembers his companion's constant inquisition about their surroundings and fellow passengers on board the ferry.

'Is she ugly?'

Such questions, uttered in ringing tones over the breakfast table, caused the young man some embarrassment. Lewis insisted on everything being described to him, 'not for his personal safety but because he was interested, wanted to know, and was ever afraid someone might try to keep something from him.'

Their destination was 'Montfieldstown', a big, 28-roomed house set in 40 acres of rich farmland, half a mile from the nearest village, Rochestown, and two miles southeast of Cork city. It was completely isolated, hidden from sight and shielded from the wind by immense trees. Visitors often spent hours looking for it. Through the trees there was a fine view of Cork harbour and the sea.

The building was about 160 years old and had been the scene of a famous local tragedy. A young bride returning from church with her new husband was confronted by a former suitor and, in remorse, stabbed herself while the wedding guests waited for her to cut the cake. Tradition had it that Charles Dickens knew the place and used a detail from its story for the creation of Miss Havisham's Satis House in *Great Expectations*: following the bride's suicide, the wedding breakfast remained uncleared for a generation. Meyrick Booth had spoken to old people in the neighbourhood with childhood memories of peeping through the dining-room windows at the mouldering banquet.

Lewis found the Booths' accommodation was not the 'dream–come–true sort of place' he had been led to expect. 'I was staying in an enormous practically unfurnished house', he told Stephen Spender on his return:

I was surrounded by violently coughing heads; for my hosts appeared unable to buy fuel. But I consoled myself by sitting in a conservatory

576

beside an Indian tulip tree, and found that the Irish sun through glass is quite respectably hot.

They stayed long enough for 'the sprightly Omar' to catch the eye of a local girl, the daughter of one Colonel Lucy. A brief flirtation ensued and Lewis was highly amused at the denouement:

> Alas, Kitty betrayed the stigma of superstition; in fact, she told him that there was a giant who lived underneath her house, whose beard grew into a table. This was too much for Omar, and he saw Kitty Lucy no more.

If a reconciliation between Lewis and his wife was needed, it was presumably achieved in Cork, because she accompanied him back to London on or about 6 June. The following week they prepared to leave Notting Hill together. The renunciation of that great barn-like studio above their living quarters, practically unused and gathering dust for the previous two years, was final confirmation, if such at this late stage was necessary, that Lewis's painting career was at an end.

Lewis and his wife moved into a fourth-floor flat in Ashley Mansions, a red-brick block on the north side of Vauxhall Bridge Road between Rochester Row and Victoria Station. It was about half a mile away from Eaton Mews North.

*

That month saw the first fruit of Lewis's latest and final publishing partnership. Methuen & Co. brought out *Tarr*, 'first of a new series of reprints', its blurb promised, by 'one of the most startling personalities in the British world of art and letters'. Coinciding with this, and with hopes that it would boost sales, came a pamphlet by Geoffrey Grigson: *A Master of Our Time: A Study of Wyndham Lewis*.

The dust-wrapper of *Tarr* was the only one of the Methuen series to be designed by the author and was probably his last effort at graphic art. Even so, his eyesight was by this time so poor that his wife had to colour in the rather confused decoration with red, blue and lime green. The job took her, she remembered, about 45 minutes.

*

Among the first visitors to Ashley Mansions were Bridson and the actor who was going to play the Bailiff, the most important and challenging characterisation in *The Childermass*. Donald Wolfit was not in fact the first

577

choice for the role. While Lewis was in Cork, Bridson had sent over the final quarter of the adaptation for his approval and, in a covering letter, had broken the news that Charles Laughton would not be back in the country in time for the broadcast on 18 June. Wolfit and Lewis, however, got on extremely well. Over tea in the Ashley Mansions flat, Lewis gave the actor the one clue he needed to build his interpretation of the character. 'The Bailiff', he said, 'was rather a George Robey sort of character.' Bridson remembered:

> Wolfit's subsequent playing of the part was one of the most remarkable radio performances that I remember. He gave anything but a George Robey interpretation to it . . . but the occasional inflection, the waggish vulgarity, the playing to the gallery and the sudden confidential aside, each were a part of the Music Hall tradition that had made Robey what he had been.

Two months after Bridson's initial approach, the Lewises attended a party to 'listen in' to the live 90-minute broadcast. The transition of his work from page to sound stage was for Lewis 'an almost miraculous event'. *The Childermass* was, he claimed, the book he set most store by and it had sprung 'into concrete life, with live actors bestowing upon it an almost startling physical reality, and a very able and ingenious living composer playing the Bailiff's barge across the mournful river and jazzing the appellants into a bacchic dance.' He gave full credit to Bridson as the magician who had brought it all into being:

> All I can do is salute you as one would some benignant spirit who had suddenly materialised and transformed one's existence.

Following the success of the *Childermass* broadcast, Bridson persuaded Harman Grisewood, Controller of the Third Programme, to commission Lewis to complete the drama. A visit was arranged to Broadcasting House to discuss the details. 'Grisewood could not have been more appreciative or encouraging', Bridson recalled:

> He told Lewis that he hoped he would always feel free to come and address the Third Programme audience on any subject he chose. Lewis thanked him, courteously but noncommittally. Did he listen regularly to the Third Programme? he was asked. No, said Lewis, he was afraid not. Had he at least got a radio set which received it clearly? Grisewood enquired, obviously prepared to arrange for the loan of one if not.

Lewis's response to the enquiry would have left Grisewood and Bridson wondering whether it was genuine or affected unworldliness. 'Oh yes,' he said gravely, 'I have a wireless set, but perhaps I had better get it *filled.*'

B. H. Gray of the BBC's Copyright Department particularised the arrangements of the commission. The author would receive an advance of one thousand pounds. Half would be paid him immediately and half after six months 'providing that the work is going on satisfactorily'. When it was finished, it would be adapted for radio and broadcast before being published in book form. The thousand pounds would be 'worked off' in performance fees of £120 for the existing part 1 of the drama, and £160 for the remainder still to be written. Repeat broadcasts within seven days of the original performances would be paid for at half the performance fee and repeats thereafter at the full rate.

Whilst welcoming this new form of patronage, Lewis was under no illusions that it would radically improve the conditions of life for himself and his wife:

> the support that I am receiving from the B.B.C. generous as it is, will when income tax has been deducted not amount to more than about twelve pounds ten a week. Since more than half of this must go on rent, heating and lighting, not much will be left for the additional expenses entailed by the condition of my eyes, not to speak of food and other normal expenses.

*

They lived at 254 Vauxhall Bridge Road for no more than two months. Lewis's only explanation for their move back to Notting Hill was that Ashley Mansions was 'too noisy'. Whether it was noise from neighbours or the roar of traffic four floors down that bothered them was not made clear. On 17 August 300 books, four bookcases, a table and sewing machine were transported to Notting Hill Gate by a removals firm for £4. On surrendering the tenancy Lewis and his wife left owing the landlady £70 in back-rent. This did not include outstanding accounts for telephone, electricity and gas. A month later Miss MacKusick instructed her Estate Agent to contact her former tenant and demand the sum of £97 15s. in complete settlement and to place on record that he had 'committed a serious breach of one of the covenants set down in the Tenancy Agreement'.

Back at 29A, the luxury of Ashley Mansions' lift was exchanged for the familiar wearying flights of stone steps. The studio above the flat remained unused, or unusable, and Lewis rented a work room some short distance away in Ladbroke Road, opposite the Mercury Theatre. The landlady was coincidentally connected with an institution recently familiar to him. Margaret Ruth Dix was a Fellow of the Royal College of Surgeons and Clinical Assistant at the National Hospital for Nervous Diseases in Queen Square. Her specialist field being diagnosis of disorders to the inner ear, however, made it unlikely she would have previously come into close professional contact with her tenant.

It is not known how long Lewis rented the work room, nor precisely what work was performed there, but at least two monthly payments of £9 changed hands and there was ample time for him to become suspicious about the visits of a housekeeper in his absence. Following remarks made over the phone and demands that no further access be granted this individual, Miss Dix wrote to reassure him that Mrs McGrath was an entirely reliable, careful and trustworthy person and that she had been given special instructions, as with Miss Dix's own papers, that no books or documents were to be touched.

*

At the time of writing 'The Sea-Mists of the Winter', Lewis claimed to be working on two books, 'one a novel, the other an art book'. These, he assured his readers, would be completed with the aid of a dictaphone. The device, trade-named 'The Tapewriter', was the latest thing in office equipment, weighing between 25 and 30 pounds and about the size of a portable typewriter. It could record up to half an hour's dictation at a time onto a tape contained in cassette form that could be unclipped and replaced without the necessity of rethreading. A small hand microphone 'for close talking' was included and equipped with a button to be compressed during dictation and released to instantly stop recording.

The impressive, wedge-shaped machine resting on a little round gate-leg table in front of him, Lewis posed gamely for a photograph, leaning forward with microphone gripped in his left hand, as if in the act of dictating prose directly onto magnetic tape. But although reliably informed that many American writers, 'possessing ordinary visual powers', found the immediacy of this method of composition useful, it proved uncongenial for Lewis. Another photograph taken during the same session showed him in more characteristic writing mode.

His armchair was backed by shelves of books, while ashtray, matches and cigarettes lay to his right on the little table with its two circular surfaces that had figured in portraits of Pound, Tangye, Symons and Eliot. To his left was a slender standard lamp, its dark metal shade reminiscent of the storm cone that had once, enigmatically, adorned the pages of *Blast*. He sat with a drawing board aslant his knees on which lay a foolscap pad.

This was the way the blind man wrote. Anchoring the top corner of the uppermost sheet with the index, middle and third fingers of his left hand, he placed the ball-point pen against the tip of his index finger. Having established the starting point, three finger breadths from the top of the page, he could move the bunched fingers down so that the third now occupied the position, against the ball-point, that the index had done. The ball-point was now poised ready to write. He wrote the words:

FINAL CHAPTER

He returned the ball-point to the tip of his index finger, being careful to keep it in position on the paper while he moved the three fingers down again until the third rested against the ball-point. He then drew a horizontal line across the page separating the block capitals from what was to come next before he placed ball-point against index finger once more and shifted the three fingers further down the page's margin.

Four words:

Lewis sat at the

comprised his first line of text following the underscored block-lettered heading. He had intended to write five words. Early ball-point pens were erratic tools and the Biro that Stella Newton had given him was apt to withhold its flow of ink occasionally for no apparent reason. He had intended to write:

Miss Lewis sat at the

but the ball-point failed to ink the first word. The Biro might cease to function altogether and, oblivious, he could scrawl laboriously across several pages of unsullied whiteness before his wife, or Agnes Bedford, came to collect the manuscript for typing and noticed the fault. Then all would have to be written again.

The ball-point once more three fingers down from the first line, he wrote the second:

tea-table under the large tree

There was a comma and he returned the ball-point to the left-hand side of the paper, against the index finger, slid the three fingers down before continuing:

and her three companions were

In this way he completed the page with another three lines:

all smiling at her in silence. Miss
Lewis's face lost its
disciplined calm and she

He dropped the page to the floor and, inscribing a number two in the top right corner of the next sheet, he was ready to carry on with:

darted a hostile look

He thought better of it and, three finger breadths down, wrote:

hostile eye at the bearded face

and below that, finished the sentence:

in front of her.

There were other ways of writing blind and ensuring the lines of script did not converge. Tomlin recalled him keeping to the line by sliding his thumb down the left margin. The distance between lines would then have been from thumb tip to knuckle perhaps. Another account has him stretching a wire across the page to slide the pen along, then lowering the wire to achieve the requisite spacing. In August he received news of the existence in New Zealand of a simple wooden frame to hold a writing pad, and a moveable wooden guide to keep the lines of handwriting from amalgamating. He may have experimented with a number of methods.

In October he wrote to Bridson explaining a long silence:

My desire to get everything out of the way in order to begin the full-scale work on Childermass II has caused me to live a hermit's life. Two days ago, I had not been out for ten days. My beard reaching an ambitious length . . . My nails . . . grown so long they kept catching in things . . . I am completing the long novel . . . My wife and I have been extremely hard at it.

The 'long novel' had been gestating since the war. In 1946 it was called *Chateau Rex* and Editions Poetry London contracted to publish it. That agreement having been cancelled in 1947, another contract was signed with Hutchinson for the same novel, this time entitled *The Victory of Albert Temple*. Then, on 14 September 1951, a month before he described to Bridson his 'hermit's life', Katherine Webb at Hutchinson wrote demanding repayment of the £225 advanced him in 1947 for the book they had now, over three years later, given up hope of receiving. The letter concluded peevishly:

> Furthermore, we note that Methuens are announcing a new book entitled ROTTING HILL from your pen, and this seems to us very unfair in the circumstances.

He was able to placate Mrs Webb, informing her that *Rotting Hill* was not a novel but a book of short stories, and assuring her that, despite his having recently lost his sight, he was 'working extremely hard, and all the time' on the novel for Hutchinson and hoped to finish it 'in one month'.

The laboriously blind-written FINAL CHAPTER, beginning with Miss Lewis's three companions smiling at her across a tea-table, was just one of a number of alternative final chapters for this same novel. When it was eventually published in April 1954, no comparable passage and no character by the name of 'Miss Lewis' was to be found in it.

*

Rotting Hill was published on 29 November 1951. The title derived from a coinage of Ezra Pound's and the stories chronicled aspects of Britain under its first Labour government, thrown out of power by the Conservatives in a general election only a month before the book was published. Most of the stories were autobiographical, all were political. 'The Rot' was a memoir of the eradication of *Merulius lacrymans* from the timbers of 29A Notting Hill Gate seen as a microcosmic class-war. 'The Room Without a Telephone' combined a fictionalised version of his experience in St Vincent's Clinic, the Catholic nursing home, scene of the bloody mass extraction of his teeth in 1950, with jaundiced observations upon the newly formed National Health Service. Some stories were the thinly disguised experiences of recent friends and acquaintances. Henry Swabey, an advocate of Social Credit, 'damn good man, one of the Few', according to Ezra Pound, was Vicar of Lindsell in Essex, where he founded an independent school when the local Education Authority closed the old one down. In 'Parents and Horses' he appeared as the Reverend Matthew Laming, enemy of 'Stateism' and leader of local resistance to the closure of a village school and transportation of children to a 'Central Rural Primary School' two miles away. And another clergyman friend, Willis Feast of Booten, near Norwich, served as the model for Samuel Rymer in 'The Bishop's Fool'.

There was even an affectionate portrait of the Lewises' neighbour in Studio C, Miss Blossom Hellyer:

> I met Blossom on her way from market who gave me a brilliant decent smile. She is a plump flower of the Cornish Riviera, a walking Matthew Smith. I loathe thin flowers and her luxurious bulk breasts the waves of Rottinghillers, flowing around the fish shop and the butcher's counter. Seen in the shops she is like a figurehead of a gallant ship, a Saxon Queen perhaps, moving irresistibly, gently cleaving the surging mass. She is my toast in her sky-blue mackintosh.

The book finished with a surreal walk through 'Rotting Hill', encountering friends, real and imaginary: Robert Colquhoun and MacBryde, Roy Campbell, Augustus John and finally:

> Britannia . . . wore . . . a 'liberty-cap' (hired from Moss Bros.). Once so robust, she was terribly shrunken: some wasting disease, doubtless malignant. The trident now employed as a crutch, she held out a mug for alms. I saw in the mug what looked like a phoney dollar bill, and I dropped myself a lucky threepenny bit. I would give my last threepenny bit to poor old Britannia. In a cracked wheeze she sang 'Land of Hope and Glory.' I must confess that this last apparition, and its vulgar little song, rather depressed me.

*

Towards the end of that year, a letter arrived from Dr C. R. Morris, Vice Chancellor of the University of Leeds. At a meeting of the Court of the University to be held on Wednesday, 19 December, it would be proposed to offer for Lewis's acceptance the degree of Doctor of Letters *honoris causa*. The conferment of the degree would take place on Thursday, 15 May 1952. Before making this proposal to the Court, the Vice Chancellor was writing to ask whether it would be agreeable to Lewis to receive this degree from the University and to come to the ceremony for it to be conferred upon him. He very much hoped that Lewis would accept and, until the Court met, he would regard this communication as private and confidential.

Lewis had, in fact, been considered for this honour twice before. In 1949 and again in 1950, Bonamy Dobrée, Professor of English Literature at

Leeds, had, in recommending him, stressed Lewis's considerable influence upon the writing and thought of his generation. The following year Professor Dobrée 'once more very strongly' recommended his candidate and suggested that 'to give him an honorary doctorate would reflect honour upon this university'.

Each year the minutes of the Honorary Degrees Committee recorded Lewis's name among those it had decided 'to omit from consideration on the present occasion'.

Curiously, Professor Dobrée had not read 'The Sea-Mists of the Winter' when he again put forward Lewis's name for the Committee's consideration in November 1951. But three days later he wrote to the Vice Chancellor:

> Since sending in my recommendation . . . I have heard that he has gone blind . . . I know, of course, that an appeal ad misericordiam constitutes no ground for an honorary degree: but at the same time I feel that to offer it to him now would be a timely act and a humane gesture.

The following week the Honorary Degrees Committee agreed that Lewis be made a Doctor of Letters. His fellow graduands for this honour were to be Miss Margot Fonteyn the ballerina, and the author of *Swallows and Amazons*, Mr Arthur Ransome.

When official notification of the Court's decision arrived, Lewis made his official acceptance to the Registrar by telegram:

> THANK YOU FOR INFORMING ME OF THE GREAT HONOUR WHICH HAS BEEN DONE ME

The Times announced the news on 28 December and described him as 'Mr P. Wyndham Lewis, American author and artist'.

The question of his nationality was of considerable importance to Lewis at this particular time. He was shortly to be the recipient of another honour, somewhat more lucrative than a Doctorate of Letters, and one for which British citizenship was a necessary prerequisite.

Civil List pensions were granted by the King or Queen on the recommendation of the Prime Minister of the day to those who by their useful discoveries in science or their attainments in literature and the arts 'merited the gracious consideration of their Sovereign and the gratitude of their country'. Under the Civil List Act of 1937, £2,500 a year was distributed by the Paymaster General's Office among such deserving cases.

During the previous year Naomi Mitchison had been instrumental, through her husband, the Labour MP for Kettering, in getting her friend's name put forward. She had sent Lewis the preliminary application forms in

April, and a month later informed him that various Honourable Members were putting their names down as his sponsors. 'You are a British citizen, aren't you?' she asked him. 'That is essential.'

So when *The Times* described him as an 'American author and artist', it was not only interests of factual accuracy that necessitated a reply:

> I am, of course, not an American. Metropolitan birth could not be assured in the days of the 'Empire upon which the sun never sets', I happened to be born in America more years ago than I care to remember.

The letter was signed, inexplicably, 'P. J. Wyndham Lewis'.

*

On 29 February 1952 he was informed that the Queen, on the Prime Minister's recommendation, had been pleased to award him a Civil List Pension of £250 per annum in recognition of his services to literature and art. Geoffrey Cass of the Prime Minister's office wrote that he would be glad to know whether this proposal was acceptable to Lewis and that an early reply to his letter would be appreciated.

FIFTY-ONE

'So lonely an honour'

In March, Katherine Webb at Hutchinson received a letter from Lewis and finally gave up hope of ever receiving *The Victory of Albert Temple*. She was sorry to learn that the novel, commissioned in 1947, was 'still hanging fire' and that he felt he could give no definite delivery date. This was a great disappointment to her 'after such a long wait'. Mrs Webb asked him for a cheque drawn in Hutchinson's favour to the sum of £225, together with his half of the contract. On his repayment of the advance, she promised to forward him, by return, the counterpart agreement, duly cancelled.

She was unaware that, on an afternoon a little less than a fortnight before, J. Alan White, at Methuen, had returned to his office after a brief absence to find a typescript lying on his desk. It was the third and final part of a novel that Lewis was now calling *A Man Cannot Kill Himself Twice*, and which Methuen would eventually publish two years later. Although it was to undergo further changes of title, Mrs Webb would have been annoyed to learn that this was, essentially, the same novel for which Lewis had professed himself unable to give her a definite delivery date in early 1952.

A story told by White in the mid-1960s suggests that Lewis had offered the book to Methuen as early as the autumn of the previous year, at the same time as he was placating Mrs Webb, urging patience and promising to have the novel finished for her 'in one month'. White's story went as follows:

> I well remember receiving the typescript of this book, and before I had finished reading it receiving a visit from Lewis demanding it back because he had thought of a better way to end it. He 'had it back' for six months: then he brought it in again, put the parcel down on my desk, remarked, 'This is as good as any book I have ever written', and a moment later got up to leave. 'That's all I think. Do produce it well.' And off he went.

Having thought of 'a better way to end it', Lewis would have only needed to take back Part III of the novel, and it was this rewritten section that, six months later, on 21 February 1952, White found lying on his desk. The publisher's recollection differs in only two respects from the facts. First,

Lewis did not deliver the revised typescript in person. And second, presumably in deference to the author's blindness, White made arrangements to visit him at home a week later to discuss the novel. Lewis's remarks about it being as good a book as any he had ever written and his urging to 'produce it well' may have been made on that occasion.

Methuen's publication of the long-awaited novel ensured a uniformity of imprint for the last six of Lewis's books, along with four reissues, published in his lifetime. But a more material consideration for the change of publisher was that the £450 advance on royalties he received from Methuen was double that which he then had to refund Hutchinson.

*

The forthcoming Leeds solemnities called for hasty qualification of a paragraph in the Conclusion to *The Writer and the Absolute*, due to be published later in the year by Methuen.

'By maintaining the highest technical standards in his work, and even more by austerely refraining from all watering down, sweetening, or in other ways rendering more popularly palatable, and of course by never departing from the truth as it shows itself to him, a writer cannot receive more than the barest worldly reward', Lewis had declared high-mindedly before learning what Leeds University had in store for him. The passage continued:

> But the place of honour, as I have never failed to recognise, is outside. Honours make any man suspect. At least of that I am blameless.

A footnote was inserted into the proofs anticipating the potential contradiction to this claim that he feared would exist by the time the book was published:

> I hope that being made a Doctor of Literature of the University of Leeds (15 May, 1952) will not be seen, by the watchful, as a symptom of demoralisation. It is so lonely an honour that it may be forgiven by the most austere.

When *The Writer and the Absolute* was published in June, however, Lewis had thereby inadvertently anticipated the honour by five months. The death of George VI in February plunged the Palace into official Court mourning until 31 May, and because the Princess Royal, sister to the late King, was to preside as Chancellor, the University authorities were forced to postpone the Congregation until the following November.

*

For the first few months of 1952, and at other times during that year, Lewis seemed to be spending occasional periods apart from his wife. Delays in maintaining correspondence were symptomatic of this dislocation in his domestic affairs. *The Times*'s description of him as an American was allowed to stand unchallenged for ten days, and tardy replies to letters sent him at Kensington Gardens Studios were excused by his having been 'moving about'.

On New Year's Day came the first indication that he was to be found elsewhere than Notting Hill Gate. He told Eliot that 44 Eaton Mews North would be his address 'for some weeks'. Making arrangements to dine at a nearby restaurant, he added: 'Froanna, by the way, may not be able to come.'

However, later in January the Lewises were together in their flat when a young student from St Martin's School of Art came to visit.

The third son of the Reverend Sir Henry Denny of Burwash Rectory in Sussex, Robyn Denny was to make a name for himself at the Royal College of Art five years later through being denounced by John Minton as an 'Angry Young Man'. Denny retaliated by scrawling 'Eden Come Home' in bitumen across a sheet of hardboard and setting fire to it. But in January 1952, unacquainted with such up-to-the-minute painting techniques, he had just embarked upon his second term at St Martin's School of Art in the Charing Cross Road when someone walked into the life room and shouted his name. Then:

Mr Wyndham Lewis is on the telephone asking to speak to you.

This, also shouted for all to hear, gave the 22-year-old considerable kudos among his fellow students. When he picked up the receiver Lewis said that he understood Denny to have a painting for him and would he care to come over and deliver it.

Hubert Hilton, formerly Herman Hildesheim, paying guest of the Reverend and Lady Denny, had entrusted the early portrait of his Slade School colleague to the Rector's son and informed Lewis it would be delivered in a day or two. 'Robyn, who is a particularly nice young fellow,' he added, 'is very intrigued by the honour of being introduced to you. I hope you will find him an agreeable visitor.'

Almost 50 years later, Denny remembers little of this, nor of a subsequent couple of visits. He thinks it strange he has no recollection of what they talked about and only the haziest memory of their surroundings. One impression remains, however, of 'a bleak domestic atmosphere' as he sat opposite the blind old man with a backdrop of bookshelves and his wife in protective attendance to one side. He remembers Lewis thanking him for the portrait and asking him to convey his apologies to Mr Hilton because he could not see and could therefore make no comment upon it.

The following month there was a further separation. Ashley Dukes knocked in vain at the door of Studio A, while Mrs Lewis stood silently inside and waited for him to give up and go away. 'My wife, unless she knows who it is, does not answer the door', Lewis explained later to his thwarted visitor. She informed her husband 'that an unidentifiable neighbour had left a parcel and a letter outside.' About the same time Bridson wrote to Lewis at Agnes Bedford's place and concluded his letter: 'Regards to Froanna. Hope she is feeling better.'

Eaton Mews was the address Lewis gave the Prime Minister's Office in early March when he wrote to inform Geoffrey Cass that the proposal to grant him a Civil List Pension of £250 in recognition of his services to literature and art was indeed acceptable to him. And he was still in Agnes Bedford's cramped quarters in mid-March when he wrote to Ackerley and told him to 'note above change of address.'

It is not clear how serious this separation was. Since husband and wife appeared, on the evidence of letters to friends, to be in regular contact, it seems to have been an amicable arrangement between Gladys and Agnes Bedford to share the burden of caring for Lewis.

Whatever interpretation is placed on the separation, it abruptly came to an end in late March. On the 27th, Lewis wrote again to Geoffrey Cass in connection with his Civil List Pension. The 'permanent address' given in his previous communication 'was not quite so stable as [he] thought' and the following week he announced to Bridson:

> Froanna and I have terminated our visits and are now at the traditional Rotting Hill address.

For about a month and a half relations returned to normal. Invitations to dinner were extended. Geoffrey Wagner, a nephew of Edward Wadsworth, was in London from the States and visited with a present of stockings for Mrs Lewis, 'American Du Pont and so beautifully dark', with which generosity she professed herself 'enchanted'. Geoffrey Grigson was summoned to 'the old address' for 'tea or dinner' and cautioned to wear footwear protective against the emissions of a neighbour's pet:

> There is a big white bullterrier, and there are large honey coloured lakes, supplying our corridors with what they have always lacked.

Then, in late June, there was another separation, more acrimonious than the last, marked as it was, this time, by a solicitor's letter. The firm of Ernest W. Long & Co. wrote to 'Mrs Windrum Lewis'. They had been consulted by her husband 'about the unhappy position' which had arisen and he had given instructions for a £6 postal order to be sent to her 'to meet any immediate need of cash for food and necessities'. Ernest W. Long & Co. promised to write to her again, when they had fuller instructions from their client, concerning collection from the Notting Hill flat of 'certain things' he would be needing 'and also about the situation generally'.

There was no clue as to what had caused the rift, although this may have been the occasion he telephoned Joyce Bridson, to say he had left home and was to be found at Agnes Bedford's place:

It's not good enough when your wife throws the frying pan at you. When you're blind you can't see when to duck.

But shortly after, the Lewises were receiving visitors as before. Gerty Cori was over from St Louis and wrote thanks for dinner, as did Geoffrey Bridson. In late July he and his wife were 'still talking of Froanna's cooking'. They were regular recipients of lavish hospitality at this time. 'Lewis prided himself upon serving the best food and drink obtainable,' Bridson recalled, 'and Froanna was a really excellent cook.'

*

Another guest, E.W.F. Tomlin, recorded an insight into the Lewises' sanitary arrangements, derived from what he described as 'paying a visit . . . backstage':

A request to go to the bathroom was always preceded by a hurried and slightly embarrassed tidying up expedition . . . Turning from the water-closet to wash one's hands, one was surprised to find no wash basin. At the same time, the sound of gushing water, quite distinct from that of the last gasps of flushing, served to direct one's attention downwards: whereupon one perceived a liberal jet of liquid issuing from the wide-mouthed bath tap, of which one was obviously intended to make use.

Unable to understand why neither Lewis nor his wife ever insisted upon having a basin installed, Tomlin put it down to 'something unpractical about both of them'. He cannot have known of the hazardous complexities in the antiquated plumbing system running through the warren of dwellings that was Kensington Gardens Studios.

On an autumn Sunday morning in 1952, the waste-pipe serving both the kitchen sink on the same floor as the abandoned studio, and the bath below it, became blocked. This had happened before and a succession of plumbers had explained that the waste-pipe was too narrow and that a section of it, underneath the Lewises' flat, unaccountably twisted up and down no fewer than five times. This, combined with the narrowness of the pipe, made blockages a certainty. That Sunday morning, the kitchen tap upstairs had been left running and eventually, unable to negotiate the blockage in the labyrinthine waste-pipe, the trapped water backed up through the bath's plug-hole. The bath filled, overflowed and leaked down through the ceiling of Studio D.

But this was as nothing compared to the major inundation that occurred only two days later. Lewis and his wife were roused by firemen pounding on their door around midnight and told they were 'flooding the people downstairs' again. This time, however, a thorough search of Studio A revealed no sign of anything untoward. Then the plump Blossom from Studio C appeared and reported sounds of rushing water in Studio B. The firemen gained access through an open window. Studio B had been empty for some time and the new tenant, one Minnie Tabor, had not finished moving in her possessions. She was not there that Tuesday night but had left the bathroom tap running. Studio B's waste-pipe also being blocked, the bath was overflowing and Studio D flooding again from another direction. It took the firemen until 4.30 in the morning to drain off all the water.

Over a year later Lewis communicated this detailed critique of domestic plumbing to his solicitor in order to forestall possible damage claims, arguing that the more serious deluge had originated elsewhere.

*

In September Miss Selby, Secretary for Hospitality at Leeds University, gave the prospective Honorary Doctor of Letters finalised details of the November conferment. Accommodation had been arranged for him at the home of the University Librarian, who rejoiced in the name of Page: Bertram Samuel Page. There was to be a small dinner party in the University refectory on the Tuesday evening, given by the Vice Chancellor, for honorary graduands, their wives, their hosts and the professors who would be presenting them for their degrees. The next day, before the ceremony, a luncheon in their honour would be held in the Queen's Hotel. Members of Senate and their wives, members of Council and their wives and a number of other distinguished guests were invited and the Chancellor, HRH the Princess Royal, was to preside. At this luncheon a toast to 'The

Honorary Graduands' would be proposed and Lewis was asked to be one of the two responders. The ceremony itself would take place in the Town Hall at 3 p.m., after which a tea party was to be provided by the Lord Mayor and Lady Mayoress at the Civic Hall opposite. Afterwards Lewis could either return to London or spend an extra night with Mr and Mrs Page.

Eliciting no reply, Miss Selby wrote again three weeks later. This time Lewis responded by return of post, addressing her, as he did throughout their correspondence, as 'Mr Selby' and proffering the familiar apology that he had 'been moving about' and mislaid her first letter. He asked her to convey his thanks to Mr and Mrs Page for their kind offer of hospitality but 'for various reasons' he and his wife would prefer to stay in a hotel.

This was the first Miss Selby had heard of a wife. She had made 'extensive enquiries', she told Page, 'and nobody seemed to think he was married.' There was, she pointed out, 'no mention whatsoever of his ever having been married in *Who's Who*!' And she blamed that all too fallible reference work for the oversight when she wrote to assure Lewis that no discourtesy had been intended in not including his wife in the invitation to the ceremony and attendant festivities.

Lewis replied that he was aware his name figured in *Who's Who*, and added, mysteriously, that if those responsible had not stated he was married, it could not be that they were unaware of the fact. He conceded that he ought to have informed Miss Selby that his wife would be coming. Indeed, he went on, if she were not coming then he should be unable to do so either, because he was blind.

Whilst regarding it as 'quite inexcusable' that Lewis had not replied until this late date, Miss Selby felt that the burden of looking after the blind old man had been lifted from her shoulders and that it was better for all concerned that a wife had been found to accompany him. 'It will make things very much easier for us,' she told the Librarian, 'and you will be relieved of the responsibility of giving him hospitality. I am sure that you and Mrs Page will not feel very upset about this.' She added that even though the Pages were not after all to act as hosts, they might still take advantage of their invitation to the Vice Chancellor's dinner on the Tuesday evening.

Lewis had asked Miss Selby to reserve him a twin-bedded room with bath and toilet, 'if that is a common thing in Leeds Hotels', he added. The University was not liable for the expense of accommodation beyond the hospitality already offered him by the librarian and his wife, and so when Miss Selby made the reservation she informed the Queen's Hotel Reception Clerk that the account would be paid by Mr Wyndham Lewis personally.

*

Back in April, Miss Selby asked Lewis to give her his full Christian names, as these would be needed for the programme. She asked for the information again three weeks later and received the reply that 'Wyndham Lewis' were the only two names he used professionally and that he did not think any other names should appear in the programme. In October he reiterated the injunction. He preferred not to be described as 'P. Wyndham Lewis', he told Miss Selby. And then came the odd proviso that, if initials had to be used, 'P.J. would have been better than P.'*

*

There is a photograph of Lewis being presented to the earnestly smiling Countess Harewood, the Princess Royal, before luncheon at the Queen's Hotel in Leeds on 12 November. As he shook her white-gloved hand, his round head was lowered deferentially to a level with her own. Behind him stood Mrs Lewis, grimly protective, wearing a formidably hat-pinned creation on her head and a large mink stole draped across her shoulders. The corners of her mouth drawn down, she appeared to be regarding suspiciously the white-haired man with his back to the camera, probably Professor Dobrée, who was introducing her husband to the late King's sister.

At the luncheon a toast to 'The Honorary Graduands' was proposed and Sir Cyril Hinshelwood, an Oxford Professor of Chemistry, was called upon to reply. When Sir Cyril sat down, Lewis was to rise and give the second reply.

Miss Selby had told him that he should thank the University on behalf of his fellow graduands for the honours that were shortly to be bestowed upon them. Thereafter he was to feel free to say exactly what he liked so long as he did not speak for longer than ten minutes. 'We work to a close timetable', Miss Selby explained:

> The lunch itself is timed to end at 2 pm, the three speeches . . . are timed to end by 2.30 pm. We have to leave at once for the Town Hall to enable people to have time to robe . . . and to form the procession.

He was told that, four years ago, Edith Sitwell had cast this delicate

* In the *Encyclopaedia Britannica Year Book* for 1952 which records the conferment of his Civil List Pension, his full name, presumably taken from official records pertaining to the award, was given as 'Percy James Wyndham Lewis'. This would seem to confirm that the signature 'P. J. Wyndham Lewis' at the bottom of his letter to *The Times* in late 1951 was not a misprint. However, these, along with the letter to Miss Selby, are the only instances of this initial or forename being used.

schedule into confusion by delivering a long lecture on the writing of English poetry. 'One of the most important things', Miss Selby gently impressed on him, 'is not to over-run 10 minutes.'

There is no record of what he said, nor how long he took to say it, when he rose to follow the Oxford Professor of Chemistry. Lewis was never the most fluent of public speakers and, in the past, would have prepared a detailed script marked with pauses, even indications of gesture. But this was the first time he had been called upon to address a large gathering since becoming blind, and written notes would now have been useless to him. It is unlikely therefore that his reply to the health of 'The Honorary Graduands' would have been more than perfunctory.

Later, gowned in scarlet at the Town Hall, he received a rousing introduction from the man who, at the third year of trying, had secured him this honour. Lewis wrote to Bonamy Dobrée a day or so later, complimenting him on the clarity and eloquence of his delivery and declaring himself 'pleased and flattered' by the speech:

> Your Royal Highness and Chancellor: For those involved in literature or the visual arts, the name of Wyndham Lewis is linked with the group containing Joyce, Eliot, Pound, Picasso and Juan Gris, which did battle against the dry, bald and sere conventions which bade fair to stifle creative activity in the early years of this century. He was their first furious publicist in his magazine *Blast*, which in 1914 applied dynamite to the dovecotes of the complacent. But his fierce intellectual vigour could not be contained in any group; and in his journal of the late 'twenties, properly named *The Enemy*, he declared implacable war on all mass-movements, on all cliques – platoons, in his view, of 'apes of God' corroding the truth of the artistic vision, ever beckoning to the dark abyss of convention against which his free spirit revolted in contempt.

At the mention of 'apes of God', some of Professor Dobrée's listeners may have recalled one of the prime targets of Lewis's satire, on whom the female 'ape', Lady Harriet Finnian Shaw, was based, and whose lecture on the writing of English poetry had kept them so long over luncheon four years before. They would have been aware that it was Professor Dobrée himself who had on that occasion proposed and presented Edith Sitwell for her Honorary Doctorate, and who was now, even-handedly, championing the enemy camp:

> Ceaselessly directing the burning light of emotional and intellectual integrity on society, the arts and criticism, in his many works ... he ruthlessly examined vulgar assumptions and the usually applauded

hypocrisies. He continues to do so with fearless satiric energy. The vices he attacks are unlikely ever to die out; what will certainly remain is his own creative work, strikingly original and seminal, as *Tarr* and *The Wild Body*; and finally that triumphant fantasy, yet to be concluded, *Childermass*, which after some twenty years is at length beginning to filter into the general mind as a masterpiece at once creative and profoundly critical. In painting, his work is original, strong and generative. Early in recognising the intuitive importance of abstract art and of cubism, he adapted them to his own purpose, awakening us to a new vision of the forms around us; and in the realm of portraiture infusing into his canvas a vivid reality which might be called stark, were it not so full-bodied, so nervously actual. In both arts he has exerted an influence, itself a tribute to his genius; thus it is because he is not only a great artist but also a great power, that, Your Royal Highness and Chancellor, I pray you to confer upon WYNDHAM LEWIS the Degree of Doctor of Letters *honoris causa*.

Knowledge that Edith Sitwell had been honoured by the same institution in May 1948 did not sour the experience. Lewis did, however, discourage friends from calling him Doctor. 'When I remember that this sort of academic honour is conferred upon every political blackguard', he told White, 'it has not the same appeal for me as it has for Miss E.S.'

Edith Sitwell was known to chide anyone leaving off her Litt.D. from the envelope when writing to her. After receiving a second honorary doctorate, from Durham, she insisted upon the designation 'Litt.D., Litt.D.'

Eliot told him that the first honorary doctorate he was awarded came from Leeds in 1939 and that, thereafter, other Universities had followed suit at an average rate of one a year. By 1952 he had fourteen. In Lewis's case the chain reaction did not occur, and this remained, as he had described it in the footnote on page 196 of *The Writer and the Absolute*, 'so lonely an honour'.

FIFTY-TWO

'Does he not mean Self-Condemned?'

In December, Lewis had been promised by Methuen that the proofs of his novel, once called *Chateau Rex*, then later *The Victory of Albert Temple*, and now sporting the unwieldy title *Are you perhaps a Fool, my son!*, would be ready for him to correct 'just before Christmas'.

When they failed to materialise he tried, throughout January, to reach Alan White by telephone. He left messages but received no response. Eventually, and the effect on Lewis's prickly sensibilities was like 'a slap in the face', a telephonist relayed his name to the Managing Director and returned with the message: 'Mr White says he is busy, and cannot speak to you.'

In February he was told that White had gone to Australia, but that proofs of the novel would arrive 'in two or three weeks time'. They did not. By the end of March, White had returned from his travels but either did not receive, or chose to ignore, Lewis's messages. Then in April, Lewis sent him a note requesting a meeting as he had 'several things' he wished to talk about. On a separate matter he enclosed a cutting from the *Daily Mirror* for 27 March. 'I think something ought to be done', he wrote and asked White to let him have the cutting back.

No more than a mile away, to the northwest of Kensington Gardens Studios, the first corpses had come to light three days before that issue of the *Mirror*. Scantily clad women, strangled and probably worse, had been stuffed into a kitchen alcove behind a flimsy partition, wallpapered over for disguise. The newspaper-buying public was already agog at the grisly revelations of what journalists were now referring to as 'The House of Murder' at the blind end of a cul-de-sac called Rillington Place.

Lionel Crane was covering the sociological background to the case for the *Mirror*. Notting Hill had a reputation for violent death, he declared, going back to the 1930s and, beyond that, to a time when highwaymen, vagabonds and murderers infested the area. As John Reginald Halliday Christie's sinister activities were exposed, Crane conjured up a seedy underworld of cafés, popular music, tea and teddy boys:

It was a big night last night in the Juke Box Cafe in London's Notting Hill district. Frankie Laine and Johnnie Ray bellowed at the top of their voices. Teenage boys in American-type drape suits lolled against the tea and sandwich counter. The balls in the pin table in the corner clicked busily.

He described the crime-ridden area as lying 'only a cosh throw from some of Kensington's most elegant streets'. He heard of a local shop being wrecked by a gang of youths, the shopkeeper's wife pelted with bottles. He saw the leader of such a gang, barely out of short trousers but carrying a car's starting handle as a weapon. 'Police now regard it as Black Spot Number One and locally they have given it a change of name to Rotting Hill.'

The headline of the article was a mock-up of a street sign:

The Royal Borough of Kensington
ROTTING HILL, W.11.

This was the cutting that Lewis sent to his publisher with the vague injunction that 'something ought to be done'.

*

There was a more pressing concern for Lewis at this time than a minor infringement of copyright. He was urgently in need of fresh funds.

He had, by now, written, 'at least in the rough', the two books intended to complete *The Childermass*. They were to be called *Monstre Gai* – 'this combination of words', he helpfully volunteered to I. A. Richards, 'from Voltaire' – and *Malign Fiesta*. Respectively of 300 and 250 published pages each, they were written in little more than a year but would require 'months of polishing'. When he managed to reach White by telephone in April, he asked for a further £100 to enable him to finish this work, for which Methuen had already paid him an advance of £300. Before White agreed to this, Lewis made a second appeal a few days later. He had, he said, given a far too optimistic account, during their phone conversation, of what he should need to properly finish the two books. 'When we wrote the agreement', he went on:

> I was so overjoyed that the 'Childermass' was at last to be finished, that I did not sit down and soberly work out how much money I should require to complete this difficult piece of writing.

At first he had thought that the £1,000 advanced him by the BBC would

598

enable him, not only to produce what was necessary for Bridson to convert into radio drama, but also to fulfil 'the much more exacting task' of finishing the writing for publication by Methuen. 'But I did not know at that time that I should be writing two full length books . . . The three hundred advance, to cover everything, would have been all right – I would even have accepted no advance at all,' he rather implausibly confided, 'if the B.B.C. money had proved adequate.' Under the circumstances, and 'dreadfully sorry', he was obliged to ask for a further £300 in advance. Of this, the £100 already requested was a matter of some urgency and he trusted White would get it to him as quickly as possible.

He was greatly dismayed by White's reply. The publisher was 'extremely sorry' but, having 'earnestly considered the problem', could advance no more on Part II of *The Childermass* than the £300 already received. In his defence, and to show that Methuen & Co. had, to date, 'not been backward in making advances', he drew the author's attention to unearned balances on the books published so far and to the advances on books as yet undelivered or, like the new novel, not yet published. This formed a total of £1,300.*

Lewis was particularly stung by mention, in terms he interpreted as reproachful, of the alarming grand total of outstanding advances. 'If a publisher is taking on a number of books of a writer like myself,' he argued, 'it is obvious that now and then, such a momentary collision of advances must occur, especially where books are commissioned and the publication considerably delayed.' And he returned to the vexed subject of his 'long novel', implying it was not his fault the largest outstanding advance was on a typescript White had by this time been in possession of for a year and which appeared no closer to being published.

In conclusion, and no doubt realising that White was immovable on the £300, he demanded £100: 'nothing to do with "Childermass", just a general advance'.

White wrote to say that, while 'a general advance' was not practicable, he was prepared to add a further £100 to the £300 already advanced so that the total of £400 be considered as the advance in respect of *Monstre Gai* and *Malign Fiesta*, and Lewis was to drop him a line if this was acceptable. Lewis would have telephoned but his telephone was out of order and it was, besides, of little importance to him if the money was described as a 'general advance' or as an advance on something specific so long as it was advanced him immediately:

Of course let it be that, if you prefer it that way.

* This did not include an extra £90 paid to Chatto & Windus, when rights were transferred to Methuen, in respect of unearned royalty balances on *Tarr, The Wild Body* and Part I of *The Childermass*.

599

His impatience for the money was apparent in the terse communication that, to save time, he had 'someone', probably Gladys, deliver to the Methuen office on 1 May:

> Would you be so kind as to send it as quickly as possible: it is, as I wrote you, urgent.

*

In a diary entry of 3 July, Dorothy Richards recorded her impressions of Lewis and his wife at a restaurant in Charlotte Street. Dorothy and her husband were in England on their regular summer visit from Harvard and, as they were to do in subsequent years, had arranged to dine with the Lewises. Between that early July in 1953 and the summer of 1956, she provided her diary with a brief annual bulletin, sympathetic but unsentimental, born as it was of no great personal liking, of his conversation, behaviour and deteriorating physical appearance.

When Mr and Mrs Richards got to the Restaurant de l'Etoile they found Lewis and Gladys waiting for them. This was not unusual as they were often early for engagements. Joyce Bridson recalled them arriving at her flat for dinner half an hour before they were expected and finding her still in her underwear. At the Etoile Mrs Lewis was sipping a gin. Dorothy found her 'pleasant' and thought she 'must have been very pretty' once. Lewis was 'very frail and faint'. Unaware she was describing characteristics of the hormonal changes brought about by his pituitary tumour, she remarked on 'that queer white skin, unlined face and hands'. The hands, she noticed, were 'beautifully manicured'. At dinner she found his expensive tastes irritating, especially as her husband would be picking up the bill. Demanding a half-bottle of 1935 or 1936 champagne for himself, she noted, he left the 'best part of a glass' untouched. Her general impression was that he had 'lost his vigour of phrase' and was a 'very pathetic shadow' and that the occasion 'all felt hollow'. There was, presumably, from Richards and perhaps from Mrs Lewis, a 'vein of flattery going on all the time'. Lewis made 'sly remarks about everybody' and Dorothy found this particularly distasteful when such remarks were aimed at Eliot, 'whom one knows has done a lot of nice things for him'. He told them more about the 'Tudor period' in Toronto, spoke warmly about his time at Assumption College and talked a lot about young Henry Ford in Detroit, 'whom', he assured them mysteriously, 'one could see a good deal of'. On matters of more immediate concern, he complained about Alan White at Methuen, who kept insulting him, and gave a progress report on Part II of *The Childermass*: he had 'got something written' of the two volumes and thought there might be another one to follow, but none were in a publishable state as yet.

At the end of the meal, and issuing from the restaurant, his vulnerability and lack of co-ordination became apparent. He was 'strangely unable to put his hat on or get into [the] taxi – a kind of complete loss of balance. Like an old frog the feeling he leaves you with.' Dorothy Richards's 1953 summer bulletin concluded: 'He seems to be completely lacking in the milk of human kindness.'

Later that month Gladys had a 'beastly accident' and dislocated her left arm. It was the second injury she had sustained within two and a half years, the first requiring a course of ten physiotherapy sessions in early 1951. X-rays were now taken of the stricken limb and it had to remain immobilised for some time. As a result of this catastrophe she was unable to type, and Lewis was still excusing lapses in his correspondence three months later: 'My wife received an injury to her arm', he told Hugh Kenner in October. 'This is rather as if I had my own right arm in a sling.' The injury was serious enough to warrant three guineas worth of treatment from Philip Newman, a Harley Street orthopaedic surgeon, and was still giving enough cause for concern at the beginning of December for her referral as a private patient to Professor Brian Wellingham Windeyer, Director of the Meyerstein Institute of Radiotherapy at the Middlesex Hospital.

*

In August, Lewis offered Methuen 'a short book on Extremism in the Visual Arts'. The matter was urgent. Having just heard White was going on holiday in two days' time, and 'owing to the economic difficulty' in which he found himself, it was imperative that Lewis 'immediately market' the work. 'Rapid publication', he added, 'would be essential for the success of the book.' This was a rather pointed reference to Methuen's far from 'rapid publication' of his novel, for which he was still awaiting proofs.

Two days later White took delivery of what perhaps proved to be his holiday reading: the typescript for a 30,000-word book concerned with a crisis in modern painting. This crisis was being brought about, Lewis believed, by contemporary artists pushing the limits of abstraction to a point beyond which art logically ceased to exist; 'driving the whole bag of tricks into a nihilistic nothingness or zero'. Methuen published *The Demon of Progress in the Arts* fifteen months later.

*

Three months after Alan White left for his holiday with the typescript of this diatribe against modernism, Lewis wrote to tell McLuhan that he had just received, 'one year after submitting the Ms', page-proofs of his novel. 'One year' was in fact a charitable estimate. It was closer to two. Then, in late December, there was a flurry of unaccustomed urgency from Methuen. White telephoned to say that the Book Society was prepared to 'recommend' the novel if publication could be in April. The opportunity of printing 'Recommended by the Book Society' somewhere on the dust wrapper was sufficient incentive to have it rushed to press without further delay. Not content with a telephone call, White expressed a letter to Lewis on 28 December to ensure it reached him the following morning. If the April deadline was to be met it was imperative the corrected proofs be returned during the following few days. The letter also contained first mention of the title which author and publisher had by now agreed on: not *Chateau Rex*; nor *The Victory of Albert Temple*; nor yet *You are perhaps a Fool, my son!*; nor even *A Man Cannot Kill Himself Twice*. Instead, it was to be called *Self Condemned*.

*

'The Hotel, first and last, is the central feature of the book,' Lewis told Michael Ayrton a month later, 'and the death of the Hotel gives you flames and ice, smoke, and ruin.' The Tudor Hotel had become the 'Hotel Blundell'. The fantastic conjunction of fire and ice which the Lewises witnessed on the morning of 15 February 1943, and which had effectively brought to an end their 'Tudor Period', now formed the climax of the middle section of the novel. Ayrton had been commissioned to design the dust wrapper and Lewis was sure it would be 'superb'. He hoped that White was 'not being too tiresome', and told his young friend that if the design required a particular colour that the publisher's budget would not run to, 'let me know, and I will see what I can do with him.'

But if Ayrton was constrained by printing costs, he made good use of the colour blocks available to him. The dust wrapper showed the 'central feature' of Lewis's book, the hotel, with one side sheathed in icicles, grey and black against white, the other side spouting a swirl of yellow flame and picked out with hot patches of red. A preliminary design had the towering building viewed from a conventional angle somewhere around street level. The finished version presented an aerial view, the vertiginous perspective enlarging a pair of upper windows to form the hollow eye sockets of a face.

Lewis pronounced himself satisfied, although Ayrton was never sure how the blind man acquired a sufficiently accurate impression to be satisfied or otherwise. He assumed that Mrs Lewis described the design in detail and Lewis, 'using his previous knowledge', constructed the image from her description.

Lewis need not have worried about White making difficulties for his protégé. There would be greater problems over the design for a reprint of *The Apes of God*.

Late the previous year Bernard Hanison, of Arco Publishers Limited, had noticed that 1955 would be the 25th anniversary of Lewis's gigantic satire. He approached Methuen in December and, having ascertained that White had no plans to publish the title, proposed to Lewis that Arco produce an edition limited to 1,000 signed and numbered copies. The author was to write an introduction and Ayrton to design the wrapper. Ayrton recalled that Hanison considered Lewis's original jacket design to be 'out of date', a judgement which drew from Lewis a grim laugh. Apart from the two innovations of introduction and 'up-to-date' jacket, Arco's would be a photographic facsimile of the 1930 Arthur Press edition. Even the retail price of the tome, after 25 years, was to remain unchanged at three guineas.

The contract, vetted by Lewis's solicitor, was signed in mid-March. He was given an advance of £175. But Ayrton's part in the enterprise got off to a bad start. Offered 15 guineas to execute the wrapper design, he demanded more, only to be told 15 guineas was all that was on offer for the job.

*

In March, Lewis received a letter from 10 Downing Street informing him that, on the Prime Minister's recommendation, the Queen had been pleased to award him a supplementary Civil List Pension of £150, with effect from 1 April, in addition to the £250 per annum he was already receiving. Again, he was asked to acknowledge the communication and to say whether the arrangement met with his approval. Lewis replied that he was grateful to the Prime Minister for recommending the increase. He added that 'to be receiving it from the hands of so personally great a man gives this public attribution an especial value'.

It is difficult to reconcile this glowing description of Sir Winston Churchill with the man he once slightingly described as an 'ex-Minister of State' and who, during a Royal Academy banquet 15 years before, delivered his 'passionate advocacy of platitude' at the expense of Lewis's rejected portrait of T. S. Eliot.

*

In the *Times Literary Supplement* of 16 April, Methuen was able to announce 'Two Book Society Recommendations' forthcoming from 36 Essex Street. One was Karl von Frisch's popular account of his discoveries in apian behaviour, *The Dancing Bees*. The other, *Self Condemned*, was published the following week in an edition of 3,000 copies, to largely favourable, often enthusiastic reviews. It was generally felt that the book's faults were far outweighed by its brilliance. L.A.G. Strong in *The Spectator* called it a 'vast novel, at its best magnificent, at its worst stupefying' and saw in it 'many signs that suggest further possibilities in the growth of an artist who, unequal though his work may always be, has lit his age with an occasional irritated lightning flash of genius.' John Biggs-Davison in *The Tablet* called it 'powerful, witty and withering'. The anonymous reviewer of the *TLS* said it lacked a satisfactory structure and that its digressions were 'tiresome' and impeded continuity. Nevertheless, he concluded, it was 'a brilliant, disorganised book, yet one which carries a compulsion to read it to the bitter end'.

L. P. Hartley welcomed it in the most glowing terms for *Time and Tide*, suggesting that, far from weakening the book, as other commentators suggested, by presenting the reader with so unlikeable a main protagonist as René Harding, Lewis had actually strengthened it:

> The fact that [Harding] can command our sympathy, as ultimately he does, by sheer integrity and without any appeal ad misericordiam, any soft spots for pity to light on, is a proof of the unswerving consistency with which Mr Wyndham Lewis has drawn his portrait.

Alan Pryce-Jones, writing for the *London Magazine*, and drawing upon acquaintance and conversation with Lewis in the late Forties to trace the novel's autobiographical roots, suggested that:

> things became too abominable . . . to be borne. The war itself, an exile not less disturbing than [his protagonist's], the Welfare State, the general collapse of good sense in international affairs, the rise of upstarts everywhere: Mr Lewis is not alone in finding all this a sore trial.

But he concluded that raw hatred was not conducive to the creation of a true work of art and that 'a point of repose' was needed, 'from which the excesses of the twentieth century can be seen with a calm satiric eye'. Lacking such a viewpoint the novel ultimately failed. Pryce-Jones nevertheless applauded its vigour, its lack of pretension and its refreshing break with the genteel tradition of the modern novel. Unable to control his instincts for tinkering with other men's prose, the literary editor of the *Times Literary Supplement*, who six years before had enraged Lewis by altering a book review and drawn down on his head sundry pages of blistering invective and threats of legal action, could not resist suggesting the insertion of a hyphen: '*Self Condemned* (does he not mean *Self-Condemned?*)'.

Patricia Hodgart also expressed mixed reactions in the *Manchester Guardian*. She found the first part 'tiresome and repetitive . . . sometimes like D. H. Lawrence at his very worst'. The middle section, however, contained some of the author's 'most astonishing and imaginative writing'. She concluded that: 'It is painful to read, but some unnecessary pain could be avoided if Mr Lewis were more critical of his prose style.'

Walter Allen, in the *New Statesman and Nation*, said it was one of Lewis's most powerful pieces of writing, 'at once terrifying and comic, comparable in its total effect to Kafka's *America*'. He ended by castigating others who reviewed it with anything less than admiration:

> It is, of course, superbly written, for of one kind of English prose, that which we associate first of all with Thomas Nashe, Mr Lewis is the modern master. This, it must be admitted, is not what one would gather from some reviewers of Mr Lewis's new novel, reading whom one can only echo Shaw's 'Really the English do not deserve to have great men.'

The Book Society's recommendation had encouraged brisk trade and substantial headway was being made in sales to the lending libraries. A second printing of 2,000 copies was published in June and a further 2,000 the following February. Curiously, nowhere on Ayrton's strikingly designed dust wrapper did the seductive words 'Recommended by the Book Society' appear.

In May, McLuhan wrote to say that he had not only read the novel himself but had been so busy thereafter evangelising the book and pressing it upon his friends that he had been unable to retrieve it for a second reading. He believed it to be a 'very important piece of work . . . The first time that anything Canadian has been given serious treatment.' It was still not available in Canadian bookshops, however. 'Toronto waits humped in silence', he reported, 'for the book to hit the stalls.'

Self Condemned received a belated response in Toronto from the novelist Robertson Davies in October 1955. Writing for *Saturday Night*, he criticised 'the boring quality of the writing, the flat-footedness of the prose, the lack of climax in the construction'. Using an imaginative but scarcely coherent metaphor, he described it reading 'as though it had been written in lemon juice, with a rusty nail, on a piece of tin'. Davies denied disliking the book because it was critical of his country. Indeed:

A good sousing satire on Canada would be a fine thing; but the Momaco of Mr Lewis's atrabilious description is not like anything in Canada, or perhaps in the world. It exists only in the bleak waste land of his imagination.

Curiously, Davies was under the impression that Lewis had had a comfortable time in Canada during the war, 'painting portraits and sniffing the incense which was liberally burned by the nobility and gentry at his shrine.' But if his experience was really anything like that delineated in his book, Davies felt heartily sorry for him.

*

The 1,000 limitation sheets for the Arco edition of *The Apes of God* were delivered to Lewis in May and he set about signing them with his blue 'Biro'. Bernard Hanison was present at the Notting Hill flat for part of this operation and remembered Mrs Lewis guiding her husband's hand to the correct place on each sheet.

Michael Ayrton completed the dust-wrapper design in the same month. A great mandrill baboon crouched on the front cover, eating a piece of manuscript with its right hand, grasping a hunting crop in its left and clutching a palette and brushes in the toes of its left foot. The lash of the hunting crop, intended as reference to Part VI of the novel, 'Ape Flagellant', curled along the lower edge of the design and around the words 'by WYNDHAM LEWIS'.

For some reason Bernard Hanison found fault and returned it to Ayrton with instructions for emendation. Lewis, according to Hanison, was mortified when he heard that his protégé's work had been slighted and insisted the design remain as Ayrton originally conceived it, even paying his friend's fee out of his own pocket. If Hanison's story is to be believed, Ayrton may not have known whence his fee finally came. Certainly, in the account he gave of the affair the following year, he made no mention of the money. 'The publishers', he said, 'were not pleased until Mr Lewis instructed them to be so.'

*

In July I. A. Richards and his wife were in London again for their summer vacation from Harvard. They came for dinner on the 21st, Dorothy divulging no details of the meal in her diary apart from the observation that Mrs Lewis was a 'striking cook'. As in the previous year's entry, mention was made of how beautiful she must once have been. Also, that she was 'a heavy drinker' and 'non stop smoker'. A tour of the abandoned studio upstairs was granted by their host. Dorothy called it 'his strange messy attic'. She found Lewis himself 'quite a different man at home' and that evening 'he was at his nicest', she thought. It was an impression much improved on that of the previous July at the Etoile, despite the scurrilous baiting of her oldest friend's husband, Robert McAlmon, as 'a homo' and suggestions that other mutual friends were probably 'homos' too.

She observed that he did not seem to 'move with any security in his own room'. She noted how pasty he looked, as if he didn't get enough fresh air, and the suspicion was confirmed by his wife. 'She said they never went out.' As Lewis talked about the two further parts of *The Childermass* all but complete, and of *The Demon of Progress in the Arts*, Dorothy's attention was drawn to his 'beautiful pale mobile hands'.

Another visitor that year remembered his hands 'swollen by illness but still beautiful'. Patricia Hutchins had come to ask him questions about Joyce and Pound. She remembered climbing the concrete stairs and negotiating the long, uncared-for passageway to his front door. Beside the door, 'typed downways, as if to be more difficult', there was a faded notice:

W
Y
N
D
H
A
M

L
E
W
I
S

Mrs Lewis showed her into a dark sitting room full of books and pictures. 'Soon a large, slow-moving man entered and was helped, or rather refused help, to settle in an armchair with rugs round his knees.' He had an invalid's fretfulness about draughts and asked if all the doors were shut. Miss Hutchins spoke from the sofa, where she sat next to a pile of reference books and dictionaries and a large pad of foolscap covered with wavering lines of thick pencilled notes. Misunderstanding his query about the doors she tried to reassure him. 'I'm all right here', she said. And Lewis remembered his customary courtesy to female visitors. 'I thought I'd be in a draught', he said. 'I should have asked if you were comfortable.' Mrs Lewis sat on a stool, forming, with armchair and sofa, a triangle. 'My husband, you know, is blind', she gently told their guest.

He wore a green eyeshade and she saw, below it, that his pupils were green-grey 'muffed like a dimmed bulb'. She noted also the skin of his face, 'curiously unmarked by the inner life'. And it was when she showed Mrs Lewis her book, *James Joyce's Dublin*, and this was given her husband to hold, that Miss Hutchins noticed his swollen but still beautiful hands. His fingers moved lightly over the binding and pages. 'Well made', he said. 'I can feel it.'

The interview began a little awkwardly, Miss Hutchins suspecting he was afraid she would stay too long. Then she got him talking about the time in 1920 when he and Eliot delivered Pound's second-hand shoes to Joyce and he relaxed into genial reminiscence of old friends: one 14 years dead, one a Nobel laureate and the other an indicted traitor or madman. 'In Paris that time', he told her, 'we behaved like schoolboys, and didn't mention serious subjects.' She told him she had heard it said that the character of Pullman in *The Childermass* was based on Joyce, and he seemed surprised. 'Oh I don't know about that', he demurred. He told her about Pound sitting for his portrait in the studio above, stretched out because he needed his rest and had not the energy he liked to make out that he had. And he recalled the poet's green eyes wide open for a instant, the only time he ever really saw them.

'Come and see me again', he told her as she left.

But the next time she entered that room she came uninvited, into a cold, windy, gutted shell. The pictures, the books, even the shelves had gone and the rain-soaked, frozen floorboards were littered with broken glass and plaster, fallen laths and old press clippings.

FIFTY-THREE

'The Vorticist whale'

Late in 1954, Michael Ayrton began work on a series of illustrations for *Monstre Gai* and *Malign Fiesta*, to be published in a single volume by Methuen after the BBC had finished broadcasting them in October 1955. Each part was to contain three illustrations. *The Childermass*, when it was published in a uniform edition in 1956, contained another three. Ayrton himself wanted to produce at least six for each book and Methuen were perfectly amenable to the increase. Lewis, however, was insistent that there should be no more than three. Moreover each illustration, through Mrs Lewis's detailed description, was, as it were, run past his mind's eye for final approval. And he was 'explicit', Ayrton recalled, 'in his requests for alterations and new versions.'

The collective title for the three books was to be *The Human Age*; derived from the idea, advanced by the character of Sammael in *Malign Fiesta*, of combining the Human and the Angelic in a quasi-divine hybrid. Lewis had, for a time, contemplated calling the series *The Human Dream* but abandoned this on the grounds that it might have been thought he was referring to Christianity as a mere dream.

*

Writing shortly after *The Demon of Progress in the Arts* was published, and incidentally questioning whether painters were really so easily led by art critics as he made out in that book, Naomi Mitchison told Lewis of a recent dream of her own:

> in full colour as many of my dreams are – of an enormous exhibition of your pictures, which were in a very strange variety of styles – more pictures than anyone could paint in a life-time. In fact, I thought some of them looked suspiciously like Matisse, but I didn't like to say so because there was a catalogue. I'm not sure what you make of that.

A month or so later Lewis received a letter from Sir John Rothenstein which gave Mitchison's dream the quality of prescience. The Trustees of the Tate

Gallery were hoping to honour him with a retrospective exhibition. It would cover 'the whole range of [his] work as a painter and a draughtsman, together with a pendant illustrative of the Vorticist movement which [he] led, including the work of Wadsworth, Roberts, Hamilton, and others'. The Trustees appreciated that the exhibition would not be possible without his own 'goodwill and assistance' and Rothenstein was writing to ascertain whether they could count on this. He added 'that, as an almost lifelong admirer' of Lewis's art and thought, he 'should be very proud to be associated with such an exhibition'.

Lewis replied that the thought of an exhibition at the Tate was 'most stirring' and that Rothenstein might rely on any assistance he could give. The Vorticist 'pendant' was, however, to prove an initial source of discontent. Lewis felt it unfair that, while other recent retrospective exhibitions, such as those of Jacob Epstein, Ben Nicholson and Stanley Spencer, spread themselves through three galleries, his own would occupy only two, the third being devoted to a class of artist to be called 'other Vorticists'. He was eventually persuaded by Rothenstein to accept the arrangement, albeit 'with a grace that did not disguise his disappointment'.

When the exhibition opened the following year, the objections of one 'other Vorticist' to this arrangement were not so easily dealt with and continued long after Lewis's death.

*

In February, Lewis addressed 'the question of obscenity' in *The Human Age* and told White that he had modified 'offensive passages' and removed 'objectionable words'. The abusive exchanges between angel and devil in *Monstre Gai* he preferred to leave untouched and the anatomically robust descriptions of the goat-men in the same chapter did not, he felt, need 'watering down'. He did, however, express a willingness to be guided by White in these matters.

As late as April, he was still making excisions. He informed White that on page 51 of the galley proofs the words 'Only had you allowed my hand to wander a little, the nature of your sex would have been revealed' might be deleted. The sentence followed Sentoryen's placing of Pullman's hand on his bare midriff and the question 'had you not known I was a man, but thought I was a girl, would you have had the same sensations as if you had been caressing a woman?' The proposition remained. But Pullman's reply, with its indirect allusion to hand and genital contact, had to come out.

*

Sir John Rothenstein had not met Lewis since interviewing him in 1951 as part of the groundwork for the second volume of *Modern English Painters: Lewis to Moore*. During their long conversation on that occasion, 'Lewis was very pale . . . his features were puffy', Rothenstein recalled, and 'he looked seriously ill.' But his energy, if only fuelled by bile, seemed unimpaired, as he raked over past quarrels and current slights. Four years later when the Tate director visited the Notting Hill flat to discuss the forthcoming exhibition, Lewis's condition had deteriorated greatly:

> I was shocked to find him aged and ill . . . utterly reduced, his features white and without form, his energy ebbed away. Apprehending how changed I found him he spoke with envy of Augustus John's health and in sudden irrelevant disparagement of Matthew Smith's painting as 'the taste of the stupid.'

Smith had been honoured with a retrospective exhibition at the Tate in 1953. With this in mind, Lewis's disparagement might not have been entirely irrelevant. If he was enviously comparing the tribute accorded Smith with that being prepared for himself, it cannot have escaped him that, in 1953, the 81 canvases representing that painter's contribution to British art, 'noble and unique' according to Bryan Robertson in *The Listener*, had occupied all three of the Tate's customary exhibition galleries, instead of only two.

*

A month after Rothenstein's visit, the BBC's dramatisation of *The Human Age* received its first complete performance. *The Childermass* was broadcast in a new production on Tuesday, 24 May. As in the first version, four years before, it lasted one and a half hours. Two days later came *Monstre Gai*, at a gruelling three and a half hours the longest play in the series, and, finally, the following Monday evening, *Malign Fiesta* went out from 6 o'clock until 8.

A party was held at Broadcasting House to celebrate completion of the seven-hour drama. Walter Allen found the author sitting alone on a sofa, 'a blind titan'. Lewis remarked that V. S. Pritchett had just been talking to him. 'Pritchett says he thinks my books are very funny.' He repeated the epithet: 'Funny!' Allen remembered 'a wealth of derision in his enunciation of that word "funny" '.

The same could not, unreservedly, be said of *The Human Age*. Dorothy Richards heard that their friends the Jack Sweeneys had been sickened, listening to the infernal torture sequences in *Malign Fiesta*, and Mrs Lewis

611

herself confessed to being 'upset by the cruelty of it all'. While it could hardly have been laid entirely at Lewis's door, the Richardses heard that audiences for the BBC's Third Programme were not on the increase. They received a similar report from P. H. Newby of the BBC Talks Department, who told them that, while the plays had caused 'a lot of discussion' and were 'worthwhile', he could not say they were a success.

All three plays were repeated in July and again in October. By contractual agreement this last sequence was completed immediately prior to the publication of *Monstre Gai* and *Malign Fiesta* in a single volume by Methuen.

Dorothy Richards and her husband visited London late in the summer of that year. Their annual dinner appointment with the Lewises was in September, at the recently refurbished Café Royal. The place had just celebrated its ninetieth anniversary but was empty, the food bad and expensive, and Lewis, 'very old, shrunk and collapsed', his face 'gone very limp and slack'. As Dorothy recorded the strained and depressing evening in her diary, Mrs Lewis, as if to compensate for her husband, was 'very vivacious':

> she played to his hand all evening – very gallantly. He unable to take part in the conversation. We all threw the ball at him as hard as we could but he couldn't see it. He slumped over the table and . . . went to sleep from quite early on. Horribly pathetic . . . It's an awful desert for the old.

Mrs Richards felt just a flicker of irritation, as two years before, at the expense incurred by geriatric caprice as Lewis ordered Moët et Chandon at £1 18s. the half-bottle and 'which he didn't finish'. She was more understanding of his lack of appetite for the 'very dull' food.

There were 'flashes' when he seemed to wake up. He spoke of the *Childermass* broadcast and called it 'a hubbub in the desert' but there was nothing the others could take up. Then, following the struggle of a visit to the lavatory, he appeared to revive and Dorothy felt he would have sat up half the night. The Richardses made an excuse of the friend they were lodging with in Hampstead and preparations were made to leave at 11 o'clock.

As they helped him into a taxi in Regent Street, Lewis clung to them both as though he thought he would not see them again. Mrs Lewis kissed her hand to them as the taxi drew away. 'One feels so sad', Dorothy wrote in her diary and she remembered something Mrs Lewis had told them earlier in the evening, beyond her husband's hearing. 'He's had a very vague day. It's the pressure on his brain – which has caused his blindness.' Then she added brightly: 'But he can do his novel and isn't vague about the details of that.'

*

The novel Mrs Lewis referred to was to be the last published in her husband's lifetime. Late in 1953, Lewis offered a synopsis to White, introducing it as 'an extremely topical' and 'a deeply interesting subject matter'. He did not feel the need to enumerate to his publisher 'the many facets, religious and political', which the narrative provided and imposed. White received the synopsis on a Thursday and Lewis expected him to give it his personal attention over the weekend in order to be able to give an account of his reactions the following week. 'I would like to stress', he concluded, 'that it is my intention to make this book extremely easy to be read by everybody.'

The potentially popular novel concerned the downfall of a charismatic High Anglican vicar with left-wing views, dubbed by the popular press 'The Red Priest'. The Reverend Augustine Card, a boxing Blue at Oxford, is an immensely powerful athlete. A fight with his curate, a smaller man with a heart condition, results in Father Card serving a three-year prison sentence for manslaughter. On his release, Card leaves his wife and child and seeks redemption as a missionary among the Eskimos of British Columbia. There, history repeats itself: he kills an Eskimo and is gruesomely butchered by other Eskimos in revenge.

The topicality of the story rested not so much on the melodramatic events, but on the identification of High Anglicanism with Communism, notable in such figures as Conrad Noel, the 'Red Vicar' of Thaxted, his equally 'Red' successor, the Reverend Jack Putterill, and the 'Red Dean' of Canterbury, Hewlett Johnson. In 1947 the Archbishop had publicly distanced himself from his Dean's political utterances and in 1951, as a friend of the Soviet Union, Father Johnson was awarded the Stalin Peace Prize.

By October 1955, only a month after the 'horribly pathetic' Café Royal dinner, Lewis had finished *The Red Priest*. White read the typescript over a weekend 'with all the pleasure and admiration' he expected to feel.

*

Immediately following the last complete broadcast of *The Human Age* on the 11th, 19th and 25th of October, Methuen published the 566-page volume containing *Monstre Gai* and *Malign Fiesta*.

Despite its size and weight, Patricia Hutchins carried it around with her 'in bus, train, underground and restaurant' because, she told Lewis, it had 'got a hold' of her. She was, however, disappointed not to find a few estate agents in his inferno. Looking for a new flat at the time, Miss Hutchins felt that members of this profession 'would have interests there!' And Naomi Mitchison wrote:

> What a terrifying book. It's like a congealed nightmare and I can't think how you could bear writing it except that I suppose it was better to get it out than have it inside . . . I must say, you do succeed in making one's hair stand on end.

A significant change had been made in the published ending from that which had been dramatised. In the climax of the broadcast, whilst admiring Satterthwaite's Japanese peony, Pullman was accidentally trodden on by an angel's foot 'the size of a German farm-cart'. There was a shrieking crescendo of music, which merged into the shrieking of Satterthwaite, and the last words, before the crash of closing music, were spoken by James McKechnie as the Narrator:

> Satters stared down where the foot had been. Upon the ground was his peony as flat as those flowers which we crush between the leaves of a book: souvenirs of a picnic. And there was what had been a head, stamped as flat as a sheet of paper into a shape which was in another dimension to the shapes of the living. He could see teeth mangled into something like a mosaic representing a fish. It was a patchwork pancake, mostly blood. Underneath came a larger unit. It was an enormous cowpat where the body and legs had been and one real boot at the bottom of that, a boot in which was a foot and a bloody section of bone.

In the published version, the giant angel's sandal crushes only the peony, while Pullman is captured and carried off by a pair of God's soldiers. His survival admitted the possibility of a sequel. *The Human Age* was not intended to remain in only three parts after all. Opposite the title page published on 27 October the complete tetralogy was listed. The dust-wrapper blurb promised that Book One, *The Childermass*, long out of print in the Chatto & Windus edition, would 'in due course be published in the same format as the present volume' containing Books Two and Three. Book Four, listed there as if already in existence, was *The Trial of Man*.

Following on from the 'Limbo' of *The Childermass*, the 'Purgatory' of *Monstre Gai* and the 'Hell' of *Malign Fiesta*, this was to be Lewis's 'Paradise'. In it, he told Hugh Kenner, Pullman finds himself 'in the Celestial Camp . . . in Divine Society'. Naomi Mitchison foresaw the obvious difficulty:

But are you going to be able to describe good as efficiently as you do evil?

It was a question about which Lewis himself was uncertain. 'God is a big problem', he told Bridson.

In a surviving fragment, the Supreme Being enters, to a rather unimaginative accompaniment of tinkling little bells. He has grey eyes, blue-grey hair and is dressed in the closest shade of pale bluish-purple to pure white. His voice is deep and gentle and he does not smoke tobacco. Predictably, the Devil has all the best lines:

I saw the shadow of the Beast of Heaven! He was there! I smelt him . . . I smelled the lump of butter which would not melt in his dirty mouth. I smelled the fug of the Goodness – of Someone who is too disgustingly inhuman to live – even in Heaven. Who calls himself All Father, but has not the guts to pup a single son. Whose Son had to be born of a Virgin! I smelled that great absence of guts – that big Nothing we call God!

During the last complete year of his life, Lewis divided his time between the resolution of that 'big problem', and the writing of a new novel about an artist.

Twentieth Century Palette was complete but unpolished at the time of his death. It survives as a 253-page typescript divided into 34 chapters tracing a painter's life from public school just after the First World War, through art school and Montparnasse, commercial success in London, marriage, divorce and remarriage, the loss of an arm at El Alamein, the establishment of his own art school in postwar London to death from natural causes in a private clinic.

Although the chronology of Evelyn Parke's life was shunted forward some 20 years from Lewis's own, certain key stages of their early careers can be noted in common. Like Lewis, Evelyn is 16 when sent to an art school on the advice of his house-master. A similar bohemian apprenticeship is enjoyed in Montparnasse. Then, reflecting Lewis's relationship with Sturge Moore, Evelyn's education is completed under the informal tutelage of an elder mentor in Holland Park.

However, it is the *dis*similarities between the real and fictional lives that are significant. Evelyn is brought up by one parent, a father, and Lewis effectively lost his father at the age of ten. Evelyn has the advantage of a relatively prosperous family and a talent for painting that is immediately recognised by the art world. He is never short of money and is a commercial success from the start. The same could not be said of Lewis. 'In one way and another', he wrote, perhaps ruefully, of his protagonist:

he was ideally placed as an artist, and encountered none of the difficulties that handicapped many of those around him.

Both of Evelyn's marriages produce offspring, two from the second being killed in a car crash along with his second wife. The only child of his first marriage suddenly confronts him, aged 20, as a student in his own art school. Whilst this encounter superficially recalls the reappearance in the 1930s of Lewis's illegitimate son Peter, Nicholas Parke emerges, not as a juvenile delinquent and unsuccessful burglar, but as a brilliant painter and, eventually, his father's loving, dutiful and favoured son, his professional colleague and his heir. When Evelyn dies he is mourned by the art world and by the entire student body of the 'Parke Academy'. He is eulogised in *The Times* and accompanied to his grave by the strains of the funeral march from *Götterdämmerung* which gives the final chapter its name. Lewis might have been rehearsing an ideal end to his own career.

*

The previous April he had been agitated to learn that another exhibition, scheduled by the Tate Gallery for the summer of 1956, might overshadow his own. Rothenstein was at pains to reassure him that no date had at that time been fixed for 'One Hundred Years of German Painting (1850–1950)' but that the Gallery had no intention of allowing the two exhibitions to overlap. As it happened, the German show immediately preceded Lewis's and so conflict was avoided. But, with only a month to go before 'Wyndham Lewis and Vorticism' opened, Rothenstein foresaw a problem when the Tate was offered an exhibition of Cubist paintings at short notice. 'Autour du Cubisme', a miscellaneous group of about thirty pictures, was made available to London because the Musée d'Art Moderne in Paris had recently been forced to close due to the building's extreme dilapidation. The proposed dates for the showing of 'Autour du Cubisme' were from 27 July to 8 September, and Rothenstein was quick to forestall any objections Lewis might have had:

> You will notice that it is not suggested that it should open until yours has had a run of three weeks entirely to itself. The effect of the addition of a small but distinguished group of paintings with a quite definite relation to your own early work, would be to enhance your own exhibition and stimulate further public interest in it. I ought to explain that these Cubist works are not available at any other time and that in my view it would be to the advantage of your exhibition and to the interest of the public generally.

He must have been relieved when Lewis raised no objections, replying with perhaps only the faintest trace of irony:

> The overlap you refer to will leave plenty of time for the public to concentrate their attention on my work, I think.

To reach the private view on 5 July, so feeble he was unable to negotiate the flight of steps to the main entrance from Millbank, Lewis had to be taken up in a service lift from the rear. He told Elizabeth Rothenstein how pleased he was with the exhibition and gratified by the consideration with which the Tate had treated him. He added that he was deeply touched by everything her husband had done on his behalf. A photograph shows him strangely isolated in the middle of a row of chairs. Eliot sits on his right, reading the catalogue, and on his left, Ayrton grins into the camera. Both men seem too far removed for conversation from the deaf old man sitting between them. On the other side of Eliot sits Elizabeth Rothenstein talking to the painter Ceri Richards, who leans attentively above her. Sir John Rothenstein stands. At that moment only one member of the group looks at the slumped, white-headed ghost in their midst. Mrs Lewis, at the extreme edge of the picture, closer to the camera than Ayrton, turns to direct a watchful, protective eye at her husband.

'The private view was a remarkable assembly of Lewis's old friends', Rothenstein recalled, 'T. S. Eliot, the Sitwells, Kate Lechmere . . . Mrs Nevinson, and many others.' In conversation with Eliot, Rothenstein referred to his oft-quoted appraisal of Lewis in the September 1918 issue of *The Egoist*: 'the most fascinating personality of our time'. Rothenstein was convinced that Eliot's response was not intended to imply the least denigration of the man they were all honouring that night. 'But that was so many years ago', the poet said vaguely. It was as if 'at that particular moment he himself was also occupied with thought of happenings of "many years ago".'

The last time Rothenstein ever saw Lewis was at the end of the evening, 'so exhausted by the ordeal that it was only with difficulty that Mrs Lewis, Elizabeth and I could get him into a taxi – exhausted, but touchingly happy.' In another account, Rothenstein noted tears in the blind man's eyes.*

The following week I. A. Richards and his wife came to dinner at Kensington Gardens Studios. Dorothy thought Lewis looked better than the last time she saw him on that ghastly night the year before at the Café Royal. She was still slightly repelled by his behaviour. He was 'irritatingly helpless' and he complained about his food, particularly the taste of the

---

* Introduction to Jane Farrington's catalogue to the City of Manchester Art Galleries exhibition, 1980.

peaches. At one point he snapped at his wife, wanting to know what she was doing with his plate. It was 'not amiably said', Dorothy thought. His deafness made conversation difficult and he did not speak much, except at the beginning of the evening. Then it was to complain that Valerie Fletcher, secretary and soon to be wife of T. S. Eliot, was interfering with his telephone calls to her employer. The Richardses were also shocked, and somewhat incredulous, at a piece of 40-year-old scandal he regaled them with concerning their friend's first marriage. He claimed that a week after the wedding, Vivien Eliot had an affair with Bertrand Russell 'which upset Eliot very much'. It may have been the cruel way he told the story, perhaps chuckling about how indignant Eliot had been, and Mrs Lewis's sense of their guests' embarrassment, that made her spit the words at him: '*You* would have been indignant!'

Apart from this and complaints about his food, the only other subject of Lewis's conversation recorded by Dorothy Richards in her diary was that he was 'pleased with the reception of his show at the Tate'. He showed them the 'excellent' *Spectator* review in which Basil Taylor declared him to be 'among our greatest portrait painters' and, furthermore, 'among the finest draughtsmen in the history of English art, as he is one of our undoubted masters of prose'. Admittedly Taylor's praise was slightly qualified by the suggestion that, in both prose and drawing, the 'precision, . . . lucidity, . . . sharpness of observation and imagery' were sometimes mixed with 'cliché and formal slackness'.

But, overall, Lewis was entitled to be pleased with the critical reception. *The Times* reported that 'in the best of the portraits, an underlying humanity warms the steely strength of the line, and turns a relentless technical precision to the service of some of the most distinguished original creations in modern British art.' In *Time and Tide*, Eric Newton devoted two glowing reviews to the exhibition, one week dealing with Lewis as a creator of images, the following week as a painter of portraits. T. W. Earp lauded him in the *Daily Telegraph*, just as he had reviewed the Redfern Gallery show in 1949 and so impressed Lewis's Viennese dentist. Even David Sylvester, writing in *Encounter*, who recognised borrowings in Lewis's work from both Augustus John and Gauguin, and who thought a comparison with the French paintings of 'Autour du Cubisme' was 'discouraging to chauvinism', conceded that the large Vorticist canvas, *Revolution*,* the portraits of the painter's wife and the semi-abstract drawings of 1925–27 were 'among the best things done by British painters in our time'.

Rothenstein remembered Lewis telephoning 'to express his annoyance'

---

* Shown at Second London Group Exhibition, March 1915, as 'The Crowd'.

about Myfanwy Piper's review in the *Sunday Times*. However, it is difficult to see what he found objectionable in that favourable, if rather sycophantic piece, unless it was that she devoted a considerable part of it to slavishly quoting his own pronouncements from the 1920s back at him.

Michael Ayrton's review, 'The Stone Guest', appearing in the *New Statesman and Nation*, was also vigorously partisan. But it may have served to trigger the only truly hostile response the exhibition was to provoke. It certainly inflamed an already smouldering resentment, and fuelled a spate of pamphleteering worthy of Lewis himself in his prime.

*

William Roberts had been suspicious about the exhibition from the beginning. Early in February he received an invitation to participate in the 'Other Vorticists' section, signed, not by the Director of the Tate, but by Miss Chamot, an assistant keeper. The letter went unanswered. His suspicions regarding the status to be accorded the 'Other Vorticists' were not allayed when he learned that a collector had offered to lend the organisers a Roberts painting measuring 4 ft by 5ft which had been refused 'because it was too big'. The largest of his pictures eventually displayed was *The Cinema*, borrowed from Violet Schiff, which measured 2ft 8ins by a little over 3 ft.

When the exhibition opened, Roberts acquired a copy of the catalogue and read Lewis's introduction. The fifth paragraph of this document began with a heavily punctuated declaration:

Vorticism, in fact, was what I, personally, did, and said, at a certain period.

When, a fortnight later, Ayrton repeated that claim in the *New Statesman and Nation* and added that 'the other Vorticists collected at the Tate look rather like a lot of sprats a whale has caught', Roberts fired off letters to *The Times*, *The Listener* and, of course, the *New Statesman and Nation*, in protest. None of these letters was printed. He than had recourse to a small printing firm at 152 Kensington Church Street. The Favil Press Ltd was just around the corner, and barely a minute's walk from the home of the man whose self-proclaimed position as sole begetter of Vorticism Roberts intended to challenge.

With only two days of the exhibition left to run at the Tate, Mary Chamot sent Lewis two small pamphlets she thought might interest him.

The first consisted of two leaves stapled in a yellow paper cover. On the front were the words:

THE
RESURRECTION
OF
VORTICISM
AND THE
APOTHEOSIS
OF
WYNDHAM LEWIS
AT THE
TATE

The message on the back cover was more succinct:

BLAST
VORTICISM

Inside, Roberts gave an account of his grievances through the letters refused publication in *The Listener, The Times* and *New Statesman*. A cartoon made heavy-handed reference to Michael Ayrton's observation in 'The Stone Guest', and to John Huston's epic film, the American release of which had been reported, coincidentally, in the adjacent column of *The Times* to a review of 'Wyndham Lewis and Vorticism'. The cartoon showed Moby Dick, standing erect on his fluke in front of an easel, holding a paint brush in one flipper and a palette in the other. It was labelled: THE VORTICIST WHALE.

The second pamphlet was a little more substantial. It consisted of four leaves in a paper cover – an identical shade of pink to the first issue of *Blast*:

COMETISM
AND
VORTICISM

A
TATE
GALLERY
CATALOGUE
REVISED

On the back cover was an abstract design. At first sight it appeared as a jumble of irregular black shapes, ellipses, and thin cylindrical forms. Closer inspection showed it to be the storm cone emblem from *Blast*, turned upside down and smashed to bits.

'I cannot understand how he got it printed', Lewis told Ayrton:

> In the main it is abuse of me. He believes that the Tate show was organised by me, that I am very proud of Vorticism, wish to make use of him, chose the pictures insisting on his own being very few, etc. etc. etc. He regards you as a bad man too . . . If you have seen this wretched little squib give me your views.

Lewis himself took the 'wretched little squib' seriously enough to contemplate legal action, and the firm of Field, Roscoe & Co. was alerted to hold itself in readiness.

*

Meanwhile, he had other preoccupations. The functioning of his bladder was causing him discomfort and, probably, embarrassment. Dr McPherson could find no trace of infection and so ruled out cystitis. However, due to the large quantity of vegetables and fruit in his patient's diet, there was a lower than average degree of acidity in his urine and this in turn was leading to weakness in the muscles of the bladder. The doctor explained that an acid condition of urine helped to stimulate the muscle and maintain its tone. In order to rectify the balance he prescribed a mixture of strychnine and dilute phosphoric acid to be taken before food and ephedrine hydrochloride tablets to be taken after. In addition, McPherson was making enquiries about the availability of absorbent pads, but thought that these might be rendered unnecessary if the medication proved effective.

The Lewises were also being threatened with eviction. The London County Council intended pulling down all the buildings on the south side of Notting Hill Gate in order to widen the road. This scheme was intended to remedy the notorious bottleneck Lewis himself had been the victim of some years before when hit by a motorcycle in the congested traffic.

He was interviewed in the *Daily Mail* under the headline:

The blind outsider battles on at 72

The correspondent, Richard Evans, finding a rather incongruously keen-eyed, avian simile for a blind man, described him 'crouched sharp and silvery as a heron in the clutter of his Notting Hill studio'. Lewis clearly enjoyed being seen as an individual under siege and standing up to the faceless authority of local government:

> The L.C.C. demolition squads are closing in on me with their picks and hammers to knock this excellent solid room down about my head if I am not out by Christmas. All Notting Hill will be rubble.

Posing as an embattled survivor from a more chivalrous age, he continued indignantly:

> Why even the little flower shop guy who makes me a posy of orchids if I am visited by a beautiful lady is being kicked out.

It was the height of the Suez Crisis, and Lewis jokingly called upon the current bogey man of the British and French governments to intervene. 'Nasser should deal with the L.C.C.', he told the *Mail*.

The interview was happily timed to publicise his latest novel, and this was given duly bold prominence: '**The Red Priest** (Methuen 15s.), just published'. Lewis gave Evans a demonstration of his laborious writing method and told him he could produce 'thousands of words a week' and was currently 'slogging away' finishing another novel. The interviewer asked if he would be writing many more books. Lewis replied: 'You insult me! I am still alive. I work up to midnight if I feel like it.' The article finished on a decidedly optimistic note, with Lewis saying: 'Life is still as rich and fascinating.' Referring to the fate he had imagined for himself in 'The Sea-Mists of the Winter', five years before, he went on: 'I am not locked up in a dark room. The mind has many chambers.'

*

The Red Priest did not receive unanimous acclaim from the press. Many were agreed that it displayed a falling off from the standards of his other recent work. *The Scotsman* felt that, after *Self Condemned* and *The Human Age*, the new novel came as an anticlimax and that it 'will not add much to Mr Lewis's deservedly great reputation'. Maurice Richardson, in the *New Statesman and Nation*, drew attention, in rather a pot and kettle fashion, to the novelist's style: 'Mr Lewis savages his farce like a werewolf decimating a stolen thigh. The style creaks and groans as if someone were wrestling with a straitjacket.' *The Bulletin and Scots Pictorial* called it 'a powerful creation, but serious reading with a lot of religious argument and some disturbingly stilted speech'. In the *Sunday Times*, John Metcalf thought that *The Red*

Priest 'isn't a total failure . . . but three fourths of this arrogantly careless book are.'

Despite the imminent prospect of losing the roof over his head, Lewis was still preoccupied with Roberts's pamphlet campaign well into September. A letter to the press was drafted, defending himself against the 'venomous misunderstandings . . . scattered abroad' by the 'little Mr X':

> I found myself given a huge exhibition . . . at the Tate. This was the work of Sir John Rothenstein and his youthful assistants . . . Anyone resenting this outburst of my work should blame them, not me. I was not responsible for Mr X being insufficiently represented . . . I cannot see to read a book or write a letter, and was quite unable to see my own pictures, and certainly am not interested enough to vote for or against Mr X's canvases. Lastly, Vorticism. . . . What does this word mean? I do not know . . . but let me say that I did not ask for this meaningless word to be revived . . . We live in a world of Art Historians: they do funny things.

But, finally, it must all have seemed too much trouble. The letter to the press was not sent. A telegram was dispatched to his solicitor, Kenneth Ewart, at Field, Roscoe & Co.:

PLEASE DO NOT WRITE MR ROBERTS WILL WRITE TO YOU – LEWIS

And Mr Ewart replied that he would do nothing until instructed further. No further instructions were received.

When 'Wyndham Lewis and Vorticism' ended its run at the Tate, the Arts Council of Great Britain arranged for a selection of the exhibition to tour. Seventeen of the 41 paintings and 37 of the 114 drawings travelled first to Manchester, then on to Glasgow, down to Bristol and back up to Leeds. Where necessary, owners were asked to extend the loan of their pictures until the end of the tour in mid-December. Mrs Lewis agreed to allow the sketch of her beloved Sealyham terrier, who had died in Windsor, Ontario, to travel. The drawing, called *Tutsi*, was the hit of the show so far as the Manchester *Evening Chronicle* correspondent was concerned. '*Don't miss Tutsi*', he urged his readers, 'the impudent pup . . . is an oasis in a stormy sea.'

On the other hand, Lewis refused to extend the loan of his *Portrait of John McLeod*, explaining that it was required elsewhere.

An exhibition of British portraiture from the 16th century to the present was to open at the Royal Academy on 24 November and Gallery number one, together with the Small South Room, were to be devoted to the achievements of modern painters. The irony of a picture by Wyndham Lewis being solicited by the Royal Academy cannot have escaped Humphrey Brooke, who wrote to thank him for the loan of the 'fine portrait of John McLeod'. Because the Tate exhibition was still on tour, opening in Leeds on the same day that their own exhibition opened in Burlington House, the Royal Academy Council was unable to obtain the portrait by Lewis that they most wanted. Nevertheless, Brooke wished him to know that their first choice had been the 1938 *Portrait of T. S. Eliot*. All was forgiven.

FIFTY-FOUR

'He's getting confused now – can we stop?'

One of the last articles Lewis wrote was commissioned by an ambitious young Harvard academic called Henry A. Kissinger. Little more than a decade away from the global political power and influence he achieved under Richard Nixon's presidential administration, Kissinger was executive director of the International Seminar Programme, conducted under the auspices of the Harvard Summer School of Arts and Sciences and of Education. He was also editor of *Confluence*, 'a quarterly designed to give European, Asian and American intellectuals an opportunity to exchange views on contemporary problems in politics, philosophy and the human-ities'. He had become friendly with Michael Ayrton during the Summer School of 1954 and it was through him that he contacted Lewis:

> The topic we have in mind . . . and for which we would particularly like to have a contribution . . . concerns the function of education at the present time.

The Spring and Summer 1957 issues of *Confluence* were to be devoted to the subjects, respectively, of the 'Role of Education' and 'Education Today' and Lewis was asked for an article of three to four thousand words, by 1 November. The $100 offered was 'not wonderful', Ayrton told him, but the brief was so wide that he could write almost anything he liked. 'Nor would any word of yours', he went on, 'be questioned by the Editor should you see fit to dig out something.' The last phrase suggests Ayrton did not expect him to go to the trouble, for a fee of $100, of writing something specially. But Lewis did.

The article came to something *under* 3,000 words. Written blind and laboriously across 70-odd sheets of paper, it reduced to a nine-page typescript – 'Elitemindedness: a policy' fulfilled the wide brief in that it was loosely on the subject of education. To be precise, the first three and a half pages were about education. Lewis then, unashamedly, changed tack. He even directed an aside to Kissinger, letting him know what was happening:

> I have now made a few desultory remarks about education . . . I have no

contacts with European universities, so can express no opinions as to developments in those institutions. But in addressing yourself to me I presume you had in mind essentially cultural problems; for the rest of this article it will be of culture that I will speak.

In the five pages that followed he rambled inconsequentially over disparate aspects of contemporary culture. The late Dylan Thomas's talent, he declared, resided in his voice rather than his words. That voice silenced, he concluded, the words had no importance. The Berliner Ensemble's visit to London in late August with *Mother Courage* served to show that England had produced 'nothing . . . of equal creative value', as did the plays of Jean-Paul Sartre. He referred to Princess Margaret's African tour in September and October, and to her royal patronage of rock and roll in adopting the parting salutation 'See you later, Alligator'. The correct response to this, as Lewis and millions of teenagers knew, was 'In a while, Crocodile!' Finally, he mentioned a debate broadcast from the Oxford Union on the motion that 'this house would abolish the Third Programme'. Less than an hour before midnight on 22 October the motion was defeated. But the abuse he heard levelled at the Third Programme that Monday evening provided a tenuous link to anti-intellectual zealotry during the French Revolution, which allowed him to finish with an 'outburst of humanitarian horror' at the Red Army's suppression of the Hungarian uprising later the same week. The article was, if nothing else, bang up to the minute.

*

Hugh Kenner visited London in November and the Lewises made full arrangements for his accommodation. Because of its proximity to Victoria Station, he was to sleep at Agnes Bedford's mews cottage on the night of his arrival. Thereafter, it seems, he would stay above the offices of Faber & Faber at 24 Russell Square. This at least was the address at which Lewis promised him free lodgings and breakfasts for ten days. The young academic from Santa Barbara College was told that he would be welcome to take his evening meals at 29A Notting Hill Gate. All this had been arranged in September.

When Kenner paid his first visit to the flat on the 18 November, it was Lewis's birthday and there were to have been more people invited to celebrate. But he had been taken ill a couple of days before and the larger gathering postponed. Kenner was the only guest, and among the last to see Lewis in his own home. 'His massive form stooped, his sparse silvery hair curling at the collar, he acquiesced in the ritual of shuffling across the room, on his wife's arm, from his arm-chair to the dining-table; but it was only back in the arm-chair of the small dark book-lined sitting-room that he seemed remotely comfortable.'

During the uncomfortable interlude at the dining-table, Kenner remembers the festive trappings of pheasant and champagne and Lewis showing little interest in either. He remembers Mrs Lewis asking her husband if he would like more pheasant. 'His high pitched 'NO' rattled the windows' and Mrs Lewis turned to their guest: 'You mustn't mind Wyndham shouting, it's just . . .', there was a slight pause as she groped for the phrase, 'high spirits!'

The day after Lewis's birthday, Kenner had lunch with T. S. Eliot at the Garrick Club. It was an occasion that furnished the young man with an anecdote for life. He told how Eliot had cautioned him: 'Never commit yourself to a cheese without having first . . . *examined* it'; how he had methodically tapped, rotated and prodded the Stilton for a long time before pronouncing it 'rather past its prime'; how he had tapped, prodded and sounded every piece of cheese on the board before proffering 'a rather fine Red Cheshire' which his guest might enjoy; how he had asked the waiter to identify a particular pockmarked, toadstool-yellow specimen that exuded green flecks; how the waiter had confessed ignorance and summoned up two more waiters with the same result; how Eliot had taken his knife and 'achieved with aplomb the impossible feat of peeling off a long slice' of the 'Anonymous Cheese' and tasted it; how he had transferred the 'Anonymous Cheese' to his plate and, without any further observations or pronouncements, and without assistance, consumed it.

That evening Kenner told his anecdote for the first time. He had returned from the exclusive splendours of the Garrick Club to the almost deserted tenement building that the LCC was impatiently waiting to demolish. It was Lewis's balloon-popping response to the anecdote, and not the anecdote itself, that made Ezra Pound roar with laughter when Kenner told it again, eight years later, in Venice.

Lewis had listened attentively to the young man's account of Eliot at luncheon and then said:

Oh, never mind *him*. He's like that with everybody. But he doesn't come *in here* disguised as Westminster Abbey.

Kenner recalls other conversations with Lewis 'in that chilly month, the last November of his life'. Having all but finished *Twentieth Century Palette*, which only required revision, Lewis was turning his mind to the last book of *The Human Age*. The theme was to be 'Pullman's slow acclimatisation to the Celestial environment. He was not merely to favour the Divine, he was to find his home at last in the divine milieu.' Kenner believes that 'Lewis's mind in those last days was taken up with Pullman, with whom his imagination had now identified itself. The infernal Sammael interested him little, as did satire. Not even God seemed by then the book's central problem; he thought that Milton had been mistaken to introduce God in person, and rather inclined to take Milton's lapse for a warning.'

In 1960, Alan White told Geoffrey Grigson that Lewis had left nothing of that final book that could possibly be published:

> At the time of his death he was still experimenting with methods. Eliot told me that in his opinion what Lewis was attempting in that last volume was impossible. Be that as it may, by the time Lewis started on Part IV [of *The Human Age*] his physical condition was such that he would dictate a few sentences, drop asleep, wake up a few minutes – or an hour or two later – and continue an unfinished sentence at precisely the point at which he had left off.

When Lewis was interviewed by Richard Evans of the *Daily Mail*, in connection with the LCC's plans for Notting Hill Gate, Agnes Bedford, identified as his secretary, was on hand. 'He remembers all he has written in earlier chapters', she told the correspondent. 'His memory is remarkable – as exact as a young man's.'

But in late November and December his condition deteriorated. A torn-off scrap of paper survives from this time. In the 1960s the item was solemnly catalogued and filed in the Cornell archive as: 'DIOR'. The tiny piece of manuscript was created by Agnes Bedford, probably while she was reading back to Lewis the typescript of *Twentieth Century Palette*. What the American archivist mistook for the word 'DIOR' was an underlined page reference, recording the point Miss Bedford had reached in her reading. Underneath she had written seven words and silently handed the note to Mrs Lewis:

> P101
> He's getting confused now –
> Can we stop?

*

The principal of the Central School of Arts and Crafts, William Johnstone, remembered two encounters he had in late 1956. The first was with Hugh Gordon Porteus, who visited his studio 'in great distress' and asked if he had heard the news, only slightly premature, and clinically inaccurate, that

Wyndham Lewis was dying from 'a cancer growing between his eyes'. What was more, Porteus told him, Lewis and his wife were being threatened with eviction.

The following day Johnstone had a conversation with Mrs Helen Bentwich, Chairman of the LCC, while that lady was visiting the Central School. She told him 'that a big development at Notting Hill Gate was being held up by an artist of no importance and that the London County Council were taking steps to evict a man called Percy Wyndham Lewis.' She asked Johnstone if he had heard of the man. 'He was holding up the whole scheme, as his studio would have to be demolished to get this great plan completed.' Johnstone replied: 'Mrs Bentwich, they can't possibly do a thing like that, because Wyndham Lewis is one of the greatest artists of our time in Britain.' He remembered what Porteus had told him the day before, and added: 'more than that, he's dying of cancer in the eyes. The time he'll live now will be very short.'

Lewis developed cardiac failure in December, necessitating hospitalisation, but by early January he had rallied briefly and was back in the condemned flat. Despite William Johnstone's protestations to Mrs Bentwich, just before Christmas the Director of Housing issued an eviction order giving three months' notice to leave. For Lewis, this would be ample time.

*

In January 1957, D. G. Bridson had his last conversation with Lewis. It was the night his adaptation of *Tarr* was repeated on the Third Programme. The production had first been broadcast on 18 July of the previous year. After listening to that performance Lewis had been enthusiastic in his praise and told Bridson how the book had come alive for him. He asked whether the girl who played Bertha Lunken was really German and whether the girl playing Anastasya Vasek had actually been drunk, in the restaurant scene, so convincing was her performance.

As soon as *Tarr* finished at 10.30, on the evening of 13 January, Lewis telephoned Bridson, who was having a dinner party. He was in great good humour, keeping the producer talking for half an hour about how the whole book had come alive for him again. And again he asked the same questions he had asked after the first broadcast. 'Was the girl who played Bertha *really* German?' Marjorie Westbury was not German. 'Had Anastasya *really* been primed with champagne for that last magnificent scene with Tarr and the oysters?' Had she not, in short, been 'as tight as a tick'? Bridson assured him, as he had assured him the previous year, that Grizelda Hervey would not have played the scene nearly so convincingly if she had been 'tight as a tick'. Lewis barked happily with laughter and rang off, allowing Bridson to return to his guests.

*

At the beginning of February a letter arrived from Henry Kissinger, apologising for not having written more promptly to acknowledge Lewis's typescript. 'I like your article very much', he wrote, 'and appreciate your having undertaken it for us.' A cheque was being sent him in payment.

The editor of *Confluence* carefully avoided committing himself to actually publishing the article. Lewis's name appeared at the back of the Spring issue, among the eight international contributors promised for the next. But when the Summer issue came out, articles by G. P. Malasekera of Ceylon, Bangalore Kuppuswamy of India and Wyndham Lewis of England were not included.

*

Later that month, Mrs Lewis wrote to Docker:

> Since I saw you a fortnight ago . . . my husband's health has become considerably worse. We have had the heart man in again and the pathologist, but they could not account for his condition and yesterday Dr Meadows the neurologist examined him. He explained to me that this tumour in his brain . . . is sapping the pituitary gland. There are certain experimental treatments that he advises as possibly having some result, they are of course very expensive, otherwise there seems little to be done about it. In his present state there is of course no question of his doing any work – he is in bed and sleeps a great deal – I am expecting our usual doctor in today to discuss it all with me – it is very difficult to know what is the best thing to do for him.

Docker's cheque for £50, sent a couple of days later, was acknowledged:

> I am most deeply touched and I know Wyndham will be too if and when he can fully understand.

Naomi Mitchison came to see him but he was barely aware of her presence. She sat at his bed and held his hand. She wrote to Gladys: 'It is terrible to see someone becoming so completely different from his real self. Does he realise how ill he is?' Later, when she heard the news of his death, she wrote again: 'I couldn't have wished him to go on like that. It wasn't really him and none of us want to remember him that way. It seems in a way a messy kind of end to such a clear cut life.'

When he was admitted to Westminster Hospital on 18 February he was semi-conscious, moderately dehydrated and anaemic, with extensive bed sores to the small of his back. He was able, from time to time, to respond to questions, but soon lapsed into semi-consciousness again. One question he is alleged to have answered concerned the last occasion he had opened his bowels. The response is credited with containing his final words on this or any other subject. 'Mind your own business!'

Two and a half weeks after his admission, on Thursday 7 March, Wyndham Lewis died. 8.30 p.m. was the time of death given in the report of the autopsy carried out the following day, although Mrs Lewis told John Adams that her husband had died at 7.30. She also told Porteus that she had not expected him to die. 'I was arranging for him to leave hospital on the following day. What happened remains a mystery. I was assured when I agreed for him to enter the hospital that there was no danger of anything happening.'

Back at the flat that night, with Agnes Bedford, Mrs Lewis picked up the nearest piece of paper to hand and drafted a note to Sir Nicholas Waterhouse for Agnes to type. It was on the back of Henry Kissinger's letter, telling her husband how very much he liked the article for *Confluence*, that she wrote:

Dear Docker. Our dear Wyndham passed away this evening.
All our love Agnes & Froanna.

Death in the subdistrict of Westminster South was registered by the deceased's widow the following day:

died seventh of March 1957, Westminster Hospital, Percy Wyndham Lewis, Male, 72 years, of Studio A, 29 Notting Hill Gate, Kensington, Artist and Author.

*

The funeral service took place on 13 March at St George's, Campden Hill, Kensington, Prebendary S.A.H. Eley presiding. Geoffrey Bridson recalled:

Like the funerals of some of our greatest contemporaries, it was depressingly flat and uninspiring. (One could imagine Lewis's disgust at being sent to rest to the strains of *Going Home* on a Hammond Organ . . . !) Most of those that one would have expected to attend the

631

ceremony, out of respect for the genius of a fellow-writer, were conspicuously absent. So were the wreaths which failed to arrive from those that one would have expected to show at least a normal interest. Apart from those sent by relatives and close personal friends, only three stood out in fitting tribute. One was the wreath from Lewis's old sparring partner Ezra Pound – cabled in from St Elizabeth's Hospital. The second was from the Slade, in memory of one of their greatest pupils. The third was from a man who had met him only twice, but one who respected him as an even greater artist, it was signed by Donald Wolfit.

The actor's tribute, of roses, tulips and daffodils, bore the lines adapted from *Hamlet*:

> He was a man. Take him for all in all
> We shall not look upon his like again.

Over 30 mourners were listed in *The Times*, and William Johnstone rather exaggerated the 'depressingly flat and uninspiring' nature of the service when he wrote years later that there had been only six.

The coffin was taken to Golders Green for cremation. The 15-shilling 'Universal' urn containing the ashes was placed in a closed niche, number 5800, set about shoulder height in the north wall on the top floor of the Hall of Memory. The marble closing tablet had the inscription, cut and gilded:

**PERCY WYNDHAM
LEWIS
7th March 1957
AGED 72 YEARS**

Below were four words from the Book of Isaiah:

Thy light is come

Niche number 5800 measures one foot high, one foot deep and nine and a half inches wide. The 50-year lease on this address, more cramped even than the Pall Mall Safe Deposit, will expire in April 2007.

Probate was granted on 3 May, and it was declared that the gross value of his estate amounted to one thousand two hundred and thirty-nine pounds eight shillings and ninepence. Following tax deductions, his widow inherited £1,045 5s. 5d.

Although for the greater part of his life he had been close to the edge of bankruptcy, Wyndham Lewis died solvent.

FIFTY-FIVE

Post mortem

Myth has it that the Notting Hill flat was demolished in his wake. Bridson wrote that 'he was finally taken away by ambulance . . . while workmen were actually tearing the building down.' A 17-day shift of the chronology provided a suitably melodramatic climax for Jeffrey Meyers's biography: 'On the day after Lewis's death, a malign fiesta, the wreckers arrived to destroy his flat. They marched through the sitting room and up to the studio . . . glanced at the drawings and threw them on the floor. When Ayrton arrived to rescue them, he found that one had the mark of a large boot and that a drawing of Pound had half the head torn away.'

In fact, Mrs Lewis stayed on for over a fortnight after her husband's death. On 25 March she moved into a tiny flat provided for her by the LCC in Sheffield Terrace, a quarter of a mile away.

She left behind evidence of burnt papers in the studio stove upstairs.

*

Despite the LCC's haste to empty the property, Kensington Gardens Studios remained standing for almost another year. In January 1958 Patricia Hutchins went to explore the place before it came down.

'It was very cold but there were huge fires at Notting Hill Gate where the new underground is to be built. The doors to Kensington Gardens Studios on the corner of the Mall were locked but at the back, a foreman sat on a pile of bricks . . . Two storeys above . . . was the wide gap which had been the window of the flat.' She climbed the concrete steps, walked along the dark empty corridor and into the Lewises' former home. She had been there only once before, in 1955, interviewing Lewis and collecting information about his former associates, Joyce and Pound.

Now, 'the interior of the flat was unrecognisable, like walls after an air raid, partitions gone, water pipes wrenched aside, a wound where shelves had been.' Picking through the rubble, pieces of coal and broken laths, she found a forgotten litter of newspaper clippings: reviews of *Paleface*, *The Apes of God* and *Self Condemned*.

633

Moving up to the studio, she noticed torn pieces of drawings that had fallen into a gully between staircase and wall. Some of these pieces she assembled into the portrait of a boy, worked and reworked, then abandoned. Also in that narrow space she found a copy of *The Egoist* dated 15 July 1914. It contained the 12th instalment of *A Portrait of the Artist as a Young Man*, an article called 'Mr Joyce Writes' by Ezra Pound, and Richard Aldington's review of *Blast*, illustrated by a Brodsky cartoon of 'The Lewis-Brzeska-Pound Troupe' blowing their own trumpets and frightening a top-hatted *Times* reader before the walls of Jericho.

Upstairs, the huge north-facing skylight was broken and chunks of glass, 'like ice from a pond', were scattered across the studio floor. Behind a disconnected water tank were pastels and worn hogshair brushes. Copies of *Vogue* and dress patterns showed the occasional use to which Mrs Lewis put the room when her husband's blindness had made it surplus to requirements as a painting studio. Also among the litter was a cobbler's repair outfit and shopping lists. Under the glass fragments lay a damp compost of papers and a few books. In a corner of the great barn of a room, untouched by rain from the shattered roof, was a postcard reproduction of Van Gogh's *Sower* from Munich.

In the ruined kitchen she found a stump of candle in an old-fashioned candlestick, and a 'Peterson' pipe. She looked out of the window, down to the bottleneck of Notting Hill Gate, soon to be eased by demolition of the building in which she was standing.

Back in the studio she examined the big 'Essa' stove, purchased in 1947, and so profligate with the inferior coal then available. A row of half-smoked cigarettes lay along its edge. Inside she found the delicate black curled remains of burnt paper. 'What memories had been consumed there on some last night of weary packing?' she asked herself.

It is idle to speculate on what documents Mrs Lewis had fed into the 'Essa' stove while preparing to leave 29A Kensington Gardens Studios for the last time. It is equally idle to wonder whether the succession of cigarettes, absent-mindedly rested there by the chainsmoker, then forgotten while she lit another, represented a single sitting or several; a cursory glance through her husband's papers as she packed them, or a more systematic cull. This, in the immediate aftermath of his death, would have been the first stage in her subsequent 20-year defence of Lewis's reputation.

When she left, Patricia Hutchins took with her all the papers she had found. At her house, 10 Kensington Church Walk, once the home of Ezra Pound, she sorted and dried out the soggy haul. She went back later, this time scouring the area behind the building, and, with considerable difficulty, retrieved more material from rubbish dumps on the site.

She invited Mrs Lewis for tea and showed her what she had recovered. Apart from the press clippings and *The Egoist*, there were a number of books and pamphlets, some of which, she surmised, 'had perhaps been hidden away behind furniture'. There was a copy of *The Borough* by George Crabbe, Arthur Kitsen's *Money*, an essay on economic reform by A. C. McGregor, Father D'Arcy's *Catholicism* and Goethe's *Campagne in Frankreich*. Finally there was a slim book entitled *Protocols of the Learned Elders of Zion*.

The full significance of this last publication may have at first escaped Mrs Lewis. When Hutchins suggested the books and papers be kept with her in Church Walk as a small archive for students and interested parties to consult in the future, Mrs Lewis agreed, claiming only the July 1914 *Egoist* for herself and taking it away with her. But a day or two later she returned to retrieve *The Protocols of Zion* as well.

She subsequently claimed Hutchins's story was 'not truthful' and warned her, through a solicitor, not to use anything 'she [was] supposed to have found in the studio.' Hutchins thought Lewis's widow was upset about what had been found abandoned to the ravages of the rain, 'as though it reflected on her care'. It is more likely, however, that Gladys was agitated about this inquisitive woman's discovery, in her former home, of one of the most notorious pieces of anti-Semitic propaganda ever published. This, at least, was what she must have been referring to when she accused Hutchins of being 'not truthful' about what she had found. 'One of the items', she assured her solicitor, 'I have never seen before and I had gone through very thoroughly the papers I left.'

As the author of a book on anti-Semitism, Lewis had, of course, an impeccable excuse for possessing a copy of the infamous text. Indeed, in *The Jews Are They Human?* he specifically referred to it, as one extreme of his own even-handed approach to the subject:

> I am proof against *The Protocols of the Learned Elders of Zion*, and also against invitations to pro-Jewish excesses. I neither regard the person of Jewish race as a devil nor as a darling.

Ironically, Lewis's little volume of 1939, deploring the treatment of Jew by Gentile, has acquired, on the basis of its too-clever title alone, as evil a reputation as *The Protocols of Zion* itself. So too the glib, under-researched defence of Hitler, published in 1931 at a time when not even the most prescient of political commentators could have imagined the full horror of the Third Reich, has, with hindsight, caused its author to be branded 'Fascist'. *Left Wings Over Europe* and *Count Your Dead: They Are Alive!* are remembered, if they are remembered at all, not as anti-war books, but as pro-Mussolini and pro-Franco respectively. Finally, even his 1939 anti-Nazi book, *The Hitler Cult*, written, it is argued, too late in the day to be at all convincing as a genuine change of heart, is seen as damage-limitation rather than recantation. 'These are long vendettas', he had written in 1933, of present and future detractors, 'a peculiar people, neither forgivers nor forgetters'.

Today, almost 70 years later, the opening of an exhibition of his paintings, the publication of a critical monograph or biography, indeed any occasion generating renewed interest in Wyndham Lewis's life and work, will still prompt the knowing question, in a radio or television discussion programme: 'And his support for Hitler, what of that?' The stigma remains. His widow had good reason to be protective. So it would hardly have been surprising if, attempting to forestall the denigration of her husband's reputation by posterity, Gladys returned home from her second visit to Kensington Church Walk and immediately reduced *The Protocols of Zion* to ashes.

Patricia Hutchins sent her the five-page typescript of the article she had written, ' "Lot Thirteen": The Last of Wyndham Lewis', for approval and permission to publish. Both were denied. But Hutchins spoke on the Home Service's *Today* programme, in the early morning of 7 March 1958, the first anniversary of Lewis's death. In conversation with Robin Boyle she described her visit to the derelict building but provided few details of the material she had found and brought away with her. The piece ended with her final salutation before leaving the wrecked shell of 29A Kensington Gardens Studios:

> knowing that in a day or two, air and emptiness would take over the man-made space there, I called, that it might be heard for the last time – Wyndham Lewis! Then I remembered his Christian name, but one does not take a liberty with so great, so strong a ghost!

ACKNOWLEDGEMENTS

Victor M. Cassidy of Chicago, Illinois, laid the groundwork for this book. When, in 1990, I mentioned in the pages of *Enemy News*, Journal of the Wyndham Lewis Society, that I was embarking on a biography, Cassidy wrote to offer me the research material he had amassed for his own, abandoned, book. He had started working on a life of Lewis in 1970 and he passed on to me the contents of one-and-a-half filing cabinets, 12 ring files crammed with xeroxes and notes on Lewis's correspondence, photographs collected from a number of sources, transcripts of interviews, card indexes, etc., etc. These papers have been my daily companion for the last decade and I can honestly say that, without Victor Cassidy's industry, scholarship and his extraordinarily generous gesture, the book, in its present form, could not have been written.

Geoffrey Ward first suggested to me the idea for a biography of Lewis in a Liverpool pub called 'The Blackburne', and Marion Wynne-Davies made initial moves towards finding it a publisher. She also put me in touch with my agent at A. M. Heath, Bill Hamilton, whose grandfather, serendipitously, turned out to have been Lewis's agent in the 1930s. Later, Marion Wynne-Davies's credit card rescued me from a peculiarly Lewisian predicament when I found myself stranded, without money, in Montreal.

The University of Liverpool provided generous financial assistance in the early stages, as did the Society of Authors. A British Academy grant enabled me to make the first of two research trips to the USA and Canada. The Wyndham Lewis Memorial Trust, comprising Jim Dolman, C. J. Fox, Graham Lane and Omar S. Pound, showed its faith in the project by buying me a computer. That machine obeyed my every command over the strenuous course of work before collapsing, exhausted and foaming, in the final straight. A. M. Heath gave me another, surplus to their requirements and already out to grass, which finally carried me past the post.

A great many people have helped gather information. Alan Munton generously shared with me the fruits of his researches into Lewis's First World War experience. Cy Fox gave me the benefit of a daunting wealth of knowledge. Graham Lane's comprehensive library of Lewis's works has been an invaluable resource and I have shamefully exploited his good nature on several occasions by telephoning and demanding the precise wording of one reference or another. I recall him, recently, scanning *Hitler* in search of a particularly elusive quotation. Michael Wood, Jean Samuel and the staff of Bircham & Co. provided access to the Lewis papers in their care and made diligent searches for birth, marriage and death certificates in the Public Records Office. I am grateful to Frank Milner of the National Museums and Galleries of Merseyside for allowing me access to the Walker Art Gallery's library of exhibition catalogues; to Pauline Rushton of Liverpool Museum's Decorative Arts department for information about gentlemen's shirt collars and ladies' dress styles, and Simon Jones, curator of the N.M.G.M.'s King's Regiment Collection, for guiding me through military records and the intricacies of trench maps. Stephen Corrie at the British Museum supplied details of Lewis's reader's card application and renewals. Stephen Chaplin, at the Slade School, showed me the signing-in books once presided over by Campion and explained the layout of the building as it was in Lewis's day. Sidney Hutchison revealed the mechanics and conventions of the selection process for the Royal Academy Summer Exhibition. Dick Humphreys of the Tate Gallery, Millbank, and Sarah Fox-Pitt of the Tate Archives also gave assistance, as did Joan Fillmore of Cumberland County Museum, Amherst, Nova Scotia, Mark Shipley of the Leeds University Archives, and Carrie Starren of the Local History Department of Kensington Public Library. My thanks also go to the splendid staff, both past and present, of the Rare and Manuscript Collections at Cornell University, particularly Joan Winterkorn, James Tyler, Mark Dimunation and Lucy B. Burgess; to Robert J. Bertholf of the Poetry/Rare Books Collection at SUNY Buffalo; to Bruce Whittman of the Department of Rare Books, McGill University, Montreal, and to the staff of Princeton University Library; also to Catherine Mastin of the Art Gallery of Windsor, Ontario, for her hospitality and for effecting an introduction to the Honourable Paul Martin and Eleonor Martin; and, in Toronto, to Hugh Anson Cartwright and Douglas LePan, and to Robert Stacey for his hospitality, the local knowledge he shared and for the $40 that enabled me to leave that city. I am grateful to Omar Pound and his wife for their hospitality, cheer and reminiscences in Princeton, New Jersey, and to Walter and Harriet Michel for a delightful and informative afternoon at their home in Ringoes, New Jersey.

For their patience in answering my morbid enquiries, thanks to: Dr Vince Chauhan, Chief M.L.S.O., curator of the Pathology Museum, Imperial College School of Medicine, and his predecessor Dr Antony Carré Branfoot Ch.B., FRCS, F.R.C.Path., curator of the Museum before its move to Hammersmith; Dr Alan Douglas Morgan MD, Ch.B., who performed the post mortem on Lewis, and Dr Swithen P. Meadows MD, MRCS, LRCP, who diagnosed his pituitary tumour; also John Clark Ch.M., FRCS, Susan

Clark M.R.Pharm.S., Dr Edward Williams Hughes MD, FRCP, and Christopher Neoh FRCS, F.R.C.Oph.

Thanks also to Adrian Henri for checking the back of the portrait of T. S. Eliot for chalk marks in Durban, South Africa; Mike Riggelsford for obtaining xerox copies of relevant pages in the Teyler Museum visitors' book; Herbert Williams, Mary Johnson, Patrick Galvin and Gerry Murphy for researches in Cork; Richard Williams for sundry trawls through the Public Records Office for passenger lists and census returns; Lilian Williams for translations and for corresponding on my behalf with Dieppe and Wuppertal; Waltraud Boxall for answering queries relating to the German tongue and Mike Boxall for a gift of *The Old Gang and the New Gang*; David Smith and Lesley Keen for the breakthrough of information concerning Olive Johnson and Peter Lewis, and for facilitating contact with Peter's daughter, Margot Lewis, and to Margot herself for providing photographs of her father; John Russ and his sister Roxanne Collins for providing information and photographs of their parents, Sidney and Mary Priestley Russ. My thanks to Robyn Denny, Naomi Mitchison, Stephen Spender and Julian Symons for sharing their memories of Lewis and to Frederick Gore RA for allowing me access to his father's papers.

For a variety of information, conversational insights and technical assistance, thanks to the following: Robin Barry, Peter Carracciolo, Giovanni Cianci, Margaret Comery, Robert Cowan, Joseph B. Dallet, Tony Dash, Arthur and Lillian Elliot, Toby Hall, Malcolm Hicks, Friedrich Hitzer, Justine Hopkins, Kate Hughes, Philip Niles Jones, David McKnight, Gordon Mills, Ian Patterson, Ian Qualtraugh, Ron Stewart, Elisa Swinglehurst, Mr and Mrs A. R. Trotter of Charterhall, Duns, Larry Tucker, Brian Wake, Catherine Wallace, Gordon Wightman, David Williams and Suzanne Yee.

Special thanks go to Paul Edwards, a learned and unselfish consultant, whose knowledge of Lewis scholarship is unparalleled and who could tell me in an instant whether an idea was truly original or already exhaustively explored elsewhere; to my neighbour, John Edmund Vaughan, whose library has yielded answers to more of my questions than I can remember; and to Sian Hughes, unfailing arbiter of grammar, syntax and sense, who had no idea, when first she heard the recorded voice intoning 'If so the man you are' through her car stereo, how long she would live with the spectre of Wyndham Lewis and even grow to quite like him.

My thanks also to Birgitte Sigmundstad for her photographic work among the macabre specimens at Hammersmith, to Steve Cox for an awe-inspiring job of copy editing and Jörg Hensgen for his invariably reassuring phone calls while co-ordinating the final stages of production. And finally, to my editor, genial lunch companion and friend, Will Sulkin, for his patience, enthusiasm and unflagging faith in this book, the warmest thanks of all.

Photographic Credits

For kind permission to reproduce illustrations, the author and publishers wish to express their thanks to the following: the Division of Rare and Manuscript Collections, Cornell University Library, for photographs of Anne Stuart Prickett, Charles Edward Lewis, Wyndham Lewis aged about six, as Bombardier, as 2nd Lieutenant, aged about thirty-seven and 'writing blind', and for photographs of Ida Vendel, Marjorie Firminger, and of Gladys Hoskins with her family in Brighton, and with Lewis aboard SS *Empress of Britain*; the Burser of Rugby School for photographs of Stallard House, 1897 and 1898; the University of London Library for the photograph of Lewis aged about twenty-five (Sturge Moore Papers MS 30/95); Ivor Braker for permission to reproduce the drawing 'Mamie', 1911; Lesley Keen for photographs of Olive Elstow née Johnson in the 1940s; Margot Lewis for the photograph of Peter Lewis; the British Library for permission to reproduce illustrations from *The Sketch*; Manchester Art Gallery for permission to reproduce the drawing of Iris Barry, 'Girl Knitting', 1920; Express Newspapers for permission to reproduce the *Star* front page; John Russ for the 1933 portrait of Sidney Russ and the photograph of Mary Priestley Russ; the City of Toronto Archives for photographs of the Tudor Hotel from the *Globe and Mail* Collection; the Tate Gallery, Millbank, for permission to reproduce 'A Canadian War Factory'; Dr S. P. Meadows for the X-ray of Lewis's skull; the Ross-Parry Picture Agency for the photograph of Lewis being presented to the Princess Royal, Leeds, November 1952; the Estate of Michael Ayrton for permission to reproduce the dustwrapper design of *Self Condemned* and for the photograph of the 1956 Tate Gallery Retrospective Exhibition 'Wyndham Lewis and Vorticism'; and Fox Photos Ltd for the photograph of Lewis in the courtyard of Burlington House, April 1938.

REFERENCES

When the identity of writer and recipient is clear from the text, only the date of letters, if known, together with the source, is given. Manuscript collections are referred to in brief and bracketed (see Bibliography). PWL denotes Percy Wyndham Lewis; ASL, Anne Stuart Lewis; CEL, Charles Edward Lewis; and GAL, Gladys Anne Lewis.

Frequently cited titles have been shortened as follows:
AIP – *America, I Presume*
B&B – *Blasting and Bombardiering*
EN – *Enemy News: Journal of the Wyndham Lewis Society*
P/L – *Pound/Lewis*
RA – *Rude Assignment*

CHAPTER 1

3 'queer white . . . old frog': *A Friendship Documented* ed. Constable and Watson, p. 42–3.

CHAPTER 2

4 'It was . . . a wharf': 'The Vita of Wyndham Lewis' ed. Bernard Lafourcade *EN* 20 Winter 1984.
4–5 'November 18 . . . Canada': PWL to Immigration authorities, 16/8/40 (Cornell).
5 'moderate . . . temperature': 17/11/1882.
6 'was ablaze . . . in telegraphy': *Daily Evening News* 18/11/1882.
'fully two thirds . . . many colours': *ibid.* 20/11/1882.
7 'Do you . . . little place': *Interviews and Recollections* ed. Mikhail, p. 107.
'gallant . . . the war': memo on CEL's military service (National Archives).
8 'ESCAPE . . . Interesting Inci-

dents': 18/2/1865.
'Most miserable . . . hotel': (Cornell).
'I sympathise . . . your own': 28/9/1877 (Cornell).
9 'longing . . . shall be': 2/8/1877 transcribed by GAL (Cornell).
'ask the nurse . . . come home': 6/9/1877 ibid. (Cornell).
'It is hard . . . look at them dear': 10/10/1877 ibid. (Cornell).
9–12 'much warmer . . . peck of apples': ASL Diary (Cornell).
13 'my mother . . . inside it': 'Vita of Wyndham Lewis'.
'My infant . . . English coast': to Giovanelli 18/10/48 (Cornell).
'the Collis boys': GAL Biographical Notes (Cornell).
'At around . . . small American': 'Vita of Wyndham Lewis'.

CHAPTER 3

15 'So it is' . . . looming ahead': *Seeds*

in the Wind ed. Braybrooke p.70.

16 'would be willing . . . afresh': ASL
to CEL 16/5/1893 (Cornell).
'the old people . . . Polly': to ASL
n.d. (Cornell).
'He looks . . . as a berry': ibid. n.d.
(Cornell).
'a thunderous roar . . . cheered':
Seeds in the Wind pp. 76–7.
'Am greatly disappointed . . .
future': CEL to ASL n.d. (Cornell).

17 'very comfortable . . . Cottage':
CEL to ASL n.d. (Cornell).
'about out of funds . . . days later':
CEL to ASL 20/12/1892 (Cornell).
'coal and things': CEL to ASL 3/1/
1893 (Cornell).
'Charley went . . . astonished': to
ASL 7/10/1893 (Cornell).

17–   'I must admit . . . Yours unfaith-
18   fully': 15/4/1893 (Cornell).

18   'As man and wife . . . that is': ibid.
(Cornell).

18–   'fondly and devotedly . . . divorced':
19   16/4/1893 (Cornell).

19   'seems . . . intercourse with him': 6/
7/1893 (Cornell).
'About Charles . . . see him again':
to ASL 14/12/93 (Cornell).
'simply . . . my brother': to ASL 6/
7/1893 (Cornell).
'But [he] bemoans . . . upon himself': 8/6/1894 (Cornell).
'I can't quite . . . wrong way': to
ASL 25/5/1894 (Cornell).
'As for yourself . . . friend': 8/6/
1894 (Cornell).

19–   'good time . . . our form': n.d.
20   (Cornell).

20   'I do not intend . . . to follow': 22/
8/1894 (Cornell).

21   'It will teach . . . as well': to ASL
10/12/1894 (Cornell).
'Mr Morgan . . . playground shed':
18/1/1895 (Cornell).
'I have without . . . impossible': to
ASL 10/7/94 (Cornell).
'a most beautiful . . . grievously':
ibid. 20/11/1897 (Cornell).

21–2 'Fair . . . on the whole': (Cornell).

22   'footer . . . was there': to ASL n.d.
(Cornell).
'Scarcely did I . . . didn't mind':
'Vita of Wyndham Lewis'.

23   'two years . . . work': *RA* p. 250.
'bunked . . . 'sixth licking': n.d.
(Cornell).
'He . . . was very proud . . . prefect's
door': 'Wyndham Lewis' *The Atlantic* December 1969.

23–   'I feel sure . . . hard to tell': 18/12/
24   1897 (Cornell).

24   'Whatever it be . . . education': 20/
11/1897 (Cornell).
'some weeks every . . . mesmerism':
RA p. 249.

25   'Instead of poring . . . normal company': ibid. p. 249.
'an old Scot . . . enthusiasm': ibid.
p. 119.
'Is not doing . . . work or go':
(Cornell).

CHAPTER 4

26–   'about fifty . . . Nor did he': 'Three
27   Teachers: Brown, Tonks and Steer'
Burlington Magazine June 1943.

27   'This was . . . we were told': ibid.
'Slade School ingenious': *RA* p.
127.

28   'treating chiefly . . . Living Model':
Slade School Prospectus 1900–1.

29   'Veal and ham . . . student': handwritten draft of *RA* (Cornell).
'my first experience . . . race': handwritten draft of *RA* (Cornell).

30   'Your brother . . . bogey for me': to
Hilton 9/6/51 (Cornell).

31–   'a hairy male . . . images': *RA* pp.
33   127–8.

33   '1899 was the year . . . School': 'The
Slade School Summer Composi-
tions since 1893' *The Slade* . . . p.
25.
'I tried my hand . . . Signorelli': *RA*
p. 128.
'I had always . . . cinquecento': 9/4/
47 (Cornell).

35   'He liked . . . never met': *Men and
Memories* vol. II pp. 26–7.

36   'My son . . . no more': (Trust).
'So great . . . watch him work':
(Cornell).

37   'giving assistance . . . younger Students': Slade School Prospectus
1900–1.

'I was seldom ... the nude': *RA* p. 250.

'The Council ... the Schools': Slade School Prospectus 1900–1.

'like many other ... himself': (Cornell).

'the same ... the door': *RA* p. 250.

38 'So bitterly ... dangerous': quoted Cork *Vorticism* ... vol. I, p. 3.

CHAPTER 5

39 'He hesitated ... daily life': *Men and Memories* vol. II, pp. 26–7.

'To Doubt' ... 16th year': note on MS. (Cornell).

'So young ... as I am': handwritten draft of *RA* (Cornell).

'strange and interesting': *Men and Memories* vol. II p. 26.

39– 'he has written ... to a man!': *The*
40 *Apes of God* p. 40.

40 'sooner or later ... by the way': Yeats to W. Rothenstein 17/10/02 *Letters* vol. III pp. 235–6.

'an exquisite ... hardly anyone': *Men and Memories* vol. II p. 19.

'so young ... three or four': *RA* p. 124.

40– 'Mr Boleyn ... lovely poem': *The*
41 *Apes of God* p. 40.

41 'Ace, tray ... space?': ibid. p. 341.

'SUICIDE'S TOILET ... unsound mind': 28/4/02.

42 'While still ... demands that': *Twentieth Century Palette* p. 77 Unpublished typescript (Cornell).

43 'How calm ... taught me that': 12/7/42 (Cornell).

'this patriarch ... biblical courses': *RA* p. 128.

'The only people ... their own': ibid. p. 123.

CHAPTER 6

45– 'I think Madrid ... lot here': PWL
46 to ASL n.d. (Cornell).

46 'studied ... Venetian grounds': to Barr 24/11/41 (Cornell).

'We ... while I'm abroad': PWL to ASL n.d. (Cornell).

47– 'very stupid ... exaggerate that':
48 ibid. 7/10/04 (Cornell).

48 'They pawned ... their pawnings': ibid. n.d. (Cornell).

49 'I can't work ... needn't detail': ibid. n.d. (Cornell).

'models more less ... in London': ibid. n.d. (Cornell).

'Italian models ... cigarettes': ibid. (Cornell)

49– 'I don't much ... difficulty': ibid.
50 n.d. (Cornell).

50 'be able ... occasionally': ibid. n.d. (Cornell).

CHAPTER 7

52 'which shows ... amusing yourself': 10/1/05 (Cornell).

'about 14/- ... 17/- a week': PWL to ASL n.d. (Cornell).

'extremely bad for painting': ibid. n.d. (Cornell).

'I am going ... of a sou': ibid. n.d. (Cornell).

53 'the after effects ... of medicine': ibid. n.d. (Cornell).

'I am suffering ... holiday': n.d. (Aberystwyth).

'Am I 22 ... return of post': n.d. (Cornell).

'I don't very ... *pour elle*': n.d. (Cornell).

53– 'The German ... bred mistress': to
54 ASL n.d. (Cornell).

54 'girls who ... so far either': ibid. n.d. (Cornell).

'You have ... visit you there': n.d. (Aberystwyth).

55 'A magnificent ... willing to lend': to ASL n.d. (Cornell).

'It wouldn't matter ... Christmas': ibid. pmk 30/9/05 (Cornell).

'She poses ... number of hours': ibid. n.d. (Cornell).

'I am ... models go': ibid. n.d. (Cornell).

'I begin ... long ago': ibid. n.d. (Cornell).

'I don't want ... my model': ibid. pmk 30/9/05 (Cornell).

56 'the proper person ... present address': 12/9/05 (Cornell).
'We were foolish ... getting it': to PWL 2/10/05 (Cornell).
'It appears ... in a store': 12/09/05 (Cornell).
'The one thing ... present': 2/10/05 (Cornell).
'a room ... 7/- or 7/6': PWL to ASL n.d. (Cornell).

57 'The drawing ... make thirty': ibid. n.d. (Cornell).

57– 'You might have ... state of fin-
58 ances': 9/11/05 (Cornell).

58 'It is a pity ... responsibilities': 20/9/05 (Cornell).
'If you get ... saving of £2. 8s.': 9/11/05 (Cornell).
'Well dear boy ... alone': 9/11/05 (Cornell).
'It is the man's ... time also': 6/12/05 trans. from French (Cornell).

59 'and the way ... much, Percy': Ida Vendel to PWL n.d. (Cornell).
'How dreadfully ... Ida's purity': 17/11/05 (Cornell).
'You want to ... what she is!': *Tarr* p. 224.

59– 'I will only ... de ses forces':
60 Simons to PWL 17/11/05 (Cornell).

60– 'I will never ... for good': Hedwig
61 Vendel to PWL 6/12/05 (Cornell).

61 'Personally I like ... very tactless': to PWL 27/6/07 (Cornell).
'I play ... nothing, nothing!!': n.d. trans. from French (Cornell).

62 'I don't think ... arrange itself': to ASL n.d. (Cornell).

CHAPTER 8

63 'this modern ... Elberfeld?': *Blast War Number* p. 9.
'The only effect ... sadder': to ASL n.d. (Cornell).

63– 'Some of the best ... may have':
64 n.d. (Cornell).

64 'The pension ... disagreeable': n.d. (Cornell).
'There is always ... 6 weeks!': n.d. (Cornell).

65 'I will never ... wear them': pmk 3/2/06 (Cornell).
'very amusing ... articles of attire': n.d. (Cornell).

65– 'and avoid *Bal Parés* ... say any-
66 thing': n.d. (Cornell).

66 'I slept well ... my life': n.d. trans. from French (Cornell).
'it's really ... freer afterwards': n.d. (Cornell).
'I want ... good for me': n.d. trans. from French (Cornell).
'it is 20 marks ... good to be true': to ASL n.d. (Cornell).

66– 'After this blow ... sure I am': ibid.
68 n.d. (Cornell).

68– 'Received your letter ... two rent-
69 als': 14/4/08 trans. from French (Cornell).

69 'I'm going ... its existence': n.d. (Aberystwyth).

69– 'I am writing ... *Faust* forthwith':
70 n.d. (Aberystwyth).

70 'matrimonial projects ... habitual padding': n.d. (Aberystwyth).
'My poet ... consulting me': n.d. (Huntington).
'although hardly knowing ... handbook': PWL to John n.d. (Aberystwyth).

71 'you always ... ashamed of me?': n.d. (Cornell).
'this cost me a little': to ASL n.d. (Cornell).
'dirtiness ... him so much': n.d. (Cornell).

71– 'He came back ... I wept': n.d.
72 (Huntington).

72 'I can't ... frustrates any effort': n.d. (Cornell).
'The poet irritates ... boundless': to Schepeler n.d. (Huntington).
'He had never ... an ox's!': *Tarr* p. 294.
'What a mistake ... each remark': to Schepeler n.d. (Huntington).
'send me ... that score': n.d. (Cornell).

72– 'laboratorical gibberish ... ex-
73 tremely ridiculous': n.d. (Aberystwyth).

73 'I felt ... stay away': 12/6/07 (Cornell).

'a convenient . . . human groups':
Tarr p. 21.

74 'I wish . . . as well': to ASL n.d.
(Cornell).
'She is abusing . . . the letter': ibid.
(Cornell).

74– 'They called me . . . a bit': ibid.
75 (Cornell).

75 'What a refreshment . . . brother': to
John n.d. (Aberystwyth).
'of peritonitis . . . other things':
PWL to ASL n.d. (Cornell).

75– 'I have roughly . . . astonishing':
76 n.d. (Cornell).

76 'To show how . . . saw Everett': to
ASL n.d. (Cornell).
'I have . . . little helps': ibid. n.d.
(Cornell).
'Ida is here . . . relationship with
her': n.d. (Cornell).
'I couldn't . . . the contrary': n.d.
(Cornell).
'I have . . . about it': n.d. (Cornell).

77 'I don't see . . . isn't it?': n.d.
(Cornell).
'An intense . . . on a beetle': *Tarr* p.
309.
'I've not seen . . . german bitch':
n.d. (Cornell).
'I think . . . this *world*': n.d. (Cornell).

77– 'Lewis announced . . . *le nigaud*':
78 n.d. (Huntington).

78 'I've come . . . without her': to ASL
n.d. (Cornell).
'Oh, so it's . . . if you can': ibid. n.d.
(Cornell).

CHAPTER 9

79 'I think . . . better terms': 27/6/07
(Cornell).
'As to Lewis . . . tergiversation': n.d.
(Huntington).

79– 'Renouncing the illusions . . . his
80 savages': n.d. (Cornell).

80 'I have begun . . . did it': 18/2/07
quoted Shone *Bloomsbury Portraits*
p. 44.

80– 'I got the 3 . . . Schelfhout days': to
81 ASL n.d. (Cornell).

81 'I really think . . . to Brittany': 27/
6/07 (Cornell).

'We arrived . . . installed myself': to
ASL n.d. trans. from French (Cornell).
'She . . . said . . . again meet': ASL
to PWL 27/6/07 (Cornell).
'I've had a lesson . . . in a hurry':
PWL to ASL n.d. (Cornell).
'Although you feel . . . goes there':
27/6/07 (Cornell).

82 'The mandates . . . see her again':
Tarr p. 207.
'the best thing . . . other friend':
PWL to ASL n.d. (Cornell).
'Lewis no doubt . . . petits Suisses':
27/7/07 (Tate).

82– 'sitting on a bench . . . receive alms':
83 quoted Paul Edwards 'Wyndham
Lewis's Narrative of Origins: "The
Death of the Ankou" ' *Modern Language Review* January 1997.

83 'I was painting . . . a complementary
creation': *Beginnings* pp. 100–1.

83– 'Don't send . . . *tiny* scratchings':
84 30/5/08 (Cornell).

84 'That devil Lewis . . . promises to
pay': 10/1/08 (Tate).
'We accosted . . . than formerly': to
Lamb 6/2/08 (Tate).
'It might be . . . delighted': 11/3/08
(Cornell).

86 'his Spanish . . . surprising people':
Complete Wild Body p. 228.
'I daresay . . . your heart': 24/7/08
and 20/9/08 (Cornell).
'It is most dangerous . . . proper
remedies': 24/7/08 (Cornell).
'I hope you will . . . tired out': 16/
7/08 (Cornell).

87 'My poor Lewis . . . Spanish frankness?': n.d. (Cornell).
'a tall . . . best of hearts': *Complete
Wild Body* p. 264.
'I have recently . . . confraternity':
6/11/08 quoted Holroyd *Augustus
John* p. 284.
'the daughter . . . hidalgo': *Complete
Wild Body* p. 196.

88 'Now I believe . . . necessary
things': 19/7/08 (Cornell).
'These fetes . . . most precious':
Complete Wild Body p. 194.

89 '*Don't* get *wet* . . . *unboiled milk*':
5/9/08 (Cornell).

'don't go . . . guide books say': 20/
9/08 (Cornell).
'Added to this . . . and dirtier': 4/
10/08 (Cornell).
'this cantankerous old woman': to
PWL 12/9/08 (Cornell).
'little airs . . . tiresome': ibid. 20/9/
08 (Cornell).

90   'get your writing . . . you can see':
20/9/08 (Cornell).
'collect all . . . departure': 20/10/08
(Cornell).
'and a few other . . . in December':
ASL to PWL 25/11/08 (Cornell).

91   'My dear Missis Lewis . . . does he
work?': (Cornell).
'Don't get . . . *any money*': 25/11/
08 (Cornell).

CHAPTER 10

92   'I often think . . . communicate
with': 18/11/08 (Cornell).
'The Brittany . . . to listen': 9/2/09
(Cornell).
'The day before . . . her children?':
Memoirs p. 214.

93   'very bad way . . . his genius': n.d.
(London).
'Unpardonably . . . carelessness': to
Sturge Moore n.d. (London).
'prepared . . . for your curses . . .
the writing': n.d. (London).

94   'Hueffer is a shit . . . for myself':
n.d. (London).

94– 'something happened . . . advertise-
95   ment for him': n.d. (Tate).

95   'at the end . . . in the face': n.d.
(Cornell).

96   'Dorelia is . . . strenuous plotting':
n.d. (Aberystwyth).
'chiefly army . . . subtle for them':
PWL to Pinker n.d. (NYPL).
'miserable pot-boiler': ibid. n.d.
(NYPL).
'not marketable . . . pot-boiling':
ibid. n.d. (NYPL).
'I can probably . . . not recur': ibid.
n.d. (NYPL).

97   'we wish to exalt . . . white teeth':
South Lodge pp. 64–5.

'I am to tell . . . Mona Lisa?': n.d.
(Aberystwyth).

98   'The clap . . . voilà tout': n.d.
(Tate).
'an "analytic novel" . . . etc': n.d.
(Tate).

CHAPTER 11

99   'On or about . . . year 1910': *Mr
Bennett and Mrs Brown* p. 4.

100 'cutting away . . . abstract elements':
'The Grafton Gallery – I', *The
Nation*, 19/11/10.

101 'By an admirably . . . his peers': 12/
11/10.
'a fine thing . . . exquisite thing':
The Builder 12/11/10.
'This show . . . British philistinism':
to Dickinson 15/10/10 *Letters* vol.
I, p. 337.

101– 'It is paint . . . sick headache': 9/11/
102 10.

102 'It is all titter . . . a monocle': 24/
11/10.
'A stout, elderly . . . fresh air': 'The
Art-Quake of 1910' *The Listener* 1/
2/43.
'The exhibition . . . bonfire of
them': *My Diaries* vol. II pp. 343–4.

103 'For a moment . . . unmanly show':
16/11/10.
'Don't go in . . . evil': *Exhibition* p.
39.
'a very small . . analytic novel': n.d.
(Aberystwyth).

104 'I suppose . . . justified this step':
n.d (London).

CHAPTER 12

106 'It has been . . . novel from me': n.d.
(London).
'The critics . . . But invariably!':
n.d. (London).

107 'I was neither . . . of archaism': 18/
6/11.
'A few visitors . . . "queer" ': 18/6/
11.
'As an imaginary . . . exhibition': 3/
7/11.

'fools will behave ... too late': 6/
10/11 (Cornell).

108 'these two psychological ... came
here': n.d. (London).

109 'I shall now ... finished it': n.d.
(London).
'a largish ... yellows and browns':
RA p. 130.
'two men ... vanished': quoted
Michel *Paintings and Drawings* p.
333.

109– 'Mr Wyndham Lewis ... pictures':
10 11/12/11.

110 'Mr Wyndham Lewis's ... criticism': 9/12/11.
'the Fishermen ... this subject': 2/
12/11 (Cornell).
'I am quite ... such rubbish': n.d.
(Ashmolean).

CHAPTER 13

111 'all things ... blended with it':
Futurist Manifestos pp. 27–8.
'WHAT DO YOU ... SERIOUSLY?':
6/3/12

112 'The Club will ... dancers dance':
(Gore).
'I admit ... unnerved me': *Chiaroscuro* p. 116.
'a sort of man hole': 27/6/12.
'even more delightful ... continuous joy': 30/6/12.

113 'enough ... till dawn': *The Times*
27/6/12.
'two paintings ... of the walls': n.d.
(Cornell).

114 'a cubistic ... red and purple': John
Quinn Sale Catalogue 1927.
'kissing ... the mouth': 27/11/13.
'two wicked-looking eyes': quoted
Robins *Modern Art in Britain* p.
137.
'some terrible battle ... murderous
insects': *Daily Telegraph* 21/10/13.
'some gigantic ... other planet':
Observer 26/10/13.
'crabs in anguish ... lobster legs':
quoted Robins *Modern Art in Britain* p. 137.

114– 'His design ... beauty of colour':
15 *Nation* 20/7/12.

115 'having shed ... achievement': 27/
7/12.

116 'we are persuaded ... not wanting':
30/7/12
'that wretched fellow ... gratitude':
n.d. (Cornell).
'an almost derelict firm': *South
Lodge* p. 61.

116– 'My good girl ... a genius': Tripp
17 to PWL 19/8/12 (Cornell).

117 'Your great fault ... view': n.d.
(Cornell).
'fire, water ... serious nature': n.d.
(Cornell).

118 'one of the most ... divested of
function': 12/10/12.

118– 'Mr Wyndham Lewis ... repres-
19 ents': 19/12/12.

119 'with the majority ... mechanical
marionette': 14/12/12.
'the honorary ... together': *South
Lodge* p. 62.

120 'with or without ... possible chance':
17/12/12 (Cornell).

120– 'One youthful person ... gets dull':
21 1/1/14.

CHAPTER 14

122 'disreputable Slav ... mouth for
you': n.d (Princeton).
'most amicable ... entertaining':
'Wyndham Lewis from 1912'.
'When the time ... his demands':
Beginning Again p. 95.

123 'all other contributors ... my vanity': n.d. (Cornell).
'a fresh impression ... arouses':
quoted *Times* 20/3/13.
'It is not ... archaic women': 24/3/
13.
'a synthesis of laughter': 27/3/13.
'If his composition ... its kind': 20/
3/13.
'a large paper-picture': to Oliver
Brown 11/2/37 (Cornell).
'an over-lifesize ... reddish': *RA* p.
130.

124 'undistinguished . . . number': *Athenaeum* 22/3/13.
'a large paper . . . Laughing Woman" ': n.d. (Cornell).

125 'I've *got* to . . . workshop': 31/5/13 *Letters* vol. II p. 369.

125– 'building up . . . Adios': Gill to
26 Duncan Grant 29/8/66 (V&A).

126 ' "Group" is more . . . no primitive': 2/8/13.

127 'stages . . . young woman': Gill to Grant, June 1966 (V&A).
' "Laughing Woman" . . . *Contemporary Art Society*': n.d. (Cornell).
'I'm afraid . . . final judgement': n.d. (Cornell).

128 'My wife . . . miscarry': to PWL n.d. (Cornell).
'The chains . . . work of hanging': ibid. 4/8/13 (Cornell).

CHAPTER 15

129– 'have been given . . . said by me': to
30 PWL 4/8/13 (Cornell).

130 'through Bloomsbury influence': *RA* p. 130.
'at any rate . . . nightmare shape': 2/2/14.
'For God's sake . . . YOURSELF": n.d. (Gore).
'in an advanced style': Fry to Gore 7/10/13 quoted Quentin Bell and Stephen Chaplin 'The Ideal Home Rumpus' *Apollo* June 1966.

131 'as you very . . . *Daily Mail*': (Gore).
'the Omega . . . various artists': (Gore).

132 'Nothing at all . . . No decorations': PWL to Bell n.d. (Cornell).
'It was . . . [wall] decoration': to Gore 9/10/13 and 18/10/13 (Gore).
'Lewis had . . . over that': quoted Cork to Cassidy 21/6/70.
'Did you know . . . in vain': n.d. (Aberystwyth).

132– 'I am sorry . . . enjoyed it more':
33 n.d. (Cornell).

133 'Ça, c'est trop fort!': quoted 'Ideal Home Rumpus'.

133– 'Understanding that . . . of the
34 Omega': n.d. (Cornell).

134 'I . . . can only . . . my things': (Cornell).

134– 'We have had . . . the writers':
35 quoted 'Ideal Home Rumpus'.

135 'you ought not . . . doing there?': quoted Bell and Chaplin, correspondence *Apollo* January 1966.

135– 'Prettiness . . . action for libel':
36 quoted 'Ideal Home Rumpus'.

136 'I am very sorry . . . supporters': to PWL 21/10/13 (Cornell).
'I have received . . . sordid intrigues': n.d. (Cornell).
'The commission . . . latter gentlemen': quoted 'Ideal Home Rumpus'.
'I think . . . shall not oblige': to Rose Vildrac 4/11/13 *Letters* vol. II p. 375.

137 'to transact . . . business': n.d. (Cornell).
'a young frenchman . . . very different': *Autobiography of Alice B. Toklas* p. 134.

138 'bustle . . . leave her "en panne" ': n.d (Cornell).
'The Strindberg . . . godless old ape': n.d. (Cornell).

CHAPTER 16

139 'zang – tumb . . . TUMB-TUUUUUM': *Marinetti e il futurismo* p. 323.
'It was . . . by comparison': *B&B* p. 37.
'Lewis was threatening . . . hand first': quoted Cork *Art Beyond the Gallery* p. 109.

140 'I don't think . . . fools come': 19/11/13 (Cornell).
'I am going . . . been put on': quoted Hassall *Edward Marsh* p. 258.
'the sick poor of all denominations': *Times* 24/10/13.

140– 'She wants . . . a buyer': n.d. (Cor-
41 nell).

141 'Exquisite . . . nightmare faces': 4/12/13.

'menacing . . . people laugh': 4/12/13.

'a good note . . . Christmas carnival': 4/12/13.

141– 'the crowd . . . exhibition of dan-
42 cing': 4/12/13 (Cornell).

142 'I saw futurist . . . "Robert E. Lee" ': 4/12/13.

'I hope . . . diminish': 21/10/13 (Cornell).

'I have not . . . something *better*': 17/12/13 (Cornell).

'You may . . . we miss': *Letters* p. 65.

143 'His bull-dog . . . M[oore]'s bull-dog': *The Cantos*, LXXX, p. 507.

'It was a solemn . . . his instructions': *South Lodge* pp. 67–8.

144 'a special night . . . "Blast Club" ': n.d (Cornell).

'The Lewis group . . . amazing thing': 26/1/14 *Letters* vol. II p. 378.

144– 'the departure . . . mediocre stuff':
45 15/1/14.

145 'You've got to . . . public': 'Talk with K. Lechmere 1 January 1954'. Xerox obtained from Victor Cassidy. Whereabouts of original typescript and identity of interviewer unknown.

'almost wholly . . . cubist pictures': 16/2/14.

'stole the show . . . an American': 'Talk with K. Lechmere 1 January 1954'.

'large decoration . . . exorbitant': n.d. (Cornell).

146 'vivid light . . . tints': *Times* 28/2/14.

'rioting mass . . . so to speak': 25/6/14.

'to see the Frieze . . . drawings': (Cornell).

'Among the exhibits . . . can tell': 5/10/58.

'a perfectly bloody show': n.d (Aberystwyth).

'Mr Wyndham Lewis . . . houses': (Cornell).

147 'American Millionaire . . . influen-

tial': Nevinson to PWL n.d. (Cornell).

'I hope . . . his pocket': 28/10/13 (Cornell).

'The Lewis gang . . . among artists': 6/3/14 *Letters* vol. II p. 379.

'black doors . . . orgies of colour': 25/6/14.

'The studio walls . . . Chinese red': 'Wyndham Lewis from 1912'. Xerox obtained from Victor Cassidy. Whereabouts of original typescript unknown.

'It will be . . . on this scale': (Cornell).

'an extra room . . . to paint in': 'Wyndham Lewis from 1912'.

'The London Group . . . Picasso': 7/3/14.

'A champagne glass . . . lady's leg': 10/3/14.

148 'quite remarkable . . . as a whole': 26/3/14.

'Epstein is Hulme, Hulme is Epstein': 'Wyndham Lewis from 1912'.

149 'There was to . . . in its place?': *A Press View at the Tate*.

150 'bloody bitch . . . be bullied!': Cassidy interview with Lechmere 28/7/73.

'Free Entrance for . . . London, to lecture': (Cornell).

151 'absentmindedly in a tail coat': *South Lodge* p. 65.

'The principal object . . . on tip-toe': (Cornell).

'Lewis . . . behind a door': 'Recollections of Vorticism' *Apollo* January 1971.

'Let me introduce . . . have in mind': n.d (Cornell).

152 'Supposing they wanted . . . heaven to himself': 18/5/14.

152– 'You are a futurist . . . an English-
53 man!': from *B&B* pp. 37–8.

154 'I assembled . . . Doré Gallery': ibid. p. 33.

'Only bad work . . . *Hurrah* for lightning!': *Manchester Guardian* 13/6/14.

'maintained a confused uproar': *B&B* p. 36.

155 'I never see . . . upside down': ibid. p. 39.
'It was verbally . . . libel in it': 25/6/14 (Cornell).

156 'At the moment . . . ever seen': 1/7/14.
'Our Vortex . . . red-hot swiftness': *Blast* p. 149.
'That what is actual . . . North': ibid. p. 34.

157 'in their . . . Futuristic . . . to be found': ibid. p. 41.
'Signatures for Manifesto': ibid. p.43.
'something between . . . sick headache': September 1914.
'pucey pink': 5/7/14.
'chill flannelette pink . . . draper's stock': 1/7/14.
'miraculously . . . tried this': Cournos *Autobiography* p. 268.

158 'languid era . . . no one did': *Ezra Pound Speaking* p. 108.
'It is like . . . why should I?': 13/7/14 (Cornell).

158– 'You make everyone . . . another
59 personality': n.d. (Cornell).

159 'You hurt me . . . be courteous': n.d. (Cornell).
'nicer . . . unshaved': n.d. (Cornell).
'Something ugly . . . formal gentleness': n.d. (Cornell).

160 'I keep trying . . . want me to do': n.d. (Trust).
'that Mr Lewis . . . these copies': Lechmere to PWL 23/7/14 (Cornell).
'I am coming . . . Lewis': n.d. (Cornell).
'After your language . . . as possible': 26/7/14 (Cornell).

161 'I couldn't . . . new premises': 30/7/14 (Cornell).
'So ended the Rebel Art Centre': 'Wyndham Lewis from 1912'.
'the turf . . . the heart good': Ford *Return to Yesterday* p. 416.
'There won't be . . . declare war': from *B&B* pp. 62–3.

162 'It appeared . . . belonged': *Blast War Number* p. 95.

CHAPTER 17

163 'I am supposed . . . German subjects': n.d. (Cornell).

163– 'I am not surprised . . . Dunkie':
64 n.d. (Trust).

164 'he had . . . three days': Aldington to Herbert Read 12/3/57 quoted Meyers *The Enemy* p. 71.
'Just now I'm sick . . . or talk to': n.d. (Cornell).

165 'Any violent . . . saved my life': *B&B* p. 91.
'a bottle . . . celebrated marks': ibid.
'some wine . . . came on again':
'Cantleman-Crowdmaster' *EN* 35, Winter 1992.
'cursing together . . . all its works': *B&B* p. 91.

166 'Think of all . . . septic ghosts!': *Tarr* p. 32.
'I have admitted . . . with my self': n.d. (Trust).

166– 'you must know . . . about kiddies?':
67 n.d. (Trust).

167 'I am doing . . . Lectures, etc.': n.d. *P/L* p. 8.

168 'complete set . . . the present': Turner to PWL 10 Aug. (Cornell).
'People ought . . . to see them ': 31/12/14 (Cornell).
'excellent . . . ribaldry': n.d. *P/L* p. 8.
'For Christ's sake . . . your ass': *Inventions of the March Hare* p. 307.
'Put on your rough . . . House Ball!': ibid. p. 311.
'to have no . . . -Unt and -Ugger" ': n.d. *P/L* p. 8.

169 'never saw . . . does it want to': 11/3/15.
'in our desire . . . enjoy it': 10/3/15.
'that to call . . . actionable': *Blast War Number* p. 78.

169– 'should disarm . . . the present':
70 4/7/15.

170 'Every penny . . . my hospital': 30 May (Cornell).
'do you really . . . no effect': n.d. (Cornell).
'very extraordinary letter . . . service to you': 23 June (Cornell).

171 'that Miss Lechmere . . . the war': 13/1/20 (Cornell).

'the poor artist ... answer the letter': n.d. (Cornell).

172 'Oh! Here's dear ... to visit us!': Wadsworth *Edward Wadsworth* p. 67.
'I am getting ... colour blocks': n.d. (Huntington).

173 'I vould do anyting for Mr Lewis': William Roberts 'Wyndham Lewis the Vorticist' *Listener* 21/3/57.
'very violent and explosive': quoted Cork *Art Beyond the Gallery* p. 209.
'too strong a book': PWL to Guy Baker 4/1/16 (Cornell).

173– 'God damn ... the novel': n.d. *P/L*
74 pp. 18–19.

174 'dealt entirely ... antipathy': pmk 27/12/15 ibid. p. 20.
'I read her ... Weaver business': Dec 31st ibid. p. 21.

174– 'I should class ... portions added':
75 11/1/16 (Cornell).

175 '£50 now ... a volume': n.d. *P/L* p. 19.
'the upkeep ... pocket': n.d. ibid. p. 16.
'that THIS IS ... Mr W.L.': n.d. ibid. p. 18.

CHAPTER 18

176 'two dependents ... School Education': 18/1/16 (BL).

177 'evidently ... Kermesse': n.d. *P/L* p. 25.
'Quinn is concentrated ... the matter': pmk 6/3/16 ibid. p. 24.
'What! GARRISON ... a church': n.d. ibid. p. 46.
'antediluvian ... and the siege ones': pmk 29/3/16 ibid. p. 28.
'I [ate] six ... on the piano': pmk 9/4/16 ibid. pp. 29–30.

178 'altered ... improved': 25/10/13.
'primitive ... paid out': pmk 12/4/16 *P/L* pp. 30–1.
'had about cleared ... Lewis drawings': 9/9/16 (Cornell).

179 'The Colonel ... of my squad': 22/6/16 *P/L* p. 38.
'might ripen ... interpretations': 25/6/16 ibid. p. 43.

'half-cracked ... well-disposed': 22/6/16 ibid. p. 38.
'that he took ... "blasting" ': pmk 16/5/16 ibid. p. 36.
'more positive marks ... elusive thing': 22/6/16 ibid. p. 37.

180 'I should be ... pedestrination': n.d. ibid. pp. 80–1.
' "the Ranks" are a trap': 22/6/16 ibid. p. 37.
'I should have waited ... done that': 22/6/16 (Cornell).
'If he's any ... promotion anyhow': n.d. *P/L* p. 46.

181 'a pleasant ... battery': pmk 16/7/16 ibid. p. 48.
'the well-known Vorticist ... original': 18/7/16.
'Bdr. Lewis ... the chapter': 23/7/16 *P/L* p. 54.

181– 'The R.G.A. ... where I am': 4/8/
82 16 (Cornell).

182 'count the money ... buttons': PWL to Schepeler n.d. (Huntington).
'I am progressing ... his place': pmk 20/8/16 *P/L* p. 56.

182– 'I nearly lost ... British Warm':
83 *B&B* pp. 103–4.

CHAPTER 19

184 'Our advance party ... unsatisfactory': *P/L* p. 59.
'Going to war ... interests': 23/5/17 (NYPL).
'quite unfit ... things': n.d. (Cornell).
'sketches ... the Front': 'Writings' *EN* 10, May 1979.

185 'a pleasant life in tents': pmk 27/5/17 *P/L* p. 71.
'Whizzing ... unfortunate conflict': 6/6/17 *P/L* p. 73.
'Many more people ... question': 6/6/17 (Cornell).

186 'an immense and smoky ... more calm': 8/6/17 *P/L* pp. 73–4.

187 'the best of *jolliest* ... provided with!': *P/L* p. 82.
'My balls ... as a book': 7/7/17 *P/L* p. 85.

'to execute . . . a will': 9/7/17 *P/L* p. 87.

'I would rather . . . children': n.d. *P/L* p. 92.

188 'Now, here . . . dealt with': 9/7/17 *P/L* p. 87.

'oxide . . . aniseed': *Tarr* p. 269.

'Un Officier, Armée . . . convalescent, sick': (Cornell).

'The food . . . Hotel like': n.d. (Cornell).

'disease . . . rays of the sun': PWL to Schepeler n.d. (Huntington).

'I have come . . . summer': n.d. *P/L* p. 93.

189 'You've come . . . from hell': *B&B* p. 147.

'I have got *Tarr* . . . expressions': 17/8/17 *P/L* p. 94.

189– 'pitch-dark, dank . . . their souls':
90 pmk 20/8/17 *P/L* p. 95.

190 'As I left . . . gun positions': n.d. *P/L* p. 97.

191 'a little extra .. humdrum': 26/8/17 *P/L* p. 100.

'I did not see . . . my back': *B&B* p. 105.

'Before going . . . pleasant country': n.d. *P/L* p. 103.

192 'Should I ever . . . flesh creep': 8/9/17 (Huntington).

'the ways . . . Sunday School': n.d. *P/L* p. 103.

192– 'We sit . . . much sense': pmk 22/9/
93 17 *P/L* pp. 105–6.

193– 'is Tarr complete? . . . Butcher': 29/
94 9/17 *Letters* p. 95.

194 'I have lost . . . poisonous refuse': pmk 8/10/17 *P/L* p. 107.

'They are perfectly . . . official task': pmk 12/10/17 *P/L* p. 108.

'like trying . . . a cloud': pmk 18/10/17 *P/L* p. 109.

'a melancholy . . . mutilated insect': pmk 12/10/17 *P/L* p. 108.

'a bulging figure . . . with mud': 18/10/17 *P/L* p. 109.

195 'It's hell isn't it? . . . retorted Orpen': from *B&B* p. 180.

'Damn Orpen anyhow': 22/10/17 *P/L* p. 111.

'I want . . . existence': 7/7/17 *P/L* p. 86.

196 'Railway Transport . . . Office jobs': pmk 18/10/17 *P/L* p. 110.

197 'That night . . . melted together': version reprinted *B&B* 2nd edn. pp. 304–11.

199 'his life . . . might have been': 18/1/18 (NYPL).

CHAPTER 20

200 'Three glasses . . . love you': n.d. (Trust).

'There was no . . . bicycling plumber': Hart-Davis *The Arms of Time* pp. 82–3.

'All is well. Relieved at Sutton': n.d. (Trust).

201 'Lewis has been . . . viceroys, etc': 29/12/17 (NYPL).

'the only . . . viceregal rank': *B&B* pp. 57–8.

'whether . . . other countries': ibid. p. 55.

'What are you in? . . . rumination': ibid. p. 58.

202 'Why return . . . OF COURSE!!!': ibid. pp. 188–9.

'I hope to God . . . execution': 28/11/17 (NYPL).

'I was in . . . side of the war': *B&B* p. 190.

203 'Arrived, installed . . . quite know': (IWM).

'a dismal . . . die in': 1/1/18 *P/L* p. 113.

'a dandy gun pit': 9/1/18 ibid. p. 113.

'contending . . . scarcity of cars': 16/1/18 ibid. p. 116.

'The Canadians . . . very much': 1/1/18 (IWM).

'no signs of Art anywhere': 9/1/18 *P/L* p. 113.

203– 'WYNDHAM . . . suppressed':
204 *London Mail* 2/2/18.

204 'unpleasant . . . the sod': to PWL 3/2/18 (Cornell).

'Have you seen . . . I fear': n.d (Huntington).

204– 'I would be glad . . . the purpose':
205 28/12/17 quoted Cork *Vorticism* . . . vol. II, p. 526.

205 'like a galley slave': PWL to Sybil Hart-Davis 9/4/18 (Trust).
'in connection . . . Government': 15/4/18 (Cornell).
'paintings . . . not overlap': 16/4/18 (IWM).
'a very charming size': 18/4/18 (IWM).

206 'the bad American *Tarr* . . . about that': n.d. (Cornell).
'a cleverish pastiche . . . beside Stavrogin': 10/8/18.
'the author . . . model too!': from *B&B* pp. 94–5.
'he will probably . . . that time.': 8/7/18 (IWM).

207 'doomed . . . plague [her]': n.d. (Trust).
'the wild dandelion': n.d. (Trust).
'not quite truthful': 1/12/17 Cornell.
'Is it wanton . . . refrain?': 20/6/18 (Trust).
'you can boast . . . genuinely sometimes': n.d. (Trust).
'Remember . . . were some': 11/6/18 (Trust).
'I dined . . . camouflages ships': *The Arms of Time* p. 90.

207– 'lots of stairs . . . nice girl': *The*
208 *Contrary Experience* p. 139.

208 'Black or Liver poolian holiday': Sybil Hart-Davis to PWL 2/9/18 (Trust).
'regards to Barry . . . terrify of you': n.d. (Cornell).
'Many kisses, little Dunkie': n.d. (BL).

209 'On looking . . . war has been': 17/12/18 *Letters* p. 102.
'My painting . . . sight of it': PWL to Quinn 8/1/19 (NYPL).
'It is . . . not his own': Royal Academy Catalogue Jan.–Feb. 1919.
'an important . . . Information': (IWM).

CHAPTER 21

210 'you know . . . swear to it': 10/7/19 Alice Parrish to ASL (Cornell).
210– 'second wife . . . assigns forever':

11 (Register of Wills, County of Philadelphia and Pennsylvania).

211 'apologising . . . twenty years': *Playboy*, March/April 1919.
'first of all . . . as successful': 8/1/19 (NYPL).

211– 'extremely well received . . . being
12 sold': 2/2/19 (Buffalo).

212 'one could not . . . pleasant': 28/4/19 (Cornell).
'very rude': Brigid Peppin to the author 1/7/95.
'staggered . . . of the hill': 8/3/19 *P/L* p. 117.
'not yet in proper . . . to another': PWL to Yockney n.d. (IWM).

213 'Percy Bark': pmk 22/4/19 (Cornell).
'How far advanced . . . photographed?': 18/9/19 (IWM).

213– 'unless your picture . . . to a close':
14 16/10/19 (IWM).

214 'Remember! . . . word round!': Osbert Sitwell *Laughter in the Next Room* p. 30.
'Four years . . . torn from his life': *The Contrary Experience* p. 141.

215 'repeated sectional . . . and so forth': 31/10/19.
'four different pairs . . . Wyndfield Lewis': Della Denman 'Kate Lechmere, Recollections of Vorticism' *Apollo* January 1971.
'the regrettable . . . his art': *The Athenaeum* 31/10/19
'the serious mission . . . World-War': *Blast War Number* p. 5.
'a great work by a great artist': 9/11/19.

CHAPTER 22

217 'Why X? . . . this group': 20/3/20.
218 'impossible . . . reasonable price': statement re Income Tax n.d. (Cornell).
'This is to say . . . cancelled': 27/2/26 (Cornell).
'PLEASE . . . LEWIS': (Cornell).
'I have led . . . with you': n.d. (Trust).
219– 'You don't know . . . a machine':
20 n.d. (Trust).

220 'I don't want . . . bearable situation':
n.d. (BUFFALO).
'I must remind . . . the contrary':
pmk 5/8/20 (Cornell).

221 'I am sorry . . . get at': pmk 5/8/
20 (Cornell).
'On the matter . . . paid handsomely':
26/7/20 (Cornell).
'best of luck . . . Semites': n.d.
(Trust).

221– 'We were both . . . certainly wish':
22 10/8/20 (Trust).

222 'which is a lot . . . all that': n.d.
(Trust).

223 'Thereupon . . . French table':
B&B p. 275.
'This is . . . second-hand clothing':
Pound/Joyce ed. Forrest Read, p.
169.
'Ought I . . . or what?': 19/8/20
(Trust).

224 'I have been . . . divine villages': 21/
8/20 (Cornell).
'W.L. has been . . . to talk to':
Letters p. 403.
'medium sized surface gash': PWL
to Barry pmk 28/8/20 (Cornell).
'The dispute . . . changing hands':
'Wyndham Lewis' Hudson Review
Summer 1957.

225 'He believes . . . lockjaw': Letters p.
404.
'what would . . . day's work': PWL
to Barry pmk 28/8/20 (Cornell).
'Your friend Mr Eliot': B&B p.
287.
'I can't decide . . . I'm helpless!':
19/8/20 (Trust).
'I don't suppose . . . the neighbourhood': pmk 28/8/20 (Cornell).
'BACK TOMORROW . . . LEWIS':
28/2/20 (Cornell).
'This is just . . . and knitting': n.d.
(Trust).

225– 'I want you to . . . Invent one, then':
26 n.d. (Trust).

CHAPTER 23

227 'was at least . . . afford': statement
re. Income Tax (Cornell).
'You must tell . . . any use':
(Cornell).

'my work as . . . my work': statement re. Income Tax (Cornell).

228 'Praxitella . . . will increase': 14/4/
22 (Cornell).

229 'We have never . . . at that': 14/4/
21 (Cornell).
'It has its points': Exhibition p. 77.
'If I sell . . . things there': 2/5/21
(NYPL).
'A Tyro . . . real life': 11/4/21.

230 'This man . . . we have!': Exhibition
p. 76.
'The point . . . expression line': 30/
4/21.

231 'but kept on . . . terrified': n.d.
(Cornell).
'Roger and Nessa . . . fear him': to
Sydney Waterlow 3/5/21 Letters
vol. II p. 467.
'I have to leave . . . to live': 14/4/21
(Cornell).
'Had several . . . like him': 31/7/
21 Letters vol. III p. 42.
'Remember . . . Ideal Giant': Ell-
man, James Joyce, p. 530.

231– 'I'll never . . . illegitimate children':
32 EN 16, Summer 1982.

232 'You may . . . write it': Olson and
Pound: an encounter . . . ed. Seelye,
p. 107.
'My journey . . . complete failure':
n.d. (Cornell).
'a similar pied-à-terre . . . experimental stuff': 2/5/21 (NYPL).
'We are now . . . the mark': (Cornell).

233 'The little margin . . . no count': 1/
9/22 (Cornell).
'I . . . paid call . . . ensuing week':
n.d. (Cornell).
'The fare 2nd class . . . holiday':
n.d. (Cornell).
'because of . . . arrangements': to
Barry 1/9/21 (Cornell).

233– 'Your letter has been . . . Sudbury':
34 n.d (Cornell).

234 'I repeat . . . work house': n.d.
(Cornell).
'If I make . . . dull town': (Cornell).
'an ex-Communist . . . thing of his':
to McAlmon 14/10/21 Letters p.
128.

234– 'Walden and . . . the West': 12/9/
35 21 (BL).

235 'journalistic inspiration': pmk 27/9/
21 (BL).
'Lewis now paints ... you enter':
22/10/21 *Letters* vol. II p. 573.
'in good ... constructed': (Kensington Public Library).
'an area ... phonetically': 'The Ape of God'. Unpublished typescript (Cornell).

CHAPTER 24

237 'not *in any* ... this sketch': 22/3/22 (BL).
238 'the days ... lighthouse lamp': 12/4/22 (BL).
238– 'The studio ... damned laundress':
39 from 'The Ape of God'.
240 'nearly finished ... concerned': to Violet Schiff 2/5/22 (BL).
'The most suffocating ... every day': 2/6/22 (BL).
'Whence £500?': 12/12/22 (Cornell).
'the importance ... development': to Schiff 2/5/22 (BL).
240– 'set aside time ... instalment': ibid.
41 28/4/22 (BL).
241 'This between ourselves': 30/5/22 (Buffalo).
'As regards ... willing to sit.': 3/7/22 (BL).
'Lewis, these ... for you.': *B&B* p. 240.
242 'I rang ... Hemingway': *B&B 2nd edition* p. 277.
'Wyndham Lewis ... unsuccessful rapist': *A Moveable Feast* pp. 108–9.
243 'I will write ... few days': pmk 29/9/22 (BL).
'rather exquisite ... *and arrive*': n.d (Cornell).
'squalid-looking ... hope so': *Diaries* pp. 265–7.
243– 'Most of the ... each other': n.d.
44 (BL).
244 'Yesterday I ... following day (Monday)': to McAlmon *Letters* p. 132.
'Oh, he's the boy ... the nose': *B&B* pp. 236–7.
245 'I wish ... train that day': n.d. (Cornell).

'Dear, dear Lewis ... very much': n.d. (Cornell).
'I ... am thinking ... ZEX-LIFE': n.d (Cornell).

CHAPTER 25

247 '*Sportsman's Engagement Book*': (Cornell).
'a particularly ... powdered eagle': *B&B* p. 214.
'a blur of erasures': *The Arms of Time* p. 117.
248 'noted ... address': n.d. (Cornell).
'Forgive ... perpetual lateness.': n.d (Cornell).
249 'age snobbery ... use to you': n.d. (Cornell).
250 'bankrupt stock ... some use': 14/12/23 (Cornell).
251 'Although hard up ... inconvenient': quoted Wyndham to PWL n.d. (Cornell).
'One night ... read Chekhov': n.d. (Cornell).
'PLEASE SEND ... LEWIS': quoted PWL to Fanny Wadsworth n.d. (Cornell).
252 'special request ... short notice': Fanny Wadsworth to PWL 17/4/24 (Cornell).
252– 'jolly glad ... continue receiving it':
53 PWL to Fanny Wadsworth n.d. (Cornell).
253 'Either I am ... enclose cheque': n.d (Cornell).
'You must not ... treacherous bounty': 29/4/25 *P/L* p. 144.
'work or works ... other influence': 2/5/25 ibid. p. 145.
254 'If I am ... regret it': 4/5/24 (Cornell).
255 'I hope that ... subscribed': 30/4/24.
'I am so ... take it': n.d (Cornell).
'WHERE'S ... LEWIS': Symons 'The Blaster' *London Magazine* June 1967.
256 'I cannot ... this rate': 15/11/24 (Cornell).
'Where are we ... your move': 11/11/24 (Cornell).

'I realise . . . playfulness of yours':
n.d. (BL).
'I now offer . . . dispense with it':
13/11/24 (Cornell).
257 'to clear up . . . points': 15/11/24
(Cornell).

CHAPTER 26

258 'I want to . . . next six months': 5/
9/22 (BL).
'for some months . . . books at
once': 31/1/25 (Cornell).
259 'the complete . . . *the World*': 2/2/
25 (Cornell).
'longer than *War* . . . and so on':
29/4/25 *P/L* p. 144.
'leave me alone . . . a year, say': n.d.
ibid. p. 134.
'Wyndham Lewis . . . the moment':
to Henry Allen Moe 31/3/25 *Ezra
Pound and the Visual Arts* ed. Zinnes
p. 294.
260 'the question of . . . Shakespeare
principally': 29/4/25 *P/L* p. 145.
'The publisher's reader . . . many
copies': 7/5/25 ibid. p. 147.
'If you have . . . uninteresting subject': 12/5/25 ibid. p. 148.
261 'I do not want . . . my career': 11/6/
25 ibid. p. 150.
'I . . . good luck': ibid. pp. 151–2.
'In writing . . . devote to them?':
24/7/25 (Austin).
262 'lately or at any . . . some sort of
job': xerox from James F. O'Roark,
Santa Barbara, California.
262– 'It is of very . . . hasten the print-
63 ing?': 16/9/25 (Austin).
263 'I am writing . . . connection with
it': 9/12/25 (Austin).
'englishman . . . chinese ': 26/12/25
(Austin).
264– 'The whole . . . disorder': *Apes of
65 God* p. 618.
265 'I am extremely . . . its completion':
27/6/2 (Reading).
266 'no legal . . . manuscript': Waterhouse to PWL 11/6/26 (Cornell).
'some remarks . . . in the matter':
ibid. 12/6/26 (Cornell).

'magnificent and disinterested . . .
generosity': 12/8/26 (Cornell).
267 'Lewis, it seems . . . see me.': *Letters*
vol. III p. 142.
'a very considerable . . . of [the]
book': Waterhouse to PWL 1/10/
26 (Cornell).
'Never again . . . with you': 11/11/
26 (Cornell).
'Least because . . . exposed to
assault': 16/11/26 (Cornell).
'building up . . . with practice':
Ackerley *My Sister and Myself* p.
156.
268 'I hope . . . in front of it': 20/2/33
(BL).
269 'like a gigantic . . . victorian world':
Enemy Jan. 1927 p. 111.
'literary horseplay . . . the other':
ibid. p. 124.
'The buyers . . . bargains': April
1927.
'I succeeded . . . American champagne': 24/2/27.
270 'mainly owing . . . *Lion and the
Fox*': to Montgomery Belgion n.d.
(Cornell).
'a stone's throw . . . Square': to
Pound 17/12/38 *P/L* p. 201.
270– 'It has been . . . parish churches': 1/
71 8/27 (Reading).
271 'The boat . . . earthquake shocks':
PWL to John 3/2/28 (Aberyst-
wyth).
271– 'Did you notice? . . . lurid and
72 memorable.': MacLeish *A Continuing Journey,* and MacLeish to Rose
25/4/60 (Vassar).

CHAPTER 27

273 'There have . . . its position': 3/2/
28 (Aberystwyth).
'*intime* . . . smallish gallery': St John
Hutchinson to PWL 5/6/18 (Cor-
nell).
'a reddish . . . muddy water': *RA* p.
121.
274 'Seizing a stick . . . disliked the
painter': *EN* 16, Summer 1986.
275 'What a pity . . . hear, however': 23/
1/28 Huntington.

'a little screwed ... particular to drink': to John (Aberystwyth).
'a fringe of crystals ... nummulitic limestone': *The Childermass* p. 1.

276 'My connection ... doubly so': 18/4/28 (Cornell).

276–
77 'as a weapon ... suit me as well': n.d. (Cornell).

277 'You will bear ... TO NO ONE': 10/5/28 (Austin).
'Modern Philosophy ... personality sketch': 5/4/28 (Cornell).
'gossipy ... words': 12/4/28 (Austin).
'with infinite ... almost unreadable': Garnett to Rose (Vassar).
'very fine things ... admirable': 29/5/28 (Cornell).

278 'a creative writer ... pure artist': 'Wyndham Lewis' unpublished typescript (Cornell).
'It is popular ... suppress it': 4/6/28 (Cornell).
'They should ... naivety': Rascoe *Art & Decoration* November 1928.
'neither good nor saleable': quoted Belgion to PWL 6/1/28 (Cornell).

279 'It is possible ... philosophical discussion': 29/5/28 (Columbia).
'In Friede's garden ... his leg': Rascoe *Art & Decoration* November 1928.

280 'It is as powerful ... surpassed': n.d. (Cornell).

281 'together with interest thereon': Waterhouse & Co. to PWL 3/6/29 (Cornell).
'half of an epic ... distressing fact': to Waterhouse & Co. 7/7/29 (Cornell).

CHAPTER 28

282 'noticed his feet ... very slightly': Marjorie Firminger 'No Quarter' p. 9. Unpublished typescript (Cornell).
'a pale ... dark eyes': ibid. pp. 10–11.

283 'There wasn't ... further still': ibid. p. 21.
'The room ... overlooked': ibid. pp. 15–16.

'Very *grande* ... in the bed': ibid. pp. 26–7.

284 '*People are there to be used*': ibid. p. 34.
'Now I must ... provinces': ibid. p. 28.
'This is my office ... bed in it': *Everyman* 19/3/31.

285 'Why shouldn't ... Why indeed?': 'No Quarter' p. 33.

286 'a ridiculous charge ... fixed abode': *Clapham Observer* 28/2/30.

287 'It had no literary ... the gingering': 'No Quarter' pp. 37–40.
'It is a ... But I ask': 19/3/30 (Cornell).
'So far the novel ... send anything': 21/3/30 (Cornell).

288 'one of the best criminal ... behind [him]': n.d. (Trust).
'would not have ... committed': Freke Palmer to PWL 1/4/30 (Trust).
'to fly ... 3 or 4 weeks': 18/3/30 (Buffalo).
'been very much ... private matter': 1/4/30 (Buffalo).

289 'The endearments ... returning it to you 1/4/30 (Cornell).

CHAPTER 29

290 'rich mountebank ... of a wife': *Apes of God* pp. 179–80.
'brilliant ... the table': ibid. p. 273.

291 'prevent ten ... egotistical state': ibid. p. 189.
'New Zealand ... kosher fist': ibid. p. 394.
'very tentatively ... Never mind': 'No Quarter' p. 48.
'I find you ... justifiable': *Satire and Fiction* p. 10.

292 'one of the best ... implicated': 2/7/30 (Cornell).

293 'GREETINGS ... APES': n.d. (Cornell).
'did not seem friendly': *Daily Express* 4/9/30.

294 'AM WORKING ... ESSENTIAL': (Cornell).

295 'except for a few sketches': 26/11/ 30 (Cornell).
'the very slightest pique': 11/11/30 (Cornell).
'I have suggested . . . to you': 3/11/ 30 (Cornell).

296 'The main reason . . . German reader': Fiedler to PWL 12/1/31 (Cornell).
'In this gigantic . . . scream': *Time and Tide* 17/1/31.
'night-circuses . . . loneliness': ibid. 24/1/31.

297 'I'm not a gold digger': Diary 1930–31 (Austin).
'a much worse book': 'No Quarter' p. 85.

298 'would lay . . . wide public': 12/1/ 31 (Cornell).
'an exponent . . . publish them': *Time and Tide* 17/1/31–14/2/31.
'anything startling . . . and vice': ibid. 31/1/31.
'I for one . . . mattered!)': ibid. 21/ 2/31.

299 'are two expressions . . . Teutonic': ibid. 7/2/31.
'nothing but satisfaction . . . whole thing': to Lady Glenapp n.d. (Cornell).
'always a rather . . . his advice': 5/ 2/31 (Cornell).

300 'a nice chap . . . finely bound volumes': 'No Quarter' p. 78.
'I have just . . . this afternoon': n.d. (Cornell).
'expressions . . . in Paris': *Snooty Baronet* p. 23.

300– 'enchanted to be . . . of *course* not':
301 'No Quarter' pp. 80–3.

301 'Saw M. Firminger . . . importance': (Austin).

301– 'The worst fault . . . a dolt': 18/4/
302 31.

302 'what do we . . . information': 2/4/ 31.
'the official representative . . . Englishman': *The Hitler Cult* p. 12.
'a racial redherring': *Hitler* p. 43.
'Hitler *himself* . . . *Judenfrage*': *Time and Tide* 31/1/31.

302– 'If you do not . . . oldest friends':
303 *The Hitler Cult* p. 14.

303 'These are long . . . infamous': *Collected Poems and Plays* p. 248.

CHAPTER 30

304 'unusually painful . . . Capital!': 'No Quarter' pp. 89–91.

305 'I sold . . . set out': *Filibusters in Barbary* p. vii.

306 'the huge, red . . . mud and sand': ibid. p. 86.
'rushing for . . . ocean valley': ibid. p. 89.
'brought it down . . . taking shape': 4/6/31 (Buffalo).
'attempting to undermine . . . Public': *Filibusters in* Barbary p. 81.
'fifty dumb . . . shadow–picture': ibid. p. 91.

306– 'upon the edge . . . Atlantic': to
307 Mitchison 11/7/31 *Letters* p. 203.

307 'whitewashed cell . . . to you': 25/6/ 31 (Reading).
'been to places . . . believed': 11/7/ 31 *Letters* p. 203.

308 'ridden . . . a mule': to Mrs John Rothenstein, n.d. (Cornell).

308– 'come along and do . . . miscon-
309 struction': 'No Quarter' pp. 97–109.

312 'The Apes . . . Osbert Sitwell!': Grayson *Stand Fast, The Holy Ghost*, p. 132.
'two or three functions . . . pop into it': to Gilman 22/11/31 (Cornell).
'a *great girl*': 17/12/38 *P/L* p. 201.
'a strange . . . deal of gin': Alsop to Cassidy 24/4/73.
'gazed into . . . parlour': 17/12/38 *P/L* p. 201.
'Boston 'is a good place': to Gilman 10/12/31.

CHAPTER 31

313 'we sat . . . of heat': *Summer's Lease* p. 130.
'sealed, locked, . . . tin can': *Stand Fast, Holy Ghost* p. 130.

314 'We are amazed . . . a novel': (Cornell).
'was I to go . . . Bloomsbury friends': 1/7/32 (Cornell).

315 'We speak . . . his solicitor': 29/2/ 32 (Cornell).
'I am awfully . . . noose': 8/4/32 (Cornell).
'The studio . . . Aga Khan!': Harmsworth to Cassidy 17/8/73.

316 'proud and mettlesome . . . equally good': n.d. (Cornell).
'I can't meet . . . afraid to say so': Grant *Stella Benson* p. 304.

316– 'Mr Winn's publishers . . . adequate
17 apology': (Cornell).

317 'My visit to . . . was not': Waugh to Cassidy 26/7/32.
'We are instructed . . . SUPPLE- MENT': 27/7/32 (Cornell).

318 'I should say . . . became a man': *Doom of Youth* pp. 113–14.
'The said words . . . sexually per- verted': 28/10/32 (Cornell).

319 'in connection with . . . completely failed': 28/7/32 (Cornell).
'Can we . . . know him?': notes by PWL 29/7/32 (Cornell).
'All the time . . . except himself': Grant *Stella Benson* p. 304.

320 'succeeded . . . occultation': p. 5.
'a peculiarly uncivil . . . all round': *The Hitler Cult* p. 11.

320– 'a coarse . . . sort at stake': PWL to
21 Neuman Flower n.d. (Cornell).

321 'We understand . . . us first': (Cor- nell).

322 'the paper . . . backs to them': 10/ 10/32.
'details . . . by lawyers': 20/9/29 (Cornell).
'say £10 . . . extension of time': Barnes to PWL 8/10/32 (Cornell).

323 'So there are two of you': (Cornell).
'Every day . . . STREET': *Letters* p. 44.

323– 'GEORGE . . . has wholly failed':
24 (Cornell).

324 'I hope that . . . engaged in filling': 20/11/32 (Cornell).
'A bug walked . . . venereal scar': PWL to Gilman 12/2/33 (Cornell).
'a roaming . . . to roost': 8/3/33 (Cornell).
'ACHTUNG . . . DANCES': *Let- ters* p. 44.

325 'These things . . . in England': n.d. (Cornell).

CHAPTER 32

326 'complicated . . . the doctors': PWL to Violet Schiff 12/2/33 (BL).

327 'You remind me . . . nothing to me': from *B&B* p. 12.
'very skilful massage': n.d. (Cor- nell).

328 'a rather alarming . . . stopped there': PWL to Violet Schiff 19/3/ 33 & 29/3/33 (BL).
'My attitude . . . successes of Sci- ence': 15/3/33 (Trust).
'there was definitely . . . about her': to Russ 13/11/34 (Trust).

329 'There was once . . . that I think': n.d. (Trust).

330 'Goebbels's eye . . . accordingly became': *The Hitler Cult* p. 11.

331 'a slight recrudescence . . . was mis- taken': 10/5/33 (Cornell).
'Mr Waugh . . . for damages': 12/5/ 33 (Cornell).
'drop the whole matter': 21/6/33 (Cornell).
'Our instructions . . . we must pro- ceed': 29/6/33 (Cornell).

332 'that we prefer . . . his company': *Times* 12/5/33.
'Herr Hitler's . . . has inspired': 12/ 5/33.

333 'Red spittle . . . call them *Jews!*': *The Hitler Cult* p. 12.
'My secret address . . . on your table': 5/2/34 (Cornell).
'two or at the most . . . prices': 22/ 7/33 (Cornell).

334 'Talking nearly . . . can't bear': n.d. (Trust).
'ever since . . . forever': n.d. (Trust).
'What has happened . . . can I come?': n.d. (Trust).

334– 'In the Autumn . . . this way': 13/9/
35 33 (Cornell).

335 'A firm . . . connection': *Collected Poems and Plays* p. 50.
'I didn't know . . . easy, Read': Grigson *Recollections* p. 12.

336 'you would . . . she is ill': quoted Russ to Mary Russ 1/2/34 (Trust).
'The rent . . . such premises': 11/ 12/33 (Cornell).

'a rapid ... capitals': PWL to Gilman 10/11/33 (Cornell).

337 'Do not mention ... Paris': 15/12/33 (Austin).

'We send you ... instituted': 21/12/33 (Cornell).

337– 'IMPORTANT ... S.O.S.': n.d.
38 (Cornell).

338 'sulking in ... days return': PWL to Gilbert 19/1/34 (Cornell).

338– 'and if he is ... background': PWL
39 to Grigson (annotated by Grigson) n.d. (Cornell).

340 'tonight the surgeon ... send you this': (Cornell).

CHAPTER 33

341 'Mrs Russ ... mince matters': 27/2/34 (Trust).

'It's 4 o'clock ... mignonette': n.d. (Trust).

'Such a queer ... shovelsful': n.d. (Trust).

342 '[It] enabled ... all no duns!': n.d. (Austin).

'They tell me ... Good!': 20/3/34 (Cornell).

'I cannot ... exceedingly ill': verso of above (Cornell).

'The pathologist ... new to me': n.d. (Trust).

343 'Ernest Hemingway is ... or bullfighting!': April 1934.

344 'to celebrate ... than that!': 4/5/34 (Cornell).

'no trifler ... beat about the bush': n.d. (Trust).

'circus ... zakuskis': n.d. (Cornell).

345 'You call yourself ... worship a leader': from *Fascists at Olympia* p. 15.

'If you want ... awful lot': n.d. (Cornell).

345– 'it's big enough ... so lonely': n.d.
46 (Trust).

346 'a good fellow': PWL to Mitchison 3 May (Edinburgh).

'Wyndham Lewis ... agreeable but touchy': *My Life* p. 225.

'I hate to think ... contribution': 28/09/34 (Trust).

'I have suffered ... physical misery': to Waterhouse 10/8/36 (Cornell).

'please come ... good talk': 29/9/34 (Trust).

347 'Cruel devil ... Cruel devil': pmk 20/10/34 (Trust).

'I'm sending ... you'd rather': 30/10/34 (Trust).

'Coming to see ... be locked': (Trust).

347– 'I thought my body ... difference':
48 n.d (Trust).

348 'If we did ... around them': 14/5/34 (Cornell).

'*Au dela* ... ideas don't hold': n.d. (Cornell).

'I find the next ... it somehow': 29/9/34 (Cornell).

348– 'It was the greatest ... self-portrait':
49 *You May Well Ask* pp. 148–9.

349 'No! ... let you go': *Beyond This Limit* p. 87.

'Once upon ... of yore': n.d. (Trust).

350 'psychological experiment ... language': PWL to Russ 13/11/34 (Trust).

'as if ... a child': Russ to PWL n.d. (Trust).

'Of course ... accepted them': 13/11/34 (Trust).

'You say that ... intervention?': 23/11/34 (Trust).

352 'at least ... my own': n.d. (Cornell).

'rhinoceros headed idiot': Mary Russ to PWL n.d. (Cornell).

'Thank you ... flames already': 27/2/35 (Trust).

CHAPTER 34

354 'in the nature ... speak of for it': PWL to Howard (Cornell).

'I had not ... had supposed': 22/2/35 (Cornell).

'I will not ... to do so': 27/2/35 (Cornell).

355 'it is nothing ... the pot': 29/4/35 (Cornell).

'You were very ... the wireless': 1/5/35 (Trust).

'I can only . . . anvil ringing': 12/6/
35 (Cornell).
'I bought his . . . might be that':
Listener 26/6/35.

356 'Your stuff . . . every time': n.d.
(Trust).
'When it rains . . . maisonette': to
Gilbert 12/7/35 (Cornell).
'I am laid . . . order again': PWL to
Mr Evans n.d. (Cornell).
'a sound fellow . . . scrupulous
hands': 22/7/35 (Trust).
'to quell . . . MIDDLESEX': 6/8/
35 (Trust).

356– 'a first class . . . confess': to Russ
57 n.d. (Cornell).

357 'the bird had flown': Russ to PWL
n.d. (Cornell).
'I hope . . hard up sometimes': n.d.
(Trust).
'It might . . . few guineas': n.d.
(Trust).
'a live . . . difficult to catch': Doro-
thy Priestley to PWL 11/9/35
(Cornell).
'Madame . . . I expect': n.d. (Trust).
'address . . . strictest confidence': 7/
10/35 (Trust).

358 'but that was . . . took it': John Russ
to the author 26/7/96.
'Well, 1935 . . . 1936': n.d. (Trust).
'The . . . avoidance . . . extremely
unfavourable': 8/5/36 (Cornell).

359 'It was . . . as ever': 6/5/36 (Buffalo).
'one or two . . . discussion?': 5/5/36
(Cornell).
'nothing but . . . difficulties': to
Neuman Flower 6/5/36 (Cornell).
'been attended . . . disagreement': to
PWL 8/5/36 (Cornell).
'I think . . . not with others': 25/5/
36 (Cornell).

360 'the necessary . . . X-Ray': 3/7/36
(Cornell).
'the size of a duck's egg': 'Record of
Life in America' 1/1/44 (Cornell).
'pulled every available string': 12/
6/36 (Cornell).
'I am wondering . . . as ourselves':
(Cornell).

361 'I can still . . . death-rattle': *RA* p.
225.

'Somewhere in hospital . . . for the
present': (Cornell).
'He must be very strong': 'Record of
Life in America' 1/1/44 (Cornell).
'The scrotum . . . freebooter': 5/9/
36 (Cornell).
'When we first . . . at that': 14/8/
36 (Cornell).

362 'There is Geoffrey . . . as reader':
The Roaring Queen pp. 104–5.
'highly amusing . . . less libellous':
27/8/36 (Cornell).
'the entire book trade . . . publish
it': (Cornell).

363 'we submitted . . . destroying the
book': (Cornell).
'the "Bloomsbury" principle . . .
individual 'Bloomsbury" ': n.d.
(Cornell).
'I am afraid . . . correspondence': 2/
12/36 (Cornell).

CHAPTER 35

364 'The political . . . the matter': *Left
Wings Over Europe* pp. 171–3.

365 'an ordinary . . . and a shave': *Count
Your Dead* p. 196.
'futile performances . . . just that':
RA p. 209.

366 'a word . . . Internationalism':
' "Left Wings" and the C3 Mind'
British Union Quarterly Jan.–Apr.
1937.

366– 'I am encouraged . . . inconsiderable
67 voice': 11/2/37 (Cornell).

367 '12 paintings and masses . . . green
eyes!': n.d. (Cornell).
'The statement . . . used to this':
quoted PWL to Loviat Dickson 21/
3/37 (Cornell).

368 'I can see . . . myself I must': 21/3/
37 (Cornell).
'Oblige me . . . objected to?': (Cornell).
'to forget its politics . . . 12 months':
n.d. (Cornell).

369 'as if to be more difficult': Hutchins
' "Lot 13" The Last of Wyndham
Lewis' (Cornell).
'without . . . gas company': coal
ration application 5/3/49 (Cornell).

'by a device ... when ready': Tomlin *Wyndham Lewis an Anthology of his Prose* p. 6.

370 'just sitting around cafés': *EN* 11, Autumn 1979.
'I felt I had ... inexpressible squalor': *The Jews – Are They Human?* pp. 42–3.
'When I informed ... always done': *The Hitler Cult* p. 38.

371 'deplorably outmoded ... upside down': 'Berlin Revisited' (Cornell).
'I watched ... quick march!': *The Hitler Cult* p. 128.
'We left ... at least': *EN* 11, Autumn 1979.
'I am so ... Germany': 18/8/37 (Cornell).

372 'in all arts ... grocery trade': 6/10/37 (Cornell).
'an embittered ... justify itself': n.d. (Cornell).

373 'the Double ... an artist': 27/12/37 (NYPL).
'What a curiously ... you aren't': n.d. (Cornell).

375 'and thumped ... with pleasure': *Twenty-Four Letters* ed. Julian Symons, p. 20.
'Dear Mr Lewis ... vitally': pmk 4/12/37 (Trust).

375– 'Would you please ... sincerely,
76 Peter': pmk 18/12/37 (Trust).

376 'Our client ... any sort': n.d. (Trust).

378 'For some time ... made': 24/1/38 (Cornell).

CHAPTER 36

381 'I am voicing ... institution" ': 22/4/38.
'in a quiet ... every year' ': 22/4/38.
'I personally ... present day art': 22/4/38.
'I do not ... were passed': 23/4/38 *Daily Telegraph*.

382 'I am glad ... Royal Academy': 21/4/38 (Cornell).
'the Council ... accepted': (RAL).
'I read yesterday ... a reason': (Cornell).

'Dear President ... I remain': (RAL).
'VERY SORRY ... JOHN': (RAL).

382– 'I very much ... a corpse': 25/4/
83 38.

383 'The Royal ... Mr John': 25/4/38.
'Mr Wyndham Lewis ... embarrassed': 30/4/38.
'There is not ... open mind': 30/4/38 *Daily Herald*.

384 'I have not ... technical tact': 30/4/38.

385 'You can imagine ... countenance': 2/5/38 *Times*.

386 'The "controversy" ... rhetoric': 4/5/38 *Times*.
'swaggered in ... cushioned chairtop': *B&B* 2nd edition p. 286.

387 'Are you free ... run to time': *EN* 16, Summer 1982.
'the portcullises ... *very* good': 17/12/38 *PL* p. 202.
'that thaaar north west corner': 20/12/38 ibid. p. 203.

388 'Tonight by rotary ... thousand times': ibid. p. 206.
'only just finished': 25/3/39.

389 'with growing ... eighteen years before': *Brave Day Hideous Night* p. 43.

CHAPTER 37

390 'No one is ... courage to advocate': Apr.–Jun. 1939.

391 'The "Jewish ... our history': *Jewish Chronicle Supplement* March 1939.
'less of a nuisance ... recriminations': n.d. (Trust).
'Help! ... pay cash': 16/4/39 *P/L* p. 209.

392 'perched above ... owls do': Grigson *Crest on the Silver* p. 187.
'Wyndham Lewis came ... round hand': Nicholson *Half My Days and Nights* p. 225.

393– 'a little at hazard ... suet dump-
94 ling': 8/6/39.

395 '"Dr John" ... unintelligent patronage': n.d. (Cornell).

'I have a natural . . . business too':
17/8/43 (Cornell).
'Where public funds . . . tradesman': 23/6/39 (Cornell).
'A submarine-like . . . oppressiveness': PWL to William Rothenstein
7/6/39 (Cornell).

396 'Have you got . . . well, then': Julian
Symons ed., *The Essential Wyndham
Lewis* p. 4.
'I shall I hope . . . some months':
17/12/38 *P/L* p. 201.

397 'She never . . . boodle': Tomlin 'A
Few More Impressions' *EN* 17,
Autumn 1982.
'the political situation . . . understate-
ment': 6/7/39 (Cornell).
'What a filthy . . . Notting Hill
Gate': 3/7/39 (Cornell).

398 'Dear Mr Lewis . . . David': 3/7/39
(Cornell).

398– 'I sent . . . catarrhal Indian colonel':
99 'Journey out of Anguish' *Wyndham
Lewis in Canada* Canadian Literature Series, 1971 (revised and
expanded reprint of *Canadian Literature* 35, Winter 1968).

399 'rather a good . . . fly buttons': 10/
8/39 *P/L* p. 212.
'man of peace': 31/1/31.
'it was like . . . epileptic life': *The
Hitler Cult* p. 5.

400 'The picture . . . America': 22/4/
38.
'time to turn . . . arrangements':
PWL to Honeyman 13/9/39 (Cornell).
'I hope . . . know when': 10/8/39
P/L p. 212.
'Everything . . . floating coffin': *AIP*
p. 36.
'Indescribable scenes . . . darkness':
ibid. p. 39.

401 'They even . . . Northwest Passage':
ibid. pp. 44–5.

CHAPTER 38

403 'like an operating theatre . . . unacceptable': 'Journey out of Anguish'.

404 'queen of the . . . United States':
AIP p. 57.

'An awful nice . . . building for
Nineveh': ibid. pp. 60–4.
'It would be . . . were mine': interview with Sir Stephen Spender 29/
1/91.

405 'baroque and . . . any drawingroom':
AIP pp. 67–9.
'a big thing . . . very fully': n.d.
(Cornell).
'I am trying . . . work of art':
'Journey Out of Anguish'.

405– 'after the minimum . . . anybody
406 else': PWL to Abbott 15/10/39
(Buffalo).

406 'hung on . . . appreciation': Abbott
to PWL 9/1/40 (Cornell).
'considered . . . his agency': PWL to
McLuhan 5/9/43 (Cornell).
'something Buffalonian may come
along': PWL to Abbott 15/10/39
(Buffalo).

406– 'You can divine . . . a poster': PWL
407 to McLuhan 5/9/43 (Cornell).

407 'the friendly Director . . . recognised': *Brave Day Hideous Night* pp.
67–8.
'apparent from . . . liveliest interest':
ibid.

408– 'let off a single . . . all this, Cor-
409 coran': *AIP* pp. 236–55.

410 'I feel that . . . burlesque form':
PWL to MacDermot 19/11/40
(Cornell).
'where he had time . . . above his
head': 'Journey Out of Anguish'.

411 'ring me . . . understand you': (Cornell).

411– 'not among his best . . . local con-
12 sternation': *Brave Day Hideous
Night* pp. 67–8.

412 'I was taken . . . doubters': Abbot to
PWL 9/1/40 (Cornell).
'If there's one . . . to paint?': *Brave
Day Hideous Night* p. 67.

CHAPTER 39

413 'grim abstract metropolis': PWL to
McDermot 15/12/39 (Cornell).
'It is a spectacle. It is immense': 15/
11/39.
'WE ARE PROUD . . . Mink year':
New York Times 12/11/39.

'extraordinary scenes . . . concourse': *Brave Day Hideous Night* p. 66.
'a rather pleasant . . . about movies': Barry to PWL 24/10/39 (Cornell).
'crowded beyond . . . anything seriously': 6/12/39 (Cornell).
'not enough': Ransom to PWL 20/10/39 (Cornell).

413– 'a protean jack-in-the-box . . . something new': 'Picasso' *Kenyon Review* Spring 1940.

414 'Pittsburgh steel . . . aunt need portraits': 11/9/39 *P/L* p. 214.
'has money . . . with money': 16/10/40 (Cornell).
'I will take . . . alive today': n.d. (Cornell).
'The ideal . . . desirable': PWL to Stone 20/12/39 (Cornell).

415 'quite hysterically . . . to be there': Dora Stone to Victor Cassidy 9/1/74.

415– 'But even where . . . book would 16 be': *Brave Day Hideous Night* pp. 70–1.

416 'Wyndham Lewis . . . of all idols': 7/2/40 quoted *A Friendship Documented* p. 11.
'overcome the chronic . . . the Fall?': 16/2/40 (Cornell).

417 'too deeply orientated . . . prewar period': 13/2/40 (Cornell).
'too obviously "dashed off" . . . author's best': 5/6/40 (Cornell).

418 'a political storm . . . was not *his*': *RA* p. 232.
'a Russian Jewish . . . mildly bold': PWL to Morley 17/10/42 (Cornell).
'a quite pleasant . . . melons and things': PWL to Tate 27/8/46.
'In the four . . . intelligent rich': 18/3/40 (Cornell).

419 'the coming portrait painter . . . work of art': quoted Fox, 'A Momaconian Rebuff' *Lewisletter* 9 Summer 1997.

419– 'Nothing . . . happened here': *AIP* 20 pp. 78–9.

420 'emulated Leatherstocking . . . to the South': 'The Do-Nothing Mode: An Autobiographical Fragment' *Agenda: Wyndham Lewis Special Issue* Autumn–Winter 1969–70.

420– 'It is the most . . . early love': 21 quoted W. K. Rose *Wyndham Lewis at Cornell* p. 18.

421 'The peace . . . experienced': n.d. (Cornell).
'the pluperfect hell': Slocum to PWL 9/8/40 (Cornell).
'too much . . . this stage': 9/7/40 (Cornell).
'slick and superficial . . . point of view': 11/7/40 (Cornell).

422 'All children . . . foreign state': Shipley (Passport Division, Dept. of State) to PWL 2/10/40 (Cornell).
'to have . . . clownishness': PWL to Stone 3/10/40 (Cornell).

422– 'resented very much . . . Mr Slo-23 cum': 'Note of transactions in Russell & Volkening's Office Oct. 1 & 2 1940' (Cornell).

423 'magnificent job . . . book [he had] written': PWL to Sweeney 27/10/40 (Cornell).
'There is . . . Arnold system': PWL to Slocum 21/11/40 (Cornell).

424 'so much nearer . . . nightmares': PWL to Sweeney 27/10/40 (Cornell).
'according to whether . . . rumbled towards it': PWL to Morley (draft) 17/10/41 (Cornell).
'I am sorry . . . "Cheerio" ': 4/12/40 (Cornell).

425 'I do not feel . . . terribly dreary': 16/12/40 (Cornell).
'being most . . . Sassenachs': 18/11/40 (Cornell).
'Wyndham Lewis . . . paint snow': 18/11/40.
'14 bucks . . . at least': 20/11/40 and 5/12/40 (Cornell).
'seedy . . . more comfort': 'The Lewis Age' (Austin).

CHAPTER 40

427 'five portrait drawings . . . the war': PWL to Stone 7/12/40 (Cornell).

428 'Wyndham Lewis – novelist . . . with *Mac!*': CBC Radio script (Cornell).
'on the portrait . . . lady': PWL to Stone 30/12/40 (Cornell).

429 'I work ... in blizzards': 15/1/41 (Cornell).
'If it is ... other work': 30/12/40 (Cornell).

429– 'The portrait is ... sitter's wide
30 reading': 18/4/41.

430 'In my portrait ... experience': 'Speech at the unveiling of the J. S. McLean Portrait' (Cornell).

431 'You have to ... for a portraitist': 7/12/40 (Cornell).
'All this tiresome ... can't be helped!': 6/6/41 (Cornell).
'I think they're ... overlooking the street': LePan *Bright Glass of Memory* pp. 114–15.

432 'I did not ... alarming place': 17/6/41 (Cornell).

432– 'the various womenfolk ... female
33 ruffian': 11/2/43 (Cornell).

433 'deliberately ... insulted': Reid to PWL 30/6/41 (Cornell).

433– 'My remark gave ... provincial
34 tonight?': *Bright Glass of Memory* pp. 113–15.

434– 'Don't think ... Lion and the Fox':
35 Reid to PWL 30/6/41 (Cornell).

435– 'GLASSES ... INJURY': PWL to
36 Greeves, n.d. (Cornell).

436 'one of the most ... the first': PWL to Morley 17/10/41 (Cornell).
'not entirely ... optimism': PWL to Barry 5/10/41 (Buffalo).
'a septic ... first order': PWL to Morley 17/10/41 (Cornell).
'it has almost ... tooth-paste': 5/10/41 (Buffalo).

437 'Things have come ... flophouse': 3/9/41 (Cornell).
'If I can ... do it': 23/6/41 (Cornell).
'I am satisfied ... 1000 dollars': 4/7/41 (Cornell).
'There is a wolf ... blizzard': 11/8/41 (Cornell).

438 'Whenever I receive ... water pipes': n.d. (Cornell).
'He is trying ... walk': PWL to Stone 26/9/41 (Cornell).
'Of course ... propitious moment': 22/9/41 (Cornell).
'My next portrait ... the map': 23/9/41 (Cornell).

439 'Here I am ... experience': 22/9/41 (Cornell).
'I am directed ... you suggest': 24/9/41 (Cornell).

439– 'These drawings ... to lose': (Cor-
40 nell).

440 'I have spent ... bloody earth': 26/9/41 (Cornell).
'The portraitist ... his brush': 25/9/41 (Cornell).

440– 'Yes, or somebody ... wasn't spe-
41 cific': PWL to Pierce 9/10/41 (Cornell).

CHAPTER 41

442 'something taking ... own work': PWL to McLeish 21/10/41 (Cornell).
'This appointment ... battered by war': PWL to Brockington 13/8/41 (Cornell).
'painters, sculptors ... creative work': Dollard to PWL 10/10/41 (Cornell).

443 'an ultra conservative ... diverse United States': PWL to Jameson 6/1/42 (Cornell).
'It will really ... charming fellow': 7/11/41 (Cornell).
'I shall have ... weekend': (Buffalo).

444 'So far no ... distant planet': 25/11/41 (Cornell).
'I was just ... in smoke': PWL to Stone 5/1/42 (Cornell).
'near the centre of things': 4/12/41 (Cornell).
'overjoyed ... the novel': 5/12/41 (Buffalo).
'A sale ... desperate': 5/12/41 (Cornell).

445 'new friends ... little party': 21/12/41 (Cornell).
'one of those ... futility': 1/1/42 (Cornell).
'good college ... small matter': PWL to Jameson 20/12/41 (Cornell).

445– 'As a matter ... Michigan': ibid.
46 28/12/41 (Cornell).

446 'After all ... a wife': ibid. 10/1/42 (Cornell).

446– 'As to the . . . just "residing" ': 30/
47 1/42.
447 'I know time . . . Oregon!': PWL to
Jameson 23/2/42 (Cornell).
448 'highly unorthodox': 16/3/42 (Cornell).
'All the colleges . . . experiment
involves': n.d. (Cornell).
'Educational jobs . . . janitors':
PWL to Grierson 7/6/42 (Cornell).
'I am not . . . painting': 25/3/42
(Cornell).
448– 'Already my life . . . "spacious"
49 days': 30/4/42 (Cornell).
449 'It isn't poverty . . . ways worse':
Self Condemned p. 175.
450 'I have to . . . at night!': (Cornell).
'She cried . . . legs': *Self Condemned*
p. 177.
'I should like . . . unreasonable': n.d.
(Cornell).
451 'A gentleman . . . bitch': PWL to
Kahma 21/10/49 (Cornell).

CHAPTER 42

452– 'Dear Mr Lewis . . . Mercury
53 defend you': Kahma to PWL 27/5/
42 (Cornell).
453– 'THIS LETTER . . . to terra firma':
54 ibid. 11/6/42 (Cornell).
454 'Mr Eric Kennington . . . investigate': (IWM).
'Any fees . . . Canadian funds':
(IWM).
455 'The Chairman . . . payments':
(IWM).
'£1 a day . . . Tudor Hotel': 5/11/
42 (Cornell).
'so unceremoniously . . . rent': 8/7/
42 (Cornell).
456 'Before leaving . . . to us': 16/9/42
(Cornell).
'As I am . . . at once': 27/11/42
(IWM).
'Am I right . . . a knight?': 4/12/42
(IWM).
'I may . . . heard about it': 4/1/43
(Cornell).
'He is . . . *not* a knight': 24/12/42
(IWM).
457 'What do you want? . . . Sir Ken-
neth': from Comfort 'Portraits from

Memory', unpublished typescript,
quoted by Mastin *'The Talented
Intruder' Wyndham Lewis in Canada, 1939–1945* p. 62.
'In New York . . . flophouse': 13/7/
42 (Cornell).
457– 'I have never . . . understand': 5/
58 11/42 (IWM).
458 'I cannot . . . light and dark': Murphy, 'Wyndham Lewis at Windsor'
Canadian Literature 35 Winter 1968,
p. 11.
459 'he saw . . . his head': *Self Condemned* p. 259.
'I think . . . further insults': 11/2/
43 (Cornell).
460 'intolerably . . . *never* work?': 5/1/
42 (Cornell).
'As I write . . . cold': 30/1/43 (Cornell).
461 'It was about . . . public library':
Daily Star 15/2/43.
461– 'The main building . . . my address':
62 17/2/43 (Cornell).
462 'VERY MUCH . . . STOP HERE':
(Cornell).
'the moment . . . set out': 26/2/43
(Cornell).

CHAPTER 43

463 'perhaps . . . spray booths': 20/3/43
(Cornell).
'PLEASE . . . LEWIS': (IWM).
464 'I do not . . . not get': 3/5/43
(IWM).
'in train': 13/4/43 (Cornell).
'an unfortunate . . . funds': Williams
to PWL 31/5/43 (Cornell).
'it was economically . . . unalacrity':
PWL to Kennington 13/9/43 (Cornell).
464– 'at a sort . . . molten glass': PWL to
65 MacDonald 25/3/43 (Cornell).
465 'I believe . . . apparatus of war': 31/
3/43 (Cornell).
'a busy scene . . . large enough':
PWL to MacDonald 19/1/44
(IWM).
'demonic casting shop': PWL to
Beatie 10/8/43 (Cornell).
'quite unsaleable . . . baloney': to
MacDonald 18/1/44 (Cornell).

466 'Have patience . . . passengers': 31/
5/43.
'My picture . . . Records': 16/6/43
(Cornell).

467 'There is nothing . . . to hand': 17/
5/43 (Cornell).
'The Tecumseh . . . demented':
PWL to Burgess 17/7/43 (Cornell).
'He points . . . reject it!': 2/7/43
(IWM).

467– 'he had simply . . . apartment':
68 McLuhan 'The Global Lewis' *Lewisletter*5, October 1976.

468 'If you are . . . with you': 24/7/43
(Cornell).
'Lewis . . . your paragraph!':
'Wyndham Lewis at Windsor' p. 13.
'We have recently . . . paid': 27/8/
43 (Cornell).

469 'an excellent small studio': PWL to
Giovanelli 5/9/43 (Cornell).
'Alas . . . to see it': 31/8/43 (Cornell).
'probably . . . flock along': McLuhan to PWL 17/8/43 (Cornell).
'a hard-headed . . . lawyer': ibid. 2/
9/43 (Cornell).

469– 'I have turned . . . mistaken': 18/9/
70 43 (Cornell).

470 'Has Mr Wyndham Lewis's . . .
please?': (IWM).
'I have got . . . picture': (IWM).
'The War Artists . . . metal tube':
24/9/43 (IWM).
'was accompanied . . . time': PWL
to Burgess 24/11/43 (Cornell).
'Father Murphy . . . College': Cassidy interview with Fr J. S. Murphy.

471 'I am instructed . . . governed accordingly': 17/11/43 (Cornell).

471– 'I have followed . . . their doors':
72 n.d. (Cornell).

472 'the day of . . . must disappear':
(Cornell).
'it really was delivered': 5/12/43
(Cornell).
'a snooty affair . . . undiscovered':
McLuhan to PWL 27/11/43 (Cornell).

472– 'frankly they want . . . will be': ibid.
73 31/12/43 (Cornell).

473 'What sort . . . these people': ibid.
27/11/43 (Cornell).

'I think . . . a lulu': PWL to McLu-
han 11/12/43 (Cornell).
'The . . . Committee . . . to him?':
16/11/43 (IWM).
'What I was . . . for granted': quoted
Williams to Pugh 23/11 (IWM).
'If it can't . . . a crate': 23/12/43
(IWM).

473– 'He maintains . . . by sea': 12/12/43
74 (IWM).

474 'Finance Division . . . Wyndham
Lewis': 31/12/43 (IWM).
'I do think . . . uncertain': 6/1/44
(IWM).

CHAPTER 44

475 'The temptation . . . to do': 13/1/44
(Cornell).

475– 'We are on . . . comfort!': PWL to
76 Giovanelli 28/1/44 (Cornell).

476 'the public . . . St Louis': McLuhan
to PWL 4/1/44 (Cornell).
'recognised . . . bargain-hunter':
ibid. 13/1/44 (Cornell).
'to have . . . other cities': ibid. 4/1/
44 (Cornell).

477 'One could . . . *des musées*': 18/1/44
(Cornell).
'some supplementary . . . weeks':
PWL to MacDonald 16/6/43 (Cornell).
'more solid . . . other things': ibid.
18/1/44 (Cornell).

478 'Latest title . . . God help us!': 17/
1/44 (Cornell).
'My Finance . . . the picture': 21/2/
44 (IWM).
'My letter . . . more news?': 9/3/44
(IWM).
'everything . . . discredited': Giovanelli to PWL n.d. (Cornell).

478– 'Will this Bergsonian . . . work
79 here': 1/2/44 (Cornell).

479 'If he wants . . . for $5000': McLu-
han to PWL 3/2/44 (Cornell).
'that palatial . . . plutocracy': PWL
to McLuhan 26/5/44 (Cornell).

480 'well afford . . . air at all': McLuhan
to PWL 1/2/44 (Cornell).
'There is nothing . . . needed': 17/
2/44 *Letters* p. 156.

481– 'Under these circumstances . . .

82 human audience': 'Wednesday Club Lecture' (Cornell).

482 'the lecture . . . halt finally!': Nagel to Cassidy 5/5/74.
'I enjoyed . . . abstract painting': 25/2/44 (Cornell).
'I was lured . . . forthcoming': 11/4/44 (Cornell).

483 'banker . . . expenses came': PWL to McLuhan 26/5/44 (Cornell).

483– 'He accused . . . friendships':
84 McLuhan to A. J. M. Smith 12/10/45 (Toronto).

484 'There is . . . matter to her': Giovanelli to PWL 22/5/44 (Cornell).

485 'choir boy . . . behind him': PWL to Martin 22/10/44 (Cornell).
'Gio had begun . . . like me?': McLuhan to Smith 12/10/45 (Toronto).
'scratching, . . . understand us': PWL to Pauline Bondy 20/4/44 (Cornell).

486 'we do not . . . quest': (IWM).
'should try . . . Massey': (IWM).
'Noted with satisfaction!': 5/5/44 (IWM).
'Yes, but . . . months sooner': 21/7/44 (IWM).
'As the War . . . tell me?': 29/3/44 (Cornell).
'extremely distressed . . . force majeure': PWL to MacDonald 11/4/44 (Cornell).

487 'Dear Mr MacDonald . . . look attractive': 30/5/44 (Cornell).
'The . . . place . . . anyway': 26/5/44 (Cornell).

487– 'Feel free . . . hidden meanings':
88 n.d. (Cornell).

488 'In view . . . the war?': 21/7/44 (IWM).
'I fear . . . the Ministry': 24/7/44 (IWM).
'two large sun-smitten windows': PWL to Gerty Cori 20/8/44 (Cornell).
'One hour's . . . before you go': 18/6/44 (Cornell).

489 'So the position . . . anxiety': PWL to MacDonald 11/4/44 (Cornell).
'measure . . . couple of pencils': PWL to Murphy 27/3/44 (Cornell).

'They're both . . . perfectly right': 'Wyndham Lewis at Windsor' p. 18.

490 'some "ham-and-egger" . . . photographs': Murphy to PWL 25/3/44 (Cornell).
'I am prepared . . . Toronto artist': 27/3/44 (Cornell).
'The little job . . . unamusing occupation': 20/8/44 (Cornell).
'I hope . . . the picture': 8/8/44 (IWM).

491 'If you know . . . extreme': n.d. (Cornell).
'for some . . . one thousand': PWL to Martin 21/2/45 (Cornell).
'got the job for Lewis': McLuhan to Smith 12/10/45 (Toronto).

492 'A pox on Stix': 24/9/44 (Cornell).
'a loan . . . and unfortunate': McLuhan to PWL 27/9/44 (Cornell).
'The phrase . . . for that': PWL to McLuhan 28/9/44 (Cornell).

492– 'Your method . . . referred': 9/10/
93 44 (Cornell).

493 'Dear Mr Robey . . . you suggest': 9/10/44 (Cornell).
'draw the file . . . month's time': (IWM).
'If you are . . . catastrophe': 24/10/44 (Cornell).

494 'really a good . . . surprised': 21/11/44 (Cornell).
'have a breathless . . . seven': PWL to MacDonald 22/11/44 (Cornell).
'I assume . . . Clark's letter': (IWM).
'This is . . . lecture on art': 15/11/44 (IWM).

495 'very temperamental . . . hustle him': 16/10/44 (IWM).
'I am afraid . . . swindled': 28/11/44 (IWM).
'I literally . . . talk about': 11/12/44 (IWM).
'the War Artists . . . good time': 18/12/44 (IWM).
'I am afraid . . . sad story': 29/12/44 (IWM).

495– 'It certainly . . . to the Treasury': 5/
96 1/45 (IWM).

496 'a paragraph . . . Mr Crossley': (IWM).
'Mr Gregory . . . Finance 19.1.45': (IWM).

CHAPTER 45

497 'Although people . . . Windsor': 21/2/45 (Cornell).
'intimate, domesticated . . . relaxed position': PWL to Martin n.d. (Cornell).
'Smile up to your ears!': interview with Paul and Eleanor Martin 7/6/91.
498 'I was very . . . yards away': 21/2/45 (Cornell).
'the Minister . . . my wife': 9/1/45 (Cornell).
498– 'Dodge millionairess . . . other two': 26/2/45 (Cornell).
99
499 'D. B. Wyndham Lewis . . . writer': 27/1/45.
'completely different . . . Ezra Pound': 3/2/45.
500 'Dear Mr McLuhan . . . to heart': (Cornell).
'You have made . . . lecture': (Cornell).
501 'would and indeed *must* . . . out of pocket': 21/2/45 (Cornell).
502 'His method . . . at Windsor': Taylor to Cassidy 7/8/74.
'At first . . . bloody fool'": Feinberg to Cassidy 24/10/71.
503 'very successful . . . very well': Valentiner to Walter Allen 9/1/58.
'It was a complete . . . somewhere': 26/5/45 (Cornell).
'I had a hard . . . gave him': quoted Meyers *The Enemy* p. 285.
'long baggage train . . . moderate thirst': PWL to John 19/6/45 (Cornell).
504 'Wyndham Lewis . . . correspondence': 29/6/45 (IWM).
'I do not . . . advance': 30/6/45 (IWM).
'WYNDHAM LEWIS . . . STRATHEDEN': (IWM).
505 'the glass roof . . . half a roof': PWL to Paige 17/8/47 (Cornell).
'I will not . . . horror of it': 17/8/43 (Cornell).
'only millionaires . . . freedom': PWL to MacDonald n.d. (Cornell).
'The number . . . Canadians!': to Lady Waterhouse 19/9/45 (Cornell).

'All I can offer . . . gin': 14/11/45 (Cornell).
'Hot soup . . . weeks or so': 16/11/45 (Cornell).
506 'devoutly thankful . . . my landlord': 27/10/45 (Cornell).
'I am tightly . . . between them': PWL to MacDonald n.d. and to 'Mr Lewis' 7/11/45 (Cornell).
507 'was extremely uncivil': PWL to 'Mr Lewis' 6/11/45 (Cornell).
'a cash down . . . owing': n.d. (Cornell).
'sitting . . . in dust': PWL to Lady Waterhouse 19/9/45 (Cornell).
507– 'As to the portrait . . . on show': 23–24/10/45 (Cornell).
508
508– 'regarding Mr Wyndham Lewis . . . necessary': (IWM).
509
509 'a shortage of labour': PWL to Gwynne-Jones 26/10/45 (Cornell).
'To telephone is not easy': 29/11/45 (Cornell).
'with much trembling': Dodd to Crossley 3/12/45 (IWM).
'SORRY . . . LEWIS': (IWM).
510 'to make . . . my being here': 13/12/45 (Cornell).

CHAPTER 46

511 My book . . . sociable again': 10/2/46 (Cornell).
511– 'Mr Gregory . . . supply fuel': n.d. (IWM).
12
512 'near the Lambeth . . . the road': 22/3/46 (IWM).
'HAVE FLU . . . LEWIS': 25/3/46 (IWM).
512– 'an account . . . matter in hand': n.d. (IWM).
13
513 'Everyone . . . your honour': 3/4/46 (IWM).
'The weather . . . work on it': 9/4/46 (IWM).
'The matter . . . settled?': n.d. (Cornell).
'and the sitter . . . chins)': PWL to Rebecca Citkowitz 24/9/46 (Cornell).
514 'As you know . . . mere stumps': (IWM).

'might be able . . . help you!': 1/5/
46 (IWM).
'But can you . . . for them': 8/5/46
(IWM).

515 'It was not . . . the nose': Tangye to
Jenkins 1/11/85 (Tate).
'When you reach . . . artist. – See?':
23/7/46 (Cornell).

515– 'The food . . . speakeasies': PWL to
16 Tate 27/8/46 (Cornell).

516 'Do, when you . . . nothing else':
24/9/46 (Cornell).
'and one cannot get new ones made':
23/8/46 (Cornell).

517 'It seems . . . developments': 4/9/
46 (Cornell).
'a slightly indented . . . discomfort':
PWL to Waterhouse 19/11/46
(Cornell).

518 'Any Nicholson's . . . Wyndham
Lewis': n.d. (Cornell).
'Charlie . . . winter with us': GAL
to Mrs Giovanelli 20/11/47 (Cor-
nell).
'He tells me . . . diarrhoea': RA
p. 203.
'We were expecting . . . desisted':
GAL to Mrs Giovanelli 20/11/47
(Cornell).

518– 'I must take . . . your return?':
19 (Cornell).

519 'I . . . advise . . . urgency': 7/1/47
(Cornell).
'Worst winter . . . in our beds': n.d.
(Cornell).
'a beautiful . . . the street': PWL to
Soby 29/11/47 (Cornell).

520 'to identify . . . crisis was at hand':
The Listener 3/4/47.

521 'Time is passing . . . hospital': (Cornell).

521– 'since the happy . . . foreseeable
22 period': 14/5/47 (Cornell).

522 'described by . . . in England" ': The
Listener 13/9/47.

522– 'kind of tory . . . pay the fees': PWL
23 to Giovanelli 2/10/48 (Cornell).

523 'Big, toothy . . . tablets': Messengers
of Day p. 149.

524 'they . . . are wafting . . . compromise': PWL to Kahma 15/11/47
(Cornell).
'While this . . . reversed': ibid. 29/
11/47 (Cornell).

CHAPTER 47

525 'I am appalled . . . the money!': 4/
1/48 (Cornell).
'I have not . . . terrified': PWL to
Waterhouse 13/1/48 (Cornell).

526 'We now . . . few goods" ': (Cornell).
'a dazzlingly . . . present': 31/3/48
(Cornell).

527 'co-ordinating . . . civilisation':
Times 14/2/48.
'To speak . . . tell me what': 29/1/
48 (Cornell).

527– 'infinite disgust . . . committee
28 meetings': PWL to Read 5/2/48
(Cornell).

528 'INDIGNANTLY . . . SUBSTI-
TUTE': 4/2/48 (Cornell).
'Should [the Committee] . . . too
many': 5/2/48 (Cornell).
'I hope . . . anonymity': 3/2/48
(Cornell).
'expressed in scarcely sane terms':
Messengers of Day p. 152.

529 'when it became . . . conjunction':
10/2/48 (Cornell).
'The impression . . . avoided': Messengers of Day p. 152.
'It is a triumph . . . grateful': 8/2/
48 (Cornell).
'big lawyer . . . terrified of me':
PWL to Mitchell 1/5/48 (Cornell).

530 'in my dedication . . . author's
hand': 19/6/48 (Cornell).
'an all time . . . mutilated': 2/7/98
(Cornell).
'Left side . . . in pain': PWL to
Giovanelli 12/7/48 (Cornell).

530– 'rather dispiriting . . . into the
31 night': 'Tarr and Flying Feathers'
Golden Sections pp. 149–50.

531 'Mr Wyndham Lewis . . . "Captain
Brown" ': Inside the Forties p. 132.
'It is a watertight boycott': PWL to
Lynette Roberts 20/9/48 (Cornell).

532 'that cross . . . his hands': The
Writer and the Absolute p. 48.
'remember . . . bubble-headed rat':
PWL to Giovanelli 1/10/48 (Cornell).
'in a nightmare . . . feverish dream':
PWL to Gene Nash 1/11/48 (Cornell).

533 'he would find . . . muscling in!':

PWL to Giovanelli 1/10/48 (Cornell).

'I cannot ... our canon': 2/10/48 (Cornell).

534 'Now, if ... background': 9/10/48 (Cornell).

'If Osbert ... annual income': 2/10/48 (Cornell).

'shake money ... careless': 21/10/48 (Cornell).

'CONTRACT ... EXCLUDED': PWL to Giovanelli (Cornell).

535 'That Bloomsbury ... write': PWL to Lynette Roberts 9/10/48 (Cornell).

'give himself ... Reading Room': *Times Literary Supplement* 16/10/48.

'Mr Wyndham ... his book': ibid. 6/11/48.

'fake-"scholarly" ... pseudoexpert': 9/11/48 (Cornell).

'Obviously ... my lawyer': 11/11/48 (Cornell).

'playing ugly ... system': PWL to Giovanelli 18/12/48 (Cornell).

536 'It appears ... maligned': 18/12/48.

'If that ... again': PWL to Giovanelli 11/11/48 (Cornell).

'The Sitwells ... enjoying it': quoted Glendinning *A Unicorn Among Lions* p. 277.

'surrounded ... girl there': PWL to Nash 21/1/49 and to Giovanelli 8/1/49 (Cornell).

'shortly after Christmas': 24/9/48 (Cornell).

'late January or February': PWL to Nash 1/11/48 (Cornell).

537 '2 or 3 ... New York': PWL to Giovanelli 6/12/48 (Cornell).

CHAPTER 48

538 'Why had I ... article!': PWL to Sargent 8/1/49 (Cornell).

'a very tough ... names': 'The Vita of Wyndham Lewis'.

539 'Acknowledgement ... broadcasting': 13/1/49 (Cornell).

'Can't make ... great man': Symons

'The King-Bull Affair' *EN* 36, Summer 1993.

539–40 'I walked ... and friendly': 'Meeting Wyndham Lewis' *London Magazine* October 1957.

540 'a paper-manufacturer in a big way': PWL to Giovanelli 20/4/49 (Cornell).

'Mister Lewis ... money': PWL to Giovanelli 12/7/48 (Cornell).

541 'not allow ... exhibition': PWL to Nash 18/12/48 (Cornell).

'papers ... expensive': PWL to Kahma 18/12/48, 18/8/48 and 18/1/49 (Cornell).

'who affect ... Curse them': ibid. 27/12/49 (Cornell).

'If we are ... of yours!': ibid. 18/12/48.

542 'Forgive ... dark from me!': Heron 'The Lost Portraits of a Poet' *Guardian* 24/9/88.

'form filling galore': PWL to Kahma 8/2/49 (Cornell).

'The Nobel ... "goes to sleep"': PWL to Nash 7/3/49 (Cornell).

'Two drawings ... Ezra studies': PWL to Giovanelli 21/5/49 (Cornell).

542–43 'the slowness ... responsive action': Ackerley *My Sister and Myself* pp. 155–6.

543 'to see ... the nose': Lewis 'The Sea-Mists of the Winter' *Listener* 10/5/51.

'they hang *tomorrow* ... painted': 7–29/4/49 (Cornell).

543–44 'Mr Lewis! ... average man's': PWL to Earp 11/5/49.

544 'now than it was then': 19/5/49.

'that if ... great artist': 19/5/49.

'One knows ... some sort of genius': 7/5/49.

'A man of undoubted ... to say': *Guardian* 24/9/88.

'not so far ... turning!': 11/7/49 (Cornell).

'ten thousand ... my property': 19/5/49 (Cornell).

'far more ... portrait': 18/5/49.

545 'I know ... *hands* were': PWL to John Rothenstein 24/6/49.

'The Board declined ... for £250': (Tate).

'When I learned ... on top': PWL to Eliot 1/7/49.

'on whom ... have fallen': *Time's Thievish Progress*, p. 39.

'by a sneer ... Bloomsbury *sniff*': *Satire and Fiction* p. 8.

546 'I shall not ... live with it': 30/5/49.

'Wyndham Lewis ... offered': *A Friendship Documented* p. 19.

'What was ... an error': n.d. (Cornell).

'perfectly placed ... properly': Levy and Scherle *Affectionately, T. S. Eliot* p. 82.

547 'the son ... could be bought': 14/7/49.

'abominable ... drop him': PWL to Giovanelli 10/7/49 (Cornell).

'a young ... talent': 10/7/49 (Cornell).

'assist him ... sort of thing': 10/7/49 (Cornell).

'urbane ... New York': Williams to Cassidy 11/10/73.

548 'to educate ... British Guyana': PWL to Williams 3/9/49 (Cornell).

'Guyana is ... hard-up': PWL to Giovanelli 10/7/49 (Cornell).

'If one ... only one': 14/12/47 (Cornell).

548– 'It was my ... married before': 4/
49 12/73 to Cassidy.

549 'people were lecture ... will "draw"': 10/1/50 (Cornell).

550 'You were inaccessible ... evaporated': 15/5/50 (Cornell).

'I have practically ... particularly': PWL to Willis Feast (Cornell).

'Tomorrow ... after Christmas': (Cornell).

550– 'generalised *very* ... bone infec-
51 tion': Lindsay-Rea notes 30/12/49 (Cornell).

551 'The doctors ... Pray for me': (Cornell).

CHAPTER 49

552– 'as a great joke ... I don't know"':
54 GAL Diaries (Cornell).

554 'All noxious ... removed': 28/2/50–11/3/50 (Cornell).

'This involves ... hitherto': to Dr Fant 9/3/50 (Trust).

554– 'Lewis told ... must be mad!':
55 GAL Diaries (Cornell).

556 'He probably ... meningioma': 31/3/50 (Cornell).

557– 'As far as ... suspect him of
58 having': GAL Diaries (Cornell).

558 'You will recall ... I assume': 8/4/50 (Cornell).

559 'one of the best ... what you have': 22/4/50 (Cornell).

559– 'She is getting ... lowest of louts':
63 GAL Diaries (Cornell).

563 'If you do not ... go blind': PWL to Eliot n.d. (Cornell).

'the star Swiss eye-doctor': PWL to Campbell 28/6/50 (Cornell).

'there were different ... right way': PWL to Eliot n.d. (Cornell).

'It might ... as possible': 14/6/50 (Cornell).

563– 'The best ... alternative': PWL to
64 Eliot n.d. (Cornell).

564 'the more ... for him': 30/6/50 (Cornell).

'The Swedish ... about it': to Feast 24/9/50 (Cornell).

564– 'The X-ray ... shaken': n.d. (Cor-
65 nell).

565 'death, total blindness ... myopic one': (Cornell).

566 'as you did ... decisive': 17/11/50 (Cornell).

566– 'that is ... medical authorities':
67 (Cornell).

CHAPTER 50

568 'You were so ... beyond words': 20/1/51 (Cornell).

'The Lefevre ... gently recoil': 20/1/51.

'My wife ... caused fire': n.d. (Cornell).

569 'It is ... too late': PWL to Booth 24/12/50 (Cornell).

'Doctor ... much use': to Kahma 24/2/51 (Cornell).

'there had been ... decided against it': D. G. Bridson 8/3/70 quoted *RA* Appendix III p. 263.

570 'Twin came ... a lawyer': GAL Diaries (Cornell).

'must be ... worded': n.d. (Cornell).

'Plenty of writers . . . expect': 9/4/51 (Cornell).

'Thanks for . . . to see': 4/4/51 (Cornell).

'What a hellish . . . Childermass': 10/4/51 (Cornell).

571 'a beautiful name': 9/4/51 (Cornell).

572 'If my eyes . . . live in': to Morley 17/10/41 (Cornell).

573 'a brilliant . . . powerful': 17/5/51.

'Yes . . . art criticism': interview with Sir Stephen Spender 29/1/91.

'I really . . . old ones': 13/5/51 (Cornell).

'beating your . . . bitch!': 5/10/51.

'I made . . . you believed': 25/5/51 (Cornell).

'Since the days . . . babies born': 9/6/51 (Cornell).

'the three . . . in England': 9/6/51 (Cornell).

574 'healers . . . intractable cases': 16/6/51 (Cornell).

'As to when . . . not stand': 15/5/51 (Cornell).

575 'Lewis . . . chocolate cream': GAL Diaries (Cornell).

'After that . . . Lyall St.': *A Friendship Documented* p. 29.

'My dear Froanna . . . blessings. W.L.': (Cornell).

575– 'However long . . . further injury?': 76 GAL to Hirst n.d. (Cornell).

576 'What kind of hat . . . from him': 'Wyndham Lewis' exhibition catalogue, City of Manchester Art Galleries, p. 31.

576– 'I was staying . . . respectably hot': 77 n.d. (Cornell).

577 'the sprightly . . . no more': 26/8/51 (Cornell).

578 'The Bailiff . . . he had been': *Prospero and Ariel* pp. 188–9.

'an almost miraculous . . . one's existence': to Bridson n.d. (Cornell).

578– 'Grisewood could . . . *filled*': *Pros-* 79 *pero and Ariel* footnote p. 189.

579 'the support . . . expenses': to Richards 5/7/51 *A Friendship Documented*.

'too noisy': to Lynette Roberts 26/8/51 (Austin).

'committed . . . Agreement': F. W.

Gapp & Co. to PWL 1/10/51. (Cornell).

581– 'FINAL CHAPTER . . . front of 82 her': handwritten draft of *Self Condemned* (Cornell).

582 'My desire . . . hard at it': 24/10/51 (Cornell).

583 'Furthermore . . . circumstances': (Cornell).

'working . . . one month': 3/10/51 (Cornell).

584 'I met Blossom . . . depressed me': *Rotting Hill* pp. 275–81.

585 'once more . . . this university': to Loach 30/10/50 (Leeds).

'Since sending . . . gesture': to Loach 10/11/51 (Leeds).

'THANK YOU . . . DONE ME': 31/12/51 (Leeds).

586 'You are . . . essential': n.d. (Cornell).

'I am of course . . . remember': 9/1/52.

CHAPTER 51

587 'still hanging . . . long wait': 5/3/52.

'I well remember . . . he went': to Jane Woolston 7/7/65 (Cornell).

588 'By maintaining . . . most austere': p. 196.

589 'Froanna . . . to come': 1/1/52 (Cornell).

'Mr Wyndham . . . speak to you': interview with Robyn Denny 3/11/98.

'Robyn . . . agreeable visitor': 13/1/52 (Cornell).

590 'a bleak domestic atmosphere': interview with Robyn Denny.

'My wife . . . letter outside': 12/2/52 (Cornell).

'Regards . . . feeling better': 18/2/52 (Cornell).

'note above change of address': 16/3/52 (Austin).

'permanent address . . . as [he] thought': (Cornell).

'Froanna . . . Rotting Hill address': 5/4/52 (Cornell).

'American . . . enchanted': PWL to Wagner 16/5/52 (Cornell).
'the old address . . . lacked': 16/6/52 (Cornell).

591 'about the unhappy . . . situation generally': 24/6/52.
'It's not good . . . excellent cook': Bridson 'Froanna at Home' *EN* 11, Autumn 1979.
'paying . . . both of them': Tomlin 'Visiting the Lewises' ibid.

592 'flooding the people downstairs': PWL to Mr Betts 16/1/54 (Cornell).

593 'extensive enquiries . . . upset about this': Selby to Page 13/10/52 (Leeds).
'if that . . . Leeds hotels': 10/10/52 (Leeds).

594 'P. J. would have . . . than P.': 14/10/52 (Leeds).

594– 'We work . . . 10 minutes': 16/10/
95 52 (Leeds).

595 'pleased and flattered': 14/11/52 (Cornell).

595– 'Your Royal . . . *honoris causa*':
96 (Leeds).

596 'When I remember . . . blackguard': n.d. (Cornell).

CHAPTER 52

597 'a slap . . . speak to you': PWL to White 25/4/53 (Cornell).
'in two . . . time': ibid. 24/7/53 (Cornell).
'I think . . . be done': 7/4/53 (Cornell).

598 'at least . . . from Voltaire': 17/6/53 *A Friendship Documented* p. 42.

598– 'When we wrote . . . dreadfully sorry':
99 22/4/53 (Cornell).

599 'extremely sorry . . . problem': 24/4/53 (Cornell).
'not been . . . advances': 30/4/53 (Cornell).
'If a publisher . . . general advance': 25/4/53 (Cornell).

599– 'Of course . . . urgent': 1/5/53
600 (Cornell).

600– 'pleasant . . . human kindness': *A*
601 *Friendship Documented* pp. 42–3.

601 'beastly accident': PWL to Ayrton 14/9/53 (Cornell).
'My wife . . . arm in a sling': 26/10/53 (Cornell).
'a short . . . the book': to White 5/8/53 (Cornell).
'driving . . . or zero': *The Demon of Progress in the Arts* p. 33.

602 'one year . . . the Ms': 9/11/53 (Cornell).
'The Hotel . . . do with him': 29/1/54 (Cornell).

603 'using his previous knowledge': *Golden Sections* p. 152.
'to be receiving . . . value': 5/3/54 (Cornell).

604 'vast novel . . . flash of genius': 4/6/54.
'powerful, witty and withering': 12/6/54.
'tiresome . . . bitter end': 21/5/54.
'The fact . . . his portrait': 21/5/54.

604– 'things became . . . *Self-Con-*
605 *demned*?)': November 1954.

605 'tiresome . . . prose style': 4/5/54.
'at once terrifying . . . great men': 8/5/54.
'very important . . . hit the stalls': 9/5/54 (Cornell).

605– 'the boring quality . . . his shrine':
606 1/10/55.

606 'the publishers . . . to be so': *Golden Sections* p. 152.

606– 'striking cook . . . mobile hands': *A*
607 *Friendship Documented* p. 44.

607– 'swollen by illness . . . see me again':
608 ' "Lot Thirteen" The Last of Wyndham Lewis'. Unpublished typescript (Cornell).

CHAPTER 53

609 'explicit . . . new versions': *Golden Sections* p. 152.
'in full colour . . . that': n.d. (Cornell).

610 'the whole . . . exhibition': 28/1/55 (Cornell).
'most stirring': n.d. (Cornell).
'with a grace . . . disappointment': Rothenstein *Time's Thievish Progress*, p. 41.

'Only had you . . . revealed': 4/4/54 (Cornell).

'had you not . . . a woman?': *The Human Age* Books 2 and 3, p. 186.

611 'Lewis was very . . . the stupid': Rothenstein *Time's Thievish Progress* p. 40.

'a blind titan . . . "funny" ': *As I Walked Down New Grub Street* p. 202.

612 'upset by the cruelty . . . details of that': *A Friendship Documented* pp. 46–7.

613 'an extremely topical . . . everybody': 18/11/53 (Cornell).

'with all . . . admiration': White to PWL 10/10/55 (Cornell).

613– 'in bus, train . . . interests there!':
14 Hutchins to PWL 24/11/55 (Cornell).

614 'What a terrifying . . . on end': n.d. (Cornell).

'the size . . . farm-cart': *The Human Age* p. 562.

'Satters stared . . . section of bone': BBC recording no. LP 25612–4.

'in the Celestial . . . Society': 29/8/55 (Cornell).

615 'But are you . . . do evil?': n.d. (Cornell).

'God is a big problem': Bridson 'The Human Age In Retrospect', *Wyndham Lewis: A Revaluation* ed. Meyers, p. 250.

'I saw . . . call God!': 'The Trial of Man', *Malign Fiesta* p. 219.

615– 'In one way . . . around him': *Twen-*
16 *tieth Century Palette* p. 85.

616 'You will notice . . . generally': 6/6/56 (Cornell).

617 'The overlap . . . I think': 18/6/56 (Cornell).

'The private . . . touchingly happy': *Time's Thievish Progress* p. 41.

617– 'irritatingly helpless . . . the Tate': *A*
18 *Friendship Documented* p. 49.

618 'Among our greatest . . . slackness': 13/7/56.

'in the best . . . British art': 6/7/56.

'discouraging . . . our time': September 1956.

'to express his annoyance': *Time's Thievish Progress* p. 41.

619 'because it was too big': *The Resurrection of Vorticism and the Apotheosis of Wyndham Lewis at the Tate*, 1956.

'the other Vorticists . . . caught': 21/7/56.

621 'I cannot . . . your views': 28/8/56 (Cornell).

621– 'The blind outsider . . . many cham-
22 bers': 6/9/56.

622 'will not . . . reputation': 13/9/56.

'Mr Lewis . . . a straitjacket': 15/9/56.

'a powerful . . . stilted speech': 30/8/56.

623 'isn't a total . . . book are': 2/9/56.

'venomous misunderstandings . . . funny things': n.d. (Cornell).

'PLEASE . . . LEWIS': 25/9/56 (Cornell).

'*Don't miss* . . . stormy sea': 4/9/56.

624 'fine portrait of John McLeod': 12/11/56.

CHAPTER 54

625 'The topic . . . present time': 10/8/56.

'not wonderful . . . something': 24/8/56.

625– 'I have now . . . humanitarian hor-
26 ror': (Cornell).

626– 'His massive . . . high spirits!': 'Stele
27 for Hephaestus' *Poetry* August 1957.

627 'Never commit yourself . . . Westminster Abbey': *The Pound Era* pp. 440–4.

627– 'in that chilly . . . warning': 'The
28 Trial of Man' *Malign Fiesta* p. 239.

628 'At the time . . . left off': 31/3/60 (Cornell).

'He remembers . . . young man's': 6/9/56.

629 'a cancer . . . very short': *Points in Time*, p. 164.

'Was the girl . . . a tick': *Prospero and Ariel* p. 199.

630 'I like your . . . for us': 31/1/57 (Cornell).

'Since I saw . . . for him': n.d. (Cornell).

'I am most . . . understand': 13/2/ 57 (Cornell).
'It is terrible . . . ill he is?': n.d. (Cornell).
630– 'I couldn't . . . clear cut life': 12/3/
31   57 (Cornell).
631 'Mind your own business!': *Prospero and Ariel* p. 200.
'I was arranging . . . happening': 15/3/57 (Cornell).
631– 'Like the funerals . . . Wolfit': 'The
32   Making of *The Human Age*' *Agenda: Wyndham Lewis Special Issue* Autumn–Winter 1969–1970.

CHAPTER 55

633 'he was . . . building down': *Prospero and Ariel* p. 200.
'On the day . . . torn away': *The Enemy* p. 329.

633– 'It was very . . . behind furniture':
34   '"Lot Thirteen" The Last of Wyndham Lewis'.
635 'not truthful . . . the studio': GAL to Underwood 26/2/58 (Cornell).
'as though . . . her care': Hutchins to Cassidy 12/10/74.
'One of the items . . . left': GAL to Underwood 26/2/58 (Cornell).
'I am proof . . . darling': pp. 15–16.
636 'These are long . . . nor forgetters': *Collected Poems and Plays* p. 47.
'knowing . . . a ghost!': BBC *Today* script (Cornell).

BIBLIOGRAPHY

Note: The excellent Black Sparrow editions of Wyndham Lewis's writings have beem used and cited where available:

Ackerley, J. R. *My Sister and Myself* ed. Francis King, London: Hutchinson, 1982

Ackroyd, Peter *T. S. Eliot* London: Hamish Hamilton, 1984

Alington, Adrian, et al. *Beginnings* London: Thomas Nelson & Sons, 1935

Allen, Walter *As I Walked Down New Grub Street: Memories of a Writing Life* Chicago: University of Chicago Press, 1981

Apollonio, Umbro, ed. *Futurist Manifestos* London: Thames & Hudson, 1973

Ayrton, Michael *Golden Sections* London: Methuen, 1957

Bell, Clive *Art* London: Chatto & Windus, 1914

Blunt, Wilfred Scawen *My Diaries* vol. II, London: Martin Secker, 1920

Braybrooke, Neville ed. *Seeds in the Wind: 20th Century Juvenilia from W. B. Yeats to Ted Hughes* London: Hutchinson, 1989

Bridson, D. G. *The Filibuster: A Study of the Political Ideas of Wyndham Lewis* London: Cassell, 1972

—— *Prospero and Ariel: The Rise and Fall of Radio* London: Victor Gollancz, 1971

Brown, Oliver *Exhibition: The Memoirs of Oliver Brown* London: Evelyn, Adams & Mackay, 1968

Campbell, Roy *Wyndham Lewis* ed. Jeffrey Meyers, Pietermaritzburg: University of Natal Press, 1985

Carpenter, Humphrey *A Serious Character: The Life of Ezra Pound* London: Faber, 1988

Chapman, Robert T. *Wyndham Lewis: Fictions and Satires* London: Vision Press, 1973

Clements, Keith *Henry Lamb: The Artist and his Friends* Bristol: Redcliff, 1985

Constable, John and S.J.M. Watson ed. *Wyndham Lewis and I. A. Richards, A Friendship Documented 1928–57* Cambridge: Skate Press, 1989

Corbett, David Peters ed. *Wyndham Lewis and the art of modern war* Cambridge: Cambridge University Press, 1998

Cork, Richard *Art Beyond the Gallery in Early 20th Century England* New Haven and London: Yale University Press, 1985

—— *A Bitter Truth: Avant-Garde Art and the Great War* New Haven and London: Yale University Press, 1994

—— *Vorticism and Abstract Art in the First Machine Age* vol.1 *Origins and Development* London: Gordon Fraser, 1975

—— *Vorticism and Abstract Art in the First Machine Age* vol. 2 *Synthesis and Decline* London: Gordon Fraser, 1976

Cournos, John *Autobiography* New York: Putnam's Sons, 1935

Cunningham, Valentine *British Writers of the Thirties* Oxford: Oxford University Press, 1988

Edwards, Paul *Wyndham Lewis: Art and War* London: Lund Humphries, 1992

—— ed. *Volcanic Heaven: Essays on Wyndham Lewis's Painting and Writing* Santa Barbara: Black Sparrow Press, 1996

Eliot, T. S. *The Letters of T. S. Eliot, Volume 1 1898–1922* ed. Valerie Eliot, London: Faber, 1988

—— *Inventions of the March Hare, Poems 1909–1917* London: Faber, 1996

Ellman, Richard *James Joyce* Oxford: Oxford University Press, 1959

—— *Oscar Wilde* London: Hamish Hamilton, 1987

Ford, Ford Madox *Return To Yesterday* London: Victor Gollancz, 1932

Fothergill, John ed. *The Slade: A Collection of drawings and some pictures done by past and present students of the London Slade School of Art, 1893–1907* London: University College, 1907

Fry, Roger *Letters of Roger Fry* vols I and II, ed. Denys Sutton, London: Chatto & Windus, 1972

Gawsworth, John *Apes, Japes and Hitlerism: A Study and Bibliography of Wyndham Lewis* London: Unicorn Press, 1932

Glendinning, Victoria *Edith Sitwell: A Unicorn Among Lions* London: Weidenfeld, 1981

Goldring, Douglas *South Lodge: Reminiscences of Violet Hunt, Ford Madox Ford and the English Review Circle* London: Constable, 1943

Grant, Joy *Stella Benson: A Biography* London: Macmillan, 1987

Grayson, Rupert *Stand Fast, The Holy Ghost* London: Tom Stacey, 1973

Grigson, Geoffrey *The Crest on the Silver* London: Cresset Press, 1950

—— *A Master of Our Time: A Study of Wyndham Lewis* London: Methuen, 1951

—— *Recollections: Mainly of Writers and Artists* London: Chatto & Windus, 1984

Handley-Read, Charles *The Art of Wyndham Lewis* London: Faber, 1951

Harrison, Charles *English Art and Modernism 1900–1939* London: Allen Lane / Bloomington: Indiana University Press, 1981

Harrison, John *The Reactionaries: W. B. Yeats, Wyndham Lewis, Ezra Pound, T. S. Eliot, D. H. Lawrence* London: Victor Gollancz, 1967

Hart-Davis, Rupert *The Arms of Time: a Memoir* London: Hamish Hamilton, 1979

Hemingway, Ernest *A Moveable Feast* New York: Charles Scribner's Sons, 1964

Holroyd, Michael, *Augustus John* (revised edn.) London: Chatto & Windus, 1996

Hutchison, Sidney *The History of the Royal Academy 1768–1986* (2nd edition) London: Robert Royce, 1986

Hynes, Samuel *The Auden Generation: Literature and Politics in England in the 1930s* London: Bodley Head, 1976

—— *The Edwardian Turn of Mind* Princeton: Princeton University Press, 1968

—— *A War Imagined: The First World War and English Culture* London: Bodley Head, 1990

Jameson, Fredric *Fables of Aggression Wyndham Lewis, The Modernist as Fascist* Berkeley and Los Angeles: University of California Press, 1979

John, Augustus *Chiaroscuro*, London: Jonathan Cape, 1952

—— *Finishing Touches*, ed. Daniel George, London: Jonathan Cape, 1964

Johnstone, William *Points in Time* London: Barrie & Jenkins, 1988

Kenner, Hugh *The Pound Era* London: Faber, 1971

—— *Wyndham Lewis* Norfolk: New Directions, 1954

LePan, Douglas *Bright Glass of Memory* Toronto: McGraw-Hill Ryerson, 1979

Levy, William Turner and Victor Scherle *Affectionately, T. S. Eliot The Story of a Friendship: 1947–1965* Philadelphia and New York: J. B. Lippincott, 1968

Lewis, Wyndham *America and Cosmic Man* London: Nicholson & Watson, 1948

—— *America, I Presume* New York: Howell, Soskin & Co., 1940

—— *Anglosaxony: A League that Works* Toronto: The Ryerson Press, 1941

—— *An Anthology of his Prose* ed. E.W.F. Tomlin, London: Methuen, 1969

—— *The Apes of God* ed. Paul Edwards, Santa Barbara: Black Sparrow Press, 1981.

—— *The Art of Being Ruled* ed. Reed Way Dasenbrock, Santa Barbara: Black Sparrow Press, 1989

—— ed. *Blast* and *Blast War Number*, reprinted Santa Barbara: Black Sparrow Press, 1981

—— *Blasting and Bombardiering* London: Eyre & Spottiswoode, 1937

—— *Blasting and Bombardiering* (2nd edn.) London: Calder & Boyars, 1967

—— *The Caliph's Design* ed. Paul Edwards, Santa Barbara: Black Sparrow Press, 1986

—— *The Childermass* London: Chatto & Windus, 1928

—— *Collected Poems and Plays* ed. Alan Munton, Manchester: Carcanet, 1979
—— *The Complete Wild Body* ed. Bernard Lafourcade, Santa Barbara: Black Sparrow Press, 1982
—— *Count Your Dead: They Are Alive!* London, Lovat Dickson, 1937
—— *Creatures of Habit and Creatures of Change* ed. Paul Edwards, Santa Barbara: Black Sparrow Press, 1989
—— *The Demon of Progress in the Arts* London: Methuen, 1954
—— *The Diabolical Principle and the Dithyrambic Spectator* London, Chatto & Windus, 1931
—— *The Doom of Youth* London: Chatto & Windus, 1932
—— ed. *The Enemy*, nos. 1, 2 and 3, reprinted (with notes and afterword by David Peters Corbett) Santa Barbara: Black Sparrow Press, 1994
—— *The Essential Wyndham Lewis* ed. Julian Symons, London: André Deutsch, 1989
—— *Filibusters in Barbary* London: Grayson, 1932
—— *Hitler* London: Chatto & Windus, 1931
—— *The Human Age* Book 1 *Childermass* London: Methuen, 1956
—— *The Human Age* Book 2 *Monstre Gai* & Book 3 *Malign Fiesta* London: Methuen, 1955
—— *The Jews Are They Human?* London: George Allen & Unwin, 1939
—— *Journey into Barbary* ed. C. J. Fox, Santa Barbara: Black Sparrow Press, 1983
—— *Left Wings Over Europe, or How to Make a War about Nothing* London: Jonathan Cape, 1936
—— *The Letters of Wyndham Lewis* ed. W. K. Rose, London: Methuen, 1963
—— *The Lion and the Fox* London: Grant Richards, 1932
—— *Malign Fiesta* (including essay by Hugh Kenner and opening chapters of 'The Trial of Man') London: Calder & Boyars, 1966
—— *Men Without Art* ed. Seamus Cooney, Santa Barbara: Black Sparrow Press, 1987
—— *Mrs Dukes' Million* Toronto: Coach House Press, 1977
—— *The Mysterious Mr Bull* London: Robert Hale, 1938
—— *The Old Gang and the New Gang* London: Desmond Harmsworth, 1933
—— *Paleface* London, Chatto & Windus, 1929
—— *The Red Priest* London: Methuen, 1956
—— *The Revenge for Love* ed. Reed Way Dasenbrock, Santa Barbara: Black Sparrow Press, 1991
—— *The Roaring Queen* London: Secker & Warburg, 1973
—— *Rotting Hill* ed. Paul Edwards, Santa Barbara: Black Sparrow Press, 1986
—— *Rude Assignment* ed. Toby Foshay, Santa Barbara: Black Sparrow Press, 1984
—— ed. *Satire and Fiction* London: Arthur Press, 1930
—— *Self Condemned* ed. Rowland Smith, Santa Barbara: Black Sparrow Press, 1983
—— *Snooty Baronet* ed. Bernard Lafourcade, Santa Barbara: Black Sparrow Press, 1984
—— *Tarr: The 1918 Version* ed. Paul O'Keeffe, Santa Barbara: Black Sparrow Press, 1990
—— *Time and Western Man* ed. Paul Edwards, Santa Barbara: Black Sparrow Press, 1993
—— ed. *The Tyro* nos. 1 and 2, reprinted in one volume, London: Frank Cass, 1979
—— *The Vulgar Streak* ed. Paul Edwards, Santa Barbara: Black Sparrow Press, 1985
—— *The Writer and the Absolute* London: Methuen, 1952
—— *Wyndham Lewis the Artist, from 'Blast' to Burlington House* London: Laidlaw & Laidlaw, 1939
Lidderdale, J. and M. Nicholson *Dear Miss Weaver: Harriet Shaw Weaver 1876–1961* London: Faber, 1970
McLuhan, Herbert Marshall *Letters of Marshall McLuhan* ed. Matie Molinaro, Corinne McLuhan and William Toye, Oxford: Oxford University Press, 1987
Marinetti, F. T. *Marinetti e il Futurismo* ed. Luciano De Maria, Milan: Mondadori, 1973
Marsden, Victor E. trans. *Protocols of the Meetings of the Learned Elders of Zion* London: The Britons Publishing Society, reprinted 1933
Mastin, Catherine M., Robert Stacey and Thomas Dilworth *'The Talented Intruder' Wyndham Lewis in Canada, 1939–1945*, Windsor Art Gallery, 1992

Materer, Timothy *Vortex Pound, Eliot, and Lewis* Ithaca and London: Cornell University Press, 1979
—— *Wyndham Lewis the Novelist* Detroit: Wayne State University Press, 1976
Meyers, Jeffrey *The Enemy: A Biography of Wyndham Lewis* London: Routledge & Kegan Paul, 1980
—— ed. *Wyndham Lewis: A Revaluation* London: Athlone Press, 1980
Michel, Walter *Wyndham Lewis Paintings and Drawings* London: Thames & Hudson, 1971
Mikhail, E. H. ed. *Oscar Wilde: Interviews and Recollections* vol.1 London: Macmillan, 1979
Mitchison, Naomi *You May Well Ask* London: Victor Gollancz, 1979
—— and Wyndham Lewis *Beyond This Limit* London: Jonathan Cape, 1935
Morrow, Bradford and Bernard Lafourcade *A Bibliography of the writings of Wyndham Lewis* Santa Barbara: Black Sparrow Press, 1978
Mosley, Sir Oswald *My Life* London: Nelson, 1968
Nicholson, Hubert *Half My Days and Nights* London: Hamish Hamilton, 1941
Normand, Tom *Wyndham Lewis the Artist: Holding the Mirror up to Politics* Cambridge: Cambridge University Press, 1992
Olson, Charles *Charles Olson and Ezra Pound: an encounter at St. Elizabeths* ed. Catherine Seely, New York: Grossman, 1975
Porteus, Hugh Gordon *Wyndham Lewis A Discursive Exposition* London: Desmond Harmsworth, 1932
Pound, Ezra *The Letters of Ezra Pound 1907–1941*, ed. D. D. Paige, London: Faber, 1951
—— *The Cantos* (revised edition., 2nd impression) London: Faber, 1981
—— *Ezra Pound Speaking: radio speeches of World War II* ed. Leonard W. Doob, Westport (Conn.): Greenwood, 1978
—— and James Joyce, *Pound/Joyce: The Letters of Ezra Pound and James Joyce* ed. Forrest Read, London: Faber, 1969
—— and Wyndham Lewis, *Pound/Lewis: The Letters of Ezra Pound and Wyndham Lewis* ed. Timothy Materer, New York: New Directions, 1985
—— *Pound/The Little Review: The Letters of Ezra Pound to Margaret Anderson* ed. Thomas L. Scott and Melvin J. Friedman, with the assistance of Jackson R. Bryer, London: Faber, 1988
—— *Ezra Pound and Dorothy Shakespear, Their Letters 1909–1914* ed. Omar S. Pound and A. Walton Litz, London: Faber, 1985
Pound, Omar S. and Philip Grover *Wyndham Lewis: A Descriptive Bibliography* Folkestone: Wm. Dawson & Co., 1978
Pound, Reginald *Their Moods and Mine* London: Chapman & Hall, 1937
Powell, Anthony *Messengers of Day* London: Heinemann, 1978
Pritchard, William H. *Seeing Through Everything English Writers 1918–1940* London: Faber, 1977
—— *Wyndham Lewis* New York: Twaynes Publishers, 1968
Read, Herbert *The Contrary Experience* London: Faber, 1963
Reid, B. J. *The Man From New York: John Quinn and His Friends* Oxford: Oxford University Press, 1968
Richardson, John *A Life of Picasso* vol. 1 1881–1906 London: Jonathan Cape, 1991
—— *A Life of Picasso* vol. 2 1907–1917 London: Jonathan Cape, 1996
Roberts, William *The Resurrection of Vorticism and the Apotheosis of Wyndham Lewis at the Tate*, London: Favil Press, 1956
—— *Cometism and Vorticism, A Tate Gallery Catalogue Revised*, London: Favil Press, 1956
—— *A Press View at the Tate Gallery*, London: Favil Press, 1956
—— *A Reply to my Biographer Sir John Rothenstein*, London: Favil Press, 1957
Robins, Anna Gruetzner *Modern Art in Britain 1910–1914* London: Merrell Holberton, 1997
Rothenstein, John *Modern English Painters* vol. II *Lewis to Moore* (revised edition) London: Macdonald & Jane's Publishers, 1976
—— *Summer's Lease: Autobiography 1901–1938* London: Hamish Hamilton, 1965

—— *Brave Day Hideous Night* New York: Holt Rinehart & Winston, 1966

—— *Time's Thievish Progress* London: Hamish Hamilton, 1970

Rothenstein, William *Men and Memories*, vol. II, London: Faber, 1932

Sassoon, Siegfried *Diaries 1920–1922* ed. Rupert Hart-Davis, London: Faber, 1981

Shone, Richard *Bloomsbury Portraits: Vanessa Bell, Duncan Grant and their Circle* London: Phaidon Press, 1976

Sitwell, Edith *Selected Letters*, ed. John Lehmann and Derek Parker, London: Macmillan, 1970

Sitwell, Osbert *Laughter in the Next Room*, London: Macmillan, 1949

Spalding, Frances *The Tate: A History* London: Tate Gallery Publishing, 1998

Spender, Stephen *Journals 1939–1983* ed. John Goldsmith, New York: Random House, 1986

Stanford, Derek *Inside the Forties: Literary Memoirs 1937–1957* London: Sidgwick & Jackson, 1977

Stock, Noel *The Life of Ezra Pound* London: Routledge & Kegan Paul, 1970

Symons, Julian *Makers of the New: The Revolution in Literature, 1912–1939* London: André Deutsch, 1987

—— ed. *A.J.A. Symons to Wyndham Lewis: Twenty-Four Letters* Edinburgh: Tragona Press, 1982

Tomlin, E.W.F. *Wyndham Lewis* London: Longmans, Green & Co., 1955

Trevor-Roper, Patrick *The World Through Blunted Sight* (revised edition) London: Viking, 1988

'Vindicator' *Fascists at Olympia, A Record of Eye-Witnesses and Victims* London: Gollancz, 1934

Wadsworth, Barbara *Edward Wadsworth: A Painter's Life* Salisbury: Michael Russell, 1989

Wagner, Geoffrey *Wyndham Lewis A Portrait of the Artist as the Enemy* London: Routledge and Kegan Paul, 1957

Wees, William C. *Vorticism and the English Avant-Garde* Toronto: University of Toronto Press, 1972.

West, Rebecca *The Meaning of Treason* (revised edition) London: Penguin Books, 1965

Woolf, Leonard *Beginning Again, An Autobiography of the Years 1911–1918* London: Hogarth Press, 1964

Yeats, W. B. *Memoirs: Autobiography and first draft journal* ed. Denis Donoghue, London: Macmillan, 1972

Topographical material

Allen, Fletcher *Cook's Traveller's Handbook to North Africa* London: Simpkin Marshall, 1933

Baedeker, Karl *Belgium and Holland* (15th edition) Leipzig: Karl Baedeker, 1910

—— *Northern Germany* (11th edition) Leipzig: Karl Baedeker, 1910

—— *Southern Germany* (9th edition) Leipzig: Karl Baedeker, 1902

—— *London and its Environs* (18th edition) Leipzig: Karl Baedeker, 1923

—— *Paris and its Environs* (14th edition) Leipzig: Karl Baedeker, 1900

—— *The Rhine* (16th edition) Leipzig: Karl Baedeker, 1906

—— *Spain and Portugal* (2nd edition) Leipzig: Karl Baedeker, 1901

Hillairet, Jacques *Dictionaire Historique des Rues de Paris* vols 1 and 2 (8th edition) Paris: Editions Minuit, 1985

Muirhead, James F., *The Dominion of Canada* (1st and 2nd editions) Leipzig: Karl Baedeker, 1894 and 1900

—— *Great Britain* (7th edition) Leipzig: Karl Baedeker, 1910

—— trans. *Northern France* (3rd edition) Leipzig: Karl Baedeker, 1899

—— trans. *Southern France* (4th edition) Leipzig: Karl Baedeker, 1902

Post Office London Directory London: Kelly & Co., 1908–1946

Adressbuch von München Munich: M. Siebert 1906
Didot-Bottin Commercial de Paris Paris: Didot 1903–1910
Toronto City Directory Toronto: Might's Directory Co., 1940 and 1943

Manuscript collections

Note: Brackets indicate the abbreviations used in the References.

Papers held by the Wyndham Lewis Memorial Trust, London (Trust)
Papers in the possession of Frederick Gore RA (Gore)
University of Reading Library (Reading)
Leeds University Archives (Leeds)
National Library of Wales (Aberystwyth)
National Library of Scotland (Edinburgh)
British Library (BL)
Imperial War Museum (IWM)
Tate Gallery Achives (Tate)
Victoria & Albert Museum (V&A)
University of London Library (London)

Thomas Fisher Rare Book Library, University of Toronto (Toronto)

General Manuscripts Collection, Princeton University Library (Princeton)
Poetry/Rare Books Collection, State University of New York, at Buffalo (Buffalo)
Humanities Research Centre, University of Texas at Austin (Austin)
New York Public Library (NYPL)
Department of Manuscripts, The Huntington, San Marino (Huntington)
Rare & Manuscript Collections, Carl A. Kroch Library, Cornell University, Ithaca, NY
  (Cornell)
Vassar College Library, Poughkeepsie, NY (Vassar)

INDEX